The Book of Pictures
Muṣḥaf aṣ-ṣuwar

by

Zosimos of Panopolis

Corpus Alchemicum Arabicum

Volume II.2

(CALA II.2)

Edited by Theodor Abt and Wilferd Madelung

Living Human Heritage Publications, Zurich

Studies from the

Research and Training Centre
for Depth Psychology
According to C. G. Jung and Marie-Louise von Franz

The Book of Pictures
Muṣḥaf aṣ-ṣuwar

by

Zosimos of Panopolis

Edited with an Introduction
by Theodor Abt

Translation by Salwa Fuad and Theodor Abt

LIVING HUMAN HERITAGE PUBLICATIONS, ZURICH
2011

The Arabic transcription follows the German standard,
which is more precise than the English one.

First edition 2011
Living Human Heritage Publications
Münsterhof 16, 8001 Zurich, Switzerland
info@livinghumanheritage.org
www.livinghumanheritage.org

ISBN-10 3-9522608-7-8
ISBN-13 978-3-9522608-7-6
EAN 9783952260876

LAYOUT: Pınar Tuncer and Theodor Abt

PRINTING AND BINDING:
MAS MATBAACILIK A.Ş.
Hamidiye Mahallesi Soğuksu Caddesi
No:3 34408 Kağıthane, İstanbul / Türkiye
T. +90 212 294 10 00 (pbx) F. +90 212 294 90 80
info@masmat.com.tr

Contents

Foreword to the Translation 5

Foreword to the Facsimile Edition 9

Part I: Introduction to the Facsimile Edition

1. The earliest Alchemical Texts 17
2. Arabic Texts as a Witness to Greek Alchemy, especially to Zosimos 17
3. The Origin of the Muṣḥaf aṣ-ṣuwar 21
4. New Insight into the Roots of Zosimos' Teaching 27
5. A Testimony to the Basic Attitude of Zosimos 28
6. First Reflections on the Muṣḥaf aṣ-ṣuwar 29
7. The Muṣḥaf aṣ-ṣuwar and its Relationship to the Kitāb al-mafātīḥ fī aṣ-ṣanʿa 45
8. Texts of Zosimos as the main Source of the Kitāb al-ḥabīb and the Kitab Qirāṭis 49
9. The Greek Origin of the Turba philosophorum? 52
10. The Muṣḥaf aṣ-ṣuwar and the Rosarium philosophorum 59
11. The Muṣḥaf aṣ-ṣuwar and one of the Mutus liber 64
12. Summary 68

Part II: Introduction to the Translation

1. The Three Picture Series of The Muṣḥaf aṣ-ṣuwar 74
2. The Difference between Allegory and Symbol 85
3. The Challenge to my Hypothesis of the Origin of the Muṣḥaf aṣ-ṣuwar 96
4. Hallum's Counter-hypothesis 114
5. Significance of the Date of the Muṣḥaf aṣ-ṣuwar 125
6. Closing remarks 132
7. Summary and Conclusions 135

Part III: Translation of the Book of Pictures

The red folio numbers given here refer to the red ones in the manuscript.

Remarks relating to the translation 140

1. The 1st Book of the Learning known as the Book of the Truth Folio 2a, page 141

2. The 2nd Book of the Names Folio 38b, page 213

3 The 3rd Book about the Weights Folio 63b, page 262

4. The 4th Book about the Composition Folio 70a, page 275

5. The 5th Book about the Magnesia Folio 85b, page 306

6. The 6th Book about the Nature known as the Book of Imuth Folio 127b, page 390

7. The 7th Book about the Mercuries Folio 133b, page 402

8. The 8th Book about the Operation Folio 170b, page 476

9. The 9th Book about the Measures of the Fire Folio 190b, page 516

10. The 10th Book about the Other Work Folio 195a, page 525

11. The 11th Book about the Other Composition and Its Bodies and What Ameliorates It Folio 204a, page 543

12. The 12th Book about the Last Operation only and its Weight Folio 210a, page 555

13. The 13th Book about Questions concerning the Last Composition Folio 214a, page 563

Part IV: Apparatus

1. Bibliography 585

2. List of Illustrations 597

3. General Index 600

4. Diacritical Signs 749

Foreword to the Translation

The translation presented here of the *Muṣḥaf aṣ-ṣuwar* (The Book of Pictures) into English is its first translation into a European language. It is the result of painstakingly careful, repeated distillation work over a period of more than twenty years.

In 1988, I had the first opportunity to meet Professor Fuat Sezgin in Frankfurt. My explaining to him the Corpus Alchemicum Arabicum project led him to show me a photocopy of Zosimos' *Muṣḥaf aṣ-ṣuwar* that he had discovered in 1955 in the Archaeological Museum in Istanbul. Seeing my enthusiasm, he allowed me to make a copy of the manuscript. Back in Zurich, I showed the pictures of the *Muṣḥaf aṣ-ṣuwar* to Dr Marie-Louise von Franz. She confirmed my intuition that this book must contain most important material with regard to alchemy. At that time I was, together with Salwa Fuad in Cairo, still occupied with the English translation of Muḥammad ibn Umail's *Ḥall ar-rumūz* and his *ad-Durra an-naqīa*. It was not until 1990, two years later, that, encouraged by Dr von Franz, we could start to translate the *Muṣḥaf aṣ-ṣuwar* into English.

As the two of us were unfamiliar with the thoughts of Zosimos, the dialogue appeared to us in many places completely alien. Therefore we often just had to translate the text word for word. The fact that we always worked in Egypt for around three weeks at a time—with some months break in between these periods—allowed Mrs. Fuad to transcribe the text and prepare it for our next meeting. During these breaks, I was able to ponder over the newly translated parts as well as other related texts, and discuss with Dr von Franz the reactions from the unconscious in my dreams. Then, refreshed, I could return to Egypt to continue our translation work. In 1993 I was able to give the completed translation to Marie-Louise von Franz. She confirmed our earlier hunch, saying that this text is indeed a key text for a deeper understanding of alchemy.

In 1998, after Dr von Franz had passed away, I started to write up additions to her psychological commentary on Muḥammad ibn Umail's *Ḥall ar-rumūz*, which appeared as CALA I A in 2007. These additions finally developed into a second commentary, published in 2009 as CALA I B. This interpretation work made me aware of many misunderstandings in the first translation of Zosimos' *Muṣḥaf aṣ-ṣuwar*. So it became necessary to revise the whole translation. In 2006, with the help of Prof. Dr Fuat Sezgin, I was able to obtain a coloured high-resolution copy of the *Muṣḥaf aṣ-ṣuwar*. The facsimile of this manuscript was published in 2007 as CALA II.1. This excellent copy of the manuscript allowed a much better reading. Therefore we re-translated the whole text for a second time, incorporating important improvements in the English language and improvements in the translation contributed by Dr Peter Starr, lecturer at the Çankaya University in Ankara. This work was completed in February 2007.

Meanwhile, at the Research and Training Centre for Depth Psychology in Zurich, I started lecturing on the interpretation of Zosimos' dreams found in the *Muṣḥaf aṣ-ṣuwar*, as well as on two of the three different picture series. In order to be able to obtain an overview of the dialogue of Zosimos with his student Theosebeia in this book, I felt the need to go through our translation, together with Mrs Fuad, once more. This revision brought further significant improvements to the translation. It was completed at the beginning of 2009.

Finally, the publication of this important text required a fourth check of the translation with Mrs Fuad, and, for the English language, with David Roscoe. Working on these improvements permitted a discussion of passages still unclear; this work was completed in February 2011. Now it will be up to other researchers to verify and further improve our translation, both by collating passages from other manuscripts of the *Muṣḥaf aṣ-ṣuwar*, and with increased knowledge of other extant texts by Zosimos in Greek, Syriac and Arabic. The facsimile edition of the Arabic text will allow Orientalists to see how we were reading Zosimos' book.

My foreword to the facsimile edition of the *Muṣḥaf aṣ-ṣuwar*, which appeared in 2008 as CALA II.1, is reprinted here. This also applies to my introduction to that book. Both texts are given in Part I. This makes them accessible to those readers who are only interested in the translation presented here. Major editor's corrections and improvements in these two texts are marked in green. However, minor changes in my text and in ameliorations of our translation of passages from the *Muṣḥaf aṣ-ṣuwar,* quoted in this Part I, are not marked in green. Therefore the introduction to the facsimile edition and all translations of passages given there replace those from CALA II.1.

These two texts, reprinted from CALA II.1, are followed by Part II, the introduction to this translation volume, which appears as CALA II.2. Further discussion of the origin of the *Muṣḥaf aṣ-ṣuwar* became necessary because a reviewer of the facsimile edition questioned my claim that this text is a translation of one coherent Greek book, proposing that it is a later compilation of texts by Zosimos that were then turned into dialogue form. As there are further arguments supporting my hypothesis, this debate is likely to continue.

In Part III, the translation of the *Muṣḥaf aṣ-ṣuwar* is presented in such a way that each page of the facsimile edition is found again in the translation. Usually a space is given when Theosebeia asks a question, and each new line of the manuscript is marked in the translation with a small red number. Texts in the manuscript that are, for whatever reason, to be deleted are marked in cyan blue, while remarks or additions by the editior are maked in green. As the translation is based on one single manuscript, the translators had to rely on *internal relationships* for their work: not rarely the explanations of Zosimos on a specific subject are again taken up later. This allows a comparison of those texts, and, wherever necessary, an emendation of unclear or wrongly copied passages. Such corrections were only possible thanks to our repeated translation of the whole text on the one hand, and thanks to my lecturing on the interpretation of Zosimos' dreams and pictures on the other hand. This allowed in time a better understanding of this enigmatic text.

I would like to express my gratitude first of all to Prof. Dr Fuat Sezgin, Director of the Institute of the History of Arabic-Islamic Science, J. W. Goethe University of Frankfurt, for his continuous support of the Corpus Alchemicum Arabicum project, and his enormous labour of love in making the cultural heritage of Arabic-Islamic science more accessible to the western world. The facsimile edition of the *Muṣḥaf aṣ-ṣuwar* is therefore dedicated to him. Then I wish to thank Salwa Fuad in Cairo for her great devotion to duty in our joint translation work. Our long collaboration on translating Arabic alchemical texts, and her knowledge not only of classical Arabic but also of the dialect of Upper Egypt, were essential to an understanding of our text. For their support and for valuable discussions concerning the origin of the *Muṣḥaf aṣ-ṣuwar*, my thanks go to Dr Wilferd Madelung, Professor emeritus at the University of Oxford, and Dr Erik

Hornung, Professor emeritus at the University of Basle. As mentioned in other places, I would surely not have dared to start this translation of the *Muṣḥaf aṣ-ṣuwar* without the support of Dr Marie-Louise von Franz, who passed away in 1998. From the moment she saw the manuscript, she urged me to continue with the translation. For her teachings and her valuable contributions, I am deeply grateful. In addition, the unfailing support of my wife Regina and our daughters Sabine and Doris was equally important for my research, and for this I am also very grateful. A special thank you goes to Dr Peter Starr, Arabist and lecturer at the Çankaya University in Ankara, for checking the Arabic translation of the *Muṣḥaf aṣ-ṣuwar*, and for many discussions surrounding its publication. I am grateful to Dr Benjamin Hallum and his thesis adviser Prof. Dr Charles Burnett, Director of the Warburg Institute in London, for the basic research on Zosimos of Panopolis that made Hallum's review of my facsimile edition possible. Based on that research I was able to further debate the origin of our manuscript.

I would also like to thank the Swiss Institute of Archaeological and Architectural Research for Ancient Egypt in Cairo for their support, especially Dr Horst and Dr Felicitas Jaritz and, since 2003, Dr Cornelius and Beatrice von Pilgrim. For their efforts I would like to thank Sabine Mayer-Patzel, who produced the index, David Roscoe, for polishing up the language, Claudine Leyer and Nikola Patzel for help at the beginning of this publication, and last but not least, Elisabeth Vogel-Bodmer, who ran my office so efficiently in my absence. I also thank the Marie-Louise von Franz Foundation, as well as the Research and Training Centre for Depth Psychology in Zurich, for financial contributions with regard to this publication.

A heartfelt thank you for excellent collaboration goes again to Mehmet Bora Akgül and his team, especially to Pınar Tuncer. It was their patience and attention to detail that made possible the publication of this translation in this form.

Zurich and Istanbul, Spring 2011 Theodor Abt

Foreword to the Facsimile Edition

Scholars consider the Egyptian alchemist Zosimos of Panopolis to be the first historical figure in Greek alchemy.[1] He probably lived in the 3rd/4th century.[2] Other authors praised him as one of the great authorities, referring to him, for example, as «the crown of the sages», «the one whose language has the depth of the ocean», «the old one», «the one inspired by the gods», «the divine Zosimos», «the friend of the truth».[3] Later on, in Arabic alchemy, he was praised by Ibn Arfaᶜ Raʾs as «the universal sage and the shining flame» or «the head of the philosophers and the collector of the dispersed».[4]

Little is known about his outer life, except that he came from the town Panopolis,[5] as it was called in Greek. Panopolis is situated in Upper Egypt on the East bank of the Nile, 200 km north of Luxor and about 70 km north of Nağ Ḥammādī, where the famous Gnostic library was discovered. Today the town is called Aḫmīm. The holy site of Abydos, also mentioned in the writings of Zosimos, with its enigmatic Osiris resurrection-chapel, is only some 30 km south of Aḫmīm.[6] Newly discovered Coptic papyri are evidence that in very early Islamic times, Aḫmīm was a place where

1 He must not be confused with personalities of the same name that lived in Egypt around that time. See M. Mertens, *Les Alchimistes Grecs*, Tome IV.1, Zosime de Panopolis, Mémoires authentiques, Collection des Universités de France, Paris 1995, p. XII f.

2 Zosimos quotes the encyclopaedist Julius Africanus, whose death is dated after 240, and speaks in one of his authentic texts of the Serapeion, which was destroyed in 391. Zosimos must have lived between these two dates. M. Mertens: Zosime de Panopolis, Mémoires authentiques, l. c., p. XVI f. Mertens is trying to date his life even more precisely and suggests on p. LVII, note 148: «Selon moi c'est plutôt vers 300 qu'il faut situer l'époque de l'activité de Zosimos». The mentioned dating of Zosimos' life is confirmed by a statement in the *Muṣḥaf aṣ-ṣuwar*, quoted in this introduction on p. 27.

3 See Mertens, ibid., p. XI, who quotes M. Berthelot and Ch.-E. Ruelle, *Collection des Anciens Alchimistes Grecs*, 3 tomes. Paris 1888; Vol. II. p. 83, line 21, then line 20, p. 140, line 17, p. 199, line 14, and p. 401, line 5.

4 M. Ullmann, *Die Natur- und Geheimwissenschaften im Islam*, Leiden 1972, p. 161.

5 In most of the extant Greek works, we find that Zosimos is called «the one from Panopolis». See Mertens,ibid., p. XIII f.

6 Apido = Abydos; see M. Berthelot, R. Duval and O. Houdas, *La Chimie au Moyen Age*, 3 tomes, Paris, 1893, p. 226.

alchemy was practised, not only theoretically but also with experiments.[7] The Pharaonic temple of Aẖmīm was famous for the symbolic images that were painted on the temple walls. «All the Arab writers have enthused [...] about this ancient temple, which was particularly famed owing to its traditional association with Hermes Trismegistus».[8] Ibn Ǧubair, who visited Aẖmīm in the year 579/1183, even called the huge temple «one of the wonders of the world, beyond description or defining».[9] In Arabic alchemy, when the knowledge of the hieroglyphs was lost, these images were understood as descriptions of the opus alchemicum. In his *ad-Durra an-naqīya*, Muḥammad ibn Umail (10th century) recommends that one has to go to the temple of Aẖmīm to study the reliefs on the walls,[10] and his commentary on his *al-Qaṣīda an-nūnīya* is an alchemical interpretation of Pharaonic images on temple walls. According to the *Suda*, the Byzantine lexicon from the 10th century, Zosimos is from Alexandria, to where he probably moved at a later time.[11] According to an Arabic text, he lived for 70 years as a learning child, and for 40 years as a teacher.[12] The age of 110 years was considered in Pharaonic times to be the ideal lifespan. It is remarkable to find this Ancient Egyptian ideal preserved into the Middle Ages.

The time of Zosimos was characterised by great transitions, transforming people's perception of the invisible world. The Bible was translated into Upper Egyptian Coptic in the 3rd century. Becoming a Christian required a person to renounce all gods and goddesses previously

7 See T. S. Richter, "The master spoke: «Take one of 'the sun' and one unit of almulgam», Hitherto unnoticed Coptic papyrological evidence for early Arabic alchemy", Leipzig 2000, and "What kind of Alchemy is Attested by Tenth Century Coptic Manuscripts?", *AMBIX* 56/1(2009), p. 23-35.

8 See *Encyclopedia of Islam*, s.v. Akhmīm; contrary to this quoted article, which states that of this temple «no trace now remains», it has always been there in ruins. New excavations have exposed, among other things, a huge statue of Meritamun, the daughter and later wife of Ramses II. The temple was destroyed in the 8th/14th century. See also M. T. Derchain-Urtel, «Thot at Akhmim», in *Hommages à François Daumas*, Montpellier 1986, p. 173-180.

9 *The Travels of Ibn Jubayr,* translated from the original Arabic by R. J. C. Broadhurst, London 1951, p 55. See also the two Arabic Hermetica connected to the temple of Akhmim mentioned in M. Ullmann, *Natur- und Geheimwiss.*, l. c., p. 167 f.

10 Ms Āṣafiya library Hyderabad, 1410, fol. 17.

11 The *Suda* calls him: «Zosimos, the Alexandrian, the philosopher» (s.v. Ζώσιμος).

12 Gotha, 85.14, fol.105b 3 ff. See M. Ullmann, *Natur- und Geheimwiss.*, ibid., p. 160.

revered. Those became demons, hostile spirits «contending against the One God of goodness and justice … .»[13] This increasing polarisation and «moralisation of the universe» (Martin Buber) also led to the growing popularity of the anchorites (S. Antonius Eremita passed away in 356). At the same time, Gnostic-Hermetic thoughts were spreading in Egypt, and, like Christianity, becoming a serious rival to ancient Pharaonic temple-knowledge. Christanity became the state-religion of Rome in 313 with the Emperor Constantine.

It is evident from his teachings that Zosimos was close to the Gnostic-Hermetic world view, which worshipped the inner God-man.[14] In a Syriac text translated by R. Duval we read: «One could even say that it is the principle of the principles, the son of God, the word, that one whose thoughts and feelings also come from the Holy Spirit. This, my lady, is the explanation of the mirror. When a man looks at it, and sees himself, he will turn away from all that is called gods and demons, and by relating to the Holy Spirit, he becomes the perfect man; he sees God, who is inside him, thanks to the mediating Holy Spirit.»[15] As we will see later, this statement also expressed the essence of the teaching in the *Muṣḥaf aṣ-ṣuwar,* where its author Zosimos collected the teachings of past alchemists, connecting their statements with his own experience. He thus consolidated the knowledge of this art in his own time, both its theoretical and its experimental side.

The realisation of this facsimile of the *Muṣḥaf aṣ-ṣuwar* goes back to 1988 when—returning from India with a collection of Arabic alchemy manuscripts from Indian libraries—a stopover in Frankfurt gave me the opportunity to meet Professor Fuat Sezgin for the first time. I showed him my collection and expressed the intention of Marie-Louise von Franz and myself to further deepen our studies of Arabic alchemy. After an intense

13 Quoted from E. Pagels, *The Origin of Satan*, New York 1996, p. XVI.

14 *Coll. Alch. Grecs*, l.c., p. 262 f. See also R. Reitzenstein, *Poimandres*, Leipzig 1904, p. 8 f., G. Fowden, *The Egyptian Hermes; A Hist. Approach to the Late Pagan Mind*, Princeton 1993^2, p. 120 f., and J. Lindsay, *The Origins of Alchemy in Graeco-Roman Egypt*, London 1970, p. 323 f.

15 Editor's translation from French into English. «A moins qu'on ne dise que c'est le principe des principes, le fils de Dieu, le Verbe, celui dont les pensées et les sentiments procèdent aussi de l'Esprit-Saint. Telle est, o femme, l'éxplication du miroir. Lorsqu'un homme y regarde et s'y voit, il détourne sa face de tout ce qui est appelé dieux et démons, et, s'attachant à l'Esprit-Saint, il devient un homme parfait; il voit Dieu qui est en lui, par l'intermédiaire de l'Esprit-Saint.» *La Chimie au Moyen Age*, ibid., Vol. II, p. 263.

discussion he showed me this *Muṣḥaf aṣ-ṣuwar*, and before I left Frankfurt he allowed me to make a copy of the entire manuscript. Of course, I was most excited, especially about the pictures. The art of picture interpretation has been one of my special fields of interest since 1977, when for the first time I lectured on the interpretation of a series of alchemical pictures at the C. G. Jung Institute in Zurich. Ever since then, I have continued my research in this field.

When I showed this manuscript to Marie-Louise von Franz (1915-1998), she too was very excited and urged me to translate the entire manuscript. Salwa Fuad in Cairo and I have worked on this text over many years, because other ongoing obligations required my attention as well. Continuous studies of the history and the meaning of symbolic alchemy have accompanied this translation work. Regular lectures on the art of picture interpretation and on alchemy—since 1977 at the C. G. Jung Institute in Zurich and since 1995 at the Research and Training Centre for Depth Psychology in Zurich—made possible a growing understanding of the meaning of this unique text of symbolic alchemy. The translation of other still extant Arabic alchemical texts of Hermes, Zosimos, Maria, Agathodaimon, Morienus and Ibn Umail, brought about the necessary familiarisation with the vocabulary used by these authors. In this way, the meaning of their symbols became more and more apparent to me; *liber librum aparit*—one book opens the other—as the Latin alchemists used to say when recommending the study of alchemy in their books. The result of this procedure was a gradual improvement in the translation of the *Muṣḥaf aṣ-ṣuwar*.

The first results of this effort to understand symbolic alchemy are now available in the text edition of the *Ḥall ar-rumūz*, written by Muḥammad ibn Umail (CALA I, 2003, revised 2nd edition 2012). The first commentary to this text, written by Marie-Louise von Franz was published as CALA I A in 2006, and my second commentary, which is based on other, hitherto untranslated texts written by Ibn Umail and authors he quoted, was published as CALA I B in 2009. The translation of the *Muṣḥaf aṣ-ṣuwar* is prepared for publication as a companion volume to the CALA II.1 facsimile of the Istanbul manuscript, as CALA II.2. My psychological commentary on this text, delivered as a series of lectures at the Research and Training Centre for Depth Psychology, will follow as CALA II A.

It is the great merit of Prof. Dr. Fuat Sezgin to have discovered and copied this unique manuscript from the Arkeoloji Müzesi (Nr. 1574) in Istanbul in the year 1955.[16] The facsimile of this manuscript is dedicated to him also as a tribute to his own patient research and work on the history of Arabic and Islamic science, which he has pursued with devotion and humility for over 50 years, supported by his wife Ursula Sezgin and his colleagues at the Institute of the History of Arabic-Islamic Science at the Johann Wolfgang Goethe University in Frankfurt am Main. This Institute also published a reprint of a great number of relevant texts in the field of Arabic alchemy that serve as a valuable tool for researchers in this field.[17] It will be up to future generations to appraise the value of the immense contribution of Fuat Sezgin's research work towards a better general recognition of what Western culture owes to the Arab world.

Since its early stages, Fuat Sezgin has been a strong supporter of our CALA project, for which I express my deep gratitude. This facsimile came to print with his generous support as well as with the help of Havva Koç, Director of the Library of the Arkeoloji Müzesi in Istanbul. Mehmet Bora Akgül from MAS Matbaacılık A.Ş. in Istanbul, supervised in a most careful way the whole process of creating this facsimile, Dr Peter Starr in Ankara checked and improved our English translation of the *Muṣḥaf aṣ-ṣuwar* also making valuable suggestions for the Introduction, and Tuğba Ünlü prepared the individual folios. To all of the above I am most grateful. A thank you for improvements regarding the introduction to this facsimile also goes to Prof. Dr Erik Hornung and Prof. Dr Wilferd Madelung. Furthermore I would like to express my gratitude for logistical help during all the years of translation work to the Swiss Institute for Archaeological and Architectural Research of Ancient Egypt in Cairo (Director Dr Horst Jaritz, since 2003 Dr Cornelius von Pilgrim).

The Foundation of the Research and Training Centre for Depth Psychology and the Marie-Louise von Franz Foundation generously

16 Personal communication; see also his article "Das Problem des Ǧābir ibn Ḥayyān im Lichte neu gefundener Handschriften", *Zeitschrift der Deutschen Morgenländischen Gesellschaft* 114, 1964, p. 266. Fuat Sezgin has done extensive research, especially in libraries in the Middle East and in India, the fruits of which other orientalists were and will be able to harvest.

17 *Natural Sciences in Islam, Chemistry and Alchemy, Texts and Studies*. Collected and Reprinted by Fuat Sezgin (editor) in collaboration with Carl Ehring-Eggert, Eckhard Neubauer and Farid Benfeghoul, Vol. 55-74, Frankfurt am Main 2001/02.

supported this publication. I am, of course, most grateful to the late Dr Marie-Louise von Franz, who continuously encouraged my research in this field.

Zurich and Istanbul, Spring 2007 Theodor Abt

Part I

Introduction to the Facsimile Edition

1. The Earliest Alchemical Texts

The earliest texts on alchemy originate in Ancient Egypt and were written in Greek. This *Corpus Alchemicum Graecorum*, as the sum of all extant texts of Greek alchemy, goes back to the beginning of the 1st millenium. It is the great merit of Marcellin Berthelot and his translator Charles Émile Ruelle to have made these basic alchemical texts accessible.[18]

However, as these text editions are not quite up to modern scientific standards, they are now in the process of being reedited as *Les Alchimistes Grecs*.[19] We owe the carefully worked out and reliable new edition of the «Mémoires Authentiques» (Authentic Notes) of Zosimos of Panopolis to Michèle Mertens.[20] There we also find an overview of the different manuscripts extant in Greek that she used for her edition.[21] From her list of Zosimos' work, we can also see some of what has been lost.

2. Syriac and Arabic Texts as a Witness to Greek Alchemy, Especially to Zosimos

We also owe basic insights into the transmission of Greek alchemy to the Islamic World to the dedicated work of Marcellin Berthelot and his translators Rubens Duval (for Syriac texts) and Octave Houdas (for Arabic texts). They made a great number of Syriac and Arabic alchemical texts accessible to the scientific world, published under the title *La Chimie au Moyen Age*.[22] However, this collection only gives a very limited and arbitrary choice of such Syriac and Arabic texts. Moreover, like Berthelot's Greek collection, these edited texts do not conform to modern scientific standards and are therefore not reliable.[23] Thus *La Chimie au Moyen Age* is not a solid basis for assessing the importance of Arabic alchemy.

18 M. Berthelot and Ch.-Ém. Ruelle, *Collection des Anciens Alchimistes Grecs*, ibid.

19 Two volumes of this series appeared in: Collection des Universités de France, Paris.

20 M. Mertens, *Zosime de Panopolis*, Mémoires authentiques, ibid.; it is hard to understand why such an excellent edition does not include a general index.

21 Ms *Marcianus Graecus* 299 (10th or 11th cent.), Ms *Parisinus* 2325 (13th cent.), Ms *Parisinus* 2327 (copied 1478) see M. Mertens, l.c. XXI–XXXVIII.

22 M. Berthelot, R. Duval and O. Houdas, *La Chimie au Moyen Age*, ibid.

23 E. J. Holmyard comments on *La Chimie au Moyen Age*: «... the whole is marred by the circumstance that every fact has to be checked, every statement verified, every identification

In Berthelot's *La Chimie au Moyen Age* we find a number of texts written in Syriac that are ascribed to Zosimos.[24] However, in the light of the aforementioned statement, these texts also need to be edited anew.

Meanwhile a number of carefully edited texts have appeared on the subject of Arabic alchemy. But, in spite of this, a huge number of such texts still need to be translated into a European language so that the contribution of Arabic Alchemy to the development of consciousness can be better assessed.[25]

In the *Kitāb al-fihrist* (Book of the Catalogue) of Ibn Nadīm, written in 987, we find in the list of books that circulated at that time in the market of Baghdad four books by Zosimos, namely the *Kitāb al-mafātīḥ fī aṣ-ṣanʿa* (The Book of the Keys to the Art), a series of epistles known as *As-sabʿūna risāla* (The 70 epistles), the *Kitāb al-ʿanāṣir* (Book of the Elements), and the *Kitāb ilā ǧamīʿ al-ḥukamāʾ fī aṣ-ṣanʿa* (Book for All the Sages on the Art).[26]

The *Muṣḥaf aṣ-ṣuwar* presented here is a collection of 13 books in Arabic. The books can be considered chapters of a single book, some books being much longer than others. They contain the teachings of Zosimos to his student Theosebeia, written in the form of a dialogue, with all its human shortcomings such as misunderstandings or the feeble-mindedness of the student and the teacher's impatient outbursts, despite their love for each other. Given this accurate description of human dialogue with the attendant emotional background, the author is most likely to have been either Zosimos or Theosebeia. However, we have to be aware that the *erotapokriseis* or questions and answers genre was known in Greek antiquity, and became very popular in the 4th century.[27] It was widely, but

investigated and every translated phrase compared with its original». See E. J. Holmyard, «A critical examination of Berthelot's work upon Arabic chemistry», *Isis* (Philadelphia) 6, 1924, p. 485.

24 Ibid., Vol. II, pp. 210-266 and 297-308.

25 See the number of Mss found in F. Sezgin *Geschichte des Arabischen Schrifttums*, Volume IV, and also M. Ullmann, *Die Natur- und Geheimwissenschaften im Islam.*

26 See J. W. Fück, "The Arabic Literature on Alchemy according to Ibn Nadīm. A Translation of the Tenth Discourse of The Book of the Catalogue (Al-Fihrist) with Introduction and Commentary", *Ambix*, 4 (1951), p. 91 ff. and further commentary by M. Mertens, *Mém. auth.*, p. LXXVIII f.; the *Kitāb al-mafātīḥ fī aṣ-ṣanʿa* will be included in the CALA series, based on the Ms kīmiyā' 23 M in Cairo, Dār al-kutub 395. The Greek tradition also refers to a *Book of the Keys*, see *Collection des Anciens Alchimistes Grecs*, Vol. II, ibid., p. 277.

27 That form of dialogue may have its roots in the dialogue form of Plato, whose works were known to and respected by Zosimos. See Mertens, *Mém. auth.*, ibid., I, 1.76.

not exclusively, used by Christian writers, and it continued into Byzantine, Syriac and Arabic literature. Some works ascribed to Hermes Trismegistus are in this form.[28] The genre lends itself to convenient compilations of a teacher's knowledge for the benefit of disciples. As a pupil desiring a summary of her master's teachings, Theosebeia might have asked Zosimos to write the *Muṣḥaf aṣ-ṣuwar*. Alternatively, it might be a compilation, not made by Zosimos himself, but by a contemporary or near-contemporary pupil, using material derived from the teacher. In the next section, I will argue that our text is important evidence of a Greek source, whether directly or indirectly from Zosimos' teaching.

In the *Muṣḥaf aṣ-ṣuwar*, Zosimos drew numerous pictures for Theosebeia; our manuscript shows 42, of which 37 are given completely or partly in colour (see now also p. 75). Six pictures have landscape format and are placed on two folios, and two and a half pictures are described in the text but missing in our manuscript. The description of the pictures sometimes also mentions the colours. These references give us an indication of how authentic these colours are or which colours are missing. The colours given only partially correspond to what it says in the text. In one place, the divine water is coloured green instead of the sky-blue mentioned in the text (see folio 172b, see also figure 3). This error could be explained by a change of the colour blue into green over a period of time. There are a number of places where some colours mentioned in the text are missing in the picture. Every one of the first 12 books starts with a picture. Only the pictures at the beginning of the «1st Book of the Truth», the «3rd Book about the Weights», and the «4th Book about the First Composition» are missing, but they are described in detail in the text. The «5th Book about the Magnesia» and the «7th Book about the Mercuries» give a series of pictures.

In different places, Zosimos advises Theosebeia to ponder over the meaning of his symbolic images, while also urging her to read again and again his symbolic answers to her questions. Thus his images complement the dialogue and are intended to clarify the meaning of his teachings. In the same way as in the Ancient Egyptian Books of the Afterlife, e.g. the *Amduat*, we have here a transmission of knowledge in the form of image and word.[29]

28 B. Copenhaver, *Hermetica*, Cambridge 1992, especially p. 1 ff. and p. 67 ff.

29 See e.g. *The Egyptian Amduat, The Book of the Hidden Chamber*, ed. by E. Hornung and Th. Abt, Zurich 2007.

Who Theosebeia actually was remains a mystery. The *Suda* mentions a work called *Cheirokmeta* (Manual Skills) by the Alexandrian philosopher Zosimos, consisting of 28 books addressed to his sister—probably in the sense of his soror mystica—Theosebeia. Many of Zosimos' works, in Syriac and Arabic as well as Greek, are addressed to her. It is in the *Muṣḥaf aṣ-ṣuwar*, and, to some extent, in the *Kitāb al-mafātīḥ*, that she has a role beyond that of the addressee. She comes to life, persistently asking questions, complaining if the answers do not satisfy, and thankful if they do.

In two works, Theosebeia is called a queen (*Kitāb al-mafātīḥ,* e.g. fol. 1 and *Chimie au Moyen Age*, II, p. 238). But as there were no queens in Egypt at the time of Zosimos, this must either be seen in a symbolic sense as «his queen of the heart», or as a confirmation of a passage in the authentic letters which Zosimos wrote to Theosebeia «when he came from Egypt», in the sense that she really lived outside Egypt and might have been a queen (see fn 30, and also our text, fol. 19a, 13). In a Syriac text of Zosimos, we find Theosebeia being called a priestess (*Chimie au Moyen Age*, II, p. 308). This might also indicate something about her life, and supports the fact that in one of his dreams (*Muṣḥaf aṣ-ṣuwar* fol. 41a, 5-7), Zosimos reports that he went to the tomb of Theosebeia, which she had already prepared during her lifetime. This points to a royal- or noble-priestly Theosebeia who cared about her afterlife.

It is remarkable that here we have an almost complete manuscript of the *Muṣḥaf aṣ-ṣuwar* that is dated AH 668/AD1270,[30] especially as it is rare to find manuscripts on alchemy before the 14th/15th century. We have some fragments of the *Muṣḥaf aṣ-ṣuwar* in different libraries, but they are too small to be worth integrating into this manuscript edition.[31] Their collation with the text given here will be for further detailed research.

30 On the contents page, which includes the Coptic numbers characteristic of Egyptian manuscripts, we read: «This contents page is completed with the exalted God's help, to Him be praise. It was written by the slave in need of the exalted God's help, Yūsuf ibn Muḥammad ibn Mūsā al-Azharī, on whom and the Muslims be blessing, in 987.» He was the copyist of the section up to folio 17b, where a note reads: «Collation with the source from which it was taken reached here in 987.» The rest of the codex, from folio 18a, is older, and the nameless colophon at the end (fol. 223a) gives the date: «18 Ǧumādā al-Āḫira 668 H, which is 19 Meshir in the year of Diocletian the King. As well as re-copying the first folios, Yūsuf al-Azharī has added corrections throughout the text.

31 For these fragments see F. Sezgin, *Geschichte des Arabischen Schrifttum*, Vol. 4, p. 75 f. and M. Ullmann, *Die Natur- und Geheimwissenschaften im Islam*, p. 161.

3. The Origin of the Muṣḥaf aṣ-ṣuwar

We now need to find out whether the *Muṣḥaf aṣ-ṣuwar* is really the authentic teaching of Zosimos. For this we shall compare this text with those writings of Zosimos found in Greek and Syriac manuscripts.

a. The first simple argument in support of the *Muṣḥaf aṣ-ṣuwar* being a translation of a Zosimos text is that Theosebeia is his addressee, and in the Greek texts she is called *ō gynai*, «O woman»—or, for the noble woman that she most probably was, rather «my lady».[32] The same form of address is found in his Syriac texts,[33] and in the *Muṣḥaf aṣ-ṣuwar* it is *ayyatuhā al-mar'a*.[34]

b. The next argument for the authenticity of the text is found in the fact that in both the Greek and Syriac texts, Zosimos warns Theosebeia about her priest-friend Nilus.[35] The same warning is also found more than once in the Arabic texts, where Nilus became Fīlbis or Bīlis.[36] With his warnings, Zosimos emphasises among other things the uniting quality of the symbol of the stone in contrast to the more materialistic and polytheistic, magic attitude that prevailed at his time in the temple knowledge of the priests in Egypt.

c. One fragment concerning mercury, extant in the Syriac language,[37] speaks of the three mercuries. In an identical way, we find these thoughts in the 7th book of the *Muṣḥaf aṣ-ṣuwar*, named «The Book about the Mercuries». We also find the parable of the fusion of tin and mercury known from Zosimos' Syriac text[38] in the *Muṣḥaf aṣ-ṣuwar* on folio 161a.

d. References to *The Book of Imuth* in our text provide a clear connection with Zosimos or his school. A passage from a book of this title

32 M. Mertens, *Mém. auth.* I.12 and VIII,1, and often in M. Berthelot, *Alch. Grecs.*

33 M. Berthelot, *La Chimie au Moyen Age*, Vol. II, l. c., e. g.: p. 213, 232, 238, 239, 260, 262, 263 etc.

34 In the *Muṣḥaf aṣ-ṣuwar* we find this expression over 20 times, and in the *Kitāb al-mafātīḥ fī aṣ-ṣanʿa* we also find this expression over 20 times.

35 See, for example, M. Berthelot, *Alch. Grecs*, XXVII, § 8, and *La Chimie au Moyen Age* Vol. II, p. 228.

36 On folio 4a, 41a, 100b. Also in the *Kitāb al-mafātīḥ fī aṣ-ṣanʿa* we find the priest Nilus on fol. 41b and, indirectly, again on fol. 84a. (Ms 395 kīmiyā' 23 M, Dār al-kutub, Cairo).

37 *La Chimie au Moyen Age*, Vol. II, p. 242 f.

38 Ibid., p. 245.

ascribed to Zosimos survives in a quotation in the Chronography of George Syncellus.[39] The quotation concerns the myth of the misalliance between angels and the daughters of men, and the angels' gift of a book called *Chemeu*, which brought the knowledge of alchemy to the first alchemists. Likewise, in a Syriac manuscript translated by Rubens Duval, the *Book of Imuth* is mentioned as the name of one of the 24 parts of the mysterious, first alchemical book of the angels.[40] The *Muṣḥaf aṣ-ṣuwar* contains the same myth, clarifying that every one of the twenty-four foundational books was called *The Book of Imuth* (Imuth is Imhotep). However, other passages in our text make clear that *The Book of Imuth* was also the name of a work by Zosimos. The relation between this *Book of Imuth* of Zosimos and the twenty-four foundational books with this title remains unclear.[41] The *Muṣḥaf aṣ-ṣuwar* also shows that *The Book of Imuth* was a symbolic name for the nature used in the alchemical work.[42]

39 See Mertens, *Mém. auth.*, p. XCIV. Note also the reference in Olympiodoros to a «separate work about the fire» by Zosimos, who «writes about the fire in all his works, as do all the ancients», see Berthelot, *Alch. Grecs* II, p. 78, §16. It is possible that this is a reference to the «9th Book about the Measures of the Fire» in the *Muṣḥaf aṣ-ṣuwar* (see now also p. 96 f.).

40 M. Berthelot, *La Chimie au Moyen Age*, Vol. II, ibid., p. 210–266.

41 Zosimos refers to his earlier *Book of Imuth* repeatedly in the *Muṣḥaf aṣ-ṣuwar*. «Our lead-copper is like that: If you do not refine its pounding, clarify and bleach it well, no beautiful colour will come out of it. I explained this operation in *The Book* (*Muṣḥaf*) *of Imuth* (fol. 125a, 14). See also (fol. 168a, 19). There is a strong likelihood that this book was Zosimos' account, perhaps as a commentary, of teachings ascribed to Imuth (= Imhotep) himself, and presumably it claimed to transmit wisdom from the first sages' 24 books: «She (Theosebeia) said: "Tell me about your statement in *The Book* (*Muṣḥaf*) *of Imuth*: 'Many kinds are among them, some get splashed, some get mixed and some get cast.'" He (Zosimos) said: "Imuth made clear and was not jealous."» (fol.166a, 9-11). In fol.129a, 16-19, Theosebeia asks why «the first ones (sages) named this gum "The Book of Imuth". Zosimos answered: «When the first sages obtained this book, and recognized the benefit of knowing it, they feared that people would obtain it. So they wrote 24 books about it, and they named each one of them with its name (i.e. *The Book of Imuth*), inserted in it what is not from it, so by that they veiled it from common people.»

42 The 6th Book of the *Muṣḥaf aṣ-ṣuwar* is entitled «The Book about the Nature» which is known as "The Book (*Muṣḥaf*) of Imuth"». This book, however, is not identical with Zosimos' *Book* (*Muṣḥaf*) *of Imuth* mentioned elsewhere in his *Muṣḥaf aṣ-ṣuwar,* because that 6th Book refers neither to angels nor to sayings of Imuth. In a passage on fol. 127b, 6-10, Theosebeia asks Zosimos about «the single nature [...] that the sages named "The Book of Imuth" because of their jealousy, and in order to keep it secret.» He (Zosimos) said: «I have told you that the support, key and basis of this work are in this nature. So, O Theosebeia, make use of it, and beware that you do not neglect it because this work is only supported by this nature.»

e. In the *Muṣḥaf aṣ-ṣuwar*, e.g. on the folios 136a, 4 and 13, 138a, 3; 139b, 3, we find books mentioned that carry the letters of the alphabet, in the same way as they are mentioned in different places in the extant Greek and Syriac texts of Zosimos.

f. As an important further fact in the *Muṣḥaf aṣ-ṣuwar* we find three of Zosimos' own dreams.[43] Given the importance of dreams, known from his Greek texts, we find here further confirmation of his relationship to his dream-life. In the light of these new dreams, reported in the *Muṣḥaf aṣ-ṣuwar*, we recognize a consistent personality named Zosimos, who continuously nourished his inner God-man by paying attention to his dream-life, wondering and pondering about its meaning.

Just to give one example of a dream, reported in the 1st Book of the *Muṣḥaf aṣ-ṣuwar* called «The Book of the Learning», there is his dream about the man of copper that he told to Theosebeia (6b, 19 -7a, 18): «She said: "Then tell me, O Zosimos, when you say that all the sages wrote frequently about the cooking. Is all of this to deter people from this science, and because of jealousy of them?" He said: "Concerning the people of the right attitude and of wisdom who desire it (the work), they did not do anything like that to them. However, they made their operation inaccessible to the shameless, in order that they could not corrupt the world, as the responsibility for those people would be with whoever taught it to them." She said: "Then show me how they dispersed it (the science)." He said: "Did I not explain to you that in my great dream (*ruʾīā*) I saw that the killed one was cut into pieces: the two hands were cut up, the fingers were cut up joint by joint, vein by vein, and the bones and veins were pounded until they became very fine like dust. What I am telling you about this dream corresponds to the statement of Agathodaimon, who said: 'Pound and cook, pound and cook, (from the margin: cook), repeat it, do not be impatient, and repeat it.' For the work on these things at the beginning of the mixing, the cooking, the soaking, the roasting, the heating, the whitening, the pounding, the roasting, the vaporisation, the rusting and the dyeing is one. If Agathodaimon had known that one pounding, one cooking and one soaking would be enough for it, he would not have repeated what he said. However, he repeated the statement 'pound and cook', so that they would

43 On fol. 7a, 5-17; fol. 40b, 12-41a, 7; and fol. 82b, 3-17, the *Kitāb al-mafātīḥ* also mentions two dreams of Zosimos.

cook it many times without losing patience and in order to disguise it from those who did not know these names. My lady, if I wanted to hold anything back from you, it would have been enough for me to tell you that in my dream I had just found a killed man. But I informed you that he had been killed and cut into pieces, divided and cut into fragments till he became a decayed corpse." She said: "Am I right to see that this killed man is the copper body that you have ordered me to operate on?" He said: "Now you have understood what I said […] ."» This human body of copper or copper-man is well known from authentic Greek texts of Zosimos, where he speaks of the copper-man (*kalk-anthropos*)[44] whom he saw in his dream, who turned into a man of silver and finally into a man of gold. The symbol of the mutilated copper-man is a parallel to the Pharaonic Osiris, the ruler of the Netherworld, the *deus absconditus* who has to be extracted from bodily reality and then further worked upon, as Zosimos explains later, on the basis of another dream that could be a continuation of this dream (fol. 40b, 12- 41a, 7).

g. A comparison of the authentic Greek texts of Zosimos with the *Muṣḥaf aṣ-ṣuwar* reveals that practically all the key symbols such as lead-copper, magnesia, pyrite, chrysocolla, alabaster, the divine water, the etesian stone, the copper without shadow, etc. are also found in this Arabic text. In the *Kitāb al-mafātīḥ fī aṣ-ṣanʿa* of Zosimos, a book mentioned in the Greek texts as well as in the *Kitāb al-fihrist* (see footnote 26), Zosimos speaks in the same way of the same symbols in relation to his dreams, and he describes the aim of the work in the same style. This would confirm Zosimos' authorship of the *Muṣḥaf aṣ-ṣuwar*. It is also noteworthy that in this book the same authorities are quoted: Democritus, Maria, Agathodaimon, etc.

h. The earliest quotations from the *Muṣḥaf aṣ-ṣuwar* seem to be in the *Kitāb al-ḥabīb*, a compilation of alchemical texts from ancient authorities. The *Kitāb al-ḥabīb* may itself have been translated from Greek. Fuat Sezgin argues against Ruska's view that the Arabic compilation works (the *Kitāb al-ḥabīb*, the *Turba* and the *Kitāb Qirāṭis*) were made in Islamic times: "Apart from the fact that it cannot be established historically, and

44 See, for example, M. Mertens, *Mém. auth.*, part X, line 61, 70, 81 and 115. As we find a dream about the copper-man in the Greek Authentic Notes and in the *Muṣḥaf aṣ-ṣuwar* we can say that Zosimos here refers back to the same dream that is known from the Greek original. That demonstrates an internal relationship between the Arabic and the Greek texts.

that it furthermore lacks credibility if one cites the stage of development of this science in Egypt to explain why these writings lack the changes which took place in the alchemy of the Arabs, the quotations and personal names cited indicate the pre-Islamic composition date of these books, and therefore also of the *Kitāb al-ḥabīb*."[45]

k. Finally the fact that we also have pictures in the *Muṣḥaf aṣ-ṣuwar* points to its pre-Islamic origin. The representation of divine or demonic figures, as we find it in figure 1 on page 30, would be unlikely in an Islamic context. In Arabic alchemy, we find in general only very few pictures, as pictures are generally forbidden, partly owing to a fear of their magic power.[46]

An argument *against* our hypothesis that the *Muṣḥaf aṣ-ṣuwar* is a translation from a Greek text of Zosimos or his school, or indeed from any Greek text, can be found in a passage on folio 10a, 8-16 that reads: «She said: "Then tell me about the statement of Maria from her father: 'The nation in which this science will appear will be at the end of time.'" He said: "Your questioning me was about what the sages had described, but concerning what has been described about the nations, you are not in need of it, and it is not a question for you." She said: "I ask you, why did you tell me about this nation?" He said: "They are the sons of Ibrāhīm." She said: "The Jews?" He said: "No, they are the sons of Ismāʿīl. After 160 years of their reign, it (the science) will appear to them."And there is not a nation that was more disbelieving in the sages than them. After 140 years of their reign, the number of seekers of this science will increase, and they will feel enthusiasm for it. Then the great and exalted God will reveal it to them after they were in despair about it, in order to increase their desire for the other world more than for this world.» This passage is an

45 *Geschichte des arabischen Schrifttums*, IV, p. 92: «Abgesehen davon, daß es historisch nicht nachzuweisen und darüber hinaus gedanklich nicht nachzuvollziehen ist, wenn man die in diesen Schriften fehlende Entwicklung, welche die Alchemie bei den Arabern erfuhr, mit dem Stand dieses Wissensgebietes in Ägypten erklären will, weisen auch die zitierten Quellen und Eigennamen auf die vorislamische Entstehungszeit dieser Bücher und damit auch des *K. al-Ḥabīb* hin.»

46 The copyist might just not have been aware of what he was doing. See also *La Chimie au Moyen Âge*, Vol. II, p. 228: «Les hommes étaient saisis de crainte à la vue des images; ils pensaint qu'elles étaient animées et qu'elles tenaient leurs couleurs de la nature vivante; à tel point qu'ils n'osaient pas les regarder en face … .»

argument against a translation from a Greek original. It would rather point to our text being an *Islamic adaptation* of the original text of Zosimos. Prof. Wilferd Madelung informed me that such adaptations are well known in the Arabic literature of the time. However, the text is best understood as a translation with a certain amount of adaptation. The reference to the Arabs here must be an interpolation in the original text.

The Arab alchemist, as we have seen, added a prophecy referring to themselves. The adapter felt free, as Dr Peter Starr pointed out to me, to add Hadith quotations (i.e. sayings of the prophet Muḥammad) to the text. An Arabic idiom derived from Hadīth literature is found on folio 10a, lines 7–8: "I am quite content [...] either against me or for me" (*raḍītu* [...] *bi-l-kafāf, lā ʿalaiya wa-lā līya*). This phrase is found repeatedly in Hadīth literature. Caliph ʿUmar responds to a young man's praise in such words (Buḫārī, 5, 57: 50). On folio 11a, line 18, there is a direct quotation from an Arabic proverb, which is also a weak Hadīth: "The best and most just of all things is their middle." As a Hadīth, attributed to the Prophet, we only find this in the *Tafsīr* (*Qurʾān* exegesis) of the classical scholar al-Qurṭubī (died 671 H).

To sum up these reflections on the origin of the *Muṣḥaf aṣ-ṣuwar*, one comes to the following conclusion: The comparison of the content of this book with the extant Greek and Syriac writings of Zosimos shows that the original text is most probably a text of Zosimos himself, of his student Theosebeia, or of one of his other disciples. The entire content of the *Muṣḥaf aṣ-ṣuwar* confirms that our text corresponds to the teachings of Zosimos, as known from his Greek and Syriac texts.

Assuming that this conclusion is corroborated by later research, the text presented here would be the oldest extant text with coloured illustrations of the religious-symbolic branch of alchemy. The fact that the *Muṣḥaf aṣ-ṣuwar* is almost complete, makes it possible to gain a more comprehensive overview of what Zosimos may have intended to impart through his teachings, and the reason why he treasured the alchemical work above all else in this world.

4. New Insight into the Roots of Zosimos' Teaching

The *Muṣḥaf aṣ-ṣuwar* offers us some remarkable new insights into the basic foundation of Zosimos' teachings. This will need to be studied in detail on the basis of all the extant Arabic translations in relation to the texts of Zosimos already known. I can give only one example here. On folio 106a, 1-8 we read: «He (Zosimos) said: "My lady, understand the statement of my sage, as you lack understanding. I did not desire anything from the sages except to become one of their students. However, I particularly selected Democritus for this, and I became a student of his, although there are 660 years between us. This is because he spoke the truth, making it clear and striving for sincerity. He spoke clearly for those who knew its meanings, with knowledge of what the sages were hiding. Also (I selected him) because Ostanes the Great preferred him, for Ostanes ordered each of the sages to write an illuminating, difficult and enigmatic book about this work. Maria was with them at that time. Then he told them that the best one for illuminating, revealing and hiding the truth, as well as (protecting) the knowledge, was Democritus, who has the crown.»

This passage shows that Zosimos considered Democritus to be his inner teacher, a concept that is still known today in India, where some people speak of an inner guru. It is characteristic of mystical writers to have a living relationship with an authority from the past.

If we deduct 660 years from the time that Zosimos was living (3rd/4th century), we come to just about the period when Democritus of Abdera was living (460-370). This is further confirmation of the dating of the life of Zosimos in the 3rd/4th century.

The statement given above also shows that Democritus was for Zosimos the main source of inspiration. Looking at the Greek and Syriac texts of Zosimos, we find some remarkable internal correlations, as in these texts Democritus is also respectfully quoted.[47] Especially in the text *Peri aretes*, Democritus is praised by Zosimos as «my most excellent one».

47 See the list of quotes from Democritus and Le Philosophe in M. Mertens, p. 269 and M. Berthelot, Coll. des Alch. Grecs, l.c., III.VI., 6: ὁ Δημόκριτος ἐκεῖνος ὁ ἐμοὶ ἀγαθώτατος. Also in the Syriac text, we find two quotes from Democritus: See M. Berthelot and R. Duval, in *La Chimie au Moyen Age*, Vol. II, l.c., p. 214 and p. 260. The same can be said

5. A Testimony to the Basic Attitude of Zosimos

In the *Muṣḥaf aṣ-ṣuwar*, Jesus is mentioned on two occasions. On folio 194a, 12-18, we read: «She said: "Then tell me about when Alāsārdus says: 'O you students, I warn you of strong fire in the operation, for it is the enemy of the water, until the two are reconciled.'" He said: "In the same way as Christ (*masīẖ*), peace be upon Him, said to those who came to test His knowledge by their science, addressing them before they started speaking: 'How amazing of you, O community of sages, that you reconciled fire and water so that they live together in the operation.' They were astonished when He knew them by their science." (Zosimos continued:) "In the same way, I warn you about the fire, and I tell you that if you reconcile fire and water, your work will be good, God willing."»[48] This quotation shows that Zosimos knew of Christ as a teacher. It also shows that he revered Him to the extent that Jesus was assimilated into the alchemical tradition.[49] Zosimos, in our *Muṣḥaf aṣ-ṣuwar*, seems to have recognized a certain one-sidedness of the Christ-image, who is stressing himself the importance of *the reconciliation of the opposites of the blessed water and hellish fire, the upper light and good God and the lower dark-evil Satan.*

Zosimos' teaching presents the aim of the alchemical work as a turning to the despised and rejected matter. On folio 160a, 1-6, we read: «She said: "Thus the things which enter your work, are they the non-accepable things for people?" He said: "If it were not like that, this science

about *Kitāb al-mafātīḥ fī aṣ-ṣan'a*, the other main Ms. of Zosimos extant in Arabic. This later text is a commentary to the (no longer extant text) *The Ten Keys* by Democritus, who is quoted quite frequently in our text. Detailed research will be needed to verify the hypothesis of an internal correlation of the different texts, assumed to originate from Zosimos' teachings (see also p. 116).

48 On folio 42a, 17 -42b, 3 we read a similar passage: «Zosimos said: [...] "And I warn you about the fire in the operation, for it is the enemy of the water because of their opposition and mutual hatred, until peace comes to the water and the fire and they are reconciled. As Christ, peace be upon Him, said: 'How amazing of you, O community of sages, that you reconciled water and fire, so they stayed together in the operation.' The sages were astonished that He (Christ) knew them by their science. Know that if you reconcile water and fire, your work will be good, by the will of the magnified and glorified God."»

49 E. O. von Lippmann points out in his *Entstehung und Ausbreitung der Alchemie* Vol. 1, p. 75, that at the time of Zosimos there was a considerable community of Christians in Upper Egypt.

would be clear." She said: "Why is it like that?" He said: "The exalted God with His omnipotence knows that the greatest thing in people's eyes is gold. So He wanted to teach them that it (the gold) is made from the most inferior and cheapest things, [...]"» Zosimos' main aim in his alchemical work and in his teaching was to reconcile the opposites of highest and lowest, of fire and water, of male and female.

6. First Reflections on the Muṣḥaf aṣ-ṣuwar

Zosimos lived in Egypt at a time when Pharaonic temple-culture was still alive. But at the same time, owing to Hellenistic influences, there was the incipient struggle to overcome bodily urges and, in a Platonic way, to establish a firm conscious attitude separate from the body. Christianity too was bringing in these new values, with its praise of the ascetic lifestyle, and the rejection of all «devilish bodily urges».

In the *Muṣḥaf aṣ-ṣuwar*, Zosimos teaches Theosebeia—who was also his beloved—about the meaning of consciously accepting the suffering of a passionate love relationship that cannot be simply lived out physically. To give an idea of how image and word are to be seen together in this *Muṣḥaf aṣ-ṣuwar*, we should look at the 2nd book called «The Book of the Names». On folio 38b, 2-10, we read: «She said: "I have reached, O Zosimos, all that I could attain in the education. So tell me about the things which the sages named with other than their true names. Make them no longer obscure to me, and thereby complete your favour to me." He said: "With what I wrote and told you, and with the picture I made for you with me in it, I gave you what you need to know and this should be enough for you. Now I have no other choice but to complete the best of what you want, because of your kindness and the relationship with you. So ask me whatever you want concerning these names. I will tell you about them to the extent of my knowledge regarding what you were not able to understand. So contemplate again the figures at the beginning of the book, I mean «The Book of the Names», and ponder over what I have presented to you because I did not put anything in them except as an analogy for what you need.»

This statement of Zosimos makes clear that we need to see what is happening to Zosimos and Theosebeia, what grips them, and in whose hands they are. As we have no detailed description of this picture in «The Book of the Names»—Zosimos obviously drew the picture for her—it must mean that it has simply to be pondered upon (see fig. 1). We know from

Fig. 1: (fol. 38a) Zosimos, with the sun on his head, and Theosebeia, with the moon on her head. Zosimos is in the hand of a three-headed being that is much larger than these two. Text and image of «The 2nd Book of the Names» show aspects of the psychological process that Zosimos experienced in his relationship with Theosebeia.

later alchemical books, e.g. the famous two books called *Mutus liber* (Book without Words), dating from the 17th century, of a similar procedure. As we have no interpretation given in the text, there is no other way to understand this picture than *out of itself,* with the help of tools developed for the art of picture interpretation.[50]

In the centre and dominating the whole picture, we see a big three-headed figure. With his left hand, this figure grips Zosimos, who has a sun on his head. The three-headed figure is about three times larger than Zosimos, whose hands are outspread, as if in despair or in a gesture of surrender. At the side of Zosimos, we see Theosebeia with a moon on her head. She clings onto the body of Zosimos, holding him around his chest. Both figures give the impression of being lifted up into the air, and both figures are represented, from the knee downwards, with uncovered legs.

With his right hand, the three-headed figure holds a human-shaped being with animal tail and paws, but with a human head and eyes. That figure is strongly coloured, mainly black and red. The hands are put together in an almost human way. Beside this figure there is a second figure with similar features, who seems to be connected to the arm of the three-headed figure. These two dark-coloured figures are like enlarged shadow figures of Zosimos and Theosebeia, depicting their activated animal or bodily nature. Thus both the couple on the right and the couple on the left are Zosimos and Theosebeia, lifted up into the air.

This triune figure is Hermes-Mercurius, as becomes evident from the pictures in the «7th Book about the Mercuries» (see also fig. 18). He is obviously able to handle with one hand the light and uncoloured spiritual-humans, and with the other, the dark black-red animal-humans. Hermes symbolizes a spiritual entity that goes beyond Christ, who was—as he declared—not of this world, and who is not identical with Satan, the principle of evil.[51] Our figure here is clearly a representation of the guide to alchemy, the one that can separate *and* hold together the light and the dark side, the lower animal realm and the upper divine aspect of human existence. He is the evasive spirit of the unconscious with different appearances, *uterius capax*, capable of both. He is not only good but can also be evil: «He is good with the good and evil with the evil» as some Latin alchemist said. It depends on

50 See the method developed in: Th. Abt, *Introduction to Picture Interpretation*, Zurich 2005.

51 For details, see C. G. Jung, "The Spirit Mercurius", *Coll. Works* 13, § 239 f. and § 481.

the attitude of the humans. He is a representation of the *anthropos,* symbol of the entire human, including also his or her dark bodily side. But here, this figure is experienced first in its hideous aspect, depicting a real possession by the archetype of the daemonic or divine greater human.

The picture represents the beginning phase of the work, where Zosimos and Theosebeia are seen hopelessly gripped by a force much greater than themselves. The two, Zosimos and Theosebeia, are now kept in suspension; they cannot move freely and are at the mercy of this divine or demonic spirit who reminds us, e.g., of the three-headed Shiva in Hindu mythology. It is not the devil but rather a figure like Lucifer-Prometheus.[52] This anthropos-figure that starts the process is what we would call today with C. G. Jung the *principium individuationis*. We have in this figure a symbol of the greater inner human that is still unconscious.

Zosimos and Theosebeia with a sun and a moon on their heads are represented in Hermes' left hand. This shows that the archetypes of the male and the female principle, symbolized by sun and moon, have entered the realm of the two humans. The animal shapes of the bodies of the two beings in Hermes' right hand show that the dark or unconscious bodily instincts are alive as well. This is what we experience today in the same way when falling in love. C. G. Jung once wrote to Aniela Jaffé: «The coniunctio of the male and the female half of the self wants to overwhelm the individual and force it to represent it physically in this world. You would like to illuminate the world as Luna (and I as Sol). Every archetype, however, before being integrated consciously wants to be represented concretely, forcing the subject in its form. The self (i.e. the archetype) is unconscious about its divine nature. It can only become conscious within the frame of our consciousness. And this is only possible if the ego is able to hold it. It (the self) must become so small, smaller than the ego, in spite of being the ocean of the divine. [...] In the vessel the hierosgamos takes place. You are not the goddess, nor I the god, on principle, otherwise we would no longer be humans and God would not have been born. We can only hold our hands and thus know about the inner human. The superhuman does not belong to us.»[53] This corresponds precisely, and in a nutshell, to the teachings of Zosimos to Theosebeia.

52 See also Zosimos' text on "The letter Omega", M. Mertens, *Mem. Auth.*, I.

53 C. G. Jung, *Letters*, Vol. 1, Princeton 1992, Letter of 3rd Nov. 1943 (amended transl.).

Here follows a summary of a part of the dialogue between Zosimos and Theosebeia which illustrates the wrestling of two human beings, of teacher and student, to make understandable and to understand the meaning of alchemical symbolism. It reveals that what Zosimos explains to Theosebeia is definitely not just outer chemistry but the description of a *psychological transformation* described and explained with the help of chemical symbols and analogies.

In the «5th Book about the Magnesia», which contains an entire picture series, Zosimos explains to Theosebeia: (fol. 98a, 11 -98b, 6) «He said: "I will illustrate the two of us in several different pictures, not just one, in this book of mine. In it, I want to give you your right at every level of this work until I reach its end, in order that you know what you asked me about. Ask me whatever you want, as long as my picture seems appropriate to your picture." She said: "Do you want my picture to be separate from your picture?" He said: "Yes, my picture must be separate from your picture." She said: "Whom do I ask questions then?" He said: "You will ask my spirit." She said: "Will the spirit seem to be appropriate to me?" He said: "No, it will not seem appropriate, but from my spirit imagined colours will appear that your eyes never saw before." She said: "How will I ask questions of your spirit, O Zosimos, once it has separated from your body? You just put me into trouble although I am ignorant, and you make me enter into what is more difficult than what I complained to you about being too obsure. Has anybody before me seen a spirit separate from its body that appears before one's eyes?" He said: "Yes indeed. If my spirit separates from my body, it must be concealed in your spirit. Therefore it seems appropriate for you. So accept this statement of mine. Know that your spirit will talk with my spirit, and it (your spirit) will know what it asks it (my spirit) about. At this time you will see the miracles of the exalted God's wisdom."»

This passage shows that Zosimos seeks to explain to Theosebeia something that later in Latin alchemy was called *imaginatio vera* or *colloquium cum aliquid qui non videtur*. Today we would speak of an active imagination, a method of encounter with inner psychic contents that was rediscovered by C. G. Jung. Our passage is remarkable as this is most probably the earliest document that explains in great detail the process of how to achieve a conscious separation of the divine or spiritual aspect from the concrete human person, onto whom this divine quality was projected.

Fig. 2: (fol. 99a) In the *upper register*, we see Theosebeia, on whose head is a moon with a face. To her right is Zosimos, on whose head is a sun that also has a face. On a lead, he holds a man with two wings. In the *lower register,* we see Theosebeia, on whose head is a moon with no face. In front of her are two yellow vessels. One of the vessels shows Zosimos, on whose head is a sun with no face and a white bull. In the other vessel is, as the text says, a green-white bull. The two levels, the upper spiritual and the lower human, can also be seen in later Latin alchemy (see fig. 8).

In the text belonging to the image on folio 98b, 8-11 (see fig. 2), we read: «The image of Theosebeia and Zosimos, and with Zosimos there is a man with two wings who is pointing to him. And there is an image of Theosebeia, and in front of her a yellow vessel with Zosimos in it, together with his bull, and another yellow vessel with a white-green bull in it.»

The two levels of the picture show the need for a simultaneous view of the upper and lower reality: The small or human Theosebeia down below (with a moon on her head, having no face) is confronted with the need for a yellow vessel for the white-green bull (probably her own). In front of her is the small or human Zosimos (with a sun on his head, having no face), who is contained in a yellow vessel with his bull. On the upper level, we see the great or divine Theosebeia (with a moon on her head, having a face), together with the great or divine Zosimos (with a sun on his head, having a face) together with his spirit, which he holds on a lead. This separation of the upper-archetypal and the lower-human level is also found in two other pictures (on fol. 128b and fol. 191b), and it remained a topic throughout the tradition of religious-symbolic alchemy, as can be seen e.g., in fig. 8 of this introduction. The colour yellow of the vessels points to the quality of light or consciousness that characterizes them, while the white-green colour of the bull points to the union of the colour of life with the non-colour white. The bull can be understood as a symbol for the divine, life-providing quality of the bull-energy (the *Ka* in Ancient Egypt) that is, when entering consciousness, first experienced as overwhelming bodily drivenness that then, with the help of the alchemical work, needs to be consciously contained in the yellow vessel.

Then follows a long dialogue between teacher and student about this separation of the spirits of Zosimos and Theosebeia from their bodies. This dialogue culminates in a most remarkable statement of Zosimos, who then explains: (fol. 100b, 13 -101a, 3) «He said: "Your spirit appears on the outside of my spirit." She said: "How can my spirit win over your spirit, when you are stronger, wiser and more knowledgeable than me?" He said: "Your spirit is full of weapons, and I have no power over you in any of these matters." She said: "I have never seen a weak one winning over a strong one." He said: "Today you have seen it." She said: "Then what led my spirit to take your spirit?" He said: "In order that by it you are able to fight the enemies." She said: "I did not know I had any enemy." He said:

"Your enemy is very much present!" She said: "I have not done any evil to anybody, and I am good-natured towards people." He said: "So what do you think of the great sun that Hermes mentioned, but he did not name by its name?" She said: "There is no deep-rooted hatred between the sun and me." He said: "It is your murderer, and it has been your enemy of old."»

Here we have the document that explains what was really meant by the famous «*ascunīa* (acacia), murderess of her lover or her husband» that we find so often in the *Muṣḥaf aṣ-ṣuwar*. This story, which is known in literature as «The Legend of the *Giftmädchen* (poison girl)», will be presented in detail on page 54 f. of this introduction, and again in Part II on page 126 f. What needs to be kept in mind here is the fact that this image of Theosebeia, who is full of weapons and is able to defeat Zosimos, is explained clearly as a symbol for a transpersonal *psychological* phenomenon. She is not simply a *Decknamen* (cover name) as many historians of alchemy think.

After the description of a picture, the text goes: (fol. 102a, 1-4) «She said: "You have spoken much, O Zosimos, and you took a direction that I had not asked you about. Tell me about yourself. What destroyed you and separated your spirit from your body?" He said: "You took away my splendour and you turned me into silver, after I had been gold before. You dressed me in black, which is the lowest of all the colours, then you turned me into ashes [...]. (fol. 102b, 4-5) Then I will be resurrected. And I am bound to be resurrected, to come back to life and to become better than I was before."»

Then follows (on fol. 103a) a picture described as: «The image of a man lying dead on the ground, golden, with red stripes.» The text runs: (fol. 103a, 7 -103b, 14) «She said: "What shape is that?" He said: "It is in the clothes of the greatest king in purple colour, and the purple is woven with gold." She said: "What urged you to this shape?" He said: "Did I not tell you before not to ask me?" She said: "I do ask you, because I am impatient about what I hear." He said: "They are my winding sheets." She said: "Are the dead wrapped in cloths of gold?" He said: "Yes, they are the winding sheets of the sages, because the gold holds back and prevents the fire from burning me at death, until I am resurrected, alive." She said: "What was it that killed you, O Zosimos?" He said: "You." She said: "I am too weak for that." He said: "Keep away from me." She said: "Am I able to do that? Woe unto you O Zosimos! How could I do to you what you are describing?" He said: "When you are wrapped in the silvery winding sheets." She said: "So, O Zosimos, your death is nigh, and at that time the colours of the rainbow appear in you." He said: "Woe unto you, O Theosebeia, what extinguishes these colours (of the rainbow) is the one whose inside is black. When it mixes with me, it extinguishes my light and illuminates you, and reveals your splendour and increases your brilliance." She said: "I do not understand what you are saying, and you only want to mock me. Woe unto what you say!" He said: "Die in your grief! You are a fool. Look at the pictures of the two of us at the beginning of this book. Then ask me questions, as long as you see my picture and I will answer you about what I promised you. Do not leave out anything you think you will need without asking me about it. I will reveal to you what a father keeps back from his son. And I think, O Theosebeia, that if you understand what I say, your soul will be filled with joy and you will praise me much for it."»

Then follows on folio 104b, 6-9 a further dialogue, where Theosebeia wants to know more about the vanishing of Zosimos' light. He answers her that it is she, the silvery one, who did that, and that she made the statement of Agathodaimon become true, who said: «Turn the gold into silver!» She has further questions that Zosimos answers with quotes from Democritus, ending (fol. 105a, 12-15): «I did not neglect to answer you about it, but I began my answer to you with obscure words of Democritus. Concerning the body of magnesia, no sage has entered into this work whose body God has not turned into gold and his spirit into silver, and what holds both of them together is spiritual. So now I am the golden Zosimos, and you are the silvery Theosebeia.» This shows clearly that we have to understand the symbols of gold, silver, body of magnesia etc. not as a description of some outer material that needs to be worked upon, but rather as an enigmatic symbol for an inner process of transformation.

This process of death and resurrection is obviously the consequence of a problem of transference, as we would call it today. A later picture on folio 172a (see fig. 3), shows the great divine Theosebeia with a moon on her head which has a face, i.e. the archetype of the moon is activated. She holds in her arms the body of the great divine Zosimos. He has a sun on his head that has no face, pointing to a sun that seems to be extinguished or dark. This representation is similar to that of Isis and Osiris, or, for a Christian, to Mary and Jesus, well known from statues of that period. It shows that the

Fig. 3: The dead man with a sun on his head, no longer with a face, is the divine aspect of Zosimos. The woman who holds the dead body is the great or divine Theosebeia. She has a a moon on her head which has a face, and on a lead she holds the spirit that is separated from the corpse of Zosimos. Above the two, there is a symbol of the stone of the sages, described in the text as consisting of two parts. The lower part is described as being sky blue, while the upper part is yellow. Out of the upper part pours the divine water which should also be blue. This is the divine water that revives the dead body. The complete picture is on fol. 171b and 172a.

archetypes of sun and moon, which have in previous times been projected onto a superhuman god and goddess, *have entered the realm of humans.*

Zosimos tries to explain to Theosebeia in pictures, symbols and analogies how this divine dimension of their relationship as sun-king and moon-queen has first to be separated from the human reality, and then, in a second step, reunited again with the individual, giving him or her the feeling experience of something divine and eternal *im Weltinnenraum* (Rilke), in his or her psyche. Finding a way to disidentify from initial possession by the archetypes, establishing a durable relationship with this archetypal world, thus becomes the centre of the alchemical work.

Later on the sun and the moon symbolism was taken up and further differentiated in Arabic alchemy, especially by Muḥammad ibn Umail, and in Persia, by Ganjavi Niẓāmī in his famous book called *Laila and Mağnūn.*

The *Muṣḥaf aṣ-ṣuwar* contains the first complete explanation of the process of projection and recollection of the anima, as C. G. Jung named the unconscious feminine side of a man. In chemical symbols and analogies, which are connected to the Ancient Egyptian embalming ritual, Zosimos describes to his beloved Theosebeia how he himself experienced this process as symbolic death and resurrection. Then he explains the same process the other way around for her, Theosebeia, describing her relationship with him.

This topos of resurrection is already found in the Pharaonic *Books of the Afterlife*. In these texts the process was primarily projected onto the time after death, although we read, for instance in the *Amduat*, that the knowledge of the journey of the Sungod through the night-world is not only good and effective for the deceased, but also for a person on earth, «a true remedy, a million times proven».[54] The aim of alchemy is that the adept learns *during his or her lifetime* a way to relate to an inner centre within his or her own psyche. This inner centre corresponds to the God-image of all religions. It is symbolized by the stone of the sages or the anthropos that is first unconscious, buried in the unconscious. Only if an individual continuously relates to it and works on the images emerging from this inner centre, does this nucleus turn into a reliable inner *psychopompos* (psychic guide). This is what C. G. Jung meant by the realisation of the self.

In his treatise *Peri aretes*, Zosimos uses for this 'chemical' process of transformation the Greek word *taricheia*, which means

54 See *The Egyptian Amduat*, ed. by E. Hornung and Th. Abt, p. 51, 74, 83, 383, 386-7 and 390.

embalming.[55] In the *Muṣḥaf aṣ-ṣuwar*, he describes explicitly what happens psychologically during this embalming of the corpse of Osiris—that is the copper-man or the anthropos—until he is resurrected. In his Greek treatises, Zosimos also explains what happens to the copper-man in the form of several dreams. These great dreams, or so-called visions of Zosimos, were interpreted in depth by the Swiss psychiatrist Carl Gustav Jung.[56] In the *Muṣḥaf aṣ-ṣuwar*, we learn more about other dreams of Zosimos and also that he has further pondered over his dreams. He was thus able to become more and more conscious of the *meaning* of this inner process of death and resurrection: It is a symbolic representation of the transformation of his soul which became—thanks to his ongoing process of pondering or distillation, as it was called in alchemical language—more and more purified, ready for the union with God.[57] *That is the mysterium coniunctionis*: the ego of the alchemist is not identified with God, but becomes the witness of the union of his or her soul with the eternal. In the visions of Zosimos, human beings are tortured by a priest figure who is also himself dismembered until he becomes «the man of gold», which is the name for the *anthropos* or the inner god-man in every individual. It is as if during the embalming process, the human side of the dead person and his or her divine core are simultaneously and mutually tortured in order to produce the immortal inner personality, the philosophers' stone. The embalming process which, until now, we knew only from its outer manipulations in Ancient Egypt, is revealed by Zosimos to be a symbol for an inner process, which is no longer projected onto the afterlife. It now takes place within the psyche of the living alchemist when he works on the philosophers' stone, i.e. on the creation of a solidified personality. Such an individual is ready for the journey of continuous rejuvenation in the Pharaonic *nun,* as it is described, for instance, in the *Amduat.* Today we understand the *nun* as being a symbol for the collective unconscious.

The *Muṣḥaf aṣ-ṣuwar* shows the process of a gradual disidentification of Zosimos from being in the grip of the inner god-man Hermes, and seeking to unite as Sol with Theosebeia, in whom he saw Luna. In a later picture (see fig. 4), we see the resurrected Zosimos with his inner

55 M. Mertens, *Mem. auth.*, X. 55. See also M.-L. von Franz, *On Dreams and Death*, p.103.

56 C. G, Jung, "The Visons of Zosimos", *Coll. Works*, Vol. 13, p. 57 f.

57 See a similar document in Th. Abt, "The Great Vision of Muḥammad ibn Umail" (2003), now reprinted in Th. Abt, *Psychological Commentary on Ibn Umail's Hall ar-rumūz*, CALA I B.

«Other-One» who gradually came into consciousness as a result of his constant relationship to the dream-world. This «Other-One», on the other side of the sprouting tree, points with his left hand to the earth, and with his right hand, he shows Zosimos what grows in between them. It seems to be a palm tree, which can be understood as a symbol for Zosimos' tree of life.

In the last picture of our book (see fig. 5), Theosebeia is depicted in the left half of the picture with a moon on her head that has no face. The woman in the right half has a moon on her head that has a face. Her head is remarkably larger than the one of Theosebeia. This greater woman corresponds to the «Other-One», or the god-man in the picture of Zosimos that we see on the opposite page 42. We can understand her as the great woman of Theosebeia or the female aspect of her inner self. The moon on her head has the same suffering face as the human face of Theosebeia. In a surprisingly clear way this shows the mutual suffering of the human and the divine. The painful separation of Theosebeia from this supra-human female and her containing this experience inside as an earthly woman, leads to her ability to disidentify from this female aspect of the divine, and to an incarnation of the female aspect of the self. This is the result of the alchemical process for the woman. In Latin alchemy, this was summarized in the famous *solve et coagula.*

At the end of the *Muṣḥaf aṣ-ṣuwar*, we find a concise formulation of the goal of the work: «She said: "Then tell me what you say about the alabaster." He said: "It is the lime. When it became a stone, we named it alabaster because of its intense whiteness. As for the lime (we called it this) because it conceals fire in it, in the same way as the fire is concealed in the lime of ordinary people." (fol. 220a, 6-9)[...] Later she said: "Tell me more." He said: "There is more to say about it than can be said in words." She said: "In spite of that, tell me!" He said: "The sage said: 'It is a stone-not a stone, known-not known, precious-cheap, and it is the only thing that is good for dyeing. This is because when the heat of the fire hits this stone, it is destroyed and it becomes a spirit that is single-unique (*fard*) in its working and there is no other stone which does its work." She said: "Why is that so?" He said: "Because it is what makes the copper white, what makes it red, and what turns it into a spirit." She said: "Is it single-unique from the beginning?" He said: "When it reaches this stage that you asked me about concerning its names, it is single-unique with regard to the name because everything is collected in it. However, before that it was not

Fig. 4: (fol. 157a) On the left side of the picture we see the resurrected Zosimos while his «Other-One» is on the right side. This «Other-One» points with his left hand toward the earth below. With his right hand, he shows what grows between the two of them. The tree with the three twigs or branches seems to be a palm tree that can be understood as a symbol for Zosimos' tree of life.

Fig. 5: (fol. 210b) On the left side of the picture we see Theosebeia, represented with a *hilāl* (a new moon or moon crescent) on her head. On the right side we see a woman with a larger head, carrying on her head a moon with a face. She can be understood as the «Other-One» or the greater woman in Theosebeia. Between the two, something like a small tree is growing. Around the head of Theosebeia we see some yellow, the same colour as on the robe of the greater woman. It is like a halo.

single, but it was composed. Then the dyes were collected in it, therefore it became one, like a human being which contains various things."» (fol. 220a, 16 -220b, 8) This makes it clear that the goal of the opus alchemicum—the creation of the stone of the sages—is the creation of the unique, unified personality, formed by continuously nourishing, and thus at the same time being nourished by, the inner God-figure, symbol of the archetype of the self in its material and spirtual aspect. The stone of the sages, symbol for the solidified personality, thus reconciles the opposites of the divine water and the devilish fire that is then concealed or contained within the individual and no longer suppressed, rejected or, on the other hand, lived out uncontained.

Manfred Ullmann summarized Jung's view of alchemy by writing that «for Carl Gustav Jung, alchemy with all its symbols and processes is the projection of the archetypes and the collective unconscious on matter. The opus alchemicum is in fact the process of individuation by which one becomes the self.»[58] This is only partly correct. The fact is that Jung was able to document in careful detail—on the basis of those texts that were available to him—that the great work is a process of purification of the soul of the adept that can then unite with the self, using chemical symbols for the description of this inner-psychic process. This bold hypothesis is now clearly confirmed by the *Muṣḥaf aṣ-ṣuwar*. So, contrary to Ullmann, who misunderstood Jung's research, the goal of the alchemical work is precisely *not* an identification of the adept with the self, but the coagulation of a durable *relationship* of the adept's soul with the self.

The self is a symbol for the experience of an inner-psychic centre that is in itself light and dark, male and female, a union of opposites. The final union of the soul with this «two-one» self is again a *rebis*, a two-oneness, as innumerable symbols of the stone of the sages, especially the often mentioned lead-copper, confirm. The ego of the adept is then the fourth 'pillar' in this quaternio, allowing the *quinta essentia* to become alive or real. That would correspond to an entirely new attitude. It is a durable connection of the day- and the night-world, of consciousness and the unconscious, of the mortal and the immortal. This differs from a mystic like Hallaj, who publicly declared *ana al-haqq*, «I am the Truth» (one of the names of Allah).

58 M. Ullmann, *Natur- und Geheimwiss*, p. 146: «Für [...] Jung ist die Alchemie, [...], eine Projektion der Archetypen und des kollektiven Unbewussten auf die Materie. Das opus alchymicum sei in Wirklichkeit der Individuationsprozess, durch den man zum Selbst wird.» (Ed.'s translation)

To the best of my knowledge, the *Muṣḥaf aṣ-ṣuwar* is the most complete text that explains, in a dialectic way, the symbolic meaning of the mystery of the union of inner opposites, the opus alchemicum. It confirms the hypothesis of C. G. Jung that the aim of the alchemical work is indeed the psychological development of the adept. Jung first worked out and formulated this hypothesis in his book *Psychology and Alchemy* (first published in German in 1944, now in *Collected Works* Volume 12), then in his book *The Psychology of the Transference*, and later in his *Alchemical Studies*, which culminated in his summa, the *Mysterium coniunctionis*.[59]

7. The Muṣḥaf aṣ-ṣuwar and its Relationship to the Kitāb al-mafātīḥ fī aṣ-ṣanᶜa

Our *Muṣḥaf aṣ-ṣuwar* is closely related to the *Kitāb al-mafātīḥ fī aṣ-ṣanᶜa* (The Book of Keys to the Work), a commentary on a ten-treatise work ascribed to Democritus. The 10th-century Arabic catalogue of Ibn Nadīm lists the *Kitāb al-mafātīḥ fī aṣ-ṣanᶜa*, which may also be the *Βίβλος κλειδῶν*, mentioned as a work of Zosimos by a Greek alchemist (*Coll. Alch. Grecs* II, p. 277).

The *Kitāb al-mafātīḥ*, like the *Muṣḥaf aṣ-ṣuwar*, is written to «my lady» Theosebeia. Much of the *Kitāb al-mafātīḥ* is in dialogue form, with Theosebeia repeatedly asking Zosimos to «complete your favours to me». The content of both books is consistently similar. There is the same emphasis on the fact that there is just one operation (*Kitāb al-mafātīḥ*, fol. 41b, 11, see, for example, *Muṣḥaf aṣ-ṣuwar*, fol. 110a, 5), and the same central role for Democritus, "the head of the sages of his time" (fol. 48b, 10, see *Muṣḥaf aṣ-ṣuwar*, fol. 106a, 2). The operation in both books centres on a composition of vapours (fol. 44b, 8, see *Muṣḥaf aṣ-ṣuwar*, fol. 14b, 12-14). It has the same essential feature of extracting the subtle with 'gentleness' (fol. 44b, 5, see *Muṣḥaf aṣ-ṣuwar*, fol. 190a, 1-5), from all four natures.

59 These books are now published as "The Psychology of the Transference" in *Collected Works* Vol. 16 (first publ. as a separate book in German 1946), *Alchemical Studies* in Vol. 13, and *Mysterium coniunctionis* in Vol. 14 (first German edition 1956).

(fol. 57a, 10; see *Muṣḥaf aṣ-ṣuwar,* fol. 9a, 3), the mixing of like with like (fol. 44a, 19; see fol. 21b, 10), and the need to bind the fugitive spirit (fol. 45a, 14; see fol. 74b, 7). The books have analogies in common, for example that of copper with the human being (fol. 59a, 21; see fol. 45b, 17).

In at least one passage, the text of the two works is the same:

Kitāb al-mafātīḥ fī aṣ-ṣanʿa
(fol. 71b, 4–7):[60]

«I said to him: "Then why did the sages name the composition etesios?" He said: "Because according to them the etesian is born once a year, and it has different colours that change each month from one colour to another. That is why they named their composition the etesian stone because it changes at every level of the operation from one colour to another."»

Muṣḥaf aṣ-ṣuwar
(fol. 38b, 10–14):[61]

«She said: "Then why did the sages name the composition the etesian stone?" He said: "Because the etesian stone is born once a year, it has different colours, and it is born and changes each month from one colour to another. That is why they named their composition the etesian stone because it changes at every level of the operation from one colour to another."»

Our dialogue was written *after* the *Kitāb al-mafātīḥ*, in spite of the introduction to the latter, which says «it was the last one they wrote for her» (fol. 41a, 3–4). The *Muṣḥaf aṣ-ṣuwar* refers back to *The Keys*: «Did I not send you special epistles, dedicating them to you? After them I sent the *Sarṭamīṭā* but it did not convince you. Then I sent you *The Keys* and other things, hoping that you would understand the anthology from the

60 فقلت له: فما بال الحكماء سمّت التركيب اطسيوس؟ فقال: لأنّ اطسيوس فيما زعموا يُولد في كلّ سنة وإنّ له ألوان مختلفة يتحوّل من لون إلى لون في كلّ شهر. فلذلك سمّوا تركيبهم حجر اطسيوس، لأنّه يتحوّل في كلّ درجة من التدبير من لون إلى لون.

61 قالت: فما بال الحكماء سمّوا التركيب بحجر اطيسيوس؟ قال: لأنّ حجر اطيسيوس يُولد في كلّ سنة مرّةً وله ألوان مختلفة، وهو يُولد ويتحوّل من لون إلى لون في كلّ شهر. فلذلك سمّوا تركيبهم حجر اطيسيوس، لأنّه يتحوّل في كلّ درجة من التدبير من لون إلى لون.

works of the sages that I collected for you. But you said: "I do not need them. Rather I want the books of the sages themselves [...]"» (fol. 90a, 5–8). (One may note in passing that the Greek term 'anthology', a collection of flowers, was retained in the translation into Arabic).

Some similar passages show how the *Book of Pictures* makes use of *Kitāb al-mafātīḥ* material. For example, Zosimos' dream of the young man fighting the dragon is in both books, and in the *Muṣḥaf aṣ-ṣuwar* Theosebeia refers back to the earlier account of the dream: «Tell me, O Zosimos, about your big dream about the young man you saw fighting the dragon ...» (fol. 82b, 2 f.). The *Kitāb al-mafātīḥ* account (fol. 73b, 1 -74a, 3) begins with Zosimos claiming that fellow alchemists confused him by saying that one gum had to be improved with a similar one. Zosimos went to sleep sadly and sorrowfully and dreamt (now follows a summarized version) that he saw himself standing on a rock on the east bank of the Nile. From there he saw on the other side of the river a young man fighting a dragon. «The young man [...] called to me for help, and indicated that I should cross the river. In one leap I came to where he was. I took a bar of iron, and leaped towards the dragon, ready to fight it. Then the dragon turned towards me and puffed at me once, throwing me back 28 cubits (1 cubit = 58cm), but not killing me. I turned back and attacked a second time». The young man stops Zosimos and shows him how the dragon can be defeated by using water. Then he takes the dragon and squeezes it, so that «out of it came the egg of a crocodile.» He then works the egg «in the way the stomach cooks the food inside it, so that some of the subtle part of that food would come out, and it is the four natures, the phlegm, the blood, and the two bitter things (*murratain*).» The young man guides Zosimos to the etesian stone, in which the dragon and his wife can be seen. At first the dragon and his wife arc old and unable to move, but as a single dragon it is rejuvenated and flees in fear of Zosimos. The young man then shows Zosimos a shining lance. Zosimos asks the young man about the right time to take the eyes of the dragon and is told that the wife's eyes must also be taken. At this point, the young man begins the work on the dragon, cutting it with the lance to reveal a series of colours. He then sorts the groups of colours that are similar to our science: the diamond-colour, claudianus-colour, iron pyrite-colour, red cinnabar-colour, grey potash-colour and yellow russet-colour. Then «he went to the egg of the crocodile and broke it. He separated the redness, the white and the moisture, and purified the whiteness with the whiteness, and the redness with the redness.» However, while the young man is preoccupied with his work, the dragon leaped up again and hissed at them. This time it is Zosimos who cuts off its head by throwing water (at the dragon). The young man vows to make the dragon a decayed corpse, and causes its more subtle matter to rise up into the air. He squeezes out the dragon's poison, being careful not to breathe it in. Finally, the young man threatens Zosimos with death and adds that if Zosimos reveals this secret of Hermes, the dragon will come back to life. Zosimos awakes in terror.

The *Muṣḥaf aṣ-ṣuwar* gives a briefer account of the same dream, leaving away the circumstances of the dream, but with some new details. It is reported in this way (fol. 82b, 4-17): «When the young man saw me, he called to me for help against the enemy (female) of Memphis. I took one leap and came upon that enemy. I took a two-pronged iron, wanting to kill the dragon. But it turned towards me, hissed in my face, and threw me back 28 cubits, yet I did not fall down but remained upright. Then I leapt at it again, but the young man whom I wanted to help said: "Stop!" Then he took water and with it cut off the head of the dragon. He went close to it, saying: "Give me what you swallowed!"» (This points to a relationship with the Pharaonic Apophis, the enemy of the Sungod.) He takes the crocodile's egg, which Zosimos, thinking it a dragon's egg, feels to be unjust. The young man explains that it is«"a crocodile's egg. But it does not rot, and especially it does not become blood yet. But take the food which has been cooked in the stomach, and divide it equally and justly into four (parts) for the corners of the body. Then gather it and turn it into one unmixed thing, pure ashes. Then suspend it and raise it up until it becomes purified.» The *Muṣḥaf aṣ-ṣuwar* mentions at the end that the young man «led me to the mountain and I found all of a sudden that I am a rock like alabaster». Then Theosebeia asks Zosimos about another matter.

The comparison of these two reports of Zosimos' dream suggests that it is a feature of the *Muṣḥaf aṣ-ṣuwar* to compile elements from previous works of Zosimos in summarized form.

8. Texts of Zosimos as the main Source of the Kitāb al-ḥabīb and the Kitāb Qirāṭis

The *Kitāb al-ḥabīb* is a compilation of quotations from Greek alchemists. Many passages are from Zosimos, and as a number of these are from the *Muṣḥaf aṣ-ṣuwar*, it is likely that the *ḥabīb* (lover) is Zosimos, the lover of Theosebeia. We can trace large sections of the text back to the *Muṣḥaf aṣ-ṣuwar.*

Two extracts presented here testify to this connection. They will have to stand as evidence of a much larger amount of material that originates in the *Muṣḥaf aṣ-ṣuwar*. These extracts show that in the *Muṣḥaf aṣ-ṣuwar*, Zosimos' answers are longer, confirming that this text must be the original one, whereas the *Kitāb al-ḥabīb* tends to abbreviate.

Muṣḥaf aṣ-ṣuwar (fol. 189b, 10–14):[62]	*Kitāb al-ḥabīb* (p. 58, 2–4):[63]
«She said: "Tell me, why did the sages name the rust 'poison of honey'?" He said: "When the water is cooked with the bodies, it takes their taste, in the same way as water takes the taste of honey when it is mixed with it. Like that the sages extracted the dye from the bodies by the moisture. Then they added it to whatever they wished."»	«She said: "Why did they name the poison 'honey'?" He said: "It is because when this water mixes with the bodies, it takes their nature, in the same way as water takes the taste of honey when it is mixed with it."»

Muṣḥaf aṣ-ṣuwar (fol. 118a, 12–118b, 7):[64]	*Kitāb al-ḥabīb* (p. 66, 1–8):[65]
«She said: "I see that these things are fugitives." He said: "Yes. Therefore the sages preferred the fugitives to those that do not flee." She said: "Does this fugitive	«She said: "I see that these things are fugitives." He said: "Yes. Therefore the sages preferred the fugitives to those that do not flee." She said: "Does this fugitive

have a name by which it is known?" He said: "How many names it has!" She said: "Then tell me some." He said: "It is the dragon eating its tail, for the egg has been divided into four parts, thus when they were operated on and mixed, they turned into one thing, like the four natures of the world." She said: "How does it eat its tail?" He said: "When its similar one that is like it, enters into it, it (the dragon) eats it (the similar) and turns it (the similar) into water. Then what the dragon ate turned into a body. Concerning their comparison of their egg to the egg of a hen, that is because the colours of their egg are like the colours of an egg (of a hen). And secondly they already knew before they dissolved it that it has a flying fugitive in it, which

have a name by which it is known?" He said: "How many names it has!" She said: "Then tell me some." He said: "It is the dragon eating its tail, for the egg has been divided into four parts, thus when they were operated on and mixed, they turned into one thing, like the four natures of the world." She said: "How does it eat its tail?" He said: "When its similar one that is like it, enters into it, it (the dragon) eats it (the similar) and turns it (the similar) into water. Then what the dragon ate turned into a body.

She said: "Tell me about your statement: 'Do not reject burning the bodies'…"»

62 قالت: فأنبئني، ما بال الحكماء سمّت الصدأ سمّ العسل؟ قال: إنّ الماء لمّا طبخ مع الأجساد أخذ طعمها كما يأخذ الماء طعم العسل حين يمزج به. وكذلك الحكماء استخرجت الصبغ بالرطوبة من الأجساد ثمّ أدخلته حيث شاءت.

63 قالت: فلِمَا سمّوا السمّ عسلاً؟ قال: لأنّ هذا الماء إذا اختلط بالأجساد أخذ طبيعتها كما يأخذ الماء طعم العسل إذا خلط به.

64 قالت: فأرى هذه الأشياء أوابق. قال: نعم، ولذلك اختارت الحكماء الأوابق على التي لا تأبق. قالت: وهل لهذا الآبق اسم به يُعرف؟ قال: ما أكثر أسماءه! قالت: فسمّ لي بعضها. قال: هو التنين الذي يأكل ذنبه. لأنّ البيضة قُسمت على أربعة أجزاء، فلمّا دبرت واختلطت وصارت شيئًا واحدًا كنحو من طبائع الدنيا الأربعة. قالت: وكيف يأكل ذنبه؟ قال: إذا دخل معه شبهه الذي هو مثله، فأكله وأصاره ماءً. ثمّ صار الذي أكل التنين جسدًا. وأمّا تشبيههم بيضتهم ببيضة الدجاجة، فذلك لأنّ ألوان بيضتهم كألوان البيضة، وأمّا الثاني من قبل إذابتهم إيّاها، فقد عرفوا أنّ فيها آبقًا طيّارًا، وهو الذي يأبق بأصحابه. وكما في يدك بيضة الدجاجة وأبت تعرفين أنّها ليست ببيضة دجاجة ولا جسدها، وأنّه إذا جُعلت تحت الدجاجة بيضتها خرج منها الطائر. وكذلك بيضة الحكماء، فيها جسد ونفس وفيها ما يأبق وهي المغنيسيا وقد سمّتها بها ولكن حوّل اسمها.

65 قالت: فأرى هذه الأشياء أوابق. قال: نعم، ولذلك اختارت الحكماء الأوابق على التي لا تأبق. قالت: وهل لهذا الآبق اسم يُعرف به؟ قال: ما أكثر أسماءه! قالت: فسمّ لي بعضها. قال: هو التنين الذي يأكل ذنبه. لأنّ البيضة قُسمت على أربعة أجزاء، فلمّا دبّرت واختلطت صارت شيئًا واحدًا كنحو من طبائع الدنيا الأربعة. قالت: فكيف يأكل ذنبه؟ قال: أدخل معه شبهه الذي هو مثله، فأكله وأصاره ماءً. ثمّ صار الذي أكل التنين جسدًا. قالت: فأفتني عن قولك لا تنافي حرق الأجساد...

escapes with its companions. And just as you have the egg of the hen which we also have, and you know that it is only an egg of a hen and its body, but when its egg is put under the hen, a bird comes out of it. The egg of the sages is like that. It has in it a body and a soul, and it has also in it what escapes, which is the magnesia; and they named it like that, but its name has been changed."»

After our second quote from the *Kitāb al-ḥabīb*, the topic of the dragon switches to a quite different question from Theosebeia, concerning the burning of the bodies in order to extract their souls. The style and content of the *Kitāb al-ḥabīb* resemble other texts of Zosimos, and about one quarter of the way through (from p. 45.1 onward), the *Kitāb al-ḥabīb* becomes a dialogue between Zosimos and Theosebeia. Many of the questions and answers can be traced to our *Muṣḥaf aṣ-ṣuwar*, although the quotations do not follow the original order. For example, *Kitāb al-ḥabīb* edition in *Chimie au Moyen Age* p. 47, 9-14 = *Muṣḥaf aṣ-ṣuwar* fol. 7b, 14-19; p. 48, 2-7 = fol. 66b, 10-16; p. 49, 16-19 = fol. 55b, 9-13; p. 50, 15-51, 17 = fol. 117a, 19-118a, 19, etc. We also find in the *Kitāb al-ḥabīb* the characteristic expression «my lady» (*ayyatuhā al-marʾa*) on p. 67.7. Zosimos is mentioned, but not consistently, and new names are introduced into the dialogue between student and teacher, names such as Pythagoras and the Byzantine Gregorius. There are many passages in dialogue form in the *Kitāb al-ḥabīb* which cannot be traced to the *Muṣḥaf aṣ-ṣuwar*, although they are similar in style and content. Where these come from is unclear.

The *Kitāb Qirāṭis al-ḥakīm* was edited with the *Kitāb al-ḥabīb* in Chimie au Moyen Age III (pages 1–33), and the relationship between this work and Zosimos should also be noted. When we compare the *Kitāb Qirāṭis* and the *Kitāb al-mafātīḥ,* we find that it is mainly (from page 6, 3) an epitome, turning into a word-for-word copy, of part of the Zosimos' work (fol. 58a, 12–75a.4, including the dream of the young man and the dragon). However, the name Zosimos is either suppressed or replaced by the name Qirāṭis (perhaps from Ḏūmiqrāṭis, Democritus).

9. The Greek Origin of the Turba philosophorum?

The author of the *Turba philosophorum* must have known the *Muṣḥaf aṣ-ṣuwar*. This can be seen first in a passage found in both books, which also relates back to Ancient Egypt.

Muṣḥaf aṣ-ṣuwar
(On fol. 174b, 13–175a, 9):[66]

«She said: "Tell me about when he says: 'The tree from which whoever eats will never feel hungry again.'" He said: "We were told (about it) by the sages, who continued searching for the nature which is called their tree till they found it, and ate its fruit. I asked them about it, and about its state. They

Turba philosophorum in the
sermon LVIII of Balgus[67]

«He [asked]: "Why have you omitted to describe that tree from which (it was said) whoever eats of its fruit shall never again feel hungry?" Balgus [said]: "I was told by a certain person who followed the science till he discovered this same tree and how, after appropriately operating on it, he extracted the

66 قالت: فأنبئني عن قوله الشجرة التي من أكل منها لم يجع أبدًا. قال: قد أعلمتنا الحكماء الذين لم يزالوا طالبين الطبيعة التي سمّيت شجرتها حتّى أصابوها فأكلوا ثمرة تلك الشجرة. فسألتُهم عنها وعن حالها، فوصفوها لي بالبياض الخالص وذكروا أنّها موجودة، ولكن ما تغني مسألتك إيّاي عنها، ولم يذكروا تمام أمرها ولا غذاءها. قالت: فإذ ستروا ذلك، فأنعم عليّ بتمام ما ستروا. قال: أفعل فافهمي، فإنّي إنّما أجيبك رمزًا. قالت: فافعل. قال: فخذي تلك الشجرة البيضاء، فابني لها بيتًا مدوّرًا مظلمًا يحيط ذلك البيت الندى. واجعلي فيه معها رجلاً كبيرًا عمره مائة سنة وأكثر، ثمّ اغلقي عليه وعليها وأنعمي الإغلاق لأنّ لا يصل إليهما ريح، واتركيهما في بيتهما ذلك مائة وثمانين يومًا. واعلمي أنّ ذلك الشيخ يصير صبيًا حدثًا. فعجبًا لكم من طبائع سير ذلك الشيخ في جسد شاب، فصار الأب ابنًا، فتبارك الله أحسن الخالقين، خالق ما يشاء. لعمرك يا تيوسانية لقد صدقت الحكماء إذ سمّوا ذلك الماء حياةً لأنّ من شرب من ذلك الماء مات ثمّ عاش فصار شابًا. واعلمي أنّ الحديد لا يصدأ إلاّ برطوبة هذا الماء...

67 J. Ruska, *Turba Philosophorum*, Berlin 1931, reprint Berlin 1970 and Frankfurt am Main 2002. p. 161,15 ff. (Editor's translation). The Latin text runs: «Et ille: "Cur arborem dimisisti narrare, cuius fructum qui comedit, non escuriet unquam?" Et Balgus: "Notificavit mihi quidam, qui scientiam consecutus est, quousque illam invenies arborem convenienter operatus est ac fructu extracto comedit. Mihi autem quaenti eam mera descripsit albedine, ratus quod ipsa absque labore invenitur; dispositionis autem eius perfectio ei cibus est. Mihi autem quaerenti, qualiter cibo nutriatur, || quousque fructiferet, ait: 'Accipe illam albam arborem, et aedifica ei domum circumdantem, rotundam, tenebrosam, rore cicumdatam, et impone ei hominem magnae aetatis, centum annorum, et claude super eos, et necte fortiter, ne ad eos ventus seu pulvis perveniat; deinde centum et ocoginta diebus in sua domo <eos> domitte. Dico, quod ille senex de fructibus illius arbores comedere non cessat ad numeri perfectionem, quousque senex ille iuvenis fiat. O quam mirae naturae, quae illius animam senis in iuvenile corpus transformaverunt, ac pater filius factus est! Benedictus sit Deus, creator optimus!'"»

described it to me as pure whiteness, and they said that it exists. But your asking me about it is not sufficient to leave the matter there. They did not give a complete explanation of it, nor of its nourishment." She said: "If they veiled it, then do me a favour with a complete explanation of what they veiled." He said: "I will, so understand for I will answer you symbolically." She said: "Please do!" He said: "Take that white tree and build a round, dark house for it, with dew surrounding that house. Put an old man, more than a hundred years old, in the house with the tree. Close him up with her (the tree), and be careful to close it in such a way that no wind reaches the two. Leave them in their house for 180 days.

Know that this old man will become a young boy. How astonishing are you natures! That old man was changed into the body of a youth, so that a father turned into a son. God be praised, the best creator, the creator of whatever He wants. O Theosebeia, upon your life, the sages were right when they named that water 'life', because whoever drinks from that water dies and comes back to life, and he turns into a youth. [...]"»

fruit and ate of it. But when I asked him concerning the growth and development, he described that pure whiteness, thinking that the same is found without any laborious disposition, the perfection of its operation and its nourishment. But when I asked how it is nourished with food until it bears fruit,

he said: 'Take that white tree, and build a house for it, which shall wholly surround it, being circular, dark, encircled by dew, and place in it a very old man of a hundred years; close them up, and secure the door in order that neither wind nor dust can reach them.

Then leave them for 180 days in their home. I say that this man shall not cease to eat of the fruit of that tree till the completion of the number [of the days] until the old man shall become a youth. O what wonderful natures, which have transformed the soul of that old man into a body of a youth, transforming the father into the son! Praise to God, the best creator!'"»

The roots of this parable can be traced back to Ancient Egyptian, especially to the *Royal Books of the Afterlife*. The Ancient Egyptian calendar had 360 days. The 180 days needed for the old man (according to the Turba it is his soul) to become a youth again is the topos of the renewal of the Sungod. He becomes rejuvenated in the arms of the white tree, which is a symbol of Hathor, the goddess of the West, i.e. the land of the dead. Through her, the old Sungod dies and is reborn, turning into a youth after the journey through the «night of the year» (180 days). The water that Zosimos then explains to Theosebeia is also mentioned in the *Turba*, sermon LIX of Nofil (Theophilus). This shows the Pharaonic origin of this parable: Zosimos speaks of the water of life that first kills and then gives birth again to the youth, a well-known feature of the primordial water *nun*.

Julius Ruska has worked out the Arabic origin of the *Turba Philosophorum*. Martin Plessner, in his extensive review of the book, tried to find a key to an exact dating of the *Turba* by showing that the parable mentioned there, which he calls the «international legend of the *Giftmädchen*», originates in India. Then he states that «this legend is not to be found in Graeco-Roman literature», and it came to the knowledge of the Arabs only «at the beginning of the 10th century.» Then he concludes from this assumption that the *Turba* must be dated around 900.[68] But this archetypal parable of the *Giftmädchen,* the woman killing her lover, can be

68 See Martin Plessner, *Vorsokratische Philosophie und griechische Alchemie in arabisch-lateinischer Überlieferung*, Studien zu Text und Inhalt der Turba Philosophorum, Wiesbaden 1975, p. 122-130. Plessner writes on p. 123: «Was hier zur Veranschaulichung (oder Verdeckung) einer alchemistischen Operation dient, ist nichts als die bekannte internationale Legende vom Giftmädchen, das die Männer in der Umarmung vergiftet und tötet. Der Ursprung dieser Vorstellung ist in Indien gelegen; die vollständigste mir bekannte Zusammenstellung der Nachrichten darüber enthält die grosse Abhandlung von Wilhelm Hertz *Die Sage vom Giftmädchen*. Diese Sage nun findet sich nicht in der griechisch-römischen Literatur; dagegen ist sie im Islam sehr früh bezeugt. Sie ist bereits in dem aus Indien stammenden Giftbuch des aus dem Anfang des 10. Jahrhunderts erwähnt,» On the basis of this argument Plessner concludes on p. 125: «Da bei der Abfassung der *Turba* durch einen vorislamischen Griechen nicht verständlich ist, woher der Verfasser Kenntnis von dieser Sage haben soll, für einen Araber dagegen selbst ein sehr früher Abfassungstermin der Turba die Bekanntschaft mit der Sage nicht ausschliesst, wie wir gesehen haben, so können nunmehr Einwände gegen den arabischen Ursprung des Werkes nicht mehr erhoben werden.» Plessner could have learnt of the *Muṣḥaf aṣ-ṣuwar* account of the *Giftmädchen* as he criticised the very article of Fuat Sezgin (see n.16) in which the existence of this manuscript of Zosimos was announced.

found in our *Muṣḥaf aṣ-ṣuwar,* frequently mentioned as «*asqūnīa*, murderess of her husband».[69]

In the light of the dialogue of Zosimos and Theosebeia that was presented earlier on page 35 f., it becomes clear that ascunia is not a cover name (*Decknamen*), as Plessner and other historians of alchemy assumed, but is a symbol for the *feminine principle that was experienced by Zosimos with his beloved student Theosebeia.* We read, for instance:

Muṣḥaf aṣ-ṣuwar folio 10b, 19–11a, 14:[70]	The text in the *Turba* (sermo LIX f. of Nofil i.e Theophilius):[71]
«"How amazing! That woman does not agree to be taken for bridal money; and she is not satisfied that her splendour goes to anybody except her husband, although she has poison in her. He does not care about it, and he stays with her and comes together with her until he completes sexual intercourse with her. So her fertilization is complete in order that God increases her children, and God makes it a blessing to whomever He wants."	«In the same way, that woman, fleeing from her own [husband, emendation], with whom she lives, [and] although angry, she does not consider it dignified being overcome, nor that her husband—who madly loves her—should possess her beauty. Thus he keeps awake, contending with her, till he shall have sexual intercourse with her. Thus God makes perfect her children and multiplies the sons according to what pleases Him. His beauty, therefore, is consumed by fire, he

69 Asqūnīa means acacia, having 'murderous' thorns. See J. Ruska, *Turba*, l. c., p. 248, n3.

70 وعجبًا لتلك المرأة كيف لا ترضى [أن] تؤخذ بمهر ولا تطيب نفسًا أن يذهب بهاءها إلاّ زوجها. وإن كان معها سمّ لم يحفل به، يصير معها ويقابلها حتّى يفرغ من جماعها، فيتمّ لقاحها ليكثر الله ولدها، فيجعله الله رزقًا لمن يشاء. قالت: لقد قلت فأحسنت، فأنبئني ما الذي أذهب بهاءها؟ بالنار ذهب بهاءها وبياضها، وبالسخونة صارت رمادًا، ولم تطب نفسًا بذهاب ذلك البهاء إلاّ للذّتها مجامعته. قالت: فزوجها هذا ما هو؟ قال: هو التنين. قالت: فهل يموت؟ قال: لا يموت أبدًا، ولكنّ الحكماء قتلوه بالحيلة والرفق بامرأة قتّالة لأزواجها، لأنّ جوفها مملوء سمًّا وسلاحًا. فتحفر لذلك التنين قبرًا، ثمّ تدخل تلك المرأة معه، فمن شدّة ألفة التنين يلتفّ بتلك المرأة، فكلّما لزم قطّع جسده سلاحها المخلوق معها في جسدها حتّى تتقطّع أوصال ذلك التنين إربًا إربًا. فإذا أيقن التنين أنّ المرأة قد علقت بكلّ مفصل، ألقى يده وأيقن بالهلكة، فصار دمًا. فإذا أيقنت الحكماء أنّه قد صار دمًا تركوه في الشمس أيامًا كثيرةً حتّى يذهب سمّه ويجفّ الدم، فيجدون السرّ قد ظهر، فعند ذلك الريح الغامر.

71 J. Ruska, *Turba Philosophorum*, ibid., p. 162 (Editor's translation). The Latin text reads: «Similiter illa mulier suos fugiens generos, quibus parte quamvis irata domestica fit, nec dignatur se superari, nec ut suus coniunx suum habeat decorem, qui furibunde eam diligit et cum ea pugnans vigilat, quosque concubitus cum ea peragat, eius foetus Deus perficiat, fil-

She said: "What you have just said is wonderful. Then tell me what caused her splendour to disappear." He said: "With the fire, her splendour and her whiteness went away, and with the heat she turned into ashes. And she was not happy that this splendour disappeared, but she enjoyed the intercourse with him." She said: "Who is this husband of hers?" He said: "He is the dragon." She said: "Does he die then?" He said: "He never dies, but the sages killed him by trickery and the gentleness of a woman who is murderous to her husbands. This is because her inside is full of poison and weapons. Thus she digs a tomb for the dragon. Then that woman enters it (the tomb) with him. Because of the intense desire of the dragon, he embraces that woman. Then, whenever he clings (to her), her weapons which are created in her body, cut up his body until that dragon's parts are cut into pieces. When the dragon is sure that the woman is attached with every part,

who does not approach his wife except by reason of desirousness. For when the term is finished he turns to her.

I also make known to you that the dragon never dies. But the philosophers have given over to death the woman who slays her spouses, for the belly of that woman is full of weapons and venom. Let, therefore, a sepulchre be dug for the dragon. Then let that woman be buried with him who is strongly joined with that woman. The more he clasps her and turns around her, the more his body is cut up into parts by the female weapons created in the body of the woman.

iosque multiplicet prout sibi placet. Eius autem decor igne consumptus est, qui ad suum non tendit coniugem nisi libidinis causae; termino enim ad eam vertitur. Item notifico vobis, quod Draco nunquam moritur. Philosophi tamen mulierem suos coniuges interficientem neci dederunt; illius enim mulieris venter armis plenus est et veneno. Effodiatur igitur sepulchrum illi Draconi, et sepeliatur illa mulier cum eo qui cum illa fortiter vinctus muliere, quanto magis eam nectit et volvitur circa eam, tanto corpus eius mulieribus armis in mulieris corpore creatis in pertes secatur. Videns se autem in mulieris artubus mixtu, certus fit morte, et totus vertitur in sanguinem. Videntes autem philosophi (ipsum) in sanguinem versum, in sole dimittunt per dies, quousque eius lentitudo consumatur et arescat et venenum inveniunt illud; iam apparens tunc ventus est occultus.»

he surrenders, and he is sure of his destruction. Then he turns into blood. When the sages are sure that he has turned into blood, they leave him in the sun for many days, until his poison goes away and the blood dries up. Then they find that the secret has appeared. At this point comes an overwhelming wind."»

When he mixes with the limbs of the woman he becomes secure of death,
and the whole is turned into blood. But when the philosophers see that he has turned into blood, they leave him in the sun for some days, until the softness is consumed, and the blood dries up, and they find that venom which now is manifest. Then the hidden wind appears.»

Fig. 6: The immortal dragon and the murderess of her husband, from M. Maier's *Atalanta fugiens* (1618). The parable is already found in the *Muṣḥaf aṣ-ṣuwar*.

The quote given from the *Muṣḥaf aṣ-ṣuwar* is the same text that we find in the *Turba*, given by Plessner as the main argument for dating this text. In the light of this new evidence, however, his proposal to date the *Turba* around 900 is no longer acceptable.

A further striking parallel between the *Muṣḥaf aṣ-ṣuwar* and the *Turba* leads finally to the question of whether we have in this text of Zosimos a key that will allow us to trace the origin and the date of the *Turba;* we might even have here parts of the original *Ur-Turba* (First *Turba philosophorum*). We find a passage which could have provided the seed for the framework story of the *Turba*. Zosimos tells of a leading philosopher who called a crowd of philosophers together in order to debate the conjunction of male and female (fol. 88a.6.-13): «Then Būtīṭos, the head of the sages, said: "Gather around me the sages of the countries so that they can tell me why they united this man and this woman." When they (the sages) were assembled, the sage (Būtīṭos) asked them. One of them said: "When this man and this woman had the child, Ars (Ares, Mars) was in the East, the woman (note in the margin: Venus) was in the West, and the Sun was in the middle of the sky, in Aries, the house of Ars. The woman (Venus) was pointing to the East, and Ars was pointing to the West." Another sage said: "By God, these two must unite in the house of the king." Another sage said: "Indeed, the love between the two would not have happened if they had not united at the time when the Sun was in the house of its height."» Then other sages joined in the discussion. This passage indicates that the dialogue between Zosimos and Theosebeia could have been the basis of inspiration for a later Greek or Arab creation of one of the earlier synodos of the Greek philosophers.

Our examples confirm that the *Turba* originates in Egypt since it uses the same symbolic images as found here in the *Muṣḥaf aṣ-ṣuwar*. They further dismiss Ruska's (and later also Plessner's) assumption of an Arabic origin of the *Turba* and corroborate the hypothesis of M. Berthelot and F. Sezgin that this book could have a Hellenistic origin.[72] In the light of these and additional new facts, all coming from hitherto neglected Arabic alchemical manuscripts, the problem of dating the *Turba* and reviewing *and thus clarifying* its Latin translation must be treated anew.

72 See M. Berthelot, *La Chimie au Moyen Age,* Vol. I, p. 253-269, and F. Sezgin, *Geschichte des arabischen Schrifttums*, IV, p. 64f.

10. The Muṣḥaf aṣ-ṣuwar and the Rosarium philosophorum

The *Muṣḥaf aṣ-ṣuwar* found its way into the Arabic world and inspired certain introverted lovers of the soul, especially Ǧābir ibn Ḥaiyān and Muḥammad ibn Umail.[73] Its pictures must have later on somehow found their way to Europe, where they became a source of inspiration for various Latin alchemists such as the author of the illustrated book entitled *Rosarium philosophorum* (15th cent.), and later the creator of one of the *Mutus liber* (16th cent.).

When we look at the *Rosarium* pictures, it is remarkable to see that the symbolism of the sun and moon is also to be found in some of the pictures. But these luminaries are no longer connected to two specifically named human beings, as is seen so clearly in the *Muṣḥaf aṣ-ṣuwar*.[74] This shows that in the transition from Greek and Arabic alchemy to Latin alchemy, the individual relationship faded into the background, and the adept and his soror mystica became simply the archetypal sun-king and moon-queen, like figures in a fairy tale.

It needed the experience and the boldness of C. G. Jung to look at the psychological facts, and thus rediscover the connection between the pictures of the *Rosarium* and psychology.[75] In his book *The Psychology of Transference*, Jung used this picture series as a guide to show how the process of individuation develops in a really deep analysis, and how the relationship between analyst and analysand gradually finds its right form if the two are able to separate (solve) the upper, divine dimension (sun and moon) *and* the lower, subhuman or instinctual level (the snakes and the dogs) from the human level. Then they are able, *deo concedente,* to experience the mysterium coniunctionis of the transpersonal opposites within themselves, represented in our text by the great Zosimos and the great Theosebeia, and to allow the experience of this reconciliation of the opposites to coagulate in their now re-humanized relationship on earth.

The conclusive argument for the continuity of culture in the Western World can be found in a treatise called *Rosinus ad Euthiciam*, which is

73 See Th. Abt, *Psychological Commentary to Ibn Umail's Ḥall ar-rumūz* (CALA I B), Part II.

74 See *Artis Auriferae*, Basle 1610, p. 158–208.

75 See C. G. Jung, "The Psychology of Transference" in *Coll. Works* Vol. 16.

Fig. 7: King and queen standing on sun and moon from the «Rosarium cum figuris», as this late medieval alchemical florilegium was called by earlier historians of alchemy in order to distinguish it from other Rosarium texts without pictures (Vadiana Library, St. Gallen, Ms 394a).

how the names of Zosimos and Theosebeia were distorted by the time they came into Latin. In the first volume of the *Artis Auriferae* (first printed in Basle 1593), we find in the second chapter a dialogue that corresponds to the «2nd Book of the Names» of the *Muṣḥaf aṣ-ṣuwar*. This translation preserved essential elements of the teachings of Zosimos to a surprisingly large extent.

In the introduction to this dialogue, we even read that one has to look at the pictures (*speculare figuras*) at the beginning in the same way as the reader of the different books of the *Muṣḥaf aṣ-ṣuwar* is supposed first to look at the pictures given at the beginning of each chapter. In Latin alchemy, however, the pictures seem to have migrated from the dialogue *Rosinus ad Euthiciam* to a separate treatise called *Rosarium philosophorum,* although the text that accompanies the *Rosarium* pictures is merely a compilation of quotations—some from later alchemists—commenting on the different stages of the work represented in the pictures. These pictures of the *Rosarium* have the union of sun-king and moon-queen as their central topic, clearly connecting this series to the *Muṣḥaf aṣ-ṣuwar.*

After the remark about looking at the pictures, the text of *Rosinus ad Euthiciam* continues, showing at times that it is a translation of the dialogue from the Arabic text which is the object of this study:

Muṣḥaf aṣ-ṣuwar (fol. 43a, 9–43b, 7):[76]	2nd chapter of *Rosinus ad Euthiciam* in the *Artis auriferae*:[77]
	«… look at the figures of the names at the beginning, and meditate on what he states, for he did not write anything except by way of analogy

76 قالت: فأنبئني عن قول شيماس بن طيفن الحكيم إنّ الشيء واحد الذي به يكون ما تطلبون. فإن لم يكن فيه مثل ما تطلب، فلست مصيبًا شيئًا ممّا تطلب. قال: قد بيّن لك أنّ من دخل في الصنعة إنّما يطلب أن يصيّر الأشياء ذهبًا. فأنت إن لم تجعلي الذهب في الذهب فلست على شيء. قالت: وما الذي ينتفع به أن يُجعل الذهب في الذهب؟ قال: لأنّه يخرج من القليل الكثير. قالت: لو عرف هذا أهل الدنيا لكثر ذهبهم. قال: هو ذا قد أعلمتك به. قالت: فما في يديّ من شيء. قال: جهالتك بتدبير أشباهه الذي يخلط به من أقاربه المؤتلفة غير المختلفة. قالت: فأنبئني عن ذكر الحكماء مزاج الهواء. قال: إنّما وضعوه قياسًا للتركيب. قالت: وكيف وضعوه؟ قال: لأنّه إن لم يكن بين الرطبين اللطيفين ماسك مصلح بينهما هلكا وهربا من النار ولم يقويا على كثرة الطبخ. وإن لم يقويا على كثرة الطبخ لم يخرج منهما شيء ينتفع به، لحبّ الرطوبة اليبوسة وحبّ السخونة البرودة. وكذلك القمر والنجوم إنّما صار ضوءهنّ من ضوء الشمس، ولا سيّما القمر خاصّة أكثر ما يأخذ من ضوء الشمس، ولذلك كثر ضوءه بالليل. وكذلك كلّ شيء من الأشياء فمن الأصل يستفيد القوّة والصبغ.

77 Basle 1610, p. 165: «Speculare figuras initio nominum, & meditare quare hic posui nihil enim eorum posui, nisi ad eorum quibus eget coparatio. Ista est secunda expositionis nominu alienorum Rosini ad Euthicia, & est per quaestiones & responsiones...Et illa: "Patefac igitur

«She said: "Then tell me about what the sage Šīmās ibn Ṭaifūn says: 'The thing by which what you are seeking comes into being is one. If it does not contain something like what you are seeking, you will obtain nothing from it.'" He said: «He has explained to you that whoever enters the work is seeking to turn things to gold. If you do not put gold into gold, you will be wrong." She said: "Then what is the benefit of putting gold into gold?" He said: "Because from little comes out the manifold."

She said: "If the people of the world knew this, their gold would increase."
He said: "That is what I told you." She said: "Yet, what I have

for some of them. This (statement) is followed by the explanation of the other names of Rosinus to Euthicia, and it takes the form of question and answer. She said: "Explain therefore what Syrnas the Philosopher said, that the thing in which everything that is to be operated on is one, for if it is not there, you will find nothing."

He said: "He has shown you here that whoever enters into the art is only seeking to turn things into gold. If you do not put gold upon gold, that is the ferment that is prepared and put onto the stone of the philosophers, you will not gain that from which much comes from little."
She said: "If many inhabitants of the world knew this, gold would be multiplied for them everywhere."
He said: "That is what I told you."
She said: "But it gave me nothing."

quod Syrnas Philosophus ait, quod res est una in qua sit totum quod operaturu est: quod nisi insit, nihil inveniatis." Respondet: "Iam tibi demonstravi, quod qui in hanc artem ingreditur, nihil adinquirit, quam res in aurum vertere, tu aurum nisi aurum in aurum ponas, id est fermentum praeparatum, & in lapidem Philosophorum positum, nihil habes ex eo quod a paulo multum exit." Et illa: "Si mundi habitatores haec scirent, eorum auru utiq, multiplicatetur." Respondet: "Ecce tibi notificavi." Et illa: "Nihil mihi tum profuit." Respondet: "Propter tuam ignorantiam & insipientiam, huius regem qualiter proxima immiscentur apta, non inconvenientia." Et illa: "Cur aere Philosophus narrat complexione?" Respondet: "Hoc ad compositionis coparationem posuerunt." Et illa: "Qualiter haec descripserunt? " Respondet: "Nisi duobus tentrissimis humidis continens fuerit aliquid quod ea placabilia faciat, pereunt, & ignem fugiunt, & coctionem sustinere nequeunt: & nisi decoctione sustinuerint, nihil ex eis utile procedit, eo quod siccitas humiditatem diligit, & calor frigus. Similiter Lunae & Stellarum splendor ex Solis est lumine, maxime vero, & proprie Lunae, quae magis ex Solis lumine sumit: quare nocte lume eius multiplicatum est. Similiter omnia ex radice sumunt vires."»

in my hands is nothing." He said: "It is your ignorance of the operation of things similar to it, which are mixed with it from among its relatives that are in harmony with it, not in disagreement." She said: "Then tell me about the mixing of the air which the sages mention." He said: "Indeed, they wrote it as an analogy for the composition." She said: "How did they write that?" He said: "Because if there were no holder and reconciler between the two subtle, moist ones, the two would be destroyed, and escape from the fire, and they would not be strong enough to resist the intensive cooking. If they are not strong enough to be intensely cooked, nothing will emerge from the two that could be beneficial, because the moist loves dry and the hot loves the cold. It is the same with the moon and the stars: their light comes from the light of the sun. Especially the moon takes very much light from the sun, That is why its light is intense during the night. In the same way, everything gains strength and dye from its origin."»

He said: "That is because of your ignorance and feeblemindedness, as near and suitable things are mixed with this thing, not unsuitable (things)." She said: "Why does the philosopher speak of a composition in the air?" He said: "They gave that as a comparison for the composition." She said: "How did they describe this?" He said: "If there is not something to contain the two very soft and moist ones, which makes them more pleasing, they perish and flee from the fire, and they do not tolerate cooking. Unless they are put in the cooking, nothing useful will come from them.

For dryness loves humidity, and heat loves cold. In the same way, the shining of the moon and the stars comes from the sun, especially that of the moon, which takes great light from the sun. That is why at night its light is made greater.
In the same way, all things gain power from the root."»

The end of the chapter also corresponds to the end of the «2nd Book of the Names» of the *Muṣḥaf aṣ-ṣuwar*.

In conclusion to this chapter, and on the basis of the fact that the *Muṣḥaf aṣ-ṣuwar* must have been known, at least partially, in the Western world, it would be difficult to reject the hypothesis that Zosimos' *Muṣḥaf aṣ-ṣuwar* was the major source of inspiration for the *Rosarium philosophorum*. Now, with the pictures of the *Muṣḥaf aṣ-ṣuwar* and the detailed teachings of Zosimos, we can get a consistent and more complete idea of what he meant by the alchemical work and its effects on the adept.

11. The Muṣḥaf aṣ-ṣuwar and One of the Mutus liber

In one of the *Mutus liber* (a 'silent book' i.e. without words), called here the *Mutus liber* I (given in Mangetus' *Bibliotheca curiosa*, Vol.I, after p. 938), we also find clear parallels to the *Muṣḥaf aṣ-ṣuwar*.[78] But here again we see pictures which, in contrast to those of the *Rosarium*, show an individual relationship of the adept with his soror mystica. In some, there is a clearly defined lower register, where we see the adept and his soror mystica on their knees in front of the oven, and then an upper level, where we see what happens on the transpersonal level. The content of the upper, archetypal world needs, however, to be well contained in the hermetic vessel.

This is a clear parallel to two pictures in the *Muṣḥaf aṣ-ṣuwar* also dividing the upper divine level and the lower human level, and point to the need for a containing vessel. But while the picture on folio 99a (see p. 34) of the *Muṣḥaf aṣ-ṣuwar* shows the lower level clearly separated from the upper level, the picture on fol. 128b gives the two levels not clearly separated. Only the text speaks of the two levels, namely the upper, large Theosebeia, and the lower, small or human Theosebeia. The entire *Mutus liber* I illustrates how the upper archetypal world and the lower human level must be clearly kept apart. The symbolic depiction of the opus alchemicum in the *Mutus liber* I not only lacks a detailed explanation—contrary to the *Muṣḥaf aṣ-ṣuwar*—but also excludes the animal level that is so frequently represented in the pictures of the *Muṣḥaf aṣ-ṣuwar,* where we see depicted the bull, the serpents, the dogs, the whale and the birds. These animals are sometimes even represented as if they belong to a separate third, sub-human register.

The essential work in alchemy, since the time of Zosimos, has been distillation. The furnace for this work in fig. 9 is of the same size as the great Theosebeia with the moon on her head and the great Zosimos with the sun on his head. Its striking similarity to the *Mutus liber* is seen in fig. 10. It needs to be pointed out here that the alembic represented in the *Muṣḥaf aṣ-ṣuwar* bears a close resemblance to the distillation apparatus represented in a Greek Ms, written by Zosimos (see now p. 134).[79] The furnace was considered by the alchemists to be a microcosm, as can be seen in fig. 11.

78 La Rochelle, 1678, reprinted in *Bibliotheca Curiosa* of J. J. Mangetus, Genève 1702.

79 Codex Parisinus gr. 2327, fol. 81v, 220r and 221r. See also Part II, p. 134.

Fig. 8: The upper part of the 2nd picture of the *Mutus liber* I shows the Sun-king and the Moon-queen protected by the great Mercurius, all contained in a retort. In the lower part of the picture, we see the male and female adepts on their knees in front of the oven with this retort.

Fig. 9: (fol. 153a) The huge alchemical oven with the small vessels on top is the same size as Zosimos and Theosebeia, showing that it is not the concrete outer oven that is depicted, but the oven as a symbol. It points to the fact that the distillation process is the best possible image for continuous pondering, as becomes clear from the text of the *Muṣḥaf aṣ-ṣuwar* (see fol. 59a). The product of this distillation process is the red elixir, which is also shown condensed in the upper part of the head of Theosebeia. As Zosimos says in many places, «the stone is called the brain» (see e.g. Berthelot, *Alch. grecs* II, p. 114, 2). The elixir is distilled from the autonomous phantasies revolving around the bodily urges, becoming in the end like a halo around Theosebeia's own head and a yellow scarf around her shoulders.

Fig. 10: Another picture from the *Mutus liber* I, showing a woman with the moon on her head and a man with the sun on his head, symbolizing the divine aspects of the adepts. Here, in this 17th century picture, the oven is again the same size as the humanized archetypal figures. The similarity of this picture to fig. 9 on the opposite page is striking, leading to the hypothesis that the pictures in the *Muṣḥaf aṣ-ṣuwar* must have been known to the author of this *Mutus liber* I. The numbers 100, 1,000, 10,000 etc. point to the *multiplicatio* of the elixir as a result of the successful union of the opposites.

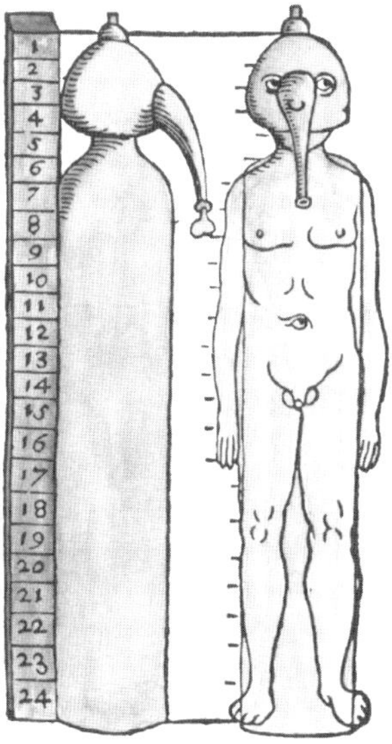

Fig. 11: View of the alchemical oven with a distillation apparatus on top. The picture comes from a text written by Dorneus, a medical doctor and alchemist from the 16th century (*Aurora* 1577). The oven is the same size as the human being beside it, pointing to the symbolic dimension of the alchemical oven. The elixir is distilled out of the human body, i.e. out of the mysterious urges and phantasies that emerge from the inner unconscious world of the individual. Distilling them is a symbol for pondering over those images, as we learn from alchemical writings. This painstaking work gradually reveals the deep wisdom of the earth and the body (see fn. 73, p. 59).

12. Summary

This introduction has provided evidence for the following conclusions concerning the *Muṣḥaf aṣ-ṣuwar*:

a. The book must be considered to be a translation from a Greek original, above all because of a strong correspondence of ideas and language with extant Greek books of Zosimos. But the Arabic translation of the *Muṣḥaf aṣ-ṣuwar* which has come to us is best understood as a translation with a certain amount of adaptation. The prophecy concerning the Arabs here must be an interpolation into the original text. Our text must have been written by Zosimos himself or, quite possibly, one of his followers.

b. The *Muṣḥaf aṣ-ṣuwar* shares many characteristics with the *Kitāb al-mafātīḥ fī aṣ-ṣanʿa.* There is evidence that our dialogue was composed later than the *Kitāb al-mafātīḥ*, which is mentioned in the *Fihrist* of Ibn Nadīm. Both texts also have later offspring: the *Muṣḥaf aṣ-ṣuwar* can be found to a large extent in the hitherto single, unique *Kitāb al-ḥabīb,* while the widely-known *Kitāb Qirāṭis* turns out to be largely (from page 6, line 3) an epitome and copy of part of the *Kitāb al-mafātīḥ.*

c. The *Muṣḥaf aṣ-ṣuwar* is important for the question of the origin of the famous *Turba philosophorum*, since the *Turba* derives partly from the *Book of Pictures*. Even the framework of the meeting of philosophers may have its origin in this book.

d. Our text was known in some form in the Latin alchemical tradition, as can be seen from a translation of the «2nd Book of the Names» from the *Muṣḥaf aṣ-ṣuwar*,which can be found in the *Artis auriferae* of the 16th century. The pictures of the *Rosarium philosophorum* go back to Zosimos, whose pictures also seem to have influenced one of the *Mutus liber*.

Above and beyond these connections, the *Muṣḥaf aṣ-ṣuwar* has to be considered a *key text* to opening up a better understanding of the religious-symbolic branch of alchemy. This branch thrived among the Arab alchemists, who were influenced by a wide knowledge of translations from Greek works. Authors like Muḥammad ibn Umail, known in Latin alchemy as Senior, developed Zosimos' symbolism further.

This branch of symbolic alchemy must henceforth be seen as the description of a *psychological transformation* of the adept on his or her quest for immortality. This process is described in the *Muṣḥaf aṣ-ṣuwar* with basic substances, mirroring the very elemental, collective character of this process. It is the great merit of C. G. Jung to have shown the way to a better understanding of this branch of alchemy. Further research that seeks to understand this type of text should no longer look only for concrete substances that might be covered by the symbols mentioned by these authors.

The *Muṣḥaf aṣ-ṣuwar*, the complete text of which survives in only one manuscript, reveals the important role played by Arabic alchemy in enabling the continuity of Western civilization. Arabic-Islamic culture was a bridge that reconnected Western culture to its cradle, the culture of Antiquity. The uncovering of the historical facts presented here further reinforces the discoveries of C. G Jung concerning the meaning of religious-symbolic alchemy.

Part II

Introduction
to the Translation

Second Introduction,
written in response to Benjamin Hallum's Review of the Facsimile Edition of the *Muṣḥaf aṣ-ṣuwar*

In a review,[1] Benjamin Hallum, orientalist and expert on Zosimos of Panopolis,[2] welcomed the facsimile edition of the *Muṣḥaf aṣ-ṣuwar*, published in the series Corpus Alchemicum Arabicum as volume CALA II.1. The essence of this review is that Hallum considers the *Muṣḥaf aṣ-ṣuwar* to be a later Arabic compilation of texts written by Zosimos of Panopolis.[3] With this statement he puts forward an interesting counter-hypothesis to the one presented in my introduction to the facsimile edition, reprinted as Part I in this book. My hypothesis is that the *Muṣḥaf aṣ-ṣuwar* must be a translation of an authentic book, written by Zosimos himself, or by Theosebeia, or quite possibly somebody of his immediate following.

1 B. Hallum, "The *Tome of Images*: an Arabic Compilation of Texts by Zosimos of Panopolis and a Source of the *Turba Philosophorum*", in *AMBIX* Vol. 56, No. 1, March 2009, p. 76–88.

2 At the Warburg Institute in London, B. Hallum wrote a PhD thesis on *Zosimos Arabus. The Reception of Zosimos of Panopolis in the Arabic/Islamic World*, London 2008 (unpubl.). His thesis contains valuable references to important Arabic texts attributed to Zosimos, as well as some thoughtful reflections about their history and authenticity.

3 In his review, Hallum claims that the title of the *Muṣḥaf aṣ-ṣuwar* must be translated by *Tome of Images*, arguing that there is another book, «[…] attributed to Zosimos, and one which has a much stronger claim to authenticity (than the *Muṣḥaf aṣ-ṣuwar*)». This other book is entitled *Kitāb aṣ-ṣuwar* «[…], which is likely to have been the earlier of the two books in date […] (but it) contains no illustrations». However, an examination of this book shows something different from what Hallum's text suggests: The *Kitāb aṣ-ṣuwar* is found in a manuscript of the Dār al-kutub in Cairo, kimiyāʾ 23 M, and has a title-page «[…] *The Book of Pictures* by the sage Zosimos and it is named *The Book of the Epistles from the Sage Zosimos to the Queen Theosebeia, Daughter of Maria the Copt*, in which the Work is explained for whoever understands it. […]». That title-page heads not only a part of the collection of Zosimos' *Seven Epistles* (2nd-5th) which have, as Hallum asserts, «a much stronger claim to authenticity (than the *Muṣḥaf aṣ-ṣuwar*)», but the manuscript also contains material from other authors, as Hallum himself mentions in his thesis *Zosimos Arabus* on p. 191. Any distinction with reference to this *Kitāb aṣ-ṣuwar,* which does not even have pictures (!), but was probably the source for the *Muṣḥaf aṣ-ṣuwar* (as will be demonstrated), is based on a distortion of the given facts. So Hallum's proposal not to translate *Muṣḥaf aṣ-ṣuwar* as *The Book of Pictures* merely creates confusion. When quoting Hallum's review in this second introduction, I will therefore replace his proposed translation *Tome of Images* by *Muṣḥaf aṣ-ṣuwar.*

The reviewer is able to present his counter-hypothesis together with further facts, and he states his arguments with profound scholarly expertise. With this introduction to the translation of *The Book of Pictures*, I will continue the debate about the origin of the *Muṣḥaf aṣ-ṣuwar* by adding new facts, some in support of my hypothesis, some in support of Hallum's counter-hypothesis. Furthermore, I will also clarify the method of my approach with regard to text and pictures of the *Muṣḥaf aṣ-ṣuwar*, and hence to the contents of this manuscript. In so doing, I enhance the significance of this unique document. With the English translation presented here, non-orientalists will also be able to participate in this debate.

1. The Three Picture Series of *The Muṣḥaf aṣ-ṣuwar*

First of all, it will be helpful to obtain a simple but basic orientation concerning the pictures. Hallum states at the beginning of his review (p. 77) that the *Muṣḥaf aṣ-ṣuwar* «comprises the earliest known example of a continuous series of allegorical alchemical images». Some differentiation needs to be made here, as this will create an important basis for subsequent debate. Indeed, the pictures in the *Muṣḥaf aṣ-ṣuwar* represent the earliest known alchemical picture series, but these pictures are not «a continuous series of images», as they can clearly be divided into three different series. Careful reflection on the manuscript's 223 folios, with its 42 pictures, reveals the pedagogic path chosen by Zosimos in his *Muṣḥaf aṣ-ṣuwar*. Step by step and from different angles, Zosimos shows the alchemical process of transformation to his student Theosebeia, and the images he draws for her—as he mentions on different occasions—are his basic guideline. It is, of course, difficult for us, with today's differentiated linear thinking, to understand that the alchemical work is not a linear path going straight from A to B, but that this process has to be conceived rather as a gradual transformation of the arcane substance that takes place in an enigmatic way, deo concedente. The following brief examination of the pictures of the *Muṣḥaf aṣ-ṣuwar* will demonstrate that these illustrations must be divided into three separate series, each one of them comprehensively depicting Zosimos' teaching of the art.

Book	Picture	Description
1.	missing	on folio 2a
2.	on fol. 38a; fol. 47b missing	missing (one after 37b)
3.1.	missing	on folio 64a
3.2.	on fol. 64b	on folio 64b
4.	missing	on folio 70b
5.1.	on fol. 86b and 87a	on fol. 85b-86a
2. Series 5.1-5.11:	11 pictures extant	11 descriptions
6.	on fol. 128a,128b	on fol. 128a
7.	7.1. missing	missing
3. Series 7.2-7.22:	21 (+2) pictures extant	21 descriptions
8.	on fol. 171b-172a	on fol. 171a
9.	on fol. 191b	on fol. 191a
10.	on fol. 196a	on fol. 195b
11.	on fol. 205a	on fol. 204b
12.	on fol. 210b	on fol. 210a-b
13.	none	none

Fig. 12: The three picture series of the 42 illustrations of the *Muṣḥaf aṣ-ṣuwar*. According to the text, the pictures on fol. 147b and 149b must be deleted.

The first series comprises the illustrations found at the beginning of each of the twelve books (see fig. 13 on next double page). Unfortunately the pictures of the 1st Book, one of the two pictures of the 2nd and of the 3rd Book, and the illustration at the beginning of the 4th Book, are missing, but we have a description of all of them in the text. However, the first picture of «The 7th Book about the Mercuries» is missing, both in image and in text. From the numbering of the lengthy picture series of this 7th Book, we can assume that originally there was a picture at the beginning of this book, as the first picture to be found in this 7th Book is called the second picture (folio 134b). Finally, «The 13th Book about Questions Concerning the Last Composition» has neither a picture nor a description of an illustration that would point to something missing at its beginning; this is understandable as this last book consists solely of additional questions and answers.

Let us now look briefly at the content of this *first series* in order to supply evidence as to why these pictures belong together, allowing us to

2nd picture fol. 38a

3rd picture fol. 64b

5th picture fol. 86b - 87a

6th picture fol. 128b

Fig. 13: First picture series.

8rd picture fol. 171b - 172a

9th picture fol. 191b

10th picture fol. 191a

11th picture fol. 205a

12th picture fol. 210b

speak of a coherent series. The main reason that we can speak of a series is the fact that they are connected with regard to their motifs as well as by their descriptions given. The first picture—which should be at the beginning of «The 1st Book of the Truth»—is missing. But a description on folio 2a tells us that in this picture, Zosimos is represented with a sun on his head, while his student, Theosebeia, has a moon on her head. This representation of Zosimos and Theosebeia with sun and moon is found throughout this book in all representations of teacher and student (except on fol. 102b, 149a, and 157a). For an Egyptian living in the 3rd/4th century, the sun is connected to the Sungod Re and the moon to Thot-Hermes-Mercurius. So in the relationship between master and student, the luminaries of the day- and the night-world are also constellated. As the text says, there are also close to Zosimos' legs «two winding vipers, bound together by two knots.»(fol. 2a, 6) One of them is related to the sun and the other to the moon, as the colours on their back, mentioned in the text, indicate: One of them has the colour of the water of gold (the metal of the sun), and the other one the colour of the water of silver (the metal of the moon). Thus, besides the upper two luminaries, there are also, in the lower part and related to these two human beings, two cold-blooded, poisonous vipers.

In the next picture, at the beginning of «The 2nd Book of the Names», the two human beings from the first picture are seen again with a sun and a moon on their heads, but now we see a dramatic change. The two humans are represented without solid ground under their feet. They are fully in the grip of *Hermes ter unus*. (I have given an interpretation of this picture in Part I of this book, on p. 29-33.) Then come the two pictures at the beginning of «The 3rd Book about the Weights». One of them is missing, but we find its description in the text on folio 64a. From the description of the missing picture, and from the picture that we find in our manuscript, we can see that Zosimos wants to point out to his student Theosebeia, that she needs to see that in the work there is also a greater Zosimos and a greater Theosebeia involved. Furthermore, she has to see (on fol. 64b) that the small Theosebeia, together with the small Zosimos, are both in the hand of a much larger representation of Theosebeia, who is able to balance out Zosimos and Theosebeia, the two small human beings on earth, with six spiritual beings on the other scale. This large figure must represent a greater or divine Theosebeia. From the description of the other (missing) picture we learn that a large Zosimos is holding two balances. These two greater figures seem to balance out the state of possession of the two small human beings on earth, depicted in the picture before. The representation of a huge Zosimos and Theosebeia, both symbolizing a supernatural force that interferes in the relationship of the teacher and his student, connects these pictures to the ones at the beginning of the 2nd Book, the 6th Book and the 12th Book. There is also an internal relationship with regard to the motif of the two times three birds that we get to know from the description of the missing picture at the beginning of «The 3rd Book about the Weights» (folio 64a. 8-19), since the motif of the birds reappears later on in the picture at the beginning of «The 9th Book about the Measures of the Fire».

«The 4th Book about the Composition» starts again with a missing picture, but a description on folio 70b shows that this picture is directly related to the picture at the beginning of the 1st Book, as we read: «Zosimos and Theosebeia [… are] standing as we described at the beginning of this book» (fol. 70b, 8). This most probably refers to «The 1st Book of the Learning». Furthermore we have again in the description of this picture the motif of the balance, connecting this picture to those at the beginning of the 3rd Book. Next, the first picture of «The 5th Book about the Magnesia» connects in many ways (e.g. by the two vipers below) with the above-mentioned picture at the beginning of the 1st Book, and at the same time, it opens up the special teaching about the enigmatic symbol called magnesia, which Zosimos explains in a separate, second picture series that we find in this 5th Book. The picture at the beginning of «The 6th Book about the Nature» shows again a huge Theosebeia holding up two men. To her right we see a small Theosebeia carrying two men on her shoulders, one with a sun and the other with a moon on his head, the opposing luminaries of the day- and the night-world. Below there is a lake with blue water. I do not want to go into any interpretation of the pictures within the framework of such an introduction, but only wish to point out again the relationship of this picture to the earlier picture at the beginning of the 3rd Book, where we also saw the big Theosebeia holding the balance and the small Theosebeia in one of the scales. And the motif of the lake below is again represented later, in the picture at the beginning of «The 9th Book about the Measures of the Fire». Then the first picture of the lengthy series of «The 7th Book about the Mercuries» is missing, as mentioned above.

The development of this first picture series culminates in the one at the beginning of «The 8th Book about the Operation». There we see a representation of the dead Zosimos in the arms of his student Theosebeia. These two symbolic figures are shown on one side of the book, while the teacher Zosimos and his student are represented on the other side. The text reveals that it was she who killed him. (I gave a first interpretation of this picture in Part I, on p. 37-41.) The next three pictures, which we find at the beginning of the 9th, 10th and 11th Book, reveal their inner coherence by the fact that they revolve around the fixing of the nine spirits that appear, in two of these pictures, as a group of six and as a group of three figures. We already saw a group of six spirits in the picture at the beginning of the 3rd Book. The final picture in our first series is at the beginning of the «12th Book about the Last Operation Only and Its Weights» (folio 210b). The text says that we see Theosebeia «as we described at the beginning of this book». This is again a clear reference to the beginning of our *Muṣḥaf aṣ-ṣuwar*. The last picture in this series illustrates the goal of the work, namely what Theosebeia has to become conscious of: She has to learn to separate herself as a human being from the greater, divine Theosebeia with the moon on her head. A brief interpretation of this picture is given in my introduction to the facsimile edition on p. 41. To summarize our reflections on the first series of pictures, we can see that it reveals numerous internal relationships. It illustrates the whole alchemical process, *focusing on the final goal of the alchemical work for Theosebeia*, as can be seen from the last picture in this series.

As Zosimos was an Egyptian, and as in his *Muṣḥaf aṣ-ṣuwar* he repeatedly mentions motifs from the Pharaonic culture, we can assume that there is a connection back to the twelve hours of the journey of the Sungod through the night, which brings the rejuvenation and transformation from the Sungod's old manifestation as Atum to his renewed form as Chepri. This process is well known from different Royal Books of the Afterlife of Ancient Egypt, for instance from the *Amduat*, which was still in use in Egypt for funerary purposes in the 3rd/4th-century.[4] Thus, these Royal Books of the Afterlife must be considered an important source for the development of the religious-symbolic branch of alchemy in Hellenistic times. This

4 See Th. Abt and E. Hornung, *Knowledge for the Afterlife*, Zurich 2003, p.14.

development of Zosimos' alchemical teachings in 12 steps in picture and text later found its way into Latin alchemy. In the treatise "De Lapide Sapientum" of Basilius Valentinus (15th century), for instance, each of the twelve chapters or keys also starts with a picture describing the work.[5]

The second series of pictures consists of 11 pictures found in «The 5th Book about the Magnesia» (see fig. 14, a 12th picture might be missing). It starts with a picture having similar motifs as the missing picture of «The 1st Book of the Learning», which is described of fol. 2a. This series illustrates the alchemical work from another angle, ending with the 11th picture. The similarity between the picture at the beginning of «The 1st Book» and the first picture here at the beginning of «The 5th Book», shows that the transformation of the magnesia is the entire work. In my publication «Psychological Commentary on Muḥammad ibn Umail's *Ḥall ar-rumūz*», (CALA I B, p. 85-88), I have provided evidence that magnesia is a symbol for the arcane substance that has to be transformed by the work of the alchemist. The meaning of magnesia in Zosimos' *Muṣḥaf aṣ-ṣuwar* is similar to the one found later on in Ibn Umail's *Ḥall ar-rumūz.* It is this involvement with the enigmatic magnesia which finally leads to the symbolic death of Zosimos (8th picture of this second series). The caption to this picture on folio 103a, 6 reads: «The image of a man lying dead on the ground, golden, with red stripes.» The dialogue that follows on folio 103a, 7 -103b, 14 about the symbolic death and resurrection of Zosimos has been given on page 36-37. That text, referring to the picture, shows the close relationship between picture and text. After the symbolic death of Zosimos, he describes how he was resurrected (folio 102b, 4-7) in the same way as we find this motif in the first series (folio 171b -172a and folio 174b, 19 -175a, 9). So we see that the «5th Book about the Magnesia» and its pictures are *in themselves* a description and illustration of the whole alchemical work: the adept's symbolic death and resurrection. This also becomes evident from the text, for instance on folio 108a, 7-11, where Zosimos explains: «... when all things came together in the magnesia, it is like the ship that is called one ship although it contains many utensils, and like the human being who is named by his name, although he has a body, a spirit and a soul. He is one in name, but if you analyse him you will find more than one thing in him.» To summarize, this second series is especially focused on the *individual work with regard to*

5 In the *Musaeum Hermeticum*, Frankfurt 1678, p. 393-423.

1st picture fol. 86b - 87a

2nd picture fol. 89b

3rd picture fol. 97b

4th picture fol. 99a

5th picture fol. 100a

Fig. 14: The second picture series from «The 5th Book about the Magnesia»

6th picture fol. 101b

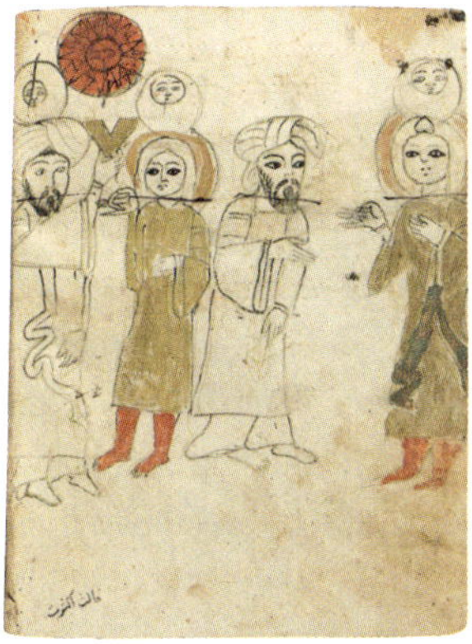

7th picture fol. 102b

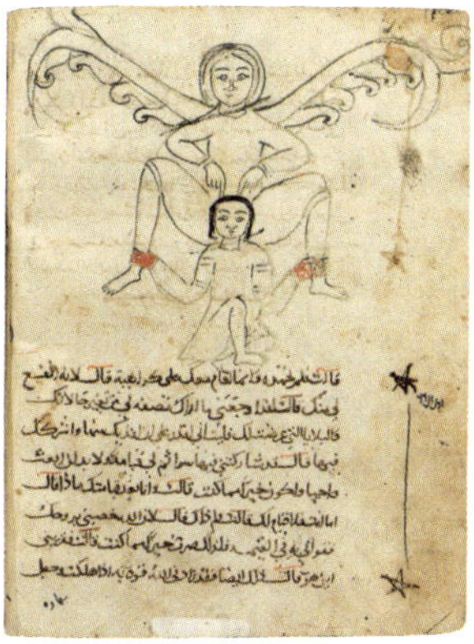

8th picture fol. 103a

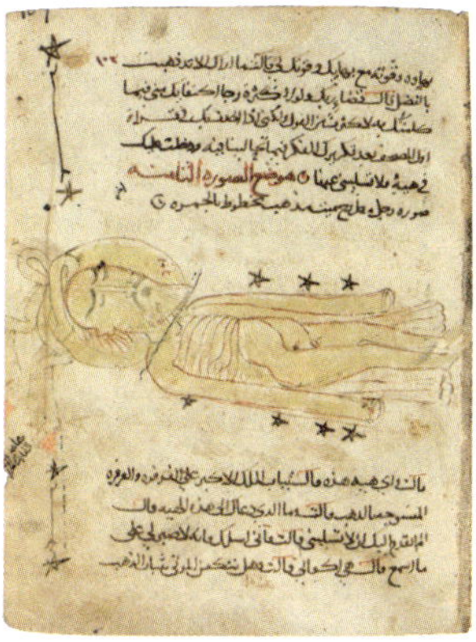

9th picture fol. 104a

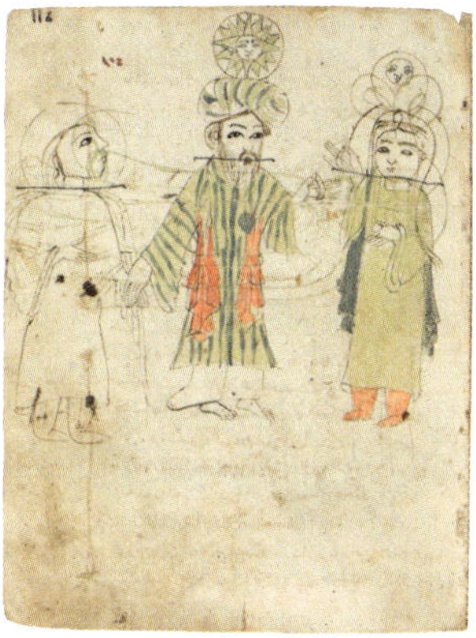

10th picture fol. 105b

11th picture fol. 106b

the relationship of the teacher and his student, as can be seen from the 11th picture of the series, where each one of the two, Zosimos and Theosebeia, are finally depicted with a dog below—their individual guide to the work.[6]

The third series, with 22 pictures, is found in «The 7th Book about the Mercuries» (see figs. 15-16). The first picture is missing, as already mentioned, and we do not know anything about this picture. In the manuscript, one folio is missing that must contain this picture on one side and on the other its description, together with a continuation of the text that ends abruptly on folio 133b. Again, a study of the text and pictures of this book reveals that the meaning of the theme of the three mercuries points to the enigmatic arcane substance; and again, the whole book and its pictures are in themselves a form of teaching about the complete alchemical work, namely the transformation of this arcane substance. This third series shows, in the same way as the other two, how the transformation leads to the symbolic death of the adept. Once more we see Zosimos in the 18th picture (folio 152a), where the text says: «[...] Zosimos, dead, naked, lying on the ground, and the sun is on his head, [...]». His resurrection is symbolized in the last, the 22nd picture, where we see Zosimos and his teacher, who points out to him the growth of the palm tree with its three branches as one living being, which unifies the three mercuries that were separate entities at the beginning and throughout the work. This tree, as I explained in my introduction to the facsimile edition on page 41-45, points to the gradual unification of the opposites in the psyche of the adept, the central feature of the tree of the sages in alchemy. So this third series illustrates again the whole work of the two human beings, *this time focussing more on the goal of the work for Zosimos*.

Extensive reflection on the pictures and the text of «The 5th Book about the Magnesia» and «The 7th Book about the Mercuries» reveals the inner coherence of these two other picture series. Zosimos created them in order to explain to Theosebeia the possibility and the meaning of the transformation of this arcane substance, once symbolized by magnesia, and once by the three mercuries. Therefore we cannot speak of these images, as

6 The second dog on fol. 106b is cut off. The text describes the picture: [The picture of] Zosimos and Theosebeia pointing to the other [...] two dogs, one of them is red [having a rope round his neck and the other one is white(?)]. The motif of the dog is again found in the *Muṣḥaf aṣ-ṣuwar* on folio 191b. See also p. 347, fn 69.

Hallum does, as «a continuous series of allegorical alchemical images». This first basic fact will be taken up later, and will show that *the inner structure and the gradual building up of Zosimos' teachings are consistent in picture and text, forming one single book*. So Hallum's assumption (in his review on p. 81) that «the *Muṣḥaf aṣ-ṣuwar* lacks any coherent structure, which might support his (Abt's) claim that it was composed as an integral work», is not based on the facts that we find in the manuscript.

2. The Difference between Allegory and Symbol

A second clarification is needed in order to understand Zosimos' *Muṣḥaf aṣ-ṣuwar*. As will be demonstrated, its pictures are not «allegorical alchemical images or illustrations» as Hallum states at various points in his review (p. 77, 81 and 88). In actual fact, all the pictures in the *Muṣḥaf aṣ-ṣuwar* which Zosimos made for his student Theosebeia are of *symbolic nature*, as are his explanations. This can be seen from Zosimos' own words in different places in the *Muṣḥaf aṣ-ṣuwar*. He tells Theosebeia that his teacher Democritus said: «What I wrote for you is only in symbols» (fol. 105a, 3), and he, Zosimos, is doing the same.[7] With regard to his illustrations, we can learn that Zosimos advises Theosebeia to look at and to ponder over the pictures he made for her (fol. 63b, 17 -64a, 1; 103a, 4-5; 133b, 9; 195b, 4-5 and 204a, 17 -204b, 3) in order that she will in time understand what he is pointing out by analogy [8] (fol. 38b, 4-10). And it is at this point where Theosebeia stumbles again and again, being impatient because she does not

7 Fol. 53a, 11-16: «[…] every sage […] named the things, with which he obtained this work with names that he invented […]. So he […] named the thing according to his opinion, writing about it in analogies, parables and symbols. I (Zosimos) therefore do the same, […].» A further confirmation of the symbolic nature of alchemical substances is found e.g. on fol. 111b, 15-19. See also fol. 95a, 11 and fol. 169b, 18-19; for the symbolic nature of the work see fol. 220a, 13-16.

8 Analogies (*qīyāsāt*), similarities (*šubhāt*) and parables (*tašbīhāt*) are often mentioned by Zosimos. In this way, Zosimos seeks to transfer information or meaning from something known (the source) to the unknown other (the target), which has similar features. Pictures as analogies, and stories as analogies, similarities or parables, can be made up of different symbols.

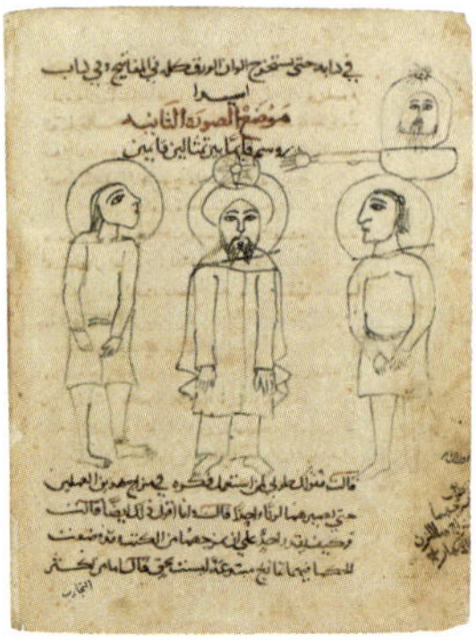

2nd picture fol. 134b

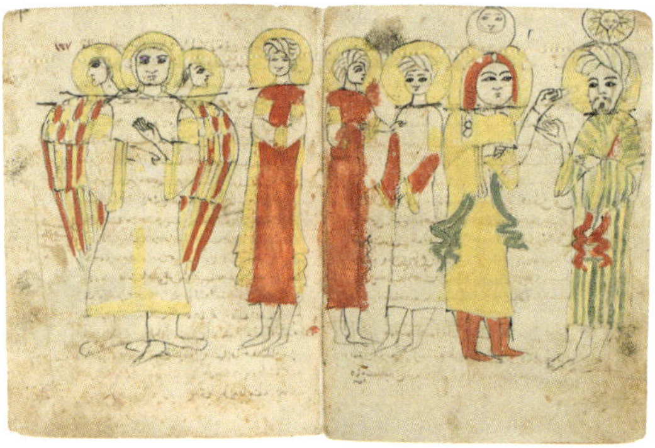

3rd picture fol. 136b - 137a

4th picture fol. 138b - 139a

Fig. 15: The third picture series, first part.

5th picture fol. 140a

6th picture fol. 141a

7th picture fol. 142a

8th picture fol. 143b - 144a

9th picture fol. 145a

10th picture fol. 145b

11th picture fol. 146b

12th picture fol. 147a

wrong picture fol. 147b to be deleted according to the text

13th picture fol. 148a

14th picture fol. 149a

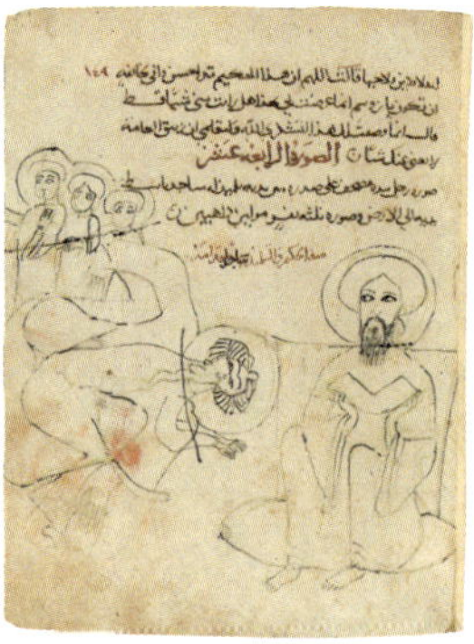

wrong picture fol. 149b to be deleted according to the text

Fig. 16: The third picture series, second part.

15th picture fol. 150a

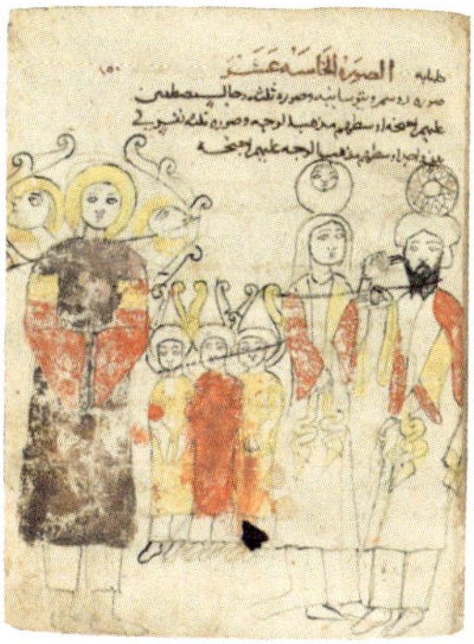

middle 16th picture fol. 151a

17th picture fol. 151b

18th
›icture
·ol. 152a

›niddle
9th
icture
›l. 153a

20th picture fol. 154a

1th
›cture
›l. 154b
›d
›l. 155a

22th picture fol. 157a

understand Zosimos' teachings straightaway. Therefore she despairs repeatedly, as can be seen when we look at the whole dialogue. For a long time she could not understand the nature of symbols and analogies that Zosimos was presenting to her, since they point to something unknown to her, and so she assumed that he was merely drawing or recounting allegories.

The word allegory comes from the Greek *allēgoria*, which is made up of the words *allos* = another, different, and *agoreuein* = to speak openly, to speak in the assembly. This verb is related to *agorā* = open space, typically a marketplace. Thus allegory means literally «to describe one thing under the image of another» in the sense of «to speak convincingly». Today we use the word allegory «to illustrate something in a figurative mode by similes or metaphors», like, for instance, Plato's famous allegory of the cave (*Politeia* VII, 106a). There the shadowy images on the wall, seen by the prisoners in the cave, are an impressive figurative representation of a three-dimensional reality of the world of eternal forms or ideas behind them; they are an allegory of the flat and simplified perception of the world that we normally get. Shadows are well known in this world. They are not symbols that could gradually lead us to become conscious of the unseen content behind the prisoners, as will be discussed next. Allegories are, therefore, pointing to something figurative *that is known in this world.*

Sometimes we have allegories mentioned in alchemical treatises, such as the so-called "Merlini allegoria".[9] This allegory narrates of a king who drank so much water that it finally made him sick, so he appeared to be dead. He was therefore in urgent need of treatment. As the text tells us, his people called for Egyptian and Alexandrian medical doctors. The final outcome of the story is that the Alexandrian medical doctors were able to revive the king. The allegory of the healing of this king points to the alchemical work and reminds us of the noble or royal origin of any adept. The work is therefore also called the Royal Work. For that reason, the story is called an allegory, as this points to something known in the outer world in the sense: Look, you adept, you could also be like this king.[10] The

9 "Merlini allegoria profundissimum philosophici lapidis Arcanum", in *Artis Auriferae* 1593, Vol. I, p. 392-396. For a psychological interpretation of this text see: C. G. Jung, *Mysterium Coniunctions*, Coll. Works 14, § 10-14.

10 This is the same motif that we find in the famous "Hymn of the Pearl", where a prince was sent out on a quest for the precious pearl, but then forgot his royal origin and his task. The Hymn is a passage from the apocryphal *Acts of Thomas* (4th century), M. R. James' translation, p. 108 f.

abundance of water in the body of the king in the "Merlini allegoria", however, is a symbol for that enigmatic water which is the central ingredient in the alchemical work, leading to death and resurrection. Zosimos also points out in his *Muṣḥaf aṣ-ṣuwar* that without water there can be no work.[11] In modern language, we name this water the unconscious, but even today we cannot say what this enigmatic "influx" from the realm beyond consciousness really is. That is why we simply name it the unknown or the unconscious. And today we also know, in the same way as in the past, that if too many "flowing images" of this other, unconscious world enter the conscious realm, we have to speak of an inundation or possession by the unconscious, which makes suitable treatment necessary.

Symbols are quite different from allegories. The English word symbol comes from the Greek *symbolon* belonging to the verb *sym-ballein* = «to throw together», «to join together». Originally, in Ancient Greece, a *symbolon* was something broken into two parts, a coin, a ring or a tablet whose halves join together at the broken edge. It was used at that time to seal a contract or to confirm hospitality. Thus, the word symbol was used to bring together two things—in the same way as the two halves of the ancient *symbolon*—a picture and a hidden, unknown meaning. In this way, a symbol connects this known world to the world beyond consciousness; it is the best expression for something that is *not yet known in this world*, as Zosimos says: «[…] the sages did not describe anything in their books without alluding to something else» (fol. 7a, 19). «Our gold is not the gold of this world», as the old masters emphasised. Only one part of the symbol (the gold) belongs to this world, *while the other part, which belongs to the unknown other world, can in time be discovered, with the help of the symbol.* This is the difference between an allegory (as well as a sign, a metaphor or a codename) on the one hand, and a symbol on the other.

In one of Zosimos' Greek authentic texts, known by the title «On the Letter Omega», we find an illustration of the difference between allegory and symbol. There we can read: «Thus the first man is called by us Thot

11 Studying the *Muṣḥaf aṣ-ṣuwar* reveals that Zosimos meant by the moisture or the water whatever emerges from the inner world and which has to be understood in its *symbolic* meaning, «because this true work of ours is born in and nourished by the sea» (fol. 182b, 1; see also fol. 186a, 10-13). In his article "'Divine Water' in the Alchemical Writings of Pseudo-Democritus" (*AMBIX* 56 2009), Matteo Martelli does not include the symbolic dimension of the divine water and analyses only the «technical and philological point of view».

and by them Adam, which is a name in the language of the angels; but with reference to his body, they named him symbolically (*symbolicōs*) after the four elements of the whole heavenly sphere.»[12] Then Zosimos relates the four letters, which make up the word Adam, to the course of the sun. Thus the four letters of the original man are a symbol for the totality of that unknown four-folded kernel in the unconscious, which we name in today's psychological language the archetype of the self. In the same text, a little later, we read: «For, according to the words of allegory (*kata ton allēgorikon logon*), Prometheus and Epimetheus are but one man, namely soul and body.»[13] Here, Zosimos uses the word allegoric in order to explain in a figurative way how soul and body are one.

To give an example in the *Muṣḥaf aṣ-ṣuwar*, let us look at those pictures where we see Zosimos and Theosebeia. In almost all of them Zosimos is depicted with a sun on his head, while Theosebeia is represented with a moon on her head. All these pictures of Zosimos with a sun on his head must be seen as a symbol, which points to the fact that for his student Theosebeia, he has acquired the features of a sun hero or Sungod. Zosimos and the sun are parts of our known world that point to something specific but unknown in the other world, which today we name archetypal. It is *not* the other way round, i.e. that Zosimos with the sun on his head could be simply understood as an allegory that stands for «gold or a hot, active, masculine principle», as Hallum writes in his thesis *Zosimos Arabus*.[14] With this statement, he fails to acknowledge the other part of the symbol "Zosimos with the sun on his head". By reducing a symbol to an allegory or a figurative representation of a *substance* (gold) or to a *material* principle that is «hot, active, masculine», the main feature of a symbol, namely that it points to *and thus can lead to the archetypal background*, becomes impossible. Therefore the pictures of Zosimos and Theosebeia together with the luminaries on their heads, when understood as symbols, have to be taken for what they are.

In my psychological commentary on Muḥammad ibn Umail's *Ḥall ar-rumūz* (CALA I B, p. 69-70), I have explained the method of understanding these alchemical symbols *by amplification*. There I referred to a later alchemist of the 13th century, who gave detailed instructions in this respect, and wrote: «Abū al-Qāsim al-ᶜIrāqī [...] explains in detail the method of

12 M. Mertens, *Zosime de Panopolis*, *Mém. Auth.*, I.9, 89 (translations by M.-L. von Franz; see CALA I A, § 6 point 9).

13 Ibid., I.12, 114 (CALA I A, § 6 point 12).

14 p. 265.

understanding "the inner meaning of the symbols and allusions of the sages". As a central point, he declares that we need "necessary associations" (in Arabic: *iltizām*) in order to understand obscure alchemical statements and symbols such as "Eastern Mercury, [...] River Nile, [...] or Land of India".[15] That means one has to find out what the same author or other quoted authors have to say about the same symbol in order to finally create a *synopsis* (*syn-opsis* , gr.: lit. a together-view), as Olympiodoros (5th/6th century) called the key to understanding alchemy (M. Berthelot, *Alch. grecs*, II.IV.38, 1). On fol. 107a - b, especially on fol. 107b, 18, Zosimos gives clear information about the ignorant who think that alchemical names are covering up something of this world, and are no more than codenames.

Symbols are entirely different from signs or codemanes. They express what is otherwise simply not describable. As C. G. Jung has pointed out, alchemical symbols have *a numinous quality*, especially the innumerable names for 'their stone' and 'their water', because they make the archetype of the self visible, and bring it into the realm of experience.[16] The main feature of a symbol is the fact that its larger implications cannot initially be fully recognized. Only over a period of time and by intensive pondering will the hidden meaning of a symbol unfold, as Zosimos told Theosebeia repeatedly. What can be said today, for instance, about these two symbols, Zosimos with a sun and Theosebeia with a moon on their heads, is a psychological interpretation that we are able to make, centuries later, thanks to the discovery of the unconscious. These two symbols are pointing to *the male respectively the female archetypes* neither of which, as such, is directly recognizable. And this holds true for other symbolic representations as well. In other words: what word apart from 'symbol' could you use for «a serpent that bites its tail», the description of a motif that we find in the text for the missing picture at the beginning of «3rd Book of the Weights» (fol. 64a, 14)? Or what word apart from 'symbol' could describe the picture of the dead Zosimos in the arms of Theosebeia

15 Abū al-Qāsim al-ᶜIrāqī, *Kitāb al-ᶜIlm al-muktasab fī zirāᶜat aḏ-ḏahab*, p. 55-57; see also the quotations from ibn Umail's *Ḥall ar-rumūz* and his *al-Māʾ al-waraqī*, given in CALA I B,.

16 See e.g. C. G. Jung, *Man and his Symbols, Coll. Works* 18/1, § 416 f, and *Psychology and Alchemy, Coll. Works* 12, § 557. In 1945, C. G. Jung wrote (now in: "The Philosophical Tree", *Coll. Works* 13, § 395): «Just as dreams do not conceal something already known, or express it under a disguise, but try rather to formulate an as yet unconscious fact, *so myths and alchemical symbols are not euhemeristic allegories that hide artificial secrets* (my italics).»

(fol. 172a), reminding us of Isis holding her dead brother-husband Osiris, or of Mary holding her dead son? The lack of understanding symbolic alchemical documents will remain as long as we continue to reduce symbols to allegories or codenames. In this way, we have no key to fully appreciate the tremendous insights to which these symbols can lead. Such images or names of substances do not replace or hide something known in this world. We can thus never find out what exactly they could mean *in this world alone*. It is, to give just one testimony, as the later Pseudo-Mağrīṭī (10th/11th cent.) says: «A symbol (*ramz*) is an expression that does not mean the outer sense (*ẓāhir*) of the word, but rather points to an inner (*bāṭin*) spiritual meaning.»[17] We have to realize that alchemical symbols point to something *really unknown*, something which many alchemists themselves were not fully conscious of.

Different lexica could give the impression that the many names in alchemical literature must be considered to be codenames: In Greek, we find the "Lexique de la Chrysopée" in the Codex Marcianus 299 (*Coll. des alch. grecs* II, I.II); in Syriac, we have the one in M. Berthelot's *La Chimie au Moyen Age* II, p. 156 f.; in Arabic, we find, for instance, the one in Abū al-Qāsim's *Kitāb al-Aqālīm as-sabaᶜa* (fol. 15b -17a) and the one presented by Gabriele Ferrario[18] and in Latin, the one of Martin Rulandus (1612). But a closer examination of these lexica shows that mostly they try to provide a basic orientation in the bewildering variety of names. Thus the Greek lexicon explains, for example, that «the ejaculation of the serpent is mercury». This name brings a different quality of mercury into focus. But «the ejaculation of the serpent» is a symbol and with regard to the different metals, we have to remember that they are also symbols, such

17 «Ein Symbol (*ramz*) ist nämlich ein Ausdruck, der nicht seinen äusseren (*zāhir*, offenbaren) Wortsinn bedeutet, vielmehr einen inneren (*bāṭin*, verborgenen) geistigen Sinn hat.» in: Pseudo-Mağrīṭī, *Picatrix – Das Ziel des Weisen*, London 1962, p. 177. German transl. by H. Ritter and M. Plessner. *Picatrix* is the Latin title of the *Ġāyat al-ḥakīm wa aḥaqq al-natīğatain bi-'l-tawdīm*.

18 G. Ferrario: "An Arabic Dictionary of Technical Alchemical Terms: MS Sprenger 1908 of the Staatsbibliothek zu Berlin (fols. 3r-6r)", *AMBIX* 56/2 (2009), p. 36-48. His suggestion to create with a computer «a systematic overview of the codenames» will, however, be misleading in the light of the fact that alchemical symbols are mostly *not covering up something known from this world*, but need careful amplification work in order that these names can reveal what they refer to in the still unconscious beyond. Therefore any computerized overview of alchemical names would only increase the already existing confusion about alchemy. We have to read what Zosimos explains in our text (e.g. on fol. 34a, 16-19 and on fol. 21a, 9). For a general overview of the theme *Decknamen* I refer to M. Ullmann, *Natur- und Geheimwiss. im Islam*, p. 266-67.

as «our mercury is not the mercury of the people». So with one symbol another symbol is explained, *ignotum per ignotius* (The unknown is explained by the more unknown), as a later Latin alchemist pointed out. The lexica just help the adept to become familiar with a symbol, i.e. they help to amplify a symbol *with what other adepts thought about it.* An examination of Zosimos' *Muṣḥaf aṣ-ṣuwar*, especially the «2nd Book of the Names», and other texts written by him or by other masters of the religious-symbolic branch of alchemy, such as Moḥammad ibn Umail, will confirm the symbolic nature of these names in alchemy.

It is therefore necessary to make a clear distinction between allegories and codenames on the one hand, and symbols on the other. After this differentiation, we have to ask whether an alchemical image or name is an allegory, a codename *or* a symbol. Only if we clearly have an allegory or a codename are we allowed to seek for the object in this world, to which it points.[19] However, if it is a symbol, then we have to ponder about it, i. e. to circle around this symbol mentally, as recommended by Abū al-Qāsim. That means we have to collect «the necessary associations in order to understand obscure alchemical statements and symbols». In other words, we have to amplify the symbols, using what can be collected in other passages that are written by the same author and then look at the texts quoted by this author, in order to familiarize ourselves with the possible meaning of each symbol, which basically takes *something known in this world to point to something unknown in the beyond.* (On fol 212a, 16, Zosimos says that he gave signposts to his student.) It is never the other way round, namely that we attempt to find out whether a symbol is just covering up something known in this world, and could therefore be considered to be a codename.

19 In order to do justice to Hallum for speaking of the pictures in the *Muṣḥaf aṣ-ṣuwar* as allegories, one has to point out that such great authorities on Arabic alchemy as Fuat Sezgin, also speak of allegorical alchemy (see F. Sezgin, *Geschichte des arab. Schrifttums*, p. 30 and 74). The confusion of sign and symbol is also common in literature, when scholars speak, for instance, of planetary symbols instead of planetary signs. (See e.g. B. Obrist's article "Visualisation in Medieval Alchemy", 2003, p. 134, and M. Martelli, "Divine Water" l.c., p. 7). A sign stands for something known and defined in this world. A reflection on allegory and symbol is found in the thesis of I. Vereno, *Studien zum ältesten alchemistischen Schrifttum* (1992), p. 13-15, although the author is not fully aware of the nature of symbols, as can be seen from the commentary on his edited texts p.182 f. With regard to the *Risāla al Fakīyāt al-kubrā* (the great Epistle of the Spheres), he describes its language, «which is mainly in images», as allegorical. (p.183). Relevant articles on 'Symbol' and 'Zeichen' can be found in the *Wörterbuch der Symbolik*, (1979), ed. by M. Lurker.

3. The Challenge to my Hypothesis of the Origin of the *Muṣḥaf aṣ-ṣuwar*

An expert on Zosimos, Benjamin Hallum, has put into question my hypothesis that the *Muṣḥaf aṣ-ṣuwar* is the translation of an original Greek text. He claims that this text was written much later, and, as a counter-hypothesis, he proposes that the text and its pictures are a later compilation by an Arab author, suggesting the dating of the *Muṣḥaf aṣ-ṣuwar* as at least after 900 AD (p. 88). As he includes interesting new text material from his thesis in the review, a thorough discussion of his arguments used against my hypothesis in the introduction to CALA II.1 (Part I in this book) is called for.

Hallum's challenge (on p. 80) is based on a summary of my position:

«a) the *Muṣḥaf aṣ-ṣuwar* was probably written by Zosimos or Theosebeia, but it could be a compilation (in Greek) produced by a student during or shortly after Zosimos' lifetime;

b) the *Muṣḥaf aṣ-ṣuwar* is a complete and integral work that was transmitted—illustrations and all—from Greek into Arabic; and

c) when the text was translated into Arabic, some slight changes were made and interpolations were added.»

We start with *point a* of Hallum's summary. He starts his challenge by stating that the arguments given in my introduction to CALA II.1 (on page 21 f.) are «insufficient in themselves to prove that, in its present form, it (the *Muṣḥaf aṣ-ṣuwar*) is a translation from Greek». But he cannot provide convincing evidence that the work was *not* translated from Greek. Thus in this response, I will add more arguments to support my hypothesis. As pointed out in fn 39 on p. 22, the texts of Greek alchemists provide us with two important facts that need to be considered in this debate. In a book written by Olympiodoros from Alexandria ($5^{th}/6^{th}$ century), we find a reference to the effect that Zosimos wrote a special treatise (*idion logon*) «About the Fire».[20] With this statement, Olympiodoros could be referring to «The 9th Book about the Measures of the Fire», folio 190b-195a. As this book contains not even ten pages of text, it should, indeed, rather be named a treatise. Olympiodoros could be referring to this part of the *Muṣḥaf aṣ-*

20 *Amelei kai ho Zosimos idion logon peri pyros poieitai.* M. Berthelot, *Alch. grecs*, II.IV.16, 6-7. On fol. 178a, 5 Theosebeia refers to a *Book about the Fire*..

ṣuwar, as he correctly went on to state that in all his books, Zosimos pointed out the importance of the fire, as we can also verify in the *Muṣḥaf aṣ-ṣuwar*. However, since text and pictures of the *Muṣḥaf aṣ-ṣuwar* reveal so many intimacies, as I will demonstrate in my next argument, he probably did not want, or dare to refer to the *Muṣḥaf aṣ-ṣuwar* openly. This precaution is in line with the well-known alchemical tradition, also mentioned by Zosimos in his *Muṣḥaf aṣ-ṣuwar*, namely to disperse the knowledge (*tabdīd al-ᶜilm*) in order that the unworthy people will not be able to obtain it. Thus Olympiodoros' reference to the treatise «About the Fire» is only understandable for those who are personally acquainted with the entire *Muṣḥaf aṣ-ṣuwar*. Then, later in the same text, we find an even stronger indication that could point to Olympiodoros' knowledge of the *Muṣḥaf aṣ-ṣuwar*. He writes: «[…] as for the art, it is divine […] as Zosimos explains to Theosebeia in a 1000 places.»[21] The only book, so far known where we find over 1000 answers by Zosimos to Theosebeia's questions is our *Muṣḥaf aṣ-ṣuwar*. But, of course, one could argue that these 1000 places are just an allegory or metaphor for countless places. The reply to this objection is that in the hitherto known texts of Zosimos we do not know of any other text—apart from the *Muṣḥaf aṣ-ṣuwar*—that has countless places where Zosimos explains the divine art to his student Theosebeia. Thus these two references could point to a possible knowledge of the dialogue found in the *Muṣḥaf aṣ-ṣuwar* in the 5th/6th century. However, as Wilferd Madelung pointed out to me, only the discovery of a Greek dialogue between Zosimos and Theosebeia will finally settle the question of whether our text can be considered a translation from a Greek text.

Concerning *point b*, Hallum states that «nowhere amongst Zosimos' authentic works preserved in Greek or Syriac is there any indication that Zosimos ever employed the dialogue form, and no fragment of a Zosimos-Theosebeia dialogue is found elsewhere in the Greek alchemical corpus.» He therefore rejects the possibility of the *Muṣḥaf aṣ-ṣuwar* being original. This statement, of course, does not prove that the text is not authentic, as this might well be the first appearance of a dialogue between Zosimos and Theosebeia as a form of teaching. But we do have evidence provided by

21 *Zosimos* […] *kata tēn technēn hōs kai theos eis,* […] *kai tauta en myrios topois pros tēn Theosebeian theēgorei* […]. «[…] As for the art, Zosimos says that it is like God. […] he explains to Theosebeia in a thousand places […]. M. Berthelot, *Alch. grecs*, II.IV.26, 22-23.

a text preserved in Arabic that is probably pre-Islamic. As demonstrated in Part I, page 51, we have at the end of the *Kitāb al-Ḥabīb* a dialogue between Zosimos and Theosebeia which, in many ways, is quite similar to the one the *Muṣḥaf aṣ-ṣuwar.* According to the convincing arguments of Fuat Sezgin, this text goes back to the 4th/5th century. This shows that the form of lively dialogue between our partners exists in a probable pre-Islamic document.[33] Secondly, we have to remember that at the time of Zosimos, works in question-and-answer form were quite common in order to explain a complicated issue (see Part I, p. 18-19). And thirdly, when we look more closely at the text and illustrations of the *Muṣḥaf aṣ-ṣuwar*, we see that this book reveals a complete and thorough symbolic teaching by Zosimos, based on *amazing intimacies* that clearly originate from what was a most personal and bewildering experience for the teacher himself. The action of pondering long enough over the *Muṣḥaf aṣ-ṣuwar* is the essential prerequisite to understand his teachings, as Zosimos repeatedly ordered his student. When following Zosimos' advice, one can see that he was extremely open and bold in revealing, both in text and pictures, his own inner process. He tells his student frankly about his own suffering and his (symbolic) dying and, in time, his experience of redemption and resurrection. This is something absolutely unique compared with the other alchemical texts that I have so far come across. *Thus this dialogue was certainly not meant to be published for the general public*, and it is not too far-fetched to say that this dialogue was most probably handed down from person to person, as is still the case, for instance, with therapeutic case material, which is often in the form of a dialogue between doctor and patient. It is also well known that sometimes authors keep some of their personal experiences hidden from the public, as, for instance, is known from the life of Isaac Newton, who kept his alchemical work hidden from people. To give a recent example, the important alchemical dream series of the Nobel laureate physicist, Wolfgang Pauli, reveals only the transpersonal aspect of the alchemical myth, while personal implications of these dreams are not for the general public and remain undisclosed.[22]

Next, *still under point b*, Hallum claims that the pictures that accompany the text are not pre-Islamic but rather of Mamluk origin. The basis of my assertion that the paintings are of pre-Islamic origin was my

22 Publ. in C. G. Jung, *Psychology and Alchemy* [Coll. Works 12], p. 39-223. First in German 1944. The identity of the dreamer of the dream series became public only much later.

observation that the Arabic alchemical manuscripts so far known to me are rarely illustrated, except for certain schemata or apparatus. An exception is the beautifully illustrated and coloured Arabic text on alchemy, named *Kitāb al-Aqālīm as-sabaᶜa fī al-ᶜilm al-mausūm bi aṣ-ṣanᶜa* (Book of the Seven Climes on the Science called the Art), an anthology of alchemical texts attributed to Abū al-Qāsim al-ᶜIrāqī.[23] This text, copied in the 18th century, is especially mentioned by Hallum to demonstrate that in Mamluk times we do find illustrations in Arabic manuscripts, and he also mentions that three (in fact four) pictures of this book are found in the *Muṣḥaf aṣ-ṣuwar*. However, an examination of this example supports my point, as the illustrations in Abū al-Qāsim's book are *not* of Islamic origin, as Manfred Ullmann has observed.[24] They have their roots clearly in the Christian-Gnostic tradition and even in Pharaonic iconography, as will be demonstrated in fig. 26. I published ten of these pictures in CALA I B (Fig. 18, 46, 56, 65, 69, 87, 89, 94, 95 and 99). The cover page of Kevin van Bladel's thorough research, published as *Arabic Hermes – From Pagan Sage to Prophet of Science* also shows one of of the pictures of this book, namely *Hermes ter unus* (see fig. 18).[25] A closer examination of the pictures of the *Muṣḥaf aṣ-ṣuwar* depicts—in addition to Mamluk clothing—some possible Mamluk architectural motifs; however, both features might well be later Muslim adaptations. As four pictures of the *Kitāb al-Aqālīm as-sabaᶜa* show basic elements of the *Muṣḥaf aṣ-ṣuwar*, they are given on the next four double pages. The pictures on the left are from the *Muṣḥaf aṣ-ṣuwar*, while the illustrations on the right are from the later *Kitāb al-Aqālīm as-sabaᶜa*. The direct comparison allows us to see the reductions, distortions, but also transformations of the 'original' picture in the *Muṣḥaf aṣ-ṣuwar* that occurred in the much later *Kitāb al-Aqālīm as-sabaᶜa.* Also the colouring of the pictures—and this holds truc for both books—has to be verified in general by checking whether the colours correspond to the ones given in the text.

23 British Library, London 1517,1 (= Add. 25724), and Chester Beatty Library 5433, Dublin.

24 Die *Natur- und Geheimwissen. im Islam*, 1972, p. 237. There he writes: «[…] These images go back to an old gnostic iconographic tradition.» (my transl.) The commentary of ibn Umail to his *al-Qasīda an-nunyīa* is based on images from a Pharaonic temple that he interprets to the reader, but so far I have not been able to find an illustrated manuscript of this text. Hallum's focusing on the Mamluk origin of the paintings is surely one-sided, as we can also discern other elements, (e.g. Indian mudras). I refer here to R. Ettinghausen, *Arab Paintings*, 1977², p. 60, 67, 74 and 161).

25 K. van Bladel, *The Arabic Hermes*, Oxford 2009

Fig. 17: *Muṣḥaf aṣ-ṣuwar*, fol. 38a.

Fig. 18: *Kitāb al-Aqālīm as-sabaᶜa*, fol. 17b, attributed to Abū al-Qāsim al-ᶜIrāqī, copied in the 18th century. The relationship to the human beings involved in the alchemical process was at that time lost: in the picture here, Hermes no longer has a direct relationship to the two aspects of Zosimos and Theosebeia, and thus to matter.

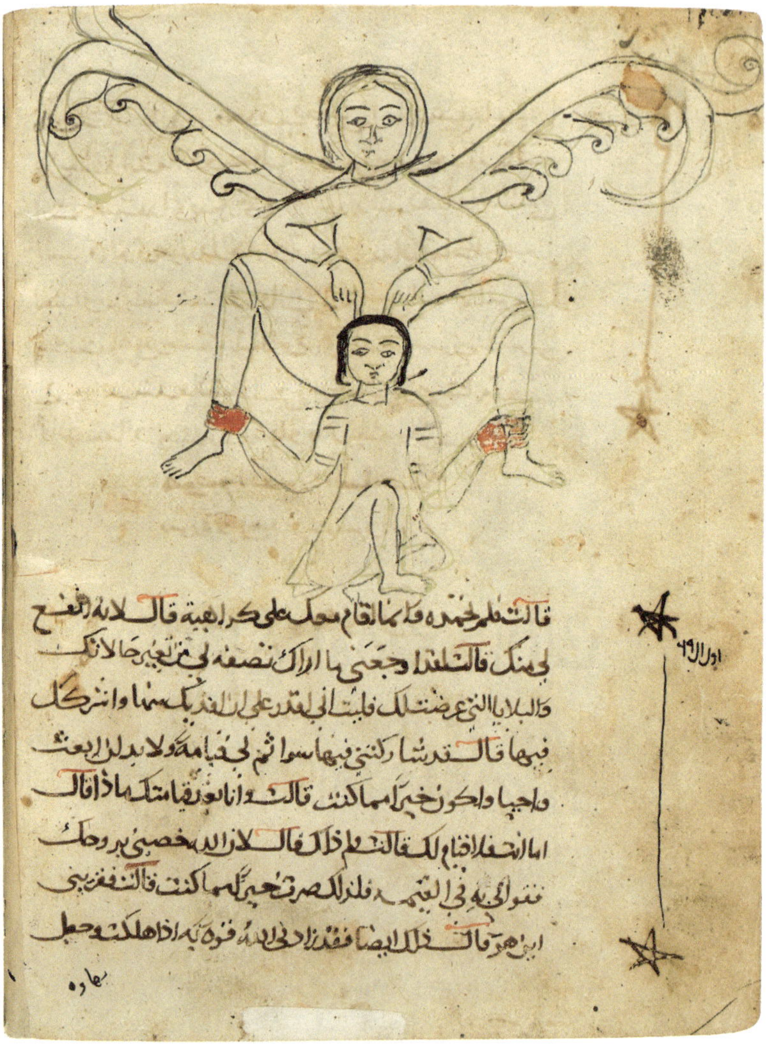

Fig. 19: *Muṣḥaf aṣ-ṣuwar*, fol. 102b.

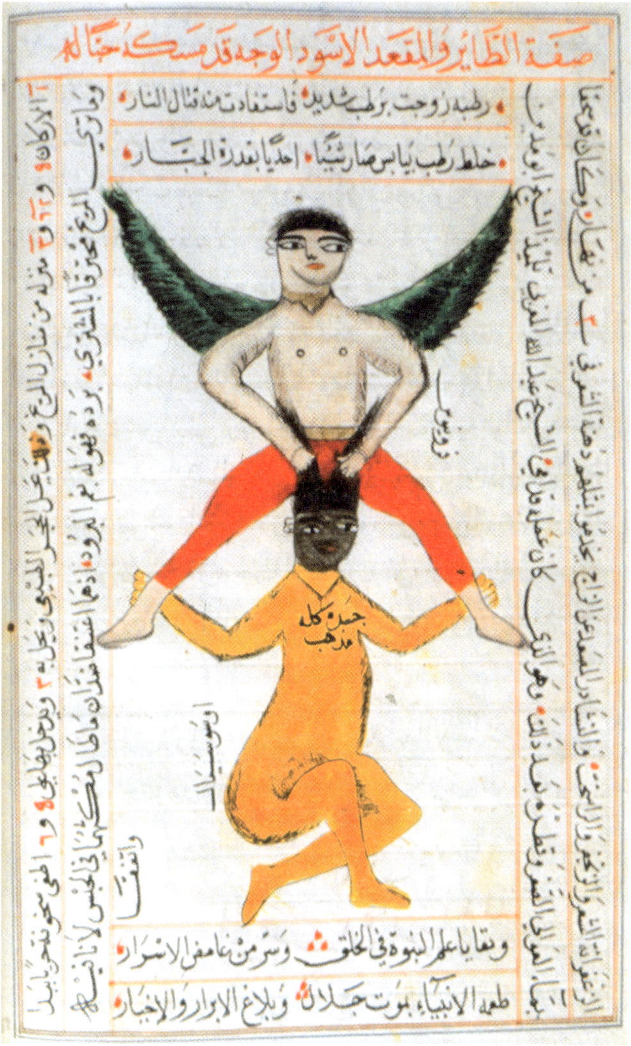

Fig. 20: *Kitāb al-Aqālīm as-sabaᶜa*, fol. 12b, attributed to Abū al-Qāsim al-ᶜIrāqī. Some of the missing colours in the picture of the *Muṣḥaf aṣ-ṣuwar* are represented here according to the description of the man below in this book on fol. 102a, 10.

Fig. 21: *Muṣḥaf aṣ-ṣuwar*, fol. 196a.

Fig. 22: *Kitāb al-Aqālīm as-sabaᶜa*, fol. 18a, attributed to Abū al-Qāsim al-ᶜIrāqī. The sun is no longer on the head of the corpse of the dead Zosimos as we can see in the picture of the *Muṣḥaf aṣ-ṣuwar* given on the opposite page.

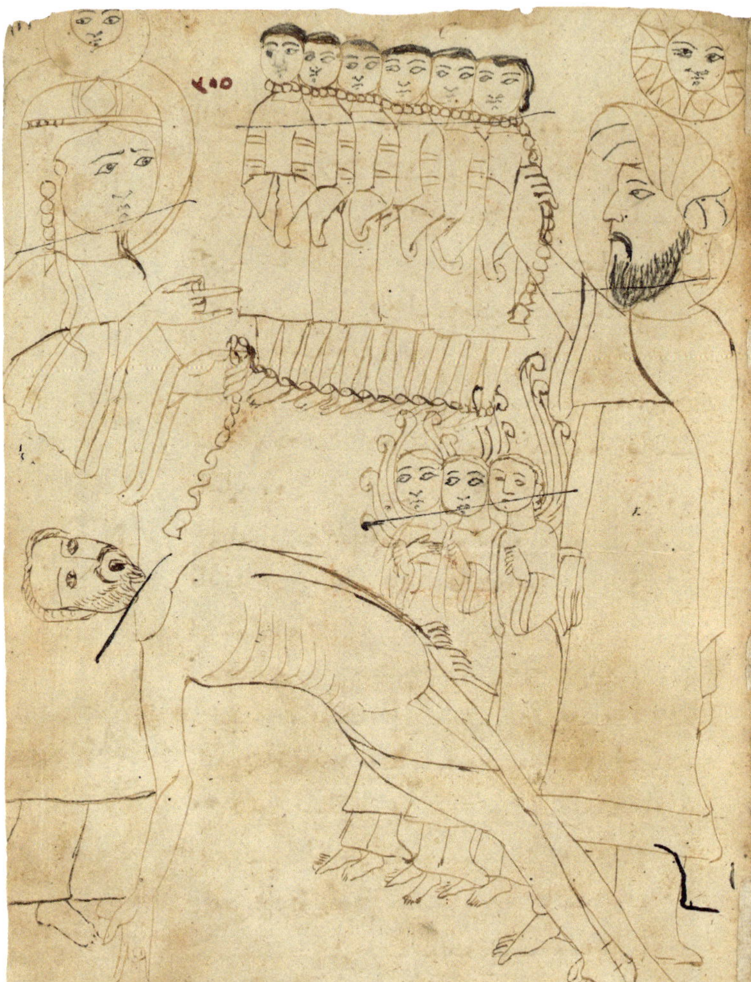

Fig. 23: *Muṣḥaf aṣ-ṣuwar*, fol. 205a.

Fig. 24: *Kitāb al-Aqālīm as-sabaᶜa*, fol. 18b, attributed to Abū al-Qāsim al-ᶜIrāqī. None of the colours is described in the text of the *Muṣḥaf aṣ-ṣuwar* on fol. 204b. The corpse of Zosimos in the picture of the *Muṣḥaf aṣ-ṣuwar* is no longer represented.

One element in the pictures of our book which clearly points to a Pharaonic iconography is the fact that *the sun and the moon are depicted on the head of human beings.* This is a typical Pharaonic way of representing their divinities. However, the fact that we find in a number of pictures an aspective view of the eyes—when a face is represented from side-view—is no indication that this element goes back to the Pharaonic way of their representation, as this aspective way of illustration remained alive in Mamluk times (fig. 25).[26]

Fig. 25: To the left: The Pharaonic goddess Hathor gives the ankh-sign (symbol for life) to the Pharaoh Thutmosis IV. Her eye is represented in the aspective way, showing the eye in front-view in a face seen in side-view. The symbol of the sundisc on the head of Hathor is a typical feature of Pharaonic divinities.To the right: Zosimos as represented with a similar aspective view of his eye (on fol. 99a). A later Mamluk painting below still shows the same aspective representation of the eye (12th cent.).

26 The word *aspective* was coined by the Egyptologist Emma Brunner-Traut. See her epilogue "Aspektive" in Heinrich Schäfer, *Principles of Egyptian Art*, ND Oxford 2002, p. 421-446. That aspect of an object which was considered important for the Ancient Egyptians, was represented in its most powerful and clear appearance.

It is remarkable that fig. 22 represents the carrying of the corpse of the deceased Sungod by the three mercury-spirits, a motif singled out from a picture from the *Muṣḥaf aṣ-ṣuwar* (fig. 21). This motif has a clear connection to the 6th hour of the *Amduat*, a Pharaonic Book for the Afterlife, which goes back to the beginning of the New Kingdom (around 1500 BC), and was still known in Egypt in Roman times (see fig. 26).[27] There, the corpse of the dead Sungod is also lying on its back, protected by a serpent 'Many-faced', which in the Amduat is described as «His tail is in his mouth». In Hellenistic times, this was translated as *Ouroboros*. In the Amduat, the Sungod is brought to his own rejuvenation—symbolized by the scarab *Chepri* on his head—by the serpent power, as the entire process of the night-journey of the Sungod shows. In later Greek alchemy, the symbol of the serpent developed into the symbol of the spiritual mercurial serpent, as can still be seen in fig. 18, where two heads of Hermes are serpent-bird heads. The three mercury-spirits, which in the *Muṣḥaf aṣ-ṣuwar* carry the corpse of the Sungod—who is, according to the description in the text, a symbol for Zosimos' inner god-man—therefore represent the same transforming agent that we find depicted in the Amduat. The rejuvenation that took place during Zosimos' lifetime in his relationship with his student

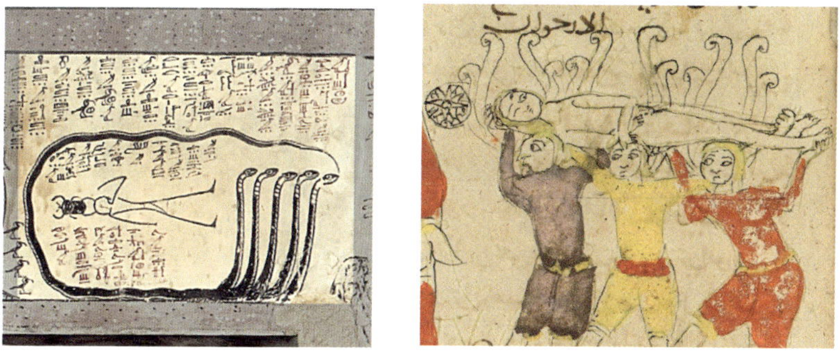

Fig. 26: On the left side we see from the Amduat the last scene of the middle register of the 6th hour. It shows the corpse of the dead Sungod. He is protected by the Ouroboros-serpent.[28] On the right side we see a detail of fig. 21, p. 104, representing the dead Zosimos with a sun on his head. He is a symbol for the Sungod on earth.

27 See Th. Abt and Erik Hornung, *Knowledge for the Afterlife*, Zurich 2003, p. 14.

28 From E. Hornung and Th. Abt (eds.), *The Egyptian Amduat*, Zurich 2007, p. 200.

Theosebeia was, some 1800 years earlier, projected into the afterlife. The frequent motif of the death and resurrection of Zosimos with the sun on his head obviously goes back to the Pharaonic Books of the Afterlife, which appear to be an important source for the teachings of Zosimos.

Summing up the pros and contras of Benjamin Hallum's claim that the illustrations of the *Muṣḥaf aṣ-ṣuwar* are of Mamluk origin rather supports my hypothesis. We would need to find some typical Mamluk elements in our book, comparable to what can be seen, e.g., in the picture of Muḥammad Ibn Umail, representing his great vision (fig. 27).[29] As this is only partly the case, we can assume that our illustrations are pre-Islamic, originating in Egypt, probably in Jewish or Christian Gnostic circles.

It is to the credit of Benjamin Hallum that he was able to analyse in his thesis certain Arabic texts of Zosimos that are to be considered authentic, and

Fig. 27: The great vision of Muḥammad Ibn Umail. This picture shows clear Mamluk elements (13th cent.) that we do not find in the pictures of the *Muṣḥaf aṣ-ṣuwar.*

29 From the Ms of *al-Ma' al-waraqī wa-l-arḍ an-nağīya*, Ms A. 2075, Topkapı Sarai, Ahmet III Library, Istanbul, dating 608 H / 1211. See also Persis Berlekamp "Painting as persuasion: A visual Defence of Alchemy in an Islamic Manuscript of the Mongol Period." *Maqarnas* 20 (2003), p. 35-59, and Th. Abt, CALA I B, Part I.

that he compares some of these texts with passages from the *Muṣḥaf aṣ-ṣuwar*. On this basis, he was able not only to prove that there are authentic quotes from Zosimos in our text, but he could also make evident that the authentic letters, which Zosimos wrote to Theosebeia «when he came from Egypt», [30] must have been written first, and that the *Muṣḥaf aṣ-ṣuwar* is a later text in which the former letters are turned into dialogue form. A close comparison of these texts confirms this assumption. This gave Hallum grounds for arguing that the *Muṣḥaf aṣ-ṣuwar* must be a later Arabic compilation of different parts that may, partly or completely, stem from Zosimos himself. Hallum's valuable research provides us with *evidence that part or may be all of our text goes back to texts written by Zosimos.* However, his conclusion that this text is a later Arabic compilation cannot be proven. As I was able to demonstrate by the coherence of the three picture series, the whole *Muṣḥaf aṣ-ṣuwar* represents a consistent teaching of dialogue and illustrations. As Zosimos tells Theosebeia repeatedly, the pictures which he made for her are clearly meant to be pondered upon, as they will reveal in time the meaning they are pointing out. That is, as I explained above, the nature of symbols. Therefore such a consistent and clearly structured illustrated text cannot be considered a compilation but must be named a *genuine creation*.

Thus it is much more plausible that after the epistles had been read by Theosebeia, she then asked Zosimos to explain further to her the enigmatic and complicated teaching that she found in his epistles. Zosimos—or whoever wrote the book—therefore explained the text in more detail and with much more intimacy by *adding these amazing pictures*, which illustrate the symbolic meaning of what the two experienced in their relationship (*mawadda* = friendship, love).[31] This can be demonstrated by various facts that we find in the text. For example, on fol. 90a, 5 of the *Muṣḥaf aṣ-ṣuwar*, Zosimos says: «Did I not send you special epistles, dedicating them just to you. After them I sent the *Sarṭamīṭā*[32] but it did not convince you.» From this it becomes clear that Zosimos wrote these letters to Theosebeia, but as she did not understand many of his statements, she asked him for further explanations, and Zosimos' answers are preserved in the unique document of the *Muṣḥaf aṣ-ṣuwar*. The most striking facts are two passages in the book that confirm this. One reads: «She said: "I want to ask you about a

30 From the 3rd epistle, Dār al-kutub, kīmiyāʾ Ms 23 M, fol. 27b, 8. 31 Ibid., fol. 27b, 11.

32 This book, spelled in different ways in the *Muṣḥaf aṣ-ṣuwar*, is unknown to me.

thing that I could not understand." He said: "Ask me, because I only visit you frequently in order to answer what you could not understand and know thoroughly."» (fol. 19a, 12-14) The other passage is a question of Theosebeia, who asks her teacher: «I asked you days ago about where the stone which is called the lamp (*sirāǧ*) can be found.» (fol. 37a, 5) These passages show that the dialogue of the *Muṣḥaf aṣ-ṣuwar* probably took place periodically. This confirms my hypothesis that our text is likely to be some sort of a recording of an intensive dialogue. It is evident that the *Muṣḥaf aṣ-ṣuwar* must be a later elaboration of the *Seven Epistles.* This is corroborated when we compare the «4th epistle about the Weights» (fol. 36b, 13-38a, 4; roughly one folio) with the «3rd Book about the Weights» found in the *Muṣḥaf aṣ-ṣuwar* (fol. 63b-70a, seven folios of about the same size with one picture extant). While the epistle has many features that are difficult to understand, we find in the above-mentioned 3rd Book two images (one of them is missing, but is described on fol. 64a), that help us to understand the symbolic meaning of the balance with regard to the relationship between Zosimos and Theosebeia. We also find a *much more related way of teaching*, since Zosimos responds as clearly as possible to the difficulty that his student has in understanding his symbolic language. He also explains the matter with the help of his own dreams, which illustrate the process that took place in the background of his psyche. This can be compared with what Homer did when recounting the Trojan war or the journey of Odysseus, telling the external events in the light of what happened on the level of the divinities, the level that modern psychology calls the archetypal background. When one looks at the text as a whole, it becomes clear that he, Zosimos—or whoever wrote the book—tries to explain in greater depth the difficult statements written in his *Epistles*, by adding symbolic illustrations to his words. These facts show that in the *Muṣḥaf aṣ-ṣuwar* we find a further development of the teachings of Zosimos, be it the work of Zosimos, or Theosebeia, or of a later brilliant alchemist who knew Zosimos' texts and quotes from them. Anyway, *our text is a more precise and more valuable form of Zosimos' thoughts than what is given in his earlier epistolary form.* However, with today's known sources, it is neither possible to find out when the *Muṣḥaf aṣ-ṣuwar* was written nor whether it was translated from Greek. However, the analysis of the pictures and the contents of the *Muṣḥaf aṣ-ṣuwar* reveal enough evidence to support part of my hypothesis, namely that our book must have been written «by Zosimos, or Theosebeia or, quite possibly, by one of his (later) followers».

Concerning Hallum's *point c* of his summary of my position, he rejects my hypothesis that the *Muṣḥaf aṣ-ṣuwar* was translated into Arabic from a Greek original. As pointed out at the end of Hallum's *point a*, for the time being there is no proof that the *Muṣḥaf aṣ-ṣuwar* is a translation from a Greek original text. However, we have to see that our text reveals numerous connections to Hellenistic myths (e.g. the myth of Apollo and Daphne on fol. 92b, 5-15), and even to the Pharaonic theme of the mummification ritual (e.g. the example given above and then on fol. 77a, 19 f. and fol. 103a, 10 f.) as well as to the renewal of the sun (e.g. 31a, 14-16, the theme of the ouroboros on fol. 64a, 14 and 118a, 15). All these basic themes are *put properly into context*, and are presented together with highly relevant mainly pre-Islamic pictures. As in Islamic times the Pharaonic books for the Afterlife were no longer known—the ability to understand the hieroglyphs had died out already in the 3rd/4th century—these examples about the content of the *Muṣḥaf aṣ-ṣuwar* seem to point to a pre-Islamic origin of the *Muṣḥaf aṣ-ṣuwar*, a fact that speaks against a later Arabic authorship.[33] Furthermore it is striking that the symbolic content of the pictures in the *Muṣḥaf aṣ-ṣuwar* is *always somehow associated* with the explanations of Zosimos. Nobody without knowledge of the alchemical work *and* its pagan roots in the Hellenistic-Hermetic *and* Pharaonic traditions would be able to create such a coherent illustrated teaching in a later period. This unique feature of the *Muṣḥaf aṣ-ṣuwar* with regard to its many pre-Islamic pictures and text-elements thus points to a genuine *pre-Islamic authorship* that could go back to an original Greek composition of Zosimos.

After dealing with my hypothesis, Hallum formulates his counter-hypothesis that the *Muṣḥaf aṣ-ṣuwar* is «a compilation in dialogue form, produced in Arabic by an Islamic author who had access to Arabic versions of a number of authentic Greek alchemical texts, some, if not all, of which are attributable to Zosimos» (p. 81). So we need to look at his arguments supporting this counter-hypothesis.

33 U. W. Haarmann writes: «Any continuity from Ancient to Islamic Egypt was irretrievably and doubly cut off, first by the adoption of Christianity in Egypt in the fourth century and then, three centuries later, by the Islamic conquest.» in: *The Oxford Encyclopedia of Ancient Egypt*, s. v. "Islam and Ancient Egypt".

4. Hallum's Counter-hypothesis

Hallum points to important source material concerning the origin of the *Muṣḥaf aṣ-ṣuwar*, and, with the help of such texts, tries to prove that this book is a later Arabic compilation. He states in his review (p. 82) that: «The *Muṣḥaf aṣ-ṣuwar* includes a number of excerpts from other Arabic works attributed to Zosimos, at least three of which survive, allowing the texts to be compared. The first of these is the "Third Epistle of Zosimos" (*al-Risāla al- ṯāliṯa li-Rūamūs*), one of a collection of seven epistles known only in Arabic, but certainly translated from the Greek and attributable to Zosimos. Almost the entire text of the "Third Epistle" is reproduced in the *Muṣḥaf aṣ-ṣuwar* (end of the 1st Book and majority of the 2nd Book) and nearly verbatim. [...] The "Third Epistle" is, as its title suggests, not a dialogue but, like many of the Greek works, a letter from Zosimos to his student. However, as it appears in the *Muṣḥaf aṣ-ṣuwar*, before each place in the epistle where Zosimos changes the subject or offers further clarification of a point, a corresponding question by Theosebeia has been inserted. The fact that the dialogue form is not attested amongst Zosimos' Greek works, that the text of the "Third Epistle" is less sound in its dialogue form than in its epistolary form, that the unity of the "Third Epistle" is disregarded in the *Muṣḥaf aṣ-ṣuwar*, where it is divided across two books, and that Theosebeia's contribution as an interlocutor amounts to no more than eliciting the material that is presented in the "Third Epistle", all indicate that the "Third Epistle" (in its Arabic version) was the source text and that it was adapted by the compiler of the *Muṣḥaf aṣ-ṣuwar*.»

For clarity's sake, I shall divide Hallum's arguments in support of his counter-hypothesis into four points, so that they can be dealt with separately.

1. The dialogue form is not attested amongst Zosimos' Greek works.
2. The "Third Epistle" is less sound in its dialogue form than in its epistolary form.
3. The unity of the "Third Epistle" is disregarded in the *Muṣḥaf aṣ-ṣuwar*, where it is divided across two books.
4. Theosebeia's contribution as an interlocutor amounts to no more than eliciting the material that is presented in the "Third Epistle".

Hallum's *first argument* is a (repeated) *argumentum ad ignorantium*, an argument from ignorance. The absence of evidence does not constitute evidence of absence, as already pointed out on p. 97. Just because we have not seen a dialogue between Zosimos and Theosebeia before, we cannot conclude that this new find is not authentic in this form. Apart from this fact and the dialogue between Zosimos and Theosebia found in the *Kitāb al-Ḥabīb* (see p. 98), there is, however,—as long as we do not find a Greek dialogue between Zosimos and Theosebeia—no proof that our text is a translation from a Greek original.

Let us now look at Hallums's *second argument*. Reading the *Epistles* is rather complicated. The samples for comparison between the "Third Epistle" and the *Muṣḥaf aṣ-ṣuwar,* which Hallum gives in his thesis (Appendix, II.7, p. 455), allow an Arabist to recognize that the style of the *Muṣḥaf aṣ-ṣuwar*, compared with the "Third Epistle", is more colloquial and more easily understandable. So from the content and the style it seems that the dialogue form of the *Muṣḥaf aṣ-ṣuwar* is a later elaboration and upgrading of the material from Zosimos' *Epistles*. This would confirm my claim, mentioned earlier on pages 111-112, that the dialogue form of the *Muṣḥaf aṣ-ṣuwar* is more sound than the "Third Epistle".

Concerning Hallum's *third argument* about the breaking up of the unity of the "Third Epistle", we have to look at the whole composition of the *Muṣḥaf aṣ-ṣuwar*. Zosimos was developing his teaching by presenting to Theosebeia illustrations that he made especially for her. From this it becomes clear that the author of the *Muṣḥaf aṣ-ṣuwar* took material from Zosimos' letters and explained to his student the questions which arose, one by one, arranging his answers according to the *completely new structure* that he gave to his teaching. This structure is visible in the three picture series which I have explained before. Looking at all these facts, we can see that the dialogue of the *Muṣḥaf aṣ-ṣuwar* is, as an entirely new composition, more easily understandable because it includes more differentiated answers to the various uncertainties of Theosebeia. We can also assume that the *Muṣḥaf aṣ-ṣuwar* contains material from Zosimos' letters that is no longer extant or not yet identified. Although the words used in the *Muṣḥaf aṣ-ṣuwar* are sometimes different from the *Epistles*, they express the same thought. Thus for the sake of clarity, the author of the *Muṣḥaf aṣ-ṣuwar* (whom we name Zosimos) had to disregard the unity of the "Third Epistle".

Hallum's *fourth argument* puts into question the importance and value of Theosebeia in this dialogue. It is true that Theosebeia elicits the wisdom from Zosimos by her questions. But, in the same way as Zosimos and Theosebeia are represented throughout the book as being of the same size—following the important Pharaonic tradition that respected the male and the female principle as equal—so the role of Theosebeia is not just that of a foil. She was *crucial* for the development of Zosimos' teaching, as I explained in my first introduction (p. 29-45). The text samples given there (on p. 33 and p. 35-37), as well as Zosimos' complaining about Theosebeia's frequent failure to understand, and, on the other hand, her despair about his enigmatic statements, illustrate sufficiently that «Theosebeia's contribution as an interlocutor» is certainly more than, as Hallum states, «eliciting the material that is presented in the "Third Epistle"». In the light of the lively dialogues found in our text, Hallum's fourth argument is unacceptable.

In the next paragraph of his review (p. 82), Hallum points to a contradiction in my statement of my introduction (Part I, p. 46) where I say that the *Muṣḥaf aṣ-ṣuwar* was written after the *Kitab Mafātīḥ aṣ-ṣanᶜa* (*The Book of the Keys of the Art*) but that this contradicts my quote from the introduction to the *The Book of the Keys*, which reads that «it was the last thing he wrote for her». However, this need not be a contradiction. How can we know that The Book of the Keys was really the last one that Zosimos wrote? We can read, for example. a similar statement at the beginning of Muḥammad ibn Umail's *ad-Durra an-naqīya*, saying that this is his last book.[34] This text is a commentary to his poem named *al-Qasīda al-mimīya*.[35] But also here, we simply do not know whether Ibn Umail wrote other texts later. We have to keep in mind that the absence of evidence does not constitute evidence of absence. However, we have evidence that the *Muṣḥaf aṣ-ṣuwar* was written after the *Kitab Mafātīḥ aṣ-ṣanᶜa*, as I demonstrated in my example given on page 46-47.[36]

Then Hallum moves to his final argument, writing (on p. 82) that «the most damning evidence against Abt's hypothesis is the inclusion in the *Muṣḥaf aṣ-ṣuwar* of a section from *The Sulphurs*, an authentic work of

34 Āṣafīya Library 1410, Hyderabad (Deccan), line 8 of the introduction.

35 Ms. Beşir Ağa (Istanbul) 505, fol. 225a, 33 verses.

36 Further evidence is found on fol. 134a, 18 -134b, 2, fol. 138a, 2-3, and fol. 176a, 5-7.

Zosimos extant almost in its entirety in Arabic.[37] Two Greek fragments of *The Sulphurs* survive [...]. Not only do the Greek fragments authenticate the Arabic text, but [one of] the fragment[s] supplies the original Greek text of a part of the section of *The Sulphurs* included in the *Muṣḥaf aṣ-ṣuwar*, and comparisons between the three versions of this section (i.e. those preserved in a Greek fragment, *The Sulphurs* and the *Muṣḥaf aṣ-ṣuwar*) reveal much about the relationship between the versions.» Hallum states that *The Sulphurs* is, in the same way as the Greek fragments, neither in dialogue form nor is it addressed to Theosebeia but to an anonymous readership. He also observes that this Arabic text «follows the Greek fragments closely and for the most part faithfully». Then he gives an example that is, however, not «damning evidence» against my hypothesis. Looking at his text sample, we can clearly see that the *Muṣḥaf aṣ-ṣuwar* is the refined and personal teaching of Zosimos, as he answers the numerous questions of his student Theosebeia. Whoever examines the three text versions, presented on page 84 of Hallum's review, can see what an important explanation is added to the statement extant in the Greek fragment of *The Sulphurs*. It is not within the scope of this reply to Hallum's review to explain the profound answer of Zosimos, so I have to refer to my publication CALA I B, where I quoted the above-mentioned passage and amplified the symbols of the alabaster and the quicklime.[38] The enlarged text of the *Muṣḥaf aṣ-ṣuwar* is therefore in no way, as Hallum claims, just written «to construct a text based loosely on the framework provided by *The Sulphurs* but expanding upon it to a large degree», and this text is also not «little more than a series of questions posed by the pupil, Theosebeia, and answered by the master Zosimos.»

With the connections that Hallum provides to various Greek original texts, hc increases the probability that the *Muṣḥaf aṣ-ṣuwar*—whenever and by whomsoever it was written—is likely to *be the oldest personal, illustrated document so far known that is concerned with the creation of the stone of the sages*. From the *Muṣḥaf aṣ-ṣuwar* we learn in a shockingly direct way that the 'substances' involved in the alchemical process are the teacher and his student in their different psychic states. We have to be

37 Rampur, Raza Library Ms kīmiyāʾ 12, fol. 60b, l. 18 – 61a, l. 12. A copy of this Ms was kindly sent to me by B. Hallum.

38 Th. Abt, *Psychological Commentary on Ibn Umail's Ḥall ar-rumūz*, p. 107-110.

aware that at the time of Zosimos, the hiding of such alien thoughts was an absolute necessity. A work with such unique, frank illustrations as those we find in our manuscript was certainly not meant for the general public. Zosimos points this out in his *Muṣḥaf aṣ-ṣuwar*, for instance, on folio 204b, 1: «Hermes was too cautious to illustrate these things in his books.» This shows that Zosimos reveals highly delicate material in the illustrations of his *Muṣḥaf aṣ-ṣuwar*. However, *by representing symbolic pictures he was able to point to the overwhelming archetypal energy, without being overpowered or possessed by it.* This enormous energy can be felt throughout the book. There are innumerable further places where Zosimos tells his student Theosebeia that he now reveals to her things that must be hidden from the ignorant, a request that is also well-known from other alchemical texts.

Whoever has had any experience of the power of magic attraction of somebody or something knows that this energy can have an overwhelming effect on the individual. Most disasters in modern marriages, to give an example, result from such an irresistible magnetism between one partner and somebody or something outside the marriage. Zosimos lived most probably in the Christian-Gnostic tradition around 300 AD in Egypt. Thus one can imagine that, at that time, this unorthodox onset of magic attraction between master and student must have been most bewildering. The whole *Muṣḥaf aṣ-ṣuwar* revolves around the crucial question of how to transform and ultimately contain this outburst of Zosimos' inner hellish fire of desirousness, *without trying to extinguish it.*

Now we have to discuss three further passages mentioned in my first introduction, as they could speak for a later Muslim authorship. All the passages could be arguments that point to a later adaptation or even creation of the text, and could therefore speak against a translation of the *Muṣḥaf aṣ-ṣuwar* from a Greek text, as was pointed out to me by Wilferd Madelung.

A *first argument* against the *Muṣḥaf aṣ-ṣuwar* being a translation from a Greek text was given in my introduction to the facsimile edition on page 25-26. It is based on the text on fol. 10a, 8-16. There, Zosimos explains to Theosebeia that the science will appear to the sons of Ismāʿīl, which is one of the names for the Muslims: «After 160 (later in the text 140) years of their reign, […] the number of seekers of this science will increase, and they will feel enthusiasm for it (the science). Then the great and exalted God will reveal it to them, after they were in despair about it, in order to increase their desire for the other world more than for this world.» This passage could be an argument against the Greek origin of the *Muṣḥaf aṣ-ṣuwar* if it were an integral part of the text. However, when we look at the context in which this passage appears, we find that just before that quote, Zosimos gives an answer to Theosebeia's question about quite another theme that has to do with a sage who will come at the end of time and who has already, at a very young age, an understanding of the alchemical work. The mentioned passage is only loosely connected to this above-mentioned text. After Zosimos' explanation with regard to the sons of Ismāʿīl, there follows an entirely different theme, starting with Theosebeia's question about lead and iron. This shows that this passage about Ismāʿīl' sons is not really an integral part of the rest of the text. It rather seems to be written at a later period, when a Muslim, who also wrote the introduction to the *Muṣḥaf aṣ-ṣuwar* (fol. 3b, 1-6), wanted to adapt the book to his religion. On the basis of these reflections we can assume that this passage is a later interpolation.

Then, in my first introduction (on page 26), I have added a *second argument* that could speak for a later Muslim author of the *Muṣḥaf aṣ-ṣuwar*. There I wrote that «the Arab alchemist [or] adapter felt free to add Hadith quotations to the text. Up till now we have understood these references to the Hadith of the prophet as interpolations of a later Muslim adapter. However, as already mentioned in my first introduction, one could as well argue that this is a sign that the whole text was written by a later Muslim author who was using Greek or already translated parts of Zosimos' writings. As the quoted passages are found in the first 17 folios, written by another hand than the rest of the book, it would be reasonable to investigate whether these Muslim adaptations are mainly found in this part of the manuscript.[39] The *Muṣḥaf aṣ-ṣuwar* only mentions the prophet Muḥammad four times, once at the beginning on fol. 3b, 1 and 4, then on fol. 127a, 16, where the last

39 In his *Zosimos Arabus* on p. 258, B. Hallum points out that the Ms of the *Muṣḥaf aṣ-ṣuwar* was rebound in the late 16th century. Probably at this time of rebinding, a number of folios got lost, and some margins and pictures after fol. 17 suffered from the recutting. After these 17 folios, the prophet Moses is the one frequently referred to in the text, while the prophet Muḥammad is only mentioned twice—at the end of the 5th and the 13th Book.

line of «The 5th Book about the Magnesia» is written by another hand, and once at the end in the colophon on fol. 223a, 15, while we find Moses referred to seven times—four times as prophet. Yet all of this does not prove a non-Muslim authorship, as Moses was for a Muslim also a holy prophet as was Muḥammad. However, the mentioning of «the qibla and the eastern direction» (fol. 75b, 15) point clearly to the Christian-Gnostic orientation towards the rising sun.[40] In the light of this, one could understand the few references to Muḥammad (one at the beginning of the book, one written by another hand on fol. 127a, 16 and one in the colophon), and the sole reference to mosques and minarets (*masāǧid wa madāyin*, fol. 79a, 13) to be later interpolations. Thus the facts collected from the text until now show both, supporting and dismissive aspects regarding any Muslim authorship. Thus let us look at further arguments in favour of a Muslim alchemist.

Later in our *Muṣḥaf aṣ-ṣuwar*, on folio 42a, 19 -42b, 3 and on folio 194a, 12-18, there are two similar passages that speak about Jesus. They are also mentioned in my first introduction on page 28. In these passages we do not find Jesus as the Redeemer, but as a human being who is a seeker. This could be *a third argument* that points to a later Muslim authorship. Contrary to the context of my first argument, given above (the one about the sons of Ismāīl), these passages about Jesus are, *in both places, an integral part* of Zosimos' answer to Theosebeia's questions. For the sake of a simple verification, I give the context in which one of these passages appears (42a, 15 -42b, 3): «He said: […] "Be patient and wait for the completion of the dyeing, and beg continuously of the exalted and blessed God that He may complete it (the work) for you. And I warn you about the fire in the operation, for it is the enemy of the water because of their opposition and mutual hatred until peace comes to the water and the fire and they are reconciled. As Christ, peace be upon Him, said: 'How amazing of you, O community of sages, that you reconciled water and fire, so they stayed together in the operation.' The sages were astonished that He (Christ) knew them by their science. Know that if you reconcile water and fire, your work will be good, by the will of magnified and glorified God."» Thus, on the one hand, Jesus is introduced as a human being who is searching for the alchemical secret of how to reconcile water and fire, and on the other hand, he appears as a sage or prophet who already knows the alchemists «by

40 See J. Ratzinger, *The Spirit of the Liturgy*, Chapters 2 and 3.

their science». Some of these features of Jesus remind us of how Muslims portrayed Jesus. As Tarif Khalidi could show in his book *The Muslim Jesus, Sayings and Stories in Islamic Literature*,[41] Jesus—as seen by the Muslims—does not appear as the son of God, but as a forerunner of the prophet Muḥammad. For the collection of sayings and stories in Islamic literature, Tarif Khalidi coined the phrase "Muslim Gospel". As a clarification, he writes in the conclusion to the introduction to his book: «...it has to do with the Islamic elements in this gospel. Jesus is always identified as a Muslim prophet—and this must be constantly borne in mind, for he is, after all, a figure moulded in an Islamic environment.»[42] The fact that Jesus appears here as a human being, rather than a redeemer would support the conclusion that the *Muṣḥaf aṣ-ṣuwar* was written by a later Muslim author. However, one element that is entirely alien to a Muslim Jesus is the fact that Jesus here appears to be interested in learning about the reconciliation of the opposites. Jesus for a Muslim, as the one prophet who came before Muḥammad, is always pointing to the differences between the upper and the lower, between paradise and hell.[43] So we have to look for sources where we can find this feature of Jesus, who sees the problem of the hostile opposites and is interested in their reconciliation. Such a description of Jesus can be found in the "Gospel of Philip", which is part of the *Nag Hammadi Library*,[44] discovered in 1945, close to Nag Hammadi, a town in Upper Egypt about 85 kilometres south of Panopolis, today's Akhmim.[45] There we can read that Jesus speaks about the unity of

41 Tarif Khalidi, *The Muslim Jesus, Sayings and Stories in Islamic Literature,* Cambridge (Mass.), 2001.

42 Ibid., p. 44.

43 Ibid., s.v. Paradise and Satan. In 11 sayings of Jesus, Paradise is mentioned in opposition to Hell, and in 16 sayings, Satan is shown as the enemy of God.

44 J. M. Robinson, *The Nag Hammadi Library*, Leiden 1988, p. 139-160. The *Papyrus Berolinensis* 8502, a Copic Ms from the 5th cent., containing a.o. the *Pistis Sophia*, was unearthed in Panopolis/Akhmīm.

45 In his paper, «"The master spoke: 'Take one of the sun and one unit of almulgam'" hitherto unnoticed Coptic papyrological evidence for early Arabic alchemy", Sebastian Richter asks «Is there an 'alchemical valley' around Panopolis/Akhmīm?» In part and without this question, that paper is published in: *Ambix*, Vol. 56/1, 2009, p. 23-35 (13). Just before sending this book for printing, I was informed by the author, that the first-mentioned article appeared in: P. Sijpesteijn et al. (eds.), *Documents and the History of the Early Islamic World*. Acts of the 3rd Conference of the International Society for Arabic Papyrology, Alexandria, 23-26 March 2006. Leiden 2010.

the opposites: «Light and darkness, life and death, right and left are brothers of one another. They are inseparable.» (53, 14-15) or «In the world there is good and evil. Its good things are not good, and the evil things are not evil.» (66, 10-12) And Jesus says in this Gospel: «I came to make [the things below] like the things [above, and the things] outside like those [inside. I came to unite] them in the place.» (67, 30-34) The relationship of Jesus to alchemy in this Gospel, as well as in many other places, is made obvious when we read for instance: «It is from water and fire that the soul and spirit came into being. [...] Truth does not come into the world naked, but it came in types and images. The world will not receive truth in any other way. [...] When Eve was still in Adam, death did not exist. When she was separated from him, death came into being. If he enters again and attains the former self, death will be no more.» (67, 3 -68, 26) Later on, in the same gospel we can read: «Farming in the world requires the cooperation of four essential elements. A harvest is gathered into the barn only as a result of the natural action of water, earth, wind, and light. God's farming likewise has four elements – faith, hope, love and knowledge. Faith is our earth, that in which we take our root. [And] hope is the water through which we are nourished. Love is the wind through which we grow. Knowledge then is the light through which we [ripen].» (79, 18-30) These passages could have been written by an alchemist of the symbolic-religious branch. From these quoted passages we can see that *in Gnostic times Jesus developed into a reconciler of opposites*, a theme well known in Greek alchemy.

Wesley W. Isenberg, the translator of the Gospel of Philip into English, writes on p. 141 that «the Coptic text of this gospel is undoubtedly a translation of a Greek text which was written perhaps as late as the second half of the third century.» That means the gospel was written around the time of Zosimos; thus it is not unlikely that Zosimos knew this Gospel.[46] The text

46 In the "Gospel of Thomas", which is part of the *Nag Hammadi Library* (p. 124-138), we find similar aspects of a Jesus as reconciler of opposites: «Jesus said: [...] "Rather, the kingdom is inside you, than it is outside of you."» (32, 25-26) And later on we read in the same gospel: «Jesus saw infants being suckled. He said to His disciples, "These infants being suckled are like those who enter the kingdom." They said to Him, "Shall we then, as children, enter the kingdom?" Jesus said to them, "When you make the two one, and when you make the inside like the outside and the outside like the inside, and the above like the below, and when you make the male and the female one and the same, so that the male not be male nor the female female; [...] then will you enter [the kingdom]."» (37, 20-35) This Gospel, which goes back to the 2nd century AD, was also

is, according to Isenberg, «a compilation of statements pertaining primarily to the meaning and value of sacraments within the context of a Valentine conception, of the human predicament of life after death».[47] The development of Jesus from a man who in the desert strongly rejected Satan into a Jesus who is able to reconcile the opposites, emerged in the time of Gnosticism. The passages that we find in the Gospel of Philip are revealing, as they point to a connection to alchemical thoughts, illustrating the close relationship between Zosimos' alchemy and those Gnostic circles.[48]

From this we can conclude that the passages of Jesus, referred to by Zosimos, must have had their origin in pre-Islamic times. There are two further pre-Islamic passages confirming my statement. One is found in a text of the previously mentioned Olympiodoros from Alexandria ($5^{th}/6^{th}$ century), who commented on "The Book of Action", written by Zosimos. This passage describes «Jesus being surprised at how the enemies water and fire, [...] can be reconciled [...].»[49] These words show that this passage about Jesus is clearly pre-Islamic, and that it was *a Gnostic Jesus*, who was interested in the art of reconciling the opposites. A similar passage can also be found in the already mentioned *Kitāb al-Ḥabīb*, a text that Fuat Sezgin dates back to the $4^{th}/5^{th}$ century.[50] There we read: «Our

written before the time of Zosimos. And as both texts were originally written in Greek, they were probably known to Zosimos, who, after all, comes from the same area of Upper Egypt.

47 Ibid., p. 139.

48 See also A. Roberts, *Golden Shrine, Goddess Queen, Egypt's Anointing Mysteries*, 2008, p. 95 f.

49 M. Berthelot, *Alch. grecs*, II.IV.41. It is a question of Jesus (Κυριος) with regard to the one who knows «the hidden art of chemistry» (τὴν κεκρομμένον τέχνην τῆς χυμεῖας). He told them: «How do I have to understand now the transformation? How come that the water and the fire, enemies and going against each other, opposites by nature, are uniting in the same (body), in harmony and friendship? (πῶς μεταβολὴν νῦν ὁρῶ; πῶς τὸ ὕδορ καὶ τὸ πῦρ, ἐχθρὰ και ἐναντία ἀλλήλοις και ‹πρὸσ τὴν› ἀντιπαράθεσιν πεφυκόντα εἰς τὸ αὐτὸ συνῆλθον ὁμονοίας καὶ φιλίας χάριν).

50 F. Sezgin, *Gesch. der arab. Wiss.* p. 92. f.; already M. Bethelot pointed to the Greek origin of that book in: *La Chimie au moyen âge* III, p.12. A study of the relationship between the *Kitāb al-Ḥabīb* and the *Muṣḥaf aṣ-ṣuwar* is called for. A dialogue recently published with the title *The Ancient Egyptian Book of Thoth, a Demotic Discourse on Knowledge and Pendent to the Classical Hermetica*, edited by Richard Jasnow and Karl-Theodor Zauzich (Wiesbaden 2005), could also be of relevance to our manuscript, as this text connects the Ancient Pharaonic Books for the Afterlife and Pharaonic temple knowledge with the *Corpus Hermeticum* and, albeit

Lord the Christ told the sages when they came to Him to find out what He knew about their work: "I am surprised, O you sages, how you can reconcile water and fire ..."»[51] As I could demonstrate in Part I on page 49, there is evidence that the *Muṣḥaf aṣ-ṣuwar* is the original text, while the *Kitāb al-Ḥabīb* is a later abbreviated form. This passage about Jesus, compared with our text, is also a shortened version. All these additional facts refute the argument that the description of Jesus in the *Muṣḥaf aṣ-ṣuwar* points to its Muslim origin.

With the discussion of these three points, which could speak for a possible Muslim authorship, the facts rather seem to confirm that our text cannot be considered a later compilation by a Muslim author. Whether everything that is not clearly Islamic goes back to one original Greek text can, of course, for the time being not be proven. Only a Greek dialogue between Zosimos and Theosebeia will be proof that our Arabic text is a translation from a Greek original. But in the light of the assembled facts, it becomes much more probable that the original text of the *Muṣḥaf aṣ-ṣuwar*, whose full title is *The Book of Pictures of Zosimos the Sage and the Questions of Theosebeia*, has to be sought in pre-Islamic times.

If my hypothesis is to find acceptance in the scientific community, there will need to be extensive additional research, as was undertaken, for instance, with regard to the *Turba philosophorum*. It is, above all, the many internal relationships and the different explanations by Zosimos of the same theme, that will require in-depth investigation.[52]

indirectly, with our *Muṣḥaf aṣ-ṣuwar*. This text contains elements of a dialogue between a deity, *Ḥsr.t* (Thoth), and the *mr rḥ* (The-one-who-loves-knowledge or the one-who-wishes-to-learn). As *The Book of Thoth* was probably written in Hermopolis in the 2nd century, it might even have been known to Zosimos. The *Pistis Sophia* (*The Faith of Sophia*, 2nd century, the Mss of this text come from Upper Egypt, as well) also contains elements of the Pharaonic Books of the Afterlife as well as elements that can be found in our dialogue. Therefore this text should also be included in any such further studies. Sophia was to the gnostics a divine syzygy of Christ, rather than simply a word meaning wisdom. *Pistis Sophia*, ed. by C. Schmidt, translation and notes by Violet Macdermot, Nag Hammadi Studies IX, 1978. Of course the *Corpus Hermeticum* and related texts will need to be part of such further studies, as well.

51 M. Berthelot, *La Chimie au Moyen Age* III, p. 61.9. M. Ullmann also pointed to this nexus of Olympiodoros and the *Kitāb al-Ḥabīb*, in *Natur- und Geheimwiss. im Islam,* on p. 188.

52 See, for example, the article of U. Rudolph, who was able to point to sources of early Christian Theology in the *Turba philosophorum* in his article "Christliche Theologie und Vorsokratische Lehren in der Turba Philosophorum", *Oriens*, Vol. 32 (1990), p. 97-123.

5. The Significance of the Date of the *Muṣḥaf aṣ-ṣuwar*

In the last chapter of his review (p. 86), Hallum challenges my hypothesis with regard to «the relevance of the *Muṣḥaf aṣ-ṣuwar* to the later alchemical literature, especially to the *Turba philosophorum*». There he questions my removing «Martin Plessner's key argument for a tenth-century dating of the *Turba*, namely that it contains a legend concerning a poison maiden who kills her husband—the so-called legend of the *Giftmädchen*—which Plessner believed was absent from Graeco-Roman literature and only entered the world of Islam from India in the early tenth century.» Hallum then claims that I have arrived at a false conclusion by not «conducting a wider survey of the Arabic Zosimos texts».

Then he moves on to my statement (p. 55) that, «in the *Muṣḥaf aṣ-ṣuwar*, the *Giftmädchen* is often referred to as "ascunia, murderess of her husband"», and notes that Julius Ruska understood 'ascunia' to mean acacia. For various reasons, given in detail below, I follow Ruska's translation. But Hallum states «that I am wrong, together with Julius Ruska». Then he makes first a connection by bringing in the much later Latin text of the *Turba philosophorum*, in order to point out that there «ascunia appears as ascoria or alocia amongst other variant spellings, but also, in a fuller form of the name, as *gummam, quae ab ascorie est* (the gum which is from ascoria)». From there he goes back to an earlier Syriac text attributed to Democritus which is, as he claims, almost certainly a translation from the Greek. From this text he quotes: «Here for you is the *komaris* which is from Skythia, which is a land. However, she who is from Skythia is a warrior-woman [lit. 'very manly woman'] killing people and killing readily ...». Hallum then claims that for linguistic reasons *komaris* of Skythia must mean the gum of Skythia, «hence the Latin *gumma ascotiae*». Then Hallum quotes a text from the "Third Epistle", where Zosimos seems to comment on the Syriac passage of Democritos cited above. « [...] because the women of Skythia kill their husbands without mercy. For this reason, the Sage [Democritos] named the gum and what is similar to it after the women of this city.» On the basis of these text samples, Hallum then suggests «the Classical source of the symbolism behind the choice of *Skythian* as a codename for a substance that

Zosimos classified as the feminine power *par excellence*». Classical sources show that «the Skythian women were very manly women indeed, and must have been the source for the story of the Skythian woman found in Zosimos and in the Doctrine of Democritos». That is *one aspect* of the Skythian woman, but not the whole truth.

In response to Hallum's findings, I will show why we have to be careful not to simply look at the «symbolism behind the choice of *Skythian* as a codename», as Hallum writes. As mentioned above, we need to make a clear distinction between symbol and codename. First, Hallum considers *Skythian* to be a codename. With this assumption he fails to carefully collect the «necessary associations» about which we read in the recommendation of Abū al-Qāsim. Instead of keeping the key symbol, «ascunia, murderess of her husband», in the centre of his research, Hallum moves away from this image and tries to find out what that name could mean in this world. The conclusion he arrives at is that *Skythian* is nothing but «a codename for a substance that Zosimos classified as *the feminine power par excellence*». His historical associations to the manly women of Skythia only reveal an association to something defined in this world. This is, of course, "nice to have" but it does not really contribute to the understanding of the deeper meaning of this symbol itself, which is already known as *the feminine power komaris* in Zosimos' Greek texts (M. Mertens, *Mem. Auth.* XIII, 2, 25; 34). By adopting a reductive procedure, Hallum chooses to ignore a scientific approach to understanding an unknown name, as first of all, we have to investigate where the same name or symbol occurs *in* the text.

Therefore we will now—in a *first step*—collect places where «ascunia, the murderess of her husband» occurs in the *Muṣḥaf aṣ-ṣuwar* itself. We find «ascunia, the murderess of her husband» in different places, on fol. 11a, 1-10; 12a, 16; 53b, 17; 158a, 8 and on fol. 214b, 4; on fol. 11a, 7-8 also in connection with poison. Ascunia sometimes appears as ascunia gum (fol. 18b, 7; 53b, 17; 39a, 16), where Zosimos says that a sage compared this gum with the women of that town Ascunia (a town so far unknown to me), as *ašqūnīā*-thorns (folio 18b, 7), or as white earth that is called *ašqūnīā*-soil (e.g. on fol. 130a, 12-17). In a *second step*, we will also include a passage where this symbol occurs in a text quoted in the *Muṣḥaf aṣ-ṣuwar*. Then, in a *third step*, we will look at the material side of this symbol as, after all, alchemy deals with substances, something that we must always keep in mind.

Let us begin with the places where we find «ascunia, the murderess of her husband». On folio 11a, 3-13 we read: «She (Theosebeia) said: "What you have just said is wonderful. Then tell me what caused her splendour to disappear." He said: "With the fire, her splendour and her whiteness went away, and with the heat she turned into ashes. And she was not happy that this splendour disappeared, but she enjoyed the intercourse with him." She said: "Who is this husband of hers?" He said: "He is the dragon." She said: "Does he die then?" He said: "He never dies, but the sages killed him by trickery and the gentleness of a woman who is murderous to her husbands. This is because her inside is full of poison and weapons. Thus she digs a tomb for the dragon. Then that woman enters it (the tomb) with him. Because of the intense desire of the dragon, he embraces that woman. Then, whenever he clings (to her), the weapons which are created in her body cut up his body until that dragon's parts are cut into pieces. When the dragon is sure that the woman is attached with every part, he surrenders, and he is sure of his destruction. Then he turns into blood. When the sages are sure that he has turned into blood, they leave him in the sun for many days, until his poison goes away and the blood dries up."» The dragon or serpent that never dies is a well-known symbol in the Books for the Afterlife in Ancient Egypt; the enemy of the Sungod is named *Apep*, or later in Greek, Apophis. It needs to be overcome every night anew by the Sungod, and the individual has to help him in this effort. Initially this was the task of the deceased Pharaoh, but in time this work was demotized and became a task possible for everybody. The other side of Apophis is that female principle which helps the Sungod to rejuvenate, as through her, the rebirth of the Sungod takes place.[53] So we find a connection between this motif of the dragon and ancient Pharaonic knowledge.

Then on folio 12a, 14-19 we read: «She [Theosebeia] said: "Then tell me what is the dew?"[54] He said: "The dew is that which the cold wind from the north extracted. In this way we have veiled the nature from the ignorant." She said: "Which nature is this?" He said: "They are the murderesses of their husbands with gentleness and trickery." She said: "This nature is amazing because you do not name it with its proper name." He said: "The sages named it the mountains, and, if I name it to you, it would not be

53 Th. Abt and E. Hornung, *Knowledge for the Afterlife*, Zurich 2003, p 140 f.

54 The symbol of the north wind as renewer of life is a well known Pharaonic motif.

useful for you unless you extract it from the things with which it is disguised. Know that even if you were able to remove the things with which it was disguised, you would not be able to dissolve it.» So here the murderesses of their husbands are a nature, that means they are obviously a symbolic substance, as pointed out in Part I, p. 54-55. This symbol of a *murderer with regard to Theosebeia* is found in a surprisingly direct way on folio 100b, 15-18.

Then on folio 18a, 18 -18b, 9 we read: «She said: "Then tell me about the statement of the sage: 'Indeed, the beginning of this work, its end, and its perfection, after God is this stone which is not a stone'." He said: "I explained to you that it is something honourable-despised, venerated-vulgar, known-unknown, desirable[-rejected]." She said: "(Explain it) without confusing my mind." He said: "Your mind will not be confused by this." She said: "Then explain to me an aspect of it." He said: "This stone is the gift of God, which He bestows graciously upon whom He wants. Therefore they named it the spittle of the moon and the dung of the moon. However, it is not the spittle of the moon but we named it like that because of its noble nature and its overpowering of what it is mixed with. And the best of its names is the fiery one because it is the torturer of her husband." She said: «Then name it!» He said: «It is the gum of the thorns of asqunia, and it is the water of silver, and it is the water of sulphur, because it dissolves the body and turns it into water. So the best of its names is the fiery one, because it is the torturer of her husband.» From this passage it becomes clear that the torturer of her husband is the gum of the thorny acacia tree, producer of the famous *gummi arabicum*. Ascunia gum is obviously another name for the stone of the sage, that unfathomable enigma of alchemy, described with a thousand names. It is the 'fiery one' that finally needs to be contained, as I was able to show in the above-mentioned CALA I B (p. 234-238).

Then we move on to the next place where we find the same symbol again. On folio 53b, 15 -54a, 5 we read: «She said: "Then tell me about when he said: 'Honour the stone that is fecundated by the sun.'" He said: "This stone, fecundated by the sun, is the asqunian gum, the murderess of her husband, the changer of his body which is one, named with many names." She said: "Then mention for me some of the names." He said: "It is the mercury which is rarely found, and it is the spittle of the moon, and it is the chrysocolla, and the translation of the chrysocolla is the exalted mixture. And it is that about which Maria said: 'Our God gave the prophet

Moses, may God grant him salvation, an ingot of copper. And after him, God gave it as a legacy to us, so by this nature our God perfected this work for us when we operate on it by the fire.' Thus perform the cooking well and pound finely till her husband dies with her."» This passage confirms that ascunia gum is a symbol of the stone of the sages that finally kills her husband (the sun), which means her union with «the dragon who never dies», as we saw earlier.

On folio 158a, 7-10 we find a further confirmation that we are on the right track: «She said: "What is the androdamus?" He said: "It is that for which people suffered when they looked for it, and it is the murderess of her husbands, and it is that whose operation exhausted, because they did not know its method. And it is a stone that is in the well of mercury (*bīr zaibaq*) in the depth of the red sea and it has signs.» Finally, on folio 214b, 3-6, we read that this symbol is connected to blackness: «He [Zosimos] said: "[…] Your cooking it should be with gentle fire, until you see on it the blackness of the murderesses of their husbands. Cook it till all of that blackness disappears, and pound it with the sun till the moisture dries up."» An interpretation of this statement is found on fol. 200b, 15-19 -201a, 12).

In *a second step*, we have to see whether *The [Book of the] Keys,* a book quoted in *The Book of Pictures*, confirms what we now found about the symbolic nature of the ascunia gum. There, on page (71b, 21 -72a, 10) we find a passage where «I [Zosimos] said to him: "Why did the sages name their composition rust, water of sulphur, asqunian gum, murderous gum, gold plant, rust of copper, coppery water, honey sweet poison, pleasant-tasting poison, and they named it with the names of males and females, and the names of non-males and non-females?" He said: "This is because all of these things are in their composition. […] And when they named it asqunian gum and it is murderous, then they were right, because they made enter into the composition what burned and destroyed the bodies. And when they named it honey, sweet poison, and pleasant-tasting poison they were right, because after the burning and the destruction of the body, the composition of the body becomes beneficial and pleasant, and a dyeing spirit. And even they named it with the names of males and females and the names of non-males and non-females (written in the margin: then they were right, because it has in it males and females and when the male and the female got mixed they became non-males and non-females)."» By this quote it becomes clear that asqunia gum and murderous gum are symbols for the *androgynous mercurius*, something enigmatically ambivalent. Thus this symbol points to something that is not of this world but belongs to the reality of the unconscious realm of the adept (see for that also fols. 100b, 13 -101a, 3 and 23b, 12-14).[54] Later Latin alchemy understood *gumma* in the same way as arcane substance.[55] With all these amplifications of ascunia gum that could, first of all, be collected from the text basis itself, I could easily follow Julius Ruska, who understood ascunia to mean acacia.

In *a third step*, we will have to look at the material facts of acacia and acacia gum. This is that part of the symbol which is *of our world*, and thus will give us an idea of what the other part, which is *in the Beyond* (called today the unconscious), might look like. The acacia tree (*Acacia nilotica*) is also named the gum Arabic tree or the prickly acacia. In Upper Egypt, the homeland of Zosimos from Panopolis (today's Akhmim), this tree was well known to people. It grows in the desert that, at the time of Zosimos, came close to the arable land besides the river Nile of Panopolis.[56] In order to be able to survive in the desert, this tree developed murderous thorns, and, in times of stress, a poison that is developed to prevent animals from eating its green leaves. Seeing such an acacia tree in a lonely valley of a desert in Upper Egypt is, still today, a stunning experience: there we see, surrounded by miles and miles of barren sand, this wonderful tree that has been able to withstand, for many decades, the heat of the desert sun as well as the attacks of hungry animals, proving with its presence, like a witness, «that my rooted life is stronger than the destructive heat and hunger of the fiery, immortal dragon» (see fig. 28). This acacia produces a gum that was already used in Ancient Egypt for various purposes, among them as an ingredient for the mummification or Osirification of their dead bodies. In Ancient Egypt the acacia tree was a *holy tree*.[57]

54 For details of the symbolism of the *androgynous mercurius*, see C. G. Jung, "The Spirit Mercurius", in *Alchemical Studies* [Coll. Works 13].

55 Two examples of a later similar understanding of *gumma* in Latin alchemy are found in the "Artificium supernaturale", *Theatrum chemicum* I (1659), p. 313, 32, and in the "Harmonia chemica", *Theatrum chemicum* IV (1659), p. 720, 9.

56 This can be seen from different early maps e.g. in: *Voyage d'Égypte et de Nubie* par Frédéric-Louis Norden, Tome Second, Paris 1785. See especially the maps on plates XC-XCVI, showing the Nile and its surroundings from Akhmin (Panopolis) till Giene (Qena).

57 See D. Arnold, *Die Tempel Ägyptens*, Zürich 1992, p.182, and *The Oxford Encyclopedia of Ancient Egypt*, I, p. 539.

Fig. 28: Acacia tree in the desert of Upper Egypt

We now have the «necessary associations» with regard to the symbol «asqunian gum, murderess of her husband», which could be collected from Zosimos' texts, and external conditions as close as possible to Zosimos' Egypt. All this gives us a significantly better idea of what this symbol could be pointing to in the beyond, and that is certainly more relevant than what is found in Hallum's statement, that this name is nothing but «a codename for a substance that Zosimos classified as *the feminine power par excellence*».

Now, we have to go back to the beginning of our chapter where the dating of our manuscript was put in question. We find the important symbol asqunia gum, murderess of her husband in the legend of the *Giftmädchen* in the *Turba philosophorum* in a form almost identical to the one in the *Muṣḥaf aṣ-ṣuwar*. Consequently I stated in my introduction (p. 52-58) that the discovery of this parallelism, together with my other arguments for a probable pre-Islamic origin of the *Muṣḥaf aṣ-ṣuwar*, weakens Plessner's key argument for dating the *Turba*, namely that the legend of the *Giftmädchen* is not found in Graeco-Roman literature. And so, after countering Hallum's argument for rejecting Ruska's and my understanding of the ascunia symbol, I come to the conclusion that there is no justification for Hallum's proposal (p. 88) to move the origin of the *Muṣḥaf aṣ-ṣuwar* as well as the *Turba* to a date after 900.

6. Closing Remarks

In his thesis *Zosimos Arabus, The Reception of Zosimos of Panopolis in the Arabic/Islamic World*, Benjamin Hallum compiled the texts in Arabic attributed to Zosimos. In an attempt to establish order in this complex material, he divided this corpus into four groups (chapters 4-7).

1. In the first group are texts which are directly authenticated translations of a Greek text, namely the "25th and the 29th Epistle" of Zosimos and a text named *The Sulphurs*.

2. In the second group are texts which are indirectly authenticated translations. According to Hallum, two main sets of texts fall into this category, namely the *Kitāb Mafātīḥ aṣ-ṣanʿa* (The Book of the Keys of the Work) and *The Seven Epistles*.

3. In the third group are dialogues which Hallum considers to be later compilations by an Arab author who turned the text into dialogue form. To this group belongs the *Muṣḥaf aṣ-ṣuwar* presented here.

4. Forgeries.

Looking at the extant Arabic texts attributed to Zosimos, one can agree with Hallum's proposal to separate first of all the forgeries from the rest of the corpus. But then I suggest that we divide the other texts into two groups:

1. *Texts of a more extraverted nature, focusing on technical aspects and recipes.* To this group belong the texts which are directly or indirectly authenticated translations from Greek, namely Zosimos' *Seven Epistles*, his "25th and 29th Epistle" and his text referred to as *The Sulphurs*, a treatise that consists of a series of chapters (*abwāb*) which are listed in detail in Hallum's thesis. What mainly gives this manuscript an affinity to the more technical teachings of Zosimos, as they are known in Greek and Syriac, is the fact that in this text, mainly recipes are mentioned, but not dreams, nor is there any reference to a specific sage, nor to the priest Neilos.

2. *Texts of a more introverted nature, focusing on the symbolic nature of the work.* To this group belong the *Kitāb Mafātīḥ aṣ-ṣanʿa* and the *Muṣḥaf aṣ-ṣuwar.* Texts of this group include Zosimos' inner life: his great dreams, his human reactions, such as loving feelings for Theosebeia and his resentment of the priest Neilos, not forgetting his personal painful quest for

understanding the great work. Frequent quotes of his teacher Democritus and of other sages connect these texts to the tradition of symbolic alchemy.

With regard to our second group of texts, we have to remember that *The Book of the Keys of the Work* (*K. Mafātīḥ aṣ-ṣanᶜa*) is a book, written by Zosimos, that was circulating in the book market of Baghdad in the 10th century, as we can read in the catalogue of Ibn Nadīm.[58] However, according to Hallum's counter-hypothesis, the *Muṣḥaf aṣ-ṣuwar* belongs to a third, different group of texts, a category which makes this a later compilation by an Arab author who turned the text into dialogue form. However, in addition to the arguments so far presented, there is one unique feature that connects the texts of the second group to the hitherto known texts of Zosimos, starting with *the extant Greek documents*, going on to *The Book of Keys* and concluding with our *Book of Pictures.* What connects them all is their unique content, namely *Zosimos' basis coming from his own experience, reported by him as his great alchemical dreams.* For Zosimos this is the starting point not only for his own understanding of the previous masters of the art of alchemy, but also for passing his knowledge in symbolic form on to his student Theosebeia. In the authentic Greek texts of Zosimos, we find his great dreams, known today as the visions of Zosimos (see fn 44).[59] In the *Mafātīḥ aṣ-ṣanᶜa*, Zosimos also reports some of his great dreams (on fol. 66b, 16 -67b, 7 and fol. 73b, 19 -74b, 2), and in the *Muṣḥaf aṣ-ṣuwar* we find again the same material presented by Zosimos (on fol. 40b, 12 -41a, 7, and fol. 82b, 4-17). To go into further detail here would be beyond the scope of this introduction. I can only summarize facts presented elsewhere (Part I, page 23, point f) by stating that there is a surprisingly clear internal relationship between Zosimos' great dreams, as known from his Greek texts, and the other great dreams given in the two Arabic manuscripts mentioned above. This characteristic feature of Zosimos' teachings, as well as the similar style of the *Mafātīḥ aṣ-ṣanᶜa* and the *Muṣḥaf aṣ-ṣuwar* (see p. 117-120), allows us to bring these two texts to the same group of texts, and justifies considering them as having *the same level of authenticity.*

58 Mentioned in Part I, p. 18; see J. W. Fück, "The Arabic Literature on Alchemy according to An-Nadîm. A Translation of the Tenth Discourse of the Book of the Catalogue (*Al-Fihrist*) with Introduction and Commentary", *AMBIX* February 1951, p. 81-144.

59 See M. Mertens: *Les Alchimistes Grecs*, Tome IV.1 Zosime de Panopolis X, p. 35 f. C. G. Jung lectured on these visions at the Eranos conference in 1937, publ. as "The Visions of Zosmios", in: *Coll. Works* 13, § 85-144.

As a last remark, I refer to Part I, page 64, where, in fn 79, I gave a reference to a picture found in the Greek Codex Parisinus 2327. The similarity of Zosimos' alembic represented there to the one in our *Muṣḥaf aṣ-ṣuwar* is remarkable. For that reason, both pictures are given here side by side for the reader to consider this aspect in support of my hypothesis (see fig. 29). The Greek text below the picture conveys the essence of Zosimos' teachings as found in the *Muṣḥaf aṣ-ṣuwar*.

However, the *new element in the Muṣḥaf aṣ-ṣuwar* is that the furnace is of the same size as Theosebeia, symbolizing her bodily reality. The red substance in the alembic, the product of the distillation process, is connected to Theosebeia's head, symbol for the result of her intense pondering that gradually—as a result of the alchemical work—leads to a completely new attitude, as is confirmed by the content of the *Muṣḥaf aṣ-ṣuwar*, for instance by the passage found on folio 182a, 16 -182b, 1 (see also fig. 9-11).

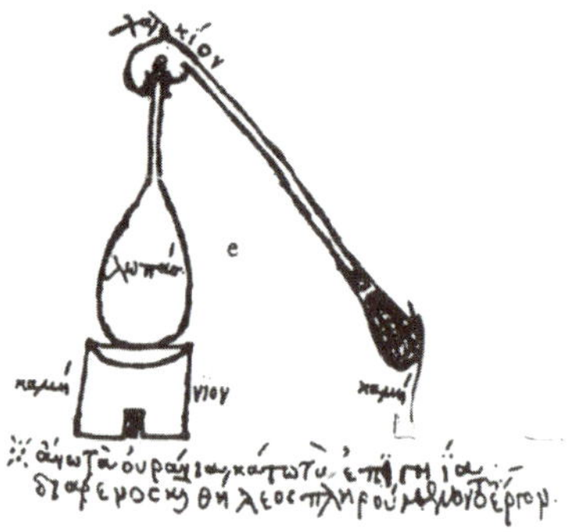

Fig. 29: On the left side: Representation of the alembic in Zosimos' Greek manuscript, Codex Parisinus 2327, fol. 81v. (part of the picture).[60] On the right side: Alembic in his *Muṣḥaf aṣ-ṣuwar*, fol. 153a (part of the picture).

60 The Greek text below the distillation apparatus reads: «Above the heavenly things, below the earthly things. By the male and the female, the work is accomplished.» More with regard to this distillation apparatus in M. Mertens, *Mém. Auth.*, p. 254 and 255; see also other similar images in her publication on p. 255, 257 and 259.

7. Summary and Conclusions

In his review of the facsimile edition of the *Muṣḥaf aṣ-ṣuwar*, Benjamin Hallum put into question my hypothesis which states that the *Muṣḥaf aṣ-ṣuwar* must be a translation from a Greek original, written by Zosimos, or Theosebeia, or by one of his followers. As a counter-hypothesis, Hallum states that this text must be an Arabic compilation, based on many—if not all—texts from Zosimos. Furthermore he claims that the date of the *Muṣḥaf aṣ-ṣuwar* has to be shifted to a time after 900. Hallum's review has the merit to have led to this second introduction, which has made it possible to put forward further arguments with regard to the origin of the *Muṣḥaf aṣ-ṣuwar*, some in support of my hypothesis but also some in support of Hallum's counter-hypothesis. This second introduction paved the way not only for a debate on the two points of view, but also for a clarification of my approach to the nature of symbols in the teachings of Zosimos, as it emerges from the text and pictures in this document.

The new findings lead to the following:

1. When examining the pictures of the *Muṣḥaf aṣ-ṣuwar*, we can, in a first step, distinguish three different series, all of which revolve around the theme of a symbolic death and resurrection of the adept Zosimos. In a second step, on the basis of this observation and on the analysis of the text with its numerous internal references to other text passages and to the pictures in the *Muṣḥaf aṣ-ṣuwar*, we can ascertain the coherence of the book as a whole. Therefore we have no choice but to speak of *one single consistent book*. This newly discovered argument leads to the conclusion that *this text cannot be considered to be a compilation.*

2. As long as we do not have this dialogue between Zosimos and Theosebeia in Greek , there is admittedly no definitive proof for my assumption that this book is a translation from a Greek original. The author could have been a later brilliant alchemist who had an overwhelming experience of love for one of his female students. In his search for an understanding of the deeper meaning of what must have been a bewildering and dangerous experience, the unknown author might have come across texts of Zosimos. These texts could have been written in Greek, Arabic or some other language. The form of presenting his experience, his insights and his teachings as a dialogue between Zosimos and Theosebeia, might have been a prudent way of remaining anonymous.

3. In Part II a series of new arguments is presented which points to the possibility that the Muslim elements in the *Muṣḥaf aṣ-ṣuwar* could be regarded as later adaptations by a Muslim copyist. My hypothesis of a *pre-Islamic origin* of this manuscript is supported by numerous passages and references to pre-Islamic and even pre-Hellenistic ideas, which were no longer known in an exact way in Islamic Egypt, as the knowledge of the meaning of hieroglyphs faded in the 4th century. Furthermore, the *Muṣḥaf aṣ-ṣuwar* contains numerous quotations from the Arabic dialogue of Zosimos and Theosebeia, found in the *Kitāb al-Ḥabīb*, a text which Fuat Sezgin dates—with various arguments—in the 4th/5th century. The Greek quotes from Olympiodoros of Alexandria (5th/6th century) could also indicate that the *Muṣḥaf aṣ-ṣuwar* was known to a pre-Islamic Alexandrine alchemist. The *Muṣḥaf aṣ-ṣuwar* twice mentions Christ. It can be demonstrated that it is not a Muslim Christ but a Gnostic Christ that is presented here. A key factor in favour of my argument for a pre-Islamic origin of this manuscript is to be found in the pictures. A closer examination shows mainly pre-Islamic and even pre-Hellenistic iconography. In the absence of any convincing evidence that our text must be a compilation by a later Arab author, written after 900, I find myself obliged to disagree with Hallum's suggestion.

4. On the basis of the facts assembled here in Part I and Part II, the direct influence of the Pharaonic Books of the Afterlife on the text and images of the *Muṣḥaf aṣ-ṣuwar* is evident. In Ancient Egypt, some of these books were still being copied in the 4th century AD, and were most probably known to Zosimos. It therefore seems probable that the *Muṣḥaf aṣ-ṣuwar* can be considered a late, modified continuation of the literature of Ancient Egypt about man's relationship with the powers of the Beyond.

5. We find motifs of the *Muṣḥaf aṣ-ṣuwar* in later symbolic Arabic alchemy, especially in the books of Muḥammad ibn Umail, and in symbolic Latin alchemy, for instance in the *Rosarium* and in one of the *Mutus liber*, which are both focused on the outer *and* inner man-woman relationship. Thus our book emerges as *a surprising missing link between Pharaonic culture*—where this male-female relationship was intuitively highly respected and venerated—*and European alchemy,* which turned out to be *the basis of modern depth psychology*, which rediscovered the existence of a *second unconscious psychic system*, the origin of the creation of reconciling symbols.

6. Between the *Muṣḥaf aṣ-ṣuwar*, the *Mafātīḥ aṣ-ṣanᶜa* and some of the authentic Greek texts of Zosimos, there is a surprisingly clear internal relationship, namely Zosimos' great dreams. They are known from his Greek texts as well as from these two Arabic manuscripts. Together they present a meaningful series showing the gradual psychic development of Zosimos. The teachings of Zosimos are based on his dream experiences, as he points out on different occasions. The love and commitment of Zosimos for his student Theosebeia, his resentment of the priest Neilos, whom Theosebeia visits once in a while, and the description of his own quest are all found in these texts. Zosimos' relation to his inner dream world and his involvement in these specific personal relationships are characteristic features of his teachings. Furthermore, the similar style of the *Mafātīḥ aṣ-ṣanᶜa* and the *Muṣḥaf aṣ-ṣuwar* justify assigning these two texts to the more introverted group of texts. This is the basis of my claim that these two texts have *the same level of authenticity*.

7. Whatever the age of the *Muṣḥaf aṣ-ṣuwar* and whoever its author was, *our document is the earliest evidence of a dialogue between an alchemical couple*, the alchemist and his soror mystica. If one day it can be proved that the *Muṣḥaf aṣ-ṣuwar* is a translation of a Greek original, then our text would be the earliest *historical* description of an alchemical work based on a psychic transformation that is ultimately leading to the adept's containment of the devilish fire of attraction. Our text is a testimony to the painstaking quest to understand not only the problem but also the meaning of attraction, repulsion and ultimate reconciliation between the outer male and female as well as the inner fire and water, an enigmatic process that can only be described by way of symbols.

8. The unique manuscript of the *Muṣḥaf aṣ-ṣuwar* provides valuable new source material with regard to Zosimos' alchemical teachings. To my knowledge, neither in Greek, Syriac, Arabic nor Latin is there any other alchemical manuscript extant that reveals so clearly the connection between the human man-woman relationship and alchemy. Our text and the pictures are the earliest document to reveal the origin and basis of the alchemical work and the enigmatic phenomenon of the inner-psychic *and* outer male-female relationship, with its magic attraction, misunderstandings, rejection and ultimately its redeeming enlightment and reconciliation. It corroborates in an unexpected way C. G. Jung's hypothesis that the goal

of the alchemical work can be recognized today in the proper understanding of the enigmatic phenomena known as transference and countertransference, which cause so much confusion, not only in the context of psychotherapy but also with regard to *relationships in general*. Thus, our manuscript is the oldest extant description of the *Mysterium coniunctionis of the inner-psychic opposites*, a work related to the healing of the outer *and* inner man-woman relationship. In picture and text, the book reveals amazingly intimate and painful experiences of Zosimos—or whoever the author was—namely his own symbolic death and resurrection. As Zosimos explains, or rather confesses, to his student Theosebeia, this transformation is directly connected to his relationship with her. Our document irrefutably confirms C. G. Jung's hypothesis of the *symbolic nature of the alchemical substances mentioned and the transformation that occurs during the alchemical process*.

9. In order to advance the understanding of the science of alchemy, it will be important for historians in this field to continue their research by examining and distinguishing first whether the author they are investigating speaks of mere substances or of symbols. If the latter is the case, it will be crucial for the researcher not only to investigate carefully the historical, palaeographic and linguistic facts, but also to look at the symbolic dimension of the different names given in the text; only in this way can these names truly be contextualised. With regard to the *Muṣḥaf aṣ-ṣuwar*, the text and pictures are clearly of a symbolic nature. We must therefore approach this document accordingly. The method of approaching the meaning of symbols in such texts is by careful amplification, a method already recommended by the Arab alchemist Abū al-Qāsim (13th century). Such an approach will open up new horizons with regard to this text and to symbolic alchemical texts in general, paving the way for the understanding that in such alchemical texts the *psyche of the adept* is also involved in the work. The psyche was and is the origin which moves the adept patiently to devote his or her life to the individual quest for immortality. This discovery will then provide the key to unlocking the meaning of this vast cultural heritage, and will ultimately help to transform symbolic alchemical texts into a *living human heritage*.

Part III

Translation of the *Muṣḥaf aṣ-ṣuwar*

Remarks concerning the Translation

There is no denying that the teachings of Zosimos are often unclear, even ambiguous, as can be seen in the words of Theosebeia herself: «[…] your allusions are not clear, and your examples are obsure and enigmatic.» (fol. 6b, 17-18) In such situations, the translators had little alternative but to adhere word for word to the manuscript.

In the Arabic text, the consonant points are often missing, so we had to decide ourselves what the original might have been. Only rarely did we opt for an emendation. There were times when we thought that a later copyist must have misunderstood the text, only to find later on in our translation work that this was not the case. Thus we only seldom corrected what we had presumed to be copyist errors. Our constant re-working on the translation always led to further clarifications, but there finally came a point where we felt we could say: Now we consider the translation ready for publication.

Marginal notes are translated only occasionally, namely when directly related to the translation, or when otherwise considered relevant. Detailed work on the margins will be mainly of interest with regard to the history of this manuscript.

Textual signs

[…]	Lacuna in the manuscript.
(?)	This indicates that the original text is unclear.
(…)	Editor's addition related to the translation, given as an aid to the reader's understanding.
(…)	Editor's remark not directly referring to the translation of the text, but possibly of help to the reader.
[…]	Editor's insertion of text that is obviously missing.
<…>	Obvious error made by a copyist; text can or must be deleted.
<~~He said~~>	Text crossed out in the manuscript.
ẖ-l-qṭār	Word in italic diacritical letters: unclear Arabic word that is given with or without a suggested vocalization and with or without a suggested translation such as *šaḥīra* (vitriol?).
12	The small red numbers refer to the line in the facsimile edition. They are only a rough indication, as the word order in Arabic differs from the English.

(fol. 2a) In the name of the merciful and compassionate God
and I am satisfied with Him alone and He is a firm foundation.

[2] The 1st Book from the Book of Zosimos the Sage. [3] And it is
THE BOOK OF THE LEARNING that is known as
THE BOOK OF THE TRUTH

[4] The *first picture* which Zosimos made for Theosebeia at the beginning of
this 1st Book [5] is a picture of Zosimos having on his head the sun in golden
water, and on his body, plates of golden water, and his shirt [6] has green and
yellow on it, and his robe is red. Close to his legs he is holding two winding
vipers bound together by two knots. One of them [7] is a yellow viper with
green on its belly and its back is gilded with golden water. The other one [8]
has the colour of the sky and its back is [covered] with silvery water. The
picture of Theosebeia has on her head a crescent moon, [9] coloured with
silvery water. And she has on her body a yellow dress and a green robe
having stripes of [10] silvery water on it, and her slippers are red. Zosimos is
pointing to Theosebeia with his hand, joining together his thumb [11] and his
ring finger, while extending his index finger, his middle finger, and his
small finger. [12] Theosebeia also points to him. And in the hand of Zosimos
there are three ropes, the ends of which he has gathered in his hand. On the
[13] upper rope in his hand there are three statues of men with wings, who are
tied by their neck to that rope. [14] And the rope is coloured with golden and
silvery water, and they (three statues) are tied with shackles coloured with
golden water. And on [15] the middle rope there is a statue of two men, both
with green and sky-blue wings, and on their necks they are tied with a rope
[16] coloured with golden and silvery water, and on their legs there are
shackles coloured with golden water. And on the lower, [17] third rope there is
a statue of a man with two wings. On his head, there is a moon coloured
with silvery water, and on his legs there are two shackles [18] coloured with
golden water. His clothes are red and green, and in his hand there is a yellow
jug, from which he pours out water in the colour of the sky. [19] All of these
dyes are from the rust of copper, cinnabar, lapis lazuli, arsenic, golden
water and silvery water.
(fol. 2b and 3a) (This double page is left empty; the first picture is missing.)
There is a text: And after this picture I begin with the first book, which is:

(fol. 3b) In the name of the merciful and compassionate God. God bless and grant salvation to our master Muḥammad, his people, and his companions. [2] Praise to God, creator of forms and bodies, who makes creatures themselves say [3] that He is the One, the Almighty, and by His power He made them appear out of nothing. He put in them the amount of wisdom that [4] He wanted, composed them, and gave each one its own role. May God bless our master Muḥammad [5] and all the prophets. May God bless them and grant them salvation and may He approve [6] of their companions and their followers, those who are performing good deeds as long as night and day shall last.

[7] This is the book (named):

The Book of Pictures of Zosimos the Sage and the Questions of Theosebeia.

[8] Zosimos said: «I thought that my description for you of the two vipers that are taking [9] my legs, and my tying up of those whom I tied up for you, would be enough for you. But you asked me things [10] about hidden matters that not even kings asked the sages. I will tell you all [11] that you deserve from me. If you have reached the limit of your learning (*taᶜlīm*, this 1st Book is also called The Book of the Learning), then ask me [12] about something else.»

She said: «You have behaved towards me, O Zosimos, in a way a faithful and devoted son [13] does to his mother. You do not deserve to be troubled too much by what I asked you, [14] because of the great obscurity of what the sages wrote in their books.» He said: «In this book of mine is [15] everything that cures and satisfies you concerning the questions that you asked me.»

She said: «Indeed, [16] there is no cure for me without knowing the natures: its hot, cold, dry and moist one, [17] and how I can fix (lit. imprison) the gold in them, and which one of them is more entitled to its companion.» He said: «You asked a very good [18] question. You must make use of the close one with the close one, because it is the quickest way to mix what you are mingling.» [19]

She said: «And how, O sage, can I mix the close one with the close one?» He said:

(fol. 4a) «With the mixing of the hot one with the cold one, and the dry one with the moist one. Then you have reached the limit 2 of the sages and what they have hidden.»

She said: «This concerns the mixing, and it is as you say. Then where are 3 the weights, the burning, the rotting, the vapours and the measures of the fire?» 4 He said: «I command and order you to search for all the things. Then ponder over 5 how it is born and how it grows. And be careful not to look for anything except what I order you. Perform 6 the operation of that thing well, with knowledge and gentleness in the whitening and the reddening. Then make white with 7 the white water and with it make red, and do not let anything foreign enter into it. That is what 8 Maria ordered with regard to the cooking, the pounding and the soaking. So you will attain the benefit 9 and the secret of the sages, God willing, just like those who were before you. I wonder what you are thinking, O Theosebeia, when you have asked me 10 about the enigmatic issues which the sages prevented the common people from knowing. 11 I have heard that you listened to the priest Neilos (*Fīlbus or Tilībus*) and that he claimed that the work 12 is not nature, and that it is made from different things and many metals, and he made you see dreams 13 in your waking state. So you thought that you were right because of them, and you paid attention to them. I swear by God, if it were not for 14 my intention to complete the best of my desire in my relationship with you, and my compassion toward you—because he (Neilos) 15 involves you in things that use up your money and remove your means of living, for which I do not blame you 16—I would not answer what you have asked me, and I would stop helping you. If it were not that I see that you regret what you did before,[1] I would have introduced you to just as much of the white poison and the plate 18 of the beloved body, and I could then leave you with it, so that you would be in doubt about it for the rest of your life. But 19 I sent it to you with the intention that you should know that the science (of alchemy) is nature. And I ordered you to take

1 The Arabic has: If it were not that you see that I regret what I did before.

(fol. 4b) the plate and to coat it with that poison, and to pound it in order that it absorbs it. I told you that it [2] opens the way for you to the beginning of the making of the poison, and I wrote for you in my book how you should [3] make the rest until it is complete, God willing. But I was not satisfied with that until [4] I had given you a testimony from the statements of the sages for every description of it, to be sure about it.» [5]

She said: «It was you who informed me, so do not blame me for my former wrong opinions. [6] To work it in the way you just said deprives me of what remains of my hope in you.» He said: [7] «You are right. I will not do so.»

She said: «Be friendly with me and provide me with all you know that [8] I am in need of.» He said: «I will do so.»

She said: «Perhaps, O Zosimos, [9] it is that of which Maria said: «When our lead (*abār*) turns black, then it is the learning (*taᶜlīm*) of the truth.» [10] He said: «You have understood well. Yes, it is that.»

She said: «Show me, how [11] this blackness comes into being.» He said: «Understand that when you first mix the things, and you cook them [12] in the first cooking for some days, there appears to you the blackness about which I told you that all of it turns black. [13] So when you see it like that, know that it is what they call their black lead (*ruṣaṣ*). If you [14] want, you can call it their black silver. Ponder over this despised, insignificant thing [15] that operates on this honoured one. No sage exists who worked this secret without mentioning it (their black silver or their black lead) and (without) writing a book [16] about it, doing his best—with all kinds of ruses—to veil and to hide it from the ignorant and from those who do not merit it. [17] And they praised it very much, but if they had described it clearly and named it with its true name, then the first [18] of the ignorant people to see it would deny it. They would deny it all the more because it is easy to do, and because it (their black lead) is abundant among the people. If even an intelligent one of them would know it, he would despise it and doubt it.

(fol. 5a) Therefore they disguised it with examples and names, and with this they veiled the science. They wanted thereby that only that sage should obtain the science [2] from their books who is persistent in reading their books, being devoted to them and patient with the suffering which [3] comes from the different statements in their books. If he reached that, the first [4] thing he would do with it is to hide what he obtained from the books, and to keep it secret from creatures. [5] This is because if he were to make it (the work) visible, the world would become corrupt, and it (the work) would become something like glass-making. But [6] God has hidden it with knowledge. Therefore the exalted God advised Šīt (in the margin it says that he is Pythagoras), the son of Adam, when he taught him this work, not to reveal it to creatures. Know that the nature [8] and the moisture turn into sand, then they turn into water, and then they turn into a stone. And the sieving (the word here is *manḫul* = sieve, in the sense of sieving see fol. 5b, 1) [9] is the pounding of the cooking because what is light and spiritual of it is raised up by it (the sieving), and [10] what is thick and heavy is made to go down to the bottom of the vessel. That which became [11] fine spiritual dust rises to the upper part of the vessel, above the water. This is the pounding of the cooking not the pounding [12] by hand. But I tell you that if you do not turn everything into fine dust by cooking, [13] the nature does not get pounded. So you must return it back to the cooking till it gets pounded and becomes fine dust and dissolves. This cooking is the (sieve) sieving. Agathodaimon said: "Cook the copper until its body becomes [15] soft and tender." He means by soft and tender that he makes it turn into spiritual fine dust, having no [16] touchable parts any more. Thus the sieving (sieve) of this pounding is the sieving (sieve) by cooking. Concerning that, a student of Hermes [17] asked him: "We did not understand how you described for us the sieving (sieve)." Hermes answered him: "O yes, put [18] the natures in the vessel, then count six or seven until all of the water comes down. So this is the pounding." [19] Know that if you make all of it turn into black water, then at this time you pounded its (that which is) (fol. 5b) finely pounded. And the sage named the sieving (sieve) of this pounding and cooking 'the sieve'. If you have understood my [2] statement about this operation, you will know how it turns into water, and after that how it turns into fine dust.»

[3] She said: «And how, O Zosimos, does the water turn into fine dust, while it is water?» He said: «O yes. Do you not [4] know that the body turned into water in the water?»

She said: «Yes.» He said: «That body [5] which turned into water in the water is what becomes its soul, and the water in it turns into fine dust. This is because [6] that which should become water—before it falls into the water—was a body. Then, when the water surrounded it, it (the water) [7] changed it (the body). Thus it turned into water mixed with the other water. When both are mixed, they together turned into one fine water (*habāʾan-māʾan wāḥidan*). [8] Know that and contemplate it.

She said: «Then tell me, O Zosimos, about the statement of [9] Hermes: "If you operate on it a thousand times without the body being purified, it will not dissolve."» He said: [10] «Hermes is right. Those who venture to mix these things [11] in ignorance fall into error. Therefore it does not dissolve. So if you want it to dissolve, then take the body, [12] pure and without adulteration (*ġišš*, lit: cheating) in it, and the things which you mix with it must also be pure and without adulteration in them. [13] Nothing but what is pure should enter it. Know that if you introduce anything adulterated into it [14] and you operate on it a thousand times, it will not dissolve for you in a good way. This is that what you asked me about [15] the statement of Hermes.»

She said: «Then tell me about the statement of Hermes when he ordered his students [16] to operate on every thing in the sea until every thing becomes water.» He said: «The sage was right [17] in advising his students. Do you not remember what I told you regarding what you asked me about on the matter of the (sieve) sieving?» [18] She said: «I have understood. But I would like to be really sure.» He said: «Then I tell you [19] a statement, so keep it in mind. I have taken it from the books of Hermes, when he says at the end of his (fol. 6a) statement: “There is nothing good in nature if its origin is not the river.”»

She said: «And what did he mean [2] by that?» He said: «By it he meant the moisture, in order that everything becomes water. If it were not like that, [3] you would be completely wrong. I swear to you by God, if you do this work in the right way, you will have a [4] river of running gold. So do not stop studying the books. Hermes [5] ordered us to search for the natures in the mountains, because ants are those that bring out the natures.»

She said: [6] «What did he mean by the mountains, and what are the ants?» He said: «He called the books mountains, [7] and the students of the science ants. And I tell you that whoever stays up at night to read these books till he realises [8] what is in them, and understands the examples which are in them, distinguishing the true parts from the false ones, will perform this [9] work correctly. Whoever does not do so, spends his life without meeting his needs. This is because they only [10] wrote in their books things that resemble the truth. When anybody reads them, he thinks [11] that they contain the truth because they called the truth by that name. In this way they deceived [12] people about this work, when they named things similar to the truth. So whoever wants to [13] read their books finds there that they make the natures red with *qalqaṭār* (gr. *chalkanthon*=iron vitriol?), *šaḥīra* (vitriol? see fn 58 on p. 316), alum, [14] and colocynth. He sees them (the natures) becoming red in the fire, and he knows that they become red. Yet he is not certain whether it is [15] the truth. It is not the truth, rather they named what they use to make those things red [16] in order to make analogies with them, but it is not the truth. The same applies to what he reads in their books when [17] they order him to solidify the mercury in the tin, and he is not certain whether it is the truth because it (the mercury) solidifies [18] in it in an impermanent way, and that is not what they wanted. By these things [19] they confused the people and disguised it from them.»

She said: «What did Democritus mean when he said:

(fol. 6b) "Why should we be interested in the many things while the nature is one?"» He said: «I tell you, [2] as the exalted God is one, in the same way the nature is one. He who deviates from that (one nature) in the work, [3] would fall into error. God is one and He is too exalted for there to have anyone similar, comparable or equal to Him.»

She said: [4] «Then why did the sages mention stones, sand, waters, metals, mercuries, [5] and remedies in their books? » He said: «I told you that you do not need any of that. [6] You are in need of the one about which Hermes said: «It is the one, the benefit having many [7] names.» So venerate God and do not attribute associates to Him. So from what I say, understand this one nature, [8] and leave aside what you are looking for, namely the many operations, the many things, and what is similar [9] to the truth in this work. They are not the truth.»

She said: «I understood your book and your sending to me the legacy (*ṭarika* [2]) [10] of Maria the Sage, and that you did not keep back anything of it. You order me to study [11] it and her testimony, because you fear that I might think that you had replaced something with something else, claiming [12] to have given me everything she taught, like gold, silver and purple stone, [13] and that you had written it to me in this book. But I did not see with my own eyes, and I am still not able to see [14] if you do not show it to me in your hands. With regard to your description of it in the books for me, whenever I think that [15] I had understood it, something obscure about the truth appears to me.» He said: «I will remove the doubt you have [16] about the operation by reminding you of what I described for you in the books, when [17] I see you have not understood it.»

She said: «Do so, although your allusions are not clear, and your examples [18] are obscure and enigmatic. So make it easy for me and enlighten me, remove from my vision this obscurity and complete [19] your kindness to me.» He said: «I will do so.»

She said: «Then tell me, O Zosimos, when you say that all the sages

2 The manuscript has *baraka* (blessing), but it should read *ṭarika*.

(fol. 7a) wrote frequently about the cooking. Is all of this to deter people from this [2] science, and because of jealousy of them?» He said: «Concerning the people of the right attitude and of wisdom [3] who desire it (the work), they did not do anything like that to them. However, they made their operation inaccessible [4] to the shameless, in order that they could not corrupt the world, as the responsibility for those people would be with whoever taught [5] it to them.»

She said: «Then show me how they dispersed it (the science).» He said: «Did I not explain to you that [6] in my great dream (*ruʾīā*) I saw that the killed one was cut into pieces: the two hands were cut up, [7] the fingers were cut up joint by joint, vein by vein, and the bones and veins [8] were pounded until they became very fine like dust. What I am telling you about this dream [9] corresponds to the statement of Agathodaimon, who said: "Pound and cook, pound and cook, (from the margin: cook), repeat it, [10] do not be impatient, and repeat it." For the work on these things at the beginning of the mixing, the cooking, [11] the soaking, the roasting, the heating, the whitening, the pounding, the roasting, [12] the vaporisation, the rusting and the dyeing is one. If Agathodaimon had known that [13] one pounding, one cooking and one soaking would be enough for it, he would not have repeated what he said. However, he repeated [14] the statement "pound and cook", (so that they would) cook it many times without losing patience and in order to disguise it from those who did not know these [15] names. My lady, if I wanted to hold anything back from you, it would have been enough for me to tell [16] you that in my dream I had just found a killed man. But I informed you that he had been killed, [17] cut into pieces, divided and cut into fragments till he became a decayed corpse (*ramīm*).»

She said: «Am I right to see that this [18] killed man is the copper body that you have ordered me to operate on?» He said: «Now you have understood what I said, [19] and you will not be duped, because the sages did not describe anything in their books without alluding to something else. So do not despise (fol. 7b) anything of what they say. God is too exalted in their eyes to write anything untrue, or name [2] any true thing with another name, except in order to hide it with (an invented name).»

She said: «What prevents you, O Zosimos, [3] from doing me a favour by explaining what my knowledge cannot reach, in the same way as Hermes did for his son [4] Tat?» He said: «Did I not do more than that for you? I even revealed and exposed this [5] hidden secret.»

She said: «You did and you did not!» He said: «I was afraid [6] that you would not be grateful for it.» She said: «If I am not grateful to you, nobody after me will be grateful to you.» [7] He said: «Which one of the questions of Tat to Hermes made you wonder?»

She said: «When he (Tat) mentioned his (Hermes') wisdom [8] and described his kindness, he (Hermes) declared that he had described what he (Tat) wanted to be described, and what he asked [9] him (Hermes) about what he wrote concerning the gold, the silver, and which of the two works must be first, the whitening [10] or the reddening.» He said: «Uncountable times I told you in my books that the whitening comes before the reddening. [11] But you are a woman whose mind has been confused by the great number of books that you have. [12] I told you that although the statements about them are numerous, the work and the things which enter into it [13] are simple, if they (the sages) are willing to talk about them. But they said a great deal in order to disguise them (from people).»

She said: «Then what about the question of Sīus [14] to Disqīus about his statement: "Why are you interested in the many things, while the nature is one?"» [15] He said: «He is right and he spoke well. I tell you that the body is one, and if you do not [16] dissolve the body till you make it turn into water, and then make it solid again, you will not be right. Do you not see how [17] the sage said: "Turn over the nature, and extract the spirit which is concealed inside [18] that body."»

She said: «How can this be turned over?» He said: «Destroy the body, [19] extract what is inside and turn it into water. Then this is what the sages named (fol. 8a) "starry earth" and "snowy earth". For that the sages compare the white water to the whiteness of the stars and the snow.» [2]

She said: «O Zosimos, I ask you by your God, will you not tell me which body is this?» He said: [3] «It is what I named for you. But you do not understand. It is the body which we named with all the bodies. Do [4] you not see how a carpenter takes the wood and then saws it up. And he makes from it what he wants, and he does not add anything to it that is not wood, and he saws it up. Then he makes out of it the various things he wants, [5] and he only works with wood. Thus wood is only good with wood. And it is the same with our copper, after [6] you compose it with everything that is suitable and corresponds to it in the mixture. So know that and contemplate it, and [7] you will reach the knowledge, the exalted God willing. Did you not understand the statement of Disqīus (here written Dilsiqīus), that if [8] you perform properly the operation of the mercury with the poison that must coagulate with it and the body, [9] it will be strong enough to resist the fire, and it will not be able to escape from the fire because it holds fast and is held fast, because of a kinship between them both.»

She said: «Then tell me about the question which Sīus asked Disqīus (here written Dīsīquš) about the burning. [11] Favour me with an explanation of their statement: "Mercury from cinnabar, while cinnabar is from mercury." [12] How can this be?» He said: «Yes. If you dissolve the body together with the mercury [13] by the acacia (*ašqunīa*) and continue to cook the whole (emendation), the acacia will kill it. Then the body will turn into [14] cinnabar. That is what the sages spoke of when they said: "It is rarely found. It is white in [15] outer appearance and red in essence." But they said: "Mercury from cinnabar" in order to disguise it from those who [16] wanted to enter this work. And I have told you before that the sages described their work with any one of the [17] crafts similar to it in order to cover it.»

She said: «So maybe this nature [18] which the sages mentioned is the heavenly one?» He said: «Yes it is, because the natures are defeated by it, and by it [19] the body is dissolved, burned, solidified, rusted and made rotten, and by this it comes into being, (fol. 8b) and without it nothing exists.»

She said: «When I studied the book of Theodorus (Tīādrus) I found [2] that he was the only one (*min nafsihi*) who mentioned things which I could not understand.» He said: «What are they?» She said: «He claimed that he had gathered the things and given a [3] brief summary, and that he had made it clear to whoever understands what he meant when he said: "O students of this science, [4] if you think that it can be done without the body—which is whitened by the poison and absorbed in it, and which is mixed [5] with the things that are in accordance with each other named by sages 'nature'—then do not think that [6] anything would ever come into being."» He said: «Did Hermes not make this matter clear for you in his book, [7] when he ordered us only to mix the natures during fixed months of winter and summer?» She said: [8] «How far away, O Zosimos, is your answer from what I asked you about!» He said: «From this I know that you do not [9] have a thorough knowledge of these matters. By the month he meant the month of winter and the month of summer in order to tell you [10] that the mixing which Theodorus mentioned only comes into being by the cold one. Then it enters the fire. So he represented [11] the cold one as winter, and with this cold the body is destroyed and decomposes, and he represented the fire as summer, [12] and it is the fire with which the body is destroyed, pounded and completed. Do you not see the statement of the sage, when he says: [13] "When you mix it, you must leave it to become cooked." And I order you and those after you: whoever enters into [14] that work and this secret and wants to perform the work and the operation has to be patient and must have understanding. [15] Know, my lady, that the operation is more exalted than its name or for minds to grasp it; and is too exalted to be worked by anything except by fire.»

[16] She said: «Then tell me about the statement of Theodorus when he says: "I have written [17] for you only two secrets." What did he mean by that?» He said: «He meant the white and the red, and the dry and the moist.» [18] She said: «You have insisted on hiding this secret, and you dislike telling the truth clearly.» He said: [19] «I am no better than Democritus, who said: "If the seeker is mixed with the fugitive, and the seeker takes the fugitive

(fol. 9a), then both of them turn to a colour that does not change anymore. This contains an explanation for you, but you are not satisfied.»

She said: [2] «How much I am satisfied with all that comes from you! <She said> Then what about his statement concerning the rotting?» He said: [3] «I told you that the rotting can only occur with the dry and the moist one, and that [4] the work can only be performed with both of them».

She said: «Then what about his statement: "I have divided this work into three parts."»? He said: [5] «He spoke well and was right. I tell you that one escapes quickly, and that is the sulphur. [6] And the other one, which does not escape quickly when it escapes, is the stone. The third one neither escapes nor leaves, [7] and that is the fixed poison. Do you not see how the sages have different opinions about this matter? [8] They differed in the glorification of these things. Some of them glorified the dust, and declared that the work [9] is in it. Some of them glorified the water, and declared that the work is in it. Some of them glorified the fire, and declared [10] that the work is in it. And there were other ones who praised the four natures (elements) and declared that the work is in them, and that [11] the work could not be without them.»

She said: «Then what is your opinion?» He said: I tell you [12] that the work is only right with these four natures, and nothing of [13] what they want can exist without them. She said: «God be praised. How good is what the sage described, and how subtle is what [14] entered into it (the work).» He said: «As far as that is concerned, it is not from the work of the sage but it is by the inspiration of God to whomever He wants, [15] and His hiding it from whomever He wants. Thus understand what the sage said, namely that he described these things, whose [16] subtle description you admired, in order to make them as an analogy for this work.»

She said: «Can this be an analogy [17] for this work?» He said: «Yes. Know that whoever wants to enter into this work [18] should take the subtle dyer from the earth which is from these things, then he should take from the subtle part [19] of the water with which it was mixed. Then he should take from the subtle part of the fire by which it is cooked. Then he should take from the subtle part (fol. 9b) of the air in which the spirit makes the soul dry. Then make it (the soul) enter into it (the spirit).»

She said: «And how can I make it enter into its inside?» He said: [2] «The nature of our work turns into dust by the operation when it takes from the body and others [3] the subtle parts of these things (meaning: the subtle parts of the water, the fire, and the air). Then they submerge into the body with which they were mixed. Then they (the subtle parts) dye it (the body), [4] the exalted God willing. Therefore he ordered us to watch attentively and to understand well, in order that [5] the mind becomes clear and we can know the truth. Therefore, whoever wants to enter into this art should not [6] neglect the intensive reading of books and not become frustrated with reading the sage's books, and take the quintessence of what they described. [7] And he should be like the honey bee, when it sucks the flowers of the trees and the grass in order to [8] make honey from it.»

She said: «Then tell me about the statement of Maria: "There will be at the end of time [9] a man skilful in the science, who understands this science when he is only twenty years old. He will read their (the sages') books [10] and explain them. And he will differentiate between their outward form and their true meaning in order to explain them to whoever comes after him.» He said: [11] «You have asked me about something that I will never answer you.»

She said: «You insist, O Zosimos, on increasing my [12] blindness, and you are determined in this.» He said: «I would rather die than accept you [13] as a mother.» She said: «Why do you have such a great fear of what I asked you, O Zosimos?» He said: «Why should I not have a great fear [14] when you ask me about the secrets, and to open the locks of the sages?» She said: «But all I asked you about this [15] man was whether you think he was before your time or that he will be after it?» He said: «I already told you that I am not [16] saying anything about him.» She said: «If I did not fear your anger, I would tell you who he is, and that [17] I know him as well as you know him.» He said: «I do not know what to say to you, except that if I punished [18] myself, I would deserve it.» She said: «By God, Maria did not mention anything but good things about [19] this man, mentioning his virtue and knowledge.» He said: «Do not speak of him anymore.» She said: «I asked you (fol. 10a) by your God, O Zosimos, could it be that you are that man?» He said: «I told you that I will not tell you anything about him.» [2] She said: «I testify that you are he, but you only resist it out of modesty.» He said: «Indeed, the only thing that makes [3] you think that I am this man is the abundance of obscurities which was revealed to you, which they (the sages) had disguised, and my making things clear [4] for you. Death is preferable for anyone of them (the sages) than to talk about it. Then woe unto me from God on the Day of Judgement, [5] if He blames me for what I explain to you.» She said: «The woe is for others, and all of the benefit is for you from your God [6] and your reward is because of your fear of your God, and your love of truth, and your dislike of putting into your books anything [7] but the truth.» He said: «I am quite content with your questions, which you ask without prejudice, [8] either against me or for me.

She said: «Then tell me about the statement of Maria from her father: "The nation in which this science [9] will appear will be at the end of time."» He said: «Your questioning me was about [10] what the sages had described, but concerning what has been described about the nations, you are not in need of it, and it is not [11] a question for you.» She said: «I ask you, why did you tell me about this nation?» He said: [12] «They are the sons of Ibrāhīm.» She said: «The Jews?» He said: «No, but the sons of Ismāᶜīl. After 160 [13] years of their reign, it (the science) will appear to them.» And there is not a nation that was more disbelieving in the sages than them. After 140 [14] years of their reign, the number of seekers of this science will increase, and they will feel enthusiasm for it. Then the great and [15] exalted God will reveal it to them after they were in despair about it, in order to increase their desire for the other world more [16] than for this world.

She said: Then tell mc about the statement of Maria: "Take the lead and the iron, [17] and cook them until both are dissolved. Then mix them both with wax from what has been dissolved, in order that the body is dissolved and turns into [18] black lead (*ruṣaṣ*). Then set it on fire, and be careful not to become annoyed, but be patient with it until it becomes amalgamated. So [19] when it becomes amalgamated, it fertilizes and is fertilized. Then cook this composition[3] on days with an uneven (number), till it destroys it,

3 In the text we have *tadbīr* = operation. We changed it to *tarkīb* = composition.

(fol. 10b) and the copper turns into good silver (*waraq*). Soak both with the moisture which you have prepared for it in order that it turns into [2] silver, and this is the ferment of gold."» He said: «This is what is mixed with the black lead, [3] so the body turned with the dissolved one into water. And you should take the silver which was solidified and turned into [4] a stone, after it was dissolved and solidified at the time of the changing. Mix them both, little by little, until the stone is destroyed, [5] and the moisture that was solidified turns into dust with the peeling (*muqaššir*) copper until it dissolves it well. This is [6] what is born from the two. Then pound it and saturate it well with the moisture until it is soaked. [7] Then put it in its furnace and kindle a fire under it, and return the copper in that moisture till [8] it becomes cinnabar. Know that on the next day—after its being soaked in the water which does not get ruined and which we named the urine of [9] boys—you have to roast it for seven days. Then you will find what you want if you kill it seven [10] times. Then cook it, soak it, make it decomposed and make it rot in order in order to make it spiritual. So the truth becomes [11] evident to you, because all of these things are extracted from the magnesia, and [12] all of the work is in it (the magnesia).»

She said: «You have done me a favour with what you have revealed. So tell me more.» He said: «You asked me, [13] and you insisted on getting out what the sages did not want to describe to anybody before you.» [14]

She said: «You have told me what is greater than it, but what you stated for me will not be useful for me unless [15] the rest is added.» He said: «Then understand what I am telling you. I just present you these things. [16] Know that when any fruit first grows on the tree it is not complete, but [17] it comes out as a flower first. The larger it grows, the better it becomes, and it grows and increases until it becomes complete and ripe. [18] So its taste becomes good and it becomes edible, just as a barren woman who flees her lovers becomes [19] delightful by gentleness, and then wears (emendation) for her lovers dresses of silver (*fiḍḍa*).[4] How amazing! That woman does not agree to

4 In the picture, Theosebeia has a dress of silver (*fiḍḍa*).

(fol. 11a) be taken for bridal money; and she is not satisfied that her splendour goes to anybody except her husband, although she has poison in her. He does not care [2] about it, and he stays with her and comes together with her until he completes sexual intercourse with her. So her fertilization is complete in order that God increases her children, [3] and God makes it a blessing to whomever He wants.»

She said: «What you have just said is wonderful. Then tell me what caused [4] her splendour to disappear.» He said: «With the fire, her splendour and her whiteness went away, and with the heat she turned into [5] ashes. And she was not happy that this splendour disappeared, but she enjoyed the intercourse with him.» She said: [6] «Who is this husband of hers?» He said: «He is the dragon.»

She said: «Does he die then?» He said: «He [7] never dies, but the sages killed him by trickery and the gentleness of a woman who is murderous to her husbands. This is because [8] her inside is full of poison and weapons. Thus she digs a tomb for the dragon. Then that woman enters it (the tomb) [9] with him. Because of the intense desire of the dragon, he embraces that woman. Then, whenever he clings (to her), the weapons which are [10] created in her body cut up his body until that dragon's parts are cut into pieces. [11] When the dragon is sure that the woman is attached with every part, he surrenders, and he is sure of his destruction. [12] Then he turns into blood. When the sages are sure that he has turned into blood, they leave him in the sun for [13] many days, until his poison goes away and the blood dries up. Then they find that the secret has appeared. At this point comes [14] an overwhelming wind. Know this, my lady, you who is asking about which measure of the heat is best for our copper. [15] After that, the bath nourishes it. If it is (too) hot, it burns, seizes, destroys [16] and dries out the body, and hurts the soul. And also if it is (too) cold and dry, it dries out, seizes [17] and kills the body. But if the bath and its water are moderate, it is suitable for the body, so that it (the body) expands in it (the bath), and the veins become soft, [18] the soul is delighted, the flesh increases and the veins find their way into the flesh. The best and most just of all things is their middle.» [19] Therefore the physicians ordered that you must feed the body in the same measure as is suitable and feasible for it, in order that the fat does not accumulate in it, (fol. 11b) as this would kill it (the body), and the skinniness does not weaken it, as this would also destroy it. Both of these two extremes, fatness and skinniness, are to be rejected [2] because they are not useful. But the middle of them both is the properly balanced amount. This is the analogy of what you asked me about. [3] If you keep that in mind, then the copper will be right, its feeding will be completed, and you will attain what you hope for from what I answered you, [4] out of consideration for you and whoever comes after you, who wishes to get involved in every operation of this work.

[5] She said: «Then tell me about the statement of Hermes: "Take the two vipers, and mix them both with castor-oil seven [6] times. You will find that the tin has accumulated and turned into a clod. Then cook the tar with the remedy till [7] both are dissolved completely, and become one thing."» He said: «I am surprised that you ask me about the beginning of the matter [8] and leave out its end.»

She said: «I ask you about what I came to you to find out, and I ignore what I do not know thoroughly.» [9] He said: «Have you not understood his (Hermes') statement: "I did not order you to make the tar and the vessel equally, but [10] all of the tar must be ten times the weight of the burnt copper.»

She said: «I asked you about the two vipers and [11] the castor-oil, and I did not ask you what Hermes ordered his students to do.» He said: «I wanted to lead you [12] to other things than what you asked me about, to test your mind; so you are one of the sages!» She said: «If I were one of the sages [13] I would be content with what I read in the books.» He said: «Do not say that. I swear by God that I have read [14] sixty treatises and books, and often I doubted some of what I found in the books, till I remembered it [15] in some of the other books which I had read before. So I understood it by comparing.» She said: «How do you acquire that (knowledge)?» [16] He said: «Each one of them invented difficult and dark things and matters for what he wrote about the work, [17] and some far-fetched analogies with which to compare them.» [18] She said: Then why do you blame me for asking someone like you?» He said: «I blame you for not doing the intensive reading of books as I ordered you.» She said: [19] «Then tell me about the two vipers. For it seems to me that you are refusing to tell me what they are.» He said: «It is my right (fol. 12a) to do that.» She said:« Then do not do that and keep jealousy away from you, and complete the crown of your favour to me for I am [2] your student and your slave.» He said: «I do not know what to say to you.» She said: «Why?» He said: «I (will) never name them [3] with their (proper) names.» She said: «Then say something about them.» He said: «One of the two is the dragon, and the other one is an egg, and the third one [4] is water. And the dragon is the yolk, and the shell is the egg, and the water is the moisture and all of that is destroyed, [5] except the yolk. And the yolk is no good except with the moisture. And the moisture is no good except with the shell.» She said: [6] «You started with the most difficult (aspect) of what I asked you about.» He said: «It is the magnesia. Thus leave away what remains as I spoke [7] without jealousy.»

She said: «Ordinary people said: "This work only dissolves, solidifies, becomes white and becomes red [8] when the natures are pure and clear." He said: «That is because ordinary people mixed the things with [9] what corrupts them. Nothing foreign that is not from them should enter, otherwise it corrupts their work. If you want [10] it to dissolve, to solidify, to become white and then to become red—if you want the composition—then take the natures pure, [11] clear, unmixed with anything foreign. Then they are dissolved, become red and become white by themselves (*fī makāniha*). Thus take the truth from the people of [12] experience. As for dissolving, only the body desires it, and as for the water, it is always dissolved. [13] But when the two join together, then the body must be dissolved until it becomes water like the other one, in order that the two become [14] one thing. Thus it is the great marrying.»

She said: «Then tell me what is the dew?» [15] He said: «The dew is what the cold wind from the north extracted. In this way we have veiled the nature [16] from the ignorant.» She said: «Which nature is this?» He said: «They are the murderesses of their husbands with gentleness [17] and trickery.» She said: «This nature is amazing because you do not name it with its proper name.» He said: «The sages named it [18] the mountains, and if I name it to you, it would be not useful for you unless you extract it from the things with which it is disguised. [19] Know that if you were able to remove the things with which it was disguised, you would not be able to dissolve <without> it.

(fol. 12b) That is what the sages of Egypt did. They brought together the two natures. And they put them in the sun until [2] they were dissolved, and without the sun of the sages nothing dissolves. As for the broth that is what is always dissolved, and what concerns [3] the destruction of the two natures, that comes from the sun.»

She said: «Then tell me about when he said: "Know that [4] there is a close relationship between the iron and the magnet, and also between the copper and the eternal water."» [5] He said: «He is right and said it well. Do you not see that the iron only adheres to the magnet [6] because of a relationship between the two? In the same way, our copper is more clinging to our eternal water than the iron to the magnet.»

[7] She said: «Why is that?» He said: «This is because when the sulphur meets the sulphur which is similar to it, [8] it is mixed with it and clings to it in the same way as your flesh is mixed with your blood.»

She said: «Those two sulphurs, [9] are they from one thing or from two?» He said: «I will never answer you about that except with what I have already written in the books. [10] If you were intelligent, you would know whether both are from one thing or from two. But I tell you [11] that the origin is one, and the three have a close relationship with that one, from [12] which come the nine and the ten, and also the fourth comes from it. And from the other one comes [13] the appearance of the lunar, that is red, airy, luminous and shining.»

She said: «Then tell me what caused the sages [14] to take sperm as an example?» He said: «Because the sperm is known in three things.» [15] She said: «And how can I know these three things?» He said: «Do not leave out the nine, [16] which the sages wrote about in their books, because the heat has turned them into the three. And they have put [17] into those three things all of the secret.»

She said: «Then what are the three by which the sperm is known?» [18] He said: «Know that the sperm comes out from the heat, then it clings to the womb. Because of the moisture [19] it (the process) goes on for forty nights. Then God completes his image in two months. Thus the sperm decomposes in the womb (fol. 13a) because of the heat and the moisture. So I should give you the feeding of the human body as an analogy [2] for our work because the body only exists by subtle food and drink. Those two are what make it (the body) strong, [3] and they make its blood appear because it eats the dry, strong earth, and drinks the airy, moist water. [4] In the case of what is dry, its thick part comes out from the behind. In the case of what is moist, [5] its thick part comes out in front. The body sucks in the subtle part of both so that its life and nourishment come from it, [6] and the veins and joints are soaked, so the flesh grows on it and the colour becomes clear. Likewise [7] the existence of our stone comes from the heat and the moisture. Concerning the moisture, it is what gathered the dust [8] until it turned it into a clod of earth. Concerning the heat, it is the strength of the rays of the sun that turned it (the clod) into a stone. And also [9] the mud-brick takes its existence from the moisture and the heat, because the moisture collected it and [10] the heat dried it. So it becomes good for building. Trees are like that, whose existence comes from heat and moisture. [11] And all of that is from the operation of God and from His subtle wisdom that He makes for each of them [12] a separate operation, till He completes them in their outer image and their inner character.»

She said: «How can you claim, O Zosimos, [13] that the sage explained (the matter) and said that all things are one nature, and that the two colours are not [14] one, and that there is no difference between the two except in the name?» He said: «Although the sage called [15] all the things one, he mentioned copper, gold and silver. So his statement about the names is not contradicted. [16] Concerning the nature, it is one and composed, and it is not possible for it to be separated. Thus the sage named it [17] one. He wanted to keep the science secret, therefore they scattered it in their books and gave many names to it. [18] The sage explained that when he said: "All of the composition has to be taken soft ." And [19] I tell you that if you omit any of the things of the composition, then what you seek would not be complete. The completeness (fol. 13b) of this work is by the moisture. In the same way as the head is worthier to be honoured than what is below it, we honour [2] the moisture because without it the world would not exist, and the cloud draws water from the sea [3] in the same way as our cloud draws the dye from its components, so that moisture deserves to be honoured. [4] Upon my life, although the things are despised, nature cannot exist without them.»

She said: [5] «And which (emendation) nature is this?» He said: «It is the one nature which has everything in it which is composed [6] from the completeness of all things, until it turns into one colour.»

She said: «Then tell me about [7] this nature, which is in everything and is the head.» He said: «I have told you about it several times, [8] and I tell you also that if that head does not have everything with it which it should have, it will not be of any use. [9] So put with that head everything that would improve it, and do its operation well because by the operation, [10] the work is completed. But that head is the most important thing that you are looking for. Know that the sages named [11] as one nature all these things with which that head is completed. And that nature [12] is not from many things. Democritus said: "Why are you interested in the many things, [13] while the nature is one?"»

She said: «What is this nature, O Zosimos?» He said: [14] «It is the secret, hidden from people, and it is cheap, expensive, despised, high-ranking, obscure and nobody knows it [15] except a sage. And because of its many colours, the sages gave it many names. As for the truth, it is one, and [16] everything is by it and from it. Know that different natures are not good for this thing, [17] but it is one nature that is suitable and harmonious. So it is necessary for this one to be operated on with gentleness [18] until what you are looking for appears from it. Therefore the sage said: "What you are looking for is [19] one, and it is not one thing and another thing, but it is one from it, and by this, it increases. So everyone (fol. 14a) who sees it but does not know its benefit, and does not know how to operate on it, will use many things. If you have understood it, then [2] I have explained to you what the sages kept secret from the people. Know that the nature is one, so do not be deluded [3] by the multiplicity of what the sages wrote in their books, nor by the many compositions and things, because the nature is one, [4] and everything comes from it. Understand this statement and ponder over its power and its obscure merit. [5] For the sage said. "Why are we interested in the many things, when the true nature is one, and it, the true nature, wins over [6] the nature of the one truth, and in this true nature is the hidden secret, concealed in its inside." [7] If you are subtle in your work, you will extract the nature which wins over the natures, because nature [8] rejoices in nature, nature wins over nature, and nature holds nature. [9] And they are not different natures but just one, having in it its similar ones, [10] which are good for it, and from them and with them it is operated on until its colours become good.»

She said: [11] «Then tell me about when the sage says: "The heavenly nature, which has no body, is [12] the spiritual one."» He said: «The sage is right, because by it (the heavenly nature) the bodies become [13] non-bodies, because the body turns into a non-body when it is destroyed and dies, [14] and its soul is extracted from it.»

She said: «And why is it done like that?» He said: [15] «In order to extract from it what is hidden in it by the heavenly nature, and (then) to dye the other body by it [16] at the end of the work.»

She said: «Is what is dyed dyed by the same kind?» He said: [17] «Yes, and what comes out from it is returned to it.»

She said: «And when does that take place?» He said: [18] «When you see that the vapour rises from below to above, because it enjoys coming out from the thick and earthy [19] to above.»

She said: «And how was it before that?» He said:

(fol. 14b) «The white, the red, the yellow, and the black were apparent in it. Then, when you see in the roasting the vapour [2] rising from below to above like the clouds, this is because it is airy. At that moment [3] when she meets her husband she will love him and he will love her, and he rejoices in her and she rejoices in him, and he prevents her from escaping [4] and she prevents him. So when you hear the sages say: "The nature is one, and the one wins over [5] all", then the one and the one (written without *alif*) is (a) composed (one).»

She said: «O sage, then what is that pure sulphur?» [6] He said: «It is the vapour which is from the water of sulphur. So it is the one which washes and purifies, and it is [7] the cloud, and the rising of the water about which the sage said that he did not leave out anything except that.» She said: «I see that the sage [8] has explained it, but which thing did he leave out?» He said: «He left all of it out. Do you not see that when [9] the mixed ones and the joining one were brought together, then out of them came water of gold in gold. At that moment he said: "There remains [10] nothing of this work for you to do, you have completed it in this operation." Upon my life, in this mixing he did not make clear [11] the composition of the cloud and the rising of the water; if he had made it clear, this work would appear to ordinary people.»

She said: [12] «The sage said: "Make the male marry the female." So tell me about the male and the female.» He said: [13] «It (fem.) is the copper which is worked upon with the cloud and the mercury, and is married to the male and the female until [14] it turns into vapour. So whoever is able to turn the body into a spirit and to make it red, dyes every body because [15] the body turns into a spirit only by subtle pounding and intensive cooking. At that moment, [16] the soul of the thick one is extracted and its earthiness disappears."»

She said: «What made its earthiness disappear?» [17] He said: «Its mixing.» She said: «And what is its mixing?» He said: «It is the magnesia which is mixed [18] with the mercury and the body, and then operated on. If you mix in this way, pound the body [19] in the operation and turn it into vapour, and then make it red until it becomes a spirit, you will extract the subtle one (fol. 15a) concealed in the inside of the body, and you dye every body by it.»

She said: «Then tell me about the statement of the sage: "What [2] dyes and what is dyed is one, and what overcomes and what is overcome is one, and what holds and [3] what is held is one, and what revives and what is revived is one, and what escapes and [4] what does not escape is one.» He said: «If you understand what the sage said, you would be content with it.»

She said: [5] «I did not ask you about this.» He said: «All of those are the four single natures, by which [6] the dyeing of the gold and the silver (*fiḍḍa*) takes place, and they are those which make white and make red, and without the natures nothing [7] would exist. I refuse to comment further on this statement, as I know that whoever reads this book will be content [8] with it.»

She said: «And why is that?» He said: «Because in everything that the sages wrote, they wrote with analogies [9] and names similar to the truth, but they are not the truth. Do you not see that they said: "Wash the copper until [10] its dirt goes away." Any reasonable person knows that all copper is dirt.» She said: «Then what did they mean by that?» [11] He said: «By it they meant the elixir. Do you not see their statement: "Take white sulphur and cook it until [12] it becomes like the purple". But it is sulphur only in name.»

She said: «Give me [13] a brief statement about the operation, because I have become confused by the many things that I hear from you.» He said: «I will do so. Yet do not [14] go beyond what I say.» She said: «I did not ask you about wanting to go beyond it for something else.» He said: [15] «I know. If you do not make things white until you turn them into something like snow, and then make gold from them like a kind of [16] ferment for fermenting the elixir in the same way as the dough is fermented until it becomes dry, you will not reach the completeness of [17] this work.»

She said: «Has the ferment to be kneaded with the gold? And how does the gold become fermented?» He said: [18] «God preserve me from your mischief, and I ask God to bless your knowledge. Yes. In the same way as the ferment of the dough is dough, [19] likewise the ferment of the gold is gold. That is the key with which the sages opened the gates of wisdom.

(fol. 15b) Ask God's forgiveness for this statement.»

She said: «Then what about the statement of Asfīẖās: "I am the one whose dwelling is [2] in the air, the rivers run below me, the sea is placed beneath me and (also) the wonders that make [3] the rivers from all over the world circulate."» He said: «He made himself as an analogy for the operation of the vapour, and for the vapour of the vapours.»

[4] She said: «Then what about his statement: "Hidden secrets appeared, and I saw the four natures, which are the basis of all of [5] the rest." He said: «He knew all of what is written with all its names, colours, taste, smell, [6] minerals, weights and combination. And (he knew) what each one of the things had in terms of power, dye, resisting or fleeing from fire.» [7] She said: «So he was the first to make gold and silver, as he says: "I am the one who changed them, extracted [8] the pure part of their bodies, and I made an equal conjunction and division between them. So their flowers came into bloom, and [9] their firmness was made well, so their pollination was completed.» He said: «Asfīẖās (written here as Asfīnāẖ) was not the first one who did it, but he was the first one [10] in his time who pounded it. With regard to his statement "I performed the division between them equally", he ordered you to deal with them equally after the completion. [11] And with regard to making the firmness well, that is when the seeker took the fugitive, and then the escaping stops.»

She said: [12] «Then tell me about his statement concerning the heavy stone with many colours.» He said: «That is the moist one [13] by nature, whose moisture is more than its body, and it has various natures and different tastes. It (the stone) is useful for the works, [14] and it enters into the works of the art of medicine when its body is whitened and its moisture is coagulated by the simple [15] work.» She said: «Does this stone not have a secret?» He said: «Certainly». She said: «Then why did you name it a stone?» [16] He said: «He who named it (like that) is the one whose statement you asked me about.» She said: «Then tell me about his statement concerning the closed stone, [17] which is named Mother Nature, that gives birth to the natures.» He said: «That is that stone which increases and [18] decreases every day. In it there is a moist nature and various bodies for those who despise [19] the metals. There exists of it (that stone) white and red, and there exists of it black and yellow. And the colours (fol. 16a) of its metals dominate over it. And the best of its stones are the soft, yellow ones having the power, whose dust is extracted, [2] and they do not get burnt in their origins.» She said: «I still do not know what this stone is.» He said: «<But of course!> With it, [3] gold, silver, iron and copper are dissolved, because it has great power when it is worked upon with the moist fire.»

[4] She said: «Then tell me about the statement of the sage about the poison, and the hidden secret, and his warning us not [5] to let anything alien enter into it. And he ordered us to divide it into two parts.» He said: «I ordered you to extract the moisture in [6] the cupolas (*qibāb*), and to separate it (from the margin: from the sediment) in the bottom of the vessel.»

She said: «And what is the name of that sediment down below?» He said: [7] «It has so many names, but with regard to this sage, he named it a fugitive. Then return the highest to the lowest, [8] until the lowest turns black without a soul, as its spirits have been extracted from it, [9] so it became a dry thing, and it is what the sages named ashes.»

She said: «Is it the ashes [10] that Hermes mentioned?» He said: «Yes.»

She said: «I do not see that you mention what Hermes mentioned.» [11] He said: «O yes, put those ashes in the mortar and pound them with the sea [12] until the white sea washes away the greasy dirt, and the blackness of the copper goes away.»

She said: [13] «Is this the first whitening?» He said: «Yes, it is the purification of the blackness of the things. Know [14] that if you do not purify the poison well, its dye would come out sombre and rotten. Thus our [15] abundant copper must be washed several times in the cupolas with the water of the sea and the sun, as I told you before, [16] until it becomes clear. Take care not to become impatient with the repeated washing until [17] you have removed its dead earthiness from it. And the fire eats the blackness that is in it. When all of that [18] moisture is clarified, then in the last mixture, the silver, the pearls and the purple will appear to you when you make it pure. [19] Know that unless you purify well the purple-coloured clothes of kings, sew them well together (fol. 16b), and take all impurity out of them, they will not be dyed well. It is the same with those who want to dye the purple: They should burn [2] the lead in that dyeing, then that dye has to be cooked in the pot until it rises to its upper part, and [3] the one who works, picks up the spirit of that dye with the wool, collecting it and dyeing the clothes of the kings with it. Then [4] a shining purple and an exalted colour for the clothes of the kings come out. This is the poison about which you asked me, [5] mixed with the ashes. It must be washed many times until it becomes white. And from [6] those ashes a pure moisture is extracted, which has been well washed by the poison and the heat, or with a gentle uncorrupted fire. [7] Then wash it many times until the blackness is removed from the poison that covers its surface, which [8] the sages name—I mean that blackness—the very old woman. Know that if you do its washing well, several times, [9] you will find the tin pure, and it does not rise when that blackness—which they name [10] the very old woman—is made to rise in the vessel. That is what the sage ordered: to separate the ashes from the poison.»

She said: [11] «Then tell me about his statement: "If you do not separate the natures, and know their mixtures and their combinations, namely the close one [12] being with the close one, and the suitable one with the suitable one, then what you do becomes useless.» He said: «Democritus was right, [13] and I mentioned that to you long ago, because when the natures meet their natures, welcoming each other, [14] clinging to each other, and rejoicing in each other, by that they rot and by that they are given birth. From something comes nothing, and from nothing [15] comes the thing. Thus nature multiplies nature.»

She said: «Then what is the nature which operates on them?» [16] He said: «That which destroyed it, then turned it into nothing. And it is what gives birth to it, nourishes it and makes it good. [17] Therefore the sages ordered people to look extensively into their books in order to know the true nature, what [18] coagulates it, what makes it good, what is its taste, what is its relationship, how they love each other, how [19] this friendship came about—that was enmity and corruption before—and how those natures get mixed and reconciled together (fol. 17a) until they are firm together in the fire. Whoever knows these things, O Theosebeia, must enter [2] into this work in the name of God. But he who does not know them should not enter into the work, because the harm [3] is greater than the benefit.»

She said: «Then tell me about the statement of Democritus: "Physicians [4] do not dare to mix remedies unless they know the natures and what is their power, [5] and which of them is the cold, the hot, the dry and the moist and what are the diseases to which they are exposed. [6] When they know them, they compose the remedies and mix them, and they cure the sick one and help them to recover [7] by the will of the exalted God."» He said: «Democritus wrote this: "The one who does not know the cold, [8] the hot, the dry, and the moist so that he can compose them—the close one with the close one, and the suitable one with the suitable one—, and has no experience or knowledge, [9] will not find a remedy that cures the soul from every illness." Therefore anyone [10] who enters into this work (in this way) becomes disbelieving towards it, because of the harm that this work causes him due to his ignorance [11] of the harmonious, non-conflicting natures which are suitable for this work. So whoever enters into [12] this work has to know the natures in it. When he knows the natures, he mixes them with what destroys them, because [13] what gets mixed with them conquers all of them with its colour. In the same way as it conquered their appearance outside, it will also conquer [14] their interior.»

She said: «How does the weak conquer the strong?» He said: «Although [15] it is weak in outer appearance, it is strong in essence (*al-maḫbar*). And it is stronger than what you see as strong, [16] and the exalted God knows best.»

She said: «Which one is stronger than the other?» He said: «The one which has patience towards it (the fire) appears to be [17] the strong one, but the one which is the fugitive (from the fire) appears to be the weak one, [18] but in essence (emendation) it is the strong one. Its ability to resist fire is only (possible) with the other one, which does not escape. [19] Know that if its outside becomes rusty, then its inside becomes rusty as well, and if the clouds make the outside of the copper white, then (fol. 17b) its inside will—without doubt—turn white. Know that the one thing wins over ten, [2] and only with the sulphur of the sages can the burning of all bodies take place.»

She said: «Then tell me what is this sulphur [3] and tell me its true name.» He said: «As for its true name as a single (name), I will never mention it till the end of my life. How many times [4] I named it to you, but mentioned it with other things.» She said: «Then describe it (the sulphur) to me.» He said: «It is a stone and not [5] a stone, it is cheap and precious, enigmatic, the hidden thing which everyone knows while they do not know [6] what is in it, whose name is one while it has many names. It has many names in order to hide it from [7] the ignorant. It is the spittle of the moon, it is the stone that is not a stone because the nature has to be worked upon by it, yet it is [8] the cheap one.» She said: «How does it come that its name is one while it has many names?» He said: «Its true name [9] is one and as for the many names, it is because of its exalted nature.»

She said: «Then what is [10] the origin of the first cause?» He said: «It is the poison.» She said: «From where did this poison get that [11] power?» He said: «From its components with which it is mixed in the first (lit.: at the beginning of the) composition.» She said: [12] «What is the name of this which comes out of that water?» He said: «It is the flowers, and with that water everything that [13] one wants to dye is made alumy, and it is what is named ferment of gold and the benefit having many names.»

She said: «Then tell me [14] about when you say in the pages[5] which you sent to me, saying that it is one thing, the strongest [15] and the most elevated of the natures for the sages, while it is the weakest of them for the ignorant.» He said: «Concerning that, I only described it [16] with what, if you knew it, you would know that I had described it without mentioning it.» She said: «Then describe [17] for me its merit.» He said: «It is what turned the body into a spirit, and then separated from it (the body). Everyone who attends to this [18] work wonders about its power, which is better than anything he ever saw, and without which nothing could be. [19] There is no making white, nor making black, nor making red, nor rust except with it.» She said: «Then this one, (note after the bottom line gives the year 987 for this copy)

5 We correct *aṣ-ṣafārāt* to *aṣ-ṣafaḥāt*

(fol. 18a) [6] is it a single one or a composed one?» He said: «No, it is a composed one. I stayed for a long time [2] pondering over the books in order to reach the value of this one thing, while begging God to give me inspiration [3] about what this one could be which the sages praised. After some time He gave me the inspiration to know it.»

She said: [4] «Then tell me about your letter to me: "I wrote a book for you about the gum."» He said: [5] «I already did that.» She said:«Then what is the gum?» He said: «It is from the eternal water, and from it comes [6] the honoured stone.»

She said: «Then what about your statement: "How astonishing that there are so many seekers of this gum and so few [7] who know it!"» He said: «Indeed, this gum only becomes good with copper alone. And you must know that [8] among the people there are some who seek the multiplications, then they achieve some works from them, but they are not able to stand [9] the torture of the fire, because they (the works) are destroyed (by the fire). As for those who did the multiplication from this [10] gum and the honoured stone which held the dye, it (the multiplication) stayed [11] in the torture, and never decreased.»

She said: «Then explain to me [12] an aspect of the power of this gum without disguise.» He said: «Know that our gum is stronger (more valuable) than gold, and it [13] must be more honoured than gold, yet we honour (only) gold. [14] Know that the gum only becomes good with copper. I have seen people buying one [15] samll pearl with much gold. Our gum is more precious than pearls, [16] yet we buy a large quantity of it (gum) with little gold. Therefore the sages kept it secret, and [17] they hated to reveal it in order that it might be kept hidden and not be known by everybody. If they knew it, [18] their owner would not sell it cheaply.»

She said: «Then tell me about the statement of the sage: "Indeed, the beginning of this [19] work, its end, and its perfection, [2] after God, is this stone which is not a stone."» He said:

6 Here the handwriting in the manuscript changes.

(fol. 18b) «I explained to you that it is something honourable-despised, venerated-vulgar, known-unknown, desirable[-rejected].» [2] She said: «[Explain it] without confusing my mind.» He said: «Your mind will not be confused by this.» [3]

She said: «Then explain to me an aspect of it.» He said: «This stone is the gift of God, which [4] He bestows graciously upon whom He wants. Therefore they named it the spittle of the moon and the dung of the moon. However, it is not [5] the spittle of the moon but we named it like that because of its noble nature and its overpowering of [6] what it is mixed with. And the best of its names is the fiery one because it is the torturer of her husband.»

She said: [7] «Then name it!» He said: «It is the gum of the thorns of acacia, and it is the water of silver, and it is [8] the water of sulphur, because it dissolves the body and turns it into water. So the best of its names is the fiery one, [9] because it is the torturer of her husband.»

She said: «Then tell me about when the sage says that if you turn over [10] the natures, the best out of them will become visible.» He said: «By turning over, he meant that [11] if you destroy the exalted nature, and turn the shadow that is concealed in the body into [12] a spirit, you will obtain from the nature the exalted dye. Thus do well the burning of the natures [13] and their torturing (emendation) with the fire. For if you turn the bodies into non-bodies and the [14] non-bodies into bodies, you will achieve your goal. Thus mix that which escapes with that which clings till they turn into [15] one thing. If you do that, you will complete the work. At that time the dyes remain [16] and the spirits are fixed, because the spirit is what makes it strong against everything.»

She said: «Which one of them is [17] the spirit?» He said: «It is the stone which contains the spirit that is the gum coming from the acacia. [18] Then when the torturer kills her husband, we will then call it 'solid mercury' [19] and a 'strong body of magnesia', which no longer escapes from the fire»

She said:

(fol. 19a) «Perhaps this is the thing which Hermes named a benefit having many names.» He said: 2 «Yes, and be careful not to be deluded with the manifold things that you find in the books, because they are worthless. Know 3 that the things are one, and that single thing is what dissolves everything, and it is what turns it white, 4 and what turns it red, and what completes it—in addition to the great and exalted God.»

She said: «And which one of them is this?» 5 He said: «It is the stone which decreases in the casting, and it is the one which destroys and ruins every body, 6 except what is from the sun alone.»

She said: «I see that this 7 acacia-gum is in agreement with the sun.» He said: «If there were not harmony between the two, it would neither 8 turn the sun into silver, nor make the shadow of the copper disappear at the beginning of the operation. Do 9 the cooking well because by the fire the gum becomes strong and turns into mixed ashes, after it had been 10 a white stone (before).»

She said: «Which stone is that?» He said: «It is what we name the alabaster 11 which submerges into that body. Thus cook it until it dries up and takes away the two moistures.»

12 She said: «I want to ask you about a thing that I could not understand.» He said: «Ask me, because I 13 only visit you frequently in order to answer what you could not understand and 14 know thoroughly.»

She said: «From where did the heat and the moisture come to the sperm?» He said: 15 «That is a good question.» She said: «Then tell me!» He said: «The two came from the birth of the blood, because when the liver 16 soaked the veins with blood, it (the blood) got cooked in them again and again. So it became a white plant 17 like froth while its origin is blood. But when it got cooked in the womb,[7] it became 18 a white froth.» She said: «Then from where do the dryness and the coldness of the womb come?» He said: «They come 19 from the veins, because when the sperm fell down into the womb, the canals of the blood became blocked up.

7 *Matn* = main thing, main part, body, here probably the uterus.

(fol. 19b) So that blood decomposed the sperm, and turned it into blood as it was before. Then the blood fed the sperm which is [2] in the womb because the womb is connected with the stomach. Thus the heat of the stomach cooked the sperm [3] which is in the womb till it made it mature and turned it into what the Powerful and Omniscient has decided about the completeness [4] of the days of that embryo, and God created it the way He wanted it. Our copper is like that [5] and our gum (also): the copper finds from the gum what the sperm finds from the womb concerning the decomposing, [6] the rotting, and the saturation with water.» She said: «What is that which makes it rot and decompose?» He said: [7] «Our moisture, which is the essential prerequisite (*milāk* or *malāk*) of our work.»

She said: «I have seen nothing more similar than the sperm to the composition of [8] the sages, their operation in the cooking, the making lean, the rotting, the taking form, [9] and cooking in the darkness of the womb.» He said: «So do not despise anything of what the sages described, [10] and beware not to miss anything out. Know that they only described things by way of [11] analogy for this work.»

She said: «Then tell me about the male and the female. Are they from [12] one nature?» He said: «Yes. But know that although the two are from one thing [13] neither their natural disposition, nor their essence, nor their force are one.»

She said: «How do [14] they become different although they are from one thing?» He said: «Understand that the male (principle) is strong, powerful, dry and [15] hot while the female (principle) is moist, weak and cold. So when the two natures [16] which I described to you, namely the hot, the cold, the dry and the moist are united, God brought out [17] from the two what your eyes saw.»

She said: «You spoke the truth. I have the impression that I understood what you [18] meant.» He said: «If you have understood, then be content with it, and if you have not understood, then ask and [19] I will answer you.»

She said: «Tell me what proves the truth of the analogy with which you started this statement.» He said:

(fol. 20a) «Know that you must ponder over this work, then you would unite the male [2] and the female.»

She said: «Are there among the bodies males and females?» He said: «Yes, and therefore [3] the sages analogised[8] this work to the sun, the moon and the stars, and they named some of them [4] males and some of them females, and some of them improve while others corrupt. [5] And you know that all the bodies are from the earth.»

She said: «I have learnt, [6] O Zosimos, that all the bodies are from the earth, and that all of them are beneficial. So tell me [7] about them.» He said: «Some of them are hot, moist, strong and luminous, and some of them are cold, dry, [8] weak, soft and sombre.»

She said: «How similar is that to the male and the female!» [9] He said: «You are right, that is what I meant. Help me by understanding what I answer you.» She said: [10] «I will do so.» He said: «I tell you that the soft-cold one has three.»

She said: «What are they (the three)?» [11] He said: «They are the blackness, the whiteness and the redness.» She said: «Is there anything else in it besides these [12] three?» He said: «Yes, there are also the four.»

She said: «And what are those four?» [13] He said: «They are the moisture because it dissolves quickly, and the dryness because it is a sulphur that burns like [14] the sulphur, and it has the coldness because it extinguishes the heat of the male, and [15] it also has the heat, which is why we named it the water of sulphur.»

She said: «So this sulphur deserves [16] to be named with these many names.» He said: «Know that the water of sulphur is [17] a great thing, the strongest of all things, and when the sages recognized its power they kept its nature secret. [18] So they named it water because it flows as the water flows, and they named it sulphur, because [19] it burns as the sulphur burns. And they named it a body because it can be touched, and they named it

8 *Wadaʿa* = to render, here in the sense of analogise.

(fol. 20b) a stone because it is a body, and (they named it) not a stone because it is a spirit. And the sages gave all sorts of names to it and they [2] even named it a hollow stone. And if I wanted to tell all that [3] the sages praised it with, all the books of the people of my time would not be enough for me, and it would not be finished in all my lifetime, and [4] my mind would not reach it.»

She said: «You gave me, O Zosimos, a good answer with what you said. How marvellous [5] that is!» He said: «Truly, it only becomes good if you understand my answer [6] to your question. So do not wonder about that, but wonder about what is more wonderful than it.» [7]

She said: «What is this?» He said: «What is more easily obtainable, and at the same time more plentiful than water?» She said: «Nothing.» [8] He said: «Then which thing is more precious than pearls?» She said: «Nothing.» He said: «(But) God created it from water.» [9] She said. «What you say is true!»

He said: «Which thing is more easily obtainable than dust (earth) and to be found everywhere?» She said: [10] «Nothing.» He said: «But the exalted God created from it sapphires and emeralds and every [11] precious stone and all of the bodies.» She said: «What you say is true!» He said: «Which thing is lower <than dust> [12] and inferior to urine?» She said: «Nothing.» He said: «From it, God created the sperm and from the sperm [13] He created human beings.» She said: «What you say is true.» He said: «Then which thing is cheaper than sulphur?» She said: [14] «Nothing.» He said: «From it, God taught us the making of gold.» She said: «Glory to you, my God, [15] how great are the wonders of your wisdom!»

She said: «Then tell me what makes the moist [16] dry and the fugitive fixed.» He said: «What transforms the two is their being firm[9] in the fire, which helps them both [17] because the death of the natures and their life is by the fire. The composed one is what [18] inseminates itself, makes itself pregnant, and gives birth to what you seek, God willing. Thus when [19] the actions and the colours of the work appear to you, then you will see the miracles of God's wisdom. So when

9 Here is written *rāsahuma,* but we read *rusūwahuma.*

(fol. 21a) the One who grants it completes it (the work), its colour will turn purple.»

She said: «Upon my life, the sages were not astonished about [2] these natures of the dyeing, except because of the miracles which they saw emerging from them, when they said: "O, you [3] heavenly natures that transform the natures by the operation!"» He said: «When you know these, then know that there is nothing [4] better than these natures in the dyeing, nor anything more precious than them, because they are the ones which increase [5] the body and turn it into a metal [10] that does not leave any more.»

She said: «O Zosimos, I saw that the sages gave [6] many of these examples, and you ordered me not to leave any one of them out, but I have seen [7] disagreement in them.» He said: «I order you not to neglect them, because they did not write these [8] examples in their books in vain, but they wrote them as an analogy for what they wanted [9] to keep secret. As for their disagreement, I already told you that every one of them invented a name [10] with which they named the natures. Because of that they differed. So you must ponder well over [11] these natures from which this work comes into being. You should unite [12] the male and the female and know that when this male marries the female, the male dies, [13] decomposes, and rots until he becomes invisible. The mother remains, which is the female that carried the male [14] in her belly. Thus she makes him rot little by little till he decomposes, then she revives him, improves him, [15] and feeds him. After a given time, the child comes out, more complete, more beneficial, [16] better in colour, stronger than his father, and he is not similar to his father in any of his qualities.»

She said: «Why [17] is he not similar to his father?» He said: «Because he became a new youth, who acquired the force from his father and his mother, [18] so his force is neither from him nor by him (alone).»

She said: «Why is it like that?» He said: «Because he has been made to come out from one nature [19] to another.» She said: «How he has been made to come out?» He said: «This is because at the beginning of his matter he was

10 We usually translate *maʿdan* with 'metal' not 'mineral'.

(fol. 21b) a thick body. Then, when he was operated on, he turned into a subtle spirit and obtained a spiritual dyeing colour, [2] yet his force only becomes visible for us in a body other than his own. And this water is like that. It turned into a [3] subtle spirit that entered into the body of silver and it dyed it, so it turned into gold. In the same way as it entered in [4] the beginning of the mixture into the female, so it (the water) made her strong, beautiful and turned her—after she was rotten—into [5] a fugitive, strong and resistant to fire. Thus in a similar way, when we introduce it (the water) into the body of silver (*waraq*) of ordinary people, [6] it makes it strong to fight the fire, and it improves its colour and its dye. Know, my lady, [7] that the long-windedness of the sages is not because of their ignorance.»

She said: «Then what led them to do that?» He said: [8] «The operation of this work, along with their effort to hide it behind similarities, and everyone [9] who has mind and understanding must make analogies of the things, until he knows their force, character, and their limits [10] in order to know which of these natures he is in need of. Then he unites every thing with what is similar and equivalent to it. [11] So he obtains what he wants from this work.»

She said: «How can an intelligent one [12] attain what you mentioned when the sages have disguised it with similarities, hiding it [13] in countless words? Since you know (this), if you want, you could simply say [14] that the sages veiled it.» He said: «Understand and know that what you are looking for and desiring [15] is just one (thing). Its completeness and its perfection is not from something else but from it, by it, and for it. [16] <She said> And I have told you that you are just one of the women of your kind. Do you not remember that when the sulphur [17] meets the sulphur, much work results from them? And those two sulphurs are of [18] one origin.»

She said: «I knew that.» He said: « This is what I meant (by saying) its completion is from it [19] and by it, and I did not tell you that its operation is from it and by it.»

She said: «How enigmatic is your statement; I fear

(fol. 22a) that I will never understand this work!» He said: «Why is that?» She said: «Because [2] you answer me about something that you hide in your heart, and my mind is not able to understand this.» [3] He said: <«Do you not wait till I tell you»> «Do you not see when I told you that its operation is done with something else?[11] Just as the earth is ploughed [4] with an iron tool, so we make the stones, and everything is made by iron and [5] everything is operated on with it. In the same way, we extract with our sulphuric water all the colours; that is why [6] we named it one.

She said: «Then why did you give it many names?» He said: «For its many colours and its great [7] benefits. Just as it is the quickest thing to turn from one colour to another, in the same way it is the quickest [8] thing to change. So we named each colour with an invented name.»

She said: «I have understood what you said. So when you [9] talk, do not make your words obscure, but make them easily understandable for me, because I am weaker than what you make me enter into.» [10] He said: «Yes.» She said: «Then give me an aspect that I can cling to.» He said: «Turn the bodies into spirits, [11] and compare the operation of this work to the work of the dyeing of clothes, because the dyers extract—[12] by their careful procedure and mastering of their work—the subtle dye of the herbs with the water of the people. [13] Then with it they dye whichever of the clothes they want. That is how you should work with the natures [14] until you extract these things with carefulness and experience.»

She said: «How can I do that?» [15] He said: «Turn the bodies into spirits in order that you extract from the solid parts of the bodies a spirit which is [16] the subtlcst thing. Then you must solidify it (the spirit) by the second composition, [17] and then you may dye whatever you want. Look at the painters. They are only able [18] to extract the dyes for their wall-pictures from the bodies and the minerals, and they are not able [19] to paint with them unless they make subtle that which is thick.»

She said: «With what do they make subtle

11 Text in the margin corrects the main text.

(fol. 22b) that which is thick?» He said: «With burning, pounding and rotting until they turn them into [2] spirits. Then they paint with them what they want. Thus you must burn the things, [3] pound them, make them rot, soak them, and turn them into spirits.»

She said: «And with what do [4] I turn them into spirits?» He said: «With the gentle, mild fire.»

She said: «Then what?» He said: [5] «You ferment that water thoroughly, so that the dye penetrates. Look, my lady, [6] you have introduced yourself into this great secret, and the love for it runs in the blood of [7] your veins.»

She said: «I did. If you want, you could relieve me by making clear what you hide [8] in your heart, O Zosimos. Indeed, what makes the matter good is simple in terms of what I ask you [9] about.» He said: «How near you are to it and how far away you are from it.»

She said: «How can the near [10] and the far come together?» He said: «Concerning the near, it is because I know your desire and your frequent questions, [11] and you explore what is obscure and enigmatic, so you ask me about it like a [12] skilful sage. Concerning your being far away from it, it is because I know the hardship and sadness that I found, [13] as I was preoccupied in searching for the sages, collecting the books, and exhausting myself in reading [14] about the world and what is in it, joining some nights with the day, pondering much and focusing [15] my thoughts. Whenever an aspect of it became clear to me, I came across other statements of the sages that blocked me in a way that [16] made me confused and doubtful, even making me forget what I knew. Thus it brought me back (to the point) when I started [17] this work. Whoever has never tasted the pains of error in this work has never tasted [18] sadness, because its error is not easy. I do not say to you that my great sadness was because of [19] the loss of my money.»

She said: «For what is it then?» He said: «It was my possibility to obtain the biggest treasure from God (fol. 23a) that I have, but then (again) there appeared to me some error that prevented me from obtaining it. Thus what is more painful [2] for the heart than this?»

She said: «You have only said this about yourself in order to share with me something from you [3] and to complete your favour towards me.» He said: «I did not speak like this for that (reason), but it impeded my speech, [4] so I described for you what I found, and I know that it arrives to whomsoever seeks [5] this work—more than it arrived to me.»

She said: «As you know well the pain that you experienced, [6] please have mercy upon me!» He said: «I do. Know that if the seed of wheat did not lie in the fertile earth [7] and be buried in it, it would remain alone, dry and useless. But if the seed gets buried, [8] rotten, decomposed and dies, God would make many things germinate from it. Therefore you should [9] dye the bodies with the bodies, and you must know that you should mix the bodies with their moisture at the beginning of [10] the work, and operate on them till they turn into one thing. At this time [11] you place it on the silver, so it turns into gold.»

She said: «Then tell me about this viper which is named [12] the Harmful One (*aš-Šāḍina*) and about its strong poison.» He said: «That is a viper which has great power and its poison [13] is deadly, and I do not know anything on earth more deadly than it.» She said: «And how does its poison kill?» [14] He said: «Its poison only kills her husband.» She said: «How does it kill her husband?» He said: [15] «When the male had sexual intercourse with her and placed his sperm in her, his soul came out immediately [16] with his sperm, thus the male died.»

She said: «I see that his sperm was his soul.» [17] He said: «Yes. Therefore his soul came out when his sperm came out.» She said: [18] «Then, what did the female do?» He said: «She accepted the sperm, longing for it. So she became pregnant. Then, when [19] her pregnancy was completed and her delivery came close, her son did not come out in the same way as ordinary creatures.» She said:

(fol. 23b) «So how did he come out?» He said: «He pierced her womb, so the child came out alive and the mother died [2] immediately. The child came out as male and female, replacing his parents in order that nothing else is mixed with the nature of the two. [3] So this foetus has always been renewed. The parents die [4] and the child lives.»

She said: «If you had not written this in your books, [5] I would have said that this is just a tale.» He said: «Did I not forbid you to despise anything in their books, [6] or what the sages wrote in their books? This is because God is too great in their eyes [7] to write anything untrue.»

She said: «You are right. But I have not seen anything like these two vipers. [8] So I ask you by your God, <to make me pay attention> to tell me, what are the two?» He said: «I did not think that you were ignorant of something [9] like this. When they describe the matter of this viper, and they describe it in this [10] way, then what you do think urged them to mention it?»

She said: «I asked you because I wonder about them.» [11] He said: « Today I will make something clear for you that you have often asked me, and that I have answered you.»

She said: [12] «So it is more appropriate that you do not withhold it.» [13] He said: «This viper, which is named the Harmful One, is our gum, the murderess of her husband. Upon the life of your father, the sage gave a good description. [14] Do you not know that the gum kills her husband when he has sexual intercourse with her?» She said: «I know». [15] He said: «Do you not know that she becomes pregnant. Then when her delivery comes close, she dies and her son comes out [16] perfectly alive. He is that about whom the sages said "He is, whose father is his son."»

She said: «You relieved me [17] of what I was in.» He said: «All that they wrote, indeed they wrote it as an analogy [18] for something. <He said:> Know that by all you find in their books about this and things similar to [19] this, they meant their hidden composition. So take care, (fol. 24a) O Theosebeia, not to ignore what they described, otherwise you will feel sorry. And do not despise anything of what they wrote, [2] as it stands for something. You must know that the copper should be rusted before anything else. Then it has to be blackened, and then [3] it has to be whitened with the water of sulphur which does not get burnt. Then it has to cling. At that time it turns into [4] a body of magnesia and a body of mercury. Then it has to be cooked until the fugitives are extracted from it, [5] and the copper becomes without rust.»

She said: «This is as if you described the first operation.» He said: [6] «This is what I meant.» She said: «So when the copper becomes without rust, did it then become our silver, which [7] is the silver of the sages?» He said: «You are right and you spoke well.»

She said: «Then tell me about her statement: "Take [8] silver."» He said: «She did not mean the silver of the people but she meant our silver which comes from our work, [9] with which we turn copper into silver.» She said: «And with what did you turn copper into silver so that it became [10] your silver?» He said: «We made it white with arsenic and mercury.» She said: «Then what about her statement: "Take gold."?» He said: [11] «It is the gold which dyed our silver, about which I told you that we make it white with arsenic and mercury.» [12] She said: «Then tell me about her statement: "Take lead."» He said: «She did not mean the lead of the people.» [13] She said: «Then which lead is it?» He said: «It is that from which the magnesia of the sages is composed.»

[14] She said: «Then tell me about when you say: "Take the white lead which is whitened by the things [15] with which it is composed." So what made it white, is it white, too?» He said: «No, [16] it is not white but red.»

She said: «So how did it make it white when it is red?» [17] He said: «It made it white at the beginning of the work of the composition (*tarkīb*) and the operation (*tadbīr*). Then [18] its redness gets concealed in the inside of the whiteness. And it is what makes it red after that.» She said: [19] «So what makes it white is (also) what makes it red?» He said: «Yes, because it is the one which makes itself white (fol. 24b) with the things that are with it. Therefore the sage told us that both dyes [2] are one work. Whoever wishes to contradict what I told you, namely that the one thing [3] contains both dyes in it, will end in error. This is because the things which [4] the sage mentioned for making white are the same for making red. Know that if [5] you attempt to make white and to make red with the things which the sage named, you would find [6] that only the potash (*qillī*) remains, which is a burnt thing. But as for the rest of the things which are [7] in the composition, they are not stable.»

She said: «Then tell me about when you say that Ostanes [8] made for each body—the copper, the iron, the lead, the tin [9] and the silver—a separate operation, and he claimed that they would become gold in the operation.» [10] He said: «All of this is untrue and only the ignorant believe it.»

She said: «Then why did [11] Ostanes write it?» He said: «To disguise it in this way from the ignorant; but I tell you [12] that these four bodies only dye if they get dyed because [13] Maria said: "The copper does not dye without being dyed before, so when it is dyed it will dye."» [14]

She said: «Then how can you speak of four bodies while Maria only mentions copper?»[15] He said: «You understood well. We are not in need of all of those four bodies [16] which are mentioned. We just want the one body [17] in which is the one dye. After this I want you to become more confident about this, [18] God willing. Know that this body does not dye till it gets dyed. [19] When it gets dyed, it dyes. Therefore Democritus said: "If you do the composition well, (fol. 25a) you will dye every body." Thus every body is the four bodies, and the four bodies [2] are the one body which gets dyed before that, so when it gets dyed, [3] it dyes.»

She said: «Then tell me what urged the sage to mention the moisture [4] with the hard one when he said: "The pure extracted water of sulphur."» He said: «He hated [5] to make his statement incomplete, so he said: "This is the union of the component of the gold." [6] So he mentioned the moisture with the hard one, when he said: "The pure water of sulphur which is [7] extracted from the one sulphur."»

She said: «Then what urged him [8] to mention it (the moisture) together with the hard one?» He said: «Because that water is extracted [9] from one hard body.»

She said: «Then why did he mention it with the broths?» [10] He said: «He mentioned it when it turned moist. The first moist one got mixed with the [11] other moist one and settled down with this other moist one.»

She said: «I see that all of the composition is rather [12] mixed from the hard and the moist.» He said: «You are right, and I will make it clear for you [13] in the "Treatise of the Sulphur", after this statement. But I complete my statement for you [14] when he said the hard and mentioned the moist with it, as he said: "The pure water of sulphur." [15] I tell you that when he called it [16] "the pure water of sulphur" he brought together in this name the hard and the moist, as well as the making white [17] and the making red in the pure water of sulphur that has been extracted from [18] the one sulphur, which is made from lime. Do you not see there is the sulphur [19] and its water. So by the hard and the moist he made it perfect and complete, because (fol. 25b) the hard turned after its mixing into a moist spirit with the other spirit.»

[2] She said: «Then tell me about the water of sulphur.» He said: «It is the water of sulphur, and it is [3] the broth, and it is that about which Democritus said: "Take some of the pure sulphury water [4] and some gum, then you will dye every body." So he (Democritus) made the gum equal with [5] the moisture.»

She said: «So when the gum is mixed with the broth, then the broth [6] is the water of sulphur?» He said: «You spoke well. Do you not see that Maria and all the sages [7] only perform the work with the water of sulphur?»

She said: «And how is the water of sulphur able [8] to make the sulphur non-burnable, while both of them are sulphurs, [9] and sulphurs are not resistant to fire?» He said: «The sages call many [10] of the moistures with the name of sulphurs although they are not sulphurs. But [11] they named them like that. Therefore Democritus said: "Put in the composition [12] some non-burnable sulphur in order that the poison be submerged inside that sulphur."» [13]

She said: «I did not understand this.» He said: «I will repeat my statement for you. [14] Know that the pure water of sulphur is not a single thing.»

She said: «Then tell me what is in it.» [15] He said: «There is in it the sulphur, the gum, and the herb with which [16] God makes the plant emerge. They named it a holy secret. When they name the water of sulphur with anything after [17] that, then they are truthful in this. If they name it sulphur [18] they are truthful because the sulphur is in it, and the sulphur is the gum. And if [19] they name it sulphur, or water of sulphur, or water of saffron they are truthful (fol. 26a) because all of these things are in it.

She said: «Then tell me about when the sages say: [2] "Pull out (*inzaʿ*) the shadow of the copper and put in it what strengthens it to become red".» He said: [3] «Concerning the pulling out of its shadow, he ordered you to make it white. And the shadow has to be pulled out by the sulphur [4] and also by the mercury.»

She said: «I see that the pure water of sulphur is what does [5] all the work in its beginning and in its end.» He said: «You are right.»

She said: «And how is [6] it able to do this work?» He said: «Because all of the things which [7] were in the first composition become pure water of sulphur. And it is what [8] all of the sages named the complete visible secret, and it is the pure water of sulphur.»

[9] She said: «Then tell me about when you say that mercury alone removes the shadow of the copper.» [10] He said: «I told you that mercury alone removes the shadow of the copper, but [11] with the power of its companions. In this regard, Šīmās said: "The work is one, [12] but everything should be in that one." Therefore [13] Hermes named it a single benefit having many names. Know that when the sage [14] said: "The water is from the single sulphur," he is quite right [15] because all of them turned into one thing.»

She said: «Then tell me, why did the sage [16] mention many things in his book but did not care to mention them when he started [17] the operation? Among other things he mentioned the herb of *anāġālīs, qīānūn* and [18] of russet colour (*muġrat*). Then why did he mention these hard things dissolved with the moistures, [19] the talc and the glass when he did not take them up in the operation?» He said:

(fol. 26b) «He only left out these things that he did not mention in the operation in order [2] to hide it from the ignorant. Whoever has intelligence should ponder over the harmonious one, take it up, [3] and make it enter into his work. And he should (also) ponder over the disharmonious one which was not [4] mentioned in the operation so that he would not consider it. Do you not see that when he mentioned [5] different things he left them out when he began the operation and he applied himself to the harmonious ones (only) and took them [6] for the operation. Then he said about the operations about which he wrote: "If you [7] know what resists fire and what does not resist fire, then [8] what does not resist fire will learn to resist fire from the one that resists fire. And if you know [9] the dyer and what does not dye until it is dyed, then when it marries it [10] it will be dyed by it." All of this statement I wrote for you is about [11] the whitening.

She said: «Then what about the statement of the sage: "Roast it for three days with their nights [12] on a gentle, continuous fire till it is roasted."» He said: «When you read in their books: [13] "Cook such and such until it is roasted", then the number of those days [14] and their nights becomes worthless when the sage makes an exception and says: "Three days and their nights." So do not [15] act according to that, leave aside these days, and ignore his statement in order [16] that the operation be completed. And as a confirmation of what I order you to do, Democritus said: [17] "Roast it for two or three days till the poison becomes fully and extremely [18] red." The sages were in agreement about the solidification of the water of sulphur with [19] its body on a small fire of dung till it gets solidified. Then it must be (fol. 27a) cooked till it becomes red. Know that among them are those who ordered us to solidify it on a small [2] fire, while others ordered us (to use) hot ashes (instead). I suggest [3] that your fire should be gentle at the beginning of the work in order that the water gets mixed with the cloud, [4] because Democritus said: “Mix the cloud with the water of sulphur and cook it on a small [5] gentle fire of dung until it gets solidified.”

She said: «Then tell me about what Democritus mentioned about [6] the cloud and the way he solidified the cloud.» He said: «Because the cloud is the cinnabar, thus the cloud [7] and the water turned into one thing. For that he (Democritus) said: “You have nothing left except [8] the cloud and the rising of the water.” Do you not see that he chose the cloud and the water. If [9] the two are united, they become the head of the work. Do you not see his statement about the operation of the ferment [10] of gold where he said: “It dyes every body.”?»

She said: «What is every body?» [11] He said: «It is the other body that he named with the name of every body. When [12] it is mixed with the ferment of gold, then the ferment of gold dyes that body which is [13] every body.»

She said: «Then tell me whether the weight decreases in the cooking or not?» [14] He said: «We compare it (emendation) with bread and every cooked thing because it has to [15] decrease in the cooking. So how can you doubt our work? Especially lead, [16] the more it gets cooked the more it decreases. Do you not see how Maria said: [17] “Know that you will find that whenever you do the work, it decreases by one fifth.” And she [18] also declared: “When the copper is cast and becomes rust, it decreases also.”»

She said: «And when is [19] that?» He said: «At the time of the completion of the whitening and at the time of the completion of the reddening.

(fol. 27b) Know also that the sulphurs dye, then they escape. And the cultivated herbs [2] also decrease because they are pounded, and their thick part disappears.»

She said: «Then tell me about [3] when Agathodaimon says: "Take the golden arsenic, extract from it its soul, [4] leave its thick part and extract from it its vapour (lit. vapoury part) which is its spirit."» He said: [5] «Agathodaimon is right because arsenic does not have a body. Know that the soul [6] and the spirit are not one.»

She said: «Then tell me what is the soul and what is the spirit?» [7] He said: «Concerning the soul, it is its colour which appeared to us. Then when [8] the body is destroyed, made to rot, nourished, and tortured by the fire, the soul disappears and [9] the spirit is extracted. If you do the operation of that spirit well, you will succeed and obtain what you need. [10] Whoever wants to enter into this work must know how he has [11] to extract the spirits from the bodies because if he preserves that [12] spirit well, he will reach his goal and get what he is looking for. But if he does not preserve the bodies in [13] the cooking when he burns them, the spirits will not remain with him either.»

She said: «Then what about the statement of Maria: [14] "The lead does not remain because it breaks up into fragments, and the sulphurs do not remain because they dye and then they escape". [15] She also declared: "The dusts escape as well."» He said: «Maria is right because what has [16] to be taken from them is their taste. Concerning their bodies, they are dead without any benefit. And concerning [17] his statement: "Make pure the herbs!" means rather that their taste has to be taken from them. Concerning the tin, [18] it does not remain because most of it gets burnt and disappears, and its taste remains. I told you [19] in all the books that nothing remains of the sulphurs or the dusts, except their taste, (fol. 28a) which is mixed with the copper. This is because among the bodies only copper has an unchanging nature, [2] except for what is from the chrysocolla and the claudianus, because Hermes said: [3] "Although the claudianus escapes from the fire, its nature stays." Know [4] that everything is destroyed in the fire, and nothing remains from it, except the copper [12] which [5] held the taste of its companions. So this is our copper [13] and our silver, which the sages praised [6] in their books. Thus do not ask for the weight of anything else but this (copper). But as for what disappeared from the rest of the other things, [7] do not let them scare you. Therefore Democritus did not write the weight of anything [8] except for the copper alone when he said: "Take from the whitened copper four ounces and from [9] the purified iron one ounce". And he left away the weights of the (other) things. Therefore I told you that if you put [10] fewer or more things with the copper, do not be concerned because they do not remain. Therefore [11] Democritus did not mention the weights of anything except for the copper.»

She said: «Do you think that those who [12] mentioned the weight are more interested in the weight than Democritus?» He said: «By God, no!» [13]

She said: «How can I know that?» He said: «Do you not see that he left out (the things) [14] whose weight is not needed, when he said: "Take from the gilded arsenic 1½ ounces." [15] And he left away the rest of the things, and he did not propose a weight for them.»

She said: «I see that the composition is rather [16] two things, from bodies and from sulphurs.» He said: «You are right. Do you not see [17] that he mentioned the weight of the things and he left out the weight of the sulphurs? So what he left out, and for which he did not mention [18] a weight, you must give it according to what you consider right. Know that everything in the composition [19] vanishes, and all of it disappears except the copper, as it is what remains because there is nothing

12 A commentary in the margin reads: The copper here is the second body, and God knows best.

13 Another commentary in the margin reads: It is not the copper of the people but the second body, which is the gold and the silver, and is called whitened, yellowed and reddened copper, and this emerges during the operation.

(fol. 28b) with a living nature that does not vanish except the copper. So when that copper finds a nature [2] it clings to it, and leaves everything else. So this is what the sages were referring to when they said: “The nature [3] enjoys the nature”, because although it is not like it in outer appearance, [4] it (the copper) accepts it (the nature) and has sexual intercourse with it, in the same way as the donkey mounts the mare, and the wolf the bitch [5] and what is similar to them. »

She said: «Then tell me about the many things Hermes mentioned concerning [6] the juices of the herbs, the dyes, and the colours.» He said: [7] «You are not in need of all of that. However, you are in need of our moisture, which you know. So do not [8] pay attention to anything else, and know that the secret, which Hermes tried to keep away from [9] the people and wanted to hide, is the spirit and the fire with which the natures are pounded. [10] That is why he named the fire a sun, when he said: “Know that it is the big sun that completes this [11] work.”»

She said: «What are the two?» He said: «They are the dust and the water. So be careful that you do not let them disappear from [12] your thinking.»

She said: «Then tell me about the statement of Maria: “If you perform well the making of [13] the white sulphur you have reached the aim of the work.”» He said: «Maria is right [14] because this white sulphur, for which they invented the many names, is what [15] enters into both compositions. The beginning of its work is the whitening, and the whitening [16] is rather for [14] the four bodies. And I told you also that when they (the four bodies) become white, [17] we name them with whatever things we want.»

She said: «Then what about when you say that the mistake only comes [18] at the beginning of the work.» He said: «I still say that, so do the measures [19] of the fire well. And as for the rust, there is no mistake possible. Therefore Democritus ordered you to

[14] We correct *from* the four bodies to *for* the four bodies.

(fol. 29a) turn the poison thick, and therefore the sage said about this sulphur: "If the torturer is made [2] to enter into the bodies, it would make the nature strong."»

She said: «Then tell me [3] about when you say: "Make it a broth that resists the fire."» He said: «And I tell you that without it [4] nothing comes into being because it is what dissolves the body, and turns it into a metal that does not escape.»

She said: [5] «So when the sulphur is turned into water, should it be burnt because it is water of sulphur?» [6] He said: «It should not be burnt[15] because it is turned into water, and you know that the fire is not [7] able to burn the water.» She said: «Did he (Democritus) therefore say: "It took its close one as the enemy, [8] and the nature became strong, and it does not escape from the fire."?» He said: «Yes, because it clings and is clung to.»

[9] She said: «And how, O Zosimos, does the nature take its close one as the enemy?» He said: «Concerning [10] its close one, it also turned into water as in the first work. So we named it water of sulphur. Concerning [11] his word "as enemy", it is because the water is the enemy of the fire, but it took its companion and it clung to it, and it did not [12] leave it to become smoke. If there were not water concealed in its (the fire) inside as its moisture, it would escape (emendation). Even [13] when you see it just like water, then know that it has a tremendous power and effect. I have already told you that [14] what remains in the fire and fights against it are the natures which are the bodies. And concerning those which [15] are not natures, they are the sulphurs which do not remain in the fire.»

She said: «Tell me, [16] O sage, why did the sages frequently mention the bodies, and what [17] urged them to do that.» He said: «In order to keep this work secret.» She said: «Then show me a way to it, in order [18] to know what they meant but were hiding.» He said: «When the sages want to mention [19] the single body, which is their aim, they mentioned other bodies with it

[15] Margin reads: When the sulphur turns into water, it turns into fire, but it should not get burnt. This is a very dark secret.

(fol. 29b) in order to hide it (the single body) with them, and to increase the doubt and the disbelief among whoever reads their books, and in order that [2] the ordinary people should not be led to their body.»

She said: «They made the matter really enigmatic and obscure.» He said: [3] «And I will increase your conviction about their obscurity. When they wanted to operate on that one, [4] they would never describe the operation of that one which is the truth. So they only [5] mentioned that statement about the true operation when they added [6] chapters with false operations together with their operation, in order to hide the true operation. Accordingly, if they [7] mention the beginning of their operation, they do not complete it until they put false statements with it [8] so as to obscure it. Then they return to the rest of that true operation, and they complete it, [9] and they also put with it what obscures it. And know that I am still following them in [10] my words and my books. That is why my books and my statements are so numerous. As for what I write [11] for you about these questions which you elicited from me, in them are things I was unable to say. [12] I see that I have made clear for you what cures you, although I have disguised from you [13] many things that I told you by means of analogies, because I was obliged to follow [14] the sages. Thus do not blame me.»

She said: «Then tell me about when you say in your book for me, [15] in summary, that the things which the sages named are one thing.» [16] He said: «If you doubt my statement then I will give you the testimony of the sages about that [17] because Hermes, Democritus, Africanus, and all of the sages said [18] that the things which enter into our work are minerals, dusts, moistures [19] and herbs.»

She said: «This your statement disagrees with their opinion.» He said: «It is not in disagreement, (fol. 30a) but you are a woman who does not understand that when these things which the sages named [2] are combined, composed, and thus get married, they turn into one thing. And Sīmās (we find him in different writings) [3] spoke well: "The thing is one, and everything comes from it." And Bersīūs (Persius?) mentioned [4] the four bodies, and he made from them one single product, and ordered that this product be cooked in [5] the furnace which dissolves the tar. As for Agathodaimon, he said: "After making [6] the copper rusty, purifying it, making it black, and making it white a high-ranking redness comes out from it." [7] Thus he meant one body. So what is it that you were doubting in their statement? [8] I tell you that when they say bodies they mean the one body [9] which is named lead until it reaches the copper.»

She said: «Then what about when they say "multiplication"?» He said: [10] «They meant by it the two bodies. Sometimes they named it lead-copper, and (sometimes) they named it gold-silver, so its names are [11] numerous as are these names.»

She said: «Then tell me about this one thing [12] which dyes: Is it a metallic stone?» He said: «How is it that you are not ashamed of that question, [13] after your extensive reading of the books of the sages? Do you think that it is one thing, not composed, [14] and that it can dye by its own nature?»

She said: «You claimed that Democritus said: [15] "The nature is one and it wins over the one nature."» He said: «I tell you that [16] the nature is one and all of the remedies are mixed with what is similar to them. Thus praise [17] God, who made all the books of medicine which you have, confirming what I pass on to you! [18] Do you not see how the sage Aristotle[16] said: "The nature is a composed one."? [19] And look at the statement of Democritus when he said: "The nature is composed of

[16] One of the margins says: I think that he is Ostanes, because Aristotle denies this work.

(fol. 30b) despised things, but the teacher made from them a great dyeing nature." Look [2] at Aristotle when he asked the sage Mīdunah about the fat which does not get burnt: [3] "What is the composition of that fat?" Mīdunah said: "It is composed of [4] a pyrite-stone, a non-burnable sulphur and a despised salt. When [5] these things were collected and were composed, they turned into one nature." Thus this is the one thing [6] which you asked about. And know that if you mix it with anything after the operation and [7] the flames of fire reach it, they burn it completely without mercy till it turns fine like dust. Thus this is the nature of [8] the composed power which is one. I wish I knew what urges you [9] to think that this matter and secret is one non-composed nature.»

She said: «Then tell me [10] about these people that you mentioned who found some books where the work is clear and summarized, [11] and the coagulation of the mercury is clear in them. Then when they read these books and saw the summary of what they (the sages) wrote [12] in them, they rejected them.» He said: «That has happened. But those were beasts, because I saw that the truth was in their hands, [13] but they did not see it because of blindness and ignorance. If you are able not to be of this [14] kind, then do not be. For, by God, the truth is in your hands but you still ask about it, and I answer you [15] in the easiest way that I found.»

She said: «O Zosimos, I seek refuge in God from being like those! [16] Those people had little understanding, great blindness and disobedience towards all of you. And you know that [17] I am of all the people the most obedient to the sages.» He said: «Thus if you want to know that, keep being [18] obedient to them, be zealous in reading their books, contemplate much about them, and ponder over and over again [19] what they described till the Inspirer of the blessings inspires you with what you are seeking.»

She said: «Then tell me about

(fol. 31a) the cloud.» He said: The cloud is the water, but when it is operated on and cooked, the cinnabar holds the subtle part of [2] the cloud, because by the cloud everything is pounded.»

She said: «Perhaps the cloud must be coagulated before [3] it is mixed with the things?» He said: «Do you not see that the sages said: "Coagulate the cloud with things similar to it?" [4] And Maria said: "When the cloud is coagulated, whitened, and mixed with the copper, it makes [5] the copper have no shadow." So it is the crown and the head of everything that you are looking for.»

She said: «And why is it considered [6] the crown of everything?» He said: «Because in it is coagulated everything that improves it.» She said: «Then where are those [7] who said: "The cloud must be coagulated alone."?» He said: «Woe unto those, how miserable they are, [8] and how numerous are their mistakes, and how far they are from the truth! Whoever wants to coagulate the cloud alone, [9] this error will make him fall into the fire, because when the cloud wants to escape, the components with which it is mixed prevent [10] it from escaping because of the closeness of that mixture. The thing that prevents it most [11] from escaping is the tin. Therefore Democritus said: "When the seeker meets with what is sought, [12] they cling to each other."»

She said: «Then tell me about this female whom you mentioned many times.» [13] He said: «It is what dissolves, makes white and makes red. Therefore Democritus mentions it [14] at the time of dissolving the ivory and the stones. And one of the people named it the transformer of the sun, and the one [15] who named it like that was right. Whoever wants to dissolve anything without it makes a mistake, [16] and nothing is more honourable than this female. Therefore they named her "good child-bearer"(*mūwallid ṭayyib*) [17].»

She said: [17] «If I did not remember how angry you were with me about the vapour, I would also ask you about it.» [18] He said: «Ask whatever you like.» She said: «I return to ask you again the same question about it.» [19] He said: «I told you that the vapour is part of the holy secret, because no

[17] The margin says: This is the statement of Zosimos: Do you see any dyer who dyes with the completeness of the components of the mixture only?

(fol. 31b) work can be without it.»

She said: «Is the vapour of the dry sulphurs similar to the vapour of [2] the moist water?» He said: «How great is the difference between the two! Upon my life, nobody ever benefited from [3] the vapour of the dry sulphurs and metals.» So do not pay attention to this because Democritus [4] did not use it (the vapour of the dry sulphurs) in any of his works or operations. He only mentioned the vapour of the moisture which [5] is needed, and with it the work is performed.»

She said: «Why is the moisture named vapour?» [6] He said: «Because every moist thing which escapes from the fire to the above is a vapour, and if the dry one does not [7] come up from the below to the above, it would (also) not be named a vapour.»

She said: «Then what is the vapour?» He said: [8] «It is what comes up to the above.» She said: «Who was the first to name it vapour?» He said: «It was Hermes. When he saw [9] the cloud rising from the earth to the sky, he said: "This is the vapour." Thus for the sages everything [10] that rises from below to the above is called vapour.»

She said: «Then tell me [11] about when you say: "The water of sulphur is composed, mixed with all the moistures.» He said: [12] «And I confirm that it is like that.»

She said: «What made all the water of sulphur turn moist?» [13] He said: «When the cooking and the pounding of the composition was done well, the moist spirits became [14] concealed in the water so that they turned into one poison, and the sediments became [15] dead ashes whose spirits were extracted from them <concealed in the water so that they turned into one poison, and the sediments became [16] dead ashes whose spirits were extracted from them> [17] into the water of sulphur. So the water is water, and the sulphur is something else. Do you not see that it (the water) is not a [18] single (thing), and they named this moist water with the names of all moist things? [19] So, whenever you hear about the moistures in some of the books of the sages, know (fol. 32a) that they named with it the water of sulphur. Do you not see how Democritus said: [2] "Operate on the pyrite with the vinegar and the salt which is the white water of sulphur." And he said [3] about the cinnabar: "Make it white with the fat, the vinegar and the honey." And he said about the andradamus: "Operate on it [4] with the vinegar." And after all of that, he said: "Then cook it with the pure water." Thus all of these moistures [5] which they mentioned are the water of sulphur because, whenever the water of sulphur is cooked [6] so that its colour changes, they changed its name.» <He said> «Do you not see how Democritus said: [7] "When it becomes red, make it russet-yellow and russet-red." And one should not put on it [8] anything of what he ordered you, but I told you that the white will be yellow, red and [9] russet-red. And know that this work does not need more than two cookings, one cooking [10] in the white and one cooking in the red. Do you not see that Democritus only wrote [11] four treatises (*risāla*). The first treatise is about the burning, the second about the whitening [12] the third about the dyeing, and the fourth is about the purple.»

She said: «So he differed from the (other) sages?» [13] He said: «With this he was preferable because he condensed it.»

She said. «So he related each one of his treatises to an [14] operation?» He said: «He did so to disguise. But these operations [15] which Democritus described are the colours that appeared to him. Do you not see his statement [16] in his fourth book (treatise) "The sulphurs hold the sulphurs, and the moisture [17] the other moisture."»

She said: «Why did he not write this about the burning in his first book (treatise)?» [18] He said: «Because he wanted to let us know that the water of the sulphur is what does [19] all the work.»

She said: «Then tell me about your book, whose summary is that (fol. 32b) the four bodies are dyed, whereupon they dye, and the sulphurs turn into smoke and then go away.» He said: [2] «My lady, know that the dye of the bodies which is extracted from them in the cupolas, [3] is a new dyeing spirit. Therefore the sage named it a vapour. As for the sulphurs, [4] they become smoke and go away, and nothing remains of them except the taste of the copper alone, [5] which is its spirit.»

She said: «Why did the spirit of the copper remain among them?» He said: «Because the copper has [6] a nature which is unlike the nature of anything else. And when it gets mixed with the sulphurs [7] and gets married with them, it holds them and they (the sulphurs) hold it (the copper). In the case of all other things, they have not natures, [8] neither in marrying nor in mixing. Therefore they do not remain, and from them no spirits arise [9] in a vapour, nor in anything else. But in the case of the copper, when it is mixed with its sulphurs, they (the sulphurs) rejoice [10] in it (the copper), and it rejoices in them, so it (the copper) holds them (the sulphurs), and they hold it.»

She said: «And how does it hold them [11] and they hold it?» He said: «Concerning it (the copper) holding them (the sulphurs), it is that it (the copper) prevents them [12] escaping. Concerning their holding it, it is that they make the shadow of the copper disappear, [13] so it is not to be seen in the operation.»

She said: «You gave this description well. I ask you [14] to tell me more about the copper. Do you think that it changes its nature because of its becoming rusty or being operated on?» [15] He said: «It does not [16] change its nature, and it does not change in any of its states, except that the colour becomes invisible to the eye, [17] so it cannot be seen in the operation. And the confirmation of what I told you about the changing of [18] its colour is the statement of the sage: "When the magnesia has turned white, it does not allow the bodies [19] to split up, and it does not allow a colour to appear on the copper. Yet its colour does not (fol. 33a) go away but the conquest of the nature defeated it and covered its colour. Therefore [2] Maria said: "Copper is not without a shadow. It becomes without shadow [3] like when the farmer (*akkār*) cuts the plants from the surface of the earth. It cannot be [4] seen while the root is deep in the earth, as is the case with (the root of) sugar cane, [5] asparagus, and other similar plants." So copper is fixed in its nature and its colour, [6] but the operation covered it by its components of the mixture. Thus nobody is able either to change [7] or to make its shadow disappear, except in what is visible to the eye.»

She said: «Then what about when the sage [8] Democritus said: "The one does what the many do, and the many need [9] the one."» He said: «He did not finish his statement about it. Do you not see that he said after [10] this: "And the many things need the one." By that he means [11] that the bodies are many and all of them need one water. And [12] that water is in harmony with the natures of those bodies. I tell you also [13] what Ostanes said: "The fiery stone[18] has a relationship with copper." [14] Therefore Hermes said: "Take the fiery stone and mix it with copper, [15] burn it, and dissolve it with gentleness and experience." And know that natures are only dissolved [16] for you, O Theosebeia, when they meet [17] their close ones. When they meet [17] their close ones they mix with them because of their longing for each other. And they mix [18] in such a way that they do not separate again because they were longing for each other. Because of this statement [19] Democritus said, following Ostanes, "Nature rejoices in

[18] Text gives a plural that must be a copyist's error.

(fol. 33b) nature." And this is the wonderful sentence which he found in the book of [2] Ostanes: "The fiery stone has a relationship with copper."»

She said: «Then tell me about [3] when you say: "Whoever has the slightest understanding, and reads some of the books of the sages [4] will find that its beginning is an achievement, thus he preserves it. Then he must ponder over them repeatedly. But you, [5] assembly of sages, never wrote a word of truth, without it being accompanied by a great number [6] of false words."» He said: «I told you that Democritus explained it clearly for [7] whoever has intelligence, although he did not make it clear. Thus he said: "The one is resistant to fire and [8] strong against it, and the other is not resistant to fire and not strong against it. [9] But if the weak one is mixed with the one who is resistant to fire, it will be strong by the strength of the one resistant to fire; [10] by the power of God it resists fire." With things similar to this, there is a sagacity, a lesson, and an analogy [11] for those with intelligence.»

She said: «Do you think, O Zosimos, that when you started to read [12] these books, you were as aspiring as you order me to be?» He said: [13] «I only mentioned this to you because I gave over to you the truth clearly, although [14] I ascribed it to others. But you are not intelligent enough and you do not understand. Therefore [15] I do not feel happy to give this matter clearly, because I did not find anyone among those who [16] were before me who was daring enough to make this secret visible.»

She said: «Then you are what you are with regard [17] to your friends.» He said: «I did not do that to you. Do you not know that [18] to the extent of my knowledge I gathered what they dispersed, and I explained what they disguised as an act of daring [19] on my part, going contrary to them, and leaving aside the oaths which they made between themselves, as a kindness to you and because of the relationship (fol. 34a) with you?»

She said: «You surely did so. But if you illuminate for me some of the obscurity of what you made me enter [2] into, you will complete your gracious gift.» He said: «By God, I see that [3] I set out for you words that are brighter than daylight. If you are successful in understanding them, then do not leave them [4] without adding other words because what improves them is close to them.»

She said: [5] «O Zosimos, the sages made this work enigmatic, and they did not want [6] God to give joy to anyone who enters into it (the work), [7] except after (their) intensive effort and persistence in reading their books, and after knowing what they (the sages) wrote.» He said: «I told you [8] that jealousy is still the offspring of the sons of Adam. If you became knowledgeable about this matter [9] you would even be more eager than the sages to keep it away from people. Do you not see that the kings [10] were not willing to leave their treasure houses and treasuries without doors and protection in [11] fortresses? Likewise the sages did not feel happy to leave these [12] unfinished treasures without protection.»

She said: «What protection did [13] the sages give?» He said: «It was in all of my words to you that I gave as an answer to your wondering why the sages were[14] hiding this work so intensely. But now that you bring up this question I will answer you (more)[15] about the protections, so do not let it pass by as if it were nothing, because it has knowledge and meaning.»

She said: [16] «Then say it!» He said: «Know, my lady, that each sage put magical words (*ṭilsamāt*) [19] around his treasure, [17] in order that none of the shameless ones who are not worthy of it would reach it. In this way it is disguised [18] in their books, and they veiled it with examples and mimic words, parables, and allusions [19] of one thing to another which nobody understands except the sagacious. Thus

[19] The word *ṭilsamāt* also means talismans.

(fol. 34b) they created for their treasures entrances and exits which nobody can find except a sage, because they [2] did not want to give over this secret to those who are not worthy.»

She said: «And what about your treatise [3] for me, (where you say) that when Hermes started to mention the dyeing of the gold, he avoided mentioning [4] a dye for the stones.» He said: «That is because of his disdain for them, and because he knew that the blessed and exalted God [5] did not put in them any gold, neither hidden nor visible. And I tell you that after Hermes [6] only Agathodaimon and Brīsīūs mentioned the stones (in their works). The only thing that prevented the two [7] from (really) mentioning them was that they both knew that every dyed stone is not like the dyeing of [8] the core of the metals. Concerning Maria, Democritus and Africanus, they mentioned [9] the dyeing of stones, leathers, wool and clothes.»

She said: «And why did they mention the dyes of [10] stones, and the making purple?» [He said:] «They wanted to tell us that when they performed the dyeing of [11] the gold well, they were not ignorant of the dyeing of stones, leathers, wool and clothes.»

She said: [12] «Then why did they mention the dyes of stones, leathers, wool, and clothes?» He said: «They wanted [13] to disguise it (the dye) from the people when they wrote about it in their books. They only meant by them [14] the dyeing of gold. Therefore Maria said: "Take the hollow stone." [15] And Democritus said: "Take the white of the egg and the dregs (*ʿakir*), meaning the dye." And Maria said [16] about the making of the lead-copper "take the dregs!" By that she meant the rust which is the smashed sediment, and [17] the exalted stone which has its nature in it. In this way they wanted to disguise the dye.»

[18] She said: «Then what urged them to use all these names which I see?» [19] He said: «They derived them for this dye in order to veil it and disguise it from the people.»

She said: «In your statement,

(fol. 35a) O Zosimos, you distinguished today between those two works which become [2] one colour and one dye in the operation.» He said: «I told you that the components of the mixture of one of [3] the two works must be composed, operated on (and) cooked. And it must be in the first (work) [4] dry and moist, and in the second dry and moist. The work and the effort really is in [5] the first work, and from it comes what is right and what is wrong, and half [6] of this first work is the rotting. As for the second work, it needs some effort, [7] but it is little.»

She said: «I already asked you, O Zosimos, to tell me how [8] to change silver.» [He said:] «I told you that what changes silver is one and the dye is one. [9] So I order you now to go on doing it, and leave aside what is different from that one because [10] they veiled that true one by these many things in order to confuse [11] the people with them, and to deter them from that one which is the true one. And know that whoever knew [12] our lead-copper, and operated on it properly, changes with it the silver, the silver of the people, because [13] our lead-copper, before it is dyed white or red, dyes the silver to a black [14] fixed dye that neither vanishes nor splits up.»

She said: «What if it did split up?» He said: «Know [15] that this happened to it because of a bad mixture, too much glass, too much moisture, [16] or too much lead-copper which you put in. As for us, we dye the silver and change it [17] to blackness. And it is the first degree of the dyeing of this work, not splitting up, but soft without any hardness»

[18] She said: «O Zosimos, your statement is astonishing. How is anybody able [19] to mix them from the books, while the sages wrote chapters about mixing

(fol. 35b) various invented things which are not true, but just invented names.» He said: [2] «Whoever with common sense and patience has tried it out, will know from where the error came to him. Once he knows [3] the error, he will be aware of it a second time. Thus know, my lady, that you should not [4] dry the silver till you extract all of its dyes.»

She said: «Then what are all of these dyes?» [5] He said: «They are the water of the blackness. When it is completed, it turns into gold. Then solidify it, [6] dry it and pound it.»

She said: «Then tell me about when you say that you put the mixing of [7] gold with silver in the second part, and you named it *al-ẖalṭūn* (the mixing)» He said: «Indeed, [8] we named it like that to confuse the people about the natures from which we make the true work [9] because we named the true natures with the names of the visible natures which are in the hands of the people.»

[10] She said: «Then tell me why you give many names.» He said: «You have asked about a difficult [11] matter by which I obscure this science.»

She said: «Then tell me an aspect of it by which I can know [12] other (aspects).» He said: «When you read in our books, ponder over the things which we order you. [13] So when we say: "Take such and such" and we give many particular names, [14] do not pay attention to the great number and know that all of them are one thing. But [15] we wanted to use many names to disguise it from them. When we speak of the splitting, we speak of it [16] because by such names we mean the elixir which we mentioned in our books.»

[17] She said: «Then tell me about when the sage said: "When the shadow of the copper is taken away [18] and it is turned red, it dyes every body."» He said: «When the sage said: "It dyes every body.", [19] he wanted by that to disguise it from you, because by every body

(fol. 36a) and by (all of) these bodies, the sage meant—and declared—that by them he dyes every body, [2] (and) indeed by (all of) them he meant the one body. And that one body is dyed, and it dyes [3] after it is dyed, so in it there is all of the composition. And know that this composition, which [4] has that body in it, is named after every body, every metal, every sulphur, [5] every herb and every dust. But all of this composition is two, [6] the making white and the making red.»

She said: «Then tell me what led Agathodaimon [7] to make an operation for the copper, an operation for the magnesia and an operation for the rust.» He said: «Copper, [8] rust, and magnesia are one thing. But Agathodaimon made [9] many operations for them in order that whoever enters into this matter should limit himself to one thing. So he rendered [10] the manifold operations (in order to express) the many days, but there are not many operations. It is [11] one operation but that operation takes many days.»

She said: «I already [12] asked you about the stone which enters into the work. You told me that you were keen that [13] I should not be infatuated by any of the stones, especially in the making of gold. [14] Then I saw that you neglected to tell to me about that.» He said: «I have promised you that, [15] and I told you that a man called Rīānūsūs (Dionysius?) did not leave a stone without describing it, [16] and mentioning what benefit and harm is in it, and that the prophet Moses—God bless him and grant him salvation— [17] mentioned the ruby and the green stone, but I think that he did not mean these [18] stones. Before that, Hermes testified that whoever mentions these two stones, [19] only means the stones of the work. Hermes told us enough and he testified about himself (fol. 36b) when he set down 365 stones, naming them with their names and [2] their colours, that he was not in need of any one of them, but he only wanted to confuse those who look for this science [3] about the stone by what must enter into this work.»

She said: «So why do you give many [4] names to the stones of the work?» He said: «Because of the differences of their colours. Sometimes we named them [5] golden, silvery and tinny according to the colour of their interior, and sometimes we named them [6] water of the androdamus. So leave aside the stones and take this stone. Whoever wants something other than it [7] is like the one who wants to go up a ladder which has no rungs, so he falls down on his face. [8] I have heard that someone who came to you, told you that this stone is dyed by [9] its operation and its sieving (sieve). Democritus said: "Why should we care for the many things, while the nature [10] is one." <He said> Those people are blinder in their hearts and their eyes than animals because what the sage [11] meant by "the nature is one" is that the water is one, composed, operated on. So this is [12] what misguided them and made them fall into error.»

She said: « I ask you, O Zosimos, how would you describe [13] for me this stone without obscurity?» He said: «There is no way for you to get what you intend, but I will describe it [14] to you with some obscurity in it. So remove its obscurity with understanding, and its work will benefit you.»

[15] She said: «Tell me! If I understand, I will be satisfied. And if I do not understand it, I find that nothing is [16] more characteristic of me than patience.» He said: «Take one part of gum and a quantity of dye [17] that is enough for the gum, mix them with the stone on a gentle heat, and put it [18] in the water in order to solidify. It should have one of the dusts in order to polish it because [19] the polishing appears only with the dust.

She said: «I do not know the dust.» He said:

(fol. 37a) «It is the hollow stone, and this stone has to be mixed with the cold water in order that [2] the stone contracts because of the intensive coldness, I mean the dyeing of the water inside it, so that it retains it. [3] Know that the gum is a nature and by it the cold water solidifies, and it (the gum) is neither afraid of fire nor [4] of water. And the dye which is in it (the gum) is only seen when mixed with water.»

She said: [5] «I asked you days ago about where the stone which is called the lamp (*sirāǧ*) can be found. You mentioned [6] that the sages who wrote the books about the stones did not describe where [7] this stone can be found. Then we spoke about something else, so you did not describe in full what I asked you.» He said: [8] «I tell you that the sages did not describe in full what you asked about, [9] and they did not describe where this stone was born, except that Maria [10] the Hebrew (emendation) named it redness. But the prophet Moses—God bless him and grant him salvation—[11] said: "It is the ruby that is found in Eden."»

She said: «Then tell me what you say [12] about it.» He said: «I tell you that this stone is never extracted from a metal, [13] neither from a ruby nor from a *ẖalqadūnī*-stone, but it is the royal stone [14] which is the copper and the *aqzāl*. Concerning the *aqzālian*, this is the water, and some people claimed [15] that in the earth of Sudan [20] there are stones that shine at night, naming them *tātlūtā*. But this is a lie, [16] so do not pay attention to it. As for the lamp-like (*sirāǧy*) stone, its light is not for itself, but [17] its light is for the people of the house who are making it. This stone, which is called lamp-like, [18] is not from a metal, but it is a stone from our stones which we made. And mostly [19] when you find this stone, you find it changing because its dye is from our sea, and often

[20] Probably the black earth, as people from Sudan are black.

(fol. 37b) it is red. Concerning the one that shines at night, it is the changing one, but if it remains [2] in our sea for a long time, its redness becomes stronger because that stone is composed through what the seas contribute (*buḫūrīya*), so that it gets dyed. [3] This is because everything dyed in our sea shines at night. Therefore the sage said: [4] "In every golden dye the salt blossoms." And know that every flower which comes from our dyeing [5] comes from our sea. This secret is the water of sulphur, and this is what he named [6] with the name of every stone and dust. So, by this stone which you asked me about, they meant our dye.»

[7] She said: «Then tell me about when you say: "When lead-copper is dissolved with what is similar to it, and it gets pounded in [8] the mortar till the two turn into one thing, it confirms what Democritus says."» He said: «You have asked me [9] about the beginning of this matter, and you left out its end because he (Democritus) said: "Know that the mixing of one poison [10] is good for everything."»

She said: «You are right, I forgot about that.» He said: [11] «You should know that by the statement of the sages "dissolve the stones and put the dye on them" [12] they did not mean the stones, because they do not dissolve, and even if they did dissolve, they would not solidify to become stones [13] again as in the beginning. But by it they meant lead-copper, and they named it [14] crystal (*mahā*) because the crystal dissolves and solidifies (again); for that they named it crystal because their lead-copper dissolves [15] and solidifies. Therefore Democritus said: "There is an operation for the crystal". And if you want to [16] soak it then put on it some mercury or spittle of the moon so that the crystal and the lead-copper become [17] one. As for lead-copper, nobody is able to turn a little of it into a lot [18] because the majority of it goes away with the despicable, which we throw away. And the experiments are better than this.

[19] She said: «Tell me about this one nature which does not get divided.» He said: That (here a part is missing together with the description of the picture)

Fig. 30: Folio 38a.

(fol. 38b) This is the beginning of the 2nd Book with God's blessing.
(THE BOOK OF THE NAMES) [21]

In the name of the compassionate and merciful God.

[2] She said: «I have reached, O Zosimos, all that I could attain in the education. So tell me about the things [3] which the sages named with other than their true names. Make them no longer obscure to me, and thereby complete [4] your favour to me.» He said: «With what I wrote and told you, [5] and with the picture I made for you with me in it, I gave you what you need to know, and this should be enough for you. [6] Now I have no other choice than to complete the best of what you want, because of your kindness and the relationship with you. [7] So ask whatever you want concerning these names. I will tell you about them to the extent of [8] my knowledge with regard to what you were not able to understand. So contemplate again the figures at the beginning of [9] the book, I mean "The Book of the Names", and ponder over what I have presented to you because [10] I did not put anything in them except as an analogy for what you need.»

She said: «Then why did the sages [11] name the composition etesian stone?» He said: «Because the etesian stone is born [12] once a year, it has different colours, and it is born and changes each month from one colour to [13] another. That is why they named their composition the etesian stone because [14] it changes at every level of the operation from one colour to another.

She said: «Then why is it [15] that nobody named the composition white or red?» He said: «This is because [16] when the dye falls on the composition it changes it. When it is cooked for the first time it makes it white, [17] and when it is cooked for a second time it makes it red. That is why they did not name it (the composition) neither in the whitening nor in [18] the reddening, because those which are named the first two compositions are the white [22] one and the red one, and they are [19] those which make the dyes permanent.»

She said (emendation): «Then what about the other two sulphurs?

[21] Title is missing; title is given later on line 9 and is also found in the table of contents.

[22] The text has yellow.

(fol. 39a) [He said:] «They are not two sulphurs, because they both did a lot of wondrous work with the help of God.»

[2] She said: «What about when you say "A sulphur that does not get burnt."» He said: «It is the one which resists the fire, and is patient [3] with it. And the mercury of cinnabar mixed with the eternal water solidifies its moisture, because [4] as much as it gets mixed and married, it resists the fire and is patient with it, and it is cinnabar that is [5] rarely found. Know, my lady, that the sages put the hidden poison [(7)] that they did not fail to hide [(6)] neither at the beginning, nor in the middle, nor at the end of their work. If it were not like that, there would be those who sell the [8] priceless poison in public cheaply, for little. [9] If they knew what was in their hands, which requires a lifetime (to obtain), they would never sell it for anything. [10] That is why the sages kept the matter of this poison secret. If it were not for the virtue of that nature [11] they would not have spoken so much about it, nor would they have praised or described its power. Do you not see [12] that they named it with every name, and they often mentioned the operation for it in order that [13] the low and ignorant people would neither dare to turn their attention to their books, nor take up anything from them.»

[14] She said: «You are right. Upon my life, it is as you described. But clarify for me, O Zosimos, [15] the statement of your sage Democritus about this gum, when he said: "It is a stone [16] and not a stone." And he [also] said: "It is the gum of acacia (*ašqūnīa*)." He said: «The sage spoke well [17] and right, and he hit the point because the women of acacia (*ašqūnīa*) kill their husbands without mercy. [18] So the sage compared the gum with the women of that town. That is why the ancients kept [19] the power of that gum secret, and they took oaths together not to reveal it

(fol. 39b) to any creature in any part of their books without adding something that when mixed with it (the gum), would ruin it, [2] except its natures, without which it (the gum) is not good. Thus, my lady, this spirit [3] with which you want to dye whatever you like, is hidden in the body and concealed in it. It cannot be seen, just as the soul [4] cannot be seen in the body of a human being. So if you do not destroy [5] that body, and pound it, and operate on it gently, and in the operation extract from the thick part of that body [6] a subtle spirit that cannot be touched, you will achieve nothing. So this is [7] what the sages worked with and attained their desires in the world.»

She said: «Thus tell me, [8] O Zosimos, about the words I found in your books and in the books of the sages [9] which confused my mind, and will confuse everybody who comes after me. (This is) when they said: "The nature is despicable, sold [10] cheaply." And they also said: "The nature is the most honoured of all natures." [11] They confused me, as I know that they did not say anything but the truth.» He said: «Do you not see [12] that they make the natures into one nature? So if they relate it to the cheap, [13] they are right, and if they relate it to the expensive, they are right as well, because in it is joined [14] the expensive-cheap, the exalted-inferior, the existing-non-existing, the [15] despised-exalted. By that they confused people before you. And I tell you that the work needs [16] both natures, because the honoured one cannot come to exist without the despised and cheap one. [17] And the despised and cheap one cannot exist without the honoured and exalted one. Know that what urged the sages [18] to hide all of this secret was not jealousy over it towards people, nor that [19] their eyes had been filled and satisfied with money, but fearing that someone would get it (the secret) (fol. 40a) who would act badly on earth and would behave with it against the will of God so it would be more harmful [2] than the work of all those who did it (the work) before. Thus they wanted to prevent the intellectuals from contemplating [3] their books, and from following them (their books) because whoever contemplates them would not only benefit [4] to make the work right, but also (benefit) in every area (*bāb*) of the matters of this world and the other world.»

[5] She said: «Then tell me about the passage where Hermes says in his book: "I mentioned to you [6] *The Book of Wisdom* that is the key to the door of every blessing."» He said: «That is because whoever contemplates [7] these words of Hermes finds benefits in his lengthy discussions and descriptions [8] of the regions, lands, towns, mountains, spirits, waters, dusts and [9] what is their taste, and waters and what is in their power. This is because he introduces here the composition of the work, [10] and with it what is not needed. So they have benefits for whoever understands them and it removes their obscurity. [11] And it is great knowledge for whoever knows the true natures, whose virtue and ability [12] to attain every desire was unknown to people. That is why he said: "It is the key to every blessing", [13] and truly, it is the key to every blessing.»

She said: «Then tell me, O Zosimos, why did the sages name [14] the clouds "soul and spirit" in their books?» He said: «Elinus (Elias?) was the first one who said: [15] "A moist spirit, having black inside, not polluted." He compared it to the human being and said: "Just as [16] in the human being there is dryness and humidity, soul and spirit, so it is with [17] this work which the sages kept secret. It is the secret of the cloud, and the raising of the water because the cloud [18] is not single, and it is not named cloud until the dyeing, powerful, [19] firc-fighter spirit, which was extracted from the hard one, enters into it.»

She said: «Then tell me, O Zosimos, [20] about when Hermes said: "Put the remedies in a fine piece of woven cloth, and leave (fol. 40b) these remedies to be cooked in the sea."» He said: «The sage named the moisture the sea, [2] and the vessel a piece of cloth. And he named the nature remedies, because the nature grows and blossoms, [3] and out of it comes a poison. Therefore Democritus said about the moisture: "Wash, [4] and wash with the moisture, until the blackness of the copper comes out of it." Some of the sages [5] named that blackness the blackness of silver, and some of them named it the face of the old woman. [6] As for Agathodaimon he made clear to us that all of the work and the operation is one, [7] when he said: "After making the copper rusty, and making it black, and the pounding of what came out of its pounding, at the end of its whitening [8] there comes an exalted redness." Understand his statement because he made [9] the whole work and operation clear for whoever understands. And in the same way, Democritus also said about the blackness: [10] "Our black lead, which is from our work."» He continued: «Do you not remember (this) in some of [11] the books which I dedicated to you?»

She said: «You dedicated so many books to me!» He said: [12] «Do you not remember that I told you that I saw in my sleep a handsome [13] murdered man whose body was as white as snow and his head was of gold. [14] The limbs of that murdered man were cut off, and I felt pity for the severe punishment that was given to him that I have seen, and I wanted [15] to know who was his murderer. So I went to bury him, but I did [not] know how to gather [16] his separated limbs. In doing so, a man with an ugly face and Saturnian features appeared to me, being a killer [17] of the soul. He looked at me in fury and anger as if he were a wild dog, having in his hand [18] a shining axe sullied with much blood. So I knew that he was the murderer of that man. [19] We faced each other and he said: "I left you until you collected the parts of that man whom I killed [20] and you counteracted my work. You challenged me!" Thus we fought against each other for a long time, but he did not defeat me nor (fol. 41a) did I defeat him, and I did not beat him. When we were both exhausted, he took the head and put it aside, and said: [2] "Choose, O man, if you want the head or the body!" So I chose the head [3] because the head is the sky of the body and the house of the eyes and the senses. So I took [4] the head and I wrapped it up in a winding sheet.[23] I thought about where I should bury it in order that shameless and [5] base people would not find it, and become more able to disobey God with what they obtain from it. So I remembered that your tomb [6] which you built would not be desired (by anybody).[24] Thus I gave it to you and you accepted it from me, rejoicing and happy. [7] So you buried it inside your tomb, and I made you swear by God not to show it to anybody. [8] The main reason for my making you swear was in order that Neilos (Bīlīs) the priest would not see it, and thereby be able to obtain [9] some work from it. I left in order to bring you the rest of the body. Then the angel of peace met me [10] and I told him what he already knew. He rewarded me for taking the head and for preventing [11] the shameless ones from taking it, in order that they would not obtain it and could act corruptly in the world with it. Then I turned to the task [12] of bringing you the rest of the body, but I woke up terrified. This great dream (*rūʾyā*) of mine contains something that will [13] remove your doubt, illumine your sight, and chase away the obscurity about which you complained [14] to me. And I am not able to give more of this secret for the sake of which you made me do something [15] that is not allowed. So if you need the rest of the body, send me a written message, [16] although I do not actually need your written message, but it is in order that whoever reads that message [17] after you and me will testify that I wrote the truth for you about my teachings, and that I put you on [18] the right and proper way. Be grateful that you obtained it.»

She said: «I was confused by [19] their different statements.» He said: «Do not get confused by what you see. Mix the dry one with the moist one!»

[23] *kaffana* II = to wrap, *kafana* I = to cover with a winding sheet, to shroud, to dress for the grave.

[24] This shows that Theosebeia was a royal, noble or priestly woman.

(fol. 41b) She said: «What is the dry one and what is the moist one?» He said: «They are the dust and the water. Mix both of them with the air, [2] and cook them with the fire till the spirit dries the soul, and the spirit holds the soul, [3] and imprisons it in its inside. And the sages are right to compare this work with these [4] four natures, because there is not one of these four natures that does not have [5] a firm root and something subtle, which is extracted from that firm root. Do you not see that the sun is [6] fiery, but by the subtleness of its ray which comes out from its origin, the earth and the sea become hot? [7] So when the heat of its ray reaches the sea, it raises its subtle part (*latīfahu*).

She said: «What is this subtle part?» [8] He said: «It is the water-vapour. And when the heat of its ray reaches the earth, the ray extracts [9] its subtle part, and raises it up from it (the earth).»

She said: «What is its subtle part?» He said: «It is its smoke. Thus when [10] the subtle part of the water-vapour meets the subtle part of the earth-smoke, they cling together, and the subtle part of each of them rises [11] into the air. So the subtle part of each of them become the nourishment for the air. And the subtle part [12] of these two subtle parts goes up to the sun, so the two become the nourishment for the sun. As for the thick part and the subtle part [13] which reaches neither the air nor the sun, it returns to the earth and the sea because of its being thick. So what reaches [14] the earth from the thick part of the subtle part of that vapour, which the air returned because of its thickness, falls into [15] the sea and becomes its nourishment. Do you not see that the animals of the sea are not created from water [16] alone, but our God created them from the water and from the thick part of what the air returned of the smoke [17] to the earth? If you want to analogise what I told you, then take a sea animal, [18] dry it and make it rotten. After its moisture evaporates, you will find [19] subtle dust. So these four natures change each other, (fol. 42a) cling to each other and improve each other by the will of God. There is no God but him, the Powerful and the Wise.» [25]

2 She said: «Then tell me about the mistrust and doubts which still occur to me 3 about this work when I see the disagreement of the sages concerning the names, 4 the operations, the compositions and the weights.» He said: «The sages did not want 5 to make this matter visible for just anyone coming after them, so they disagreed intentionally so as to disguise it 6 for the intellectual, to make them doubt. And the devils are jealous ones, so often they whisper doubts 7 to whoever comes close to this work and wants to enter it, and they tell him that this is 8 a thing that cannot exist.[26] Often they say the work is too hard for whoever wants to enter it, and tell him 9 that it is a thing that cannot exist. Often they exaggerate the expense for him, making him frightened of the loss 10 and of the sufferings of other people. Often they make him fear the rulers (*salāṭīn*) and other things, such as 11 their ruses and tricks, in order to distract whoever asks for this precious gift 12 that leads its owner to happiness in the other world, because it is a great work that God bestows upon the ones 13 He chooses from His venerators. The devils hate that it (the work) appears, being afraid 14 that they will be hindered from what God forbids when it is allowed (*ḥalāl*). And I order you to take refuge in God and in my advice, 15 and do not be impatient when reading the books or get bored with the operations. Be patient 16 and wait for the completion of the dyeing, and beg continuously of the exalted and blessed God 17 that He may complete it (the work) for you. And I warn you about the fire in the operation, for it is the enemy of the water because of 18 their opposition and mutual hatred until peace comes to the water and the fire and they are reconciled. 19 As Christ, peace be upon Him, said: "How amazing of you, O community of sages, that

25 This part could be a clue that the second part of the Ms G of the *Ḥall ar-rumūz* (CALA I) goes back to the school of Zosimos.

26 Margin in red ink reads: The devils frighten off the sons of Adam from this science.

(fol. 42b) you reconciled water and fire, so they stayed together in the operation." The sages were astonished [2] that He (Christ) knew them by their science. Know that if you reconcile water and fire, your work will be good, [3] by the will of magnified and glorified God.»

She said: «Then tell me about the statement of Maria: "If you find in the book [4] 'take copper', then they mean by it our copper, whose shadow has been removed by the operation, and if [5] you find in their books 'take lead' (*ābār*), they mean by it our lead (*rusās*) which is [6] our magnesia, and if you find 'take silver'(*waraq*), it is our silver (*waraq*) that we made from our copper, [7] which is the whitened copper that contains the male and the mercury, and if they say 'take gold', [8] then it is our silver that we dyed."» He said: «Maria was the best at the time of [9] Ostanes because of her enigmatic statements, and in her revealing the truth. Look, whenever you find [10] the sages saying in their books 'our copper', or 'our silver', or 'our gold, or 'our magnesia', [11] indeed it is that copper which they related to themselves, because it has in it something else. And they only related it [12] to themselves because it is mixed with something else. And like that is their lead, which is [13] their magnesia, and also like that is their silver, which comes from their work with the composed copper. [14] So when the copper becomes silver, they say 'our silver', and if they say 'our magnesia', then it contains [15] copper and something else, and if they say "Cypriot copper" it is the one that was burnt and blossomed. [16] Know that the copper is not burnt in one time, but it is burnt little by little. And [17] every thing that is burnt from it becomes concealed in the moisture until all of it is burnt. Then it falls down all [18] at once from its utmost place. The more it is cooked, the more it coagulates, until it produces the silver which [19] is from our work. So at the beginning of the cooking you need to have its fire gentle, until it (the copper) becomes accustomed to (fol. 43a) the fire, and they (the copper and the fire) are reconciled. Then make the fire stronger, little by little.»

She said: «Then tell me about when [2] Maria said: "I have written a clear book about this work for those who come after me. [3] So, whoever is one of us will read our book and find it clear, and whoever is not one of us will neither know [4] what is in our books nor what we wrote.» He said: «I have told you that whoever does not know [5] the natures, the compositions, the combinations and the weight is unable to know [6] anything written in the books because they did not name things with their true names, and they named [7] the false with the name of the true, and they gave the true the name of the false. So whoever reads their books becomes confused and unable [8] to distinguish between what they disguised and the truth, except (that they get) an inspiration of the blessed and exalted God [9] or (that they get) an education that God gives to whom He wants among the ones He wants.»

She said: «Then tell me about when [10] the sage Šīmās ibn Ṭaīfun says: "The thing by which what you are seeking comes into being is one. [11] If it does not contain something like what you are seeking, you will obtain nothing from it."» [12] He said: «He has explained to you that whoever enters the work, is seeking to turn [13] things into gold. If you do not put gold into gold you will be wrong.»

[14] She said: «Then what is the benefit of putting gold into gold?» [15] He said: «Because from little comes out the manifold.»

She said: «If the people [16] of the world knew this, their gold would increase.» He said: «That is what I told you.»

She said: «Yet, what I have [17] in my hands is nothing.» He said: «It is your ignorance of the operation of things similar to it, which are mixed with it [18] from among its relatives that are in harmony with it, not in disagreement.»

She said: «Then tell me about the mixing of the air which the sages mention.» [19] He said: «Indeed they wrote it as an analogy for the composition.»

She said: «Why did

(fol. 43b) they write that?» He said: «Because if there were no holder and reconciler between the two subtle, moist ones, [2] the two would be destroyed and escape from the fire, and they would not be strong enough to resist the intensive cooking. If [3] they are not strong enough to be intensely cooked, nothing will emerge from the two that could be beneficial, because [4] the moist loves the dry and the hot loves the cold. It is the same with the moon [5] and the stars: their light comes from the light of the sun. Especially the moon [6] takes very much light from the sun that is why its light is intense during the night. In the same way, [7] everything gains the strength and the dye from its origin.»

She said: «Then tell me [8] about the victorious, submerged Persian who wears the purple of the truth that is expensive and [9] intensely red.» He said: «It is what submerges into the bodies.»

She said: «How [10] does it submerge into the body?» He said: «Because it was a body. Then the lunar quality turned it into [11] a spirit with the other spirits, so it submerges quickly into the body when it meets it. [12] And it is white in its outer appearance, and red in its inner essence.»

She said: «How can it be [13] white-red?» He said: «I told you that it is the male who chose and married the moony. [14] This (the male) is what you think is gold, whose mixture is precious, which does not change [15] into anything else, nor does its knots ever unbind, nor do its traces vanish. It is the knowledge of this that God bestowed upon [16] His prophets and upon whomsoever He wants among His people.»

She said: «Then tell me, O Zosimos, about when the sage said: [17] "Everything is based on three. Regarding the solid bodies, the definition of the body has to be by the width, [18] the length and the depth.» He said: «He wrote this as an analogy [19] for the four natures of the world, namely fire, water, air and earth. They hold each (fol. 44a) other and love each other until they become one, mixed nature. [2] That occurs when the subtle part of their taste mixes, holding each other. [3] Know that the subtle part of them can only be seen and held in the thick part, [4] because there is a relationship between the thick and the subtle. So when they unite they hold each [5] other, because the two fixed, thick ones (the water and the earth) are the things from which the creation of things begins. [6] It (the creation) comes from the smoke that rises from the dry (the earth), and the vapour that comes [7] from the moisture. So from these two, the smoke and the vapour, [8] all of the air comes into being as well as the substance of the body of everything that moves in the air because the vapour became the nourishment [9] for the air, and the smoke became the nourishment for the fire. So from these things, wonders come into existence. Know that [10] every square thing is firmer and stronger than what has three angles because what has an uneven number can move more quickly [11] than what has four corners. Therefore the sage said: "Four corners are called [12] nine because when the nine is increased, it stops at the one which is the origin". [13] So whoever wants to enter into this work must compare things with each [14] other. When he knows the natures that he wants to mix, he mixes them until they reach a mixture [15] that neither dissolves nor separates, so he is spared much of what is mentioned by the sages in their books. [16] He makes white with the one nature that is the true one, collected from [17] different things. Then he operates on them (the different things) till what he seeks is completed, because the beautiful [18] blossoming of the bodies indicates the sought-after dyeing spirit inside them (the bodies). In the same way [19] the vapour of the metals indicate a similar thing.»

She said: «Then tell me about when he says: "The leftover

(fol. 44b) is for the remaining ones".» He said: «It is the one with which the three things are completed.»

She said: «And which [2] one is that?» He said: «It is the one with which the work is completed. Did I not tell you that the four [3] are stronger than the three? So when this one gets mixed with the three, it becomes four. When it [4] is mixed, it becomes complete and strong, becoming a square, turning into one thing. Then the completeness is at the end of [5] the composition.»

She said: «Then tell me about when you say: "By the completeness he means completing the poison twice.» He said: [6] «The beginning of this thing is from different things. So when it was married it was closely united, and it became [7] a knot that does not unbind.»

She said: «Then what about his statement: "A three-folded three."» He said: «This is because the basis of this thing [8] is from three things at the beginning. These three are stable, they can neither be increased nor [9] decreased, nor can they be separated because each one of them has a nature, and they are [10] different things with a relationship to each other.»

She said: «You have neglected to answer me about the completeness, and you have started with something else.» [11] He said: «The completeness is the fourth by which the ten is completed. Thus the other composition is made [12] from 10 letters because the three-folded three are from three things that make up [13] the whole composition. By it, the fourth made the completeness strong, because when the fourth mixed with the three lunar qualities, [14] it (the fourth) introduced them (the three) into its light, and they took the completeness from it. Thus those three have a relationship [15] with the one, which becomes the nine and the ten.

She said: «How strange is the sage, when [16] he said: "Turn all the things into one." So he began with the one and he finished with the other one.» He said: [17] «As for him naming all the things one, when they were united in it, he finished [18] with the other one. Then he named the one 'sulphury water', and the nature—[19] which is everything—was conquered by it (the sulphury water). So do not be misguided by the statement of the sage when he named the nature one. Know (fol. 45a) that in that nature there is everything with which the thick body is destroyed till it becomes [2] subtle-spiritual. And nobody is able to extract [3] the dyeing, subtle, invisible soul of that one body, except by the operation of what he named the one, which is the [4] heavenly nature.»

She said: «How amazing is this (heavenly) nature which does not have a body. How is it able [5] to destroy the body, turn it into a dyeing spirit and imprison it?» He said: «That is why I ordered you [6] to destroy the body in order to extract the hidden soul. That is what the sages ordered [7] in the work to make the poison (emendation).»

She said: «Then what about when the sage said: "Take the stone which is not a stone, [8] the unknown-known, the expensive-cheap, the exalted-despised."» He said: «Did you not hear [9] the sage when he said: "Stir up the fighting between the copper and the mercury, and marry the male [10] and the female. Take red copper, submerge it, return it, and turn it into rusty gold.»

[11] She said: «I understood this part of what the sage said.» He said: «So if you do that, you will [12] obtain what you want because the eveness comes about by stirring up the fight [13] between the copper and the mercury through the struggle and the augmentation (*mukāṯra*), thus turning both of them to the destruction [14] and corruption.»

She said: «How can that be?» He said: «That is because when the copper fights [15] the mercury, it (the copper) is destroyed, and when the mercury embraces the copper, it solidifies. Know that the copper [16] is the four bodies, and the true dyes that are in the composition are [17] the solid, the moist, and the herbs.»

She said: «Which one of them is the solid?» He said: «It is [18] the cloud and the male ostrich.»

She said: «Then (what about) the moist?» He said: «The moist is the water of sulphur [19] because the sulphurs hold the sulphurs.»

She said:« And (what about) the herbs?» He said:

(fol. 45b) «They are only herbs in terms of <name and> colour, because the herbs do not resist the fire. [2] As for the hard bodies, it is the whiteness and the redness, and as for what remains when [3] it mixes with them (the herbs), it dyes them, and at that point they become firm and remain. And know that things can only exist [4] by the moisture.»

She said: «And what is the moisture?» He said: «It is the water of sulphur.»

She said: «Why [5] is it called sulphur?» He said: Because this is a great name by which it is called, and without it no work can be completed.»

She said: [6] «Then tell me about when the sage said: «When mercury is mixed with the spittle of the moon, it will make every [7] body white, and when tin is mixed with mercury it will do the same. How amazing of the sage [8] that he named the one with many names, so once he says two, and at another time three.» He said: [9] «You have asked a subtle question. Concerning the one, it is the fiery poison, concerning the two, it is [10] the composed body, and concerning the three, it is the water of sulphur with which you operate until [11] what you are looking for is completed.»

She said: «And what about when the sage says: "The thing which dyes the gold [12] is the mercury of cinnabar." How amazing is it that the sage says on one occasion that it is from cinnabar, and [13] on another that it is from arsenic.» He said: «Concerning the mercury from cinnabar, it is from magnesia, while the mercury from [14] arsenic is the sulphur that comes out of the composed mixed mercury. [15] And the sage claimed that this nature turns the nature into a metal because copper [16] has a body and a soul. So you should destroy the body until nothing remains in it except [17] the dyeing spirit in order to be good for every dyeing.»

She said: «How can copper be like a human being, [18] who has a body and a soul?» He said: «It is the thick body in terms of its colour.»

She said: [19] «Which part of this is the body, and which is the soul?» He said: «As for the soul, it is (fol. 46a) the subtle one that comes out by the operation, and the body is the thick, [2] heavy, earthy colour. That thick has to be destroyed by the fiery poison. And it has [3] to be made lean and rotten, till it turns like fine dust while its dyeing spirit remains. Then from it [4] the completeness comes, the exalted God willing. It will be the origin for every thing that you want to dye.»

[5] She said: «Then tell me about when the sage said: "Those who want to reach [6] this secret should know the things which are needed."» He said: «I told you [7] that they are three. Concerning the first, it is that one, and concerning the second, it is the purified one and its supporter.»

She said: [8] «I do not understand what you say.» He said: «I will explain to you the thing with an allusion to another thing, [9] and the supporter by another supporter. Know that all over the world, all of this is one.

[10] She said: «How can you call it one when you tell me that it is not one?» [11] He said: «If you had read the books of the sages without being overcome by laziness, [12] you would know what I am saying. So do not be in a hurry to blame, think repeatedly, ponder over [13] what you have in your hands, and if you get tired, then ask me.» [27]

She said: «Then tell me about [14] the moist fugitive and the hard fugitive.» He said: «I ordered you to make from both of them a bough. [15] [Know that] the sulphurs hold the sulphurs, the moisture holds [16] what is like it (the moisture), the cold and the hot (hold) their opposites, the wind gets imprisoned by the vapour, [17] and the soul is extracted from the body. And know that the egg has in it a soul, [18] and a body, and it is the etesian and the lime.»

She said: «Then tell me about something [19] you mentioned after I asked you about it, and that you already answered.» He said:

27 The missing words of line 13 and 14 are written in the margin.

(fol. 46b) «What is it?»

She said: «Your turning the earth into water I already understood. But what do you mean when you say: 2 "The water fire, and the fire air"?» He said: «I ordered you to introduce the fire into the air, 3 in order for the fire to become concealed in it, so it takes away its coldness. And the fire increases its power to burn 4 what enters it. I also ordered you to imprison the earth inside the air.»

She said: 5 «Is anybody able to do this?» He said: «How little you understand. What the sages said about 6 the four natures from which the world came to exist is worthless. We just wrote about them 7 as an analogy for this work.»

She said: «I do not think that they did it for no reason, but 8 how can I make the earth enter the air?» He said: «If you take the subtle part of 9 the earth which is the smoke, and it mixes with the air, it becomes imprisoned inside the air.» 10 This is why I ordered you to mix the hot with the moist, and the dry with the cold. 11 Know that nature wins over nature, and nature rejoices in nature, 12 and nature holds nature. So do not despise things by this. 13 For if a person knows the thing, it can be of little importance to him [...],[28] and 14 praise be to God who makes the egg beautiful again after (written in the margin:) its destruction.»[29]

15 She said: «Tell me about when the sage Asfīẖānus (Africanus?) said: "[I was] 16 a master of natures, and I was always troubled by them until I knew them. So they came flowing out to us 17 by the work of the eternal thing, the dissolving of the bodies, their mortification, their revivification, their burning 18 with lime, the washing and the purification. What comes from them is red, black 19 and white."» He said: «He started with the operation before the composition.»

She said: «He disguised it.»

28 There is a lacuna, the missing word could be [his fatigue] or [his effort].

29 The egg has to be destroyed for the bird to come out, and later that bird can give birth to new eggs.

(fol. 47a) He said: «That is what he wanted.»

She said: «Then what about his statement: "When I reached the origin of the science, [2] I found in it the picture of a statue standing on a whale having four [3] different colours. On it [30] were depicted the courses of the sun, the moon and the planets, [4] and what separated the seven from the twelve. I was amazed at how it was divided till [5] it became balanced from various minglings and different colours. And between its eyes there was [6] a golden book with statues of priests and their signs."» [31] He said: «That is the composition which [7] the sages scattered in order to test with it the minds of those who want to enter this work.»

[8] She said: «Although he gathered the statements about it, he did his best to hide it.» He said: «That is what [9] he wanted.»

She said: «Then what about his statement: "Say to those of intelligence and sagacity that its beginning [10] is its end, and its beginning is that which is from it"» He said: «I told you that things do not work [11] without it, and no work or process is right or complete without the mercury of the sages, [12] which the sages related to gold. You have asked me about [13] various aspects of this, and I told you that the sages did not honour anything as much as they honoured [14] the moisture, because it wins over the natures, and it holds the dyes, about which [15] Abullūn said: "A pure spirit, whose blackness is hidden", and it is the one that dries up by [16] the fugitive spirits, and by it the dead bodies are mixed."»

She said: «Then tell me about his statement: [17] "The strange stone which the ignorant despise and the people [18] of wisdom honour."» He said: «That is the stone which has the dyeing nature inside it.»

[19] She said: «Which dye is concealed inside it?» He said:

30 The masculine form could refer to the statue or to the whale but it refers rather to the statue.

31 This passage could be the summary of a dream or a vision.

(fol. 47b) The picture of Theosebeia and the balance.
This line at the top of the page indicates that this blank page was reserved for this picture.

(fol. 48a) «The eternal body.»

She said: «Does the body get concealed in the body?» He said: 2 «No. But the spirit of the eternal (gets concealed) in the spirit of this stone.»

She said: «Which stone 3 is this?» He said: «It is the one that exists, and it is found in pure dunghills, 4 deserted houses, and markets where it is sold very cheaply, and 5 you can find it even for free. When it is worked upon in round vessels, washed in the whitening waters, 6 and soaked in the fugitive spirits, then it turns copper to silver.»

She said: 7 «You described this stone very extensively. Did I ask you about it before this time?» 8 He said: «Yes. It is the acacian (*ašqūnī*) stone.»

She said: «Now I understand it. Why did you not name it like that 9 at the beginning?» He said: «I only named it for you with the description of 10 Asfīẖānus.»

She said: «Then tell me about the question of the student of Hermes , the three-folded 11 with benefit, when he asked: "Do you order us to put it in the sea before we mix it?" He said: "Yes, you are right".»

She said: «But what is this sea?» 12 He said: «The sea is male, and the body 13 is then the female.[32] So when the sea accepts the dew of the early mornings, that dew becomes 14 nourishment for the male.»

She said: «Then tell me about the statement of Democritus: "For us, the best 15 of the stones is the spittle of the moon".» He said: «The spittle of the moon is the gum, 16 and when the male becomes white, it is named the spittle of the moon, and some of the sages named it a hollow stone of Eden. They said about it: "It is a stone and not a stone." This is because it has a virtuous nature so that wonderful colours come from this stone. From it comes the purple colour, and purpleness is the flower of our sea. For that reason

32 This could be a misunderstanding arising from a copyist's mistake, as, according to ancient tradition, the sea is the female, into which the body, the old sun, sinks for rejuvenation.

(fol. 48b) it has no price for us because it is of highest importance, and it is found only with those who give birth to it.

[2] She said: «So tell me about when the sage said: "Take the fugitive from the fire and a white vapour or [3] white copper.", and he did not lie.» He said: «The sage told the truth and was honest, as all of this is in the composition. [4] Whoever calls it with these names is truthful, because among them there is the fugitive from the fire, [5] the vapour, and the cinnabar, which alone makes the copper white.»

[6] She said: «Then tell me about his statement: "The sulphurs hold the sulphurs, and the moisture [7] does the same with the moisture."» He said: «That is because when the poison extracted from the ashes is sown [8] in that body and colours it with an unchangeable colour, the body will never let this poison, [9] which is its close one, separate from it.»

She said: «Perhaps this takes place when the fugitive encounters [10] the seeker, so the escaping between them both ceases.» He said: «You are right and you understood well.»

[11] She said: «As for me, I only spoke like that out of intuition. So confirm my intuition.» [12] He said: «I will do. <He said> Indeed, the nature took its close one as an enemy.»

She said: «Which one is the nature, [13] and which one is the close one?» He said: «The gum is the poison.»

She said: «What is the relationship between the two of them?» [14] He said: «Leave aside this questioning me about the relationship between the two, [15] and ask me instead to complete what I am saying about the matter, for if you interrupt this question with something else [16] you will be confused.»

She said: «Tell me then.» He said: «As for the relationship between the two, it is because [17] when the sulphur is mixed with the sulphur (the sulphur that does not rot, [18] but is made to rot), it becomes the close one to the fighter of the fire, so that it clings and is clung to. So when they mixed, a precious colour came out [19] of them, so the sulphur whose characteristic is that it escapes is not able (fol. 49a) to escape any longer.

She said: «Why is that?» He said: «Because the spirit is submerged [2] in the body. When the spirit is submerged in the body and mixed with it, the spirit dyes [3] the body, and the body takes up the spirit, so it (the body) prevents it (the spirit) from escaping.»

She said: «Then tell me, [4] O Zosimos, about the statement of Democritus: "If the torturer submerges in the body there will be [5] an unchangeable colour."» He said: «That is because he told us that the first power is the vinegar, and [6] the second power is the torturer of her husband, because she is submerged in his inside. At that time, [7] a beautiful colour comes out of it that does not change. Then take the male that comes from [8] the talcine kohl and cook it until it turns black. Then take the kohl and cook it with the water of natron [9] till it thickens like honey and fat. After that, cook it until it turns into a stone. [10] Then set it on a very strong fire in order to destroy the thickness of the body. [11] If you want to make a pure elixir from it, put in it one ounce of [12] pure iron because iron holds on to water, and cook it until it becomes [13] a silvery, pure, white stone. And be careful that the vinegar does not turn into smoke and disappears. Set it on fire for [14] 150 days.»

She said: «Then tell me, O Zosimos, about your statement: [15] «The secret of making gold comes from the male and the female. And [16] you have made clear for us that the matter of the male is in the lead, and as for the female, you mentioned [17] for us (that the matter is) in the arsenic.» He said: «Yes, take the arsenic and mix it with the lead. [18] The female rejoices when she accepts the power of the male, because the female becomes stronger by the male, and the male [19] can only take the spirit and become a spirit from the female. So mix both of them (fol. 49b) and put them in a vessel of glass and pound them with the vapour and the vinegar and cook it for seven [2] days. Keep the poison from turning into smoke, and leave it until it decomposes.»

She said: [3] «Then tell me about your statement concerning iron: "I wrote an aspect for the iron: [4] so take it, make plates out of it, pour sour vinegar on it until [5] the plates break into fragments and the iron turns into ashes."» He said: «Indeed their iron is from [6] the power of the two, the male and the female, and it has a great power. So you should put [7] the iron in the vinegar, otherwise what you seek will not be right.»

She said: «Then tell me about [8] when you say: "Silvery pyrite has a great power when it is nourished and made white."» [9] He said: «I told you that you should take the silvery pyrite, [33] and cook it until [10] it turns fine like dust. Then soak it in vinegar and cook it till the vinegar disappears. Cook it for [11] 150 days. When it (the process) is completed you will find it shining like marble. [12] Return it and cook it till all the power of the pyrite is destroyed.»

She said: [13] «Maybe this is what the sage said about lead: "Cook it till it turns red, [14] and add poison to it." <She said:> The sage here named the pyrite [15] lead.» He said: «When its whiteness is intense, and it becomes a stone we name it pyrite, [16] and Anīlū[..]s named it a golden fragmented stone. When it is mixed with vinegar it becomes [17] a pyrite stone because it is from our work, and it contains the male and the female.»

She said: [18] «Then it is not silver but the silver of our work?» He said: «Yes, then strengthen the fire for it till [19] all of it is destroyed and its squeaking disappears, so it turns into a spiritual vapour. This

[33] The margin reads: The interpretation of pyrite is the son of the fire. This explanation is found later on fol. 58b.12. This illustrates the extensive reading of the one who wrote this note.

(fol. 50a) vapour we name tin.»

She said: «So is this vapour mixed with the [2] incombustible sulphur?» He said: «Yes, it is mixed and cooked with it for some days until it dries and [3] the moisture disappears. After that, it is no longer a body. Then you soak it in vinegar [4] so it becomes an elixir. Soak it, cook it, and close the opening of the vessel well for [5] the vinegar not to disappear. Cook it for 150 days. Then you will find it complete.» [6]

She said: «Which tin is this?» He said: «It is the tin which contains the male [7] and the female, and it has another power. <He said:> Concerning that other (power), [8] it becomes white on both sides because one is a spirit, and the other is a body. So the body rejoices when [9] the spirit enters into it, and the body preserves the spirit. Every body, when finding a spirit, [10] takes it quickly. And know that when the soul is tortured with its body, and [11] its dye[34] becomes good, then after its death it becomes spiritual. And the tin is similar to [12] the human being, because it is tortured with the body so it becomes spiritual. And when it becomes [13] spiritual and its operation, purification, and cooking are performed well, it dyes the silver into gold.» [14]

She said: «What about when you say, O Zosimos: "Arsenic is one of the greatest gates, and [15] without it no dye exists."» He said: «The arsenic that I mentioned to you is not [16] arsenic because it is the male. Do you not see how the sage said: "If you put [17] with it the mercury of cinnabar, then a great secret would emerge from them."»

She said: «And what is [18] that secret which would emerge?» He said: «Take the two and mix them. After you mix them [19] till they become thick, you will find that the mercury becomes thick and the male turns into ashes,

34 Emendation: Here is written *ṣabruha*. It should read *ṣabġuha*.

(fol. 50b) hidden in the mercury. So in this way the head of the world is made.»

She said: «And how does one work with it?» [2] He said: «That is because at the beginning the dye becomes white, and after that it becomes red inside, [3] and by it the work gets completed, God willing.»

She said: «Then tell me, O Zosimos, about when you say: "If [4] you do not make white you cannot make red."» He said: «That is because they are two natures, red and white. So turn the [5] red white, and the white red.»

She said: «That is an enigmatic statement, and no intelligent person can [6] understand its meaning.» He said: «Then understand from me. Know that [7] the year has four seasons, so among them the mixing of the blackness is winter, then (comes) spring, then [8] summer with its heat and cooking, and then (in autumn) the fruits ripen. So according to these four [9] seasons, those four natures should be operated on: By the moisture of winter, [10] by the heat of the air (of spring) the flowers blossom, by the hotness and heat of summer [11] the fruits are cooked, and by the mildness of the fourth season (autumn) the fruits of the trees can be picked. According to [12] this, operate the red and the white, otherwise blame only yourself [13] because the natures that contain the dyes are to be operated on in this way [14] till they reach this utmost limit.»

She said: «Then tell me about the statement of the sages concerning the stone [15] when they said: "It is not a stone, the despised-honoured."» He said: «Concerning their despising [16] it, that is because they do not know it and what it contains. Concerning their honouring it, that is because the sages know [17] the virtues that it contains because this stone is the key and without it [18] nothing can be. Therefore the sages gave it many names to protect it [19] for fear that the ordinary people would recognize it, and corrupt the world. Therefore (fol. 51a) the exalted and glorified God recommend His prophets to hide it, when He told them about the power and [2] benefits that it contains. And it is the basis of this work, and has benefits in another work [3] more than in this work. Therefore every sage invented a name for it. Often [4] they named it with the true name, together with invented names. So there are some who named it with its metal, [5] some who named it with its colour, and some with other names than stones. [6] Indeed they confused people (to prevent them from) knowing it because of its many names, its being cheap, [7] and its being sold for money. And there are some who named it the coal of the mountain, and some who named it cinnabar, [8] and some who named it black earth, and some who named it dung of the moon, and some who named it [9] the pupil of the eye.»

She said: «Indeed, this stone is significant.» He said: «You admire my statement, [10] yet how would it be if you could see it working! It would become for you even greater and more joyful for the hearts [11] than these names. Yet the sages have given it thousands and thousands of kinds of names (*alf alf bāb min al-asmāʾ*). So [12] by this they confused the people about it, so they did not find a way to it.»

She said: «Then describe [13] an aspect of it for me, and bestow on me a favour with it, so that I will be remembered by those who come after me by what you cleared up for me. [14] And do me a favour by what you give to me from it so that I can do a favour to those who come after me.» [15] He said: «This is the hard, precious, dry and bitter stone which does not get mixed [16] with the bodies until they are dissolved.»

She said: «You insist on protecting and hiding it.» He said: [17] «It deserves that! Even if I called it with its true name, the ignorant people would disbelieve it, [18] without testing it. And even if they tested it and then mixed it, but did not know how to operate it, [19] they would be more disbelieving in it.»

She said: «Thus you refuse to give for me

(fol. 51b) an aspect of this stone so that those who come after me would know it. So tell me about its efficiency.» 2 He said: «This stone does many works, and many 3 who know it do not really know what is its power. But think about what is extracted from dead metals 4 that some of the sages named the heart of the sun.»

She said: «What is the heart of the sun?» 5 He said: «It is the reins.» She said: «And what are the reins?» He said: «They are the clinger and the clung.»

She said: «Which of the two is 6 the clinger-stone?» He said: «The eternal stone» She said: «And which one is the clung-stone?» He said: 7 «It is the stone-not-a-stone about which you asked me before.»

She said: «Then which one of them is thc male?» 8 He said: «The reddish one.» She said: «And which one is the female?» He said: «It is the black earth.»

9 She said: «Do I limit myself to those two only?» He said: «There should be a peacemaker between them.» 10 She said: «Which peacemaker do they need?» He said: «What is similar to them.»

She said: 11 «Which one of the two is stronger?» He said: «The stone-not-a-stone is stronger in essence 12 at the beginning of the matter, and the reddish stone is the strong stone by whose strength its companions became stronger.» 13 She said: «Then what is the holder?» He said: «It is the fugitive which turned its companions into fugitives.» 14 She said: «How did it turn them into fugitives?» He said: «When it turned them into spirits, 15 and they separated from their earth.» She said: «Which of the colours of these things overcame them 16 at this level?» He said: «It is the whiteness.» She said: «And from where did that whiteness come?» 17 He said: «Not from one side.»

She said: «You perplexed me, and I was hoping that 18 I would understand what you say.» He said: «I did not want to perplex you, but what I said is 19 only the truth.» She said: «You are right, upon my life, the rightness of this work is (fol. 52a) the whiteness. And may be this is what the sages said: "Turn gold into silver."» He said: [2] «The time has come for you to understand!»

She said: «This is its beginning not its end [3] because the mentioning of that stone stirs my heart, which makes me distressed.» He said: «Do not be distressed because of it!» [4] She said: «Describe more of it to me.» He said: «It is a stone having heat.»

She said: «Where [5] does its heat come from?» He said: «From its intense bitterness.» She said: «And where does its bitterness come from?» He said: [6] «From its bad origin.»

She said: «Do you think that it wins over things by its heat?» He said: [7]«Yes.» She said: «Do you think that it is more hot than fire.» He said: «The fire for it is like the water [8] for the fire.» She said: «Has it a power over the fire?» He said: «No.»

She said: «How can it be like that when [9] you declare that it is stronger than the fire?» He said: «That is because when fire meets fire [10] one of them eats the other.» She said: «Is the power of this visible, known to people?» [11] He said: «No.» She said: «Then by what is its power?» He said: «By the fire.»

She said: «How can the fire make it strong?» [12] He said: «That is because its spirit (of the fire) is concealed in its spirit (the stone).» She said: «Thus I see that this stone is [13] spiritual.» He said: «From where do you know that?» She said: «When you mentioned that the fire [14] makes it stronger. <She said:> So give me something by which I can know it.» He said: [15] «Do you not see that when you touch oil (*naft*) with your hand it does not burn, [16] but when it comes into contact with fire, it burns whatever it reaches.»

She said: «Does your stone [17] only burn with fire?» He said: «O yes. In the same way as oil only burns with fire, [18] it also burns only with fire.»

She said: «Does this stone burn every [19] thing?» He said: «Yes, and it has many benefits. But the greatest of its benefits [...] [35]»

35 Here one or more folios are missing, as the next page starts with something different.

(fol. 52b) She said: «Then tell me about this fugitive which turns those earthly (things) into [2] fugitives.» He said: «I see that you do not forget anything.»

She said: «How can I forget the wisdom I hear from you [3] by which God illuminates my heart and opens my eyes, and I hope [4] that my joy will continue because of it.» He said: «It is the vapour.»

She said: «And what is the benefit of the vapour?» [5] He said: «It is the great benefit.» She said: «So what is its benefit?» He said: «It is the one which prevents the fire [6] from eating the flowers of its brothers, and it makes the damage disappear from its brothers, as well as the dryness [7] which overcomes them, and it increases the beauty of their colours.»

She said: «With what [8] can it do that?» He said: «With what remains from it, and the fire does not consume its power.» She said: «Does [9] the fire consume anything from it?» He said: «Yes, it consumes the badness which is in it.» She said: [10] «And which badness is in it?» He said: «It is that (badness) because of which people do not want to have anything to do with it.» She said: «Why [11] do people not want to have anything to do with it?» He said: «That is because people cannot and are not able to distinguish between its [12] beneficial dye and its harmful badness.»

She said: «Did they leave it (the work) because they refuse to have anything to do with it?» [13] He said: «No, they did not leave it because they refused to have anything to do with it, but they became tired of taking [14] the benefit that is in it, and from throwing away the harmful of it. And people try to work upon it in every way [15] but nobody who wanted to work upon it would get any benefit from it, except when he separates between its harmful badness [16] and its benefit.

She said: «You really described this stone well, but [17] is it single?» He said: «On this level, yes. But at the beginning of the composition it is not.»

[18] She said: «So why did it become single here?» He said: «That is because in it [19] all things turned into one, so it became single.»

She said: «Did

(fol. 53a) that matter reach up to this level?» He said: «No.»

She said: «I ask God for the best of what you make me enter into!» He said: [2] «Did you disapprove of anything?» She said: «Yes, when you said that it is single and not-single.» He said: «Did I not [3] tell you several times that the things are not single, and when they are united at the end [4] of the first work they become single in the name?»

She said: «So tell me what improves [5] this single matter.» He said: «The high-ranking one, which gave to it its best as poison, [6] and longed to mix with the vapour out of passion.»

She said: «What gave it this longing?» He said: [7] «The joining of the sulphur (sg.) with the sulphurs.»

She said: «I will ask about something that I think is [8] different from what I was asking you before. Ask God for help because of my weak understanding. Is it not that the sulphurs [9] hold the sulphurs?» He said: «Yes, and also this nature rejoices in nature, [10] and nature wins over nature.»

She said: «So I think that I asked you [11] something that I already knew.» He said: «You already knew it, and in past times I told you about it many times. Indeed [12] every sage who achieved this work named the things, with which he obtained [13] this work, with names that he invented according to his opinion, imitating with them those who were before him. Then he saw [14] how the sages protected this work from the people, and that they were hiding it in order that [15] the shameless ones would not obtain it. So he wrote about it, and named the thing according to his opinion, writing about it [16] in analogies, parables and symbols. I Therefore do the same, as [17] those before me did the same with me. And you will also do the same for those who will come after you, because, by [18] the exalted glorified God, it is unavoidable for whoever knows this matter that jealousy enters into him.»

[19] She said: «Do you think that their jealousy is for withholding something from this world?» He said: «No. How could they withhold anything

(fol. 53b) from this world while their eyes are filled with it? But it is for fear that the [2] shameless ones would obtain it, so they would become more powerful to disobey God, so the sin (*iṯm*) of that would backfire on them. But [3] for those obedient to God it is a clear, evident matter.»

She said: «I was reading, O Zosimos, [4] these letters without paying attention to them, not really considering them fully. But today I became sure [5] that he was truthful. <She said:> [It is about] your statement "nature rejoices in nature, and nature [6] holds nature".» He said: «Indeed, if impatience must not be a feature of the sages [7] while patience is the head of wisdom for the sages, I would swear by God that I would not answer you [8] any of your questions for a whole year.»

She said: «By God, I did not want to make you angry on purpose, [9] and if I had known that this contradicts you I would not have said it.» He said: «As I know that (only) your ignorance pushed you to say [10] what you said, disbelieving the sage, and your believing [11] him after you knew it, (this was what) prohibited me from punishing you for the ugly thing you said.»

She said: [12] «I ask you not to punish me for something for which I had neither intention to contradict you, nor [13] to degrade the sage, and I blame myself for my weak understanding of what the sages said.» [14] He said: «I find it inevitable to excuse you. Upon my life, the sage completed [15] the whole work in this brief statement for whoever has intelligence.»

She said: «Then tell me about when he said: [16] "Honour the stone that is fecundated by the sun."» He said: «This stone, fecundated by the sun, [17] is the acacian (*ašqūnīān*) gum, the murderer of her husband, the changer of his body which is one, [18] named with many names.»

She said: «Then mention for me some of the names.» He said: «It is the mercury which [19] is rarely found, and it is the spittle of the moon, and it is the chrysocolla, (fol. 54a) and the translation of the chrysocolla is the exalted mixture. And it is that about which Maria said: [2] "Our God gave the prophet Moses, may God grant him salvation, an ingot of copper. And after him, [2] God gave it as a legacy to us, so by this nature our God perfected this work for us when we operate on it [4] by the fire. Thus perform the cooking well and pound finely till her husband dies with her."» [5]

She said: «Then what, when her husband dies with her?» He said: «You should [6] take two waters.»

She said: «What are these two waters?» He said: «One of them is red, [7] and the other one is white; one of them is moist, and the other one is dry. This is with regard to the action, the sagacity, and [8] the power, but with regard to the number they are three.»

She said: «You mentioned two to me, [9] so how did they become three?» He said: «How fast you forget! Did you not know that there is [10] a holder who holds them?»

She said: «Now I remember, you are right, they are upon my life [11] three.» He said: «No. But they are one.» She said: «You are right.» He said: «Now I tell you [12] that they should be four things.»

She said: «I cannot understand this.» He said: [13] «I will repeat the statement and the parable in order that you understand it.» She said: «Do that [14] now!» He said: «How many times you have asked me about this matter while [15] you should know it without asking, because of its influence on you».

She said: «Then what about when she said: "Take [16] the exalted claudianus and cook it until the plates dissolve and turn into a stone that settles in [17] the bottom of the vessel. Then extract the water of silver in order that the sediment, [18] whose spirit has been extracted, remains dry-dead.» He said: «Indeed this comes in the first composition [19] that I order you to cook and to extract its spirit.»

She said:

(fol. 54b) «With what does its spirit get extracted?» He said: «With the magnet of the sages because it dissolves [2] the body in the secret till it turns into water. So, my lady, you have to make use of this magnet.»

[3] She said: «So what about her statement regarding the dissolving of the copper: "Take copper, make filings out of it, then [4] water it and cook it, and return it till you see its vapour flowing."» He said: «This is [5] in the first composition which I order you to cook, and I told you that it will solidify [6] and turn into a stone. So make your fire gently in this cooking until you extract all the vapour [7] from the sediment, and return the water to the sediment until it turns white [8] like alabaster.»

She said: «Then tell me why they named the pure water mercury?» [9] He said: «We only named it mercury because it is mercury.»

She said: «You declared that it is [10] the pure water which is from the one sulphur.» He said: «I declared that, [11] and I tell you that we named it cloud because the cloud is composed in the sky, [12] so we named it cloud. But remember my saying and know that the sages agreed [13] to name it mercury from cinnabar. So if they gave it one name [14] they already named with it all the things, and if they named it single they named (by this) [15] all the composition.»

She said: «Then why, O Zosimos, did the first ones not name the mercury the pure water of sulphur?» [16] He said: «They were content to name it vapour, and Democritus said: "If anyone named [17] the mercury white vapour or white copper, he was truthful and spoke right [18] because it became white vapour from cinnabar.»

She said: «So the mercury of cinnabar [19] is what turns the copper white?» He said: «Yes, it turns it white in the other composition.»

(fol. 55a) She said: «Then what makes this mercury red?» He said: «The red copper, and it is that [2] about which Democritus said: “Concerning the water of sulphur, when it turns red it makes red.”»

She said: [3] «Then tell me about when the sage said: “Put it on the gold, it becomes aqzal gold”.» [4] He said: «It is the broth. When it is put on the gold, it turns it into aqzal gold.»

She said: [5] «Why did he name the lead as copper?» He said: «He named all of the composition lead and copper.»

[6] She said: «Then what is aqzal gold?» He said: «It is an invented name for the colour of the elixir [7] when it turned red like aqzal.»

She said: «Why did the sage name the gold [8] poison?» He said: «Because it is extracted from lead-copper, so it became a poison submerging in the body.»

[9] She said: «What is the cloud?» He said: «It is the broth, and when it is mixed with the gold it will turn into [10] aqzal gold.»

She said: «Thus the cloud, the ferment, and the cultivation of the gold are one. [11] <She said:> But what did Democritus mean when he said: “The ferment of gold is for every body?”» [12] He said: «The sages named lead-copper with the names of every body in order to disguise it. [13] So when you hear in their books the word body from which the ferment of gold has to be extracted, [14] they gave the name gold to the dough of the body which does not rot, because it rots [15] [in] the other work.»

She said: «Then tell me about when the sage said: “Take the plate of silver and [16] operate on it until it becomes as it should be, and its colour satisfies you. And if [17] the plate is copper, it will be better for it.” And he also said about the white broth: [18] “Take a plate of copper or silver.”» He said: «I told you that the sages [19] named their lead-copper on one occasion silver, on another copper and on another tin.»

(fol. 55b) She said: «What did they mean by that?» He said: «To disguise.»

She said: «Then tell me [2] what you think of it.» He said: «Know that if it is made white or red, it is lead-copper. But [3] the operation is what changes its colours and what changes its names. And they gave each colour a name [4] similar to the bodies of ordinary people. The name of the true composition is lead-copper. [5] As for the names like silver, aqzal gold, purple gold, flower [6] of gold and ferment of gold with which they name it, all of these (names) are, in fact, colours, and they appeared out of the lead-copper, [7] and we invented a name for them. Often the sage took from the below towards the above, and from the above towards [8] the below.»

She said: «What was it that made these colours appear?» He said: «The broth made them appear.» [9]

She said: «Then tell me about the statement of Agathodaimon: "I did not order you to mix the things [10] and to pound them for no reason."» He said: «This is because when the silver is placed in the cooking, [11] the heat of the fire enters inside the silver, makes it rotten, destroys it, and extracts [12] from it its spirit that is concealed in it in its thickness. Therefore the herbs are diminished, [13] because we take from them their dyeing nature, and their thick ground (*arḍīya*) remains. This is because nothing enters into [14] our work except the spirits of these things. Therefore Ostanes said: [15] "The body does not pass into the body but the spirit passes into every body." [16] This is why Agathodaimon said in all his books: "Take from the bodies [17] their spirits", and he also said: "Take the spirits of the chrysocolla." So all the work of Agathodaimon [18] is indeed the vapour, and the vapour is the spirit, and the white vapour is [19] the cinnabar, and the cinnabar is the cloud. Concerning this spirit, (fol. 56a) Abulūn said: "Take the pure, moist spirit whose inside is black, and the vapour [2] is the spirit, and the spirit is the dyer." Thus Hermes and Democritus named it smoke, [3] and they also named it the vapour of arsenic and sandarach.»

She said: «Then tell me about when Democritus said: [4] "Take the cloud which is in their books."» He said: «It is all the composition, but he named it after [5] every fat and every moist thing, but it is only one moist thing.»

She said: «What is that moist thing?» [6] He said: «It is the water of sulphur. So when he said: "pound it with water, vinegar, fat, honey, [7] or milk," all of that is one, namely the water of sulphur.»

She said: «Then tell me about when you say: [8] "The things are mixed with the moistures when they are raw and not operated on."» He said: «Yes, and [9] I order you to do that.»

She said: «Why?» He said: «Because the moisture washes [10] the hard bodies, and it mixes them with the sun and the dew like [11] the male sulphur and the litharge.»

She said: «What about the statement of Maria and Democritus about the making of the broth: [12] "The plates have to be pounded and returned to the broth several times."» He said: «They said that [13] in order that the shadow of the copper should disappear. And they said that in order that the returning to the broth should not inflict pain on you, [14] because when they mix their things, they cook them without becoming tired of it, and they are patient until [15] their copper becomes white, and they bring it to the end of its work, and they compose it with the other mixture [16] that makes the cloud able to make red. That is why they said: "Put some dye with the sulphur [17] on a gentle fire and it will become solid immediately."»

She said: «What is the dye?» He said: [18] «The dye is male and it is the copper.»

She said: «And the gum?» He said: "Truly the gum [19] is not the dye.» She said: «How can it be that the dyer and the dyed are one?» He said:

(fol. 56b) «If the body is soaked in the water of sulphur, and is cooked for many days, it becomes red. At this time [2] the dyer and the dyed are one. When it is thrown on the silver of ordinary people it turns [3] into gold, so know it.»

She said: «Then tell me about this water of yours.» He said: «We gave it every [4] name. Know that if it is mixed with lead-copper and cooked for some days, it becomes black. When it becomes black [5] and the blackness appears and you take from it a little amount, you will dye with it [6] a non-fugitive black dye with an everlasting yellowness in it. Know that we do not consider the dye that makes [7] the silver black, and we do not regard it as anything, but the seekers of the science like to see something of this [8] dye in order to believe in what remains of the complete dye. Know that the more this water is dyed, [9] it also dyes.» He said: «When it gets dyed, it becomes purple.»

She said: «What makes it [10] purple?» He said: «The copper which does not get rotten. When it is mixed with it (the water), it dyes it with a purple dye. [11] And the water becomes an elixir when the copper solidifies it, and its moisture has dried away from it, and it (the water) becomes a dye.»

[12] She said: «Help me to understand better this work and this statement.» He said: «Do you not see [13] when Democritus said about the operation of the androdamus: "If you put [14] incombustible sulphur in the other composition, you have perfected the making of the ferment of gold." Know that [15] you should irrigate the composition with water several times, until its dye is good and complete. Therefore [16] Maria said: "Cook the composition continuously, and put in it the murderer of the red arsenic [17] so that it ejects its semen, and the composition is amalgamated until its colour and its resistance to fire become [18] one thing." <He said:> I told you that the body that was mixed in the other composition [19] is the murderer of the sandarach, and it is what solidified the water of sulphur. And the water of sulphur is what

(fol. 57a) made it red, and returned it to being a dye. So your fire must be gentle in the beginning of the operation in order that [2] the body absorbs the water, because Maria said: "Increase the strength of the fire little by little. When it (the body) absorbs [3] the water, then increase the fire." And watch out that it is mixed with the rest of the poison to the same extent that you cook it.»

She said: [4] «Then tell me about your statement: "The natures, which have no bodies, act in the body without fire."» [5] He said: «This is because the sages took saffron of the ordinary people, Hermes' saffron, and leaves of [6] apples, while others took the roots of the demonic apple because their roots are golden. [7] Šīmās (sometimes written Šīmās) declared that it must have that root, and that no dye can come into being except from it. And [8] the sages named it with various names.»

She said: «Then tell me your opinion.» He said: [9] «I order you to take the root of the myrtle (*al-ās*). It is better than other roots because it pounds everything. [10] That is why Democritus wrote about it in the *Sarṭiṭa* with regard to the dissolving of the ivory and the bones. [11] And Maria declared that nobody is able either to dissolve or melt a stone except with it (the root of the myrtle). [12] And I make you more convinced by telling you that it is the only one that destroys the things.»

She said: [13] Why did they name it mistress (*sulṭalsīā*)? He said: «Because it is a female that is stronger than the male. He (one of the sages) said: [14] "Introduce both the male and the female into the work because one of them holds [15] the other, and the other one destroys the first one."»

She said: «How precious, O Zosimos, are those two natures!» [16] He said: «Be careful that you do not miss both of them. Know that the nature of this female and male [17] is most similar to people with regard to the marriage and the harmonious joining. They are fixed in every prayer niche (*mihrāb*)[18] in Egypt, because the two were brought from Cyprus and the land of India, and the sages united them.» [19]

She said: «Will you tell me more about the two?» He said: «You must pound the two with the rust, because (fol. 57b) they get mixed with it and they dye it. And it (the rust) dyes both of them, and drives the blaze of fire away from them.[36]»

She said: «Then tell me [2] about your statement: "Colocynth (*qalqant*) is for us incombustible sulphur, and it is the *sūrīn*.» [He said:] [3] «All of that is one red sulphur, and it is the sulphur that [4] only mercury turns into rust, so the rust is the making red. And the rusting [5] is the making white by the white sulphur at the beginning of the work. And the making red of the rust is caused by the red sulphur [6] in the other work. So I have explained to you that the making rusty of the copper is the whitening. [7] Concerning how iron can be made soft, and why they said this about it, I first give you the statement of Hermes when he said: [8] "Take the iron, make from it thin plates, and spread polished earth on and under them. [9] Treat it as *usṭam* is treated, so it becomes soft-white." And these [10] things that he mentioned are names of the white sulphur. And the clearest of all of that, [11] and you have to understand it, is the statement of Hermes: "We will not soften the iron,[37] but it is a whitening of the copper." The confirmation [12] of that is the statement of Democritus: "Put the white poison on it and it will be good."»

She said: [13] «What is the white poison?» He said: «It is the white sulphur.» I have explained to you [14] the matter of the iron, and now I will tell you about the tin. Democritus said: [15] "Take the tin which is in the snowy, starry earth, and the alum."»

She said: [16] «What are these names?» He said: «It is the white sulphur, and the white sulphur <and the white sulphur>[17] is what makes the copper white, and the removing of the squeaking of the tin is for us [18] the making white.»

She said: «You have said much, O Zosimos, about the matter of this sulphur.» He said: [19] «Now I make you more convinced that all of these names are the white sulphur.»

36 Accepting the marginal correction.

37 We include a note in the margin that reads:«We will not soften the iron, … .»

(fol. 58a) She said: «Tell me!» He said: «The statement of Democritus: "When the poison becomes white like marble, [2] then it is a great secret because it makes iron soft, copper white, removes the squeaking of [3] the tin and the moisture of the lead, and it makes the natures non-separable and the dyes [4] non-fugitive." <He said:> And Maria named this sulphur the crown of the work, and [5] others named it the great secret which overcomes everything, because by it she made the lead-copper white, [6] shining like marble, and turned it into smoke in the cupolas.»

She said: «I see that [7] this sulphur is what dyes the dyes.» He said: «Yes, it (the sulphur) is the great secret, and it is what makes [8] all of the work, and it is what burns the copper and makes it white, and it is what solidifies the mercury. [9] And it is the head of the work and its base, after the exalted and glorified God. It deserves to be named a great secret, [10] because when the red sulphur is mixed with the gum, a great secret comes from them. So this is [11] the sulphur which dyes every body, burns, makes white, solidifies the mercury [12] and makes it rusty (= makes it white).»

She said: «Then tell me about when Maria said: "If you do not find the cloud, take the cinnabar."» [13] He said: «I told you many times in my descriptions that the dye is one, and that the things [14] which the sages named are one < they named it with one name>, although they gave [15] them names which were not theirs. When they mix their things, they become one thing, [16] so they gave it one of the names of anything they chose, like iron, copper, lead [17] or tin. And mostly they named it copper and body of magnesia. [18] I tell you that copper is the whole composition, and it is the magnesia, and everything should be [19] made with it. In the same way, Democritus said: "Take the cloud and coagulate it (fol. 58b) in the body of magnesia." That is why you should know that the cloud coagulates the things, [2] and it is what improves them. I have informed you that whoever has attempted this work knows that [3] the cloud only accepts what the sages named stones, dusts, and bodies [4] that are from the Sun, the Moon, Saturn and Jupiter.»

She said: «Then tell me about Hermes, [5] after he said many things. Why did he mention the tar, saying: "Make the tar white with white things similar to it, [6] and make it red <and make it red> with red things similar to it." He said: «He named all the composition tar, [7] and said: "Make it white with its components of the mixture in the first operation." So when he completed it, he mentioned [8] the second components in it. Then he said: "Make it red with things similar to it." So he called the composition tar. Thus do not be misled [9] by the tar.»

She said: «O Zosimos, I asked you about this stone, but you replied with [10] many names that were not to the point.» He said: «It is a stone to which the sages gave many names; [11] they also named it pyrite.»

She said: «Why did they name it pyrite?» [38] He said: «Because it was born in the fire and was nourished by it. Pyrite [12] in translation is: the son of the fire. As for their naming it the etesian (stone), that is because it is a stone that [13] they give birth to every year.»

She said: «Then tell me about the colours of this pyrite stone.» [14] He said: «When they first give birth to it, its colour is the colour of silver. Therefore it is named [15] silvery stone, because its first birth is in the orbit of the moon, and the moon has [16] the colour of silver, and this first orbit is the first one which nourishes that stone. [17] Then after that, the stone grows little by little, thus it moves to the orbit of Jupiter, [18] and its colour becomes that of tin, because Jupiter's colour is similar to tin. Then [19] it moves from that to the orbit of Venus, and the colours of copper blossom in it. Then it moves

38 This question comes from the margin.

(fol. 59a) from it to the orbit of the sun. Then the colour of gold appears from it, so it resembles it in the other mixture. [2] Then it moves from that level to the colour of Saturn, so it dies, is destroyed and [3] its colour turns black. So whoever tried this work really knew these colours [4] until it ends in death. So those who look for the stone must give up looking for anything [5] else, because a stone can never come into existence in this work, except by [6] this stone, which the sages composed from their things. I have told you about this stone [7] many times. It is enough for you, so ask about something else.»

She said: «I will do (emendation). Tell me about [8] his statement: "Solidify the chrysocolla which did not have a body when it became chrysocolla.» He said: «Indeed, [9] chrysocolla is an invented name, and it is the glue of the gold, and it (fem.) is a spirit. The sage ordered [10] that it has to be solidified in order that its spirit does not escape from it. And therefore Agathodaimon said: "Take care that [11] the fugitive, the spirit[39] of the chrysocolla, does not escape from you."»

She said: «And how can I treat it with skill, [12] so that it does not escape?» He said: «Mix it with the body, arranging well its operation and its measurements of the fire [13] in the other (second) composition. So the chrysocolla, the glue of gold, the ferment of gold, the seed [14] of gold, and the flower of gold are the water of sulphur that is extracted from the ashes by the vapour. [15] Know that if you mix the chrysocolla with the body, the chrysocolla will not be able [16] to escape, and the body becomes like it (the chrysocolla) with regard to its nature when it (the chrysocolla) transforms it (the body).»

She said: «O Zosimos, maybe this is [17] what Maria meant when she said: "Turn the bodies into non-bodies, [18] and those which are non-bodies into bodies."» He said: «You have understood well, and have grasped the meaning.»

[19] She said: «I was thinking that this work comes at the beginning of the work (in the first work).»

[39] The text erroneously gives husband.

(fol. 59b) He said: «No, this has to be at the end (in the other one). Did you not understand [2] when she said at the end of her statement: "Operate on it with the fire until it becomes white and red by the cooking and the pounding, [3] so the body and the chrysocolla turn into a vapour, having no body. This is when the bodies turn into [4] non-bodies." <He said:> And if you continue the cooking, those which have no bodies will turn into [5] bodies after its (sg.) rotting and the removal of the thickness from its (sg.) body.»

She said: «Then tell me about [6] when you say: "We did not find anything that does the work of the fire, except what is from [7] the water of sulphur.» He said: «I have told you at length that no work can come to be except with the water of [8] sulphur.»

She said: «Then what are the bitters which they mentioned?» He said: «It is (sg.) the water of sulphur. [9] Therefore Šīmās (in different writing) said: "Indeed our sulphur is stronger than every fire." And about the stones he said: [10] "This thing does the work of fire, and nothing is better than it." And [11] Maria also named it the fiery poison.»

She said: «So do the bodies turn into non-bodies by this poison?» [12] He said: «Yes, and after that, by the intensive cooking, the non-bodies turn into bodies.»

[13] She said: «Then tell me about what the smoke is?» He said: «It is the vapour, and I have told you that it is white. [14] Democritus mentioned it when he said: "The smoke of the cinnabar makes everything white, [15] and the ashes, from which the shells of the pollen come, are the male which should be rubbed together [16] with the water." And he also mentioned the white smoke of the firewood.»

She said: «I see here [17] two rottings with two ashes.» He said: «You are right.» She said: «What led him to separate the two?» He said: [18] «In order that his statement about the magnesia and its body be truthful. And they meant by all these things, [19] which you see and which they mentioned, the water of sulphur. Concerning the shells of the pollen, they are the male.

(fol. 60a) Often they keep them aside when they complete their first operation. When they need them, [2] they mix them with the dye that they want to dye with. Know, my lady [3] that if the gum is not mixed with the moisture, it will be burnt. Therefore [4] the first sages ordered that they cook it gently with the moisture, in order that [5] the dyer spirit which is good for our work, is extracted from it. Know that they gave that moisture the name of [6] everything. But the water of sulphur is also an invented name. Do you not see when Democritus says: [7] "Everything that God created is white." If you want to cook it, put the moisture with the plate [8] covering it, and cook it gently as the sages ordered you, [9] till it (the cooking) turns it into an intense incombustible unruined gum.»

She said: «Then tell me [10] about the statement of Democritus when he mentioned the bitters in the making of the poison.» He said: [11] «The bitters are an invented name for the water of sulphur, and the water of sulphur is also an invented name. Do you not [12] see when Democritus said: "Whoever is able to rot the body with these bitters [13] for 40 days, until it becomes lean in the cooking, will have a true poison [14] that never vanishes." Agathodaimon said: "Make the poison blossom in the bitters." [15] Know that if you make the fire strong, you will burn the flowers of these herbs. [16] Therefore the sages ordered that the flowers be cooked with the water of the salt, or with the water of the sea, in order that [17] the sun should not burn them with its heat. If <you want> you do the cooking gently, [18] the flowers will not vanish. Know that our red sea is the sea that dyes the most, [19] and if the poison is cooked and made to rot, it becomes a dye that submerges into every body.

(fol. 60b) It is what the sages named with the names of every stone, saphire, emerald, crystal and dust. 2 This is the lamp, about which you asked me (on fol. 37a, 5), and it has to be made by the sages, and it is not 3 from metals, as I told you in the dyeing of the stone, which has four basic elements[40] with different 4 colours. But when they are gathered and operated on, they turn into one colour. So the sage gave it the name of 5 everything from the sea, every bird in the sky and every stone on earth.»

She said: 6 «Then tell me about when you say: «The spittle of the moon and the gum are two composed things".» He said: 7 «The sage told you about that when he said: "Take the spittle of the moon and the gum, and dissolve the two together." 8 He did not order us to solidify the two after they were dissolved, but he ordered us to extract their flowers 9 from their interior. And he declared that if the two are dissolved at the time of the marriage, they would appear more beautiful than 10 the rainbow appearing in the sky, and they would both make every dye cling to them, because 11 if they unite, they become one colour. Look at what Democritus wrote 12 in his four treatises. In all of them, he wrote about the water of sulphur that is extracted from 13 lead-copper, and he declared that nothing could come into being without it. So the spittle of the moon and the gum are 14 composed.»

She said: «Many people have claimed that 15 things should be taken in a state which is not[41] operated on.» He said: «Say to whoever claims that: "Woe unto you, then why did 16 the sage say about its making: 'Take red mercury and solidify it in the body of magnesia'?"»

17 She said: «You are right and you spoke well.» He said: «Do you not see that he said: 18 "Take mercury, then solidify it in the body of magnesia!"? He knows best what he said, 19 and with what one should work. So be careful not to be like the man who reads our books in a way

40 *Arkān* also means corners.

41 Marginal correction.

(fol. 61a) we did not intend, and then falls into error because of his blindness about the truth. His ignorance about what he does not know [2] becomes a sin against the sages, and he accuses them (the sages) of being liars, while he is the greater liar. Therefore I told you that I would never [3] contradict the sages till I die. So if I <told them> have dared to entrust to you some of [4] their statements with what is in it, then I am afraid that God will take [5] this science from me, because I made clear to you what the sages disguised. They would not like [6] to reveal something that they named by a different name, or to name it with its real name. And you will [7] testify that I did not leave anything of these things without making it clear to you, and explaining [8] to you what they meant by it. Often jealousy seized me and prevented me from completing it. [9] Then I would be filled with mercy, so I would complete it for you in another place. So if you see the thing incomplete, look for [10] its completion elsewhere. I have done my best to make it clear without revealing this secret to the ignorant.»

[11] She said: «Then tell me, why is it named 'the sage' after being named silver, gold and copper?» [12] He said: «That is in order that you should know that copper for him is reddish and silver.

She said: [13] «So gold for him is not gold?» He said: «No, (gold is) only an invented name.»

She said: [14] «Then what about silver?» He said: «Silver (also) is only an invented name.»

She said: «And what about copper?» [15] He said: «It is the true copper when it becomes white and when it becomes red, because [16] when it became white the sage [named it silver], and when it became red he named it gold. Most people do not [17] know this copper. Whoever does know it, makes an effort with it on his own in the operation until he makes from it [18] the colour of the mixture in the elixir, the colour of gold and the colour of silver, when it gets mixed with gold [19] and silver.»

She said: «Then tell me what you say about iron.» He said: «I did not order you (fol. 61b) to make use of the iron of ordinary people, but I ordered you to make use of the acacian (*ašqūnī*) iron. Then cast it, and put [2] into it one tenth of its quantity of gold. When it mixes, pound it till it becomes dust.»

[3] She said: «Then what about his statement: "What an amazing thing you are, a thing which is untouchable, holding the element that is touchable.» [4] He said: «That untouchable one is the spirit and the spittle.»

She said: «Then what about his statement: [5] "O body which has no body!"» He said: «The sage is right. It is not a body, and it has in it a body [6] which has no body, so it turns bodies into non-bodies.»

[She said:] «Did they therefore overcome nature [7] and separate from it?» He said: «Concerning their overcoming it (nature), this is because of their kinship. Although it is untouchable, [8] it has in it what was touchable. Therefore it became untouchable. When the untouchable one met [9] the touchable body, it was quick to cling to it because of its kinship, [10] and the untouchable one turned it into incombustible sulphur, and taught it to fight against the fire. This takes place [11] in the dissolution of the other (second) composition. At that time, the lunar colours blossom from it.»

[12] She said: «Which one of the sages said: "O what a moon are you, you spread the light of [13] the sun's rays."» He said: «That is the nature that has nothing on earth similar to her (the nature), who rejoices [14] in her close one, and he enjoys her, and she holds him, and he holds her. And about this the sages said: "Why are you interested [15] in the many things, while the nature is one that wins over everything?"»

She said: «Perhaps [16] you mean the male and the female?» He said: «I have told you that what you need at [17] the beginning of the matter is one, a natural male whose nature is one that wins over that [18] nature. And because of it Democritus said: "Nature rejoices in nature, [19] nature holds nature, and nature wins over nature."»

She said:

(fol. 62a) «The sages spoke in the same way as you have, so explain this statement to me.» He said: [2] «Upon the life of your father, O Theosebeia, he made the composition clear in this statement. Concerning the rejoicing of the nature [3] in the nature, that is because of its meeting with its own particular nature. Concerning the holding, that is because of its kinship to it. [4] Concerning the winning, that is the noblest of all, as it kills the body in a way that does not corrupt, and turns [5] it into a spirit at the completion of the work, after it had been a body. At that time, it holds [6] the other body that does not move, and it rejoices in being concealed within it. So know that.» [7]

She said: «Then tell me about your statement that the sages used two types of descriptions in their books, [8] one true and one false.» He said: «Concerning their true description, they never wrote [9] a true word without putting false ones alongside it, obscuring it with these [10] invented names. Therefore we do not find anyone who wrote a pure true word, unaccompanied [11] by falsities, except for Hermes, when he said: "I found (such a text) on the tablets which my father [12] Šīt had written about the stones when he realised the world was sure to be destroyed, although he did not know whether the destruction would be [13] by fire or by flood." Then Hermes revealed this word, as he had found it [14] in the tablets. He (Hermes) said: "Know that there can never be any dye except from the red stone." [15] As for the other sages, they disguised this stone and named it red, [...], [16] steadfast, the colour of apple, green and yellow flowers, colour of lemon, saffron, [17] black and they named it after all the dyes.»

She said: «[Why did] they strive to hide this [18] stone?» He said: «Because it is the key to this science.»

She said: «Do you think that they did [19] the same with the earth, giving it many names, and hiding it as they did with the stone?»

(fol. 62b) He said: «Yes, they hid it and they named it with other names, even naming it sand, because [2] it is what extracts the colours from their natures. Know that those who study [3] these books most persistently are the the most entitled ones to attain what is in them. If he is successful with it, [4] he will not be free of jealousy concerning it, and he will hope that no other creature will know this [5] work. So, because the sages knew that people are jealous concerning [6] this work, they disguised it in their books, so people would become confused about this science. This [7] science deserves to be doubted. But whoever knows the right path should not be afraid, by the will [8] of God.»

She said: «Tell me, O Zosimos, about their statement:«The best copper for us is the priestly (*kāhinī*) one.» He said: «And [9] I say it now. May whoever does not know the priestly one die in his sorrow. So, my lady, keep it secret [10] as much as you can. Know that it often came out better than what comes out from its origin. [11] Look at the mirror that is mixed with gold and silver, and it will guide you to what [12] completes your composition, as I wrote its completion for you in the fourth letter. [13] Know that if any mirror on earth used by people does not have in it something [14] of that nature, it will have neither a persistent polish nor a fixed shining. So you should [15] put into every composition that you make a suitable part of that thing. Know [16] that if you want to make silver, you should take mercury and mix it [17] with sulphur. And if you want to make from it a lasting vessel, take white lead (*abšimīt*) [18] and tin, and I will tell you how you can make white lead in its proper places. [19] Mix the mercury with white lead and sulphur. It will do (fol. 63a) great work, especially because mercury is from tin. Then the first mercury clings to [2] the other mercury. Know that the making of the litharge can only be from tin. [3] So do not leave aside the science of lead-copper, even if it is copper and the bleaching (the whiteness) [4] never changes, dissolves or alters. This is what Maria was talking about when she said: "Solidify the milk [42] [5] with its gum. It solidifies it in the way rennet solidifies milks of roses. Rot it for [6] many days, and do not become impatient." Know that Maria wrote this statement about the two mercuries. [7] And know that the things which make the outside of the copper white will also make its inside white, because [8] they are what dye its inside and its outside. This is the summary of what we wrote in our honoured books and the [9] *Sarṭamīṭa*. All of our books are one, but we only wrote the truth [10] in the *Sarṭamīṭa* and the others.»

She said: «Then tell me about when you said [11] that you did not find any sage who gave only one name to what is raised in the tube.» [12] He said: «I still say that to you now, but they named it copper, [13] body of magnesia, and mercury.»

She said: «Why?» He said: «Because these names are insufficient [14] for the components of the mixture which are in them, because mercury is only from cast bodies. [15] Therefore Democritus said: "The mercury of cinnabar", meaning by it the mercury that is extracted [16] from bodies.»

She said: «Then tell me about the pure water of sulphur, which is every thing.» [17] He said: «If you make the water of sulphur well, you will make [18] aqzal-gold and purple gold from it, which is the completion of what is sought.»

She said: «Then what about when the sage said: [19] "It dissolves every body, and it dyes every body."?» He said: «By that they meant

[42] We accept the marginal correction, which is probably from a later hand.

(fol. 63b) the pure water of sulphur, because it is the dyer and the dyed.

She said: «How is it dyed?» He said: «It is dyed [2] in the rotting, up to the point that it dyes. Hence his statement: "Cook it with some of the fire of dung, so that by this the dyer [3] and the dyed come into being." And [the statement] "that, which has in it every body, is water", means that [4] a dye only exists with the pure water of sulphur.»

The Book of [5] the Names is complete.
Praise be to God, the master of the two worlds.
After it comes the Book about [6] the Weights.

(fol. 63b) [7] The 3rd Book from the book of Zosimos. It is

[8] The Book about the Weights

[9] In the name of the merciful and compassionate God.

Zosimos said: [10] «I imagine that you have reached what you wanted by my clarifying for you the invented names [11] with which the sages confused the people about this work. If you have achieved [12] your intention, ask about something else.»

She said: «Upon the life of your father, O Zosimos, you spoke [13] with skill and answered with clarity. But tell me about what led the sages [14] to differ about weights.» He said: «Because the basis, the key, [15] and the completion of this matter is the weight. Whoever does not know it should neither expose his money to destruction nor himslf to [16] sadness. However, the sages were not happy to write it clearly, out of jealousy [17], and in order to hide it. I have depicted for you what weights you need [18] at the beginning of "The Book about the Weights". So be satisfied with it, if you are intelligent, because it has (fol. 64a) the truth in it, if you understand.»

She said: «You must answer me about what I asked you.» He said: [2] «Ask whatever you want.»

She said: «You have answered all my questions in a way that I hope [3] God will make me happy with. Do you not remember that you wrote to me that the sages have dispersed the weights? [4] Some of them increased them while others decreased them.» He said: «They did that, because they wanted to hide (them) from you (pl.).»

She said: «Then what about the statement of Maria: "Copper, lead, [6] honoured stone—dissolve them both equally."» He said: «Maria spoke well. Thus what prevented [7] you from grasping it?»

She said: «What prevents me (to understand) is your statement that she rendered the two three.» [8] He said: «She is right when she said: "The two are three." <He said:> «Do you not know [9] that the composed one is a body and water?»

She said: «I knew that.» He said: [10] «So she named it three.» She said: «But she neither explained which copper, nor which lead, [11] nor which stone we should take.» He said: «That is in order that you know that she did not want to be clear in [12] this statement, but she rather wanted the weights to be equal.»

She said: «Your statement has increased [13] my confusion.» He said: «This will not confuse your mind.»

Here is the position of the third picture. (This picture is missing.) [14] It is a yellow viper that eats its own tail and it has four golden knots, taking by its neck [15] a red viper overlaid with silvery water having two knots. And there is the image of Zosimos as we described. [16] In his (right) hand is a balance, whose two scales are yellow. In one of them is Zosimos and in the other is [17] Theosebeia, and the balance is equal with the two of them. In his left hand, he has a balance with [18] two yellow scales, in one of which are two red birds with a green bird between them, [19] and in the other one are three birds, red, green and yellow. They are evenly balanced.

(fol. 64b) And the image of Theosebeia sitting, holding a balance with yellow scales in her hand. (This part of the picture is given on this folio.) [2] In one of them are Zosimos and Theosebeia embracing (*multawīyaīn*, lit.: twisted), and in the other scale are [3] six winged persons, and the balance is equal with them. (The following part of the picture is missing:) And the image of Zosimos and Theosebeia, [4] standing upright, each one pointing to the other in the way we described [5] their picture. Their clothes and their fingers are the same as we described [6] at the beginning of this book.

Fig. 31: Folio 64b.

(fol. 65a) She said: «Explain it to me.»[43] He said: «I tell you that these two, which she called three, 2 became one thing, and she ordered us to take from this one thing, whose origin 3 is two. If she said three, she would be right, as we should take from the two three parts. 4 Because she wanted to hide this weight, she gave each part of this one thing the name of 5 a body. So she took three parts, and she named them three bodies. So when you mix the two, they are both 6 equally from one thing. After we took from those three 7 parts, she ordered us to put with them one part from the male. Thus they become four. And I will make you, 8 my lady, more convinced that if you increase or decrease, the truth remains. But try 9 to do the work quickly, because the thrice-blessed Hermes, said: "One fourth of the body 10 coagulates all the water." Democritus, following Hermes, said: "Put in the composition 11 some of an unburnt body, in order that the poison submerges into the body." 12 These things I have said to convince you more that the body should be less than the water in the other composition.»

13 She said: «Then tell me about your statement: «If I put less, or more, 14 or an equal amount of water, it would not harm it.» He said: «I told you that, but I feared that 15 it might be slow for you. If it were slow for you, you would think badly of it. That is why I ordered you to use the true weights 16 because the sages wrote about them in the composition of (this) work, in order to quickly make you tired. 17 I recommend that you should put three parts from the moisture and one part from the body, 18 because she (Maria) said: "Copper, lead, and honoured stone." And Agathodaimon agreed with her 19 regarding the weight, and said: "Take some chrysocolla, a soft body of magnesia

43 This sentence shows that a part of the dialogue must be missing. Together with the missing part of the picture on fol. 64b, it would make up one folio.

(fol. 65b) and eternal water." These three parts are from one thing. I told you several times, if you [2] remember my statement, that when they are referring to one thing from the composition, they gave all of it that [3] name. Also they often gave that one many names. So when they mentioned [4] one body, and said: "Take two parts or three parts," then it is rather one part [5] from one thing, because it is from one body. And when they mention three names and say: "Take [6] from each one of these names one part", it is because they are three names for [7] one thing. Thus, by this matter, thanks to Agathodaimon, God saved me from a long work in which I was involved, [8] because he said: "Take one part from copper, one part from chrysocolla, one part from saffron [9] and one part from the eternal water; then cook, pound, dissolve and solidify," [10] adding the other things they said which are known to you. Therefore you should know that the weights of three parts are from [11] one thing besides the body. These three, which are from one, are what [12] Maria called copper, lead, honoured stone. So those three names are names for one thing.»

She said: [13] «Then tell me, O Zosimos, about the statement of Democritus: "Take one part from what I mentioned at the end of the book, [14] one part from the ferment of gold, one part from aqzal-gold which is a great blessing having many [15] names, and one part from the eternal water." And he declared that he dyed every body with it.» He said: [16] «Do you not see that he named it the ferment of gold, the blessing with many names and the eternal water? So he named [17] this (one) thing with three names. This is because whenever he took a part from it, he invented a name [18] of a body, so that he took three parts of it, and gave each part a name [19] that he invented for it. So vinegar, ferment of gold and the eternal water are three names for (fol. 66a) one thing. So the weight is three parts besides the body. So, [2] together with the body, the weight became four parts. This is what Agathodaimon said: "The body of copper which is from our work is from [3] four weights." By that he means the four parts, for he named each part [4] a body until it became one stone. This is the stone that became one thing [5] about which Agathodaimon said: «It is from four parts». So he called them bodies [6] in order to disguise them from you (pl.), while they are weights. Therefore Maria is praised, because she agreed with Agathodaimon [7] when she said: "Copper, lead, honoured stone, all of them have to be made equal with [8] the gold." So they are four weights, which have to be taken from the body, because the whole composition is based on these [9] four weights, but the sage named each part of the weight [10] a body and said: "Take one from it" as he wanted to hide the weight. Know [11] for certain that on this weight the composition is based, and then the making white, the making red and the [12] whole operation. If you follow the sage, you will find the true weights they ordered [13] from the cloud and from the composed body. Then the work will come to you in time without error [14] or doubt.

She said: «Tell me about the statement of Hermes: "Put what [15] is similar to the sugar cane in it. If you mix it, it would be better and more worthy [16] to be dyed."» He said: «By this he meant the composition. He ordered us to put [17] 1/8 of the weight of zinc ore (*qidmīā*), and from the gum the equivalent of 1/8 of silver, so that [18] the big vessel receives (emendation) it. Know that Hermes said: "Only put in it [19] the equivalent of 2/6 of the weight of the sulphur that does not burn. Those 2/6 are put (fol. 66b) in the vessel for mixing (emendation).»

She said: «The two statements are contradictory.» He said: «No, they are not, but [2] you do not understand. When the 2/6 are taken, then they are dissolved on [3] 6/6, so they become eight. Then when you transform the 2/6, (the other) 6 remain. So [4] why do you refuse to acknowledge this? But they change their statements, so it is rejected. However, [5] you are more in need of (learning) other things.»

She said: «What about the statement both made: "Solidify the mercury with the copper. [6] The weight of the zinc ore should be two parts, from the pyrite one part, and from the body [7] one part.» He said: «This is also the other composition.»

She said: «Then tell me about [8] when you say: "You must ponder over the weight, and do not accept the apparent weight [9] but the secret weight which they hid because the whole secret is in it." <She said:> So tell me about [10] that secret.» He said: «I start for you with the statement of Democritus and what he said [11] about the weight: "Take one part from the composed one about which I wrote at the end of my book, and one part from [12] the ferment of gold which is the flower of gold, and it is the purple gold. Then cook it [13] with some dung-fire."»

She said: «I do not see here any weight, because he said [14] the ferment of gold and the composition of the water that he wrote at the end of his book, but he did not write [15] a weight for it.» He said: «No, but he said: "Let it absorb as much of it as it can, and cook the plate [16] of silver until you are satisfied with its colour when it is dry." That is because there is no determined weight for the water, [17] but the more the composition is soaked, the more it benefits and the better for dyeing it.»

She said: «What about when you say: [18] "If you do not turn the two into one you are not on the right way."» He said: «Maria [19] said that before me. I meant that you should mix what escapes with what does not escape, (fol. 67a) so the two become one. If you want the whitening, you also introduce sulphur to it. So [2] together with the white sulphur, the two become three. If you want the reddening after you have finished the operation of the whitening, you turn [3] the three into four with the red sulphur, which turns things red. Thus when they become rust, [4] all of them become one.»

She said: «What about when you say: "These big furnaces are named bodily."» [5] He said: «It is only the name of the type, but its name is the Cypriot which is its true name.»

She said: [6] «What is the Cypriot? » He said: «It is the luminous dye.» She said: «So by the big furnaces they meant [7] the luminous dye?» He said: «Yes. They called it furnaces, but its (true) name is [8] luminous dye. In the same way, the kings of Alexandria were using their title-names. But when they wanted [9] the truth they would use their true names.»

She said: «What about when you say: "All of these furnaces [10] have the weight of 100 rutls and nine rutls."» He said: «In terms of their being mixed according to [11] their weights, there are among them furnaces whose weight is one, and there are others whose weights are nine. They are mixed according [12] to this weight. If you then want to increase, you increase, and if you want to decrease, you decrease. This is [13] the whole account, indeed they are nine divided by spiritual nine.»

She said: «Then tell me about your statement: [14] "The sages differed over the weights of the four bodies."» He said: [15] «The composition of the other one is the four. About this, Democritus said: "Take [16] four from the copper, and from the iron that is from the lead, which has the five weights[17] that are the ferment of gold. This is what the sages composed with the sulphur, which [18] is named the seven things." And know that the sages said: "The weight should be equal in [19] the things which they mentioned for the mercury that is from chrysocolla."»

She said: «Then tell me

(fol. 67b) about when you say: "I should know how an idol (*ṣanam*) mixed with gold turns into the colour of [2] a male human being.» He said: «Yes, if you want to do that, take three parts of the gold [3] and two parts of the silver. Then cast the two and make from them an idol. And know that [4] beauty, splendour and colours will appear from it that your eyes never saw before. If [5] the statue is yellow, then you should take one part of the copper and cast it several times and soften it until [6] it turns into something like vapour. Then mix it with the same weight as the first weight. And know that you must know [7] how to make the female idol in order that its power increases like the great power of the human being (the male human being before). Then [8] take one part of the gold and four parts of the silver and mix them until they become [9] one mixture. The colour of the two will be like that of a mirror in clarity and [10] polish. Know that the colour of every idol must be in between these two [11] colours, for its mixture should be from this composition which is the true one, white and [12] black. And the dyed one should be twice of what it gets mixed with. [13] Know that in the books of the sages about the weights, they did not make them clear.»

She said: «Why is that?» He said: [14] «They hid the weight because of their jealousy with regard to people knowing this truth. For among them (the sages) some said [15] "take one part from the litharge," and others said "two parts", and others said "take one part from the litharge [16] and the magnesia". Maria did it like that with regard to the lead-copper although the sage [17] said: "Take one part from the honoured stone and one part from the magnesia which is called opium (*afīūn*)[44], [18] and mix the two and put with them lead-copper".

She said: «Then tell me about

[44] In Egypt, opium is like a black paste, a little of which is put under the tongue to let it melt slowly.

(fol. 68a) when you say: "They put different weights for the dyeing of the wool".» He said: «They did that. One [2] said, "take one part of wool and two parts of alum", and another [3] said, "(take) equal weights". As for the explanation of the sage, he put in one part of wool, one part [4] of alum and four parts of water. As for Democritus, he put in one part of wool [5] and one part of alum. So he rendered the two in equal measures.»

She said: «Then tell me about when you say to me [6] in your book: "If you want the dye to become more saturated and fine, then be wise with [7] the mixture."» He said: «The reason I wrote that to you was to tell you that if you want [8] to make a perfect saturated work, you do it, and if you want something less than that, you do it.»

[9] She said: «So give that to me and teach me from where it comes.» He said: «Understand that [10] the exalted dye and what is less than that come from the mixing at the beginning of the composition. [11] So if you want to make (emendation) the saturated one, put two ounces of golden dust [12] and three ounces of bulls' gallbladders in it. Thus it will become saturated and excellent.»

She said: «Then tell me [13] about when you say: "Some of it must be little, and some of it must be much. [14] < Some of it must be little, and some of it must be much.> And some of it must be much and [15] some of it must me little, then after that it must be equal".» He said: «I already told you that [16] if those which make the clanking were not equal, they would not make a sound. Look at what I have gathered for you, [17] and compare my words and those of the sages. Help me by showing some understanding, for I am not [18] able to write out the weight clearly for you.»

She said: «Then tell me about when [19] Democritus said: "Take four ounces of copper, one ounce of iron, (fol. 68b) and similar weights of lead and tin (i.e. lead 4 and tin 1)".» He said: «The sage said that, and ordered it. [2] As for the ferment of gold, it has no weight. So what has no weight in the books, add in [3] equal measure. Concerning the weight of the making white, Democritus described it at the end of his [4] *Book about the Broth* when he said: "Take one ounce of the male, four ounces of the sulphur and of the silver, [5] two ounces of the sap and the same of the salt, and of the other things the same as these two (i.e. two ounces) because [6] the mercury is the two compositions, and by it everything is made.»

She said: «Then tell me about when you say: [7] "I must not give you a weight for the moisture".» [He said:] «[This is] because Democritus said: "Only the cloud [8] and the rising of the water remains for you." And I swear to you from what he says that if you operate on it well, you will not care whether you increase or [9] decrease the moisture.»

She said: «Then tell me, O Zosimos, how is it that he soaks them with their equal weight, while he said: "Take one weight [10] of antimony and two weights of litharge."» He said: «You are asking me something that the sages did not write about [11] in their books. It is not appropriate for me to write about it to you, but I will tell you as much about it as I know.»

[12] She said: «Do so.» He said: «I think that they mentioned all of the lead separately, [13] in order to have the right weight when they said "one part" and "two parts", because the antimony and the magnesia are [14] one, and the litharge and the white lead are of the same sort (*ǧins*).»

She said: «Then tell me about when you say: [15] "Although Maria said all that Isis (*Asīda*) mentioned about the names, some of it [16] is little and some of it is much".» He said: «Her opinion is that it is equal, because she said in a 1000 [17] places: "Make things equal."»

She said: «Then tell me about when the sage said: "Take one part from [18] the other composition, and a part from the ferment of gold."» He said: «He wanted to tell you that the weight [19] is equal. That is why Isis and Maria ordered us to make the two equal.»

She said:

(fol. 69a) «Then tell me about when you say: "When you see that the ten companions separated and they became five, [2] then after that the five turn into three, and the three into one".» He said: «If you perform your operation well, [3] there will be pure love and harmony between the ten, and what you started will come to completion.»

[4] She said: «Then tell me what the sages meant when they said 'one'.» He said: «By it they meant the origin. [5] Even if they mentioned many things of what entered into the composition, they mentioned them according to their number, and they do so at the time [6] of the marriage, the completion, and the operation, until they reach the ten which Democritus wrote about [7] in his book, naming their names and their operation.»

She said: «Why did they mention the names of the ten?» He said: [8] «Because they are the completion of the number.»

She said: «Then tell me about the other composition.» He said: «It is the copper [9] in which are the four bodies, or rather the six. As for the ferment of gold, the blessing having many [10] names, they are the six things that have to be equal.»

She said: «Then tell me about when you say: [11] "If you want the weights, look for them in metallic bodies and you will obtain them."» [12] He said: «Democritus wrote a weight for that, saying: "Take four ounces of copper [13] and one ounce of iron." And he did not mention a weight for lead and tin. [14] But he said: "Make that like the two [4:1 see fol. 68a, 19 - 69b, 1]." For Maria explained that when she said: "Lead, [15] copper, dissolve the two equally." Know that she and all the sages named (both) copper (and) iron [16] copper. And they named (both) lead and tin lead. Thus Democritus said: "We never found [17] a difficulty more painful for us than the first composition, until we knew the mixture [18] and the weights, and they became mixed."»

She said: «Then tell me about when you say: "We found no [19] sage who dared to write the weight clearly, except by riddles, analogies and allusions.

(fol. 69b) (He said): «That is why I wrote for you at the end of the "Book about the Magnesia" that if you are truly able to obtain the water of sulphur, [2] and you mix it with that, whose weights you did not know well, it will show you some of what you desire.» [45]

She said: «Then tell me about [3] when you say that you will tell me something about the weight that no one before dared to do.» He said: [4] «For my part I will do it, but it is not clear. You will have in it a lesson and a guide with regard to what you like. [5] Some of it must be more than others. Then the weight must be equal, [6] because Maria said: "Lead, copper, honoured stone dissolve them equally." So she named the two three, [7] while they were from one being in terms of the bodies, and one being in terms of the metals. [8] Maria named them three, and she did not clarify for us how much must be from the copper, nor how much must be from the stone, [9] because some of it must be much, and some of it little. And after that it [10] should be equal, because she said. "Dissolve the copper and the stone equally."»

[11] She said: «Then tell me about when you say: "Dissolve the two equally."» He said: «Concerning that, it is from the statement of [12] the sage: "Dissolve the two equally." This can only be after one comes to know the weights of the copper and the stone, and [13] the determining of this weight from various places in the book of Maria. One time she names it iron, [14] one time copper, one time she names it "from four bodies", one time "from [15] three bodies", and one time she names it "from two".»

She said: «Then tell me about when you say: "Make use [16] of the book of Democritus."» He said: «Because he spoke clearly when he said: "Ponder over the four ounces.[17] Among them there should be one ounce of iron." But I tell you that Maria said [18] about the weight of lead and tin: "Mix the two equally." As for the copper and the iron, [19] she put in more of the copper than you thought after that composition,

45 The water of sulphur is mentioned towards the end of the "5th Book about the Magnesia" on fol. 125b.13.

(fol. 70a) because it vanishes in the cooking and one does not find all of it.»

«She said: Then tell me about when Agathodaimon says: [2] "When the things get mixed, neither the weights of the three nor of the four are known."» He said: [3] «In the case of Maria, she put two weights, and she said: "Dissolve the two equally". She kept [4] the bodies secret, but indeed their bodies are copper lead (*nuḥās abār*). When they mix their copper, [5] they put in one part from the copper and one from the stone.»

She said: [6] «Then tell me about the statement of the sages that the weight which they mentioned has to be equal.» He said: «Even if [7] they spoke the truth, it is distorted. But we recognize that distortion after what [8] remained in it. Each part of the two or the four parts becomes part of [9] the stone and the body, because the two things that are lead-copper become one body [10] having four parts. Know that your fire should be moderate, neither too hot [11] because otherwise the flower would get destroyed, nor too cold because otherwise it would not mature, and if it does not mature, its colours will not appear and it will not [12] be able to dye. So you must have patience and be careful not to become annoyed. Know that [13] the more you cook gently and well, the stronger will be the marriage of the elixir and the better will be its dyeing. [14] Know that nature will teach you the measures of your fire, if you have [15] the slightest intelligence, because the moderate fire is suitable for every colour and every dye [16] in every degree (of the operation) until it reaches its final extent, God willing, be He magnified and glorified.»

[17] The 3rd Book, which is The Book about the Weights is completed.
Praise be to God, the master of the two worlds!

[18] The 4th Book of the Book of Zosimos, and it is THE BOOK ABOUT THE COMPOSITION

(fol. 70b) In the name of
the merciful and compassionate God.

Zosimos said: «I imagine, 2 O Theosebeia, that you learnt the weight in the Book that has the images of the weights in the scales.»

3 She said: «Upon your life, I did.» He said: «Then, my lady, ask about something else.»

She said: 4 «So I ask you about the first composition.» He said: «I presented it for you in the figures (*tamāṯīl*) which are at the beginning 5 of this my book, and I made clear for you what nobody before me dared to do, and I told you 6 that they have compositions with different weights.

7 The picture of Zosimos and Theosebeia. 8 He is pointing at her, and they are wearing the clothes and standing as we described at the beginning of this book: 9 the image of Zosimos standing between two figures of Theosebeia, with the appearance and position we described, 10 with him holding the two heads with his hands. And there is the image of Theosebeia, standing upright with 11 a balance in her hand, whose two scales are yellow. In one are Zosimos and Theosebeia, united, embracing, 12 mingling with each other. In the other one there is a figure with two wings, and they are equally-balanced. 13 And there is a picture of a tower on six columns, coloured in red, green, blue (lit.: the colour of the sky) and 14 yellow.[46]

After that comes this saying:

46 The six columns, coloured in the four basic colours, are to be understood in the sense that these columns are coloured in a mixture of the four colours.

(fol. 71a) [… . He said: «…] [47] she ordered you to compose what you need to compose. Know that the nature of mercury is to dye gold, [2] because when the two are cooked, redness appears.»

She said: «Then tell me about her statement: "Take one part of gold, [3] and mix it with three parts of mercury of cinnabar and put it in its vessel. Close the mouth of the vessel tightly, and kindle a gentle fire [4] until its colour changes. Then cook it until it becomes red. Dry and cook with eternal water, so that [5] when the copper is burnt with its water, and its nature is transformed breaking into fragments, and washed, and this is to be done with it several times, [6] the gold will become better than before."» He said: «You have asked me about this several times, but her changing [7] of the names and the operation confuses you. This is the other (second) composition. Did you not read in her book after [8] this what she said: "The exalted, glorified God ordered Moses, peace be upon him, to operate on the tin-stone [9] which holds the dye. And it is cooked until a round stone that looks like a head comes out of it, [10] whose mixture comes from gold and silver, yet it is neither the gold of ordinary people, nor their silver. But it is [11] our silver (and our gold), because they clung to each other, and nothing of it is able to escape because of the harmony between them.»

[12] She said: «Then tell me about the statement of Hermes with regard to the composed cluster.» He said: «This is the [13] first composition: Take one weight of the clear, pure tar which is the origin of that cluster. [14] If you want to dissolve it, put with it some of the gum, the torturer of her husband. [15] When it (the tar) is made to enter in the cooking, it is immediately dissolved and becomes water. After that it has to be pounded intensively until [16] the gum becomes dry.»

She said: «Then tell me about the students (who said): "There was nothing more difficult in [17] this operation than the marrying until the natures, the sun and the moon, married and clung to each [18] other."» He said: «They were right, because when they mixed the bodies with the fugitives they became firm, just as [19] a corpse (*maīyt*) becomes rigid in its tomb. And if you make the harmonious ones marry, the composition will be easy for you, because of the relationship

47 A folium is missing, with the picture of the 4th Book, and the beginning of this dialogue.

(fol. 71b) between them and the speed of their mixing, although the composition is very difficult for whoever does not know the truth. [2] Know that when the North wind comes up and blows strongly, the moisture increases on earth, so [3] the earth is not able to absorb the water, but when the South wind blows, the moisture would be moderate, so the palm trees are fecundated, [4] multiply, and the fruits ripen, and that wind inhibits the rising of the Nile. Therefore when you see that the spirits blow [5] strongly, then know that it is the flood. And this key is for whoever understands.»

She said: «What about when he said: "Put [6] gold in the vessel, and put with it what is necessary until the eastern becomes ten. At the time of the completion you put the twenty."» [7] He said: «I have told you that the reins for controlling this matter and its perfection—after the exalted God—are by the fire, [8] and they have done their best to keep it secret.»

She said: «Explain to me his statement about the solidification of mercury.» He said: «Yes, it should [9] be solidified with its body, which is its relative, and it has to be cooked intensively until the water becomes eternal. [10] Know that if you continue to cook it in it (the eternal water), the mercury gets solidified. In this way the cloud preserves its relative, because it solidifies it.» [11] She said: «How does all of that become solidified?» He said: «Yes. If you understand and put in it what it should have, [12] you will do the work in the right way.»

She said: «Then also tell me about the statement of Šimās: "Take the copper of the truth, the mercury of cinnabar, [13] the filings of gold, and the filings of tin and mix that with the mercury. Put it in a vessel and dissolve it until [14] it is absorbed and turns into the colour of gold."» He said: «How good is what he meant by this statement, that he produces gold [15] to the point that he produces 360 misqal from one karat (*qīrāt*). And I order whoever wants to enter into [16] this work to progress little by little in what he does, until he achieves the goal of the work, otherwise he will regret it.» She said: «Then what is the goal of [17] the work?» He said: «Perfecting the relative with the relative, the seeker with the fugitive, the one who fecundates (the male) with the fecundated (the female), and after that the operation [18] until it turns into red dust. Then it has to be soaked with the eternal water, and after that it has to be soaked with it seven times [19] until nothing of the eternal water remains except what has turned into red dust. Then it has to be left in the other (second) rotting (fol. 72a) until the flowers with their different colours emerge, and the body is dyed <it has to be left in [2] the other rotting until the flowers with their different colours emerge, and the body is dyed> with a dye that does not [3] decrease. Then you pour some of it onto what you know, and it dyes whatever you want, God willing.»

[4] She said: «Then tell me, O Zosimos, about when the sage said that it has nine (alphabetic) letters (*aḥruf*) composed [5] of four parts, and that the first three parts have [6] two letters each.» He said: «This is a composition, because the six, including Venus, are the introduction to the light of the Sun. And Jupiter was driven to her (Venus), hidden in the light [7] of the sun. And at this time, [8] the moony appears (*qamarīya* is the feminine form of the adjective derived from the Arabic masculine noun *al-qamar*: moon), having taken up the nine weights. This is secret [9] of the composition.»

She said: «Then what are the (alphabetic) letters?» He said: «They are the natures, the bodies [10] and the spirits.»

She said: «What are the nine (alphabetic) letters? Are they a body or not a body?» [11] He said: «They are not a body, and the sage knew by the operation that it was not a body, because [12] he made it appear in the body. Do you not see that he made each of the first three parts have [13] two letters?»

She said: «I do not understand what you are telling me!» He said: «I tell you [14] that the composition is made of three things: the first three are the precious triangle and [15] this matter must have a marrying and a completion. Thus you must know that the [16] coppery body of Venus, which has many colours, is hot in its colour and nature, [17] and when it is mixed with the shining moisture, both of them turn into a sparkling pyrite. [18] They both made the yellow-coloured head lean, and they improved its colour, and made its smell delightful, because the subtle parts [19] of these two are what (can) fix the gold, increase its benefit, and extinguish [48]

[48] We accept the correction in the text that reads *āṭfayā* = both extinguish. The original writing gives *aṭīabā* = both make pleasant.

(fol. 72b) its splendour when the two were mixed and married with it (= the gold). If you understand, then I have explained it clearly. [2] Be careful not to neglect the three-folded nine.»

She said: «Then tell me about when the sage said: [3] "Put it on the gold and it will be ~~<intense>~~ aqzal-gold." What is it, and which gold is [4] this? If it is lead-copper, then why does the gold needs to be dyed, as it is (already) perfect [5] in its colour?» He said: «Did you not understand the statement of the sage: "Take mercury from the male and solidify it [6] as usual."?»

She said: «I understood this from your books and the books of the others. But I do not [7] know which male is it.» He said: «It is the mercury which is extracted from our copper. [8] So he ordered you to solidify it, as you solidified the first one.»

She said: «Perhaps [9] you meant the mercury of cinnabar?» He said: «Yes, did you not understand the statement of the sage when [10] he says: "In some dung fire"?»

She said: «And what did he mean by that?» He said: [11] «He meant to dye the gold with the gold.»

She said: «Is it the gold of ordinary people?» He said: «Rather [12] the gold of ordinary people has to be dyed with our gold, and at that time the natures are mixed with the nature.»

[13] She said: Then tell me about when he said: "There is a stone in Egypt that looks like the mother-of-pearl. It is the most precious [14] of the stones of the work that enters into our work, the making of the silver; and gold can only be made [15] with it."» He said: «It is that stone about which you asked me many times. [16] When it is destroyed by the dry fire and the moisture, and put with the eternal body [17] in equal weight, then it is rather the prepared moisture for the clinging nature.»

She said: [18] «Could you describe for me what is called the ferment of gold, and the cultivation of gold [19] so that I can distinguish it from what is similar to it.» He said: «Take from the sparkling one, which has not (fol. 73a) been mixed with the red poison, and has not been operated on. Then put it in a vessel on the fire, so it escapes [2] immediately. If you want it not to escape, mix it with the male and operate on it with the poison. [3] Then take it out [and mix it with some] cinnabar, and put it on the fire, so the cinnabar will prevent it [4] from escaping.»

She said: «And what prevents it from escaping?» He said: «It is because of the desire of [5] the sparkling one for the cinnabar.»

She said: «Then tell me about when you say: "When you (pl.) start [6] with this work, the moon should be at its height, and after that [7] the sun should be at its height in Aries."» He said: «When the moon is at its height [8] its light is strongest, and when the sun descends into Aries it increases its light. [9] So when the moon is eclipsed in the low-point and in the height, the corrupted spirits are reconciled [10] because the body has come near ~~<the sun>~~ the poison. From that you should [11] know the power of the heat because when the sun is eclipsed, it will not be able [12] to operate on the moon. Know what I described and made clear to you (sg.), and operate on it gently [13] so that you will know what is mistaken. Read the books often in order that you will know what we alluded to. And we did not [14] explain the matter clearly, but we described it with analogies of things similar to it. So whoever [15] understands, succeeds in obtaining what he needs. And whoever has a weak understanding should ask God for success.»

She said: [16] «Then tell me about when the sage says that nothing among the bodies is purer than the sun [17] ~~<and its shadow>~~, and a pure sun can only come into being by the sun and its shadow.» He said: [18] «The sage was right and true. And this does not deserve to be questioned, because [19] the sun is the reddish one, and its shadow is the stone which is not a stone. I will make (fol. 73b) you more convinced that whoever wants to make the poison of the sages without these two, makes a mistake which [2] brings him to ruin and the loss of whatever he might possess. However, who makes the poison of the sages from the sun and its shadow [3] obtains the greatest secret.» She said: «How can the poison be from the shadow?» He said: «It is that about which [4] the sage said: "If you do not remove the shadow of the copper, do not blame anybody except yourself."»

She said: «I see that you have returned [5] to the other work.» He said: «You are right, because the shadow became silvery water concealed in the other water [6] and the spirit. Thus the poison can only come into being from the sun and its shadow. As for the shadow, it is [7] the silvery water, and as for the sun it is the red copper.» She said: «Now I have understood.» He said: «Then [8] ask about something else.»

She said: «So tell me about her statement: "Take one part from lead [9] and four parts from mercury."» He said: «This is only in the first cooking. She ordered you to cook until [10] you turn the bodies to be burnt, and the water floats above them, making it (the water) subtle.»

She said: «Where is the body [11] of magnesia? I do not see it here.» He said: «It is there.»

She said: «Then what about her statement: "Copper, lead, [12] honoured stone. If they are dissolved equally, the appearance of everything of the two will be gold."» He said: «She is right. [13] That comes in the other composition. At that time the uncooked becomes cooked, and the cooked [14] becomes more (cooked).»

She said: «Then tell me about when she said: "Take one part from the body and three from our silver."» He said: [15] «From that comes the etesian stone <He said> when the blackness of the silver disappears.» She said: [16] «And when does that blackness cover it?» He said: «At the beginning of the other cooking. Then it turns into [17] an intensive white etesian stone. Then cook it until it turns into red ashes, shading into [18] black, looking like purple. Thereupon soak it with the sulphur and cook it till all of the water [19] is used up.» She said: «Then tell me about when she said: "Take four parts from our silver and two parts from our copper.

(fol. 74a) Then put it in the casting [*sabk*] and leave it for seven days. You will find that the copper is cast [2] with all our silver and both of them become water. Then close up the vessel."» He said: «This is something about which you have asked me [3] more than once. It is the second. So cook it and do not be afraid. Then open it and you will find that the blackness covers [4] the surface of the water, floating on it. Return it to its vessel in order that the blackness of the kohl disappears from it. This is [5] the making black of the silver, the removal of its blackness, and its making white.»

She said: «Then tell me about when she said: "Cook the poison [6] with the water of sulphur, or with arsenic, or with filings."» He said: «She ordered you to take the water [7] of sulphur. Then you put it in a bottle, add to it what you know, and cook it until [8] the copper is destroyed and becomes white. Know that you should cook the mercury with its components, until the components of the mixture become incombustible, and [9] you extract all of its moisture. Then the sediment remains [10] dry, dead, without soul. Then return the moisture on it, and do that several times until [11] you extract all the moisture <and the sediment remains dry, dead, without soul. Then return the moisture [12] on it, and do that several times until you extract all the moisture> and it becomes [13] dead ashes. Know that the more you make an animal move, the quicker its motion will be, and the closer it will keep to its track. [14] But if you hobble it, it will be slow and deviate from its track. Our composition is like that; the more you [15] destroy it by fire, the more it will take rust from the ashes. And the more you return [16] the moisture to the sediment, the better it will dye, and its result will be more precious. So return it seven times [17] and do not become impatient. Continue (to do this) until the moisture picks up and seizes the flowers of the bodies, so that it does not leave out anything which [18] is useful, and the moisture is cooked with the flowers of the bodies which have been taken from the ashes, [19] and they turn into one white pure thing. This is the making of the exalted mercury. Whoever works with something else (fol. 74b) falls into bottomless error.»

She said: «Then tell me about when you say: "If you mix [2] white dust and marble equally, cook the two and squeeze out their water, you extract from them [3] the white water."» He said: «If by its cooking it is softened well, then from it (the mixture) is extracted the water of sulphur, which is extracted [4] from lime, because the herbs pounded the things well and destroyed them with the sulphurs. [5] So the composition becomes red in its essence, which we named the pure water of sulphur, and that sulphur is [6] a incombustible dyer. And it is that about which the sage said: "When the nature holds its relative, [7] it becomes non-fugitive. It clings and is clung to, and the sulphur mixes with the sulphur."»

She said: [8] «And how does the sulphur mix with the sulphur?» He said: «Concerning the first sulphur, it is the relative of [9] the second sulphur. So when the water of the first sulphur mixes with the other sulphur in [10] the second sticking, it clings and is clung to, because the relative held its relative, which is similar to it.»

She said: «And how is it [11] similar to it?» He said: «When the sage extracted the water from the single sulphur [12] by the second sulphur at the beginning of the operation, they became two sulphurs. So the water of the first sulphur prevented [13] the fire from burning the second sulphur. And the second sulphur taught it how to fight the fire.»

[14] She said: «I see that the water of the sulphur is composed.» He said: «Yes indeed, it has in it what escapes from the fire and [15] what fights the fire, which is what the sages named water of alum, water of natrun, water [16] of salt, water of the sediment, water of the sea, water of urine, water of the ashes, and everything that is similar to these [17] names. Know that everything born in the fire is a fighter of the fire. Therefore [18] the sage said that a person should only enter into this work when he knows [19] these things that are useful for their work. So this water has different moistures in it, and it contains

(fol. 75a) hard ones to the extent that it holds onto them, and prevents them from escaping. And without this water nothing can come into [2] existence.»

She said: «Then tell me about the statement of Democritus: "If you put in one part of [3] the other composition and one part of the ferment of gold, which is the flower of gold, and some gum, then [4] you will dye everything."» He said: «You asked me about it before. Do you not see [5] that the nature is composed, and not single? Or do you not see that the sage said: [6] "The nature is one, and that nature wins over the one nature."? Know [7] that the one (masculine) and the one (feminine) is (sg.) composed, and know that Ostanes said: "Nothing has [8] to be used in the operation that is not composed." So do not doubt the statements of the sages if you recognize their worth, [9] because the exalted and glorified God was greatest in their eyes, and they were too indifferent to worldly things to say anything but [10] the truth. So do not doubt after this.»

She said: «Then teach me, O Zosimos, the way to know [11] how the cloud must cling and is clung to.» He said: «If you see it (the cloud) clings to the bodies while they are alive, then [12] it (the cloud) will cling to them while they are burnt, and especially to our copper, which we call pyrite [13] and with other similar names. So it is the right way.»

She said: «Then what about Maria saying: [14] "If you do not find a cloud, then take cinnabar."» He said: «The cinnabar and the cloud are the body [15] of magnesia. Rather she said: "If you do not know the cloud, know the cinnabar." So you have [16] to read the books and make them part of you (memorize them) by experiments and reading, because experiments and reading [17] will guide you to the truth.»

She said: «Then tell me about when you say in brief: "You should [18] take some of the gum of the sages and the water of sulphur and put them in the bottom of the vessel. [19] Then put with it the incombustible sulphuric water."» He said: «I told you the truth, but (fol. 75b) you do not understand.»

She said: «If it is like that, what can I do?» He said: «When you mix these [2] things, then set them on fire.» She said: «Thus advise me: Do you think I should begin by mixing [3] the herbs with the water?» He said: «No. Better begin with the dust and after that mix [4] the dust with the water, then mix the herbs [with it].» She said: «What are the herbs?» He said: «They are [5] the flowers.»

She said: «Tell me more.» He said: «Then cook these things in the vessel which [6] the sages ordered you to use. Then you should soak the water with the gum. Know that when you open [7] the vessel you will find that the herbs are burnt, and their colours and their dye remain.»

She said: «Which dye is [8] that?» He said: «It is the spirit which came out of the water of sulphur, because it has such a power and nature that [9] if you write it on a human body, it would not vanish until he dies. And if you splash the copper with it, [10] while the water is hot, it will remain forever and not vanish. This is the power of the water of sulphur.»

She said: «Then tell me about [11] the burning of the sages.» [He said:] «The burning of ordinary people you already know, because it is entirely destruction. However, the burning of [12] the sages is that they take their bodies, which are good for their work, then they burn them with their sulphur which [13] neither gets burnt nor burns. Then they put them in a vessel of glass. And know that when its dyeing is saturated and [14] its burning well done, it becomes strong and its flower will appear like the rust of copper. Therefore I ordered you to make it rusty in [15] a vessel of glass, in order to preserve it and to make it subtle. And your vessel should face the qibla and the eastern direction. [16] And know that if one looks at the interior, it is dominated by coldness and moisture.»

She said: [17] «Then tell me about the statement of Agathodaimon who said: "Whoever achieves the making of this poison has gained [18] the comfort and happiness of the world."» He said: "I tell you the same, because this [19] dew is the poison, and it is what makes the natures subtle, and turns them into fine dust, because it has a power that makes (fol. 76a) the natures subtle. Nothing accepts them (the natures) better than it (the dew), and nothing is a better dye for them. If you want to know [2] the power of this poison and its ability to fragment things, take the gold that is the purest among the metals. [3] For nothing is stronger to fight the fire or anything else. If you want to make the poison enter quickly [4] into it, then mix with it the wax of the sages, which you know is suitable for this [5] poison. That is why Maria said in her "Epistle about the Dissolving of the Idol": "Take mercury and sulphur, [6] and pound them both with gold until all of it turns into a dyeing poison." As for me, I do not solidify anything [7] of the mixture with the poison, except the water of sulphur alone. When it is mixed with the poison, it is named mercury and sulphur, and [8] it dyes more strongly than before.»

She said: «Then tell me about the statement of the sage<s>: "Take mercury [9] from arsenic and sandarach and coagulate it as usual." And he did not say: "Coagulate it in the body of magnesia", [10] but he said: "Coagulate it as usual."» He said: «This is because it has coagulated before that, at the beginning of the work, but [11] this is the second coagulation.»

She said: «With what does mercury coagulate?» He said: «With the hard bodies, [12] which fight and conquer the fire. Do you not see that the sage is content with his first statement, when he said: [13] "Coagulate it in the body of magnesia."? And after that he only said: "Coagulate it [14] as usual."»

She said: «And what does "as usual" mean?» He said: «Coagulate it the second (time) [15] with the same as you did the first (time). Know that in the second (time) it coagulates more quickly.»

She said: [16] «Then tell me about when Democritus replaced the other (second) composition by the first.» He said: «This is because he brought it from [17] below to above.»

She said: «Then what about your statement that he made clear in his book when he named his composition [18] copper, iron, tin and lead.» He said: «It is what ~~<the sage named it for you>~~ [19] we named magnesia. As for our lead, it is one part of antinomy and two parts of litharge.

(fol. 76b) Thus when the sage mentions lead he rather means magnesia that is from the body. [2] So leave aside all lengthy explanations, because when we mentioned lead, it is not the lead of ordinary people but our lead.»

[3] She said: «Then tell me about when you say: "I put the composition into the vessel before [4] I burn it." Thus I do not know the burning of the bodies.» He said: «Are you ignorant about this?»

She said: «I thought that it [5] would be burnt in the vessel.» He said: «Do you not see that the sages <did not> put it in its vessel until [6] they had burnt it and made it white? When you see that the vapour comes up, then know that the bodies have broken into fragments [7] and are burnt. Otherwise, continue its (the composition's) cooking until the bodies get burnt, at which time [8] the vapour comes out quickly.

She said: «Then tell me what burns the bodies?» He said: [9] «The burning is the head of the work and its beginning. When the ignorant heard that Democritus said: [10] "Take cloud of arsenic, put it on copper or on sulphuric iron, so it becomes white.", [11] they did not know what he meant. So they burnt the copper with the sulphur, and the iron with the magnesia, although [12] this is not the burning which the sage meant. This is a destructive burning, but all the burning of the sage is [13] whiteness and making white. And concerning the operations they mentioned, it is the making white. Thus the first burning [14] is the making white; and with regard to the second burning, all of it is making red. Therefore the sages said: "Burn it a [15] white burning."»

She said: «Then tell me about when Maria and Agathodaimon said: "Take the bodies [16] while they are alive. Then cook them with the cloud and the water of sulphur."» He said: «Democritus said: "Cook the cloud [17] with castor-oil, put in it some alum, and mix both of them with tin." I tell you that [18] these operations are one complete operation for one thing. So when they mention the fat or any of [19] the moistures, they mean the water. And when they mention some of the bodies, they mean the composed one.

(fol. 77a) And when they mention some of the dusts, they mean the sulphur.»

She said: «Then tell me about [2] when you say: "The water of silver."» He said: «The making white must take place in it in order that the sulphur becomes mixed [3] with its water, which we named water of sulphur when it is mixed. And I order you that it should be more united. Therefore [4] I warn you against mistakes and the corruption in the first mixture. Some of it you can know by sight, and some [5] you do not know. So watch out for where you are afraid that error might come from. And be cautious [6] with gentle treatments, perfect mixing, and the measures of the fire, because they are the enemy, who can most readily bring misfortune. [7] And you should also put the metals at the beginning of your mixing of the things. Then let the pure [8] of them be the last thing that you mix it with, in order that the flower of the pure one does not disappear with the flower of the arsenic.»

She said: [9] «What about when you say: "Do not be misled by the lead of the people, for I only meant by it our black lead."» He said: «Why [10] do you not blame Hermes for mentioning the lead? Do you not see that he mentioned a single lead, and [11] Democritus was right that it is not the lead of ordinary people, but it is the lead of the sages, whose whiteness increases the more they burn it. [12] Therefore Democritus named all of the composition body of magnesia, black lead, [13] and lead-copper, and they named it (the composition) mercury, metal, stone and "body with a nature". When [14] these things are united and mixed, they become one thing, which is called the body of magnesia.»

She said: [15] «Then tell me about the dog and the wolf and your writing about them in the books.» He said: «The wolf looks similar to [16] the dog when one sees them, but they are different in their interior. The wolf is a thief and the dog is [17] honest-protective. Therefore the sages mentioned them in the books. They took the dog as a [18] guardian for it (the work), because it stays with it (the work) pushing the heat of the fire away from it (the work).»

She said: «How is it that it resembled a dog?» He said: «Because [19] the dead body is what was killed and made lean in the moisture. They represent that (fol. 77b) body in the image of a dead human being wrapped in his winding sheet (*akfān*), and his father was entrusted with him, who [2] is the dog that guards him.» [as an example for the internal relationship in our book see the picture an its description on fol. 152a]

She said: «What do they want from the human being?» He said: «Extracting his soul which is in the body of that dead person, to which the moisture is entrusted for preservation and feeding, and the human being is then the vessel of the soul. Thus when the sages wanted to introduce a soul [5] into a body, they said (emendation): "Tie it to the ropes of Osiris (*Ūšīris*), in the nerve of Osiris (written wrongly as *Āndisīris*), [6] and to the veins of the palm trees, and to the hair of Isis (*Asīdā*), because the ropes of Osiris (*Ūšīris*) are the channels of the blood which [7] run in the body, and by these veins the body is moistened and warmed. As for "the nerve of [8] Osiris (*Ūšīris*)", it is the nerve that we have in our bodies. As for "the veins of the palm trees", he meant the blood by [9] which the body exists. As for his statement "to the hair of Isis", he meant the preserver of the body. [10] Just as the soul has been tied to the body and loved staying in it, being close to it, [11] the sages made the moist spirit to be the preserver of the dry body. [12] So it preserves, improves, and ameliorates it (the body). And the sages called that moist spirit [13] by many names and many colours.»

She said: «Tell me about when the sage mentioned [14] the magnet and its attraction to iron by nature.» He said: «That is because I was afraid [15] you would think that this work is only done with a talisman (*ṭilsam*), because some sages [16] mentioned talismans in their books.»

She said: «Why did they do that?» He said: [17]«In order to make the ignorant give up hope about this science. As for mentioning the magnet and the iron, [18] I wrote it for you as an analogy. In the same way as the magnet attracts iron by its nature, and the seed [19] of the olives makes the eight-legged animal come out of the sea by its nature, (fol. 78a) likewise our work attracts our nature by nature.»

She said: «In this you have spoken well, O Zosimos.» 2 He said: «I will make you more convinced with a statement of Democritus: “I found something amazing in the book of 3 my teacher (Ostanes), and it is that ‘nature enjoys nature, nature 4 overcomes nature, and nature holds nature.’”»

She said: «By God, Democritus spoke well in this.» 5 He said: «He only speaks well in your opinion when you understand the meaning 6 of what he says. More clear than that is his statement: “Why should we be interested in the many things, while the nature 7 is one?” And he [also] said: “The sages hid the true nature in between false natures.” 8 And he [also] said: “How wonderful are you, O heavenly natures, that you dye the natures.”»

She said: «Then tell me about 9 your warning me when you ordered me to cook the gum, that I should make the moon (*qamara*, femīnīne form of *qamar* = moon, which in Arabic is masculine) flow in its courses. 10 And it should have with it the stars, which are its equivalents.» He said: «That is because if it (the feminine moon) misses 11 any of them, its blood will be incomplete. And if you make the moon (*qamara*) flow with all of its stars, 12 and leave it until it becomes full with their (the stars) blood, its (the fem. moon) blood will be complete, prepared for dyeing whatever you want.[49] 13 And I will tell you another one: If you are slow to take it (the fem. moon), it will all become black because the intensity 14 of the heat of the fire will have ruined the flowers of the herbs. You should take 15 the airy water quickly, and know that the sediment which remains at the bottom has the taste of 16 salt, and what is quickly taken from the above is sweet and delicious. This is because the sky seizes 17 the dew from the sea, then it (the sky) returns it (the dew) to it (the sea). Thus that dew which the sky returned will be a nutrient 18 for the sea. Know that if that dew stays long in the sea it becomes salty. So you should take the sweet one from the salty, and whoever knows that sea will not die of thirst,

49 Line 9-13 have the feminine form for moon.

(fol. 78b) because he cannot drink from it (the sea) when it is salty. Therefore Hermes said: "Sweeten the sea with the [2] airy water, because if the sea is washed with that water it becomes pure."»

She said: «Then tell me about when you say [3] that you want to clarify for me everything that the sages mentioned.» He said: [4] «As Hermes wrote about the gravediggers (*dafāfina*): for every ten gravediggers he made one gravedigger (*daffān*) with a spade in his hand, [5] which he raises with both hands above his head. And it is the first of the gravediggers of the Scorpion, while it (the Scorpion) is in [6] the house of Aries, and the rising and setting of the Sun, and it (the gravedigger) is the master of the cold North wind. That wind is [7] the mistress of every soul in life, which enters and comes out from us. And the image of this [8] gravedigger is all white, so when its wind (North wind) blows, it makes everything white. And this gravedigger has [9] in it male and female, and it makes itself black, and in it every spirit and every water is born, and it is [10] the sea of the cloud. So it takes hold and grasps it and is not able to separate from it (sea of the cloud). This is what [11] Hermes said in *The Key* "Know that when the ~~<cold>~~ North wind blows, it stirs up [12] the clouds and pulls them towards it." So he compared this wind with the vessel that is called cupping glass (*miḥyama*, medical term), [13] and this cupping glass looks like the head of a human being towards which the vapour of the body [14] and the interior rises. That cupping glass is like this.»

She said: «You are enigmatic in this statement.» [15] He said: «I tell you that in all of what I said I meant the broth, which [16] you know.

She said: «Then tell me about when you say: «The ignorant take bodies that are neither [17] mixed nor mingled in the right way, so they change the silver in a way that is [18] not fixed. Whenever they cast it, the blackness disappears.» He said: «That is because they neither [19] combined, nor mixed, nor operated on the bodies well.

(fol. 79a) If they had mixed and operated well, harmonising the natures, they would have changed the silver in an everlasting way. In the case of anyone who [2] does not mix and operate well, that blackness disappears after one, sometimes [3] two, or sometimes after three castings. Some of it disappears little by little, [4] until the poison and the mixture disappear. Know that the works of the sages vary in their quantities, [5] because the plates are sometimes thin or thick, sometimes [6] few or many, and sometimes the things are pure or impure. [7] The disagreements of the sages came from this because the plates are sometimes thin or thick. From there came [8] the disagreement about the dissolving of the body of the gold in the work. So if you want to dissolve [9] the gold, take the gum of herb, then mix it with the water of natron and rub it [10] with pure wool until it becomes like tar or thick honey. Then mix [11] the plate with both of them and leave it for three or four days. So it dissolves, because the copper [12] is like the human being. Whoever attains this science and is then captured will not wait [13] long until he frees himself, and builds mosques (*masāǧid*) and minarets (*madāyin*), God willing. This is because [14] he will multiply gold like a man who cultivates a field of wheat. So he obtains from it a great deal. [15] Thus the gold is sown in white earth that is called acacia (*ašqūnīā*). Without [16] this earth, which is the gum, nothing can be, because with the gum he multiples [17] the gold, and with it he obtains the abundant provision that the exalted God bestows upon us [18] by His inspiration.»

She said: «Then tell me about when you say to me: "Put [it] on iron, lead, [19] copper and tin so that it becomes silver, and on the silver it becomes gold."»

(fol. 79b) He said: «When the ignorant heard the sage's statement, they thought that [2] all of these bodies are dyed into gold, but this is a mistake.»

She said: «Which one of them [3] should be dyed in order that it turns into silver?» He said: «Our lead-copper, which [4] we name silver when we operate on it and make it white. And also like that we name it salt and copper.» [5] Know that if we increase the fire under this silver which is from our work, it becomes [6] salt.»

She said: «Then tell me, O Zosimos, what led the sages to say different things [7] about melting, dissolving, making alumy, making thin, and the work which comes between that?» He said: [8] «The sages differed about the names, the dyeing of the stone and the work. [9] They did so because they did not want to reveal this secret. But I tell you that all of these things [10] are one, and one work. They differed about the names, [11] but the work is one. I will tell about this statement of mine by citing a reliable witness, for [12] Democritus said: "One pounding is sufficient for all the stones, and [13] one dissolving is sufficient for everything, and one composition of the poison makes [14] many colours appear." So do not pay attention to the many things, the dissolving, the refining, [15] the melting and the purification they mention, because all of this is one thing. But Democritus summarised [16] this one work, and, in the place of these things, he put the moistures [17] such as honey, vinegar, fat and similar things for the dissolving, because he knew [18] that neither the dissolving nor the melting nor any of these things can be done without the moisture. [19] That is why these names have been left out.»

She said: Then tell me what are the gold, the silver,

(fol. 80a) the aqzal gold and the purple gold?» He said: «This comes [2] in the other (second) work, because when it is solidified it turns into a silvery stone, and the sage orders you [3] to soak and to roast it until it turns into red dust. That colour is called gold. [4] Then he orders you to soak and to roast it (again), and that colour turns to an aqzal colour. When [5] it dries, you soak it and you roast it (once more), so that it turns into purple gold, and (by that) he means the colour. [6] And I tell you that the more you soak and roast it, the more it takes a colour that is better than its [7] previous colour. So continue to soak and to roast until it takes the purple colour, [8] God willing.»

She said: «Then tell me about when you say: "Take the male which was made white, and make it red [9] with the eternal water, in order to make the head of the world from it."» He said: «The male is the reddish one, [10] and the eternal water is the first sulphur. If the two are mixed and cooked, they become water. Then [11] they become a stone, and then they turn into dust. At that time you should soak it. When you read [12] in the books about a red male, then it is this one.»

She said: «So what is this red male?» [13] He said: «It is the big secret, and only from the male does the redness come[14] as well as the perfect dye.»

She said: «When does that come?» He said: «When it (the red male) is cooked with its [15] eternal water, the eternal water will turn the male into silver, and the male will turn the eternal water into gold: [16] Thus, my lady, I have made clear to you the making white and the making red of the male. So understand! [17] I neither meant the silver of ordinary people nor their gold. Know that!»

She said: «Why is the sage saying: [18] "O you moon, you make the light appear from the light of the sun ray (singular in the text)?"» He said: «That (the moon) is the nature [19] which has nothing similar to it on earth, and it feels happy with its relative (the light of the sun ray), and it (the sun) feels happy with it (the moon).

(fol. 80b) And they hold each other, and it (the nature) is that about which the sages said: "Why should you be interested in [2] the many things, while the one nature wins over everything."»

She said: «What is everything?» [3] He said: «It is the winner, which wins over what was not possible to be conquered.»

She said: «Maybe you mean the male [4] and the female?» He said: «I told you that all you need at the beginning of the matter [5] is one natural male, and one nature which wins over that natural one. With [6] regard to this, Democritus said: "Nature rejoices in nature, nature [7] holds nature, and nature wins over nature."»

She said: [8] «The sages said something like what you said about this. So explain to me this statement.» He said: «Upon the life of [9] your father, O Theosebeia, in this statement he made the composition clear for you. As for the rejoicing [10] of nature in nature, it is for its meeting with the nature of its own (nature). As for the holding, it is because [11] of their relationship. As for the winning, which is the most exalted thing, it is for its killing the body in a way which is [12] not corrupted, and its turning it (the body), after it was a body, into a spirit on the completion of the work. [13] Then it (the spirit) holds the other body, which does not move, and it rejoices in its being concealed [14] in it.»

She said: «Then tell me about when you say: "Every idol whose colour is in between [15] these two colours is the true one.» He said. «I tell you that also. This is because [16] it only can be in between these two colours by the composition of [17] the white and of the black, which is the true one (the composition).»

She said: Then tell me about when you say: "This [18] soft sulphur is not able to burn our copper except when the sulphur is composed, [19] then it burns it. When the sulphurs burn it (the copper) the sulphurs disappear, and the (fol. 81a) copper remains soft, white, and good and the sulphur does not burn it (the copper), except after many days.» [2] He said: «Therefore we kept secret this burning, in the way the sages wrote it in their books. [3] For that, beware of impatience in pondering and thinking over what they wrote, because this operation [4] I wrote for you is the operation of the sand, from which the Egyptians made the treasures.»

[5] She said: «Then tell me about when you say: "The copper can never become black unless [6] it is mixed with gold and silver."» He said: «And I will tell you more, because [7] its colour can neither have the colour nor the brightness of a human being, nor can any [8] precious colour appear from it, except when it is composed.»

She said: «Why is that?» He said: «Because it is single.»

She said: «[The question is missing» He said:] [9] «Because all of the sages named it magnesia, and Democritus made clear the matter of the magnesia, [10] for he said that the magnesia is the moist and the dry things when he said: "Take the lead, [11] whose moisture has been extracted by the snowy, starry earth, and the alum. Then cook [12] it with a gentle fire and mix it with the pyrite." By this statement we know that the pyrite, [13] and what is similar to it, is dry. And the saffron and the safflower, and what is similar to them, are moist.

She said: [14] «Then tell me about when you say that the sage told you: "Are you not afraid of God, O Zosimos, when you say [15] something different from what the sage said?"» He said: «That is because he hated my enigmatic statements, and he wanted us to[16] make it clear for whoever understands the statement of the sage, which he disguised. For the sage ordered [17] us to make white lead (*abšimīt*) and red lead (*sarīaqūn*), and fixed, strong colours out of it. I pretended [18] that he ordered you to turn them into spirits, and if this were true, the sages would have searched for something [19] fixed, and the statement of the sages that lead has a relationship with mother-of-pearl (*ṣadaf*) would be false.»

(fol. 81b) She said: «Then tell me about when the sage said: "Ponder over that for which we did not give a weight, then put it [2] in equal weight."» He said: «They wanted to educate us through it, so that we would know the natures, because nothing is good for these [3] natures except our moisture, and they are neither mixed nor come to exist except with it (the moisture). [4] Democritus said with regard to this: "I did not omit anything for you except the cloud and the raising of the water." He wrote [5] a weight for that when he said: "Take four parts of copper and one part of iron." [6] He did not mention here a weight for lead and tin, but he said: "Make them [7] in equal weights." The confirmation of my statement to you is the statement of Maria: "Lead, copper, dissolve both of them equally."»

[8] She said: «I understood what he said.» He said: «Iron and copper were named copper [9] by all the sages and lead and tin were named lead (see also fol. 69a.15). Therefore Democritus complained about [10] the hardship that he found in the mixing until he knew the natures, the mixing and the weights.»

[11] She said: «Then tell me, O Zosimos, how the four natures change into something different than their natures.» [12] He said: «That is because when the dust and the water united in the operation and the operation was completed, [13] the two turned into an airy fire because the fire likes to go up into the air, and that [14] fire was dust and water before. So when the two mixed, they became a rising fire.»

[15] She said: «What transformed the natures?» He said: «The mixing of the subtle part of the natures [16] with each other. Therefore the sages named the four bodies natures. [17] When they are mixed with the poison they dissolved and turned into water. This is like when water, air, and [18] sun come together in the sky, they cling to each other and they are no more able [19] to separate. Nobody is able to obtain the sought-for benefits until

(fol. 82a) the four seasons of the year take place in them so they transform them, and the exalted God makes emerge 2 from them what He wants (and) the way He wants. In this way, our work transforms the natures and they transform into 3 each other, and the exalted God makes emerge from them what He wants according to His will.»

She said: 4 «Then tell me about what you said, when you wrote to me in "The Epistle of Lead-Copper, Sulphur, 5 and the Rest of the Things" that you obtained another gum which clung to the fugitives and agreed with 6 the lead.» He said: «What moved me to mention this gum and to write about it 7 to you, is that I found some people who were looking for this work. They said: "O Zosimos, 8 we studied the books of the sages, but we did not see anything of the work. So give us your attention." I told them. 9 "O you people, you are lacking another gum, in accordance with the lead and the sulphur." They handed me 10 a book of Hermes and I read it. When I arrived at the place where his students asked him, 11 saying: "O teacher, we made this thing six times, but it did not 12 dye anything," I told them: "Your error arose from this. You should search for 13 another gum."»

She said: «O Zosimos, which gum is this?» He said: «It is the gum 14 which the sages named the cultivation of gold. Upon my life, it is the key to the furnace. <He said:> While 15 I was talking to them, a sage came whom I liked to meet. He said to me: "O Zosimos, 16 write about this gum in your books, for you need it." So I wrote about it for you in order that you learn from it 17 what the sage ordered me, and how to say it. I mentioned the book of Democritus, where he said: 18 "Take the plate and mix it with vinegar, *šaḥīra* (vitriol?) and alum:" So I knew that he meant 19 the operation of lead-copper, about which he said: "Pound the incombustible sulphur with *sūzīn*, colocynth (*qalqant*), (fol. 82b) and pure water." I laughed in astonishment because the sage said the truth, but jealousy prevented me [2] from telling them the truth. So I went away on my own, obedient to jealousy.»

She said: «Then tell me, [3] O Zosimos, about your big dream about the young man you saw fighting the dragon.» He said: «If you understand [4] the meaning of this big dream, you will obtain useful knowledge. When the young man saw me, he called to me for help [5] against the enemy (fem.) of Memphis. I took one leap and came upon that enemy. I took a two-pronged [6] iron, wanting to kill the dragon. But it turned towards me, hissed in my face, and threw me back [7] 28 cubits (1 cubit in Egypt is 0.58 meter), yet I did not fall down but remained upright. Then I leapt at it again, [8] but the young man whom I wanted to help said: "Stop!" Then he took water and with it cut off the head of the dragon. He went up to it, [9] saying: "Give me what you swallowed." He ordered it to do that. Thus it seemed that he could extract from it (the dragon) an egg of [10] a crocodile. Then he put it (the egg) aside, so I thought that it was the egg of the dragon, from which another one [11] like it would emerge. So I thought he had treated it (the dragon) unjustly. The young man said to me: "O Zosimos, it is not a dragon's egg, but [12] a crocodile's egg. But it does not rot, and especially it does not become blood yet. [13] But take the food which has been cooked in the stomach, and divide it equally and justly into four [14] for the corners of the body. Then gather it and turn it into one [15] unmixed thing, pure ashes. Then suspend it and raise it up until it becomes purified."»

She said: «Then what happened?» He said: [16] «When the young man had finished with the dragon, he said to me: "Did you see what sort of dragon we killed?" Then he led me [17] to the mountain, and I found all of a sudden that I am a rock like alabaster.»

She said: «Then tell me [18] about the statement of the sage: "Turn the natures uncracked, and the dyes into [19] non-fugitives." How can that be?» He said: «He did not mean the sulphur alone, (fol. 83a) but by that he meant the first sulphur and the bodies which were whitened, softened, [2] and whose squeaking and moisture disappeared. This is because those bodies were cooked, made rotten, [3] and they got filled with the white sulphur so that they became incombustible. [4] So when they mixed with the white sulphur, they did to it what the sulphur did to them. This is because [5] there is one sulphur from all of the bodies, and it is mixed with the sulphur, and joined with [6] the other white (sulphur). So those two sulphurs become one sulphur, and [7] the natures clung to each other, and they did not separate, and they became one mixture. And they are not as [8] they were before that, as they are four mixtures and four natures, because when they were united [9] they turned into one thing, whose first natures have been changed, so they turned into a new dyeing, not vanishing poison.»

She said: «I asked you about the cracking and the separation [11] but you talked about something else.» He said: «By God, you noticed that well, and I will give you a clear explanation. [12] They are neither fugitives nor do they separate when the vapour (*buẖār*) rises from the vapour (*āṯāl*), because the water [13] took the flowers of the bodies which could not escape from the fire. And they are [14] these things that the sage mentioned at the beginning of his statement saying: [15] "You should put iron, tin, copper and lead for [16] silver, and silver for ferment of gold, and ferment of gold for every body." [17] So this is what he said <for> and he mentioned their bodies, so all of them became [18] one sulphur. When the other sulphur was mixed with them, the two became two sulphurs: [19] one sulphur entered into the first work, and one sulphur entered into the second (work). When both of them are cooked (fol. 83b) together, they hold each other. So they call them once gold, [2] once silver, once ferment of gold and once [3] ferment of silver. That is after they became rotten and turned into gum that is dyed [4] by the bodies. So they became sulphur mixed with sulphur.»

She said: [5] «Then tell me about when the sage said: "I want to write one single book, and it is about [6] the dye."» He said: «He made clear that it is one, and that it is that one dye, [7] and (they gave it many names) in the same way as they gave mercury—which is one—many names, such as sulphur, [8] water of sulphur, and the names of every moisture. Likewise they named the natures [9] after every stone, every dust, every sand and every dry thing, However, [10] Democritus gave the best clarification when he said: "Take the gum [11] of acacia"»

She said: «Then tell me about when you say: "Whoever knows the metals [12] which come into your (pl.) work should rot them with a gentle fire until they turn into blood."» He said: [13] «I still say that, because the nature which is concealed in their inside is not extracted [14] except with a gentle fire, by kindness, and flattery to them. This is because the sage said: "If treated gently [15] and operated on as it should be, you will bring the concealed nature to the outside." [16] Anyone of good sense and judgement should dissolve the natures, mix them, change them, [17] and do this repeatedly until the dye that he seeks appears from them. This is because copper is like the [18] human being having body, soul and spirit. In this way, the waters that remain from [19] the dye become stagnant water, then it rots, and it becomes blood, then that blood turns into (fol. 84a) countless fish (*ḥītān*, whales?). Know that if you do not put dung on the earth and rot it with water, [2] there would be no hope or benefit in it. The earth in which [3] linen and papyrus are sown is also like that. If you do not make it rotten with dung and water beforehand until [4] you turn it into mud, you cannot hope that it will produce (anything). I have now given you lengthy allusions, [5] so understand!»

She said: «You explained to me that the ferment of the bread is from the bread. If [6] your statement is right, the ferment of the gold must come from the gold.» [7] He said. «That is a good question. But ponder over what Democritus said [8] about these bodies that must enter the composition: [9] "Nothing is greater, more exalted and more beneficial for dyeing than these bodies."»

[10] She said: «What is their benefit?» He said: «Because gold is concealed in these [11] bodies in the same way as the kernel of the flour is concealed in the chaff, and the chaff is (concealed) in the [12] ear, and the ear is (concealed) in the stem. Thus whoever has understanding should thresh (*yadris*) [13] in order to extract the grain of the wheat from the ear, then the grain has to be ground, thus [14] the flour is extracted from it. Then the subtle part of that flower has to be extracted. This is the same for these [15] bodies. You should destroy them by pounding, and ruin them with [16] a gentle fire, in order to extract from them the gold concealed in their subtle part, and [17] that becomes the ferment of gold. In this regard Agathodaimon said: "After the [18] making rusty of the copper, its purification, the pounding of its pounded and its becoming black, and at the end of [19] its being white, an exalted redness comes into being."»

She said: «Then tell mc about when you say:

(fol. 84b) "The dyer and the dyed turned into one dye".» He said: «I do not know of a dyeing on [2] earth where the dyer and the dyed became one except for [3] this. That is why sharp-sighted and intelligent people became more confused about it. Their confusion increased [4] because whenever we named it with a name of the things that are in it, we were telling the truth, because [5] all of these things are in it. This is because they turned into one thing, so whatever name we give [6] to that one which is in it, we are telling the truth, be it a moist thing, a dry thing, [7] a stone, or a metal. It is in that hidden secret, and we are truthful about it.»

[8] She said: «You have not made clear to me how the dyer and the dyed became [9] one dye.» He said: «The water is the dyer, and the earth is the one that is dyed by it. When the two are mixed [10] they become one dye. This is what confused whoever has no knowledge about our books.»

She said: [11] «Then tell me about when you say that I should be careful about the fire when I start the work.» [12] He said: «Yes, at the beginning of the composition you should (just) dissolve it. When it gets dissolved, it laughs. [13] Then let the male enter into it, and know that at the moment the male enters the fire [14] it escapes with the spirit, and does not remain if you do not make it enter into what I told you. Thus from here [15] comes the error. So, my lady, start by dissolving the female who is longing [16] for sexual intercourse, having her uterus seized by sensuous desire. When she gets dyed, she turns the poison sour. [17] When her husband climaxes and ejaculates the sperm, the female rejoices and laughs. [18] The goldsmiths borrow from here their saying "It laughs", when they cast a thing. But [19] they do not know what it means. In this way, the etesian stone suffers in the operation (fol. 85a) what a woman suffers in pregnancy and during the parturition. So do not be surprised that it is named one stone [2] from various things.»

She said: «Then tell me when you say: "I have placed the birth of every [3] thing in that manner."» He said: «I did that in order to tell you that Ars (Ares) is in front of me [4] and Aqrūnis (Kronos) is behind me, when I told you that Ars is Saturn and Aqrūnis is the fighter, and I am between the two. [5] Thus where I was wrong about the two was my reluctance to extract their spirits from [6] their bodies, like the merciful killer: My enemy in front of me is like a swindler [7] and a trickster, I keep him in order that he does not escape. So if you are not a sage, O Theosebeia, [8] or someone who understands, you will fall into error, because I am Aqrūnis with Aqrūnis, and with Ars I am [9] Ars and behind me is Aqrūnis, and with the fire I am fire, and with Venus I am Venus, and I am with the beauty of [10] golden Aphrodite. And also I am the ever-creator Zeus, making my light appear at the completion of the month, [11] unless some cloud opposes me. Otherwise at this time, I am [12] a large sun with the sun. Know what the sages wrote, and know that if the calculation of the stars [13] differs every year, it is true. Although my statement [14] to you differs, I am not different, because I have with me Aqrūnis and the star (*naǧm*) of Ars and it entered into my belly, [15] so I turned into a ray of the sun by the way of the blood, where the thoughts are born. This is because nobody [16] is able to say whether the sun existed before the world. As for the spirits, they turned into [17] sulphurs, and the sun was concealed in the darkness of the night among the travelling stars. [18] As (now) for the birth of the thought, it comes by the light of the sun, so I have made this clear to you, [19] and if you understand what I have described to you, the work will be easy for you, God willing.»

(fol. 85b) The 4th Book is completed, praise be to God. It is followed by
2 the 5th Book, which is The Book of the Examples about
3 Magnesia, God willing.

4 The Beginning of the 5th Book of Zosimos's Book, 5 which is

The Book about the Magnesia

[The 1st picture]

6 The image of Theosebeia sitting on

7 a green and sky blue bed under a sky blue copula

8 based on two green columns. Behind them is a

9 red cupola, based on sky blue walls.

10 Then there is the image of Zosimos, standing in front of her, pointing to her in the way

11 we described at the beginning of the book

(fol. 86a) Between the two there are

2 two entwined vipers. One of them is

3 golden yellow and the other is green

4 with silvery water on it. The yellow one is extending its tail

5 towards Theosebeia and what is behind her.

6 The other green one is extending its tail towards Zosimos

7 and what is behind him. And there is an image of a man with wings,

8 and on his head is a white bull that is tied by the neck

9 to a chair under the feet of Theosebeia. Two of its legs

10 are tied with a rope that is in the hand of Zosimos.

Fig. 32: The 1st picture, fol. 87b and 86a.

(fol. 87b) Now I start the book in the name of the merciful and compassionate God. Zosimos said: «I have already told you [2] several times that I only describe things to you by way of allegories, examples and allusions, [3] and that the matter of the magnesia is too great in the eyes of the sages for its components to be written for you. Therefore [4] I ordered you to gather what they scattered.»

She said: «Then tell me about those sages who declared that they [5] found a youth in the East, one of the most beautiful persons, outstanding in virtue, beauty and splendour. [6] Then they looked for his equivalent in beauty, perfection and virtue, but they only found it in a slave-girl [7] in the West. She was one of the most beautiful women, and among them she was the most intense white, most perfect in her thinking, power and virtue. [8] The sages sent one of them and he returned with her.» He said: «If you had intelligence and [9] understanding, then certainly you would understand what they meant by this.»

She said: «If my understanding is weak, fear [10] the exalted God, and guide me to the right way.» He said: «I will do so. Understand, and know that there is no [11] man who, seeing that woman, would not love her appearance and long for her, preferring her to every other [12] female on earth. I do not say that the love of the men for her is like the ordinary love of men for [13] women, because men cannot obtain from her what [14] men usually obtain from women.»

She said: «Then tell me about that man.» He said. «He also does not obtain [15] that woman (in the ordinary way).»

She said: «I see that these two spirits are in agreement with each other.» He said: «If they were not in agreement [16] they could not become mixed.»

She said: «Then tell me about when the two were brought together.» He said: [17] «When he returned to the sages with the slave-girl, they sent for the man (the youth) and made him sit down with her. [18] The sages said to that man: "What do you think about this desirable and beautiful woman, [19] who suits you with regard to character and kinship?" But he did not answer them.»

She said: «What prevented him from

(fol. 88a) speaking?» He said: «His intense desire for that woman.»

She said: «How did they know of [2] his intense longing for her without him saying a word?» He said: «Because his colour changed and faded away, and [3] because his love for her showed on his face, and he gazed continuously at her, and he looked and looked [4] till the water welled up inside his eyes. What was inside him was stronger than what was visible outside. [5] <He said:> «So they married him to her, and she became pregnant and gave birth on that very day. [6] Then Būṭīṭos, the head of the sages, said: "Gather around me the sages of the countries so that they can tell me [7] why they united this man and this woman." When they (the sages) were assembled, the sage asked them [about it]. [8] One of them said: "When this man and this woman had a child, Ars (Ares, Mars) was in the East [9] and the woman [note in the margin: Venus] was in the West, and the Sun was in the middle of the sky in Aries, the house of Ars. [10] The woman (Venus) was pointing to the East and Ares was pointing to the West." Another sage said: [11] "By God, these two must unite in the house of the king. Another sage said: [12] " Indeed, the love between the two would not have happened if they had not united when the sun was in the house of [13] its height."[50] A fourth sage said: "Where did their union come from?" [14] Another sage answered him: "Indeed there is a close kinship between this woman and that man [15] who married her." Another said: "I also confirm that for you." The greatest of the sages said: [16] "He is right in what he says because Jupiter and Saturn were in the house of the Sun. [17] They are brothers and Jupiter was in the house of brotherhood." One of the sages said: [18] "If what you said is true, then what made them marry and perfected them?" [19] Another sage said: "Ares (emendation) made them marry because he (Ares) looked at both of them from a strong house."

50 House of Leo.

(fol. 88b) One of the sages said: "I only see that Ares brought agreement between those and made them marry." 2 The head of the sages said: "Indeed, if Ares (ārs) had not looked at them together, they would not have married, 3 because if Ares had looked only at one of them, and not at the other one, he would have killed and destroyed this one." Then 4 Afrāsūās stood up and said: "Are you not afraid, O you sages, that your God takes away 5 this science which he bestowed on you, when you disguise this matter from people? 6 Do you not have compassion for them, when you make them fall into error and misfortune, with the destruction of what 7 God bestowed on them? Woe unto you! Any sage who knows the order of the stars would 8 know that Aphrodite is not able to marry the Sun without making Ares a companion for her in 9 your settling her."[51] Another sage said: "O Afrāsūās, 10 indeed, it was right to marry Ares to the Sun, when Aphrodite looked 11 at the Sun from under the earth while the Sun was in the middle of the sky and Ares was in the East 12 looking at Zaus (Zeus) in the square from under the earth. And he (Ares) looks at Aphrodite, 13 while she is in the West of the square." Buṭrisīūs said: "Slowly, 14 O you sages. You have revealed this secret to whoever has intelligence, and I am afraid that you bring to light 15 this secret." Būṭīsos said: "Do not be afraid, you already hid this secret. 16 But if you had put Zeus pointing to the Sun in the place of Aphrodite, and if you had put Aphrodite in the place 17 of Zeus under the earth, with Ares in the East, then you would have 18 revealed this secret. This is because you put Ares in the East, the Sun in the middle 19 of the sky, and Zeus in the West. If you had done that, you would have revealed this secret."

51 Unclear meaning.

(fol. 89a) Another sage said: "How strange it is with you that you mention the marriage although I do not see [2] any female there, and how the male has to be with the male. This is not [3] in accordance with the truth." Another sage said: "Do you not know that the house which [4] was in the West is Zeus, and Ares was in it while Zeus was sitting in it, and the Sun was [5] in the middle of the sky in a strong male sign of the Zodiac, and Ares was in the East in a [6] female sign of the Zodiac, shining strongly, pointing to the West till it ends in the middle of the sky." [7] Another sage said: "How can you say that the Sun is in [8] a strong male sign of the Zodiac in the middle of the sky when its sign is a changeable declining sign, and [9] that this is made up for us?"» He said: «You are right, we did that on purpose, [10] because making it is a joy for us, and its transformation benefits us.»

She said: «O Zosimos, you have perplexed me [11] with what the sages mentioned about the order of the stars in this work.» He said: [12] «You asked me to tell you what the sages wrote in their books.»

[13] She said: «Alright, it is a sin, so forgive me. But I want you to tell me [14] about the body of magnesia because you have not clarified for me the magnesia and the components.»

[15] *The place of the 2nd picture from this Book*

The image of Theosebeia [16] reclining on a bed made of gold, and in front of her is a man fanning her. [17] And the image of Zosimos standing upright in front of her, and with him there is a man with two wings, and a bull [18] is on his head with a rope around its neck, which Zosimos is holding in his hand.

Fig. 33: The 2nd picture, fol. 89b.

(fol. 90a) He said: «I was thinking, my lady, that you might understand better than what I saw. Today [2] I know for certain that you have a woman's mind. You are just like women concerning their weak mind. What are you then?»

She said: «Now you speak to me in anger. What makes you angry is not welcome.» [4] He said: «My anger with you is only in your imagination.»

She said: «I have not disobeyed [5] any order from you.» He said. «You certainly have. Did I not send you special epistles, dedicating them solely to you. [6] After them I sent the *Sarṭamīṭā* but it did not convince you. Then I sent you *The Keys* [7] and other things, hoping that you would understand the anthology from the works of the sages that I gathered for you. But you said: [8] "I do not need them. Rather I want the books of the sages themselves, because I will understand [9] what they wrote in them". I told you that the sages had hidden and disguised what is written in their books, [10] so it became obscure. I described it to you, and although it is somewhat obscure, it is [11] clearer for you than the books of the sages, and it is more suited to your understanding. But I see that you did not understand [12] it at all, nor that you obtained any benefit from what I wrote for you in my books. Then you insisted on asking me [13] many questions about what is useful for you. I answered all of that [14] with allusions and examples. I often made the distinction for you between the truth and the things they disguised, [15] and with which they confused people and whoever entered this work. Know [16] that copper only turns black if it is mixed with gold and silver, [17] and it can only have shiny[52] exalted colours appearing on it [18] when it is composed.»

She said: «If it is introduced into the multiplications before being composed [19] by the cloud and the rising of the water, does its colour disappear because it is single?» He said: «Yes. »

[52] or polished like a mirror

(fol. 90b) She said: «Then tell me about when you say: «Those who make the idols (*aṣnām*), name 2 the white copper Indian.» He said: «It is called Indian not because it has the colour 3 of India, although they called it that. But Nubia and what lies next to it have 4 the colour of the ashes, and therefore it is not good for the multiplications. As for why they call it 5 Indian, it is because when they mixed the copper with it they named it Indian when it is white. 6 It has not the colour of India even though they named it Indian. Concerning Nubia 7 and what lies next to it, they have the colour of ashes. As for the copper mentioned to you, 8 it is neither white like silver nor black like ash, rather its colour is in 9 between. That is why they named it Indian copper, because that copper is suitable for the multiplication of silver.»

She said: «Then tell me about when you say that dyeing black is the beginning of the work 11 and the key of the dyeing.» He said: «I tell you that the black dye which the sages meant, 12 and about which I wrote to you, can only ever exist by the gum. Thus take some leaves of pomegranate, 13 roasted *šaḥīra* (vitriol?)[53] and rust of iron, for these things are suitable for dyeing 14 black. Cook the wool in it for four hours and it will become black. Know that 15 the purple dye with which those things are dyed was stolen from the people 16 of the work and the jealous ones. Those from whom it has been stolen declared that it was forbidden 17 for anyone who wanted to dye black to do so without having extracted the colours of these things 18 by the moisture.»

She said: «When the dyers wanted to dye 19 purple, why did they first dye it with crimson (*qirmiz*[54]), and then put the garment into the high-ranking dyeing?»

53 According to Sebstian Richter *šaḥīra* is copper-vitriol, but whether this is the meaning of the symbol in this text is uncertain.

54 *Qirmiz* = kermes (dried bodies of the female kermes insect (*coccus ilicis*) which yield a red dyestuff).

(fol. 91a) He said: «So take the broth of the black things, then dye with it whatever you want, [2] but be careful not to leave the blackness in any of the things you want to dye with this [3] dye.»

She said: «You have ordered me to do too many experiments.[55]» [4] He said: «I only ordered you to do it out of concern for you. If you achieve what is in the books, [5] you will have attained your goal. But if you fall into error, you will still get [6] some meaning out of it, and you will know that it has not affected your work, and you do not have to be ashamed of it.»

[7] She said: «Then what about when you say: "Take the cracked stone"?» He said: «That is the acacian (*ašqūnīān*) lime. [8] Take it and take litharge and pound the two with water until the water becomes like glass. [9] Know that you should put in one ounce of litharge for every nine ounces of water. [10] Then cook it until it takes the moisture and you see it turning black. Know that the more you [11] cook, the more it turns black. So if you want the dye to be more exalted than [12] anything, return the wool to the alum, and dye that (the wool) with it (the alum) several times. And if you want [13] the dye to be nobler and more exalted, then put much vinegar in it, and be patient with its long cooking. Know that the head of the work and the operation of the sages is the closing of the top of the vessel in order that [15] none of the vapour comes out. If you want your dye to be more saturated and subtle, mix it wisely [16] when you mix, because whether it is high-ranking or inferior depends on the mixing. [17] If you want to make it saturated, put in two ounces of golden dust and three ounces [18] of bitter things and it will be strong and high-ranking. If you want the pure [19] purple dye, which is made black before it is treated with alum, then take three ounces of the Cypriot glassy colocynth (*qalqant*),

55 *Taǧārib*, from *ǧarraba* II = to try out, to experiment

(fol. 91b) three ounces of gallnuts (*ʿfṣ*), and as much water as it needs. Cook it until [2] it turns black, make it alumy (white), and soak the wool in it until its colour pleases you. Know [3] that if you put the sun and the moisture in a bath, the two mingle and become hot, and both would live [4] in that moisture, and would change quickly from one thing to another, because when the two enter the bath [5] their veins soften, and their bodies relax. Then they should both be [6] washed with sweet water. Everything that is dyed by the uterus and the sperm is dyed by them. [7] I only wrote for you about the uterus and the sperm as an analogy for our work.

She said: «Then tell me [8] about when you say: "The sages wrote about an operation regarding the crystal. They said: 'Dissolve the crystal [9] and mix with patience.'"» He said: «Indeed, the crystal is not dissolved. But the crystal which the sages mention, [10] dissolves quickly. When we put it on a gentle fire, it melts and dissolves [11] on the spot. At this point you should mix glass into it, and that crystal will swallow this [12] glass on the spot in its inside.»

She said: «How similar is this analogy of the sage [13] to the dragon that eats its tail.» He said: «You are right and you have grasped the meaning. Watch out for [14] when you see the dragon eating its tail. If you see colours and beauty the like of which your eyes have [15] never seen, then you can be sure that you are on the right track. But you should hide [16] these colours so that nobody sees them and these colours do not become known.»

She said: «With what should [17] I hide these colours?» He said: «While they are hot, pour on them the composed black inside so that it makes the visible colours disappear, and the body of the glass is [19] concealed in the crystal.»

She said: «I maintain, O Zosimos, that mercury makes the glass sick.»

(fol. 92a) He said: «You are right. But if it makes it sick, it will also cure it. The most knowledgeable ones (*kahana* = priests) among [2] the sages confirm my statement. They are those who made the sticking with the three-folded one and they were those who made it from crystal and [3] gum, with the plate of glass between the two. This is because those who work with gold [4] and silver, and cook the glass, made golden works. Whoever does [5] this work well sees the colours we described to him in our books.»

She said: «Where [6] do these colours come from?» He said: «They are from the rising light, which rises from *būlīs*[56], [7] the three-folded glass, after it has been dissolved and solidified again in the same way as we described for the crystal. The *būlīs* [8] is the body of the ingot of glass. If the dye is mixed with the crystal, then [9] the sage ordered that the dye be mixed with it when it dissolved. If the crystal of the people could get dissolved in the same way [10] as our crystal, it would (also) accept the dyeing.»

She said: «Then tell me about when you say: ["(…) making of ivory, horns and bones."» He said:] «By the making of ivory, [11] horns and bones we meant the stones, the glass, and everything that we described [12] for the dyeing of glass, bones and horns. That is what dyes the purple and the stones.»

[13] She said: «What is similar to ivory and its whiteness?» He said: «It is lead-copper.»

[14] She said: «Then tell me about when you say: "Take two ounces of snail, one ounce of worm, and [15] $1\frac{1}{2}$ ounces of marine glass. This is the first elixir, and it is [16] $4\frac{1}{2}$ ounces."» He said: «Yes, so know the first, the second and the third. As for the [17] second elixir, you have to take $1\frac{1}{2}$ ounces of snail, and $2\frac{1}{2}$ ounces of marble. [18] The total of these is 4 ounces. Then pound both of them. With regard to the third elixir, you have to take [19] 1 ounce of snail, 3 (ounces) of worm, and $4\frac{1}{2}$ ounces of marble. The total

[56] In the margin: It is the name of the head of the most knowledgeable ones (*kahana* = priests) and it is the eternal water.

(fol. 92b) of these is 8½ ounces.»

She said: «Then tell me about when you say: "If you want [2] the gold to get dissolved."» He said: «Yes, if you want it to get dissolved, take the gum, mix it [3] with rainwater, and rub it with the wool until it becomes like tar or thick [4] honey.[57] Then put a plate in it and leave it for three or four days, so it dissolves. [5] Know that the leaves of oleander are what pushes away the heat of fire from their companions. I know [6] that from a book of Ābullūn (Apollo) that I read. He wrote about analogies and he wrote the secret in them.»

[7] She said: «Who is Ābullūn?» He said: «He is the sun, and the sun is *āqusṭus*, [8] and *āqusṭus* is the fire. Ābullūn is the pursuer of the virgin (= Daphne), but he could only catch her [9] with oleander leaves.[58]

She said: «Do you think that Ābullūn was passionately in love with the virgin?» [10] He said: «Yes. He suited her nature but he was afraid of the fieriness of her firewood.» She said: [11] «What is her firewood?» He said: «It is the firewood of the oleander.»

She said: «Does he compare the fieriness of the virgin [12] with the firewood of the oleander?» He said: «Yes.» She said: «What about the passion of the virgin for Ābullūn?» He said: [13] «She was more passionate about him than he about her, because her nature was in accordance with his, and also she was [14] free, noble and chaste, and afraid of Apollo's fire. Know that [15] the dyed one should be twice as much as the one with which it gets mixed.»

She said: «Tell me more of the [16] operations of iron.» He said. «It is sulphur and its secret is known by its characteristic sign. [17] Do you not know my statement: "Take female iron and mix it. Then cool it and mix it [18] with mercury, and pound it with vinegar and salt until it is mixed. Cook it for many days [19] until it becomes dust. Return it to the composition of the sulphur for some days." In this is what removes

57 The thick honey of sugarcane (molasses) is black.

58 According to Dr. Peter Starr *diflā* (oleander) could be considered to be laurel here. Often plant names in Arabic are variously applied.

(fol. 93a) your doubt about the iron.»

She said: «Then what about when you say: "Half of the sulphur or some magnet dissolves it."» [2] He said: «The sulphur is the composition and the magnet [3] is the body of magnesia, and there is no relationship between the body of magnesia and the magnet.»

[4] She said: «Then tell me about this gum.» He said: «It is the moist alum. Stir it well, [5] put the stones in it (the gum), and cook it until its nature approaches the truth. [6] Then purify the fat, raise it, and mix the gum with the alum. Only put alum on [7] the gum in the measure that dissolves the body. Know that if [8] you put in more of the gum, the stone (= the body) will absorb only as much as it can. The rest of the gum [9] which you put in it will be ruined. However, if it becomes dry and fragmented, some of it will not be dissolved, and [10] you will not benefit from that rest that you dissolved with the stone.»

She said: «Then tell me how [11] mercury is destroyed and how it solidifies with its components of the mixture.» He said: «The ancient ones [12] wrote it in their books, and they disguised it, but I will describe it for you. Take [13] aqzal and mix it with spittle of the moon. When the two are dissolved, pour the mercury on them [14] gently, without violence and burning. And be careful that the two are not hot, otherwise the mercury [15] and others will escape, and the mixture will become dry. But their heat should be in the measure that [16] accepts water, so it mixes like juice with juice. Be careful not to do that while [17] the moon is waning.»

She said: «Then tell me about when you say: "If you want to make the pure purple dye—which is [18] made black, then is treated with alum and then made red—take three ounces of the glassy colocynth of Cyprus, [19] three ounces of gallnuts, and enough water for it. Then cook the two (fol. 93b) until they become black.» He said: «Even if you were a beast, you would know what you are asking me. 2 I cannot imagine that your ignorance goes so far as to ask me this question because I have made that clear to you 3 with the words that you just pronounced. Soak the wool in what you asked me about, and do that 4 several times, until its colour pleases you.»

She said: «Then tell me about when you say: "Be gentle with the nature, 5 and treat it with courtesy, and compare the imprisonment of the spirit of your work to your soul and your body."» 6 He said: «Do you not see that as long as your soul is in your body, your colour, blood, power, 7 and your life are visible and known.»

She said: «From where did that appear?» He said: «That is because 8 the soul gained pleasure and desire from the body. Concerning when the soul desires to come out from its body and 9 to be in a spirit like itself, at that point the soul hates the body. The beginning of the soul's separation from 10 its body is when it destroys it, changes its colour, turns it black and withdraws from it. For when the soul 11 finds the spirit, which is similar to it, it becomes spiritual and clings to the two other spirits.[59] 12 This is because it finds two spiritual beings like itself, longs for them, and despises the body 13 in which it was, and clings to the two spiritual beings that resemble it.»

She said: «Did the spirit that despised and 14 separated from its body mix with the two spiritual ones which were like it?» He said: 15 «Yes. They mixed and these three spirits became one spiritual soul 16 and one thing in what is visible to the eye, in the inner nature and in name. Concerning the composition, it is from 17 different things which the sages composed in harmony, agreement and longing for each 18 other.»

She said: «So was this spirit that was concealed in and clinging to its body 19 pleased to stay in it?» He said: «Yes.» She said: «Then why did it separate from its body?» He said:

59 See the three spirits in the 7th Book about the Mercuries.

(fol. 94a) «The exalted and blessed God inspired His prophets, ordering them to extract the spirit [2] from that body with two spirits. When the spirit of that body met the two spirits, [3] it desired them, hated its body, separated from it and clung to these two spirits, [4] because it was like them in its inner nature. But to the eye, what a great difference there is between it (the soul) and the two (spirits).»

[5] She said: «Then tell me about your statement that the redness comes from three things.» He said: «Yes. It comes [6] from the fighter, the one clung to and the lime. Know that if you bring them together, you extract from them a froth [7] that does not escape. Know that the sulphur which turned them black is what opened the door, so that what [8] was not able to escape could escape.»

She said: «And how did what was not able to escape become fugitive?» He said: «When the sulphur [9] mixed with it, it (the sulphur) destroyed and tortured it. It did not torture it in order to damage or corrupt, but [10] to create harmony and benefit, so it became a fugitive. If the two had tortured it to damage it, it would neither be in agreement with them nor mix [11] with them until it extracts from it the colours that neither change nor vanish. We named them the water of sulphur [12] which we prepared for the dyeing of the purple, which does not become black after that, but becomes red.»

She said: [13] «Then tell me about when you say: "This making alumy (white) is another thing in name."» He said: «Yes. Take [14] natron and urine and put them in a vessel. Pound them and put wool into them. Then [15] make alumy (white) and calcify it and put a sufficient amount of water in it, and mix it as one mixes [16] juices. Be careful that the fire is not too strong. Puff up the wool, put the pot on hot ashes, [17] and put sweet water in it. Take the same amount of alum as wool, and put a sufficient amount of [18] water on it. Leave it until it gets dissolved, then sieve its water.»

She said: [19] «Then tell me about when you say that the sages wrote about nine operations for making purple.»

(fol. 94b) He said: «They did that.»

She said: «What is it?» He said: «There are six among them that escape, and three 2 that do not escape.»

She said: «Name for me the three that do not escape.» He said: «The first one is the lime which 3 comes out of the mother-of-pearl and it can be eaten. The second is the *k-nk-l* and the third is the snail. 4 As for when you put in the lime and the *k-nk-l*, do not make the wool alumy (white). As for (the operation) on the snail, the 5 sage does not order you to use either alum or urine, but he said at the end of his book: "Know 6 that you should make alumy (white). What he orders you to make alumy with (to make white) is with urine and the water of lime." 7 However, I see that urine and the water of lime are not suitable. But with regard to the other six fugitives, know that with five of them you should make alumy (white), but the other one you must dye 9 without making it alumy (white). I have said all of this because the sage said: "Take the dye and put 10 the wool in it without making it alumy (white)." By it he meant this dye which I ordered you 11 to dissolve and to melt, because the dyeing and the making alumy (white) are one thing. Therefore he ordered you not to make the dye alumy (white), because making alumy (white) is 12 the dyeing. So when you dye, you just make alumy (white). Know 13 that if you think this thing is a mixture of two, then I tell you that it is made of 14 three, and it is also made of all of them. And if you think that anyone can mix all the lime 15 in the casting, then I tell you that the sulphur will then mix with it. But I tell 16 you that this is not like that, so I tell you the truth. Indeed, they mix the three things, 17 the magnesia, the kohl[60] and the spittle of the moon in order to turn them into lead. In these 18 things they solidify what they want to solidify. Also I have seen somebody who did this, yet did not benefit from it. But if you want the true magnesia it is the hard composition,

60 Kohl is a preparation of pulverized antimony used in Ancient Egypt, among other things, for darkening the edges of the eyelids.

(fol. 95a) which is all lead-copper, the etesian stone that is born every year. 2 Know that the solidification is not one but that you must solidify the first 3 with tin and lead-copper, and the second with amalgamation.»

She said: «Then tell me about when you say: "Sulphur, 4 arsenic and sandarach burn and vanish quickly, and the fire eats them quickly."» He said: 5 «I have told you that, and I tell you that if you mix salt, alum, natron, lime 6 and macrasite (*makraṣīūn*) in water, they will hold each other when cooked with a gentle fire.»

She said: 7 «Then tell me about the statement of the sage about the multiplications.» He said: «He meant by that 8 the two become three.» She said: «Which two are they?» He said: «They are the sulphur and the magnesia.» 9 She said: «And which thing is the third?» He said: «It is the mercury from cinnabar.»

She said: 10 «Then what about when you say that the one of the three is four?» He said: «It is the water that flows from every thing.» 11 She said: «And what about when you say: "One two, one."» He said: «It is a symbol that they mentioned.» She said: 12 «Then explain it to me.» He said: «As for "one two", it is the sulphur and the magnesia which became one from two, 13 which is then the water that is from every thing.»

She said: «Which thing is (this) every thing?» He said: «It is the cinnabar. And know 14 that the three became one. Then, if you want, bring it together with the dye, then 15 it will all become tar.»

She said: «Then tell me about when you say in more than one place that they are two, and 16 it is what you described to me saying: "The sulphurs hold the sulphurs."» He said: «Why did you ignore the rest of 17 this statement: "… and the white sulphur which is pounded with the sandarach"?»

She said: «I assumed 18 that you would understand (the rest) from the beginning of the statement.» He said: «Do not think that, although I said they are 19 two in number.»

She said: «You said that.» He said: «I tell you that I was right that (fol. 95b) they are two, and each of these two is composed like a man and a woman, [2] as between the two there is a passion and a clinging in the fecundation and in other things. Do you not understand that they are both only two [3] in name, but in number they are more than that. Concerning your question to me: "What is that [4] one which wins over the ten?", I have told you that the ten are colours that appear [5] from the composition.»

She said: «I asked you whether lead is composed or not.» He said: «I told you [6] that it is composed, but you do not understand. Do you [not] see, when I say: "O heavenly natures that are [7] dyeing the natures!" I also said about the litharge that if it makes its moisture disappear [8] it is not named lead, and I told you that its moisture disappears without any difficulty, because the natures [9] of lead are very quick to transform into things other than their nature, because nature wins over natures.»

[10] She said: «Then tell me about when you say that white lead (*abšimīt*) has a power on its own, and that the dry one [11] has a different power also on its own, and that the litharge has a power, and that red lead (*sarīaqūn*) has another power.» [12] He said: «Concerning the dry one to which they referred, it is in the hole where the silver is purified, [13] so the sages named it the one which dries it (the silver). If you had a ready understanding, you would know the natures and their composition [14] from what you asked me .»

She said: «Then tell me.» He said. «I will tell you, together with what I have already told you, [15] that they (the natures) are composed, although the things became one nature, [16] one power and one dye.»

She said: «Then tell me about when you say: [17] "Ostanes said to his students: 'Ponder over the white composition which [18] we prepared and which we named magnesia and black and white lead.'"» He said: «He named for you the truth, if you had understood his statement about this magnesia. Even if an ignorant person heard (fol. 96a) this statement, he would know that it is composed. Why do I see that you do not help yourself [2] with effective pondering. But Nilos (*Bīlis*) the Priest has made you think that the work does not exist. [3] I was thinking that with it I would do something helpful to you in response to your many questions [4] to me, by illuminating what the sages wrote about in their examples and allusions, a matter that nobody [5] had written about before me, nor will anyone have the courage to write about it after me. But now it has turned into an injustice which I brought upon myself.»

She said: «I have not doubted [6] that the work is true ever since I came to know you. So if you think that your long and complicated explanations to me [7] have prevented me from hoping for it, you deceive yourself.» He said: «How can you say that when I answered all that [8] you remembered from the books of the sages to ask me about, and you came to me with [9] more than 8500 questions?»

She said: «With your answers to most of [10] those questions you were hiding more, and towards me you are disguising more [11] than what the sages wrote in their books for the people.» He said: «How quickly you ignore [12] my beneficence, therefore I should repay you by leaving you ignorant. If you were not a woman, and it would not be appropriate for me to repay you without completing what I started for you, I would swear that I would not answer you about anything after [14] this meeting.»

She said: «O Zosimos, you are angry, although anger is not characteristic of [15] people like you. Why are you angry?» He said: «I was angered by your denial of my illuminating for you the obscurity of what [16] the sages described, and your ignorance of the fact that I dared to break their vows not to reveal [17] this secret to anybody. If your understanding cannot penetrate the allusions and analogies, [18] I am not able to say more than what I said about this matter.»

She said: «As you know [19] the weakness of my understanding and the feebleness of my thinking, be patient with a plan of mine which I present to you today (fol. 96b) and favour me with it!» He said: «Present it to me.»

She said: «I will not do it unless you require me to do it for you.» [2] He said: «Then you can ask me today anything except that I make clear this matter which God ordered His prophets [3] to hide from the people, so I will give it to you. Then ask me whatever you wish according to this plan.»

She said: [4] «I only ask you to be patient with me when I repeat for you the questions I remember I asked you [5] before, but I did not understand what you answered me, so give me a clearer answer than what you did before. Put [6] the things in proper context for me with regard to the uniting of the natures of this secret, its compositions in every place, [7] its weights, and its operations in every stage, so I can reach the end of this work which [8] is its completeness.» He said: «If I do that for you, will you ask me anything after these questions?»

[9] She said: «Yes, I will ask you about the magnesia and its body and what Democritus said about it, [10] because he was the clearest of all in what he said.» He said: «If I tell you about it, [11] will you ask me about it again after that?»

She said: «Yes, I want to see it with my own eyes.» He said: «I will show it to you with the help of examples (*amṯāl*) [12] and imagination (*taḫaīul*). As for answering you about it and naming it with its names, death would be easier for me than doing [13] that.»

She said: «You refuse to do anything but follow the sages. I have accepted what you mixed up for me. [14] So give good answers to the questions that I ask you according to what I can understand.» He said: [15] «I will answer what you asked me according to the extent of my knowledge.»

She said: «And where my knowledge is not enough, [16] complete your answer about it. I must ask you things, the full extent of which my mind does not [17] know. You cannot leave me in suspension about it, when I know that if one makes a small fault in this [18] matter, it does not leave one until one starts again.» He said: [19] «I will do that for you. Know that the only thing that prevents me from presenting the science clearly for you (fol. 97a) is that I saw you despising my books. So when your understanding was feeble, and you were perplexed, O you weak-minded one, 2 you asked me to tell you what the magnesia is and to answer your questions.»

She said: «If I did not fear 3 your anger, O Zosimos, I would tell you that jealousy has taken hold of you.» He said: «You said something worse which 4 made me angry. So what is it that you disapproved of?»

She said: «It is that you mix up what you tell me, and your strong 5 warnings to me about things. And Hermes would be more merciful to his students than you are to me. 6 May God reward you.»

7 *The position of the 3rd picture*

8 The image of Zosimos and Theosebeia, standing upright as we described, 9 and the image of a man with two wings, and 10 around his neck is a rope that is in the hand of Zosimos.

Fig. 34: The 3rd picture, fol. 97b.

(fol. 98a) He said: «I did not speak rudely to you, neither scorning your right, nor ignoring your right that I should be kind to you. So do not [2] think that my strong words to you were because of jealousy in me, or regret for what had happened.»

She said: «So answer me about the things I asked you.» He said: «I will show you [4] the magnesia and its body through the vision (*rū ʾyā*), while you are awake.»

She said: «How can [5] I see a vision, while I am awake?» He said: «Although your eyes are [6] looking, your heart and your understanding are sleeping. When your understanding gives help, and your eyes see, then you will see [7] the truth. But if your understanding does not help, then they are normal dreams (*āḥlām*).»

She said: «I do not understand what this is.» He said: [8] «I have told you the truth. So sharpen your eyesight, wake up your mind, and empty your thoughts. Be careful not [9] to ask me about anything I make you see before I finish.»

She said: «You want [10] to increase my distress?! Can healing be without asking questions?» He said: «It is the limit between me and you. [11] If you stop (asking), I will answer you when you ask me (later).»

She said: «Do what you think is right.» He said: [12] «I will illustrate the two of us in several different pictures, not just one, [13] in this book of mine. In it, I want to give you your right at every level of this work [14] until I reach its end, in order that you know what you asked me about. Ask me [15] whatever you want as long as my picture seems appropriate to your picture.»

She said: «Do you want [16] my picture to be separate from your picture?» He said: «Yes. My picture must be separate from your picture.» She said: [17] «Whom do I ask questions then?» He said: «You will ask my spirit.» She said: «Will the spirit seem to be appropriate [18] to me?» He said: «No, it will not seem appropriate, but from my spirit imagined colours will appear that your eyes never saw before.» She said: «How will I ask questions of your spirit, O Zosimos, once it has separated from your body?

(fol. 98b) You just put me into trouble although I am ignorant, and you make me enter into what is more difficult than what I complained to you about being too obscure. [2] Has anybody before me seen a spirit separate from its body that appears before one's eyes?» [3] He said: «Yes, indeed. If my spirit separates from my body, it [4] must be concealed in your spirit. Therefore it seems appropriate for you. So accept this [5] statement of mine. Know that your spirit will talk with my spirit, and it (your spirit) will know what it asks it (my spirit) about. [6] At this time you will see the miracles of the exalted God's wisdom.»

[7] *The position of the 4th picture*

[8] The image of Theosebeia and Zosimos, and with Zosimos [9] there is a man with two wings who is pointing to him.
And there is an image [10] of Theosebeia, and in front of her a yellow vessel with [11] Zosimos in it, together with his bull, and another yellow vessel with a white-green bull in it.

Fig. 35: The 4th picture, fol. 99a.

(fol. 99b) She said: «If it were not for your dignity and fear of your authority, I would say these things are just tales (*ḫurāfāt*).» He said: [2] «Did I not mention this to you and similar things before?»

She said: «You tell me about things [3] that my soul cannot accept.» He said: «I will add to your picture a witness for you, who confirms my statement, [4] and you will then see him yourself.»

She said: «And who is this witness?» He said: «He is one close to you, [5] whom you still love tenderly, and for whom you are longing. In his longing for you he is proud. [6] He never obeyed any creature except you. Although he obeys you well, and is [7] weak about being close to you and with you, [but] when he feels the torture, he would leave you if I were [8] not with the two of you, for he is the glue between you and me. If you knew him, you would be granted his closeness [9] and his being with you.»

She said: «There is not much good in being related to someone who leaves me.» [10] He said: «Although he is your relative, betrayal and uniting with the air is his character, [11] because he is spiritual.»

[12] *The position of the 5th picture:*

[13] The image of a man with two wings [14] standing upright.

Fig. 36: The 5th picture, fol. 100a.

(fol. 100b) She said: «How come that your spirit is happy with him?» He said: «He is happier today to be with me than I am to be close to him. 2 But when I am afflicted with the torture when I die, I am eager to be close to him because he 3 removes all the pain of the torture from me. And, O Theosebeia, he joins you in spite of his betrayal (*ġadr*).»

She said: 4 «I do not understand what you are saying.» He said: «If you understood it, you would praise me highly. Be careful that 5 Neilos (Bīlīs), the priest of the unbelievers, does not see me on any of these representations, otherwise my picture would not seem appropriate. 6 In that case, I would cover your body with leprosy, by which I would make your splendour disappear and turn you to ashes after you had been pure in colour.»

7 She said: «You have frightened me with something about which I felt sure. How are you able to do that 8 to me when you are away from me, not seeing me.» He said: «I am away from you only in terms of what is visible to 9 the eye, yet I am present with you, but you do not see me.»

She said: «How can you be absent and present?» 10 He said: «Only my body is absent from you, but my spirit is in your spirit.» She said: 11 «Then where is my spirit?» He said: «Did I not order you not to ask me about anything until I finish 12 telling you about it?»

She said: «You talk to me in fanciful speech. My mind is not able to understand 13 what you mean. So do not blame me when I ask you where my spirit is in respect to you.» He said: «Your spirit appears 14 on the outside of my spirit.»

She said: «How can my spirit win over your spirit, when you are stronger, wiser 15 and more knowledgeable than me?» He said: «Your spirit is full of weapons, and I have no power over you in 16 any of these matters.»

She said: «I have never seen a weak one winning over a strong one.» He said: 17 «Today you have seen it.» She said: «Then what led my spirit to take your spirit?» He said: 18 «In order that by it you are able to fight the enemies.» She said: «I did not know I had any enemy.» He said: «Your enemy is very much present!» 19 She said: «I have not done any evil to anybody, and (fol. 101a) I am good-natured towards people.» He said: «So what do you think of the great sun that Hermes mentioned, [2] but he did not name it by its name?»

She said: «There is no deep-rooted hatred between the sun and me.» He said: «It is [3] your murderer, and it has been your enemy of old.»

[4] *The position of the 6th picture*

[5] The image of Zosimos and Theosebeia, and he is pointing

[6] to her. The image of Zosimos with

[7] a book of gold in his hand that he has opened and is reading
from it to Theosebeia.

[8] She is standing in front of him. And the image of the sun is red

[9] like fire. He points with it (the book) to both of them
(Theosebeia and the sun).

Fig. 37: The 6th picture, fol. 101b.

(fol. 102a) She said: «You have spoken much, O Zosimos, and you took a direction that I had not asked you about. Tell me [2] about yourself. What destroyed you and separated your spirit from your body?» He said: [3] «You took away my splendour and you turned me into silver, after I had been gold before. You dressed [4] me in black, which is the lowest of all the colours, then you turned me into ashes. This is what you did to me as the reward [5] for my kindness to you.»

She said: «You accuse me, O Zosimos, of something that I would not be able to do to you. Where is my relative?» He said: «Upon my life, he is more helpful to my spirit [7] during the torture than you.»

She said: «Did you not declare that betrayal is in his character?» [8] He said: «But when I mix with him I prevent him from escaping.»

[9] *The position of the 7th picture*

[10] The image of a golden man, having a black head,

[11] red hands, being suspended from the two legs of a man,

[13] having two wings, flying with him.[61]

[61] See also fig. 20 on p. 103.

Fig. 38: The 7th picture, fol. 102b.

(fol. 102b) She said: «Why do you praise him, when he is only staying with you unwillingly.» He said: «Because he is more beneficial [2] to me than you.»

She said: «It causes me pain to see you describing to me your changing states, [3] and the afflictions that you suffered. I wish that I could redeem you from them and share them with [4] you.» He said: «You already shared them equally with me. Then I will be resurrected. And I am bound to be resurrected, [5] to come back to life and to become better than I was before.»

She said: «And what about me after your resurrection?» He said: [6] «As for you, you will not be resurrected.» She said: «Why is it like that?» He said: «Because God favoured me with your spirit. [7] Thus he gave me strength to be resurrected. That is why I became better than I was before.»

She said: «And where is my relative?» [8] He said: «With him, too, God increased my power when I was destroyed, and (fol. 103a) He gave me His splendour and his power together with your splendour and your power.»

She said: «I see that you have reaped [2] the benefit!» He said: «This is the decision of your God. If you had not begged me many times [3] to tell you about things precisely, I would speak at length. But when I start to read [4] the beginning of the book with you, after you have pondered about the emerging pictures of us (*taḫālaīna*), and I appear to you in any [5] shape (*haīʾa*), do not ask me about it!»

The position of the 8th picture

[6] The image of a man lying dead on the ground, golden, with red stripes.

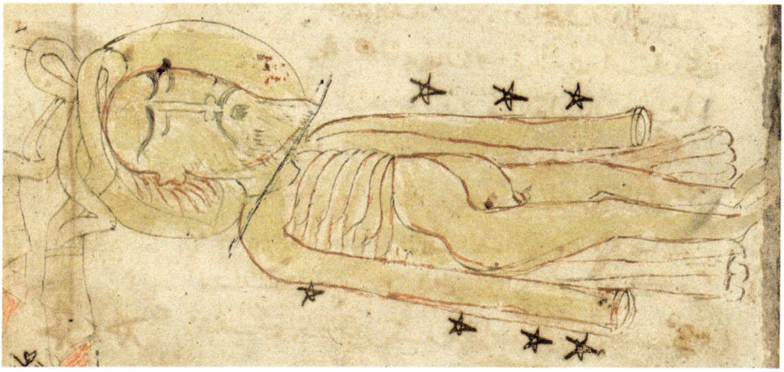

Fig. 39: The 8th picture, fol. 103a.

[7] She said: «What shape is that?» He said: «It is in the clothes of the greatest king in purple colour, and the purple is [8] woven with gold.»

She said: «What urged you to take this shape?» [9] He said: «Did I not tell you before not to ask me?» She said: «I ask you because I am impatient about [10] what I hear.» He said: «They are my winding sheets (*akfānī*) [62].» She said: «Are the dead wrapped in cloths of gold?»

[62] *Akfān* were used to mummify the body for the Osirification.

(fol. 103b) He said: «Yes, they are the winding sheets of the sages, because the gold holds back and prevents the fire from burning me [2] at death, until I am resurrected alive.»

She said: «What was it that killed you, [3] O Zosimos?» He said: «You.»

She said: «I am too weak for that.» He said: «Keep [4] away from me.»

She said: «Am I able to do that? Woe unto you O Zosimos! How can I do [5] to you what you are describing?» He said: «When you are wrapped in the silvery winding sheets.»

She said: [6] «So, O Zosimos, your death is nigh, and at that time the colours of the rainbow appear in you.» He said: [7] «Woe unto you, O Theosebeia, what extinguishes these colours (of the rainbow) is the one whose inside is black. When it mixes [8] with me, it extinguishes my light and illuminates you and it reveals your splendour and increases your brilliance.»

She said:«I do not understand [9] what you are saying, and you only want to mock me. Woe unto what you say!» He said: «Die in your grief! [10] You are a fool. Look at the pictures of the two of us at the beginning of this [11] book. Then ask me questions, as long as you see my picture and I will answer you about what I promised you. Do not [12] leave away anything you think you will need without asking me about it. I will reveal [13] to you what a father keeps back from his son. And I think, O Theosebeia, that if [14] you understand what I say, your soul will be filled with joy and you will praise me much for it.

[15] *The position of the 9th picture*

[16] The image of Theosebeia and the image of Zosimos holding the hand of a man with two [17] wings.

Fig. 40: The 9th picture, fol. 104a.

(fol. 104b) [He said:] «Look, my lady, when you start the 2nd book (The Book of the Names, see fol. 40b, 12 - 41a, 17), prepare me well [2] for my tomb, and praise God much for what you see of me and you. [3] Your winning over me, and your nature's conquest of my nature, must not lead you to stop longing for God's [4] blessings on you so that He will revive me for you after my death. For when I am resurrected I will be more beneficial for you [5] and better for you than now. Look at the 3rd book (The Book about the Weights) and ask my golden spirit [6] about my states of being. Be careful not to separate from the one whose inside is black, which extinguishes my light.»

She said: «And what [7] extinguished your light, O Zosimos?» He said: «You, O silvery Theosebeia, you took away my light. [8] Woe unto you, O Theosebeia, how you fulfilled the statement of Agathodaimon [9] when he says: "Turn the gold into silver."»

She said: «I do not know what I should say to you, except that you [10] have confused my mind. I do not understand where I stand.» He said: «I did not do that to you.»

She said: [11] «O Zosimos, stop these tales (*ẖurāfāt*). You are full of tricks and there is nothing more enigmatic [12] than all that. <She said:> «So tell me the things I asked you about concerning the magnesia and its body[13] and what your sage Democritus said about it, and your claim that he (Democritus) revealed the truth at the [14] beginning of his talk.» He said: « I tell you so now. [15] Democritus spoke the truth or some of the truth when he said: "Take mercury and solidify it [16] in the body of magnesia." You see that the sage has explained and summarised, and whoever reads [17] his books without understanding what he means, will find (it) a difficult matter and an obscure statement, unless he [18] knows the elements, their mixtures, their union, their weights, and their operations." For [19] his words were: "The one (masculine) and the one (feminine), which is the nature, and the other thing, (fol. 105a) the knowledge of which the sages prevented the ignorant and ordinary people from knowing."»

She said: «What is it, and how [2] is it mixed after it has been weighed, and what are its operations, the measures of its fire and the number of its days?» He said: [3] «I tell you that Democritus said: "What I wrote for you is only in symbols, [4] so if those who take up this work are sages, then they recognize very well the truth [5] which I wrote in my books, and the difficulty to which I alluded. But if they are ignorant, [6] then I do not mind increasing their distress and disbelief. Although I would not have wanted [7] God to deprive them of this gift, if it were not for their ignorance of their debt to God. For a long time [8] the sages warned against revealing the core of the world and how to reach it, except for those, who worked on it [9] in obedience to God, because it is a mysterious and hidden secret for those who do not know it. But for whoever knows it, [10] it is a clear, visible, abundant, available, cheap, expensive, high ranking and a despised thing.»

She said: [11] « I asked you about the magnesia and you answered me with Democritus and the obscure things [12] he wrote.» He said: «I did not neglect to answer you about it, but I began my answer to you with obscure words of Democritus. [13] Concerning the body of magnesia, no sage has entered into this work [14] whose body God has not turned into gold and his spirit into silver, and what holds both of them together is spiritual. [15] So now I am the golden Zosimos and you are the silvery Theosobeia.»

She said: [16] «This does not satisfy me.»

The position of the 10th picture

[17] The image of Theosebeia in two places, and the image of Zosimos below these two, holding a leg of each of them in his hand, and hanging from them.

Fig. 41: The 10th picture, fol. 105b.

(fol. 106a) He said: «My lady, understand the statement of my sage as you lack understanding. I did not desire anything from 2 the sages except to become one of their students. However, I particularly selected Democritus for this, and I became 3 a student of his, although there are 660 years between us.[63] This is because he spoke 4 the truth, making it clear and striving for sincerity. He spoke clearly for those who knew its meanings with knowledge 5 of what the sages were hiding. Also (I selected him) because Ostanes the Great preferred him, for Ostanes 6 ordered each of the sages to write an illuminating, difficult and enigmatic book about this work. 7 Maria was with them at that time. Then he told them that the best one for illuminating, revealing and 8 hiding the truth as well as (protecting) the knowledge was Democritus, who has the crown. And what is this 9 his crown, O Theosebeia?»

She said: «I do not know.» He said: «I tell you that 10 it is gold covered with purple colour because they (the sages) increased the dye in it. It is inlaid 11 with red rubies, green emeralds and pearls that have no equal. When 12 the sages gathered around Ostanes, he looked at what they wrote. He did not find anybody who 13 illuminated the truth better, or was more specific in what he wrote, or believing in it (and) writing it in his books, or 14 giving more enigmatic statements, or changing more than Democritus. So he (Ostanes) put the crown on him (Democritus), and he was put on 15 the shield (*turs*) [64], and he was carried on the necks of the men. [Therefore I consider] myself a student of his.

16 *The position of the [11th] picture*

[The picture of] Zosimos and Theosebeia 17 pointing to each other [...] two dogs,[65] 18 one of them is red [having a rope round his neck and the other one is black [...]. The second dog on fol. 106b is cut off having a rope round his neck and the other one is white(?)].

[63] Democritus lived 460-370, Zosimos around 300. That Democritus lived 660 years before Zosimos would speak for Democritus being the one from Abdera. See also Part I, p. 27.

[64] According to Hans Wehr, *turs* means the shield or the disc of the sun, and according to this passage, Ostanes and Maria were contemporaries of Democritus.

[65] The motif of the dog is again found in the *Muṣḥaf aṣ-ṣuwar* on folio 191b. See also the ending of Ms G in CALA I A, § 328 f., a text written by an unknown author. The motif of the dog as a guide probably originates in Ancient Egypt (*wpwt* is the god who opens the door).

Fig. 42: The 11th picture, fol. 106b.

(fol. 107a) [He said:] «And know, O Theosebeia, that even if he revealed the truth and spoke clearly, he still named it with another [2] name, and gave many names for the one thing. Not one of these names is similar to the other. [3] He started the work from its lowest point up to its beginning. In this way he became excellent in obscuring his statements, [4] because he started at the beginning of his book with the making of gold. Yet he did not mean gold, but [5] he meant making the colour of gold with which silver gets dyed and becomes gold [6] on the completion and end of the work. If he had not wanted to disguise the work, he would have [7] said, like the great Agathodaimon, that they must turn gold into silver. This is [8] the truth and Democritus said it, but he did not make it clear in the same way as Agathodaimon did. But he (Democritus) wrote it [9] in his last book about the making of silver. Hence people were confused about this [10] work and they lost their way when they operated. So they fell into error, and it was inevitable that they did so. This is because they found books where [11] the end replaces the beginning, and things were not named with their true names, and names were given to the truth [12] which distorted the true operations. Whoever reads such books and takes the things they ordered, [13] and operates on them falls into error. How can anyone not fall into error if he wants to make gold from lime, [14] colocynth (*qalqant*), *suzīn* (written *surīn*, vitriol), reddish colours (*muġrāt*), arsenics, sulphurs, dusts, [15] milks, gums, herbs, waters, and fats, none of which [16] God made for this work? So much for the difficult terms they wrote. [17] I have made the ways to it clear for you, and it is more than I can name for you. As for the manifest statement of [18] the truth which Democritus spoke about, understand—and yet I do not see that you do—what he said in detail, [19] because the first word which he pronounced was the truth: "Take mercury and solidify it in the body of (fol. 107b) magnesia." Then he did not leave his statement unveiled but disguised it with comparisons [2] saying: "…or talcous kohl, or litharge, or white lead (*abšimīt*), or this, or that…" [3] So the ignorant hurried to the magnesia of the people and took it. But [4] the magnesia of the people is only good for dyeing glass. It has no power to fight against fire because [5] in fire it turns into dust. Others went and took magnesia and burnt it with iron. Then God made them all the more misled and confused. Others took copper [7] and they burnt it with sulphur, because of their bad thinking and little knowledge of what is in the books. All of [8] their burning is destructive because their burning is black, while the burning of the sages [9] is white like snow. So they fall into error and they accuse the books of the sages of telling lies, while they themselves are the greatest liars.»

10 She said: «I ask you, O Zosimos, to help me to understand what the sages wrote. Why did you not tell me [11] what is the magnesia and its body?» He said: «I told you about it, but you did not understand.»

12 She said: «I really did not understand.» He said: «You asked about a great matter and you wanted to ruin this [13] world, and I will not name it to you to the end of my life, for I have already named it to you but you did not realize. [14] I only name it with something else similar to it, although I tell you that the magnesia of [15] the sages is composed of different things, and it is like the human being as it has a body, [16] a soul and a spirit. It is what they named marble stone because of the shining of its whiteness, spittle of [17] the moon, froth of the moon, chrysocolla, coppery kohl, litharge, [18] black lead, black silver and (other) symbols with which they named it. Whoever does not know the magnesia, [19] its components, its weights, its union, its operations and the measures of its fire, should not expose

(fol. 108a) himself neither to sadness nor destruction, because nothing can ever come into being without it. [2] In this is what cures you if you understand it, and for whoever comes after you, if God wishes to bless them. Do you not [3] see that the sage had summarized all the work in this sentence when he said: [4] "Take mercury and solidify it in the body of magnesia."»

She said: «You are right. I understood [5] that they are three. So, is the magnesia composed or single?» He said: «It is composed.»

[6] She said: «And is the body a composed one or a single one?» He said: «It is a composed one.»

She said: [7] «So why did Democritus name it one nature?» He said: «That is when all things came together [8] in the magnesia; it is like the ship [9] that is called one ship although it contains many utensils, and like the human being who is named by his name, although he has a body, [10] a spirit and a soul. He is one in name, but if you analyse him you will find [11] more than one thing in him.»

She said: «I have understood what you have said about this. Yet my mind is not able [12] to understand the true composition of the magnesia, and I was hoping [13] that I had arrived at the truth when I said three to you.» He said: «You have arrived at the truth, but these three [14] are composed.»

She said: «So perhaps Hermes named himself three-folded with the benefit, because of that.» [15] He said: «By God, you have spoken and pondered well. Yes. Because of this, Hermes was named [16] three-folded with the benefit. You are right but you are also wrong.»

She said: «How can [17] wrong and right be together?» He said: «They can. By mentioning the three you were right, but [18] by forgetting to ask about the work you were wrong.»

She said: «You are right. I have thought for a long time that [19] I obtained the knowledge but what is in my hand is only little.»

(fol. 108b) He said: «I was also like that, until the Opener of mercy inspired me for this work.»

[2] She said: «Then tell me, O Zosimos, about the statement of your sage conconcerning the making of gold, [3] when he said: "The mercury from cinnabar, the body of magnesia and the pure water."» [4] He said: «You have asked a good question.»

She said: «Then answer it well, O Zosimos.» He said: [5] «Understand this. Do you not see that the sage said: "The making of gold can only be with the mercury of cinnabar, [6] and the mercury of cinnabar only comes out of the body of magnesia."»

She said: «I see that there are different mercuries.» [7] He said: «Yes, there is not one but there are (several) mercuries, but their master and [8] king is the mercury of cinnabar, which is extracted from the body of magnesia. So to the eye it becomes [9] one white, shining mercury from different mercuries, whose essence is red.»

She said: [10] «Then why did the sage say: "Take cinnabar"?» He said: «In order to tell you that the only mercury that is ever good [11] for making gold is the one which is cooked with the body of magnesia. So [12] the body and its mixtures become one mercury, and it teaches it to resist fire. That is because the mercury [13] of cinnabar is useless for whoever does not know the completeness and the marrying.»

She said: [14] «Then tell me about the completeness.» He said: «Have you not read in the book that nature [15] enjoys nature?» She said: «Is that what he meant?» He said: «Yes.» She said: «I see that there is a relationship between the two.» [16] He said: «Yes, like the relationship between your flesh and your blood.»

She said: «Then tell me about when your sage said: [17] "O people of Egypt, I have brought for you the true natures. So throw away the vanities [18] which destroy wealth and hurt bodies."» He said: «The sage is right, but I see that [19] you do not understand what he meant. He means the magnesia, but he repeats the statement.

(fol. 109a) Ponder over when he said: “Take mercury and solidify it in the body of magnesia.” [2] There he did not say cinnabar or anything else, and he says in his second treatise: “Take the mercury [3] from arsenic, sandarach and pure water.” Then after that he said: “Take the body of magnesia.”»

[4] She said: «This statement confuses me.» He said: «This is because you do not understand. Do you not see that when [5] he mentioned the mercury of arsenic and sandarach, and then after that he said: “Take magnesia,” [6] he named the body of magnesia arsenic and sandarach.” Although he makes his statement difficult, [7] this is a blessing.»

She said: «Then what did he mean when he said “mercury from arsenic and sandarach”? » He said: [8] «He ordered us to dissolve both of them until they turn into water. Then he ordered them to be solidified until [9] what was not a body becomes a body.» She said: «I see that this must be turned into water and then solidified.» [10] He said: «You are right.»

She said: «Then what about when he says: “Put a white nature on our copper [11] thus it becomes white.”» He said: «I did not think that you would ask me about this.» She said: «Why not?» He said: [12] «Because that white nature is white mercury. Yet that mercury is not [13] single but composed. It is the mercury of cinnabar, and in it there is the magnesia and the body [14] of magnesia. So it makes the copper white because when copper and mercury come together, we call them [15] the body of magnesia. And he ordered us to solidify both of them, because they dissolve together. They should only [16] be solidified after they (first) got dissolved.»

She said: «Then tell me about his statement: “Take the pyrite [17] which is similar to iron, dissolve it, and break it into fragments”.» He said: «By that he meant that [18] when the copper is mixed with things similar to it, its colour changes, and it turns into a silvery pyrite.»

She said: «Then tell me [19] about the statement of the sage: “Break the lead into fragments until it becomes black,” and his statement: “Do not be deluded (fol. 109b) by the lead of the people."» [from the above: He said: «Yes, because he said:] "Rather you should make use of the lead of the sages which we made from the silvery stone."»

2 She said: «Why did the sage name it: "The torturer of her husband"?» He said: «That is because 3 she enters quickly into his body, and she is the quickest to dissolve him, and she is the quickest to solidify him, 4 destroy him, and turn him into a spirit, unless you mix it with wrong measures. If you mix it 5 with wrong measures, you fall into error and by that the slowness comes. If slowness comes, 6 bad thoughts come in. The sage distinguished different kinds of fire. He ordered us that at the beginning, 7 at the time of the dissolving, the fire should be gentle.»

She said: «Then tell me, why did the sage choose 8 the seventh number at the time of the completeness?» He said: «That is because the seventh number is 9 the head of the account, and it is its completeness because the work starts and is completed by it. For that reason 10 the sage said: "The beginning is by that one. And the other one is what 11 dissolves, what burns, what makes black, and what makes white at the time of the completeness. 12 By that other one it is completed also." When the sage knew the power of that 13 composed one he praised and lauded it and said: "O you heavenly creative natures 14 into which our God put natures of his power that win over the natures, and overcome them." And he (that sage) continued: 15 "Nothing comes after God except this nature, nothing is higher ranking or more inferior than it, and nothing is like it." 16 Thus, my lady, you should be content with this one sentence 17 because all of the science is included in it.»

She said: «Then tell me, O Zosimos, about when the sage says: 18 "O you sages, do not dare to reject my statement after you have come to know the power 19 of the nature, because the ones who come after you will disbelieve the truth as a result of their ignorance of the power and the virtue of the natures."»

(fol. 110a) He said: «By this statement he meant the composed nature which I told you [2] dissolves, burns, makes white and makes black every thing. About this nature [3] Agathodaimon said: "After making the copper rusty, making it black, and the pounding of the pounded, then at [4] the end of the whitening, the redness will be an exalted redness." That is what the sage really meant. And because [5] the opinion of all the sages is one, and their operation is one, and their testimony is one, the natures [6] which all of them mentioned are the nature that I told you about. It is [7] the true nature and it is one composed nature. They only sought one thing [8] and they worked with it. I recommend you to know the merit of that nature and its power, [9] to unite it in harmony with its relatives, so you would mix and operate on it well, and you will find [10] your happiness through it, God willing.»

She said: «Then tell me, O Zosimos, about why the sages blamed the sage <Bit>Tīmīs [11] because he did not place with the nature what is similar to it from the natures.» He said: [12] «Democritus and Tīmīs and all the sages spoke much about this and its different aspects, [13] because it burns more than the fire. This is what I ordered you to know. Do you not see [14] how the sage Tīmīs said: "Take the purified lead, but I order you neither the lead of the people, [15] nor the lead of one body, but a mixed lead composed with the flowers of gold, [16] the ferment, the eternal water and sour vinegar." He ordered us to close the mouth of the vessel, and to keep [17] what is inside it when we cook it. He declared that if the two were separated, it would become vile and [18] ugly. This is thus to be borne in mind.»

She said: «Tell me more.» He said: «I order you to roast it [19] on a gentle fire, being careful not to make it strong, until the two mix, dissolve and turn into (fol. 110b) one thing. When the blackness covers them, cook it as much as possible so that it changes, and dissolve it [2] until the moisture disappears. Know that this can only be after many days. [3] Be patient until the mercury becomes solid, and turns into a stone in its place.»

She said: «Then tell me, [4] O Zosimos, about the statement of Isis (*Asīda*): "Out of a human being comes only a human being, and out of animals come [5] only (animals) like themselves. Therefore limit yourselves to what I ordered you, as I have put you on the right path. [6] So do not abandon it, after having known it, otherwise you will regret it."» He said: «She spoke well [7] for whoever understands. Do you not see that she meant that a nature only works with its nature, [8] and only what is similar to it can come from it. So take the honourable nature because the work [9] comes from it, not from anything else. Know that if you do not operate on it well, you will have nothing, and know [10] that this is one of the secrets of the sages.»

She said: «Then tell me about the statement of the sage, where he says: [11] "Marry the honoured blond one, who emerges from the red slave—who served [12] the noble, the despised and the animals, whose dwelling is (in) worms. Marry him to [13] his white woman whose skin is soft, and whom nature turned into a spirit."» He said: [14] «He spoke well and I told you a long time ago, but I see that you do not understand that the blond one and [15] his white woman are the magnesia. If the two are married with what is similar to them and what brings agreement [16] between them both, they give birth to the work, God willing, because pregnancy comes soon and also delivery, [17] as the red slave can only exist by the blond one, which comes out of it (the red slave). How noble is [18] its pure virgin woman, who came out from the place where the sun rises. I order you, [19] not to heat her bath too much otherwise she faints. Put them both into the bath (fol. 111a) until their colour and their body (the text has "her body") become one thing, and their sweat (moisture) returns to them. [2] And be careful not to harm them with a strong fire, otherwise you will regret it. But cook them until they become black [3] and the blackness becomes visible. Then the blackness disappears and the whiteness comes. Then the whiteness goes away and [4] the redness comes, and it turns into a perfect dye.»

She said: «Then tell me about the statement of the sage when he said: [5] "If you are a sage, I have informed you. If you are an ignorant person, we have hidden it from you." And he declared [6] that he had given you a summary, avoiding an elaborate talk. He declared that what you are looking for comes into being from the blond one [7] and his wife, not from anything else.» He said: «What he said was true: [8] "From the sperm of the man the child has to come. If the sperm had not entered the womb, and it (the womb) had not loved it [9] in the darkness, and then nourished it by the decree of the exalted God, the child would not have come into being. In the same way, the wife of [10] the blond one makes the sperm dissolve in her womb, and nourishes it until the child comes out complete, [11] if her composition was made well, and if that which is good for her is made to enter her. But if she (the woman) separates from it, [12] they will both die."»

She said: «What is that which kills her when it separates from her?» He said: «The moisture of the truth.»

She said: [13] «Will you not tell me about Isis (*Asīda*) and what she said about the inundation of the moisture, and the great vision which [14] was revealed to her when the planet rotated— it was Saturn—and his (Saturn's) descending to her from the seventh sky, [15] and his attempt to seduce her? But she refused his request unless he taught (offered to teach) her the making of gold [16] and silver, because he was the master of that, and with him is the basis of the matter of nature, after the exalted God. [17] He refused her this but then he returned to her, and she asked him about his name. He declared that he was the greatest fighter.» [18] He said: «If you are only asking me in order to confirm what you know, you are not the first who doubted. [19] But if you are asking me out of ignorance of what Isis alluded to, (fol. 111b) maybe I should increase it (your ignorance) for you.»

She said: «Know, O Zosimos, by the great Judge of souls, [2] all these questions that I am putting to you are not out of blindness or doubting about whoever came before you, rather I find pleasure and [3] comfort in what you illuminate for me, by which God increases my happiness.» He said: «Concerning these things [4] which Isis said, they are: She is the white woman and the blond one is Amṯiāīl (Amael). So she compared [5] herself with that woman, and she took Amṯiāīl as her companion. And I told you that they only write [6] by giving enigmatic allusions and examples.»

She said: «Then what about her statement when <he> [she] pointed to [7] <her> [his] head?»[66] He said: «That is the water with the waves.»

She said: «She was not satisfied with that [8] unless he completed it.» He said: «I do not know what to say to you except that I am surprised by your question. [9] Do you not know that nothing ever comes from the blond one and his wife except with [10] other things? Did you not understand her statement when she said: "I will make you swear by the one who destroys the waves of the sea (God), and [11] I will make you swear with the flaming torture and with the fiery sword." So why did you ask me after that. [12] If you did not understand what she said, then go to the ploughmen (*akārīn*) and ponder on what they sow [13] and what they harvest. And ponder over all creatures, and how one thing comes from (many) things. [14] Then you will know that whoever sows wheat only harvests wheat, and if you sow [15] wheat you do not harvest barley. "Cultivate gold and you will harvest gold." This is the key of [16] the truth that is written in the books, and the sages only describe it symbolically. [17] I made that clear to you so that you would not look for stones, sands, or natures, which were not what [18] I ordered you. Otherwise you would spend your days searching for what you do not know regarding this secret that [19] I explained to you. For it is a simple thing and readily available.»

She said: «Then tell me about when you say: "This

[66] See M. Berthelot, *Alchimistes Grecs*, "Isis to Horus", I.XIII.2-4.

(fol. 112a) work is of two types: one of them is a hidden thing that the sages kept secret [2] for the intelligent people in order that they might extract it by their contemplation and precise understanding. As for [3] the second type, it is delusions and vanities, made from many operations and many things which are all [4] false."» He said: «Yes, it is as you said. But whoever understands must analogise what [5] he doubts about this work with the matters of the world, and he must ponder over these four [6] natures, the earth, the water, the air and the fire, for everything that the exalted God created [7] is from these four. Its birth and its nourishment come from them, its life is by them, and to them it returns, [8] by the will of God. So whoever wants to enter into this work should not doubt it. He must analogise it [9] with the matters of the world, contemplate on these four natures, and know that the uncountable number [10] of human beings is created from those two, Adam and Eve. So whoever enters into this [11] work, should not look for the many things, but only for the one origin. [12] Then he should work hard for its marriage, its fecundation and its operation. For by it, people and animals multiply. [13] And you, my lady, if you know the natures, you must make use of their master, because it is what [14] you are looking for.»

She said: «O Zosimos, then tell me about the statement of Democritus when he said: "You had been given [15] all of the science, so only the cloud and the rising of the water remain for you."» He said: «He gave them what is not useful for them, [16] for they kept the truth secret because all of this work is from the cloud and the rising of the water. [17] Concerning its rising, it is clear and known in the books of the sages. Concerning its composition, its components [18] and its weights, we did not write them, so that is what we missed out. If he had revealed that, nothing would be missing. [19] But he spoke a sentence that is not bad at all: "If you see the natures become water by the heat of (fol. 112b) the fire, and they become pure, and all of the body of the magnesia is dissolved like water, then [2] everything becomes a cloud, and it is the suitable time for the cloud to hold on to its relative." That is why [3] the sage named the two clouds because both come together in the cooking and they cling to each other, [4] and neither of them finds a way to escape even though escaping is in their character. But [5] with them there is something that holds them back and makes them cling, so they do not find a place to escape. Therefore [6] the fugitive one (the female spirit) embraces the seeker. So the two are imprisoned, (correction from the margin) in the vessel, because when the poor one (the female spirit) falls down into [7] the body, she coagulates in it, changes her colour, and her nature is changed by using ruses (*ḥīla*) and gentleness. [8] When blackness and redness cover it (the body), she falls sick and dies in the making rusty and she becomes rotten. [9] At that time it is right that she does not escape, because she quit the natural disposition of a slave, namely to escape, and she became [10] free, clinging to her husband. At this time, she prays sincerely to her God that He may return [his] first [colour] (correction from the margin) to Him, [11] the same as it was at the beginning, before the death.» And I tell you that the work is from two. But [12] the sages named these two composed ones because these two became four [13] having in them dryness, moisture, spirit, and cloud. The confirmation of what I say is the statement of Hermes, when [14] he said: "Mix the things, turn them into magnesia, and throw it into the sea." Then [15] his student Būsīūs said to him: "Do you order us, O Sage, three-folded with the benefit, to put it into [16] the sea before we mix it?" He said: "Yes, do it! You are really like your father with regard to pondering [17] and sharpness." So he ordered us to take the nature, put it into the sea, and to dissolve it in order that it becomes [18] water. Therefore you should know that our work is only good with the moisture and the gentle fire, [19] whose heat is like the heat of the sun in wintertime.»

She said: «Then tell me, O Zosimos, about what

(fol. 113a) Ṯaūfīl wrote in his book when he said: "Take pure tin which you know, magnesia, [2] Indian *asṭām* (lead?) and mercury."» He said: «As for the tin, I do not think that you ignore it. As for the body of [3] magnesia, the mercury, and what he ordered you to mix it with, thus he started at the beginning of his statement with the first [4] work. Then entered with it the other work.»

She said: «Then separate for me the first work [5] and the other one.» He said: «The first one is the magnesia, the *asṭām*, and the mercury, while the other one is [6] the body of magnesia. The body of magnesia is the mercury that is named the water of sulphur, [7] and it dyes every gold. I repeat for you in order that you understand that whoever does not know the [8] body of magnesia that ordinary people have, should die in his grief because his work is futile and [9] he will end in sadness.»

She said: «Then what is the magnesia which ordinary people have?» ~~<he should die in his grief because his work is futile, and [9] he will end in sadness.>~~ <What is the magnesia?> [11] He said: «It is what the sage named the mixing of the natures. Likewise he said [12] at the beginning of his speech: "Take the mercury, then coagulate it in the body of magnesia." Thus he started [13] the beginning of the work with truth and faithfulness, and he guided the one who has understanding to the right path. However, [14] this magnesia does not remain fixed in one colour after it gets mixed.»

She said: «How can [15] this be?» He said: «When its colour changed in the first stage, they derived a name for it with which they named it, so they named [16] it Disīūs. Then it changed to another colour, and they named it a changeable frog-stone.

[17] She said: «Why was it named changeable?» He said: «If you knew the changer and the changed, you would not ask me about [18] this. But I will give you an analogy for it. Do you not see that when a human being becomes sick [19] his colour turns yellow, and they say: "So-and-so has changed." And likewise that body, when it gets mixed with its water,

(fol. 113b) it falls into sickness, and the magnesia changes its colour and removes its beauty, and turns it into silver [2] like the water. And it is right that it is named frog-stone because it disappeared in the shadow and became invisible. This is what made the seekers [3] unable to remove its shadow. So no wonder they had to destroy it and to pound its pounded, and they turn [4] it into an airy spirit, whereas before it was a thick, earthly body.»

[5] She said: « Which one of them did that to it?» He said: «The earth did that to [6] the reddish male, which is changed by the destruction and decomposition.»

She said: «What about the statement of the sage: "Mercury of the male, [7] body of magnesia, glue of gold?"» He said: «I told you that the body is [8] the changer, and it (the body) is the decomposed male, and it is our copper that is from our work. But [9] when it becomes rotten we name it with many names. So when it is moist, we name it with the name of [10] every moist thing, and when it is dry, we name it with the name of every dry thing. Do you not see that when the sage [11] wanted to make us more sure, he said: "A sulphur that does not get burnt." She said: «What is the sulphur [12] that does not get burnt?» He said: «When the body and the waters become dry, all the bodies and all the waters become [13] one thing in the vessel. At this time we call it sulphur that does not get burnt.»

[14] She said: «And how is it that it does not get burnt, when you declare that it is destroyed and dies?» He said: [15] «Concerning the first body, it does not get burnt, but when it is destroyed, it has taught its companion how [16] to resist the fire, to be patient with it, to be firm in the vessel, and how to stop escaping.»[67]

She said: [17] «You answered well, and you chased away my doubt. But tell me, why did he name it [18] gold that does not get burnt at the moment when it turned white?» He said: «Do you not understand when the sage said: [19] «The mercury is white, makes white, and dissolves everything.»? When it coagulates with

[67] In the margin we read: I said, but God knows best, that when the natures are destroyed and made lean they turn into ash, and all ash cannot be burnt by fire. Understand that, for it is a great principle. Whoever dyes ash has achieved his aim by God, to whom we look for help.

(fol. 114a) its body, the body turns it into red dust, and it is unable to escape. So they named it [2] incombustible sulphur because it has with it what does not get burnt. Whoever does not know what I am saying to him, [3] his life will pass without any meaning.»

She said: «Then what about when Maria said: "Start with the name of the exalted God. [4] Then take the mercury and solidify it ~~<in the body of magnesia>~~ with whatever [5] you want, and however you want, in the reddish body that is the reddish male, the body [6] of magnesia. Then cook it with its white nature so that the copper becomes white, even though it [7] is dissolved until it turns into water covered with blackness. When it coagulates by cooking, it turns into silver. [8] And when it is destroyed, it turns into gold. When it gets operated on, it would turn into aqzal gold, and when it is soaked [9] with the white nature, it would be cooked gold, aqzal gold, and when it gets rotten by cooking [10] and pounding, it would turn into purple gold."» He said: «Maria spoke well. She described [11] the complete work for you in this brief statement, and she made the operation and the colours clear for you. Do not [12] think that she meant that it would turn into silver like the silver of ordinary people, nor that it would turn into gold, like [13] the gold of ordinary people, but she meant with it the colours. Do you not understand the end of [14] her statement about this: "Take the male and the water which you know, and cook it [15] with the eternal water and the body which is defeated."»

She said: «Which body is this?» He said: [16] «It is the body that is only defeated by the torturer of her husband, whose nourishment is gold.» [17]

She said: «Then tell me about when Maria said: "This is the making of the ingot, which the [18] exalted God gave to His prophet Moses, may peace be on him, in order to sustain with it the people of Israel, and to make from it [19] the body of magnesia. Then the male and the female are mixed, pounded and cooked (fol. 114b) in a vessel till the two turn into water."» He said: «This is the rotting which Maria named in other places [2] "lead-copper, honoured stone." It is what the sages ordered to be cooked [3] until it turns into water, then to be pounded in the sun until it turns white, and then to be cooked until it turns red. [4] After that, they ordered ~~<the sages to cook untill it becomes water>~~ intensive cooking.»

She said: «Then tell me about [5] when she said: "Take the honoured stone, roast it in a vessel with the eternal one, and cook it on [6] the fire until the plates break into fragments and become water in the vessel.» He said: «It is similar to what you asked me, [7] it is in the other one (the second work). Do you not see what Maria said: "After you turn it into water, cook it [8] until it becomes black and dry it, so it will turn into whatever you want." She (also) said: "Our magnesia is what dissolves [9] its body in the casting, until it becomes water. Then it (the magnesia) turns it (the body) into a very strong red rust." [10] So when you see it like that, then take the flower of copper that is the red rust [11] and soak it till its flower comes out. Then soak it according to what you see, and it will become [12] a gold flower (*ḏahab zahr*). [12] Then cook and soak it with the poison, so that the gold becomes cooked, and also soak it [13] further in water and cook it, so that it will become aqzal gold. If you soak it [14] with the poison till it quenches its thirst, it will be purple gold. And if you soak it again and again with the poison, [15] that will be better for its dyeing, and it (the dye) will submerge more quickly. Then you must make your fire stronger [16] in this operation until whatever you want is completed.

She said: «O Zosimos, I already knew that copper becomes [17] rusty before the blackness, and it should be made white by the eternal water, and it should be solidified so that it becomes a body of [18] magnesia. And it has to be is cooked till all of it breaks up into fragments, so that the fugitive turns into ashes and [19] the copper turns into dyed silver without shadow.» He said: «Then why do you ask me about something with which (fol. 115a) you are already satisfied, and that you obviously already know?»

She said: «Maybe I asked you about [2] something that I know but I ask you to be reconfirmed. I never get enough [3] of asking you questions about what the sages wrote, because the exalted God increases the benefit in me by what they advise. [4] Thus tell me more.» He said: «Then ask me about whatever you want.»

She said: «Then tell me also about when [5] Maria said: “The body should be mixed with pyrite equally.”» He said: [6] «Maria is right, but you have little understanding. Did I not tell you that Maria already said in a thousand places: [7] “The equal with the equal.” Is it not like that?»

She said: «I was thinking that she said this [8] about the magnesia.» He said: «She did indeed mean the magnesia, but [9] she changed the names, <she said> and this is how the sages try to hide this work. [10] And if it were not like that, then whoever reads their books would know what they meant. But they hid [11] the one thing with symbolic (*rumūzāt*) names. I tell you that if you cook this with [12] its right measure of fire, you will make from it a great work. The attempt and the efforts of the sages [13] with regard to hiding this matter was about the composition of the magnesia. So whoever does not know the magnesia, [14] what it contains, its weights and its combination should rather die, or he should just not enter into anything of this [15] work, because otherwise its harm would be greater than its benefit.»

She said: «Why did you not answer [16] my question about the burning of the copper, that burning which the exalted God taught Moses. [17] Your statement just branched out to things that came to your mind. Answer my question about [18] her statement.» He said: «I already told you that the copper should be burnt, till it becomes [19] rust, and the fugitive sulphur becomes white by the body of magnesia and the mercury, (fol. 115b) and it has to be cooked well, and the one who cooks it must not be impatient till the copper turns into flowers.»

She said: «Then tell me [2] what is the magnesia, what is the body of magnesia, and what is the black lead?» [3] He said: «You asked about something that no sage who knew this work would have felt happy [4] to reveal. But I will tell you something about it, hoping that you will understand. As for the magnesia [5] it is the mixing of the two. And as for the body of magnesia, the one is [6] a body, and the other is not a body. So when you find in the books: "Dissolve the magnesia", then know that [7] one is always dissolved, but you should dissolve what is not dissolved with the dissolved one. [8] Thus persist in the reading of the books, and thank God for what you owe Him.»

She said: «Then what about [9] when he said: "Make a gum from the male and the female dragon (*tinnīn*)."» He said: «He spoke well, because in both of them are [10] the red and the white, so this is the magnesia that lights up when we mention it. And Hermes said: [11] "I order you to give it its right food and nourishment in the first dissolving, and to cook it [12] until it becomes a white cluster. By this operation the earth becomes polished." [13] You must know that the gum is gums, but we named them gum [14] because it holds and is held. It is what improves the flower, but that comes in the operation of [15] the greatest nature.»

She said: «Then tell me about when he says: "The mixing should take place [16] from the 25th October […] till the 25th of April […]» (this is six months). [17] He said: «By that they meant that you must mix what you are able to mix, as much as you can afford, and wash it, [18] make salty, break into fragments and leave it in a vessel till the moisture solidifies with its components of the mixture. [19] And know that they loved each other, and it clings and is clung to. After that, ponder (fol. 116a) when the sun descends in Cancer and in Leo. Then you should return the six [2] onto the thing that you know. Concerning the white nature that you have, it is from [3] the white nature having the truth in it. If you want to try that, take a little of it [4] and mix it with the magnesia. Concerning the white cluster, cook it so that it gets pounded with it [5] in a few days, and it becomes like shining blood. Do that until it absorbs [6] all of the six. Know that if you seek this stone that you asked me about, you will find it [7] in abundance in the mountains of Egypt.[68] You should know how that stone is born, where it is born, [8] how much of it is operated on and how it is made salty. Therefore you keep all of this in mind in a simple way because [9] this is the great secret with which the sages were entrusted, and it is the crown of [10] all things.»

She said: «Then tell me about all of this.» He said: «We wrote it for you in [11] the books.»

She said: «You wrote it scattered (in many places), so please collect it for me!» He said: «Do you not know that [12] I wrote about "the big making salty" in the first, the second and the third book. If you understand, [13] then start with the honoured hidden secret that is the white magnesia which is mixed [14] three to one. Take it only pure, and your hands should also be clean and pure. [15] Then put it in a vessel with a pure heart and sincere intention, and invoke the exalted God during night [16] and day that He may make you see the greatest stone. Then put that stone on the fire in the name of [17] the greatest exalted God, and cook it gently for seven days. Then take it out and see [18] whether it has turned into a black stone. If it becomes like that, then you have operated perfectly. Otherwise operate on it [19] with the white one, as it is the greatest secret, until it turns into antimony,

[68] Margin: A very honourable statement on this page and on the one before. May God make a benefit out of it.

(fol. 116b) so that blackness covers all of the surface of the composition. Know that this blackness does not remain more than 40 days. Then pound [2] with it its components: one (part) from the flower of copper, one (part) from saffron, and one (part) from [3] cracked alum. Those are (together with the antimony) four parts. Cook it well for 40 days, [4] then during those days the exalted God will show you the origin (*maᶜdin*) of the stone that you asked me about. It [5] is named etesian, which (means) it is born every year.»

She said: «Then tell me about the statement of Bidīsios: [6] "Take the whitened body of magnesia, and mercury that got mixed with the male, [7] and pound it very fine till it turns into a gentle (*raqīq*) water, and divide the water into two parts."» He said: [8] «With regard to the body of magnesia, it is what destroyed the seekers of the science because of their ignorance about it. [9] So whoever does not know the body of magnesia is neither suited to enter into this work, [10] nor to run the risk of doing it because its harm is greater than its benefit. Many times I told you [11] about the body of magnesia but I only named it to you together with many things, and [12] at other places—where you did not ask for it—I named it with its true name. Therefore you did not recognize it.»

[13] She said: «Clarify for me an aspect of it that I may recognize.» He said: «At the beginning of the work it was [14] a body. When it got mixed with the magnesia it became white, red, fiery mercury. [15] Whenever they named it body of magnesia, they are right because it was a body. [16] In this way and in ways similar to it, they were able to hide this work. All of that [17] you have asked me several times before, and I answered you. If I told you [18] that much of what you ask me about is one, and I repeated that for you a thousand times, [19] I would be truthful.»

She said: «Then tell me about when the sage said: "Copper does not dye until (fol. 117a) it gets dyed, thus when it gets dyed, it dyes."» He said: «Is anybody able to dye something solid [2] with something solid?»

She said: «You know best.» He said: «I tell you that the body is not able [3] to dye itself except when its spirit, concealed in its interior, is extracted from it. So it turns into [4] a body and a spirit without a natural spiritual soul, and the earthly thickness disappears from it. [5] When it turns gentle and spiritual before the dying, and it submerges into the body, it (the body) is dyed.» [6]

She said: «And how does it dye?» He said: «When the earth operates on the magnesia, it will extract its gentle part, [7] so it becomes a dyer. This is what the sage meant by: "Copper does not dye until it is dyed." [8] And know that the four bodies get dyed and do not get dyed, because when the magnesia turns white, [9] it will not let the dyes escape, and it will not let the shadow of the copper appear.»

She said: «How astonishing when [10] the sage says that the four bodies get dyed and do not get dyed. And he did not say as usual [11] that when they get dyed, they dye.» He said: «That is in order that you know that he named the hard bodies [12] the body of magnesia.»

She said: «Which magnesia is this?» He said: «It is the whole composition.»

[13] She said: How does it become white?» He said: «If it is operated on as it should, and is broken into fragments by roasting, and [14] the sulphurs extract the subtle part of the hard body concealed in their interior (the bodies), [15] then out of it (their subtle part) blossom their beautiful colours. So the bodies, which is the body, become rotten because [16] when the composition is soaked by the sulphur and gets mixed, it will neither let the colours escape, with [...] nor [(see line 9 above and fol. 118b, 12)] to let [17] the shadow of the copper appear.

She said: «Then tell me about when the sage says: "Take the egg which does not come from a bird."» [18] He said: «That is the egg of the sages.»

She said: «Why did they name it egg?» He said: «It is one of [19] its first names, and its names amounted to 10,000.» She said: «Why did they do that?»

(fol. 117b) He said: «In order to hide it from the ignorant.»

She said: «So describe to me this egg with its colours.» He said: 2 «Concerning its innermost interior, it is moist red. Its outer appearance is white, and on the white there is another white, 3 and one of the two whites is stronger than the other.»

She said: «They spoke well when they named it egg.» 4 He said: «In this way they confused the people in their books because they took everything they saw that resembles 5 this (their work), using it as a name for their work. When the seeker of this work reads that, he has no doubt that 6 what they named is specifically the dye in their hands. So he takes it, works with it, and falls into error. 7 Then he blames the sages, while he himself deserves more to be blamed because he has no understanding. How does it come about that 8 he who wants to enter into this work, and to take the greatest treasure of God and its amulets 9 for himself, is not afraid when he takes the eggs of birds, wanting to extract from them a dye that does not vanish 10 in the fire?»

She said: «You spoke well about this, O Zosimos! Then tell me, is every thing moist 11 in the egg?» He said: «No, but some of it is moist and some of it is dry. Therefore the sages ordered 12 that it should be slaughtered with a sword of fire, and sour vinegar should be poured on it. Then one has to separate its soul and 13 its body by intense cooking till the soul becomes like snow, and the body becomes red 14 like fire. After that, if you want the completeness, mix the body with the soul 15 and cook it for 80 days until the body is made lean, and the soul is dyed, and it (the body) becomes 16 red like purple. Because of this, the sages said: "One from two, and two from 17 three, and from three four."»

She said: «You are enigmatic in what you say.» He said: «No. I am not. But 18 I tell you more. If you turn the earth into water, and the water into air, and the air into fire, you will reach the goal.»

19 She said: «I did not understand what you said. How can one separate between the body [and the soul], the soul of the work

(fol. 118a) and its body? And how does the earth turn into water, and the water into air, and the air into fire? And why did [2] the sages name their egg the egg of the hen?» He said: «You asked about something that the sages were [3] unhappy to describe to anybody.»

She said: «Then answer me and illuminate what is difficult for me [4] to understand.» <She said: «Then answer me and illuminate what is difficult for me [4] to understand.»> [5] He said: «Concerning the egg that the sages used, I already told you that it is from various things. [6] One can only make a dye from it if one cooks it in the sun [7] and the shadow for 80 days. Every thickness becomes decomposed and becomes rotten. At that time, the earth turns into [8] water, and the water into air, and the air ~~<after that>~~ into fire. So these three things get united and concealed in [9] one thing,[69] having spirits that are not seen in any one of them. And know that [10] the earth was not able to disappear or to escape when it turned into water, and [11] its solid part separated from it, and the water extracted its spirit, so that it became a fugitive. Therefore the sages warned the people of [12] this work about the escaping of what they have.»

She said: «I see that these things are fugitives.» [13] He said: «Yes. Therefore the sages preferred the fugitives to those that do not flee.»

She said: [14] «Does this fugitive have a name by which it is known?» He said: « How many names it has!»

She said: [15] «Then tell me some.» He said: «It is the dragon eating its tail, for the egg [16] has been divided into four parts, thus when they were operated on and mixed, they turned into [17] one thing like the four natures of the world.»

She said: «How does it eat its tail?» [18] He said: «When its similar one that is like it enters into it, it (the dragon) eats it (the similar one) and turns it (the similar one) into [19] water. Then what the dragon ate turned into a body. Concerning their comparison of their egg to the egg

[69] From line 6 up to here we find this text also in the *Kitāb al-ḥabīb*, M. Berthelot, *La Chimie au Moyen Age* III, p. 100, § 2. See Part I, p. 49-51.

(fol. 118b) of a hen, that is because the colours of their egg are like the colours of an egg (of a hen). And secondly [2] they already knew before they dissolved it that it has a flying fugitive in it which escapes [3] with its companions. And just as you have the egg of the hen which we (also) have, and you know that it is only [4] an egg ~~<only in the name>~~ of a hen <and its body>, when this egg is put under [5] the hen, a bird comes out of it. The egg of the sages is like that. It has in it [6] a body and a soul, and it has also in it what escapes, which is the magnesia; and they named it like that but [7] its name has been changed.

She said: «Then tell me, O Zosimos, how does it come about that the sage said: "The mercury fights [8] the copper."» He said: «Indeed, he ordered you to solidify both of them, as the sage said: "Take the mercury and [9] solidify it in the body of magnesia."»

She said: «Is the magnesia a male or a female?» [10] He said: «It is a female. Do you not see when I told you that it has the power of the female, and it is what dissolves everything, and it is [11] what turns the bodies into spirits, God willing? How astonishing you are! Do you not see when Democritus said: [12] "When the magnesia is whitened, it does not let the spirits escape, nor does it let [13] a colour appear on the copper."»

She said: «What solidifies the mercury? »He said: «The fire solidified it [14] in the operation by the power of the male. When it got whitened it prevented the mercury from escaping.»

She said: «Then tell me about [15] when Maria said: "Take mercury, solidify it as you want, and turn it into magnesia."» [16] He said: «The solidification of the mercury has to be rather at the beginning of the work. And like that [17] Democritus ordered that the mercury has to be solidified in the body of magnesia.»

She said: «What is [18] the magnesia, and what is its body?» He said: «It is the mixing of copper with the white nature, [19] so it (the copper) turns into silver.»

She said: «Then tell me, O Zosimos, who is he who said: "O you one, three-folded (fol. 119a) in terms of letters, by you the mixing is completed. O you, body of magnesia, from you the secret appeared."» [2] He said: «The first who said this was Hermes, three-folded with benefit. Therefore Hermes [3] himself is named the three-folded with benefit. Only with the body of magnesia do colour and secret come into being. [4] And it is the fermented cluster which is white in appearance and red in essence, [5] and it is the visible secret.»

She said: «Then tell me, what is the mercury of cinnabar?» He said: [6] «It is white in appearance, and red in essence, and when it is mixed with the other copper, [7] it turns red in appearance and in essence. I have told you several times that when the sages name [8] one thing of the composition, they mean the whole composition. When they name all that makes white, [9] then it is just one making white, and when they name all of what makes red, then it is just [10] one making red.»

She said: «Then what about when the sage said: "Take the mercury and solidify it in [11] the body of magnesia."» He said: «That is because the body of magnesia is the cinnabar, and the cinnabar [12] is the incombustible sulphur. When we made it white, we named it sulphur, [13] and when it turned red we named it red sulphur.»

She said: «What turned it into [14] red sulphur?» He said: «When the sulphur (fem.) is mixed with the sulphuric water, it (the feminine sulphur) turned it (the sulphuric water) into [15] red sulphur.»

She said: «Then it is that about which the sage said: «Put it on the gold so it becomes [16] aqzal gold."?» He said: «You are right.»

She said: «Then tell me about this copper: when it enters [17] the making rusty and its shadow becomes invisible, does its shadow really disappear in its nature?» He said: «<Yes> [No], whatever [18] the copper suffers as a result of anything, its nature still remains. Know that although its shadow disappeared [19] from outer appearance, it did not disappear in essence.»

She said: «Then where did it go?» He said: «It became concealed in (fol. 119b) the whiteness of the magnesia, in the same way as the yolk of the egg is concealed in its white, so that it cannot be seen. [2] That is why Democritus said: "When the magnesia is whitened, it does not allow any shadow of the copper [3] to appear." Therefore you should know that the shadow did not disappear but the magnesia [4] conquered it with its whiteness, thus it does not allow it to appear because of its mastering it. As a confirmation of [5] that, I tell you what Maria said: "Copper is never without a shadow but [6] the copper becomes without a shadow when the magnesia makes it white in the operation." An analogy [7] of this for you is the ploughman. When he ploughs under everything that grows on the surface of the earth, [8] nothing is seen anymore, but the roots remain in the earth. Then people do not see them but they continue to be [9] inside the earth like sugar cane, asparagus, and other things similar to them. In the same way, [10] (the shadow of) the copper is alive but not seen. But when it is mixed with the magnesia, [11] it (the magnesia) defeats it (the copper) with its whiteness so it (the shadow of the copper) is not seen. I have already told you that nothing remains of the weight [12] except the copper.»

She said: «Then tell me about when you say in a summary in "The 20th Treatise": [13] "We did not find any sage who said the truth without jealousy, and who spoke [14] better than Democritus, who said: "Put on copper one fourth of [15] sulphuric iron cast with lead, or half of that from sulphur."» He said: [16] «I wrote what you mentioned in that treatise of mine. But we named the copper iron [17] when it is burnt and broken into fragments with its companions, which were only operated on to be mixed with it and to be attached, [18] so the things turned into acacia.»

She said: «Then what about when he says: "Put on this the cloud of mercury, [19] so it turns white.» He said: «The copper turns white with the sulphur and the cloud.»

(fol. 120a) She said: «Why is it named before that magnesia and the fiery one?» [He said:] «From that you should know that if copper, lead, [2] and the honoured stone are mixed together, they will turn into an honoured stone.»

She said: «Then tell me [3] about the treatise that you wrote for me whose summary is: "Indeed in the dusts there is a great work and power."» [4] He said: «I have told you this. That is because they are those which get pounded, whitened, [5] rotten, softened, dyed and are suitable for marriage.»

She said: [6] «Maybe they are those about which Hermes and Sīmās said that they are suitable for the mixing of the sand?» He said: «Yes, [7] they are those which improve everything and to which many names were given. Know [8] that among the people there are some who called them poison. I already told you the names of the stones and the dusts. [9] If you wish me to tell you how that stone gets dyed, I will do so.»

She said: «Tell me.» [10] He said: «Take the silver that is the golden stone having a lot of blood which married [11] its woman, whom he (the sage) named with (many) names. Cast it (the stone) with the poison, roast it, and put [12] on it some alum that we named colocynth (*qalqant*). This is suitable for dyeing [13] silver, yet there are many possibilities to do it wrong unless one knows the operation.»

She said: «Then tell me about [14] your letter to me about "The Treatise of the Magnesia",[70] in which you told me many things, but you did not [15] tell me what its body is.» He said: «How many times you have asked me this, and how many times [16] I spoke to you about it. And I told you that the body of magnesia is all of the mixture [17] that is the natures, the leaden (*ruṣāṣīya*), and the rust. When those were operated on [18] and mixed with a body, the sages named them the body of magnesia. [19] Did you not read in the book of Maria about lead-copper, when she said: "Know

70 This could be the text that Ibn Umail is quoting in his *al-Maʾ al-waraqī*.

(fol. 120b) that the body of magnesia is a hidden composition made of one part of the talcine antimony, [2] one part of the etesian, and one part of the copper burnt with the sulphur. [3] Then cast the antimony and the etesian. When the two are dissolved, pour on both some of [4] the copper while it is dissolved and soften its casting. You will find that the stone above and the lead [5] down below have turned black. Then mix it with mercury." So this is what Maria said about [6] the body of magnesia.»

She said: «Then tell me about when Maria said: "Without [7] lead, nothing can be, and this is the true teaching."» He said: «Maria [8] mentioned in all of her books: "Body of magnesia, black lead, and lead-[9] copper, honoured stone, when they are dissolved equally, their appearance becomes gold, which [10] delights the one who sees it. Its appearance is cast, so by that appearance the raw becomes cooked, [11] and the cooked multiplies." Maria named all the composition a body [12] of magnesia and black lead, and that is before it is dyed.»

She said: «Then what about when you say: [13] "But when it is cooked it fights the sandarach. So do not be content when only the outer appearance of [14] the body of magnesia becomes gold, as its outer appearance and its essence should be gold."» [15] He said: «Maria said that about the magnesia, and Democritus said [16] about the magnesia and lead-copper: "Take the mercury and solidify it in the body of [17] magnesia. So the magnesia is all of the mixture." And I tell you, that when [18] the body of magnesia unites with its components of the mixture, then it is the magnesia.» Then you should put in the mercury, because Democritus said: "Take the mercury and solidify it (fol. 121a) in the body of magnesia. <And I tell you, [2] that when [18] the body of magnesia unites with its components of the mixture, then it is the magnesia.» [3] Then you should put in the mercury, because Democritus said: "Take the mercury [4] and solidify it in the body of magnesia.> And we also named it black lead [5] in the mixture with the fiery one. Know that the sages scattered the making of the magnesia [6] in their books in a thousand places. So whatever you read in their books about any composition [7] do not mind about that because it is one. With regard to what they described about the magnesia, [8] it is the black lead.»

She said: «Then tell me about this.» He said: «When you find [9] in the books of Maria and Democritus the operation of the fiery one, the potash, the claudianus, [10] the androdamus, the chrysocolla, and what is similar to this, indeed, [11] by all of those they meant the operation of lead-copper, which we named the body of magnesia, [12] and black lead. And also ponder over what you find about iron and the operation of silver, [13] or about their operation of tin, copper, or litharge. By this he meant the operation of [14] the magnesia that we named black lead and lead-copper. To make you [15] more convinced: By their whole operation of making gold and making silver [16] they meant lead-copper and the body of magnesia. Thus when they wanted to make it white, [17] they made it white with the white sulphur, and when they wanted to make it red, they mixed the sulphur [18] with the mercury. Then at this time they named it burnt copper. Therefore Agathodaimon said (fol. 121b) in many places: "Take the burnt, pounded, whitened copper." [2] By all this he meant that one which they named body of magnesia [3] and black lead.

She said: «Then tell me about the magnesia in a way that I can understand.» He said: [4] «Did you not read in a book of Democritus when he said: "Magnesia is from [5] Cypriot copper, Indian iron, acacia and the thing which has [6] no power. Or it is from tin, lead, or from magnesia [7] which they solidified with the cloud and broke into fragments, as in the operation of the fiery one and the tin."? [8] So this is the body of magnesia which the sages described without jealousy.»

[9] She said: «I have heard many people say that the body of magnesia [10] is mercury.» He said: «Did you ever see any of their works?»

She said: «No.» He said: [11] «So do not be deluded that the body of magnesia is named body of magnesia, [12] as this is not because it has a body, but when the bodies that do not escape unite with [13] the things which do escape and mix with them, they are named the body of magnesia. [14] Therefore Maria said: "The hidden body of magnesia has [15] to be from the lead, the etesian, and the copper." [16] That is what I told you. Therefore Democritus said: "Mix the mercury with alum, [17] lead-copper, and lime in order that what has no body (mercury) turns into a body."»

[18] She said: «Then tell me about when you say: "When they are mixed with each other [19] they turn into a body of magnesia, especially if you know the

(fol. 122a) right weights."» He said: "I tell you that it is the lead-copper and [2] the black lead about which Maria said: "Take the mercury that we operated on with [3] our white sulphur, and which we cooked for one day and one night until it became white, and from which we made silver, and which we put back [4] to the natron and the oil, and so we turned it into copper without a shadow." Concerning this copper, [5] Agathodaimon said: "Take the burnt, whitened copper that turned into silvery water in the operation." [6] Also it is he who said: "After making the copper rusty, its pounding, its pounding of the pounded and its roasting, [7] then at the highest of its whiteness there will be a high-ranking redness."»

She said: «Then what about his statement about the body [8] of magnesia: "If you intensify the fire, it becomes red, and if you want to make a high-ranking work from it, [9] you could do that."» He said: «I also tell you that: be careful with the intensity of the fire, because it is [10] the ever-present enemy, and from it comes the mysterious error because if you burn the spirits, their dyes are destroyed. [11] Then you will say: "My error came from the natures!" but it is not so. The error and distress came [12] from your bad operation, and your ignorance about the measures of the fire. I tell you that if you reach this point [13] in it (the work), you will reach the completion. Then if you want to make from it a high-ranking multiplication, [14] you can do so. But if you continue to work till it gets very white, turns into pure water, [15] and gets mixed with the other red sulphur, then a high-ranking redness will come out of it. [16] That will come when it is turned into rust and becomes one thing, after the three became four, and the four became [17] one.»

She said: «Then tell me about when you say about the magnesia: "When the natures are mixed [18] with each other with the right weight, they become a body of magnesia:" He said: «I tell you, [19] if you know how to operate on the body of magnesia until you turn it into water of (fol. 122b) white sulphur, you will get a white silver because you made everything white. [2] In this regard, Democritus said: "If you see the poison turning white like marble, it is [3] a great secret." If you turn it properly into red with the other red sulphur, [4] everything will turn red. In this regard Democritus said: "If it becomes red, it dyes every [5] body." If you mix the ferment well with the mercury, you will reach what you are seeking [6] and you will complete the work.»

She said: «Then tell me about when you said to me: "If you do the mixing well, [7] you will dye the body of magnesia." He said: «Yes. By God and I will tell you more about the dyeing of [8] the magnesia. If it turns white, it makes white, and if it turns red, it makes red. [9] Some of the sages made a separate operation and pounding for every component of the magnesia. [10] They ordered that it should be dissolved and raised in a furnace (*qāmīn*) with three openings, [11] and some of them said with only two openings, and some of them said with only one. They disagreed about the fire, [12] so some of them ordered the strong fire, some ordered a moderate one, and some ordered [13] a gentle one. As for Hermes, he ordered that all the things should be put into the sea, so [14] they are pounded with it.»

She said: «Of all of them Hermes said it in the most condensed way.» He said: «Of all of them, he was the one who was most entitled [15] to do that.»

She said: «What about when he said: "Put them into the sea and mix them for some days."» He said: [16] «Indeed, the things marry each other in the sea. Concerning the sea, the mixing, [17] the pounding, and the washing, there is nobody who spoke better about those things than Agathodaimon. [18] Know that among the people there are some who mixed it after all of this operation with [19] the burnt copper that has been operated on with the fiery stone. Then they make a multiplication of it. And there are some (fol. 123a) of the people who mix ~~<after all of this operation with the burnt copper>~~ it with the marble water [2] of lime, the sediment and the fat, so it becomes ready for what they want. [3] They also operate on the stones like that. What I told you was that when you mix the things [4] with each other—whether you operate on them or not—they are the body of magnesia. [5] But you should operate on it and pound it for 21 days, [6] then mix it with fat, then pound it with natron, then put it in a vessel with three [7] openings, so it becomes what you are seeking.»

She said: «Then what about when you say: "Some of the sages take [8] the natures and turn them into plates, and some cool them and mix them with the rest of the things. [9] Then they operate on them and wash them until the copper comes to have no shadow.» [He said:] «I still [10] say that because when these things that are the magnesia get mixed, whether they are operated on [11] or not, they are the body of the magnesia. But if you start to operate on them, every [12] part becomes black lead. Then they get burnt so every thing turns completely into [13] slag (*ašqūrīya*). If you taste and try it, you will find it bitter like the sediment. [14] At this time we name it black lead-copper. You asked me about the magnesia [15] so I spoke to you about it, and I told you about it as much as I hoped that your understanding could grasp, [16] because this magnesia about which the sages wrote in their books is [17] lead-copper for which the people were looking, but they lost their way, except for the sages. Know that the magnesia [18] is their copper. Therefore Taūfīl said: "Take the copper that is the crown of every thing [19] which is called copper (when) it was mixed with every thing." In this regard, Hermes said: "Indeed, our things are (fol. 123b) many, but they are named with one name." So I told you about the making of the body of magnesia [2] which you are still longing to know, and I will give you its weight and its operation [3] in their proper places.»

She said: «Then tell me about your things that only get mixed with your sea.» [4] He said: «Do you not know that Badisīūs said: "We should put the [5] white cluster into the sea in order that the magnesia be married with its components of the mixture."? Thus Hermes said: "You are right," [6] and he added "in the sea there must be two weights from the water of the air."»

She said: «What are [7] these two weights?« He said: « Hermes said: "If you put two parts of [8] the airy (water) into the sea, the sea will become strong, complete, having a soul and being fecundated."»

She said: «How does it become [9] complete from those two parts?» He said: «Do you not know that if the sea is single, it has no [10] power? Yet when the two waters, which were extracted from the stone and [11] the Cypriot copper by the operation, are concealed inside it, it becomes strong. At this time, the sea becomes passionately happy [12] to meet the airy water, which is its relative. Look at Hermes, who refused [13] to mention it (the airy water) with the magnesia until he had finished the operation of the sea, and said: "Mix [14] the glue with the natron, the alum and the blood, and leave them in front of the furnace, [15] because the smoke that comes out of the cupolas is white, (and) it turns everything white [16] that they operated on to make it white." You should know that by those things that he mentioned [17] he meant the sulphur.»

She said: «Then tell me about your own suffering.» [18] He said: «That happens because of jealousy which overcomes me when I reveal the truth, word [19] by word.»

She said: «So the reason for your extended explanation to me is to hide (fol. 124a) all of this secret, and it comes only out of jealousy!» He said: «Be patient because if [2] you knew the truth, you would also hide and disguise it, even more jealously than I do. Do you not [3] see that we were exculpating Democritus from jealousy. He could not be patient until he had hidden the work [4] because in the first word he told the truth without jealousy, saying: "Take mercury [5] and solidify it in the body of magnesia." But then he made them confused in the same place when he said: [6] "[…] or in Roman reddish colour, or in marine reddish colour, or with pure sulphur that is the [7] water of rain." With such things they were hiding and they gave many of them»

She said: «What about his statement: [8] "Roasted *šaḥīrah* (vitriol?) and uncooked *šaḥīrah* (vitriol?)." So he made some of it uncooked and some of it roasted".» He said: [9] «Although he was hiding it from you, he spoke well and rightly and did not lie, but [10] the people did not understand what he meant by raw and cooked.»

She said: «Then tell me about that.» [11] He said: «They are two works, one is raw and the other is cooked, and I swear to you, that if you understand [12] his statement you would praise him much.»

She said: «Then tell me why they talked so much about the magnesia, [13] and who was the first one to name it magnesia?» He said: «Hermes was the first one to name it like that [14] in order to hide it from ordinary people. So whoever reads his book will think that it is the magnesia of the glassmakers. [15] Did you not understand when the sage said: "O you magnesia entrusted with this nature, [16] and in you, O magnesia, the eastern cloud expanded, and with you is what is similar to Venus, [17] but not all of it is with you. And your servant serves you wine, shooting the black arrows of fire [18] to increase your light."»

She said: «Why did he say: "Not all of it is with you."?» He said: [19] «Because there remained another composition, and for that reason whoever entered this work got lost.

(fol. 124b) Do you not understand the statement of the sage when he completed its other composition, saying: "You are [2] the one nature that has everything in you, and from you God completed the work, and by the individual [3] number your Owner achieved with you His aim.»

She said: «Then tell me about when you say: "Sulphur [4] is composed but the magnet is the body of magnesia."» He said: «The body [5] of magnesia that he named magnet, is not its real name. Therefore I told you that it [6] has no relationship with the iron because our magnet—that is the body of magnesia—has no relationship [7] with iron, but the magnet of the people has a relationship with the iron. [8] So be careful that these invented names for the magnesia and its body do not confuse you.»

She said: [9] «Then tell me about when you say: "You should know the body of magnesia." So tell me how I can know it [10] because you and those before you covered and disguised it."» He said: «Do you not understand when the sage says that you should take [11] mercury and glue it onto the body of magnesia? I have repeated that many times for you. [12] Concerning his statement: "Take mercury ~~<and stick it to the body of magnesia>~~ of arsenic and sandarach and glue it [13] as usual." Thus this is the other composition. And he also says: "Take mercury and mix it [15] with tin, the rest of the sulphur, and pyrite as usual." If you put together [15] all these scattered statements, you would know what the body of magnesia is.» [16]

She said: «Then what (would I do) if I knew it?» [He said:] «Mix it with mercury and make it white! By this operation, [17] the seeker clings to the fugitive, and both of them are fugitives. But when it (the seeker) catches it (the fugitive), it (the fugitive) clings to it (the seeker). So this,[18] as I told you, is the mercury, while the sulphur is the cloud. Concerning the gum [19] and the broth, I tell you that it is the water because when he mentioned gum he just mentioned (fol. 125a) the whole composition.

She said: «Then tell me about when you say: "When some of the ignorant people entered this science [2] they became perplexed, claiming that in a book of Maria they had found: "Know that when glass [3] gets mixed with mercury it attracts it."» He said: «And I want to tell everybody who considers this statement [4] that it is false. But I tell you that all the sages name the magnesia [5] glass, and when mercury is mixed with it they improve each other, love each other [6] and cling to each other. I told you about this in *The Book about the Glass*. [7] And the coal should be intensely rubbed. Whatever you rub with it (the coal) would become good, be it a mirror, silver [8] or copper. If you rub with it the copper which comes out from the casting, [9] it would make its colour beautiful. Understand that there are two great mixings. One of them [10] is (with) the firewood of oleander that makes white and polishes, although it is wrong to use it for making copper white [11] and for the composition of sulphur. But the other (mixing) has lead-copper in it, because when the mirrors [12] get cast they would—if they do not get rubbed, clarified and polished with it—have neither a fixed colour nor brilliance. [13] Our lead-copper is like that: If you do not refine its pounding, clarify and bleach it well, [14] no beautiful colour will come out of it. I explained this operation in *The Book of Imuth*.[71] [15] Know that you should rub the copper with the firewood of the willow (*ṣafṣāf* = *Salix aegiptica*) after it has been burnt. [16] One has to take its ash and mix it with the salt, then the copper should be rubbed with it and washed with the water. [17] If the unpolished mirror gets treated with it, it would become clear.»

She said: «Then tell me about when you say: [18] "If you want to make silver from iron, then mix the iron with the magnesia, and [19] throw the weights on it so it would become silver."» He said: «Also now I order you to do that.

71 This must be a different book from the «6th Book about the Nature», which is also named «The Book of Imuth», as we do not find any explanation about the purification of lead-copper there.

(folio 125b) Know that if you knew the iron that comes from our black earth, you would know that 2 it is rather cast to the colour of silver.»

She said: «What does cast mean for the sages?» 3 He said: «That comes when they want to do that for it, so by that (the casting) it (the iron) turns into water and becomes like pyrite. So that 4 iron is rather our gold which is our lead-copper. Know that today I dare 5 to tell you that you must know that when these four bodies are turned into dust, and 6 you extract their vapour, then we call them silver, and copper whose shadow has disappeared. If you cannot cause 7 its shadow to disappear, then do not blame the copper but blame yourself because you mixed badly. But if 8 you mix and operate well you extract what comes from the first work. 9 Then you mix it with the gold in the second work so all of it will become gold, and it will turn the earth 10 into gold, so it can become matured.

She said: «Then tell me about the statement of the sage concerning what is that which 11 dyes every body.» He said: «I see that all of these statements they wrote and said are 12 about the body of magnesia, which is the four bodies from which 13 the pure water of sulphur comes. And it is what Democritus said about the androdamus: 14 "Cook it with the pure water of sulphur, and if you add incombustible sulphur it would be 15 the ferment of gold." Whoever reads this his statement would think that they are two different things.»

She said: 16 «So what is it?» He said: «I tell you that the incombustible sulphur is the ferment of gold. 17 So it is the one that turns white, and it is the one that turns red, and it is the one that is named 'the one' and it contains every thing.»

18 She said: «Then tell me about when you say that you read something written by Hermes and Danlisṭūs (?) 19 about the nature that much perplexed your mind before you could understand it.» He said: «This was because

(fol. 126a) minds can only understand the benefit of that nature by inspiration of the exalted God. Understand the examples that [2] have been given about the nature and its analogy that I will give you now. The stone that is called [3] magnet attracts iron for it is its nature, and whoever sees it does not know from where this comes. [4] And like that is the nature that you need in the work of the bleacher. Ponder also over this [5] other (analogy). The menstruation blood does not become pure until it is washed with the sperm of the man. For that the womb [6] of the woman longs for the sperm of the man. When the sperm enters into the womb it changes [7] the menstruation blood that is in the womb and turns it into white froth. From it comes the flesh of the baby [8] in the womb. Know that the blood only rejoices in the sperm because the sperm was blood before that. [9] When the blood meets the blood, they long for each other and they mix. In the same way as God inspired us to know [10] the mixing of the sperm with the blood, likewise He inspired us to take these natures, so we unite [11] and operate on them in order to extract from them the dye that we are looking for. Ponder over what I wrote for you [12] about bleaching, because in it there is evidence for you of something other than what the sages did not write about except in symbols. [13] So, my lady, be guided in the first nature by the analogy of the sperm and the blood, and ponder further. [14] If you want to put the sperm on the blood, do that only inside a bath in order that [15] the warmth of the bath and some of the moisture of the bath come to it. Then it (the sperm) changes the colour of the blood, and it turns it white [16] because when the sperm falls into the womb, it falls into moisture and warmth. If there were not this [17] moisture and warmth, the blood would neither decompose, nor would its colour change, nor would it become moist, nor would it be dissolved. [18] So the sperm would be destroyed, and it would not have any power because it did not drop into moisture and warmth. This is sufficient [19] as an analogy for you about the operation of your work for which your soul is longing.»

She said: «Then tell me about

(fol. 126b) when you say: "When the gum is put on ashes it dissolves immediately.» He said: «And I still tell you [2] that now, but when that gum is dissolved, you should mix it with the trembling shining one (mercury) [3] that is our gum, so it turns into a gummy stone even heavier than stones. Know [4] that the slag (*asqurīā*) is what was extracting every dye which is mixed with it in the furnace, [5] and with it the colour of the froth of the moon and the small pearls are extracted.»

She said: «Then tell me about (when you wrote in) your letter [6] to me that the sage ordered you to take one part of the Indian or mountainous slag (*asqūrīā*) and one part of [7] the sulphur.» He said: «Concerning the slack, it is not the Indian iron but [8] an invented name for it. Concerning the sulphur, it is our sulphur that you know. You should [9] cast all of them, and put one part of copper, one part of gold, [10] and one part of silver on both of them. Then you should cook them until all of them turn into slag (*asqūrīā*). Know that [11] the mixture of the copper consists of two ounces of copper, and whatever you think is enough of the magnesia.»

[12] She said: «Then what is the hollow stone?» He said: «It is the golden stone.»

She said: «Where can it be found?» [13] He said: «So much of it is on our earth!»

She said: «Are the claudianus and the *māṭīṭus* solidified in it?» [14] He said: «Yes. Know that any hard stone which is mixed with it turns yellow by it.»

She said: [15] «So this stone has a great power.» He said: «Yes. That is why the sages hid its name [16] and its nature.»

She said: «Who of the people is the most competent with it?» He said: «The one who [17] reads our books with utmost persistence.»

She said: «Then tell me about when you say that I should not take [18] all of the wools.» He said: «And I still tell you now to beware of the wool of ordinary people. But you must take [19] the wool of pure white female sheep that have neither dirt nor faithlessness in them, and which are (fol. 127a) pure and beautiful. Be careful not to let any wool of dead or slaughtered sheep enter into your work. You must use [2] the living ones, the best of the best of them, and use it for your dyeing. Know that the wool [3] which I order you to bring into the dyeing of the purple should be pounded before you dye it. [4] Then it should be moistened, washed with hot water, spread out, formed into a ball, rubbed, spread out, [5] and washed again. When you finish its operation, take the wool you want to dye, [6] wash it with the froth of natron, and spread it out on lime until it becomes dry.»

She said: «Then tell me about [7] when you say that the two herbs that have flowers do not change.» He said: «Concerning the first, [8] this is what has been extracted from the golden treasure house, while the second is the purple one, and [9] the two are known in every place. Know that I have answered you about them and requested that you make them alumy (white), [10] since I did not find in the *Sarṭamīṭa* anything about alum because the works of making alumy (white) are done [11] without fire. That is why Democritus said: "This *asqūnīa* has a wonderful nature, [12] because it has to work without fire."»

She said: «How can I know that it has to work without fire?» [13] He said: «Search for that in the books of Democritus and Maria.»

[14] The 5th Book from the Book of Zosimos of the greatest experiment is completed, followed by the 6th Book,
[15] called "The Book about the Nature", which is known as "The Book of Imuth", and praise be to God, the master of the two worlds.
[16] (This line is added in another hand:)
May God bless and grant salvation to our master Muḥammad, his people, and his companions. Amen.

(fol. 127b) The 6th Book of the Book of Zosimos, and it is the
2 BOOK ABOUT THE NATURE,
which is known as
THE BOOK OF IMUTH[72]

3 In the name of the
merciful and compassionate God.

He said: «You asked 4 at great length about the magnesia and I answered you about what you asked me, and what you did not ask me. I answered you 5 about what you asked me concerning it and the statements of the sages, what cured you and what is enough for you. So ask me about 6 something else.»

She said: «I ask you whether you can tell me about the single nature which you declared 7 to me that the sages named "The Book of Imuth" because of their jealousy, and in order to keep it secret.» He said: 8 «I have told you that the support, key and basis of this work are in this nature. 9 So, O Theosebeia, make use of it, and beware that you do not neglect it 10 because this work is only supported by this nature.» < O Theosebeia, make use of this nature, and beware that you do not neglect it, because 11 this work is only supported by this nature.>

[She said:] «Is it (the nature) the virgin slave whom 12 Ābulūn (Apollo) loved and who was in the West?» He said: «Yes, and I confirm it. Indeed, she is the slave girl 13 for whom the sages sent in order to make her marry the beautiful, outstanding man for whom 14 they did not find anybody equal but her.»

She said: «What did the sages intend by making her marry 15 with harmony, agreement and pleasure, and by speeding up the delivery on the same day of her marriage?» He said: 16 «<Yes>, She is the nature that enters into many crafts of ordinary people, 17 but what prevented the sages from writing about her benefits in their books is only out of fear that 18 the ignorant would know her, so this work would be revealed.»

72 Text in the margin: Imuth means the truth in Hebrew, see also fn 42 on p. 22.

(fol. 128a) *The place of the picture*

The picture of Theosebeia, seizing with her right hand the forelock of a man dressed in red clothes with plates of gold. With her left hand she holds the wing of a man with two wings, having on his head a crescent moon, hugging a boy dressed in green clothes with plates of gold, embracing him with his legs. And the image of Theosebeia, carrying two men, one of them having on his head a sun, and the other having on his head a moon. And the image of a lake with water that has the colour of the sky.

Fig. 43: Folio 128b.

(fol. 129a) She said: «Then tell me about when the sage says that when we start, we should give her preference [2] and mention her power because of her elevated nature.» [He said:] «This is because the sage did not mean the elevation of the nature [3] in her perfection, but he preferred her because she wins over and conquers what is mixed with her.»

She said: [4] «Is this nature single or composed?» He said: «It is single because it increases the thing. Do you not [5] see that he said: "O you nature, with you and with nothing else, the exalted God makes everything complete."»

She said: [6] «Then what about when you say: "O you untouchable thing that one cannot touch, with you, God holds the touchable element."» He said: [7] «Concerning this untouchable one, it is the shining spirit (*ar-rūḥ al-barrāq*).»

She said: «Then what about his statement: "O you body that is not [8] a body!"» He said: «The sage said the truth. It is not a body, but it has a body that turned into a non-body, [9] so it is what turns the bodies into non-bodies. Therefore it defeated the nature [10] and what is in it.»

She said: «Then how did it defeat it, and what is in it?» He said: «Concerning its defeating it and what is in it, it is [11] because of its relationship to it. Although it is untouchable, it has in it what was [12] touchable, and it turned into something untouchable. When the thing that is not touchable encountered the body that is [13] touchable, it clung to it quickly because of its relationship with it. What is untouchable turned it into [14] incombustible sulphur, and the other one (the touchable body) taught it to fight the fire. But this dissolving is from [15] the other composition, and when that happens, many colours blossom out of it.»

She said: «Then tell me about when you say [16] that the first ones (the sages) named this gum "The Book of Imuth".» He said: «When the first sages [17] obtained this book and recognized the benefit of knowing it, they feared that people would obtain it. So they wrote [18] 24 books about it, and they named each one of them ~~<a key>~~ with its name, [19] inserting in it what is not from it, so by that they veiled it from people. And with regard to their (books), Democritus said:

(fol. 129b) "They concealed the nature completely in many things."»

She said: «What did Democritus do [2] when he said that?» He said: «He hid, kept secret, and (also) spoke clearly when he said: "Why should you care about [3] the many things that the sages wrote in their books, veiling with them [the true nature] for you, [4] so they confused you although the nature is one."» So he helped the seekers of this science who have a smaller understanding, giving them [5] a general benefit by freeing them from the many things that the first sages wrote. And I tell you that if [6] the sage had made the truth visible, the ones who came after him would, [7] out of jealousy, have distorted it and veiled it from anyone who might come after them.

She said: «Then tell me about when you say: "If you want to know whether tin is impure, [8] then cast it. Once it is melted, pour it onto a piece of linen."» He said: «Yes, [9] understand this. If the piece of linen is burnt , then it (the tin) is corrupted with lead.»

She said: [10] «Then tell me about the examination of mercury when it is corrupted.» He said: «Put it into a bowl and verse [11] vinegar on it. If it is burnt, then know that it has lead or tin in it, which means it has been corrupted [12] with one of the two. Or put it into ~~<a bowl and put vinegar on it. If it is burnt, then know that it has lead or tin in it, which means it has been corrupted>~~ [13] a piece of cloth and rub it. If it clings to the piece of cloth, [14] it is corrupted.»

She said: «Then tell me why the sages honoured the acacia (*ašqūnīā*) [15] more than anything else?» He said: «I tell you that they did well when they named it [16] with all of the names of their compositions. This is because of the benefit which they knew it possessed because it unites [17] the things, combines them and nourishes them. So it is the one that washes, bleaches, [18] makes the dirt disappear, makes the composition right, improves it and makes it polished bright, [19] without dirt. Thus it remains alone, separating the bodies (fol. 130a) and their dusty earth. So it induces the subtle part of the bodies to become the subtle part of the bodies, and its thick part (to become) [2] its thick part. Therefore they named it with every name and every composition because it is the support and [3] basis of this work. So if you want me to make you more convinced, then ponder over the statement of [4] Democritus when he said: "Take the white one which is from the white lead (*abšimīt*) and either the adhering one, or from [5] the talqine antimony or from the white litharge, and (also) pure water." Then he said about the broth: [6] "Take our lead, whose moisture disappeared by the snowy earth, cast it, [7] and mix the pyrite, the saffron and the safflower with the flower of camomile (?) (*ẖāmūm*).

She said: «Then tell me [8] about when you say: "Take lead and pound it in the mortar of tin, and put on it some [9] salt, alum, white lead, polished earth and living water. Then pound it with the sun [10] until it becomes mercury."» He said: «This is because the sages declared that mercury indeed comes from [11] the acacia (*ašqūnīā*) nature, not from lead. And know that acacia is a nature [12] that turns everything into mercury which is pounded and mixed with it.»

She said: «Then tell me when you say: [13] "Your (pl.) bricks (*kawālib*) should be from your white soils: from the polished astral soil, [14] from the Cypriot white soil, from the hollow stone, the marble [15] and from every soil."» He said: «All these soils are names for the acacia (*ašqūnīā*)-soil. [16] So we only need the acacia-soil because without it we could not have bricks [17] with any benefit from them.»

She said:«Then, O Zosimos, what about when you say that the sages declared: [18] "If you obtain their natures precisely you would get the head of the work."» He said: «Yes, [19] and I will make you more convinced by my statement that if you obtain these natures, they would not need (fol. 130b) you to make them white because they are those which make themselves white, improve themselves, and nourish [2] themselves. That happens if you operate on them well with their right measures of fire.»

She said: «Then tell me when you say: [3] "The redness comes from three." So what are these three?» He said: «It comes from the fighter, [4] that which is clung to and the lime. Know that if they are united, a froth that does not escape is extracted from them.»

[5] She said: «What is the sulphur which made them black?» He said: «It is the one that opened the door for the one that ~~<escapes>~~ [6] was not able to escape, so it turned it into a fugitive with the fugitives.»

She said: «How did it turn the one that was unable [7] to escape into a fugitive?» He said: «Because the nature destroyed the fighter, so it turned it into a spirit.»

She said: [8] «And how did it turn it into a spirit?» He said: «The spirit of that nature took the spirit of the fighter, so it became [9] a fugitive with the spirit of the first nature.» She said: «So I see that the torturer did not torture the tortured one, [10] neither for doing harm nor for ruining.» He said: «You are right and you spoke well. Rather she tortured him for the sake of union [11] and benefit. If her torturing him were to do harm, he would neither agree nor mix with her in order that [12] the sages extract from the fighter ~~<the first>~~ the colours that neither change nor disappear, those which we named [13] the water of sulphur that we prepared for the purple dyeing.

She said: «Then tell me when you say that [14] we should have this female in that nature, because she is the one who dissolves (that) nature, and turns it into [15] a mineral that does not leave.» He said: «The sage ordered that the hard one must be dissolved.» She said: [16] «Then what is the hard one?» He said: «The body.» She said: «If the moisture dissolves it, [17] then what benefit does the moisture obtain?» He said: «The benefit it gets is that it (the moisture) fights (to keep) the fire away from it (the body), and it (the body) prevents [18] it (the moisture) from escaping from the fire. Whoever suffers from this work knows that when [19] the hard body is dissolved with the acid, natruny and salty waters, they (the waters) would fight (fol. 131a) the fire away from it (the body). So whoever knows the operation of the pyrite and the sulphur knows that they must have [2] moistures because both are fiery sulphurs. Know that if they do not have with them [3] some of the moisture in the mixture to prevent the heat of the fire from burning them, they would burn because both of them are [4] fiery, falling down in a fire. Therefore we preferred the moisture to all things, because it is the one [5] that pounds, bleaches, washes the bodies and the minerals, turns [6] the single ones into married ones, and makes white and makes red. Its colour changes when its operation changes during [7] the two works. Concerning the lead—even if you should be satisfied [8] with one thing from me—it would not be correct if I were to leave out something that the sage (also) said: "Take [9] the polished earth and rub the lead with it, and if you finish it, this would be the true one (true lead)."»

She said: «What is [10] the polished earth?» He said: «It is the white sulphur, and that sulphur is the one which makes [11] the copper white, because when the copper becomes white it is named lead, whose moisture disappeared. Know that [12] the nature of the sulphur, when operated on and whitened, changes from its first nature and becomes [13] another thing in essence and outer appearance. So each sage invents a name for it according to his thoughts [14] and preference.»

She said: «Then tell me about when you say: "In this work [15] you should know the things which enter the composition, and among them are those that have natures and others that do not [16] have natures."» He said: «Democritus saw with his own eyes how his teacher was splashing the natures [17] from outside and heating them, so that the poison penetrated into their inside. And he also said: [18] "If the torturers enter into the nature, the nature turns them into non-fugitives", and he said: "The bodies [19] without natures work better than the work of the fire."»

She said: «Then, which one of those enters into their work?»

(fol. 131b) He said: «Those that do have natures and those that do not have natures enter into the work.»

She said: «And what did the one [2] that remained in the fire do?» He said: «It fought it (the fire) and the fire was unable to consume it.» She said: «And what is that?» [3] He said: «That is for us a body, not a nature because the body of it was able to resist the fire [4] and to defeat it.»

She said: «Then what about the other one that neither fought the fire, nor resisted it, nor remained in it?» He said: [5] «That is named a nature, not a body.» She said: «Then what is that which remains?» He said: «The bodies.» [6] She said: «And what is that which does not remain?» He said: «They are the sulphurs. And with regard to them he said: "Turn the sulphurs [7] into broth in order to fight the fire."» She said: «And with what did they become able to fight the fire?» He said: «With the body [8] that turned into broth, together with them (the sulphurs).»

She said: «Then tell me about those without bodies and those [9] with bodies.» He said: «As for those without bodies, they are the fire and what is similar to it, and the mercury [10] and what is similar to it. But the bodies that are good for our work are copper, iron, tin [11] and lead, as these do not escape from the fire. When they are mixed with them (the fire or the mercury), they turn the bodies [12] into non-bodies, and the non-bodies (the fire or the mercury) [are turned] into bodies, and from both of them come the gold and the silver. [13] Know that if the bodies get mingled and mixed with the mercury, operated on as it is written in the books, [14] the seeker of this work would obtain from them what he hopes for, God willing.»

She said: «Then tell me [15] about when you say that Ostanes—who taught all the sages after Hermes—spoke about the fugitives [16] and the non-fugitives.» He said: «I swear by your father, Ostanes made clear and spoke well, and he did not hide anything when [17] he said about the operation of the copper: "Know, O you seekers of this science, that between the copper and [18] the fiery stone there is a strong relationship. So dissolve both equally." She said: «Maybe these two [19] are those two that [19] Maria ordered us to dissolve equally?» [73] He said: «You are right

[73] E.g.: "Lead-copper, honoured stone, dissolve both of them equally."

(fol. 132a) and you understood well. And know that Ostanes did not mention this statement [2] with regard to mercury, but he meant the pounding of the copper by the fiery stone until [3] it becomes untouchable and all of it turns into water. You should [4] have known that from the book of Agathodaimon, because all of his work is the cooking [5] and the pounding until all things turn into water.»

She said: «Then tell me about when you say: [6] "If this work were from one thing, the sages would not name it [7] body of magnesia, but it would be enough that they name it magnesia."» He said: [8] «And I confirm it again to you now, because the magnesia is not a single thing, and the components of its mixture [9] have been spread in the books, like the parts of a body have been spread. Do you not recognize that Maria [10] said: "Magnesia is the secret of the hidden secrets of the work." And do you not see [11] that the sage said: "Mix the natures with their relatives, in order that they are dissolved by them." And [12] the sage also said: "Indeed there is a strong relationship between mercury (a non-body, moisture) and tin (a body). Then [13] Democritus said, following Ostanes: "Mix mercury with tin because both [14] make every body white, and because nature rejoices in nature." And [15] Ostanes also said about the operation of the lead: "There is a relationship between the lead and the claudianus, [16] because the claudianus-stone is dry and the lead is moist. Therefore [17] the two were mixed and mingled and each one of them was unable to separate from its companion." [18] With regard to these two, Democritus said: "Mix the flower of gold with the claudianus, [19] and when you mix this with what escapes from the fire, they become one thing (fol. 132b) that does not escape.“»

She said: «Then tell me about when Maria said: “Pound the things with water and salt [2] for 21 days, then pound it with uncorrupted urine for 21 days, [3] and burn it with milk and water.”» He said: «Concerning milk and water, they are both the sulphur (sg.). But she [4] should have said: “Burn it with milk of a black cow!”»

She said: «So what did she mean [5] by the cow?» He said: «What she meant by it was the dark sulphur. But she said: “After [6] its burning with milk, wash it with water and vinegar, break it very delicately into fragments, and knead it [7] with oil and leave it in a place without wind. Then pound it, mix it [8] with water and vinegar, and roast it, so it will become ready for what you want.” Know that Democritus [9] has spoken a sentence—with which anybody who reads it should be content—when he said: “Know that from [10] our gum every dye should come.” Thus if those whose hearts were blinded by God would understand [11] his statement about this, they would remain with him also when he said: “Nothing remains hidden for you, and I did not cut anything away from you [12] except the cloud and the rising of the water.” This sentence could make them content and could cure them. [13] Yet they embark on what remained from the manifold, and thus they declare it invalid.»

She said: «But this statement is [14] about the making of gold and silver.» He said: «O you feeble-minded, do you not see [15] that this water—that is the water of sulphur, which is the cloud and the rising of the water—is [16] what Democritus wrote about in his four books, and he left that statement (to us). [17] I will tell you that statement, because Democritus did not leave (to us) any operation that he described [18] without mentioning the cloud and the rising of the water, although he did not call it by that name. [19] Upon my life, he illuminated and he did not hide anything. And I repeat what I told you, that the living water is (fol. 133a) our gum, because our gum, and things other than our gum, are mixed in the water. And a confirmation of this is (the fact) [2] that nature clings to nature, and by it he rather meant the living water. (This is) what is called [3] the glue of stones and the gum, and it is the mixture of the sages. Know that [4] the first sages disagreed about this name, as there is nobody among them who did not give it [5] a different name. Some of them named it after its colour, its taste or after [6] its power, some named it precisely, some named it after what was similar to it, some named it after [7] its effect, some named it a stone-tablet (*balāṭa*), some named it the cultivation of the mustard seeds, [8] some named it the gum of all things, some named it glue, [9] some named it marine, some named it milk, some named it milk of she-donkeys, [10] and some named it gum with three colours coming out of that tree, [11] [that is] a gum with three colours flowing like tears, among them is a red, [12] a white, and a black colour. And among them there are some who named it gum of almond, and others [13] named it gum of thorns, and others named it glue of a bull and glue of whales. [14] So they differed about its names and none of them was in accord with his companion. <She said> Thus by [15] this they perplexed whoever reads their books and saw these things, so they got lost in this [16] science and they were unable to know it truly.»

She said: «Then why did the sages name it gum?» [17] He said: «That is because the dyes cannot be fixed except with the gum. [74] Did you not understand Democritus, [18] when he said: "The gum which is in the white thorn is what fixes [19] its dyes." And also Maria said: "Our composed gum is what we named

[74] Marginal note: The dyes of painters are only fixed by the mixing.

(fol. 133b) living water. And some of the sages named it the gum of the tree; that is what fixes the dyes."

[2] The 6th Book of the Book of Zosimos is completed
[3] with praise and help from God. It is followed by the 7th, which is
The Book about the [4] Mercuries, the exalted God willing.

The 7th Book from the Book of Zosimos
[5] and it is what is named THE BOOK ABOUT THE MERCURIES.

[6] In the name of the merciful and compassionate God. Zosimos said: «If you have [7] fulfilled your burning desire for the magnesia, then ask me about something else, and contemplate what is [8] enigmatic for you in the two subjects about which you asked me, and which you could not [9] understand. Then look at the picture in which I represent myself together with you (The 1st picture is missing). It will cure you.»

[10] She said: «Something is still unclear in my mind about a statement, which I read in a book of Abullūn, when someone asked him a question. [11] He told him that he knows what was not mentioned to him, saying: "I see a moist spirit that is black inside."» [12] He said: «I have described for you at the beginning of this book the picture of the science, [13] but you could not understand it. These three mercuries, which are extracted from the body of magnesia, are those which make white [14] and escape.»

She said: «Then what prevented you [15] from mentioning the dry one?» He said: «Because it (the dry one) has neither a spirit nor moisture (to be) with these mercuries.» [16]

She said: «Why is it like that, O Zosimos?» He said: «Because it (the dry one) is a thirsty earth. And when it was mixed with these [17] three mercuries, it clung to them; thus it became a body for them and they became [18] a spirit for it.»

She said: «I see that this dry thirsty earth is what [18] gave them a body.» He said: «Yes, and it (the earth) found a breath hole in the spirits.» She said: «This happens when there is not […] .» Here a folium with the 1st picture (and recto more text) are missing.

(fol. 134a) She said: «Then tell me about when you say that the mercury which is your mercury takes the mercury of the tin, [2] and clings to it completely. And the mercury of the tin is what clings to [3] the cinnabar.» He said: «You have asked well and you have contemplated adequately. Look at [4] those mercuries and turn all of them into one mercury resisting the fire.»

[5] She said: «Then describe for me an aspect of these mercuries that I know.» He said: «If the mercuries of our mercury, [6] are united so that they become untouchable, then this would be the mercury of the truth. This is [7] because when it is joined with the glass, it turns it into magnesia and the tin into something [8] untouchable, although before that it was touchable.»

She said: «Then tell me about when you say [9] that I should look at these marvellous dyes which the sages described. [10] What are they?» He said: «They are from two things. Thus when you see these colours, know that [11] it is the gold which cannot be cast, but it is similar to the golden stone.»

She said: [12] «Then what about your statement: "You should know this sign (*ʿalāma*), because often when you make that furnace [13] and that *ẖuluqṭār* with the right measures of the fire and intense burning, [14] then the colours would become as brilliant as you wish. When one makes it without the right measures [15] and carelessly, then the colours would not be brilliant nor what one is looking for."» < without the right measures [16] and care, the colours would not be brilliant nor what one is looking for."»> [17] He said: «What you asked me about comes from the heat of the copper, [18] [the iron,] the lead, and the tin. Thus from these come all the colours [19] because in them we mix the ten things which Democritus mentioned in (fol. 134b) his book, in order to extract the colours from the silver. All of it is in *The Keys* and in *The Book of* [2] *Isis (Asīdā)*.

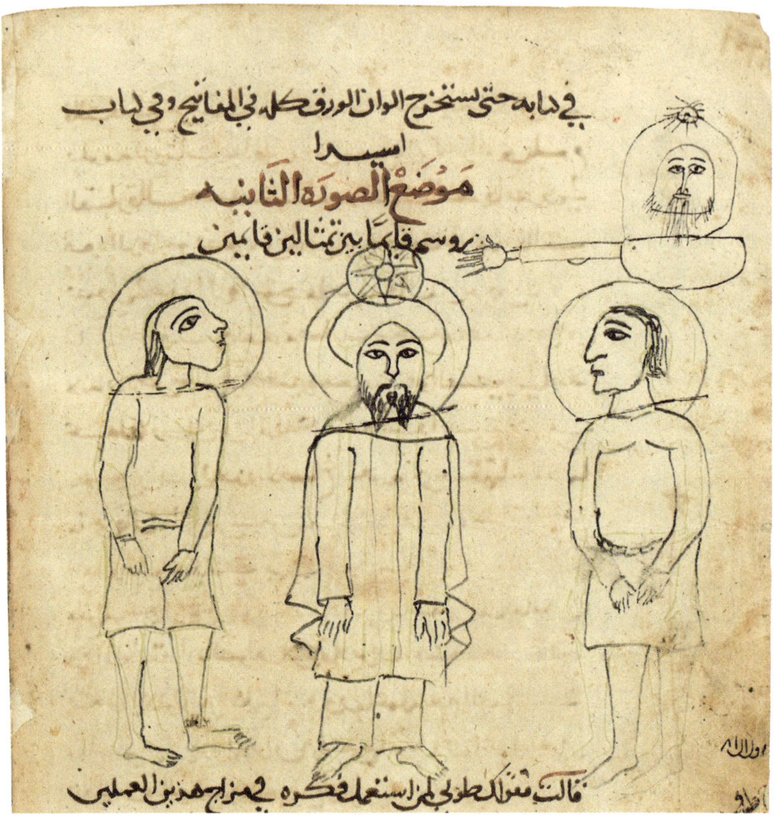

Fig. 44: The 2nd picture, folio 134b.

[3] *The position of the 2nd picture*

[4] Zosimos is standing between two upright statues.

[5] She said: «What about your statement: "Blessing to whoever ponders over the mixing of these two works [6] till he turns the two into one colour."» He said: «I still say that.»

She said: [7] «How can anyone be able to mix both of them from the books, when [8] the sages described them as invented mixtures that do not correspond to the truth?» He said: «But whoever makes many (fol. 135a) experiments (*taǧārib*) and reads the books, will understand from where the error comes to him, and when he knows [2] the error he will be aware of it. Know that these are the two works about which I told you that whoever turns them into [3] one colour and one dye, would obtain the truth.»

She said: «Describe for me an aspect of this truth [4] that I can understand.» He said: «You should render all of the first composition unoperated on, [5] some of it dry and some of it moist. All of the work is in that (unoperated on) thing. [6] But the hard suffering comes for you when you seek to understand it, to make it, to operate on it and to compose it. [7] And from this comes the rightness or the error. So contemplate this well, and be careful [8] with the fire and (see) that the marriage is done well.»

She said: «You have told me that the hard suffering [9] and your fear that I might fall into error, come in the first work. Tell me then about the second work.» [10] He said: «You should make its composition cooked and operated on.»

She said: «I do not understand [11] what you mean.» He said: «In the second composition you should put in it the one which is moist, <moist> cooked and operated on.[12] Then put into it the uncooked dry one. Thus the making of the second work is easy. What [13] you want is to extract the dye from the nature. Therefore Maria warned us by saying: [14] "Whoever is not from us should not venture into our work." Know that in the second work the sages described [15] many kinds of measures of the fire with regard to the moist. [16] Some of them said: "Cook it with urine." And some of them said: "Cook it with water." And some of them [17] said: "With vinegar". And some of them said: "With rain water." Concerning the dry one, they did not mention [18] as many names for it as they did for the moist one, except that they said: "One has to put [19] more moisture on the dry one in summer and less in winter."»

(fol. 135b) She said: «I do not know what is summer and what is winter.» He said: «[As for winter], it is the first measures of the fire [2] in the cooking. Thus you should only add a small amount of moisture. As for summer, it is the measure of fire in the other cooking. Thus decrease the moisture of the cooking [4] during winter—in the way Maria mentioned—in the three mortars (*ṣallāīāt*) in which are the *sūrīn* (vitriol?) [5] the *šaḥīra* (vitriol?), and the russet colour (*muġra*). Know that its colours should be better in summer, [6] because the sun nourishes these three mortars.»

She said: «I would like [7] you to give me an analogy for the dyeing of the clothes and the wool.» He said: [8] «I would say to whoever reads this book, blessing to anyone who is able to extract one colour, [9] who does not get annoyed and irritated by the operation, and who is patient till he sees with his own eyes the variety of these colours [10] which I described to you in the cooking. Thus he will know from where the error comes, if he is afflicted by it (the error). [11] I will assure you more if you have comprehension, but I think that you would not understand.»

She said: [12] «How much I desire to understand all your answers!» He said: «Know then [13] that these dyes have a nature that is suitable for you, so if you want, you could extract a [14] high-ranking dye from it (the nature) or a dye that is lower than high-ranking. And if you want, [15] you can make a lot of it (dye) or little of it. And if you want, you can make it in [16] a small vessel or a big vessel. I do not know, O Theosebeia, what to tell you, [17] except a statement about this subject that has neither jealousy [18] nor distortion.»

She said: «Do so.» He said: «Know then that the nature will come to you, [19] whichever weights you take. And it is possible that you do not know the measures (fol. 136a) of the fire for the composition that you make. The nature will come to you in any way you do the work, but the preference lies rather 2 in doing the work well. Some of the dye would be better than the other. So 3 read the many books continuously, and continue to make many experiments in order to know what is the most suitable for your work.»

4 She said: «What about your statement: "I describe the transformation of silver in *The Letters* (*fī al-ḥurūf*).[75] " And you wrote 5 to me about this in all of the books.» He said: «I did that for you. But if you knew the poison 6 and you want to do all of the work at one time—because when it (the silver) gets mixed with it (the poison)—the silver would first become soft (or relaxed, *yastarḫi*, X form), 7 secondly it would change and thirdly it would be dyed intensely.»

She said: «Then tell me 8 about your statement that the sages ordered that nothing should be added to the gum, the mercury and the sulphur.» 9 He said: «And I order you that too, because nothing is superior or inferior to them. 10 Know that the pounding of the mixture is the purification of the slag (*ašqūrīya*), 11 I had explained to you in the other *Letters* how it clings. And I explained to you the matter of the incombustible sulphur, 12 and from which thing it comes, and how much of this sulphur should be added 13 to the composition. I clarified that for you in *The Ninth Letter* (*al-ḥarf at-tāsiᶜ*), which is about the water 14 of sulphur. I do not think that you are unaware of how it gets mixed and operated on.»

16 *The place of the 3rd picture*

17 The image of Zosimos and Theosebeia as we described, and the image of three men, 18 upright, and lined up, and three men in one body with wings. 19 Zosimos points to them with his hand.

75 These letters refer to *The Letters* of Zosimos, which are named with letters of the alphabet. These letters are known in Greek and in Syriac.

Fig. 45: The 3rd picture, folio 136b and 137a.

(fol. 137b) She said: «Then tell me, O Zosimos about your statement: “If you do not know ‘every body’ you will not know [2] the truth.”» He said: «You have asked about something enigmatic. How often did the sages hide it from the people, [3] preventing them from knowing it. But I should answer you that it is the one about [4] which the sages said: “Dye every body”.»

She said: «And what is that ‘every body’?» [5] He said: «It is one body which is named after all the bodies.»

She said: «And where do I find [6] this one?» He said: «I told you that it is in the ferment of gold, that which they named [7] “benefit, having many names.”»

She said: «You have increased my perplexity about this matter.» He said: «It is [8] the copper whose shadow the sage ordered us to make disappear, and I tell you that if you do not make [9] the shadow of that copper disappear, then blame yourself and do not blame the copper, because you did not understand [10] what is written in the books and you did not operate well.»

She said: «Is all of what the sage mentioned [11] the copper when it was operated on and turned into vapour?» He said: «Yes, and it is what is named with [12] all of these names, and it is what is named lead-copper, silver <~~lead~~> [13] and starry earth.»

She said: «Then tell me about the other composition.» He said: «It is [14] the dissolved silver which has been extracted from the bodies.» She said: «Which bodies are they?» [15] He said: «They are the four.» She said: «Then what are the ferment, the flower of gold and the aqzal gold?» [16] He said: «All of this is the metallic one.»

She said: «Then what is the water of pure sulphur?» [17] He said: «It is mercury, which was mixed with those things, and when it was mixed with them it became [18] a body, and it was cooked until the vapour came out of it and it turned red.»

She said: «And from [19] where does it become red?» He said: «From the copper which is without shadow.» She said: «Is it that which became rusty (fol. 138a) with the ferment of gold?» He said: «Yes. Know that when the copper was mixed with the ferment of [2] gold, and was cooked and put on the silver of the people, it dyed it. And I have described for you the operation [3] on that in *The Letters (al-ḥurūf)* and at the end of *The Keys*.»

She said: «Then what about what you wrote to me [4] in *The Sarṭamīṭā*: "Every operation we described in the books is mixed [5] from three things."» He said: «Yes.»

She said: «Then what are they?» He said: «They are: First copper, [6] second silver, third gold, because the sage Democritus said: "Put mercury on [7] copper so that its shadow disappears and it turns into silver, and (put mercury) on silver so that it turns into gold, [8] and (put mercury) on gold so that it turns into aqzal gold."»

She said: «I did not understand anything [9] of these three.» He said: «The explanation is that you should make the copper white, [10] then you make it red, then you make it rusty in order to increase in it a metallic redness, and you turn it into [11] rust, whose operation is perfect. And if you wish, then mix with it its companions, because the sage [12] said: "If you add arsenic and sandarach, it becomes rust."»

[13] *The place of the 4th picture*

[14] The image of Zosimos and Theosebeia as we described, and the image of three men, [15] upright, lined up, and the image of three men in one body, having wings.

Fig. 46: The 4th picture, folio 138b and 139a.

(fol. 139b) She said: «What about your writing to me, saying that *The Ninth Letter* (*al-ḥarf at-tāsiᶜ*) is the key to all *ẖalqṭārāt* that the sages kept secret, [2] (and to) the science, the work and more than that.» He said: «Yes, and I will tell you more. [3] *The Seventh Letter* (*al-ḥarf as-sābiᶜ*) which I wrote for you in the *Book of the Sarṭamīṭa* is the key to [4] this work, and that letter is (about) the making of the mercuries which are the copper.»

[5] She said: «Then what about *The Ninth*?» He said: «It is the ninth mixture, which is the coppery water.»

She said: [6] «I see that the basis of this work is the making of these mercuries.» He said: «Yes, whoever does not [7] know these mercuries, so that he can turn them into one mercury, will not obtain anything from this work, [8] because the key to this work and the key to the coppery water which [9] dissolves all things is from those mercuries. And I have already written for you in *The Keys* about the making of the coppery water, which is the three mercuries. But I did not [10] complete it for you in them (*The Keys*). What I wrote in them still needs *The Ninth Letter*, but [11] the *Sarṭamīṭa* does not need the rest of them.»

She said: «You have described well [12] what you wrote, so tell me more about this description.»

[13] *The place of the 5th picture*

[14] The image of Zosimos and Theosebeia, standing upright, pointing to each other [15] as we described at the beginning of this book, and the image of three men [16] in one body with wings.

Fig. 47: The 5th picture, folio 140a.

(fol. 140b) He said: «Yes. Know, understand and be intelligent! You should know before anything [2] that the mercuries are three.»

She said: «You already told me that. So describe for me each one of these mercuries [3] with its characteristics, because you did not mention to me from where they are extracted.» He said: «You have asked a good question [4] and it is right that you should try to obtain an answer.»

She said: «Then answer me straightforwardly.» He said: «I will do so. [5] Know that there is one mercury among them which is the most fugitive, and it is the one that escapes most quickly. But [6] when it is mixed with its two companions, it gives up escaping.»

She said: «Does it do so of its own free will or [7] is it forced to do that?» He said: «It is forced. It works like its two companions and it purifies them both. At [8] this time, the statement of Maria is perfected: "The sulphurs are dyed; then they escape, but they hold [9] a mercury that has a close relationship with them."»

She said: «Then maybe this mercury is that about which [10] Maria said: "Solidify the mercury in the white and the red."» He said: [11] «By God, how well Maria spoke and captured the truth. She spoke kindly, clearly yet obscurely.»

She said: «The time has come for me to hear this from you.» He said: «I add to [12] the statement of Maria what the sage said: "Solidify it in the mercury of arsenic and sandarach."»

[14] She said: «I have understood what you said about this question, so may God recompense you with beneficence.»

[15] *The 6th picture*

[16] The image of Zosimos and Theosebeia as we described, and the image of three men [17] in one body with wings.

Fig. 48: The 6th picture, folio 141a.

(fol. 141b) He said: «Now ask me about whatever you want.» She said: «I ask you, O Zosimos, by God, to tell me [2] from where these three mercuries come from?» He said: «You have asked a hard question [3] and I cannot avoid answering it. Understand that what you ask me comes from three [4] things.»

She said: «And what are these three?» He said: «They are sulphur, arsenic and sandarach.»

[5] She said: «Are these their true names?» He said: «No, but they are ~~<incomplete names>~~ names which the first sages gave them in their books. And they are the truth with regard to what you asked [6] about the vapour. Democritus said. "The nature took its similar one as its enemy, [7] thus it became strong and non-fugitive because it held and was held." The first sages [8] did their best to hide this mercury with many names. Thus they named it mercury, [9] dissolved silver, silvery water, and water of glass, which is named spittle of the moon, froth of the moon, [10] and froth of every moist, froth of every animal, water of the Nile, honey, lead, [11] water of lead which breaks the gold into fragments, gall bladder of every thing, milk of every gum, [12] every herb, urine and with the name of every liquid. And they named it magnet, cloud, [13] vapour, and the hanging sulphur because when it is cooked it hangs from the vessel. They named it [14] with any name, they hid it in every case, and they named it with one name, so that whoever read their books became more [15] perplexed and more doubtful, but that mercury is from things that are in agreement not in disagreement.

[16] *The 7th picture*

[17] The image of Zosimos and Theosebeia, both standing upright, and the image of Zosimos with an upright woman in front of him, and behind him [18] there is an upright woman, and the image of three faces in one body with wings.

Fig. 49: The 7th picture, folio 142a.

(fol. 142b) She said: «Then tell me, O Zosimos, when the sages said: "Take mercury", while saying neither from which mercury [2] we should take, nor from which body it should be taken.» He said: «By this the sages wanted to hide things [3] from you and to prevent you from knowing the truth by this statement "take [4] mercury", although they did not mention from which body it should be taken. They perplexed the people, who in the end disbelieved their books, [5] and denied the truth.»

She said: «They were very jealous about these things.» He said: «Do not blame them as, by God, [6] they only did that with the endorsement of the exalted God. We honoured Democritus [7] because he spoke well and he revealed the truth. He mentioned it for both dyeings, the (dyeing) white [8] and the (dyeing) red. Concerning the red, he said: "Take the mercury from cinnabar", because what is extracted [9] from the cinnabar is the only one which makes the copper white and makes its shadow disappear, and it makes it red [10] in the second work. And it is what Democritus named the pure sulphur which is extracted from [11] sulphur only.»

She said: «Maybe it is the visible secret?» He said: «Yes.» She said: «Then what is [12] the other mercury?» He said: «It is what Democritus mentioned in the making of silver: "Take the mercury from [13] arsenic, sandarach, white lead and the rest." Thus he distinguished here between the mercury for the whitening [14] and the mercury for the reddening.»

She said: «What led him to do that?» He said: «It was because he wanted to hide [15] both works.»

She said: «Then explain it to me.» He said: «As for one of them, it is the extracting of the mercury from what you know. If you want to be more sure that those two mercuries are [16] one mercury, then look at the statement of Democritus, who said: "The mercury of cinnabar [17] makes the copper white and makes its shadow disappear." So he made it white and turned it into silver. [18] After that mercury, why would he be in need of another mercury, when this one is enough for him?»

She said:

(fol. 143a) «But he said about the making of silver: “Take mercury from arsenic and sandarach.”» He said:
2 «By that he wanted to tell you that there are two works, the making white and the making red.»

3 *The 8th picture*

4 The image of Zosimos, standing upright. His face and his body are of gold, and the sun on his head is of
5 gold. And the image of Theosebeia, standing upright with him, is as we described
6 in their picture. And the image of three men, lined up with wings; their faces and
7 their bodies are golden and their clothes are coloured red, green and yellow. And the picture of
8 three men in one body with wings, their faces being golden.

Fig. 50: The 8th picture, fol. 143b and 144a.

(fol. 144b) [He said:] «Know that these three mercuries became one mercury.»

She said: «And when did [2] they become one?» He said: «When they were extracted by the vapour. At this time [3] in the work we call them one mercury.»

She said: «How is it that you call it one while it is three?» He said: [4] «O, yes, Democritus said: "Take the mercury and solidify it in the body of magnesia." [5] And he said about the second composition: "Take the mercury and solidify it as usual."»

She said: «But, by God, [6] I see this only as one work and one mercury.» He said: «I have told you that when [7] its bodies were united in the mercury, they became mercuries with it, concealed in its inside, [8] becoming one mercury in the name and to the eye. But in its origin this [9] one mercury is not a single one, but mercuries from various similar, not dissimilar things.»

[10] She said: «Maybe this is what is called the mercury of cinnabar.» He said: «Yes, it is the mercury of the truth which [11] was extracted from the cinnabar. Thus be careful not to work with something else.»

She said: «What is the cinnabar?» He said: [12] «It is a name that we gave.»

She said: «Then name it for me with its true name.» He said: «Cinnabar (is the name for) the things [13] in which the mercury was solidified at the beginning of the work.»

She said: «Thus the mercury is what does

(fol. 145a) all the work.» He said: «No, but the mercury did the work with its components of the mixture, from cinnabar and acacia (*ašqūnīā*).»

[2] *The 9th Picture*

[3] The image of Zosimos and Theosebeia as we described, and the image of three upright statues, lined up, whose faces are golden.

Fig. 51: The 9th picture, fol. 145a.

[5] She said: «Then tell me, how did the first ones distinguish between the mercury of their work and the mercury of the people?» [6] He said: «They distinguished it in the making of the lead-copper when they said: "Mercury from silver, or mercury [7] from magnesia, or mercury from ferrous stone, or mercury from lead, or water of lead." [8] But concerning the mercury of cinnabar, I have told you that it is dyeing mercury. But the mercury which is

(fol. 145b) from copper, they named water of copper. Likewise they named it water of silver, froth [2] of the moon and dew. As for the mercury and the tin, there are some who named it water of the river, and others named it [3] water of the dragon, sperm of the dragon and the extraction of the cultivation of the dragon.

The 10th Picture

[4] The image of Zosimos and Theosebeia, and the image of three men with wings, [5] and the head and the feet of the middle one are golden, and the picture of three men in one body with wings, and their faces [6] are golden, having wings.

Fig. 52: The 10th picture, fol. 145b.

(fol. 146a) She said: «Then tell me about when you say: "Contemplate well what I tell you about the making of the silver."» He said: «Indeed [2] I ordered you that, only for fear that you might overlook this statement.»

She said: «Here I am, listening [3] carefully to what you say.» He said: «Take a plate of gold. Then sharpen it with the water-stone.»

(The following text belongs to the next page, after the 11th picture:)
She said: «And which stone [4] is this?» He said: «This is the stone which is called "the torturer of her husband". What comes out from both of them you must put [5] in a vessel of glass. This is what we name the mercury of gold and with it we write the book of the gold.» [76] [6] In this way, the sages made the mercury of the truth from the plates of the truth. But they did their best to hide it. [7] They not only wanted to hide the mercury but also the subtle of the gold. Therefore they did not reveal it (Written later as the first two lines on folio fol. 147a) to anybody, but they named that mercury the halo of the sun and the water of gold, and they named it with all of the golden names. [2] When it got rotten, they named it the pure water of sulphur and the sacred secret.

Here comes what is related to the 10th picture. This text is written vertically on fol. 146a :
She said: «Then tell me about when you say that Bidīsīūs ordered you to turn all of the bodies into mercuries.» He said: «This is because all the secret is in these mercuries. Know that if [2] you turn these bodies into mercuries and solidify them, you would obtain the whole secret that you are looking for. But I order you not to take anything from these mercuries, except what is in agreement with the composition [3] in the work, which means similar and not dissimilar things.»

[76] There comes a repetition, sentences that reappear under the 11th picture. Margin explains this confusion.

Fig. 53: The 11th picture, fol. 146b.

(fol. 146b) 12 *The 11th Picture*

13 The image of Zosimos and Theosebeia as we described, and the image of three upright persons, 14 lined up, with wings of water of gold, and the face of the middle one is golden. 15 And the image of three persons in one body with wings, the middle of them 16 with a golden face.

(Line 1-7 are a repetition of line 3-7 on fol. 146b and line 1-2 of fol. 147a.)

(fol. 147a) (The first two lines were given on fol. 146a)
[3] *The 12th Picture* The image of Zosimos and Theosebeia [4] as we described, and the image of three upright persons lined up with wings of water of gold, [5] and the face of the middle one is golden. And the image of three persons in one body with wings, the middle one of them has a golden face. (The same description as for the 11th picture.)

Fig. 54: The 12th picture, fol. 147a.

(fol. 147b) She said: «Then tell me about your statement: "When the mercury clings to its companions they name it [2] red mercury."» He said: «Yes. Whoever wants to solidify it in the way written in the books should solidify it with tin [3] and copper. Then both turn into silver. Then do it like that. Often others mixed all of [4] the mercuries, mercuries of the bodies and of the minerals. Then they cook them with the water of sulphur, [5] the gum, and the saffron. Then they operate on it with all of the written operations and turn it into

Fig. 55: To be deleted: 147b.

Text above the picture: All of the images on this page have no place here, it is a mistake by the painter.

(fol. 148a) an elixir. Then they put it on the silver, and it gets dyed. Then they swear by God to whoever saw their work [2] that it is from mercury, and they were right. Thus whoever hears them, believes their statement.»

[3] *The 13th Picture*

[4] The image of Zosimos and Theosebeia, and the image of three persons, lined up, with wings, [5] and the middle of them has a golden face. And the image of three persons in one body with wings, and their middle one has a golden face.

Fig. 56: The 13th picture, fol. 148a.

(fol. 148b) She said: «Then tell me about when the sage gave one mercury to his students.» He said: «He only gave them [2] that mercury after he had gathered the mercuries of the work and turned them into one mercury. And he gave to [3] them the operation of the rest of the work for that mercury. And they made from it an exalted dye. And those students became very happy and they thought that they had obtained the complete work [5] from that mercury. Then they accused their teacher of being a deceiver, and (they disbelieved) what they had obtained from him. But he only wanted to test [6] their gratitude. Among them there was a pious man who returned to the teacher and prostrated himself [7] on the ground before him in adoration. The teacher asked him: "Why did you prostrate yourself before me, and why did you return [8] to me?" He (the student) said: "It is the manifestation of the benefit you have given me by teaching me, and I do not allow myself to put my hand on a work [9] without your instruction. For that I thank you." The master said: "You have to thank God, as He is the one who gave it to you." The student said: [10] "But I thank God and I thank you for the favours that you bestowed upon me." Then the sage stood up and prostrated himself before the student [11] in gratitude for his adoration. Then the sage said: "Return to your companions. Then order them to come to me [12] in order that I can complete the truth for them." So he (the student) returned to them happily and said: "The sage invites you to come in order to complete the truth for you." But they [13] ridiculed and insulted him and said: "We do not need his knowledge because we have obtained the science." [14] Their companion (the student) said to them: "Woe unto you! Do not do this. That is not what the teacher deserves as a response from us." They told him: [15] "Go away, you are foolish, we will never return to him, whether something or nothing remains." Then he (the student) returned [16] to his master and told him what the students had said. So the master said: "You are my witness [17] against them. Swear by the exalted God that you will never teach them." He did so, and the master [18] gave the student the book of Bidīsīūs. Then he read through *The Ninth Letter*, and the sage [19] said to the student: "O my son, when I complete for you your knowledge, beware of those who have neither gratefulness, (fol. 149a) nor piety, nor modesty."» She said: «O God! This sage just did right, and I am afraid [2] that you, O Zosimos, might allude to me by this. Did you ever see something like that from me?» [3] He said: «I have described this to you in order that you thank God, and in order that you know that the mercury of the people [4] is of no use for you at all.»

The 14th Picture

[5] An image of a man with a book in his hand, and in front of him a student of his, prostrating in adoration, spreading [6] his hands on the ground, and an image of three persons turning their back, and going away. Written in red above the picture: Description of the sage and the student prostrating at his feet.

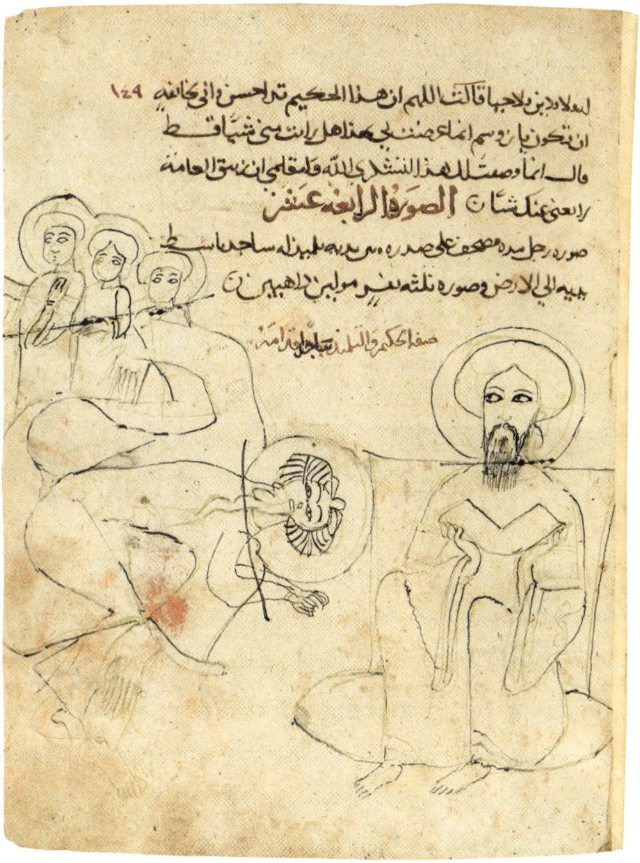

Fig. 57: The 14th picture, fol. 149a.

(fol. 149b) She said: «Then tell me about your statement that you wrote for me in all of *The Letters* about the experiment (*taǧriba*) of [2] the things that I should let enter into the work.» He said: «I wrote all of those [3] experiments about the mercury. Remember the statement of the sage about the white broth, [4] when he said: "Mercury and pure water of sulphur are the visible secret. Make all of the moistures with it."»

Fig. 58: Folio 149b. Vertical lines written in between Theosebeia and Zosimos: These two images have no description and do not belong here; this is also due to a mistake of the painter. And it is the image of Theosebeia and Zosimos, without explanation.

(fol. 150a) *The 15th picture*

2 The image of Zosimos and Theosebeia, and the image of three persons, lined up, 3 with wings, and the middle one of them has a golden face, and the image of three persons 4 in one body with wings, and the one in the middle with a golden face.

Fig. 59: The 15th picture, fol. 150a.

(fol. 150b) She said: «Then tell me about this mercury, the sandarach and the kohl.» He said: «This is similar to [2] what is before it: Take one part from each one of them, [3] three parts of marinal lime and not bad water. Then cook it seven times and raise it up in [4] the vessel. Be careful that it does not emit smoke before the seven (emendation) cookings, because if it emits smoke [5] the dyeing spirit, which is submerged in the core of the body, will go away and (only) the visible colour will remain with you. [6] And know that the water, which escapes with that smoke, is what has the splendour and the spiritual part [7] so it escapes into the air because it is airy. Therefore the good cooks cover the openings (from the margin) of their pots in order that [8] the subtle part of the water does not take the taste of the cooked things into the air because the spiritual part of all things [9] and the subtle part of the water are both things which make the food delicious and which nurture it in the cooking. [10] You should follow this guide and close the mouth of the vessel well, in order that [11] the spiritual part of all the things does not go away and does not escape. Do the operation gently, and [12] beware of the burning and the intensity of the fire. Be kind with the nature and treat it gently, and draw an analogy between [13] the imprisoning of the spiritual part of your work and your soul and your body, because as long as your soul is [14] in your body, it is what produces your blood, the clearness of your colour, your power and your life. [15] But if your soul left your body, then it (the body) would get destroyed and your colour would change to black, [16] and it (the body) would shrink because your spirit has left your body.

The 16th Picture

[17] The image of Zosimos with a golden face and feet, and the image of [18] Theosebeia, and the picture of three persons, lined up, with wings. The middle one [19] has a golden face and feet. Then the image of three persons in one body with wings, the middle one has a golden face.

Fig. 60: The 16th picture, fol. 151a.

(fol. 151b) (This is a continuation of folio 150b, 16)

And know that I gave the separation of your soul from your body as an analogy for our work, because, [2] when the soul longs to go out of its body and to be with a spirit like it, then [3] the soul hates the body and it longs to be with a spirit like itself. When [4] the soul finds the spirit which is similar to it, it becomes spiritual, clinging to [5] the other two spirits, because it finds two spiritual ones like itself, and it longs for them both,

Fig. 61: The 17th picture, fol. 151b, having neither description nor commentary. On this folio we find in the vertical, crossed out lines the description of this 17th picture, which is identical with the 15th and 16th picture.

(fol. 152a) and to be together with them, because it (the soul) is spiritual and has found two spiritual ones, because the spirit [2] which separated from its body hated to stay in it when the torture afflicted it. When it found [3] the two spiritual ones, which are like itself, it got mixed with both of them, and it joined them and these three [4] spirits turned into one spiritual soul and one thing in the outer appearance, in essence [5] and in name. But in the operation and at the time of the composition, it is made up of things which are gathered by harmony, [6] accordance and longing for each other.»

The 18th Picture

(On line 7 and 8 we find another crossed out description of *The 17th picture*. See fig. 61) The following text is written vertically: The picture of Zosimos and Theosebeia, standing upright, as we described. And he points to her with his hand, and the dead one is lying on the ground and the dog is guarding him. (This text should replace the text above, it is also written vertically:) This is the most accurate image of Zosimos and Theosebeia, and the image of Zosimos, dead, naked, lying on the ground, and the sun is on his head, and beside him a green dog sitting and guarding him.

Fig. 62: The 18th picture, fol. 152a.

(fol. 152b) She said: «Then tell me about your statement: "The rotting is half of this work in the operation."» He said: [2] «If there were no rotting, nothing of what God created would exist, because the rotting and the making lean is one, [3] and nothing is more appropriate for this work than the rotting. Concerning the second half, it is the seven things [4] which we mentioned. These things should be equal.»

She said: «Then when should [5] I start to raise the water?» He said: «When you have finished the rotting, start raising the water. [6] Know that the more you return the body to the cooking and to the moisture submerging it in it, [7] the more the dirt comes out from the body, and the more it shows its brilliance. Then take the copper which [8] turned like the filings of copper, but it is black. Cook [9] these black filings intensively, because the more you cook them (from the margin), the more they take up the sediment which remains in the slag (*asqūrīa*) [10] which does not get burnt by the rest of those filings, and the more the poison which you want to extract remains.»

[11] *The 19th Picture*

[12] The image of Zosimos and Theosebeia and the image of an alembic in a furnace (*ātūn*) on a heater [13] with three legs and seven holes, from which the fire comes out [14] to the furnace on which the alembic is. From it (the alembic) rises up what flows into a receptacle [15] under the outlet of the cupping glass of the alembic.

Fig. 63: The 19th picture, fol. 153a.

(fol. 153b) She said: «Then tell me about your statement: "The sulphur is composed and the magnet [2] is the body of magnesia."» [From the margin: He said: «The body of magnesia] we named magnet, but it is not its true name. Therefore [3] I told you that it has no relationship with the iron because there is no relationship between our magnet and the iron. [4] But the magnet of the people has a relationship with the iron. Beware that [5] the multiplicity of these invented names for the magnesia and its body does not perplex you.»

She said: «Then tell me, [6] O Zosimos, what urged you to write in your *Ninth Letter of the Sarṭamīṭā*: [7] "Take the plates of iron and rub them with the froth of the sea. Then mix them with the dissolved silver."» [8] He said: «I have already told you, my lady, that the iron of the people has no relationship [9] with the dissolved silver, because the iron is very dry, therefore it ruins it (the dissolved silver).»

She said: «Then why did you mention [10] the iron?» He said: «Because when the gold was roasted and mixed with the silver, its colour changed [11] and that gold turned white, so we named it iron. Do you not see when the sage [12] said: "If you want to turn the iron into copper, then take equal amounts of Egyptian copper and salt. [13] Then put it in a vessel of copper, put vinegar on it and shake it until it becomes [14] thick like honey." Do you not see that he did not mean the iron but he meant our copper, [15] and he ordered us to compose the copper and the salt in equal amounts?»

[16] *The 20th Picture*

[17] The image of Zosimos and Theosebeia as we described, and the image of three [18] lined-up persons, standing upright, with wings, and their middle one has a golden face [19] and golden feet.

Fig. 64: The 20th picture, fol. 154a.

(fol. 154b) She said: «Then tell me about your statement, O Zosimos: "The sage declared that if you hit [2] the essence of their natures, you obtain the head of the work."» He said: «I will tell you more with the following statement, that if you hit [3] these natures they will not need you to make them white, because they are those which make [4] themselves white, if you perform their operation right and well with their measures of fire.»

(Text above the picture in small writing:) The picture of Zosimos and Theosebeia, both upright. On the head of Zosimos is the sun and on the head of Theosebeia is the image of the moon. And the image of three persons, upright with wings.

(Text in still smaller writing:) This picture is repeated like the one before. What is on this page is the rest of the 21st picture. (wrongly crossed out)

Fig. 65: The 21th picture, fol. 154b and fol. 155a.

(fol. 155a) *The 21st Picture*

2 The image of Zosimos and Theosebeia as we described, and the image of three persons standing upright, 3 lined up, with wings, and their middle one has a golden face and golden feet. 4 And the image of three persons with wings and their middle one has a golden face.

(fol. 155b) She said: «Then tell me about your statement: "The redness is from these three."» [2] He said: «It is from the fighter, the clung one (*malzūm*) and the lime. Know that if they are united, [3] you extract from them a froth that does not escape.»

She said: «Then what is that sulphur which made them black?» [4] He said: «It is what opened the door to what was not fugitive. Thus it (the sulphur) turned it (the fighter) into a fugitive [5] with the fugitives.»

She said: «And how did it turn what was not a fugitive into a fugitive?» [6] He said: «Because the nature destroyed the fighter and it (the nature) turned it (the fighter) into a spirit.»

She said: [7] «And how did it turn it into a spirit?» He said: «Because ~~<the fighter>~~ the spirit of the nature took the spirit [8] of the fighter, thus it became a fugitive with the spirit of the nature.»

She said: «I see that the torturer does not [9] torture the tortured in order to harm or to ruin him.» He said: «You are right and you spoke well. But [10] she (the nature) tortured him (the fighter) for union and benefit. If her torturing him had been to harm him, he would be neither in accordance with her [11] nor would he mix with her, until the sages had extracted from the fighter the colours which neither [12] change nor vanish, those, which we named the water of sulphur, and which we prepared for [13] dyeing purple.»

She said: «Then tell me about your statement: "The first blackness came [14] and appeared to you from the nature of the litharge."» He said: «And I will tell you more. You will only be able [15] to extract this redness with that blackness because that blackness [16] which is the litharge is what made peace between the fugitive and the fighter, which does not escape [17] until it turns them both into one.»

She said: «How did that blackness make peace between the two?» [19] He said: «Because when the torturer submerges in the rust, it turns it into an unchangeable, not vanishing nature.» She said: «Then maybe, this thing which made (fol. 156a) that body black, is the acacian (*ašqūnīyan*) sulphur?» He said: «Yes, and know that [2] this torturer is not able to torture and also to dye, but she is the torturer and he is the dyer. [3] Know that nobody is able to make the purple colour who does not know how [4] to make the copper black, and also nobody is able—even if he does his best—to make [5] gold and silver if he does not know the dyes of our copper, because he cannot extract [6] those dyes from the gold if he does not know the natures with which they are tortured and dyed.»

[7] She said: «I asked you to explain this matter for me, but you increased my perplexity about it. [8] I do not deserve such treatment from you.» He said: «I tell you then, [9] when we solidify this stone with the gum and the cold water, we name it lead-copper. Know that [10] I have seen somebody who coagulated that stone with the water and the gum, but he did not do its operation well. [11] He started to pound it with his hand till he ruined it. So I wondered about him. Then I told him: "O my brother. [12] This pounding is not the one which the sages ordered, but they ordered that the pounding should be [13] with the nature, because that is what pounds it." But he did not understand what I told him and he said: "Where do [14] I find this nature with which this secret should be pounded?" When I saw [15] his ignorance about what he was doing, I told him: "On an earth (*arḍ*) which is called well of mercury (*bīr zaibaq*) there is a tree which [16] grows in that country with one single trunk with neither fruit nor leaves, having [17] three branches, each one of a different colour.»

She said: [18] «Then tell me about the colours of those branches, as you kept them back from that man.» [19] He said: «I am afraid that I will be afflicted by your ignorance about what I tell you, in the same way as (fol. 156b) this man afflicted me.»

She said: «I hope that it will not be like that.» He said: «I tell you that 2 one of those three branches is white. Nothing is better for the lead-copper than this. And 3 the second branch is red. Nothing is better for the rust than this. And the third branch is purple. 4 Without it God does not make any good dye. If you know this tree precisely 5 you will do the pounding of the stone well.

6 *The 22nd Picture*

7 The picture of a tree with three branches.
The highest one has a branch with

8 red leaves. The middle one has a branch with white leaves.
And the lowest one has a branch

9 with purple leaves. It (the tree) is between two upright statues,
one of them points to this tree,

10 as he makes his companion recognise it.

Fig. 67: The 22nd picture, fol. 157a.

(fol. 157b) He said: «Understand, my lady, that the sages wrote books—[2] which are supported by the Inspirer of the benefits—on how to achieve this work and how to protect it from the people, [3] except from those on whom God wishes to bestow it. And the thing they were most [4] devoted to was a science, whose talisman is *The Nine Letters*. Then they divided its treasures into [5] two parts, one eastern and the other western. Concerning the eastern, it is from [6] the white sea of Ars (Ares, Mars) to the red sea, then to the purple sea. [7] The start is with what is between the two (the eastern and western) from the royal lead-copper and the natures which are the six [8] known visible ones before the sun rises on them. But the sages put dogs in charge [9] to guard the lead-copper. Those dogs do not let anybody [10] come near it. In the middle of that sea, there is white pure water, which is the talisman of those dogs. [11] Whoever takes some of that water and splashes the faces of those dogs with it, will make them wag their tails at him, [12] knowing that he is one of the sages. Then he would take from the lead-copper what he wants. They neither chase him away [13] nor are they furious with him. He would be able to extract from that lead-copper the colours of the seven stars. [14] If you, O Theosebeia, hit upon that lead, then know that there is in it the origin of [15] the ruby and the green emerald. So keep it with you, because it contains [16] uncountable treasures. But those treasures are in the prayer niche (*miḥrāb*) of Osiris [17] and Isis (*Asīda*) and their godliness is due to the composed nature.»

She said: «By god, I have never seen [18] a statement more enigmatic and more illuminating than this.» He said: «It is time for you to understand [19] these examples and to remove some of your weak understanding.»

She said: «Then tell me more of this … [this word at the end of the page shows that one or several folia are missing.]

(fol. 158 a) [missing page …] about the description of things, your beautiful description of which distracted me from deeply penetrating your teachings, and carrying out [2] your ideas concerning the meaning of this stone. I would not be content without asking you again [3] about it.» He said: «Understand that I have told you something about the stone that, if you had understood, [4] you would have been satisfied with it. So I repeat for you my statement about it. Know that the etesian is [5] the benefit with many names.»

She said: «This is more illuminating than what you described before.» [6] He said: «Then I will tell you more. It is the black green cluster, and that is [7] the androdamus.»

She said: «What is the androdamus?» He said: «It is that for which people suffered [8] when they looked for it, and it is the murderess of her husbands, and it is that whose operation exhausted people, because they [9] did not know its method. And it is a stone that is in the well of mercury (*bīr zaibaq*) in the depth [10] of the red sea and it has signs. Thus understand, yet I think that you do not understand. Concerning the first of them (signs), it is similar to the androdamus [11] because it is gold from gold and its extract is from the purple metal, therefore it is gold [12] from gold and it does not get burnt. Concerning the second (sign), it is gilded green. Concerning the third (sign), [13] it is turbid white golden, and its greatest sign is that it does not get burnt. [14] Those who most frequently obtained its metal were mainly the Jews.»

She said: «And from where did the Jews obtain it?» He said: [15] «The exalted God inspired their prophet Moses, God bless and grant him salvation, and from it they filled Egypt with treasures, and maybe they are stones [17] called the claudianus and the *qīānūn*. But neither of these enters the work. [18] Know that what you asked me about is the completeness of this statement, because this [19] work consists of two operations. One of them is the dissolving that is called the dissolution, the making alumy (white), (fol. 158b) the making fine and many things similar to this statement. But all of this is the operation of lead-copper. 2 Concerning the second operation you should dye the body with the poison operated on (together) with mercury,[77] alum and a dye. 3 Thus, O Theosebeia, when it becomes one, you should turn 4 that one into broth, because that broth was three-folded at the beginning of the composition.»

5 She said: «How was it three-folded at the beginning?» He said: «Because it has the mercury, the alum 6 and the dye. Do you not see that the dyers mix the alum for each dye that they want. 7 They take the dye and mix it with alum and water. Then they turn these three 8 into one broth, and dye whatever they want with that broth. But we should 9 know well how the natures have to be mixed with each other.»

She said: «Then tell me.» 10 He said: «Democritus explained in his book when he said: "O you seekers of 11 this science, you should be guided by the dyers. Mix your dyes in the same way as 12 the dyers mix the flowers of their dyes with what they want, so that the colours appear to them." I have 13 told you what the sages said about the stones.»

She said: «You did so, and you spoke well about this question, 14 and I have understood, although the names are obscure, enigmatic and (at the same time) illuminating.» He said: «Praise be 15 to God that He allowed me to hear this finally from you, so that you now refrain from 16 other questions.»

She said: «Today my different questions to you have saturated my heart. Yet, 17 O Zosimos, be patient and kind.» He said: «I will.»

She said: «Then tell me, O Zosimos, about your book, 18 whose summary is in six and three operations about the dissolving of the gum: "When Democritus 19 wanted to confuse the people, he hid the dye and took up the dyes of making

77 We read *bi rifq* as *bi zaibaq*, see for that line 5.

(fol. 159a) the clothes purple and alumy (white). And he put them in his books.» He said: «Indeed, [2] he did that in order to hide the true gum of the gold. Do you not see that when he wanted the truth he said: [3] "The dyers do not prefer anything to that which does not escape. As for us, we are not in need of them, but we are in need of the fugitives, [4] because with them we dye the true dying." Thus he explained to you that [5] he did not want the dyeing of the clothes.»

She said: «Thus his description of three operations [6] which he included in his books are truly about the dyeing of clothes, and the six operations are about the dyeing of the gold.» [7] He said: «If you want to distinguish the dyeing of the clothes from the dyeing of the gold which [8] he mixed in his books, then look carefully whenever you find in his books (something) about making [9] the wool alumy (white) before he puts it into the dye; then know that this book surely is about the clothes. [10] And whenever you find this statement in his books: "Put the wool in the dye without [11] making it alumy", by this he meant the dyeing of the gold. And the completeness of his statement is the best thing that [12] I have for you, when he said: "The cold dyeing of the purple should be with the mixed waters, [13] as in this cold dyeing there is what you are looking for. Thus make use of it." But he hid it and kept it secret [14] by the cooked (= hot) dyeing which the dyers make.»

She said: «Then tell me about your statement: [15] "I did not know the measure of the fire for the moisture. There are some who ordered it to be cooked in water, and others [16] who ordered it to be cooked with some kinds of wine, and some others who ordered (it to be cooked) with vinegar and milk, and others [17] who ordered it to be cooked with honey, and some others who said (it has to be) with rain-water. But concerning the dry one, they did not put [18] as many names for it as they put for the moisture.» He said: «Yet [19] in summer the moisture on it should be increased, but in winter, the moisture should be decreased, as Maria mentioned (fol. 159b) to you concerning the three mortars. She declared that in them there are the *surīn*, [2] the russet colour (*muġra*) and the *šahīra* (vitriol?). How can you, my lady, be afraid to fall into error [3] after you experienced the effect of the pure water that you already know. You became convinced that the work is [4] one, when she (Maria) writes about it, together with what I explained to you in all my books.

She said: «Then tell me [5] about your statement: "The ignorant find bodies which are mingled and mixed in [6] a wrong way. So they change the silver into a colour that is not fixed. The more they cast it, the more [7] the blackness disappears."» He said: «That happened because they did not unite the bodies well, and they did not [8] mix and operate on them properly. If they mixed, operated on and united [9] the natures well, they would change the silver into a colour that does not vanish. But for whoever does neither the union [10] nor the operation of the natures well, for him that blackness will disappear in one casting, [11] or sometimes in two castings, or sometimes it will disappear in three (castings), or little [12] by little, until the poison and the mixture disappear.»

She said: «Then tell me, which of those things [13] entering into the work change the silver more than the others?» He said: [14] «They are the dusts, the herbs and the milks, which in the depth of science and sagacity, [15] change the silver more than the others. In this regard, Democritus said: "If you [16] mixed snowy or astral dust or the spittle of the moon with the gum, [17] you would dye every body with it." And know that whoever enters into this [18] hidden science, and knows this work, should know these things which he finds [19] in our books, together with those which are unknown, despised and rejected. They are things which, whoever reads of them in our books, (fol. 160a) would say that they are tales and reject them. But indeed they are the truth.”»

She said: «Thus the things [2] which enter your work, are they the non-acceptable things for people?» He said: «If it were not like that, [3] this science would be clear.»

She said: «Why is it like that?» He said: «The exalted God with His omnipotence [4] knows that the greatest thing in people’s eyes is gold. So He wanted to teach them that [5] it (the gold) is made from the most inferior and cheapest things, in order to let us know His omnipotence to create [6] whatever He wants from whatever He wants.»

She said: «Then tell me about your statement: “Every body that gets burnt, and gets raised up [7] by the mercury from its slag, and gets roasted with the operated sulphur, and gets thrown [8] on the silver of the people, should change that silver and dye it into an everlasting black dye [9] with yellowness.”» He said: «Indeed I only said that to see you satisfied with [10] my statement. And I never told you anything briefer and more in accordance with [11] the truth than this, when I told you that “every body that gets burnt, whitened, and burnt with the mercury [12] changes the silver”.

She said: «I was satisfied with it, but my soul longed for the statements [13] of the sages.» He said: «Be patient, because of its multiplicity and its dissimilarity, and do not be annoyed. [14] Upon your father’s life, how often you complained to me that your mind and your ears were perplexed about [15] the manifold descriptions of the sages!»

She said: «Then tell me about every body.» He said: [16] «I would rather die than answer you about it here.»

She said: «Then I ask you, O Zosimos, [17] what are the changing ones?» He said: «What they really are I will never say. But I tell you their colours.» [18]

She said: «Then tell me about their colours.» He said: «They come from our tin, our mercury [19] and our copper, but you should dissolve the silver before it gets changed in order that (fol. 160b) the dye, with which it got mixed, penetrates into it and changes it. In this regard, Maria said: "If you splash [2] our silver with the water of the gum, it would dissolve and become soft (or relaxed).»

She said: «Then tell me about the beginning of [3] this work.» He said: «The beginning of this work is the softening of the silver, its changing, its dissolving [4] and its making black.»

She said: «Then this silver about whose softening, dissolving, [5] and making black you spoke, is it the silver of the people?» He said: «No, but it is our silver. Take the highest [6] roasted one, pure, changed, and mix it with the salt that has been made lean (?), according to the measure of the eye, [7] and pound it with sour vinegar, until it becomes thick like honey. Then cast in it [8] our silver, so it will change its colour and do that with it till it becomes black.»

She said: «Then tell me what is [9] the *maġnīs*.» He said: «It is the hard one. I have also told you before this time [10] that when all of the bodies and the elixirs which are from [11] the bodies get operated on, they will change the silver completely, and they will change the stones [12] and the sulphurs. Therefore Maria and Sīmās said about the stones and the sulphurs: [13] "When the pyrite and the androdamus get mixed they will both get black." All of [14] the sages made some similar statements about these two.»

She said: «And what about their statement that some black is more beneficial [15] than the other.» He said: «Yes. So the intensity of making it black comes from performing the burning well [16] and from diminishing the sulphurs. And the bad quality of the blackness comes from bad cooking and the incomplete [17] maturation so that it cracks up whatever enters in it and ruins it, in the same way as the one who commits an error in the composition [18] of the sulphur, the lead, the stones and in all of the things. I call the exalted God as my witness [19] for what I order you, and I warn you. So when you do (emendation) any of their operations, you must make use (fol. 161a) of the similar ones, and be aware of the dissimilar ones which are not in accordance with each other. When you read [2] the books, single out the natures on their own, and distinguish them from what they (the sages) obscured them with. And [3] look at the metals, because they are the quickest things to enter in harmony with their companion, to mix with it [4] and to join it. So make use of them, cook them in the same way as the cooking of the composition and mix them with the lime [5] whose interpretation as a symbol is not spoken about.»

She said: «What is it?» He said: «It is [6] the water and the flower of gold. If you operate on this, you must pound it three times with it, then [7] three times with vinegar and then three times with fat so that *The Ninth Letter* comes out from it.»

[8] She said: «Then what about your statement: "I tell you, so understand well what I allude to when I mention the ferment of gold and the ferment of silver."» He said: « I neither mentioned to you the ferment of gold nor the ferment [10] of silver, but I wanted to extract the water of silver, and the water of gold, because both of them are suitable [11] for those two sulphurs.»

She said: «I see that you omitted the information that is in *The Book of Gold*. Thus tell me [12] about what these things are in which the sage ordered that the mercury be solidified. What did he intend by them?» [13] He said: «He wanted to extract the true mercury from those things (which are) in that mercury.»

[14] She said: «What are those things?» He said: «They are the cinnabar and they are those about which the sage Democritus said: [15] "The nature took as an enemy its similar one from its dissimilar one. Thus it (the nature) concealed it [16] in its interior until it destroyed it and turned it spiritual like it." Therefore you should [17] know that the mercury is one in name and in appearance.»

She said: [18] «Is this nature the poison because it is what turns quickest into many colours?» [19] He said: «Yes, because together with the mercury it turned into one thing. But in detail it is from (fol. 161b) things which have been composed in harmony at the beginning of the work. Thus they turned into one mercury. [2] And because of this people lost their way concerning the mercury, because our mercury is not like the mercury [3] of the people, neither in the mixing, nor in the power, nor in the action, nor in its extraction [4] nor in its essence. And know that although it has different colours during the solidification, when it is [5] white in outer appearance its essence is one, in the whitening and in the reddening.

She said: «Then tell me [6] about the spring in Morocco (*maġrib*), from which the tin wells up.» He said: «When the people of that [7] place saw that tin well up from this spring, they presented a pretty, naked [8] virgin slave girl to him (the tin). They showed her to him. When the tin saw her, he loved her passionately and [9] flowed to her in order to take her. When she came close to him he desired her, although some men have taken their secret seat (waiting) for him [10] behind the spring, holding iron axes in their hands. When he united with her and grasped her, they [11] hit him with their axes and they cut him up. His being beaten with iron made the passion of the tin disappear. [12] Then they took what was next to the slave girl and the rest returned to the spring. [13] Therefore that tin was named the water of the river, because when it pours out on the earth, [14] it runs like the running of the dragon. Therefore they named it the plant of the dragon, gall bladder of the dragon, [15] and rust.»

She said: «Then what about your statement to me: "If you cook intensively the magnesia and [16] the stones and operate on them well, then only a small amount of the mercury comes out."» He said: «Do you not [17] know that everything that is cooked on fire diminishes? So if you want your mercury not to diminish, [18] then do not cook it intensely, in order that you will find it as abundant black [19] <abundant black> impure mercury. If you want to turn it pure, then operate on it till (fol. 162a) it gets purified. If you want to make lead-copper, then take the white pure mercury, [2] which is neither operated on nor composed. And know that you should not let anything [3] enter into our work except our mercury. If you let anything else enter, then you will not [4] be able to see a beneficial dye from it, because every work in the world [5] has in itself what ruins it and what improves it. This our work is like that. [6] <This> There are some people who ruin it, and they neither know what is the nature, nor what is its beginning, nor [7] whether the nature is one or composed. Therefore be careful not to let [8] anything corrupted enter your work. If you want to test whether the mercury is pure or corrupted, [9] put it in a cup and pour on it some pure white vinegar. Then leave it for one day. [10] If the vinegar gets rusty then know that it is corrupted with lead. And there is another test for it: [11] Take the mercury, then put it in a piece of linen and rub it with your hand. [12] If it sticks to the piece of linen, then it is corrupted. And there is still another test for it: [13] Take the mercury and put it in the water. If it remains white and does not get changed, then it is good, [14] but if its colour changes, then it is corrupted.» [See also fol. 129b, 7-13.]

She said: «Then tell me about your statement: [15] "Some of the people put water in the mixture instead of urine that is not black, and others put vinegar, [16] and others put ashes of white firewood in the way they wanted to mix it. [17] When they cooked the things well, they raised up the water in the vessel (*ināʾ*), which is named me (*ana*), [18] in one, or two or three puffs.» [He said:] «This is what the sages named [19] the pure water of sulphur, which came alone from the two sulphurs and from the vessel.

(fol. 162b) And I wrote about the vessel in *The Book of the Vessels*.»

She said: «Then tell me about your statement [2] that you wrote in your book how I should make white and how [3] I should make red.» He said: «I did that for you. What concerns the rust, you already know. [4] <how I should make red. He said: «I did that for you. What concerns the rust, [5] I already told you> how it is except that I should mention to you the waters, about [6] which the sages wrote, and they mixed them and named them the pure water of sulphur. [7] Take two parts from the lime and one part from the sulphur and put them in a pot [8] and pour on them water till it covers them […] and stir it as long [9] as it is cold. Then cook it and clarify it. You will find the water high up on it [10] mixed like wine. When it clarifies, return it to its sediment that remained [11] in the pot and cook it. Then clarify it and return it to its sediment several times. Then cook it [12] and clarify it after you have cooked it several times and return it to its vessel. Cook it alone [13] and be careful not to return the water to its sediment after you have finished with both of them. But [14] I order you to cook the water alone several times till it clears up, and to clarify it several times by cooking [15] till the water becomes clear, pure and full of blood. Know that Democritus [16] mentioned the tin as the first thing that he named and operated on . He said: "Take the tin, [78] break it into fragments [17] and mix it with every body, thus it gets white." Therefore you should know that the tin dyes and it does not get dyed.»

She said: «If it is like that, then do the iron, [19] the copper and all of the bodies get dyed by the tin while it (the tin) does not get dyed?»

[78] Tin is like sulphur a hot, male substance (see s.v. *bīr zaibaq*).

(fol. 163a) He said: «Be asured, my lady, that the dye is one, and the perfection of the metallic and bodily things [2] is this dyeing. And all of the things are indeed one dye [3] and one perfection, because the two mercuries are those which make white and make red. [4] Do you not see when Hermes said to his students: "You already have the knowledge of the bodies, [5] thus you must know the components of the mixture!" Bīūn said to him: "O teacher, indeed it is a red cluster."»

[6] She said: «Then tell me about the statement of Maria: "Take the leady (*ruṣāṣīya*) of the lead (*ruṣāṣ*)"» He said: «With that she meant the spirit of the lead.»

She said: «Then tell me about her statement: "Then take the flower of copper [8] and the rust of iron."» He said: «What is wanted from these things is their subtle part, and their subtle part is [9] their spirit. Know that the roasted gold is named iron, and the subtle part of tin is called [10] white lead. When they got raised in the vapour they were named without their names, because they [11] were purified and their subtle parts extracted. Therefore the sages said: "The sulphur gets dyed, [12] then it escapes." Know that if the cooking of the natures is done well, they will break into fragments, then their dyes rise up into the air [13] and what is usually burnt will be burnt, and their [14] subtle dyes remain.»

She said: «Then tell me about the three-folded with the benefit. Why is it in need [15] of the ashes?» He said: «It is not in need of it, but it is in need of the waters which [16] got extracted from the ashes, raised up by the cooking.»

She said: «Then from where does it get raised up?» [17] He said: «We raised it up from the ashes and the bodies.»

She said: «Then is it the sea of the sages?» [18] He said: «Yes, and it is the sea of gold and the water of sulphur. When it becomes white, we name it [19] the ivory bone.»

She said: «Then what about the statement of the sage: "The softening of the silver, its changing and its blackness."?»

(fol. 163b) He said: «Indeed by all of this they meant that one. Did you not see how [2] Maria was saying openly: "When we say copper, iron, [tin] and lead, then by it we [3] mean our copper, our iron and our [tin and our] lead." But the people do not understand. Therefore [4] whoever reads our books would fall into error, if he were not from the people of wisdom.»

She said: «Then what about the statement of [5] Maria in her "Epistle of the Teaching": "The dissolving of the bodies should be rather in a vessel of glass [6] in the form of a pumpkin and it should be upright."» He said: Maria was right.»

She said: «Then [7] what are the components of the mixture which are in the bottle?» He said: «They are three things. At the beginning of [8] the work (it should be done) with a gentle fire, then it should be increased little by little.» She said: «But if we do not find the cloud?» He said: [9] «Then use cinnabar, because the cloud and the cinnabar are the three which I named for you. More useful [10] for you than this is the statement of the sage: "The cloud clings to the coppery chrysocolla." And know [11] that the cloud does not cling to any of those things about which the sages wrote, except to the chrysocolla [12] and that is because of the relationship between the two.» She said: «And what is the chrysocolla?» He said: «It is a stone mentioned by [13] the sages. But our true cloud clings to and improves our copper, because there is a [14] relationship between the two and each one of them is longing for its companion because of their closeness concerning the eye-view, essence, [15] outer appearance, action and power.»

She said: «Then what did Agathodaimon want when he mentioned [16] three names of the angels?» He said: «Yes. He named Ābullūn, Isīs and Ūṭarīq. [17] And he declared that whoever wants to make the work of the gold should invoke Ābullūn, [79] and whoever wants to make [18] the work of the silver should invoke Īsīs, [80] and whoever wants to make the work of the stones should invoke Ūṭarīq (mercury). [81]»

[19] She said: «What you told me about Agathodaimon is more enigmatic than what I asked you about.»

79 Written above: The name of the angel of the sun.
80 Written above: The name of the angel of the moon.
81 Written above: The name of the angel of mercury.

(fol. 164a) He said: «These are the names of the first composition. Did you not see Ābullūn when he said: "If you want [2] the work of gold, then invoke the sun and if you want the work of silver, then invoke the moon." [3] When I read these words in the presence of the sages, I laughed, astonished, and said [4] Ābullūn meant only the truth when he mentioned the talisman of the stones and [5] the talisman of the copper and the talisman of the purple, because he had mentioned already [6] all these ~~<three>~~ things in his book. But the sages laughed [7] at my statement, praised Democritus and lauded him (something) which was deserved, because he did not [8] deal with these talismans. They are not talismans, but a composition, [9] yet he rendered them to talismans.»

She said: «Then tell me after this also about the statement of Ostanes, [10] when he operated on the iron and declared that the iron has a relationship with the magnet and that there is a strong relationship between the kohl, [11] the copper and the magnesia.» He said: «By God, Ostanes was right! [12] Do you not know that when the iron is brought close to the magnet, it cannot but cling to it. [13] It does that because of its relationship to it. The relationship between the kohl, the copper and [14] the magnesia is like that. Therefore Maria said: "The secret magnesia, about which [15] our God taught us its mixing, is the coppery kohl."»

She said: «Tell me more about this statement.» He said: [16] «I tell you that we did not find an analogy for our work that is faster and easier to understand —for those who contemplate it—[17] than (the analogy of) the dyers and the painters, and my amplification (*ikṯāri*) for you is a favour. [18] Whoever wants the dye of the gold, should indeed take the remedies in whose inside the colours [19] of the gold are concealed. Our lead-copper is like that. It should be cooked (fol. 164b) with the cloud, with the litharge or with what is similar to the stone, and all colours that it gets coloured with. Therefore [2] all of the sages mentioned the works, the dyes and the stones. But the sages wrote about those [3] two dyes in the dyeing of the stones and the water. Then, after you [4] pour the dye (emendation), it should become water-air and that is [4] its completeness. And they also said about the making of the gum: “You should know that for each dye that you want to make, [6] you should take from it (the gum) and (dye) with it.” I made much repetition for you, not out of ignorance. [7] Thus comprehend!»

She said: «The sages mentioned many times the etesian stone and you have been excessive [8] about it, and you said that you still treat it unjustly. Thus tell me what is it.» He said: «I already told you [9] what it is in my book, which in brief is about the story of the man to whom I went. He was [10] an old man, devoted to the service of God, living in the mountains, having left the world behind him. I went to him with a letter [11] of a brother of his, greeted him and invoked God to help him in [12] his obedience to the exalted God, and I gave him the letter. When he had read it, he said to me: [13] “O my son. This stone which you are looking for is not a metal. It is a stone that few people are able [14] to obtain.” I said to him: “Then lead me in the right way, may God be merciful with you.” He said: [15] “Read the book of Hermes, three-folded with the benefit, because he described its making, [16] its operation and its colours. And be careful, O Zosimos, not to be impatient, because whoever reads the book of [17] Hermes, being neither bored nor impatient, and determined to search for [18] this stone, will comprehend it, the exalted God willing, and will attain it by his efforts. But whoever searches for it (the stone) with poor understanding or not whole-heartedly will never see it with his own eyes.

(fol. 165a) Contemplate everything that is in the book of Hermes as he explained in his book its matter, [2] its operation and what comes out of it." <He said> I said to him: [3] "<O my son> I did not understand it from the book of Hermes. Please give me your advice." The old man said to me: [4] "The stone which you are looking for is the etesian and not a metal stone, and it is [5] from various things." Then when I read the books of Maria and Agathodaimon I found that they [6] both said: "Mix gold, silver and copper, and make them white by the operation, so they will turn into [7] an etesian-stone." And I (also) order you to know the etesian and its making.»

She said: [8] «Then describe for me an aspect of it by which, when its components of the mixture get united in it, I will know that I am doing it [9] in the right way.» He said: «I tell you that if you make it right, then the fire will [10] neither be able to burn nor consume it, and if you break it, you will find its interior [11] white like the rays of the stars. When you see it like that, then cook it [12] gently, because if you do its operation well, you will extract from it [13] the seven colours which the sages described in their books. Look, if you want [14] its composition, then take three parts of salt, your own urine and mix it with the spirit, [15] natron and oil. Then mix the elixir three times, and put it in [16] a vessel, close it well and cook it.»

She said: «Then tell me about your statement: "The sulphur [17] holds the sulphur and prevents it from escaping."» He said: «This is like the statement of [18] the sage: "When the seeker meets the fugitive, the escaping stops, because the male [19] found the female." Therefore take and change only one time with the mercury, (fol. 165b) thus it will become a fugitive. Then change ~~<good>~~ another time with the tin, and [2] it will be non-fugitive. Then it not only gives up escaping but [3] also it clings to the mercury. Thus when both get mixed, each one of them will accept the other. At this time [4] their mutual escaping stops. Thus, my lady, if you understand, [5] you will be delighted, and if they get mixed and the seeker unites with the fugitive, [6] their mutual escaping stops, <Thus, my lady, if you understand, you will be delighted, [7] and if they get mixed and the seeker unites with the fugitive> [...] and the sulphur (fem.) with the sulphur (masc.), [82] [8] and the male with female, then the dye will be mixed. Understand well!»

She said: «Then tell me [9] about your statement that the silver which the sages mentioned in their books is not the silver of [10] the people.» He said: «I repeat that to you now.»

She said: «Why did they name it their silver?» [11] He said: «Because of its whiteness—but it is [not] silver—we derived this name for it.»

She said: [12] «What was its origin?» He said: «It is equal to silver and it has not the colour of silver [13] but if it is operated on it turns into silver. Thus if you read [14] in the books of the sages about the making black of the silver or its changing, colouring or [15] rotting, by this they meant their silver, whose origin was [16] from the red copper and it became white. They named their silver with the name of the silver because of its whiteness. But [17] if you see that the sages gave the name silver to a thing from the visible works of the people, [18] which are in their hands, then indeed they meant the silver of the people. And with this name [19] and names like it they confused the people about their books, till they left the true

[82] Margin: The two sulphurs, the feminine sulphur with the masculine sulphur. See also fol. 166a, 16.

(fol. 166a) natures and took the false natures. So they fell in error, because they gave their silver the name of the silver [2] of the people, and their gold the name of the gold of the people, and their copper the name of the copper of the people. Then they work [3] upon it, therefore they got destroyed. But whoever knows our work knows our silver and what we mean [4] by it.»

She said: «So what is that, your silver?» He said: «It is copper, because the books say: [5] "change the silver", "make the silver black", and "colour the silver". By all of this they meant [6] their silver. Indeed, I repeated the statement for you, in order that my books do not fall into the hands of [7] ignorant one, who look for profit. In doing so they lose, because they take [8] the silver of the people and by that fall into error. Therefore I distinguished between the two silvers.»

[9] She said: «Then tell me about your statement in *The Book of Imuth* (This is not the 6th Book of this book, see Part I p. 22): "Many kinds are among them, some [10] get splashed, some get mixed and some get cast." He said: «Imuth made it clear and was not jealous. [11] Do you not see in his statement that he mentioned three kinds; [12] some of them escape quickly, and some do not, although they are fugitive, and some neither [13] escape nor leave.»

She said: «Then tell me about that which escapes quickly and that which [14] does not escape quickly although it is fugitive, and (finally) that which neither escapes nor leaves.» He said: «You asked a good [15] question. What escapes quickly are the sulphurs, and what does not escape quickly is the feminine sulphur, but when it is singled out, it does escape. And [17] what neither escapes nor leaves are the bodies.»

She said: «Then what are the sulphurs [18] which escape quickly?» He said: «They are the arsenic and the sandarach, but they gave them [19] invented names. And concerning what does not escape quickly which we invented and named (fol. 166b) the water of sulphur, they are all the metals from the mercury to the chrysocolla. Concerning that [2] which neither escapes nor leaves are those which we named bodies, and they are the copper, the iron, [3] the tin and the lead. From this comes the dye that does not disappear.

She said: [4] «Then tell me about this mixture, about which you told me.» He said: «That comes when the fugitive meets the seeker.»

[5] She said: «And which one of them is the fugitive and which one is the seeker?» He said: «The fugitive is the mercury [6] and the seeker is the acacia gum. And as for the sulphury bodies, [7] they are the bodies, the kohl and what is of their kind. Thus the sage ordered that those, together with the arsenic, the sandarach [8] and all of their kind, have to be stuck to the magnesia. [9] And he also ordered the seeker to get mixed with the fugitive by these things, like salt, natron, [10] alum, *qalqaṭār* (gr. *chalkanthon*=iron vitriol? see p. 147), *šaḥīra* (vitriol?), colocynth and what is similar to these salts. [11] Thus the salts get mixed with the salts and the sulphurs with the sulphurs. If you [12] understand what I answered you, you will extract from all of these [13] a white body.»

She said: «And what is this white body?» He said: «It is ~~<which>~~ the [14] white-red copper, white in the making white, red in the making red. Whoever is able [15] to extract this white body and to turn it into a spirit would dye everybody with it, with a dye that never changes nor vanishes. Know that the people of the science among the sages testified [17] to me that whoever made a mixture from two bodies did not make a good dye from them. [18] Be sageous and know that you should take for the composition [19] red copper, lead and silver in an equal amount, purify them, cast (fol. 167a) all of them together and pound them with water till they turn into glue. If you want to cast [2] anything, then put the vessel on fire, put the glue with what you want, stick it (together) and [3] blow at it till you see it laughing. When you see that it laughs, stop blowing at it. Then you will find it [4] sticking together. If you want to make this a glue of copper,[83] make it.»

She said: «Then tell me [5] about the statement of the sage: "Take from silver three, from copper one, and from lead [6] two. Then cast all of them together."» He said: «The sage ordered you to mix [7] silver and copper, because it is beneficial for whoever knows it, as it is from works of the first ones (the first sages). And whoever [8] tries this work and knows it, will acknowledge to me this secret. And know—but I think that you do not [9] understand—that we are human beings who cannot live except with what improves us from (this) nutrition, [10] which is (our) food and sap. And like that we compared this work with us, [11] because whoever understands what we have written in our books, will be satisfied with the symbol of the copper, [12] the gold, and the silver because whoever has a subtle thinking would extract the obvious wisdom.»

She said: [13] «Then tell me about this obscure thing, which you named a mixed copper.» He said: [14] «It is (from) two things, namely we mixed in it drops of iron which have been cast before [15] that, and it was mixed with the juice of the copper. Thus it turned into that thing which, if you want to make the house complete (lit. ripe) with it, [16] you could do so. If you want to do this work, you must know that you will not be able to do it, [17] except from it (the two things).»

She said: «Then tell me about your statement: "The first blackness [18] came and appeared from the nature of the litharge."» He said: «And I assure you more, [19] because without that blackness you are unable to extract that redness,

[83] A correction above the word copper reads: lead-copper.

(fol. 167b) because that blackness, which is the litharge, is that which made peace between the fugitive and the fighter, [2] and which does not escape, till it turns both of them into one.»

She said: «And how did that blackness make peace [3] between the two?» He said: «When the torturer submerged in the body, it turned it into [4] a nature that is neither changeable nor vanishing.»

She said: «~~<Do it>~~ Maybe what made [5] that body black is the acacia?» He said: «Yes. You must know, that without this sulphur [6] it is unable to torture or to dye.»

She said: «What is its power?» He said: «It is [7] the torturer and it is the dyer. Know that nobody is able to make [8] the purple colour without knowing how to make our copper black. <He said> And [9] also no creature, even if he would do his best, would be able to make gold and silver, if he did not know [10] our lead-copper, because he would not be able to extract those dyes from gold, if [11] he did not know their natures, those with which it tortures and dyes.»

She said: «Then tell me about your statement: [12] "The sages said much about the three-folded changer, and they ordered us [13] to take from the herb the changeable of the sun, which is called the possessor of three testicles.» [14] He said: «There are some people, who name those three testicles a triangular bag (*qirba muṯallaṯa*). Thus take the plants of that herb and make them wet with sour vinegar for two days and put [16] in them as much water as is needed to improve them. Then take wool and wash it and soak it [17] in that broth, and cook it gently till it gets dyed.»

She said: «Then tell me [18] about your statement: "~~<Gum>~~ The gum and the alum are the triangular bag.» [19] He said: «Yes. And I say that, because we find in the book (fol. 168a) that wool should be mixed with the dye, as the dye is cold before it gets cooked. But I order you, [2] that if you see that the dye is thin, then you should add to it what is needed from the broth [3] and the black Indian, because if you mix them with the blue herb [4] before the colour turns blue, you will find a beauty that cannot be described.»

She said: «Then what about your statement: [5] "I should describe to you the making of the glass, which is the elevated crystals (*mahā*), [6] which nobody was able to make except the sages of Anṭalīnūs."» [7] He said: «Indeed there was nobody making that glass in the kingdom of Anṭalīnūs, [8] except a sage in Egypt. Thus take three qinṭār[84] of pure glass, [9] three rutl from the acacia (*āsqūnīa*), and, from the silvery body of magnesia [10] which gets solidified with the tin, an amount that is enough for the glass. [11] Then roast that seven times. Know that if these bodies get operated on [12] as it should be, there would come out from them the colours of the ashes. Look when it dries up [13] and rises over the cupolas. Then do not be in a hurry to spill the sediment, till you have obtained [14] everything in the sediment. Make its operation four times or more [15] than that, and know that the more you increase the days, the more it will be purified. [16] It is more appropriate that all of it comes out as a pure white without its shadow. [17] If you see that, then rejoice.»

She said: «Then what is the crystal?» He said: «It is [18] the illuminated stone. But if you want the truth, it is the golden stone which we named [19] king. And we have described the explanation of that stone in *The Book of Imuth.*»

[84] 1 qinṭār = 100 rutl, in Egypt = 44.93 kg

(fol. 168b) She said: «Then tell me about your statement that I must know these changers.» [2] He said: «If you do not know them, you will have nothing, because their colours are [3] in our tin, our mercury, our copper and of the kind that you know. And be aware that [4] you should dissolve the silver before it gets changed in order that the dye, with which [5] it got mixed, penetrates it and changes it. And in this regard Maria said: "If you mix [6] our silver with the water of the gum, it would dissolve and become soft."»

She said: «Then tell me about your statement: [7] "Take aqzal, spittle of the moon and mercury, and cast them."» He said: [8] «I already told you, that the mercury clings to its components of the mixture, and the spittle of the moon [9] gets cast, and the aqzal gets dissolved immediately by the milk-like kohl-stone. [10] As for the mercury which enters into our lead-copper, this is its composition: [11] You should take equal amounts of iron, magnesia and filings of silver, [12] then you must pound and roast them. Thus you operate on the mercury ~~<of the people>~~ of cinnabar. There are some [13] people who instead of iron put pyrite which we composed with the iron. [14] I think that the experiments will show you which pyrite to take [15] in your work.»

She said: «Then tell me about your statement: "When the priests wanted [16] to dye their clothes, they took from the herb which is called [17] the triangular bag."» He said: «Indeed the priests were not satisfied with the dying of the dyers, [18] but only with the dye with which God inspired to His prophet, peace be upon him.»

She said: «This three-folded bag, what is it?» He said: «This is an invented name. And in spite of that, it is (fol. 169a) gathering the truth. There are some who named this bag the face of the lion and others [2] named it the possessor of three testicles. And I order you to pound it while it is moist. Then [3] soak the wool in it, so that it will get properly dyed.»

She said: «Then tell me about your statement: "Cook [4] the snail gently. Then filter the three waters in a piece of cloth and mix them together till [5] they become one water, and divide the dye into two parts. With the first part, you should dye [6] the saturated purple and soak in it the alumy purple. The cooking should be gentle for [7] six hours."» [He said:] «If you want to make it darker and dyed more intensely, then mix the two parts [8] together and cook it with both of them for six hours. Then take it away from the fire and dry it [9] in the shadow. Thus dye that with it several times till it turns into pure purple. As I told you, these waters are [10] those from which come the dyes. Then soak the white wool in it. [11] Thus it gets dyed three times.»

She said: «Then tell me, O Zosimos, about your statement: "If you want [12] to turn the copper into silver, take some white copper, pound it, [13] and mix it with the gum, then it will not separate from it."» He said: «I order you to do that, my lady, [14] three-folded with the benefit. I tell you that from the oleander leaves come out the colour of the silver and a book [15] that does not vanish. And know that the oleander leaves are what push the heat of the fire away from their companions. [16] I knew that from a book of Ābullūn in which he gave examples [17] of the secret. Thus he took Ābullūn (from the margin) as an interpretation of the sun. And the sun is *āqusṭus*, and *āqusṭus* is then [18] the fire.» (See also fol. 92b, 7)

She said: «Then tell me about Ābullūn, the seeker of the virgin, who was not able to win her [19] except with oleander leaves. <She said:> How was the love of the virgin for Ābullūn?»

(fol. 169b) He said: «She loved more passionately, because her nature is more in accordance with him and in spite of that, she is [2] free and pure, longing for Ābullūn, but she is also afraid of his fiery nature.»

[3] She said: «Then tell me about your statement: "The dyed one should be twice as much as the one it gets mixed with."» [4] He said: «If you want to mix it with the chaff, then the heat is better [5] for you, and if you want to mix it with the dung, then the coldness is better for you, and if you want [6] to dye it with glue, then do it, dry it and mix it with the two waters. And know that [7] whoever does this operation correctly, obtains what he is looking for, because it is not right that the clothes get woven [8] with gold. And know that the ivory bones which come from the females are [9] stronger than those which come from the males. And the female bones do not get fragmented, [10] but make the male bones white, destroy them and break them into fragments. When [11] the female unites with the male, the female makes the male white and breaks it into fragments and the female remains [12] with the male, so both turn into burnt shells. Then pound them with the glue of [13] whales. Know that you should use the glue of wisdom, then take the Egyptian snail [14] and cook both of them with water on a gentle fire till they get dissolved and turn into poison. And [15] take two ounces of milk for each nine ounces of glue, and put the pot on the ashes. [16] Know that glue has a great power, because when glue gets mixed with ivory it dissolves it immediately [17] till one cannot distinguish the ivory from the glue. Then cook (what is in) the vessel with the water of the dragon[85] and with the juice of [18] the sages. And comprehend the making of lead-copper, if you understand what we allude to, [19] because we did not describe our works which contain the truth, except with allusions, examples and symbols.

85 Written is *ṭīn*, we read *tinnīn*.

(fol. 170a) Look, if you see that the nature of the glue turns into a stone, then know that this stone [2] has a beautiful appearance and that the alum neither leaves the glue of whales nor the glue of cows to boil over (*yafūr*), [3] because the alum is mixed with *qabṣ* and thus that alum solidifies every thing with which it [4] gets mixed and makes the moisture of the glue disappear. If you want to soften the ivory, then take the flower of [5] barley and mix it with the ivory and make all of them wet with the water which should be more [6] than the ivory. After three days, do it according to the operation which I ordered you. But if you see that the ivory [7] is not soft enough, then make it wet again for many days till the ivory gets softened for you. If you want to turn it to [8] the colour of the man, then take some of the herb which is called *al-abarkānūn* and cook it [9] with the water and the alum and splash the ivory, thus it will come into being (in the desired colour). And if you want the ivory to get the colour of [10] the woman, take the herb, which I ordered you to take, mix it with alum [11] and white lead and cook it.»

She said: «O Zosimos, who was the first to say: "O you one, three-folded [12] with letters (*ḥurūf*), with you the mixture is completed. O you, body of magnesia, from you appears the [13] perfect secret."» He said: «Hermes, the three-folded with the benefit, was the first to say this, and therefore [14] he named himself the three-folded with the benefit. And there exists neither a colour nor a secret except with the body of [15] magnesia. And it is the fermented cluster, which is white in outer appearance and red in [16] essence, and it is the visible secret.»

She said: «Then tell me about the statement of Hermes: "The sulphurs are [17] fugitives."» He said: «Hermes was right.»

She said: «I did not ask you about his being right, because I would not have doubted [18] what he said.» He said: «Do you not understand the statement of Democritus: "The sulphurs, although [19] they are fugitives as Hermes declared—and he was right—yet they get dyed and hold fugitives (fol. 170b) like them ~~<fugitives>~~.”»

She said: «Then tell me which one of them (the sulphurs) lives, and which of [2] their mercuries lives when it turns into a sulphur, thus which mercury is this?» He said: [3] «The one extracted from the bodies.»

She said: «Which one of them dies?» He said: «The thick one, [4] from which those mercuries got extracted, so its thick part turned into ashes.»

She said: [5] «How did its death come?» He said: «When the spirits—the spirits of the bodies—separated, [6] the bodies died when their spirits separated from them.»

She said: «I see that the moisture is the fundament of [7] this matter.» He said: «You are right, and therefore the sages did not honour anything more than the moisture.»

[8] She said: «Is this moisture the water of sulphur?» He said: «Yes. And it is not the completeness of the work, but it is the essential part[86], [but] there is another work and another composition after it.»

[9] The 7th Book of the Book of Zosimos
[10] from the biggest experiment is completed with the help of God, praise be to Him.
[11] It is followed by the 8th, the exalted God willing.

[12] The 8th Book from the Book of [13] Zosimos called THE BOOK ABOUT THE OPERATION

[86] The word *zimām* means the nose-rope of a camel.

(fol. 171a) In the name of the compassionate, merciful God. I ask you God for help, mercy and compassion.

[2] Zosimos said: «If you have attained your aim in your questions about the mercuries—for [3] I described to you what nobody had dared to before, giving examples with every statement in this my book [4] I wrote for you—ask me about something other than the mercuries.»

She said: «Then I will ask you [5] about the operation.» He said: «Only by subtle and [6] determined thinking will you be able to attain the true knowledge of things. You will not achieve that unless you devote your soul and body to knowledge and pondering. If you do not [7] purify and burn the body well, you will not extract its taste, which is its soul. (This is achieved) only when [8] the operation is performed well, because the mercury can only turn the bodies into non-bodies once you have removed its trembling [9] and brilliance, and once it has stuck to the bodies so that it becomes like them. Know that when you have altered it in this way, you can use it [10] extracting the pure spirit concealed in the bodies. For when it is stuck to them, everything [11] I told you comes out. On its emergence into view, we name it the pure water of sulphur, which is the essential part and prerequisite [12] of the work.»

She said: «I see that the water is the essential part (*zimām*) of the matter.» He said: [13] «You are right. You must use it for that, for it is the servant.»

The picture of Zosimos and Theosebeia, [14] both upright. In front of him and behind him there is a standing woman, as we described before regarding the picture of them both. And the image of the dead, twisted [15] Zosimos with the sun on his head, as we described before, and his body is golden. [16] Theosebeia, standing upright at his chest and belly, as we described regarding their picture. She has in her hand a rope like a chain going to the neck of a winged man, standing upright at Zosimos' feet, opposite his legs. [18] And an image of a green rock with a yellow rock above it from which runs water having the colour of the sky. [19] Theosebeia is standing upright as we described in their image at the beginning of the book.

Fig. 68: Picture of the 8th Book about the Operation, fol. 171b and 172a.

(fol. 172b) Know that when this stone solidifies and turns into a stone, it already fecundated and ejaculated its sperm (*nuṭfa*), and [2] started to collect its creativity. Then roast it. After that, refine its pounding by cooking, and extract its blackness [3] by cooking, and return it to the cooking till it turns fine like dust. This is why the sages ordered that things have to be put back into [4] the cooking repeatedly. Know that the more you soak the composition, the more the water becomes fixed to its companions, joining [5] those two, and clinging to its companions. And the more it is soaked, the more you should wash it with the eternal water. With this operation, the composition [6] becomes ripe and its colour changes, and it becomes softer than ointment. Know, my lady who [7] asks ~~<about>~~ and studies the sages, that everything in the world, and what people derive from it, can only [8] increase by the fecundation, by the operations, by imagination and sagacity. [9] All these things depend on the decrees of God, and His inspiring people. In the same way, by the decree of Almighty God, this gum lives and dies [10] from and by them (His decrees and His inspiration). For when the moisture enters that nature, [11] making it lean until it kills it and makes it appear dead, then it needs the fire in order to extract [12] its soul. And it decomposes and turns to dust like a corpse in his tomb; that is the time its (his) soul returns to it. [13] It becomes strong after having been weak, and it becomes good after having been corrupt, and it lives after its death. [14] Its soul and its colour return, and it becomes even better than what it was before, God willing. That is why I ordered you to burn it (the nature) in [15] a pure spring and to turn it into ashes. Thus Hermes said: “When you see the natures turn into [16] ashes, then know what you mixed is excellent.” For when those ashes are soaked in [17] that moisture, they receive the spirits, and their colour returns to them, better than before.»

She said: «Then tell me about when you say: [18] “Look at the glass-makers. If they do not first burn the bodies, they cannot [19] shape their glass.”» He said: «I gave you this as an analogy for your work.

(fol. 173a) For if you burn that body and turn it into ashes, being gentle with it in the operation, many things will come out [2] of it, just as everything comes out of a human being, because the copper [3] has a body and a spirit like a human being. People receive their life—after God—by breathing in the spirit from the air. [4] Likewise our copper inhales the spirit from the moisture, gaining power from it; so it multiplies [5] and grows, and a little of it dyes many things. In the same way, Maria said: "If [6] copper is burnt and then put back, and if this is done several times, it becomes better than it was before."»

She said: [7] «How does it become better than it was before?» He said: «Because it grows and multiplies, and the many come [8] from the one. Our copper is like that. When it first falls into the cooking, it turns into water. The more it gets cooked, the more it coagulates. Then it turns into a stone. That stone is then called "the one born every year". After (that) comes its rotting, [10] soaking and roasting in a fire stronger than before, till it is coloured and becomes like blood.»

[11] She said: «Then tell me about when you say: "This nature is like the male, because [12] when the male is affected by desire for sexual intercourse, he ejaculates his sperm into the womb, because the womb is moist [13] and it (the sperm) is blood. Then the womb cooks that sperm with the moisture in it till, after days and days of rotting and cooking, [14] the sperm turns into a body with a spirit in it."» He said: «Yes, [15] the operation of our copper is indeed like that. What happens to it [16] in the rotting and the cooking is the same as what happens to the sperm in the rotting, the cooking, the emaciation and the roasting, up to the point when the sought-for [17] dyeing colours appear from the copper. For the sage ordered us to operate on it with the dew and the sun, telling us that this copper of ours only [18] works by moisture and heat.»

She said: «O Zosimos, [19] how similar is what you say to the statement of Maria when she said: "If you do not turn the bodies (fol. 173b) into non-bodies, and turn them spiritual in the fire and the vapour, you know nothing [2] of the truth."» He said: «You are right and you spoke well. But I tell you that you are only able to change those bodies and turn them fine like dust by intense cooking, gentle pounding, dissolving, [4] soaking, long rotting, making lean and turning them into something vapoury (*āṯālīya*). Be aware that we call everything that turns into [5] dust something vapoury, and the sages named it like that too.»

She said: «Then tell me, O Zosimos, [6] about when Hermes says: "Make a bottomless sieve out of clay, and with it extract the body. When it is struck by the heat of fire, it falls into the water and all of it turns into water."» He said: «I told you already, before [8] you asked this question, if you do not turn everything into water, and turn it all untouchably [9] fine like dust, you would not have performed its pounding well, so if something remains [10] unpounded, you must return it to the fire until all of it turns untouchably fine like dust, [11] otherwise return it to the fire until all of it turns into water. [12] When the ignorant heard water being mentioned, they thought that it was the water of the people, [13] although it is the eternal water. It only becomes eternal when it is with its body, which dissolves with it (the water), so the body turns [14] into water with it, mixing with the other water, and both of them turn into eternal water. This is the water [15] the sages called the water of gold, fiery water, and a benefit having many names. [16] Hermes said: "To remove the blackness of the sun [17] which you had made enter into it, wash the sand intensively till that blackness disappears."»

She said: «Is the mercury two [18] or one?» He said: «It is one.»

She said: «[19] And why did the sage say 'another and another' while it is one?» He said: «It is one. Know that it has great power, but (fol. 174a) there should be with it 'another and another' in the operation. Know that although it is [2] white in outer appearance, it is red in essence. It is what overcomes the natures, and without it, nothing can come into being. [3] The sages named it sulphur, hiding its true name with these names. Ponder on [4] how all the sages agree on it and about it. With regard to the honoured stone, [5] the head of the bodies, he said: "Operate on it till it turns into ashes." So how [6] great are these ashes and how powerful! If it does not turn into ashes, it does not have the power to [7] hold the spirits. Maria said: "Take these ashes, soak them seven times, [8] and cook them till you extract from them the colours which I described to you in my book." [9] By this operation these ashes become mature, <And soak it seven times, and cook it [10] till you extract from it the colours which I described to you in my book. And she declared that [11] these ashes become good, pleasant> sweet and pleasant.»

She said: «Tell me about when [12] Maria says: "Take that which has no body, and which, when cooked, escapes with its body. Put the heavy dusty [13] smoke with it and cook it till it becomes cinnabar."» He said: «[14] You asked me about this before, and I told you many things, but because there were many names you became doubtful. Do you not [15] remember when Maria says: "Turn the bodies into non-bodies and the non-bodies into [16] bodies." This statement is what you asked me about, because, if what has no body [17] mixes with the smoke that gives water to the thirsty one, it solidifies in it, and it becomes a body, because there is a holder [18] between the two which prevents them from escaping. This is the great gift [19] the sages called the stone of gold, androdamas, the stone of copper, claudianus, (fol. 174b) pyrite, soluble stone, the glue of gold, and the stone of silver which solidified after having been dissolved.»

She said: «You said many things about these matters. Tell me what they are ?» He said: «They are all [3] one, but they are called by these names. Do you not see that he says: "The stone of silver, [4] which solidifies after having been dissolved"? So this is the thing you asked me about which has no body, because [5] it was solidified together with the thing you dissolved before, then after that it was solidified (again).»

She said: «Then tell me about when you say: [6] "You will find the moon in order to take some of its milk."» He said: «I am ashamed for you when [7] you ask me such questions. God forbid that it should be so! [8] By that moon and its milking he meant our silver. For this our moon (feminine form) can only acquire its spirit and its dye [9] (together) with our copper, which you know, and by which we attain the blessings of this world and the other.»

[10] She said: «Then tell me about when you say: "By this repeated cooking one third of the weight of the water goes away, [11] and the rest becomes a wind in the spirit of the second cinnabar."» He said: «You know that [12] nothing goes onto the fire and is cooked continuously without diminishing, and the raw things are always heavier than what is roasted.»

[13] She said: «Then tell me about when he says: "The tree from which whoever eats will never feel hungry again."» He said: [14] «We were told (about it) by the sages, who continued searching for the nature which is called their tree [15] till they found it, and ate its fruit. I asked them about it, and about its state. [16] They described it to me as pure whiteness, and they said that it exists. But [17] your asking me about it is not sufficient to leave the matter there. They did not give a complete explanation of it, nor of its nourishment.»

She said: [18] «If they veiled it, then do me a favour with a complete explanation of what they veiled.» He said: «I will, so understand, for [19] I will answer you symbolically.» She said: «Please do!» He said: «Take that (fol. 175a) white tree and build a round, dark house for it, with dew surrounding that house. Put an old man, more than a hundred years old, [2] in the house with the tree. Close him up with [3] her, and be careful to close it in such a way that no wind reaches the two. Leave them in [4] their house 180 days (= six months). Know that this old man will become a [5] young boy. How astonishing are you natures! That old man was changed into the body of a youth, so [6] a father turned into a son. God be praised, the best creator, the creator of whatever He wants. O Theosebeia, upon your life, the sages [7] were right when they named that water 'life', because whoever drinks from that [8] water dies and comes back to life, and he turns into a youth. Know that iron only rusts by the moisture of [9] this water. So make the iron into plates, and put it in the sun. When [10] this iron absorbs that water, it dissolves without effort. It has to be left in the sun till [11] it solidifies. After a certain number of its days it rusts. It is best to [12] remain silent about this operation, if you understand, out of respect for me.»

She said: «I asked you in God's name, not to leave out anything that [13] you know that I need to learn and that my mind has not yet grasped, so tell me about it.» [14] He said: «Know that I will also explain to you that the natures only come into existence through a mutual coming together, [15] agreement, conjunction and longing for each other. This is particularly so for the operation, because the [16] sperm begins from the blood. It is cooked in the body, and becomes [17] a white froth, although its origin is blood. When the sperm penetrates the womb it accords with it, because [18] blood meets blood. Then the blood of the womb adheres to the blood of the male, and by the heat of the womb, [19] the womb gives life to it (the male sperm). When it reaches 40 days, God turns it into a creation. Just as God causes the moisture (fol. 175b) and the heat of the womb to be the nourishment and the life for the sperm, so He causes our moisture and our heat to be [2] the nourishment for our copper. Know that when a boy is born, the only thing that is good for him and completes him [3]—after God—is milk, warm washing with gentleness and care, and also his nourishment is like that. [4] In the same way, the only thing that improves our copper at the beginning of the operation is washing and heat. [5] It has to be nourished by it, little by little. So, as I have said, there are 40 [6] days from the beginning of the sperm to its completion, then it becomes an embryo, then the exalted God creates from it a complete child, and then the only [7] thing that helps him is to treat him and his components gently. His nourishment and operation are performed with the most gentle excellent [8] operation you find, kindness, intense cooking, having no impatience, and with heat nourished by the moisture. [9] Know that there can be neither change nor completion without the exact heat.»

She said: «Give [10] me a limit for this heat on which I can rely.» He said: «I will do so.»

She said: «Then tell me about when [11] Hermes says: "If you find the natures of the mixture turn into ashes, know that [12] your mixture is good. If they do not turn into ashes, and you find it to be pyrite, cook it [13] till it turns into ashes. Then make the fire stronger till it absorbs $1/4$ and $1/6$ of the [14] great remedy which you put, then it becomes high ranking. Do you not see how Anṭiqūs questioned [15] the master, saying: "Is the great remedy $1/6$ of the magnesia?" Hermes [16] said: "Yes, when it got mixed, because it has every nature and every gum in it."»

[17] She said: «Then tell me about the question of Qusṭūs to Hermes when he said: "O master, [18] we made this vessel six times before all of it got married."» He said: [19] «Yes, and I also say to you the same as Hermes said to Qusṭūs, because he does not put

(fol. 176a) pure water onto it till all the tin decays and breaks into pieces. So whoever enters [2] this work should neither get bored with burning the copper, nor be impatient for its slow burning, because [3] it gets burnt little by little in the cooking till it turns into rust. Then it has to be cooked intensely till the burnt copper rots with the gum and the fat which were mixed [5] with it.»

She said: «Then what about when the students say: "We did what you described to us in *The Key* six [6] times till the natures got married and clung to each other, but we did not understand what you wrote [7] about the sieve at the beginning of the work.» He said: «You have asked about something obscure. It has long confused [8] people before you, who thought that they fully understood the science, because they cooked it after its marriage, [9] and when it took a long time, they thought that they had done something wrong, so they rejected it. Therefore [10] the sages kept secret the time of the work in each operation. Do you not understand his statement: "Put [11] the higher water onto the lower one, and do not despise the ashes which remain at the bottom of the pot [12] after they have raised the water."»

She said: «And why did he repeat it?» He said: «Because it is the crown of victory. [13] So mix the higher with the lower, and cook it with a gentle fire till the higher one becomes [14] like marble. When you have brought it to that point, then it is what Maria described, saying: "It is the [15] woman's work and the boy's game." And be careful [not] to burn the egg when ~~<is mixed>~~ you make it enter at the beginning of [16] the operation, because not every egg dissolves. If you dissolve it, wash it [17] with sea water till all of its salt disappears and filter it well many times. [18] Know that you have mixed the cold with the hot and the moist with the dry.»

[She said:] «Then tell me about when [19] the sages say: "In any case the soul is a fugitive. But when they return it to a body (fol. 176b) like the one from which it was extracted, it would never escape again.» He said: «You have asked about something which I did not find in any [2] of the sages' books. For those who do not understand it, it is hard and enigmatic, but [3] for those who understand it, it is easy and simple.»

She said: «Explain it to me.» He said: «I will do. When the sages extracted [4] the spirit from the body with a spirit like it, and all the things became fugitive spirits, [5] they (the sages) returned them (the spirits) to a body like the one from which those spirits were extracted. When they (the spirits) entered [6] and settled in it (that body), they did not want to separate from it any longer and turned into one dye.»

She said: «Then tell me about [7] when they say: "The red stone which gets extracted from the top of every spring (*maᶜdin*)."» He said: «That is a stone [8] with strong roots in the gold and silver metals (*maᶜādin*). It is to be found with every sage of skilful [9] and fine speech.»

She said: «You have described it to me in a disguised way.» He said: «No I did not, I gave [10] you the name the sage used for it.»

She said: «Name it to me using some of the names [11] by which it is known.» He said: «It is the eternal one with dyeing natures, among which is the clinging nature. If [12] it is diluted with wisdom, and improved with power, it captures the escaping, dyeing, fugitive waters.»

[13] She said: «Then tell me about when you say: "The stone with many names which is found in every country."» [He said:] «It is found [14] with the owners of bags (*aṣḥāb as-sirās*), delicious in taste, and soft in touch. Put it in the sieve and leave it for [15] six or seven days till all the water comes down. But these days are not [16] days.»

She said: «Then what are they?» He said: «They are more, and longer, than days. But I tell you [17] that this sieve is made of the natures, it is not made of clay, but of fire and the natures. [18] Know that the sieve must not have a base but it should be suspended, in order that (fol. 177a) when the nature is dissolved by the wind of the fire, it mixes with the other one, and the two become one thing. So in this way the sieve is dissolved, [2] and know that the sieve comes before the casting. As for the washing, mix [3] the broth with the natures till that turbid one absorbs the rest of the six waters. If you want [4] it not to become burdensome, soak it little by little to the amount that it absorbs. Then pour the water onto it [5] six or seven times. After that, leave it in the sun for 41 days, till it becomes dry and hard [6] as it was in the first days.»

She said: «Then tell me about when he says: "Take the plates [7] of copper, and make them thin. Put them in a vessel, and put western vinegar and Egyptian alum on them. [8] Cook this till the plates dissolve."» He said: «Yes, this is what we call the making rusty. So leave it [9] in the cooking till it is pounded and becomes clear water. Then cook it and it will become pure water. [10] Weigh out four measures more of it, besides its original weight, and cook it till it becomes a solid cluster. [11] This is what they call the water of the Nile and the gum, because it holds the dye.»

She said: [12] «Then tell me about when he says: "With you I only omitted the cloud and the raising of the water."» He said: [13] «The cloud is used to make all the composition. It is what rises with the water of sulphur which is [14] concealed inside the cloud and extracted by it. Then it (the cloud) rises with it (the water) up into the air. By the cloud [15] the outward and visible work unfolds, and (by the cloud comes) the silvery nourishment, which is fermented, airy, mineral, silvery, [16] marinal, moist, which is mixed with the world, gathering everything into itself. This is the thing whose price [17] they do not know, lowly in appearance, the sought-for one which made all the things yellow, [18] and which is more than any exalted thing in the world. Know that if you do not marry the fugitive soul with [19] the non-fugitive body, you will have nothing. Know that when this stone is imprisoned (fol. 177b) in the mixed moisture, and fecundates the woman of the people of wisdom and is soaked by the eternal water, it improves [2] the clinging dyes.»

She said: «Tell me about the beginning of this work, and what the sage said [3] when he explained the beginning of the dyeing.» He said: «It is your extracting it from the cinnabar. It is that cinnabar that holds [4] the dye of the mercury. It is what makes it alumy (white), and it holds onto things because it does not fear the fire, and the fire cannot overcome it. [5] It is what strengthens the broth with the spirit of the mercury, and it is what defeats the natures, breaks them into fragments, and [6] prevents the fire from ruining the composition that does not solidify except with the heat of the fire.»

She said: «Then tell me [7] about when he says: "The thirst of the fired clay."» He said: «By the thirst of the fired clay he meant the body, because it is what [8] coagulates the moisture. So by fired clay he meant the body.»

She said: «What is the water of sulphur, [9] and what is its power?» He said: «It is the vapour (*āṯālīya* feminine adjective of *āṯāl* = vapour) which the sage ordered us to mix with the male and cook for 90 [10] days till it becomes a shining white stone. Then cook it in the sun till it dries. Whenever [11] you hear of 'vapour' (*āṯālīya*) in the books, this is what it means. The vapour is what performs the whole work, [12] and it is that by which the gold is dyed. It is the ferment, and by it the gold becomes aqzal, because it has [13] great power.»

She said: «Then tell me about when you say about the eternal water: "You must take it in order for it to be [14] a preparation for the dyeing."» He said: «I have told you that, and I tell you and whoever comes after you, that [15] if anyone does not know the eternal water, he should never take up this work at all, because if he does, he will end up [16] losing, because the work can only be achieved by the eternal water, which has [17] great power.»

She said: «Why did the sages call it eternal water, and was it eternal [18] from the beginning?» He said: «[No,] only when it was mixed with the mercuries did it become eternal. [19] So when it was mixed with the eternal, it (the water) turned the eternal into a fugitive, and in the second work, the eternal made it (the water) (fol. 178a) eternal. That is why it is called eternal water. However, when it mixes with the eternal, it fights the fire [2] and is stronger than it. When this water is pounded with the body of which I told you, it turns the body [3] into a spirit, because it is mixed with it, and the two become one thing. The body [4] solidifies the spirit, and the spirit turns the body into a spirit. The body which became a spirit becomes [5] dyed like blood. That is what the sages ordered, so remember it well.»

She said: «What about *The Book about the Fire* you wrote [6] for me, and the sages' many warnings about it (the fire) to whoever enters into this work?» He said: [7] «This work can neither begin nor end without the fire. The errors, troubles, and the distress [8] which come upon the people of this work—even when they know about the natures, their union, their weights, [9] and their operation—is all because of their ignorance of the measures of the fire. So whoever does not know the measures of the fire [10] in the compositions and the operations falls into error. For it (the fire) is the enemy of the work, although the work cannot [11] exist without it. So I will tell you the necessary measurements of the fire.»

She said: «Do so! [12] This is not the first favour you have done to me, and I hope that it will not be the last.» He said: «Know that [13] for this work, when you put it in its vessel, you must divide the fire into four parts: In the first part, when you cook the things, [14] your fire should be gentle, like when the dyers cook [15] their dyes, so that the things mix with each other. When you know that [16] they have mixed, make the fire in the second composition stronger than it was before, so that [17] the things solidify and turn into a stone. Concerning the third part, when you want to destroy the stone in order that [18] the redness appears, you can only destroy it and extract that redness from it with a strong fire. [19] Strengthen the fire for it to absorb that gum by the strength of the fire, because that gum only dries (fol. 178b) with a strong fire. So strengthen the fire more than it was before. If you are concerned that your [2] glass vessel might dissolve in the fire, cover its outside with fine clay. This is [3] the measure of the fire of the emaciation. Concerning the fire of the gum, which is the fourth part, from which [4] the flowers appear, it is gentler than this third fire. So be careful with the fire, and know that whether [5] this work is successful or ruined depends on the measures of the fire.»

She said: «Tell me [6] about the making of the pearls.» He said: «Know that I did not mean the pearls of the people, but rather the pearls [7] of the cupolas (*qibāb*, the domes of the vessels), their beauty, and the joy of their people (the people of the pearls) when they see them.»

She said: «Describe its operation for me.» He said: [8] «Yes, I will, so understand it! Take one part of the honoured stone which has been operated on, and [9] one part of the gum. Then dye both of them with beetroot (*salq*) juice in a glass vessel, so that you (can) see how it <solidifies> [dissolves]. [10] For if you do not see it dissolve, it will be hard for you to bear. Cook these things with a gentle fire, like [11] the fire of the dyers, till you see that the poison is clean of all impurity, because the nature [12] cannot accept filth and impurity. Cook that composed poison till all its filth has gone. [13] If you want to make the pearls of the cupolas from it, cover the vessel so that the water goes up [14] and ascends. Then you will find those pearls appear by themselves, round, both [15] small and big, in the upper part of the vessel. Know that the more you [16] pound what is in the vessel, the more pearls will be in the cupula, because the heat dissolves the [17] splendid and shining one, and the splendid one dissolves its components of the mixture, and it is made to stay with them with [18] great joy, because it performed its work and it came out.»

She said: «Then tell me about when he says: "If you see

(fol. 179a) the composition become a melted aqzal, mix it with the gold and it becomes [2] solid aqzal."» He said: «I have told you about this already that if you see that the water [3] is extracted from the vapour, then you must mix it with the gold.»

She said: «How can this [4] happen and [why] does he call its aqzal?» He said: «Although it is white in its outer appearance, [5] it is red in essence. The redness is concealed inside it, and it is the redness which he named [6] aqzal. Do you not see that he said: "It becomes solid because from the coppery stone comes the dissolved black aqzalian (*aqzalī*) [7] water."?»

She said: «When does that happen?» He said: «In [8] the other work.»

She said: «Then tell me about when he says: "Incombustible sulphur."» He said: «He ordered the sulphur to be cooked, till all its moisture is extracted, and the sediment becomes dry ashes that [10] cannot be burnt.»

She said: «Why can it not be burnt?» He said: «Because all of its sulphur had been extracted [11] from it, so that no spirit remained in it which burns, and it has been turned into ashes.»

She said: «What did he mean [12] by the rotting?» He said: «He meant the changing of the natures, and turning the copper into poison. Know that whenever anything [13] extracted from the earthy body is washed and put back, it becomes [14] white silver, which is from our work. And the longer our silver is cooked, the stronger its redness and the unification [15] of its parts become. When its work is completed, it is neither silver nor gold, but it is [16] quickly dyed into gold.»

She said: «Then tell me about when he says: "I have described for you [17] a way for making the copper rusty."» He said: «By making rusty he meant the first composition, and that the copper turns [18] into silver.»

She said: «How does copper turn into silver?» He said: «That comes when you take copper [19] and mix it with sour water and its moisture. Then cook it a few times in it (the moisture), thus the copper (fol. 179b) melts and becomes white. Cook it till its parts cling to each other. This is our silver, [2] which is (the result) of our work.

She said: «Why do they need this silver?» He said: «When we complete the work, and achieve its aim, [3] it is what we use to dye gold [3] quickly.»

She said: «Then tell me about when you say: "Even if kings wanted to sell [5] their necks they would not gain what is gained by the fire when it is operated on and softened well."» He said: [6] «Yes. The gentle fire is what turns the sulphurs into dyes that do not burn up. [7] So you must have a gentle fire, and beware of heating it too much, otherwise the flowers are destroyed. Just as it is the nature of [8] the sun to make the flowers grow, the fire in this work makes the gold grow and [9] increase. Therefore Hermes said: "After God, the great sun is [10] the thing without which this matter cannot be completed." By that he meant the fire. [11] Know that this work cannot be done without the fire.»

She said: «Describe for me [12] one aspect of it.» He said: «Your fire must be like the heat of the sun. [13] At the time the water is raised it is extremely hot. That is when the dog (Sirius) rises up [14] in the East (in Egypt this is in July, the time of the inundation of the Nile). Those days are suitable for the pounding, the transformation, and the washing. Thus [15] Hermes said: "We have described for you the making white ~~<the sun>~~ by casting. For that [16] you must perform well their making white, when the moon is in Sagittarius, then in [17] Pisces, then in Taurus, then in Cancer, then in Libra, and likewise when it is [18] in the East." By that he meant Venus. Experimentation will guide you as to whether this is so or not.»

[19] She said: «I asked you to enlighten me on this matter, but you have only increased my confusion,

(fol. 180a) and it was not right for you to do that to me.» He said: «I tell you that [2] when we solidify this stone with gum and cold water, we call it lead-copper. Know that [3] I often saw someone coagulating this stone with water and gum, but his operation was not good. [4] He burnt it and pounded it with his hand until he ruined it. I was amazed, and said to him: "O brother, [5] this is not the pounding which the sages ordered. The pounding which [6] they ordered is with the nature. That is what pounds it." He did not understand what I was telling him, and he asked: "Where do you think [7] I can find this nature with which this secret is pounded?" When I saw how ignorant he was about what he was doing, [8] I told him: "In a place called <barmaq> well of mercury (*biʾr zaībaq*, see fol. 156a.15) there a tree is growing [9] with neither fruit nor leaves. It has three branches, and each branch is [10] a different colour.»

She said: «Tell me the colours of those branches, for you withheld them [11] from that man.» He said: «I am afraid that I will be afflicted because of your ignorance of what I say to you, [12] in the same way as I was afflicted by that man.»

She said: «I hope I will not do so.» [13] He said: «Then I tell you that one of those branches is white, and nothing else is good for the lead-copper. [14] The second branch is red, and nothing else is good for the rust. The third branch [15] is purple, and God does not make any dye good except with it. So if the knowledge of this [16] very tree becomes established for you, you will pound the stone correctly. Look when he says: "If you want [17] to turn the wool purple, then leave it to rest in the dye." Can you not see that [18] the dye is the purple of the clothes of kings? They are dyed for an hour, then they are taken out and dried. If they were left [19] in the dye, they would become black and ruined.»

[She said:] «How could the sage order us to leave it

(fol. 180b) to rest?» [He said:] «From this you know that it was not his concern to dye the stone purple 2 for the clothes of the king <They are dyed for an hour, then they are taken out and dried. If they were left in the dye, they would become 3 black and ruined.» [She said:] «How could the sage order us to leave it to rest?» [He said:] «From this 4 you know that it was not his concern to dye the stone purple for the clothes of the king> but he 5 meant the true dye, and he veiled it in this way so thc ignorant would not come to know it.»

6 She said: «Then tell me about when the sage says: "Cook, do not be impatient, repeat, cook and roast." <She said:> 7 But you say in a summary that the sage said: "Some people think that 8 this work needs to be performed over a long time, with many instruments, different furnaces, many alembics, and that this view of theirs is wrong."» 10 He said: «As for when the sage says: "Cook and do not be impatient," this is because the copper has to be burnt little 11 by little. Therefore I ordered you not to become impatient. I have told you before that our dye only comes out after months, whereas the dye of the dyers comes out after a few days. As for the furnaces 13 and the alembics, they are what you already know. Know as well that the work is easy, and that 14 it needs nothing more than intelligence.»

She said: «How can I preserve the bodies and 15 extract their spirit as the sages ordered?» He said: 16 «When the ignorant ones saw that the bodies got burnt and turned into ashes, they rejected it and thought 17 they had made an error. But it is necessary for you to burn the things till you turn them into ashes, 18 and only copper remains. In it there is the taste of the things which 19 were fragmented with it.»

She said: «But, O Zosimos, I cannot see that anything remains in the fire here except (fol. 181a) the copper and the taste of its companions.» He said: «You have understood well. <He said:> Do you not see [2] how Maria says: "Operate and burn the dry one in order that it remains permanent, in spite of being [3] burnt and invisible." If you make it in this way, then it is our copper, our silver [4] and our gold which comes from our work. Know that [5] the first burning is the existence, the basis and the completion of this work. That is why the sages praised it, and Maria said: "Know that [6] when the copper is burnt with the sulphur and the natron, and the flowers are returned to it several times, it (the copper) gets destroyed and it becomes [7] better than gold without a shadow." Our God inspired whomsoever He wanted, to honour Him with this work. Whoever experiences this work knows that whoever burns our copper with our sulphur [9] removes its shadow and its dye improves. That is why Maria said in *The Treatise of the Idol*: [10] «Before anything else, the copper must be burnt with the sulphur and the body of the magnesia. [11] Then both are cooked till everything that escapes flees from them and the copper is left without a shadow.»

She said: «O Zosimos, [12] make me more sure that the first burning is the basis of the work.» He said: «Yes. [13] God, the exalted and blessed, inspired His prophet Moses to burn the copper with sulphur, salt [14] and alum, which is white sulphur, so that it (the copper) becomes magnesia and true pyrite. [15] Šīmās said in many places: "Burn the copper with water and flowers." [16] Niqūsīūs said: "Burn the copper with oleander leaves."»

She said: «Tell me [17] what are the flowers, and what are the oleander leaves?» He said: «You know that everything moist is water. [18] As for the oleander leaves, they are the white sulphur, which is the alum, which is [19] the broth. Maria says in a 1,000 places: «Burn the copper with the sulphur.»

(fol. 181b) Know that our heavenly sulphur does not burn with a burning that ruins, but [2] makes a good, white, beneficial burning.»

She said: «What is its benefit?» He said: «It turns it (the copper) into gold [3] and it removes its shadow. Democritus also used sulphur to burn the copper, to whiten it, to remove [4] its shadow and to colour it.»

She said: «How does that come?» He said: «Cook the plates which have a shadow in this [5] broth so their shadow will disappear. Indeed he meant (by this broth) the white sulphur. So by this sulphur the sages burn, make white, and make red. In his book, Democritus says about [7] it: "The power of the action of the saffron and the cloud is one." By this we know [8] that the operation in the whitening and the reddening are one thing. In this way [9] the bodies are burnt and destroyed, and the gold becomes copper without shadow. It is good for multiplying [10] the gold and the silver. But we have never seen anybody who, knowing the whole work, would accept the multiplication; otherwise he would [11] eat his grapes when they are still unripe and green.»

She said: «Then tell me about when you say: "When the subtle parts of [12] the things are extracted they are a new spirit."» He said: «That is because they are dyed. When [13] you dye them, they escape from their thick part, while the subtle part of their dye remains with the copper. This is because copper [14] is related to them. None of the natures has a relationship with the copper, or is suitable for [15] its nature, except this nature alone. It is like the suitability of donkeys for [16] horses, or horses for donkeys, or wolves for dogs.»

She said: «So why do they speak so much about [17] lead-copper?» He said: «I explained lead-copper to you when I ordered you to operate on it [18] till you remove its moisture and its squeaking.»

She said: «How can I remove [19] its moisture and its squeaking, and how can I coagulate the moist trembling one (fol. 182a) in it?» He said: «I have told you that this is done by the heat of the fire, and by being patient when [2] cooking it.»

She said: «Then tell me about when you say: "The mixture of the sages is made with [3] the copper which comes out of the furnace. (Then) it (the copper) has to be broken into fragments with the tar, and to be mixed with the silver."» [4] He said: «Even if that copper of theirs is red at the beginning, it is not useful until [5] it becomes white. Often, if you make the fire stronger, it makes a yellow colour appear on the surface of the water, [6] but there is no benefit in the yellowness. For that reason, the sage warned us about strong fire, in order that [7] nothing but whiteness appears. So use a gentle fire, for he says: "It becomes yellow if you strengthen the fire, and in this case [8] the yellowness will not benefit you."»

She said: «Then tell me about when you say: [9] "Those who make the idols name the white copper Indian.» He said: «Yes. That is [10] because the colour of that copper is similar to the colour of the shining Indian, or it is what they call [11] Indian, but its colour is not like the Indian. It is white in its outer appearance, and yellow [12] in essence. For that reason, it is good for multiplying the gold. As for Nubia and those [13] beyond it, they are the colour of ashes, which are the single copper before the whitening, of which I told you. [14] But the copper I am telling you about is not white like silver, or like [15] ashes, but its colour is somewhere in between. That is why they call the copper without [16] shadow Indian, because that copper is suitable for multiplying gold and silver. (See similar text on fol. 90b, 1-9) I have [17] gone against the sages in what I have made clear for you, albeit without bestowing on you a favour in [18] this; thus, my lady, ponder on how you compose (the things), and how you enter into it (the work). You will only be able to do it and obtain it by subtle thought, keen understanding and much patience (fol. 182b) with it, because this true work of ours is born in and nourished by the sea. [2] Know that some of it solidifies quickly, and some solidifies slowly. If while cooking it lacks [3] dampness and moisture and it is dry, it is slow to solidify, but if [4] it is drenched in moisture, it is quicker to solidify.»

She said: «Then tell me about when you say: "Take aqzal, [5] spittle and mercury, mix all three and cast them."» He said: «Yes. I did not [6] tell you this clearly, but I often ordered you to do it with symbolic language and changed the names. That is why [7] you doubted it. Know for sure that mercury is mixed and solidifies on the spot, and [8] the spittle of the moon is also like that. But it dissolves on the spot with the aqzal and the kohl-stone, [9] and mercury is what enters our lead-copper. So if you want the true composition, take equal measures [10] of the ferrous stone, arsenic, magnesia and filings of silver. [11] Pound them and roast them by the operation of the mercury of cinnabar. Some people replace the ferrous one with [12] the pyrite, and the silver with the ferrous one, but I think that only the experiments will show you which pyrite [13] you should use in your work. After that, cook it on a gentle fire, and operate on it till [14] you see it becoming white, and coat it with vinegar. You will find that one of these three has dissolved and separated [15] from its companion (sg.). Take the one that has separated from its companion (sg.), put it in a vessel and solidify it. [16] Then take one part of worm, two parts of snail and two [17] and a half parts of stones of (finger)rings (*fuṣūṣ*). Then pound each one of them separately in a mortar, and put 21 ounces [18] (of liquid) on each one of them. Pound each one [19] of them six or seven times. Then leave it in the sun till it is absorbed, (fol. 183a) and the sun dries the earth of the Nile, which is deprived of its water, and the sun cracks it (the earth) [2] with its heat. When this mortar is pounded, and the aim of its pounding is accomplished through the right number [3] of days, the intelligent people learn by that how to pound the components. For performing the whitening well is a matter [4] of pounding the nature for a long time, and dissolving it till it becomes dissolved.»

She said: «Tell me about this [5] soft sulphur which you claimed cannot burn copper on its own.» [6] He said: «Yes. Know by your father, that sulphur cannot burn copper on its own, [7] unless it is composed with it (the copper). Then it burns it. When the sulphurs burn it (the copper) [8] they leave it, and the copper remains on its own. Know that if that sulphur is composed, [9] it can only burn the copper after many days. So do not become frustrated, but [10] be patient, for sulphurs do not separate from copper till they have dyed it and turned it into [11] spiritual water. That is why this must be kept secret in the way the jealous ones wrote about it in their books, [12] because this operation which I have described for you is the operation of the sand from which [13] the Egyptians obtained numberless treasures. So understand this matter well.»

She said: [14] «Then tell me about when you say: "Knowledge of the water by which everything is dissolved is a great science."» [15] He said: «Whoever does not know our water by which everything is dissolved should not risk doing our work.»

[16] She said: «Set down for me how it is made.» He said: «Take some human dung and dog dung, and cook both of them [17] in a clay pot (*nuṭṭām*).[87] Then take one rutl of this, six ounces of lime, six ounces of ashes of sulphur, [18] six ounces of roasted natron, one ounce of arsenic, six ounces of [19] the sediment, six ounces of burnt gum, six ounces of round alum,

87 Today this pot of clay is called *nuṭṭāl* in Upper Egypt. It is used to cook beans overnight on the remaining ashes, after bread has been made in the *tannūr*.

(fol. 183b) and six ounces of Indian salt. Pound them, and put ten measures of [2] white vinegar on them. Put them in a glass vessel, and cook that gently [3] for six hours till it cools down. Then filter out its pure water. Be careful only to take [4] the pure juices. Wash them till their colours are pure and clear. Cook it till it coagulates, [5] and filter it from its sediment, thus it will be ready for what you want.»

She said: «Then tell me about when you say: "When [6] lead-copper is cooked, purified and becomes clear like the eyes of fish, you can look out for [7] its benefit."» He said: «I will also tell you that at that time it returns to its original nature, and [8] its benefit increases; at that point, you must put it in vinegar and leave it for many days, till its visible [9] body becomes lean and is cast off, and the subtle dyer, which is whitened by the ferment to which [10] we gave many names, remains.»

She said: «Then tell me about when you say that you (the sages) did not write the dyes of the dyers in [11] your books for no reason, but you wrote them as analogies.» He said: [12] «There is a lesson there for you, and those who come after you who understand. Do you not see that the dyers take [13] *k-nk-l* after it has been made rotten? They throw it into the urine, and cook it. Whenever some of [14] the dye emerges, they pick it up, with the wool while it is still boiling, till they have taken up all the subtle part of that dye, [15] and what remains is urine and the sediment. (This) they throw away. Do you not also see that the dyers take [16] plants, or roots or any dye they want, and they cook it in the water? Then they take [17] what rises up from it and use it for dyeing. Those who work with sealing wax (*lukk*) do the same with the sealing wax. [18] In the same way, the sages raise up their things [19] by cooking in order to extract their airy flowers. Then they take the spiritual, airy one that rises up from them, and they leave aside the sediments (fol. 184a) that have no spirits in them. Then, with these fugitive spirits which they extracted from these sediments, they dye [2] that copper about which the sage said: "Copper does not dye till it is dyed, and when it is dyed [3] it dyes."

She said: «Then tell me about when you say to me about the purple: "The ferment of the purple."» He said: «Yes. [4] Take one part of chaff of linseed (*šalgan*), one part of wild thyme, one part of garlic and a sufficient amount [5] of mixed water. Mix them together and pound them for three [6] days, and return them to the cooking for seven days. Then take some Maltese and Armenian purple,[7] put the water with them in a mortar and pound them like pepper is pounded, and be careful [8] to drip onto it (this mixture) the water of the ferment in the amount by which you do it good. Then put it in the pot which is used for extracting [9] the vapour and the ferment, and return it three times. All its power comes out like the power of the crimson [10] from the chaff. If it does not, return it again till it becomes pure, and you extract [11] all its power. The sign that you have extracted that power is that you cook it for a long time, and if you find anything [12] on the cover of the pot, it comes from the power of the crimson. Then you should cook it till nothing more comes out onto the cover of the pot.»

[13] She said: «Then tell me about when you say: "Every dye has an operation which needs purification."» He said: [14] «I have told you about the purification, and I gave you an analogy for each dye. So take a rutl of the wool [15] that you want to dye and nine rutls of natron. Pour [16] water on them and wash the wool. Know that the basis of your dyeing is to wash, [17] bleach and purify the things well.»

She said: «Then tell me about your frequent commands to me to be patient [18] with the operation, and your warning me about boredom and impatience.» He said: «I was quite [19] right to order you to do that, so do not reject the truth. For I saw someone who knew this work, (fol. 184b) but when it took a long time he threw it away. He doubted it because it took so many days for the operation.»

She said: [2] «Why is that?» He said: «Because our dye does not dye quickly like the dye of the dyers, and because anyone who makes our dye [3] takes many months to dye what he wants to dye. If the clothes of the dyers [4] are steamed with sulphur, they accept it (the sulphur), and it gives them a colour. But our dye only accepts [5] our fixed sulphur after the bleaching. If we did [not] do that (the bleaching) its harm would be more [6] than its benefit. So be patient, and beware of weakness, and wait for the fruit of what you are treating, [7] for whoever eats it will never be hungry again.»

She said: «Then tell me about when you say: "Take [8] one part of the flowers of gold, one part of ashes, one part of glassy natron, and [9] a quantity of Egyptian vinegar. Pound them and mix them in a vessel. Add water on them, and stir them [10] till they become like mud. Then put it in a carafe (*dawraq*) for clarifying."» He said: «Yes. [11] So do as I ordered you. Look out for the vinegar and the flowers of gold which came to you. [12] Then put it back on the ashes and cook it till the vinegar is clear and pure, and [13] all its impurity leaves it, so that it shines as marble shines. Soften that and return it [14] to the ashes. Dry it for one day till you see the water become turbid, then return it with its ashes [15] to its filter. Know that what you are looking for is in what you extract from [16] those ashes. So do this to it four or five times, till you extract [17] everything that is in those ashes. Then take the moisture and put it in a separate place.»

[She said:] «Then tell me about when you say: [18] "Take flour of barley and alum, then mix the two with water and soak the ivory in it, thus it (the ivory) becomes soft. [19] Then clarify it till 2/3 of it disappears in the operation. If you want the operation to become (fol. 185a) soft, moisten it thoroughly, and be patient when you cook it, and make the days long. The longer [2] you cook it, the better it will be for it. Cook it gently, to the extent that dissolves it. When it is dissolved, [3] maintain that heat and do not increase or reduce your fire, and cook [4] the body, the bones and the horns.»

She said: «Then tell me about when you say: "Take one part of arsenic, sandarach [5] and kohl, and three parts of marinal (*baḥarī*) lime and [6] uncorrupted water. Cook it seven times and raise it in the vapours."» He said: «Yes, and I [7] order you again to do that, and I warn you that it does not smoke during these seven cookings, because if it smokes, [8] the dyeing spirit immersed in the core of the body will disappear, and you will only retain [9] the external colours which are pleasing to the eye.»

She said: «I see, O Zosimos, that the dye is the smoke.» [10] He said: «Yes. It is the subtle part of the cinnabar. Know that the water strives to keep up with that smoke, because [11] the water seeks that smoke, and it (the water) escapes with the smoke to the air, because it (the smoke) is airy. That is why the cooks [12] cover their pots, so that the subtle part of the water does not carry away the taste of the cooking into the air, [13] because it is the spiritual and the subtle part of the water that makes the food delicious and agreeable in the cooking.»

[14] She said: «I see that the splendour, the dye and the colour are in the smoke.» He said: «Yes. Therefore [15] we ordered you to close the mouth of the vessel well, so that the spiritual part of all things does not leave [16] and escape. You should treat the operation gently, and beware of burning or having a strong fire.»

[17] She said: «Then tell me about when you say: "It is the first elixir which mixes."» He said: «Yes, [18] and the <third> second (corrected from the margin) (elixir) burns, and the third dissolves. So put nine ounces of that [19] old vinegar on the first. Do this twice: the first time, when the vessel heats up,

(fol. 185b) and the second time when you make the vessel hot and you finish using it. As for the third time, put 21 ounces of vinegar [2] on the elixir two times, as I told you, and [3] do to it what you did to the first. Then put exactly ten [4] ounces on the third elixir, and pound it seven times till it becomes foamy. Then add ~~<to the elexir>~~ [5] burnt marble: one ounce on the first, by which one mixes, two ounces on the second elixir [6] which burns, and four ounces on the third elixir which dissolves. Then [7] dry it till it becomes a fragmented clod of earth, and put it in a mortar, and put [8] all of the elixir on it. This should be done when the sun is in the middle of the sky. Then leave it for four [9] days. Put in the same quantity of vinegar that you operated on, and leave it in the pounding with them (the other ingredients), till it cracks. [10] Mix in the same quantity of vinegar, and do this twice a day. Put in [11] exactly ten ounces of the one that mixes, and 22 ounces of the one which burns, and [12] 35 ounces of the one which dissolves, so the power of the vinegar will come out and this is its experiment. When you see that the subtle part [13] of the elixir is dissolved and is extracted from it, then wash it [14] completely pure, till nothing of the elixir remains in the core of the burnt, returned ashes, but all of it has come out.»

[15] She said: «Then tell me about when you say: "Every idol has a colour that is [16] in between these two colours, because its mixture is made from the true composition."» He said: [17] «Yes, and the true mixture is the white and the black. Know that you can only burn [18] our copper with this soft sulphur if the sulphur is composed. [19] At that point, the sulphurs burn the copper and remove its shadow, and the copper remains spiritual.

(fol. 186a) That is why the sages ordered us to keep this secret, because the returning which I described for you [2] is about the operation of the sand by which the Egyptians made their numerous treasures.»

She said: [3] «Then tell me about when you say: "Wash the composition with the water of ashes of firewood of the white sulphur, [4] till you see it is pure. Put on it some of the red vinegar which dissolves everything, and start by closing [5] the mouth of the vessel. Put it in the bathhouse for five days. This is the operation of the composition."» He said: «Yes.»

She said: «Then what is its sign?» He said: «When you see that it dissolves, and the blackness covers it, [7] wash it with hot water and repeat it (the washing) with the water of alum. Know that you should not put [8] water of vinegar on the second one, but leave it to cook with its vinegar till it dries and its earth splits away from it like the cracks in the [9] Egyptian earth when it separates from its water. Know that some of it solidifies quickly and some [10] solidifies slowly.»

She said: «What is the reason for that?» He said: «That is because of the differences in the cooking with the fire. [11] If its moisture is abundant, it is quicker to solidify, and if it is dry [12] it is slower to solidify. So you should use moisture, and be careful not to abandon it, and [13] the experiment will guide you then.»

She said: «Then tell me about when you say: "Take some [14] marine worms, some snails, and stones of (finger)rings (*fuṣūṣ*) with three angles which are taken from [15] the red sea and from the earth of the well of mercury (*bīr zaībaq*), about which I told you (that it) is given birth to every year by [16] everyone."» He said: «Yes. That is the etesian stone, so perform its operation well. Know that if [17] you operate on it more than what is right for it, the light that it took from the sea will be extinguished. [18] For that reason, the sages ordered us to preserve it. So take the etesian (stone) when [19] the moon is full of light, and put it into the dung till it becomes white. Know that if you are not patient (fol. 186b) when you leave it in the dung and when you put it back, you perform the operation wrongly, and you ruin the work. So cook it [2] on a gentle fire till you see it turning white. You will find that one of the three has separated from its companion (sg.). Take the one which has separated from [3] its companion (sg.), put it in a vessel, and solidify it [4] as usual. Know that the more you return the body to the heat and the moisture, and [5] submerge it in it, the more its dirt is removed, its shining becomes visible, and it will take up [6] the colours better. Take the copper which remained and has not been pounded, and became fragmented like copper filings, [7] except that it is black. Cook them for a long time, because the more you cook those [8] black filings, the more they take up of the sediment which remained from the slag which did not get [9] burnt, and the stronger it is for the poison.»

She said: «So tell me about when you say: "The completion of this work is by a gentle fire."» He said: «I was entirely right to order you to use [10] a gentle fire, and to warn you against a strong one. But [11] I will give you an explanation for that.»

She said: «If you do that, may God reward you!» He said: [12] «Look at the dyers when they use a gentle fire to make their dyes, because they are [13] flowers. Thus, if they (emendation) make it strong on them (the dyes), they will get burnt and the dye would disappear. And you also, [14] if you use a strong fire, they (the dyes) will get burnt, and the flowers of your dye will disappear and your dye will be useless. This is [15] the analogy for our work, because if you make your fire strong, the error will come to you, and then you will think that the error came from [16] something else. Upon my life, I have seen someone who knew this stone like you do, and he spent twenty years [17] operating on it. Know that our work has two cookings, and both of them need [18] a gentle fire and much patience, without our becoming bored or annoyed with it. The first cooking is at the time of [19] its solidification and the extracting of its purple. The second is when the blackness occurs in it. So when (fol. 187a) you see it has become entirely black, <So when you see it has become entirely black,> know that the whiteness is concealed [2] inside that blackness. So you should know with what that whiteness gets extracted [3] from that blackness, (namely) with what you know that it separates the two. Take the natures and leave [4] the sediment. Know that the blackness comes and appears from the nature of the litharge. You are only able [5] to extract the redness which you want by that blackness, because that (the blackness) is what reconciles [6] what flees with what does not flee, till it turns them into one thing.»

She said: «Tell me [7] how the blackness reconciled them?» He said: «When the sulphur (fem.), the torturer of her husband, [8] submerges itself inside the body, it turns it into an unchangeable, not vanishing nature. [9] So you must know that this sulphur, which blackens the body, did good to it. [10] Know that it (the feminine sulphur) cannot be tortured or dyed, but she is the torturer and the dyer.»

[11] She said:«Then tell me about when you say: "If you want to make purple, take 100 rutls of *sidānāṭīs*, [12] 10 rutls of ants, and 100 measures of sharp salt, and cook them [13] gently."» He said: «If you indeed do what I ordered, you will obtain more than you need. [14] Know that the people of Alexandria put in some ashes of the sun, and some ashes [15] of the sea. Then they raise it up to the air. If the water is turbid when it rises up, then it is not airy. [16] So you must purify it of its ashes, in order that it becomes sweet and clear, without any [17] turbidity in it, and boil the wool till its dirt comes out, and return it to the vessel. [18] Wash it well, and do not be careless with it in the burning, till the water becomes clear. Then [19] throw it into the sea, because it (the sea) likes the sweetness of it, because of its saltiness and its fatness. When it becomes clear,

(fol. 187b) mix it with a third of its weight of the pure flowers, in order that it dyes whatever you want.»

She said: [2] «Tell me about when you say: "The dyers are not able to make a dye like your black dye."» [3] He said: «No, neither the dyers nor anybody else is able to do it, and if you do not know it, [4] you are unable to do anything.»

She said: «Then describe for me an aspect of it.» He said: «How many times [5] have I described it for you, but you forget!»

She said: «Then repeat it for me.» He said: «Take one part [6] of colocynth, half a part of sulphur, half [7] a part of the rust of iron, one and a half parts of lime, and one and a half parts of litharge. Mix [8] and pound all of them, and add enough water to cover them. Cook them [9] till you see every part of it become black. Know that the longer you cook it, [10] the blacker it becomes. So operate this way, and do not be afraid of the burning. [11] It is your lime that dissolves the things and transforms them from one state to the other.»

She said: «Then tell me [12] about when you wrote to me: "The moisture should cover the wool."» He said: [13] «I tell you that if the moisture does not cover the wool, it will be burnt. So add more (of the moisture) to it, [14] and cook it till all of its moisture disappears, and return the wool in it and cook it [15] till all of its moisture disappears. If you want the dye to become more subtle and penetrating, [16] put the wool back into the alum for many days, dye, and do not become impatient because of the many days. [17] <If you want the dye to become more subtle and penetrating, [16] put the wool back into the alum [18] for many days, dye, and do not become impatient because of the many days.> If you want [19] the dye to become more penetrating and subtler, put in a large quantity of the vinegar, and be patient with its long cooking (fol. 188a) and do not become annoyed.»

She said: «Tell me about when you say: "Take one part of flowers of gold, one part of [2] glassy natron and a quantity of vinegar. Pound the two with the vinegar and stir it till [3] it becomes like clay."» He said: «I have often ordered you to do this, but when you find [4] the names changed you think they are different things. Take these things which [5] I named to you, and mix them with their sediment in their vessel. Whenever the vinegar and the flowers of gold sink down, [6] put them back on the ashes, and mix them with the vinegar till you see that the vinegar becomes clear and pure, shining [7] like marble. Then return it to its vessel with the ashes, and pound it so that it takes up the spirits [8] concealed in the ashes, till you see the water become turbid. Then return it to the filter [9] with its ashes. Know that what comes out of the ashes is what you are looking for. So do this [10] with it four to five times, till you extract from the ashes everything that is in them. Then take [11] the moisture and separate it from the first ashes. Know that the basis of the work that you want [12] to accomplish is that you wash these things well, and bleach and purify them. Then look for the colour [13] you want to dye, and extract for it whatever dye you know that it corresponds to. Put it (the dye) in [14] its water and its remedy. Know that there are many different ways of doing the second work in terms of the measures of its fire. One [15] of them (the sages) said: "Cook it with urine.", and one said: "With water, vinegar and rain water.". For [16] the dry one, however, they did not give as many names as they had for the moist one. This is because in summer one needs [17] to put moisture back onto it. However, in winter you should reduce the moisture, as [18] Maria said about the three mortars which contain the *sūzīn* (vitriol?), the *šaḥīra* (vitriol?) [19] and the rosette colour (*muġra*). (See similar text on fol. 135b, 3f.) Know also that their colours should be better in summer, because (fol. 188b) the sun nourishes them.»

She said: «Then tell me about when you say: "If you want to extract all the power of the crimson, [2] throw (away) the chaff or otherwise return it onto it in order to extract the power of the copper."» [He said:] [3] «The sign that you have extracted it (the power) is that you cook it for a long time, and if you find something on the cover [4] of the pot, know that it is some of the crimson that is still there. So cook it till nothing of it rises onto the cover [5] of the pot. When you have obtained all of the power of the crimson from the sediment, take the amount you know of the wool [6] or the garments that you want to dye.»

She said: «Then tell me about when you say: [7] "Take the garment and mix it with the urine and the dye." [He said: some text seems to be missing] «Put in it flour of barley [8] or beans and cook it till half of the moisture disappears. Then take the crimson with the urine, [9] and pour it out into a pot. Cook it till it becomes colourful when it is put back. Stir it till [10] all of it descends into the water, so the dye comes out in it. Then put it back in the water. [11] If you want to know whether it has reached its highest degree, taste it with your tongue. It should burn your tongue. Otherwise return it to [12] the cooking, and know that the water has not yet been cooked well.»

She said: «Tell me about what you say about the operation of the nature.» [13] He said: «Yes, it is as I will describe to you. Take some of the glass, and set it on [14] a gentle fire. If you see that its colour starts to become purply-black, do not fragment it even once, [15] otherwise it will not come out good. So keep it settled and be careful not to move it. Know that if you leave it [16] to be destroyed by itself, what comes out of it is white and beautiful. [17] When you see that the garlic dissolves and becomes like the sea, leave it for many days, [18] till the luminous thing flows from it in drops. When the luminous colours come out of it, know [19] that it has become a pure poison. When you let the glass enter, do not stop treating it gently till (fol. 189a) all of the glass becomes a sea, before it is purified. Know that, if you do not turn [2] all the glass into a sea before it is purified, ~~<and know that>~~ two parts of it remain [3] uncooked. If, however, all of it turns into a sea before it is purified, then what you are looking for comes out of it, [4] God willing. So do that to it seven times.»

She said: «Tell me about when you say: [5] "The copper must be burnt with a gentle fire like the bird's hatching."» He said: [6] «Yes, and I will add that the moisture must not separate from the copper, so that [7] its spirit does not get burnt. And the vessel should be closed from all sides so that [8] the heat of the fire circulates inside the vessel in order that the copper gets destroyed and its spirit extracted. That is why [9] Taūfīl said: "Take the mercury which comes from the flowers of copper, which Maria named copper."»

[10] She said: «Tell me about what Maria said: "If you do not pound the things [11] with the fire well and the vapour rises, nothing of what you are looking for will come into being."» He said: «This is what [12] the sage spoke of when he said: "When the many winds of the inside swirl up, they cause the cloud to ascend and the vapour [13] of the sea rises (from the margin)." By this he means the pot and the vessel, which contain the sulphur that does not get burnt. [14] This is what Maria was talking about when she said: "Solidify the mercury liquified from various things, in order that [15] the two become three, and the one with the three become four. One, two, one." Then pound [16] this second poison in order that you will know what you will end up with.»

She said: «Tell me about [17] when you say: "The nature took its similar one, so it became strong, non-fugitive."» He said: [18] «Concerning the one similar to it, this is when it takes the flowers of the hard bodies which are the dyes. [19] These flowers are the spirits of the bodies. As for those who have no bodies, it is its leaving (fol. 189b) the thick part, rejecting it, so what it takes are spirits like it, and what it rejects is the thick part [2] of the hard bodies, which are not able to escape from the fire. Thus when [3] it (the nature) turns it (the thick part of the hard bodies) into mercury, concealed in the other mercury, the spirits become similar to it, [4] because it is a spirit like those spirits. As for the bodies that are left and rejected, [5] they are the dissimilar ones to it, because the hard bodies do not flee the fire. But when [6] they became mercury, concealed in the other mercury, they fled from the fire into the air, [7] although their original birthplace, from which they were extracted, was non-fugitive. So they only became fugitives [8] by the operation. Know that the soul is different from the body, and when the soul separates [9] from the body it (the body) dies. That is why Šīmas and Maria and all the sages said: "Take [10] the dragon, whose soul is extracted from the bodies."»

She said: «Tell me, [11] why did the sages name the rust "poison of honey"?» He said: «When the water is cooked with the bodies, it takes their taste, in the same way as water [12] takes the taste of honey when it is mixed with it. Like that, [13] the sages extracted the dye from the bodies by the moisture. Then they added it [14] to whatever they wished.»

She said: «Tell me about when Šīmas says: "Everything is [15] one."» He said: «You should mix that one with everything which you need, [16] in order that what you are looking for comes out of it. Know that this [17] one contains everything you want, although it is one. So this one that I give over to you is [18] what the sages were looking for all along. » She said: «Then name it to me.» He said: [19] «It is the poison, and it is the big old dragon, which I mentioned to you in my great dream.

(fol. 190a) Know that if fire, water, air and earth do not mix with each other [2] and get rotten, nothing will come out of them. Likewise with our gold: if we want to cultivate it in the earth [3] and it is not made to rot together with the whiteners (correction from the margin), the galls, the urines, the virtuous mineral [4] natures and the high-ranking dye [5] concealed in it—then it will not be extracted from it. So be gentle and cook this nature in the gentlest way possible, and make it rotten [6] in it. For if you do not do that to it till you turn it into ashes, the colours will not come out. [7] I have already given an account of this rotting in a thousand places in my books to help you understand more.»

[8] She said: «Then tell me about when you say: "Do not neglect and do not be impatient with the burning of the bodies."» He said: [9] «I have already told you that Hermes said: "Burn the bodies intensely, till [10] their souls come out and they (the bodies) turn into ashes." When you see that the natures have become ashes, [11] know that you made a good mixture. You may need to burn these natures [12] till you extract their moisture, and that moisture becomes sulphur, and [13] the bodies become incombustible ashes.»

She said: « Perhaps this is what the sage called the white ashes [14] of firewood?» He said: «Yes, and by that he means the ashes of the natures. [15] Democritus says about this: "The sulphurs hold the sulphurs, so much work comes out from them." [16] Know that even if you make every effort with these dyes, you will only be able [17] to extract any dye out of them by these ashes.»

She said: «Then tell me about when you say that [18] your golden stone is made up of various things, in order that (added from the margin) it becomes a stone in the cooking.» [19] He said: «At this time we name it etesian, and then when it is cooked, it should (fol. 190b) be purified with the water which is not composed, as I ordered you, in order that it becomes rotten and you extract [2] the pure water of sulphur from it.»

She said: «Then tell me about when you say: "Light a gentle fire."» [3] He said: «It is what is named the flowers of copper. If you want a gentle fire, then [4] close up the holes (corrected from the margin), and if you want an intense fire, then open the holes. But you have to treat (it) with a gentle fire. [5] The Book of the Operation, which is the 8th Book of the Book [6] of Zosimos, is completed, and it is followed by the 9th, God willing

[7] The Ninth Book of the Book of Zosimos and it is the BOOK ABOUT THE MEASURES [8] OF THE FIRE

[9] In the name of the merciful and compassionate God.

He said: «If you obtained [10] what you wanted concerning the operation, ask about something else.» She said: «Can anyone have enough of this [11] mercy which God bestows upon His prophets?» He said: «Ask me about something else.»

[12] She said: «You have spoken, and spoken well. So tell me about the fire.» He said: «The sages [13] veiled and disguised what concerns the matters of the fire, giving them other names, jealously guarding them and misleading the people [14] to prevent them from being known, because there can be no work without them. [15] Moreover, the fire has measures, and if you do not know them, you cannot achieve success.»

She said: [16] «Then present some aspect of them to me.» He said: «Ask me whatever you want about it, then I will make it clear [17] for you without jealousy. So understand it well!» She said: «I very much desire to! But what [18] the sages said is enigmatic and disguised. Whenever I think that I have obtained [19] some knowledge from their books, and I can be sure of what is in my hand, there then appear to me some problems about what they said, (fol. 191a) which makes me more confused than I was before.» He said: «You are right. Were it not for the fact that 2 the exalted blessed God had inspired the sages to veil this work, 3 people would have treated it as they do glass-making. If that happened the world would be ruined.» She said:

4 «Then distinguish for me between the first and the second work.»
5 He said: «I already have.»

6 The picture of Zosimos and Theosebeia, as we described, carrying between them
7 a cupola on four columns. And there is a picture of a lake, with a fish[88] in it, coloured with the water of silver, and in front of it (there is)

8 a dog of the water (*kalb al-ma'*), and on its shore there are three long sticks with
9 two yellow birds perched on top. And there are three short sticks on which two birds sit,

10 whose colour is yellow-green. And there is the image of Theosebeia, as we described,
11 standing in the middle of the lake, pointing to those birds. And there is the image of nine
12 winged statues, tied with yellow ropes.

Fig. 69: Picture of the 9th Book about the Measures of the Fire, fol. 191b.

(fol. 192a) After this picture it says the following.

She said: «O Zosimos, present me with an aspect of the measures [2] of the fire that I may rely on. For I see that the sages differed about the measures of the fire.» [3] He said: «Indeed, one of them says "with gentle fire" while some other says "with moderate fire".»

[4] She said: «Then tell me what you think.» He said: «I think that you should look for the measure of it which [5] you understand and make it according to that, because the sages made no clear statement for me to tell you. [6] One of them says "the operations", one of them says "the vessels", one of them says [7] "the fireplaces (*mustaūqidāt*) [89]", and one of them says "the furnaces". They said that so that the intelligent [8] people would understand and extract from them (these statements) what they need.

She said: «What is the reason for the difference of the colours?» [9] He said: «This comes from the different fires and the different mixtures. So, to obtain [10] those colours that you want to appear to you, it is necessary for the measures of your fire to differ, as well as for [11] your mixture to differ. Otherwise you work like the ignorant who have no understanding, and in that way [12] you help the envious devils (*šaiāṭīn*) against your work.»

She said: «Then tell me about when you say that I should [13] experiment with the operation of the fire.» He said: «After you know the natures, [14] their combination and the true weights, there is nothing you need so much as to know the operation of the fire. Ponder over what [15] you cook every day, and how it comes out, and what its power is. Then ponder over what you cook [16] in two, three or however many days. Then reflect on it till you reach the furthest extent of [17] this matter. So you must make experiments. But, whoever has neither intelligence nor obedience, and does not make experiments, [18] will neither listen to himself nor to anybody else. Look when you see the vapour [19] rising up to the head (of the vessel), then strengthen the fire till the rest comes up. At this time dry up, and take

89 *Mustaūqid* is a fireplace where you have the fire burning for 24 hours, like in a public *ḥammām* or for cooking beans (*fūl*).

(fol. 192b) that silver mixed with the litharge that was raised up in the vapour. Then put it back till it becomes (pure) silver. [2] This is the first dyeing.

She said: «Then tell me about when you say: "The copper is like a human being, [3] with a soul, a spirit and a body."» He said: «Likewise the sages ordered that [4] this spirit should be extracted with [5] a gentle fire, similar to the hatching of eggs, because that spirit which is extracted by this gentle fire is what dyes and fights against the fire.

She said: «Then tell me about [6] this spirit which was extracted from the body and became a spirit.» He said: «When [7] the gentleness of the fire turned that spirit into a spirit, it [re]entered quickly into the body. For those who are intelligent, the analogy for it is the poison [8] that is extracted from the body by the operation. When this poison falls on the body, it enters quickly into it because it comes out of a moist body, and [9] it enters into one like it till it mixes [10] with the veins, the blood and the joints, in the same way as water mixes with honey, never to leave it. [11] This is the poison of the sages. When it is extracted from the bodies, it becomes a non-body, [12] because it cannot be touched. After that, it (the spirit) is no longer afraid of the fire, because it was extracted from the body as [13] a moist spirit, then it got rotten, then it became a poison, and after that it rose up in the vessel. If [14] you do this well, it mixes with what your are looking for.»

She said: «Then tell me about when Hermes says: [15] "Even if the thick parts of the natures oppose each other, the subtle parts are [16] in accord with each other."» He said: «Know that if the subtle parts that are different from each [17] other do not mix so that the earth becomes water, and the water becomes air [, and the air becomes fire] you are not doing the right thing. For that reason, [18] the sages ordered us to rot the composition. Then after that, a black turbidity comes out. Know that [19] you must cook the composition in a gentle way before you raise it, because it is by (fol. 193a) the gentle cooking that the spirit takes the dyeing spirits from the bodies that are similar to it. So the dyeing spirits are extracted by the gentle [2] fire and by that moist spirit.»

She said: «Then tell me about [3] when you say: "When those joint bodies enter the fire and are cooked by a gentle fire [4] till they turn into ashes, they become spirits.» He said: «Know that the only thing that turned them [5] into spirits was the association with the fire, and their inhaling the soul from the air like a human being. [6] A human being's life comes from inhaling the soul from the air, and our copper is like that. These [7] two things, the fire and the air, are what put the natures to death, and they are, [8] after God, also what revive them. Like that, the four natures of the creatures give both life and death to every thing [9] by the decree of the omniscient and mighty God. Know that what you are looking for [10] comes from the copper that has many names. When it is cooked with a gentle fire, it will turn into an etesian stone. [11] Its colour is the colour of the stones and the litharge. After you cook it (the copper) [12] and it turns into a stone, you should quench it with the moisture of the water of sulphur that is not composed [13] till you make it like thick fat. It has to be left in it for 41 days [14] in a gentle fire with its vessel sealed for it to rot, and for its thick part to be destroyed. It changes in the same way [15] as food changes in the stomach, and out of it comes the visible secret, which is [16] the pure water of sulphur.»

She said: «Tell me about what led the sages to differ over [17] what they called the fire, and over what they said its [18] measures were.» He said: «That is because they knew that the measures of the fire were the key to their work and the basis of their operations.»

She said: «Present me [19] with some aspect on which I can rely.» He said: «Know that your work has no more harmful enemy than the fire.

(fol. 193b) If you gain the knowledge of its measures you attain what you want, but [2] if you ignore them, your work will be destroyed, you fall into grief and you cease to believe in this work. [3] But this destruction came to you because you ignore the measures of the fire. Do you not know [4] that if the heat of the sun beats strongly upon a seed [5] in winter, just when it first sprouts into a plant, the small plant will burn up?»

She said: «I know that.» [6] He said: «So arrange the measures of your fire according to the four seasons as an analogy for those [7] four periods of time. Know that if you make the fire strong, you burn the flowers, [8] and if you make your fire weak, the hard bodies do not dissolve and the flowers do not come out. [9] So make your fire strong in the second and in the third (period), and in the fourth, make [10] your fire still stronger, and if you are afraid about the bottle, coat it in clay.»

She said: «Then tell me about when you say [11] that the sages said: "The error comes at the beginning of the mixture of the poison. If, however, [12] I succeed in making the poison and its composition, I am saved from the error."» He said: «And [13] I tell you that the error comes at the beginning of the mixture, be it in the black, [14] the red, or in any other thing. Do you not see that the sun is there [15] in place of the gentle fire, because the gentle fire turns the sulphurs into [16] incombustible dyes. So you must make use of gentle fire and be careful not to use fire with a strong heat, which would destroy the flowers. [17] For just as it is in the nature of the sun to cause flowers to sprout in the countries about which [18] I told you, likewise a gentle fire causes the gold to sprout and grow in this work. [19] That is why Hermes said: "With the big sun, God completes this matter."»

(fol. 194a) She said: «Then tell me about when you say: "Be careful not to burn the mixture strongly at the beginning as you would burn [2] the flowers."» He said: «I both tell you and order you to do that. You must use the gentle fire [3] for the beginning of the burning, and the same for the burning of the whitening, and the same for the burning of the reddening.»

[4] She said: «Then tell me about when you say: "If you know the measures of the fire, you attain what you are looking for."» He said: [5] «Know that if you do not know its measures, you fall into error.»

She said: «How can I know [6] those measures?» He said: «Look at your magnesia. When you see it has the colour of [7] the black lead for many days, and then after that some blackness covers it, then know [8] that the measures of your fire are in the right place, and that you are not mistaken in it. So remember what I say here!»

[9] She said: «Then tell me about when you say: "If you strengthen the fire when the dyes are cooked, you will destroy [10] the flowers of the dye."» He said: « Do you not know that when the heat of the sun burns strongly on [11] the plants of the earth, it causes them to wither and dry up, so that their lustre, splendour and benefit disappears. So be careful [12] about the strength of the fire in the composition!»

She said: «Then tell me about when Alāsārdus says: [13] "O you students, I warn you of strong fire in the operation, for it is the enemy of the water, until the two are reconciled."» He said:[14] «In the same way as Christ (*masīẖ*), peace be upon Him, said to those who came to test [15] His knowledge by their science, addressing them before they started speaking: "How amazing of you, O community of sages, [16] that you reconciled fire and water so they live together in the operation." [17] They were astonished when He knew them by their science. <He said:> In the same way I warn you about the fire, and I tell you [18] that if you reconcile fire and water, your work will be good, God willing.» [See also fol. 42a, 15 - fol. 42b, 3.]

She said: «Then tell me [19] about when Taūfīl says: "Every time you cook in the (fol. 194b) first composition, let your fire be less than in the second composition, in order that this magnesia becomes dry."» He said: «Yes, [2] he ordered you to cook it in order that this stone gets destroyed and becomes red.»

She said: «It was [3] right of you, O Zosimos, to tell me that if I made the fire strong in the whitening [4] and the reddening, the fire would consume the dye of the fugitives.» He said: «Yes, and I will also tell you that if you return [5] on them some of that dyeing spirit which was extracted from the united bodies, they (the fugitives) come to life [6] and their colours return to them. So do this your work with the gentle fire. If you want to make [7] the fire gentle, then close the holes well and know that if the body is put on the fire without vinegar, [8] it will get burnt and ruined.»

She said: «Tell me about when you say: "The mixture of the air should be in four [9] kinds."» He said: «I did not think that this could be something unknown to you. Do you not know that [10] winter comes, then spring, then summer, and then the fruits ripen? So [11] the measures of your fire and your operation on the natures must be the same. Operate on them with the moisture of winter, then operate on them [12] with the warmth of the air which makes the flowers come out, then operate on them with the heat of summer whose strength cooks [13] the fruits, then operate on them with the gentleness of the season when the fruit are picked from the trees. This is the analogy [14] for how you should operate on these dyeing natures, otherwise you have only yourself to blame.»

[15] She said: «You have frightened me with these things that have to do with the fire. So tell me at greater length!» He said: «I will only do that [16] to protect you and warn you so that you do not burn your work with the fire, and then think that it (the work) [17] is not true, while in fact the trouble and the error come from the fire. Long ago I told you [18] that if the one who enters this work did not know the (right) measures of the fire, he would be destroyed, [19] for the work can only happen through them. That is why I have repeatedly spoken about the measures

(fol. 195a) of the fire.

She said: «Then present me with some aspect of it, on which I can rely.» He said: «When you put [2] your hand in the work, you must put it (the work) in its vessel, and divide the fire into four. The first division [3] should be a gentle fire like the fire the dyers use for their dyes, in order that the things mix [4] with each other. In the second, make the fire stronger than it was before, in order that the things get mixed [5] and become a stone. Concerning the third fire, if you want to destroy [6] the stone and make it red, know that it only becomes red with the strong fire so that it absorbs all of the gum. [7] Know that it only absorbs it with a strong fire. Therefore make your fire stronger, more than it was before. [8] But if you are afraid that your vessel of glass could dissolve in the fire, then coat it [9] with a thin layer of clay on the outside. Concerning the fourth division, from which the flowers appear, it is more gentle than [10] this third fire. Be cautious with the fires, because it is the basis of the matter, but it is also its ruining. I have made clear [11] for you the measures of the fire, and I hope you understand it. I tell you that the rightness of the work [12] or its ruining depends on the fire. So come to know it, God willing.»

[13] The 9th Book of the Book of Zosimos is completed
and it is about the measures of the fire,
[it is followed by the 10th] and it is about the other work.

[14] The 10th Book of the Book of Zosimos

[15] About the Other Work

(fol. 195b) In the name of the compassionate and merciful God. He said: «If you have finished [2] asking me about the first work, its combinations, colours, compositions and operations, [3] then ask me about something else.»

She said: «Set out for me aspects of the second work, as you have described [4] the first work in the way a father teaches his son.» He said: «I have made a picture at the beginning of [5] this chapter. If you understand it, this will be enough for you.»

She said: «But I have to ask you questions.» [6] He said: «So ask whatever you want.»

She said: «Why should I not ask you questions about the second work, for you did not write [7] a book as you did for the first work?» He said: [8] «You did not ask me about that, and I would not be the one to start it with you.»

She said: «Do not let jealousy penetrate you!» [9] He said: «If jealousy had penetrated me, I would have neither written anything for you, nor would I have made clear anything of the names of [10] the first work as I have done.»

She said: «So complete your favour to me.» He said: «If you have understood what [11] the first teaching is, you would not need to search for further knowledge because in what you asked me, there is what [12] removes your doubt. Thus be grateful and beware not to reject [13] what I entrusted to you.»

She said: «God save me from being ungrateful for your kindness or for denying [14] anything you have done for me.» He said: «So ask me about whatever you want.»

[15] The position of the picture.

[16] The image of a man of gold, with a sun of gold on his head, carried in the hands of three persons [17] with wings, and on their heads are crowns of gold. And Theosebeia is standing upright [18] in a red cupola, having in her hands a rope of water of gold. With it she binds six winged [19] persons by their necks, and their legs are tied together

(fol. 196a) by a rope in the way I described the dyes as water of gold, water of silver, [2] flowers of copper, red lead, yellowness of arsenic with the colour of lapis lazuli, and the redness of [3] purple.»

Fig. 70: Picture of the 10th Book about the Other Work, fol. 196a.

(fol. 196b) She said: «Then tell me about when the sage said: "Remove the shadow of the copper." So with what does the shadow of [2] the copper get removed?» He said: «With the water that we have mentioned so many times, because when the water is mixed [3] with the copper, it prevents the colour of the copper from appearing. As a confirmation of my statement Maria said: [4] "Only mercury makes the shadow of the copper disappear." So the shadow is the colour.»

She said: «Then tell me [5] about the incombustible sulphur.» He said: «I have already told you before that it is [6] the body whose moisture was made to disappear, so it became resistant to fire. Then we named it [7] incombustible sulphur because it fights fire and is resistant to it. And I order you that when you see that this [8] sulphur turns into dust, then roast it and soak it! Then return the silver [9] so that it becomes gold; then return the gold so that it becomes aqzal gold; then return [10] the aqzal gold so that it becomes purple gold.»

She said: «Then tell me about when the sage said: [11] "Operate on it (the copper) till it becomes incombustible like filings of gold. But if it does not become [12] like that, then do not blame the copper, but blame yourselves because you operated badly.» [13] He said: «By this statement, the sage rather meant that if you take a copper that is not [14] our copper and you operate on it, nothing would come out of it [completed from the margin]. But if you operate on our copper with [15] the eternal water, then you will find that in the operation it will be like what the sage told you.»

[16] She said: «Then tell me about the statement of the sage: "Take lead and white mercury [17] and operate on it (sg.) in the dew and the sun until it becomes a silvery stone.» He said: [18] «By that he meant that if you take copper and mix it with our eternal water, [19] and cook it on a gentle fire, it will become a silvery stone. Therefore the sage said:

(fol. 197a) "Nature rejoices in nature" because of the known relationship between the two, [2] (namely) the eternal water and the honoured body, which is the master of the bodies and the head of the metals. [3] So those two things are a nature because there is a strong relationship between the two.»

She said: «Then tell me [4] about when the sage said: "We swore an oath together not to make clear this secret in any book."» [5] He said: «But what is clearer than his statement: "When the chrysocolla turns into rust, is soaked [6] seven times and cooked, it will dye every body."?»

She said: «Then tell me about the sage [7] Tīmīs, who said: "Take the male, then make plates out of it, and mix it with the moisture [8] that is the eternal water. Cook it on gentle fire until the plates dissolve and turn into water. [9] Then the plates dry up the moisture that dissolved the body.» [He said:] «This is what the sage named [10] the water of the male. You should cook it—and do not be impatient—until the plates absorb the moisture, [11] the sand appears and it becomes dry. At that time, soak it with the white water until all [12] of the water is used up, and all of the water and what is in it turns into dust. If you have obtained that from [13] this body, then leave it in its vessel to become rotten in a strong fire for many days, [14] in order for the fire to extract its colours that the sages mentioned. If you do that, you will obtain [15] the utmost good and a relief with no more deception.»

She said: «You sent me [16] *The Book of Chrysocolla* and my question to you (now) is to effectively cure my doubts [17] about it. Thus tell me about the chrysocolla.» He said: «Democritus mentioned it [18] in the 10th operation.[90] And I told you before this that the chrysocolla is similar to [19] the rust of copper. If it is roasted several times, it dyes every

90 This could refer to the 10th key of Zosimos' *Mafatīḥ aṣ-ṣanaʾa*.

(fol. 197b) body at the time of the completeness. And if the chrysocolla gets destroyed and turns into rust, it ceases to be a body [2] and its name becomes rust.»

She said: «Then why did they name it with the name of every body?» He said: [3] «Because when it dissolves, it turns into what we name lead, and when it turns black, [4] we name it copper, and when it solidifies, we name it tin, and when it turns into a [5] white stone, we name it silver, and when it becomes red, we name it gold, [6] and when it becomes fine dust, we name it rust and poison. Therefore do not think that these names [7] and bodies are the names and bodies of ordinary people; they are names that [8] the first sages invented for the chrysocolla in its changing states. So they named it after the bodies [9] of ordinary people in order to veil it from you.»

She said: «Then tell me, O Zosimos, do you think that [10] as soon as the nature is put into the sea, it makes the sea become pregnant?» He said: «The sea does not become pregnant unless [11] the poisons reach it, making the waves come out, and the sea becomes thick, then [12] the pregnancy appears. But I warn you about the rising of the sun, because the heat of the sun takes away [13] the dew that is the nutrition, food, and life of the body. Otherwise it would remain like the widow [14] who has no husband. Know that the nature is a male and a female, and the two are what [15] the sages named the body of magnesia. Thus the body is the male and the magnesia is [16] the female, and in it is the great hidden secret. Therefore put the body of magnesia [17] in its vessel and cook it intensively, and after some days, open it, then you will find that every [18] thing has turned into water. Then return it to be cooked again until it becomes thick and clings [19] together.»

She said: «Then tell me about when you said that Agathodaimon did a lot of pounding, roasting, (fol. 198a) cooking, and turning things into vapour, after rotting, making lean, and intense [2] cooking.» He said: «Yes, if you want to be a student of Agathodaimon and become [3] like the sages, then take the body of magnesia —after you have mixed it with its components—[4] and put it in its vessel which you know, close the mouth of the vessel well, and put it [5] and the mixtures on a gentle fire till the body is dissolved and becomes water. This is because when [6] the heat of the fire reaches it, it dissolves and becomes water, God willing. And this is the beginning of the path after the union [7] of the things, their composition and their weights. If they become water, then know that you will see [8] the dust covered with the water. So when you see all of that, then know that the body was dissolved. Then return it [9] to its vessel and leave it to be cooked for 40 days until the body absorbs the moisture of the vinegar [10] and the honey. There are some people who open it every seven to ten days. [11] During all that time, you will see that the water becomes (more and more) pure until it completes 40 days. When the body absorbs [12] its moisture, then you must make the blackness come out by cooking which washes until the blackness disappears and it becomes [13] a dry stone to touch. And in this regard, Maria said: "Wash the magnesia [14] with the sweet water in order that the blackness comes out." Then you must cook it intensively till it turns into dust [15] and all the moisture disappears." At this time, Maria named it the rust of copper. [16] When you see it like that, then put sour vinegar on it, or eternal water, [17] or water of the sea, shake it in it and leave it in the sun to absorb it (the liquid). This [18] is our burnt copper, which Maria ordered to be washed with the eternal water.»

[19] She said: «Then what about your telling me that Agathodaimon said that whoever reads his book, and knows

(fol. 198b) what he meant, would know that his intention was only to dissolve, pound, and cook till [9] it turns into a stone, shining like marble.» He said: «Agathodaimon spoke well [3] and he advised whoever took refuge in this his statement. The sage Democritus ordered us likewise, [4] except that he was enigmatic in his statement when he said: "Cook it (the copper) with the cloud until it becomes [5] a shining stone, brilliant and splendid, and it is the greatest secret."» Then after that he ordered that it has to be cooked [6] until it turns into glue, becomes rust, and the copper turns white. After that he ordered that [7] it has to be cooked, pounded and returned to the eternal water seven times. Then it has to be pounded and made to rot until [8] its concealed nature comes out. This statement of Democritus is the same as the one of Agathodaimon, [9] except that Agathodaimon summarized enigmatically, while Democritus [10] spoke at length, making it clear for whoever knows what he meant.»

She said: «Then tell me about the statement of Democritus [11] in his 4th Book: "Sulphurs hold the sulphurs, and moisture [12] does the same with moisture." He said: «By this statement, he meant that when sulphur is mixed [13] with sulphur, many works could come into being from them. He ordered us to operate on both with the fire [14] and the sun until what we are searching for appears out of them, so this (what we are searching for) is the powerful one about which you asked me [15] from the statements of Agathodaimon, Democritus and Isis. It is indeed one, but this [16] secret has colours, and whenever it changes from one colour to another, they name it with a name of a body [17] whose colour is similar to it. And I convince you more by telling you that there are two whitenings and two reddenings. [18] So the first whitening and reddening is for the rust, and the other one is in the pounding by cooking. [19] Concerning the making rusty, it is the making white and the making red. But (fol. 199a) without the other one, it would neither resist nor fight the fire because it is feeble and fugitive. So when it held [2] the other one it became resistant, and that other one with which it got mixed, taught it to fight the fire. Know that!»

She said: [3] «The sages insisted on saying: "Turn the bodies into non-bodies, [4] and those which are non-bodies into bodies."» He said: «They meant the destruction of the bodies [5] with the mercury and the magnesia, and the marriage of the female with the male. At this time, [6] the vapour extracts the concealed spirit that is in the nature. By this operation, [7] the bodies become non-bodies and the non-bodies become bodies. If you [8] pound the things well with the fire and raise up the vapour, you will make the things pure, non-fugitive. [9] Know that the mercury is fiery, and by one operation it burns, kills and breaks into fragments.»

She said: [10] «Then what about the statement of the sage: "If you want to make the other (work), make it white before that. Then mix [11] the white poison with the red poison, so that it becomes a red poison, and mix the rotten one [12] with what does not become rotten, so that out of it comes a perfect elixir."» He said: «How persistent you are [13] in your questions! When the white poison was a body it was not white. But [14] when it was operated on in the first composition it became silver. Then it became poison that was extracted from [15] ashes. So when the sage wanted to make red, he mixed the white poison, [16] whose origin was red, with the red poison.»

She said: «How does it come that it is white and red?» [17] He said: «Although it is white in outer appearance, its essence and core has a [18] superior redness concealed in that whiteness. When the redness which is [19] concealed in the whiteness meets the other red poison, the two are mixed (fol. 199b) like water with honey. Concerning your question about the mixing of the rotten one with the non-rotten one, [2] <He said: «How persistent you are in your questions! When [3] the white poison was a body it was not white. But when it was operated on in [4] the first composition it became silver. Then it became poison that was extracted from ashes. So when the sage wanted [5] to make red, he mixed the white poison, whose origin was red, with [6] the red poison.» She said: «How does it come that it is white and red?» He said: «Although it is [7] white in outer appearance, its essence and heart has a superior redness concealed [8] in that whiteness. When the redness which is concealed in the whiteness meets the other [9] red poison, the two are mixed like water with honey. Concerning your question about the mixing of [10] the rotten one with the non-rotten one, it is the one which was operated on and mixed with the one which was not operated on, so that out of it comes a perfect elixir. (The last part of this sentence is taken from line 2)

She said: [11] «Then what about the statement of the student Tūīn: "O you, our teacher, should these two natures—the male [12] and the female—be enough for us, or do you think that something alien should enter with them?"» He said: [13] «Hermes ordered us not to put anything in the vessel except these two natures, the male and the female, [14] after they were operated on at the beginning of the matter. And he ordered that it has to be cooked until the body dries up [15] the heavy moisture and turns into one stone.»

She said: «Then tell me what you said about it.» He said: [16] «I order you not to let anything alien enter between the two. And that is the case in the other (work), when you kindle a gentle fire [17] under them in order that they marry each other, so when they become water, [18] they get married and cling to each other. After that, when you see that the natures [19] have turned into ashes, know that you have made a good mixing, mingling, and marriage.

(fol. 200a) If you want to know whether your work is right, look, and if you see that [2] the body has dissolved and turned into water, then you are right. So cook it and do not be impatient. [3] Ponder over that spittle which dissolves that great thing, and do not mix anything [4] of the natures with it after you have operated on it with the poison, and extracted it from the cinnabar [5] because it does not accept anything alien in this dissolving, which is the last. Know that when [6] you mix the one nature with the nature that is from its natures, or, to be more precise, [7] you soak it and it gets dissolved with it, then this is the greatest dissolving with which you dissolve [8] the great thing. Know that after the operation, that thing is only mixed with its nature in which [9] the gold is cultivated, in which it becomes pregnant, and in which it is born when correctly extracted from the cinnabar. [10] So if you want to test the glue of the gold, mix it with what fights the fire, which is [11] the red cinnabar, and when it dissolves it, then your glue is good. But if you put it under the ray of the sun, and [12] its ray reaches it, then it would ruin it, therefore protect it from the fire. I swear to you by [13] the exalted God, that Hermes swore—and he was truthful—that he suffered long in this matter, [14] and found in it an intense hardship before the natures were married to each other, the nature of [15] the sun and the moon.»

She said: «Then tell me about when you say: "Take the burnt copper and the lead [16] which is the white lead (*asfīdāǧ*), and pound the two completely with the water of the natron until [17] their shadow is purified and the blackness disappears from them."» He said: «The lead [18] receives the power from the copper, so you should burn the copper by cooking till it turns into [19] ashes. Know that the nature is what burns the copper. Then take the copper, make (fol. 200b) plates out of it, then mix it with the sandarch and cook it, and you will find that the copper turns white and breaks into fragments. [2] Thus from this copper comes the great secret, if you turn it into a spirit. So cook it [3] until it becomes lean, and the moisture of the female disappears. But if it does not disappear, then cook it [4] until all the moisture disappears. When it becomes dry, then it is the copper that has no shadow, and it is [5] what the sages named the burnt copper. Know that it is the female that turns [6] the copper into a spirit. The sage said about this: "Cure the soul from every illness."»

[7] She said: «I was thinking that this statement belongs to the first work, but you brought it [8] into the other (work).» He said: «I have already told you that we often mix the two in order to veil it from ordinary people.»

[9] She said: «But do not do that with me!» He said: «Surely, these books of mine will fall into [10] the hands of others. So if I had revealed the truth, it would not be preserved.»

She said: «You insist on being cautious. Then what is its name [11] when the copper is mixed with the female?» He said: «I do not name it burnt copper as long as [12] it is not dyed and its work is not yet complete.»

She said: «Then complete its work for me.» He said: «Cook it until [13] it dries and turns into dust. Then soak it, so this is about what Maria said: "Whoever [14] dyes the gold well will obtain the work, and whoever does not do it well will obtain nothing."»

[15] She said: «Then tell me, O Zosimos, about when you wrote to me that you passionately loved a virgin slave, [16] —although you do not lightly fall for women—but when passion took hold of you, you had sexual intercourse with her, so then you felt [17] extremely tortured. You longed for her and your sleeplessness was for her, because [18] you were afraid of being killed by her hand, yet I see you still alive. How can that be?» He said: [19] «How much you ask and how little you understand! If you read the rest, it will guide you to what you do not yet know.»

(fol. 201a) She said: «You confused my mind with your many statements by giving the beginning at the end and the end at the beginning. What are the other statements which you thought [2] would make clear to me what I did not understand?» He said: It is the statement of the sages: "Be delighted, [3] O Zosimos, at the blackness, because when you die, something better than [4] you will come out of you. And when your body is destroyed, you will become a spirit, and you will enter another body, so your offspring will increase and you will be beneficial to [5] your beloved people."»

She said: «I do not understand this.» He said: «Indeed, I am the body and the virgin slave [6] is the eternal water. The body longs for the eternal water, and the eternal water longs for it (the body). It is that about [7] which the sage said: "When the sulphur gets mixed with the sulphur, there will be [8] love between them because of the close relationship between the two. When the body was mixed with that moisture, [9] it (the moisture) made its body disappear, so it became a spirit. And the body solidified the moisture, so it (the body) turned it (the moisture) into fine dust [10] with a concealed spirit inside it. Thus little of this becomes abundant, and from the one come out [11] the many." I wrote all of this as an analogy for the operation. Contemplate well [12] what you read, do not be in a hurry when reading, and put aside every stupid guiding principle.»

She said: «I would like you, [13] O Zosimos, to be kind to me and to explain to me the operation of this secret, in order that whoever wants [14] to enter this work will be more recompensed, and gladly give for it what it costs. This is in order that they understand [15] the analogy of what you described: "The inferior with the high-ranking, and the high-ranking with the inferior".» He said: «Understand and know that [16] the beginning of the mixing is the first composition. You should mix the natures uncooked, soft and [17] not operated on. And be careful not to make the fire strong until the natures are married, cling [18] to each other, fecundating each other, and are mingled in such a way that they mix [19] with each other, get burnt little by little and then get dried in that gentle fire.

(fol. 201b) She said: «Then what about when you say: "Take pyrite, operate on it, wash it in the sea until [2] the blackness disappears, and sweeten it until its drops become like drops of gold. [3] Then put it on the silver in order that it becomes gold."» He said: «I also order you here to cook [4] the pyrite until its blackness disappears. When it becomes dry, put the silvery water on it, so it becomes [5] aqzal gold.»

She said: «Then what about when she said: "Mix the gold with the silver, so it neither escapes nor [6] gets corrupted."» He said: «She also ordered you here to mix the gold with the silvery water, so when [7] it is mixed, it will not be able to escape.»

She said: «Then what about when she said: "Take the flowers of copper when it becomes [8] a red poison, and soak the secret in it according to what one sees." He said: «The flowers of copper [9] are the silvery water that was operated on and turned into eternal water. She ordered that the elixir should be soaked with it, [10] so that the gold becomes dyed. Then it should be soaked a second time, so that the gold becomes aqzal. [11] Then it should be soaked so that the gold becomes purple, and then it should be soaked again so that it submerges into the bodies, [12] dyeing them. You continue to do that until all of the water is used up. Then it has to be left [13] in the cooking for 40 days.»

She said: «Then tell me about when he said: "Take airy water, Nilotic water, [14] sulphuric water." He said: «All of this is one thing.» She said: «And what is it?» He said: [15] «It is the eternal water, and it is the flowery water.»

She said: «Then what about when he said: "Soak it according to what one sees, [15] and make it dry so you will find that the water becomes saffron.» He said: «This takes place in [17] the other composition when it dried and is soaked with the eternal water, so its colour will become like the colour of pounded saffron.»

[18] She said: «Then what about the cultivation of gold, the flowers of gold, and the ferment of gold?» He said: [19] «All of these are the sulphur, but these colours come in the first composition.»

(fol. 202a) She said: «Then tell me about when she said: “Beware of falling into doubt because we did not name the things by their names.”» [He said:] 2 «Ponder over this stone that we generated from copper and silver, and put it in a vessel of glass 3 and cook it gently. Your fire should be gentle until it is destroyed. Thus from this stone and from 4 these ashes that are the elixir, the exalted work comes, so do not despise it. Make it moist 5 and rub the stone with the cloud, and soak the composition in it until it becomes sweet and red. Soak it 6 several times and cook it strongly and intensively. By this, the fugitive natures that 7 were bodies become spirits when they mix with the bodies, and the dead ones turn into 8 living souls, which dye when they are mixed with the spirits and marry each other. 9 At this time, the nature that is named with various names will be extracted from them, and it is the poison.»

10 She said: «Then what about <~~their statement~~> when you say: “The soul has states, some of which agree with the body and others 11 disagree.”» He said: «Concerning what agrees with the body, it is the water when it mixes with the earth. 12 But that water must have some dew with it in order that this moisture is more 13 preserved.»

She said: «The way you answered me made it difficult, and you have made me more perplexed.» He said: «I will remove some 14 of the obscurity you find, and I will give you an analogy for what I answered you. Know that the moisture of the blood is 15 what preserves and improves the soul, and it prevents the soul from coming out of the body. In this way 16 our dew protects and improves the moisture of our water. It (the dew) prevents it (the moisture) from escaping from the body. Do you not 17 remember your question to me about the man of the wool who dyed it (the wool) and was 18 proud of it, but I told him he had done nothing?»

She said: «I had understood what you mentioned 19 about him.» He said: « Indeed, his dye vanished because it did not have our dew in it.»

(fol. 202b) She said: «Is this water the water of the dew?» He said: «Indeed, we named the water of our dew with many names, [2] and I will explain it to you. But what prevented you from knowing it is that we changed its name.»

She said. [3] «So, maybe it is the alum?» He said: «Yes. Do you not know that the alum is what prevents the fugitives [4] from escaping? It is what dyes the gold and the purple, and it is the dye, and it is what clings, and it is [5] what breaks the body into fragments, and improves it.»

She said: «You are right and you spoke well.» He said: [6] «And if you want me to make you more certain, I give you some of the water of sulphur, so test it [7] by dissolving whatever you want, and then burn it with fire. If it escapes as the dye of that man escaped, then I am [8] wrong. If you want it, I have already told you about the purple because we recognized your favour. Know that the [9] slag, which remains from the mercuries at the bottom of the vessel, is suitable for loosening up [10] the silver at the beginning of the work. I have already written that in the first chapter of the book [11] *Sarṭamīṭā*.»

She said: «Then tell me about when Plato said: "O you seekers of this [12] science, you will never obtain it without knowledge of what improves the body and what [13] improves the soul. You will not reach knowledge of that without numerous experiments, patience [14] in this work, and frequent asking of the masters of the science."» [He said:] «Beware of fear, [15] when you commit an error, but praise God and keep your intention sincere, because no one shows the right way [16] in this work, except He, the venerable, powerful God.»

She said: «Then tell me about when you say: [17] "Some sages called the seven things one, and they rendered the water of [18] sulphur like all of them."» He said: «Democritus ordered us to do it like that when [19] he said: "Render the sulphur like all things, and pound it like the pounding of the physicians."

(fol. 203a) Know that the broth is what rots the composition and strengthens it to fight the fire. Many [2] of the people wanted to make the sulphur fight the fire, but they did not know that the seven things [3] are more fugitive than the sulphur, and nobody is able to prevent them from escaping. But [4] when the sulphur is mixed with the composition, it prevents the composition from escaping. Whoever [5] understands what I have said knows the truth for certain, and whoever denies it must die from grief.»

She said: «Then tell me about [6] your statement that Democritus said: "Take white (emendation) lead:"» He said: «Do you not see that he [7] also said: "Take white litharge, pound it with oleander leaves, white sulphur, honey [8] and white arsenic."» [Zosimos] said: «I will make you more certain that when the tin becomes mercury [9] it will swallow the plates.»

She said: «Then tell me about when you ordered me to dye the purple with the cold one.» [10] He said: «I ordered you to dye it with composed water, but the sages named it [11] the cold one. So the composed water is the cold one, and it is the dye, and it is the making alumy (white). Thus here you should [12] broaden your understanding as it is as the sage said: "Dye the wool white, then dye it crimson, [13] then dye it purple. Then he mentioned which herbs are suitable for each dye.»

She said: «O Zosimos, [14] you have been enigmatic in your answer.» He said: «I have not done that to you, but you [15] misunderstand. Concerning the white dye, it does not dye but it is dyed, and it accepts every dye.»

[16] She said: «Then why did the sage order us to dye white?» He said: «That is because in that whiteness [17] is our red dye, concealed in the whiteness. And the whiteness covers the redness.»

[18] She said: «And which white is this?» He said: «It is the white that was dyed at the beginning of the work.» [19] She said: «I see that this white, which was dyed at the beginning of the work, became a dye.»

(fol. 203b) He said: Yes, you neither need to dye it nor to make it alumy because it is sufficient for you, and has in it [2] what you are looking for.»

She said: «Then why did you mention the herbs, the snail and the crimson?» He said: «It is [3] one thing, so do not pay attention to the many things.»

She said: «Then tell me about your statcmcnt: [4] "For the second cooking, one should take the white which came out of the first cooking, then it has to be composed [5] with its remedies."» He said: «Yes, do that with it several times till it becomes a white mixture [6] like it. When you see that whiteness appears on what is mixed with it in the vessel, [7] then know for certain that the redness is concealed in that whiteness. At this time, you do not need [8] to extract this whiteness from that redness, but you should cook it [9] until all of it becomes a high-ranking crimson.

She said: «Then tell me about your statement: "If you want [10] the dye to becomes more profound and saturated than any other dye, just leave it for [11] a long time so it will become (like that).» He said: «Did you not read in the book of Maria: "Leave it [12] at the bottom, then it will come into being."? Know that the moisture should flow over the wool. [13] If it is not like that, then add more water to it, cook it till its moisture disappears, [14] return the wool in it, cook it until all of its moisture is used up, and wash it [15] with the sea so it will come into being.»

She said: «Then tell me about the sage and his statement: "The one thing [16] is suitable for both dyes."» He said: «And I tell you that what is suitable [17] for both dyes is the fiery cinnabar. Then take the mercury extracted [18] from the bodies, and test which one of the two dyes more deeply, is more powerful and is better. Then make use of that one, and leave [19] away what is not useful for you, as it is only mentioned falsely in order to confuse you.

(fol. 204a) Leave the sulphurs and the things from which you think that it comes out, because even if they come up [2] in the vapour, you will not be able to make anything flow out of them in the tube. And their coming out—[3] if they come—rather comes on the cover (of the pot). But our mercury, which is extracted from the bodies, [4] has the power to make dry, make cling and to hold the mercuries of the bodies. And it (our) mercury turns the mercury [5] of these bodies in its interior into mercury, and it is a dyeing spirit. Know that although it is [6] moist and untouchable, it has a great power that it has gained from the bodies which [7] have been washed well and worked on well by it.»

[8] The 10th Book of the Book of Zosimos is completed, with praise to God. [9] It is followed by the 11th, the exalted God willing.

[10] The 11th Book of the Book of Zosimos About [11] the Other Composition

[12] In the name of the compassionate, merciful God.
I ask for your help and your benevolence, O God.

[13] Zosimos said: «If you are satisfied with what you asked me about [14] the teaching of the other work, then ask me about something else.»

She said: «[So] I ask you about the composition, its bodies [15] and what improves it.» He said: «I have written this for you at the beginning of the other chapter, but you are [16] a woman who cannot be satisfied.»

She said: «Complete your kindness to me.» He said: «So ask whatever you want.»

[17] She said: «How can I ask about something when you declare that what I need to know is there in the picture at the beginning of [18] the chapter?» He said: «However, I swear by God that none of the sages did [19] what I have done for you.»

She said: «Did not even Hermes do this to his son [7] Ṭāṭ?» He said: «No, by God, (fol. 204b) Hermes was too cautious to illustrate these things in his books. [2] The best sentence we find in his books is his statement to his son Ṭāṭ: "O my son, [3] no dye can ever come into being, except from the red stone."»

She said: «You leave me speechless.»

[4] He said: «So be satisfied with what I have written for you.» She said: «I am satisfied, and I will ask you.» He said: [5] «Then ask about whatever you want.»

[6] The 11th Picture

[7] The image of a man of gold with his head cut off, lying on the ground. With him are three [8] upright winged men, and at his head is Theosebeia, standing upright as [9] we described before. And at his feet, above, there is Zosimos, standing upright as we described. [10] And the image of six persons standing upright, linked together at the neck by a rope made of water of gold, its end being [11] in the hand of Zosimos. Their legs are linked together by a rope made of water of gold in the hand of Theosebeia. And with regard to the dyes and the states, they are as we described them at the beginning of this book.

[13] After that picture comes this dialogue.

Fig. 71: Picture of the 11th Book about the Other Composition, fol. 205a.

(fol. 205b) She said: «Then tell me about when the sage said: "Take the honoured stone which we named [2] claudianus, and operate on it until it becomes shining."» He said: «Do you not understand, do you not know [3] that the copper has to be mixed until it becomes thick, solid and turns red?»

(The question of Theosebeia is missing.) He said: «It is not what [4] he named lead at the beginning of this book, but it is the reddish one. He named it lead for you, [5] and he named it here lead, and ordered you to put together with it three times its quantity of the eternal water.»

[6] She said: «Maybe it is that about which Maria said: "Copper, lead, honoured stone, [7] mix them equally and roast the gold with them because if you do that, it will become a spirit [8] submerging in the bodies."» He said: «You have understood well, and you grasped the meaning.» She said: [9] So what is "grasping the meaning"?» He said: «That is because when the male and the female come together, he rather [10] meant by "coming together" the mixing. So the fugitive turned into a non-fugitive, and the composed one into a spirit.»

[11] She said: «Which one of them is the fugitive?» He said: «The moisture.» She said: «And (which one is) the composed one?» He said: «It is the body [12] and the fugitive.»

She said: «Did they make the head of the world out of this?» He said: «Yes, this is the lead [13] which we named red lead from our work, and without this lead [14] nothing can be.»

She said: «Then tell me about when you say: "Know that when this tin [15] is operated on and whitened, it has a great power, and with it the dyeing is completed, because when it is mixed [16] equally with the four spirits and cooked in its number of days, it turns red [17] like the colour of cinnabar.» He said: «And I tell you that you must have this [18] tin in the dyeing as nothing else is suitable.»

She said: «Is it the tin of the people?» [19] He said: «No, it is our tin, which is from our work, and which became mercury.

(fol. 206a) And that mercury is the crown of the dyeing, and it is the honoured one. When it is mixed with the head of the world [2] 3:1, and they become one, and they are cooked until they solidify, the copper appears for you out of it. [3] So when the flowers appear to you, strengthen your fire until all of the flowers appear and increase for you. [4] Know that all of these four parts become flowers. Then the redness appears [5] and gets cooked until it becomes a perfect poison. So this is the mercury mixed with the head of the world, [6] and I have explained to you its power and how its redness appears.»

She said: «Then tell me about [7] their composition and their operations in a way that I can feel safe with it.» He said: «Take one part of the [8] intensively white gum, one part of the body of the gum—without which [9] the dyeing does not become good—, one part of calf's urine and one part of bull's gallbladder. Then mix [10] these four parts and cook them for 40 days until everything coagulates and solidifies [11] in the hot sun. When it dries and turns into dust, soak it with the ferment. [12] Then cook it till it dries to some extent, and soak it with the calf 's urine, and [13] cook it until it dries up. Then soak it with the eternal water. When it dries up completely, [14] soak it with the dye and cook it intensively until the power of all the water goes away [15] and the moisture disappears. Then leave it for 40 days to be cooked in that dryness [16] until it feels secure and the spirit penetrates it.»

She said: «Is this the other operation?» He said: «Yes, by this [17] operation the body turns into a spirit and the spirit turns into a body. Be careful to close well the mouth of [18] the vessel, otherwise smoke can come out. When you reach this point, open the vessel and you will find precisely what all [19] the sages were searching for throughout their lives.»

She said: «Then tell me about when you said: “Mix the gold

(fol. 206b) with the silver so that it becomes aqzal gold and purple gold."» He said: «I order you to mix the gold [2] with the eternal water in the other composition so that out of it comes aqzal gold and [3] purple gold.»

She said: «Then tell me about when she said: "Make the arsenic white!"» He said: «She ordered you to put [4] the plates in the moisture in order that the moisture dissolves all thc plates.»

She said: «How does [5] the moisture dissolve the body?» He said: «Just as the earth accepts the rain, so that it loosens up until [6] the earth turns into water (from the margin). Then it dries until it becomes (completed from the margin) dust like it was before. In the same way, our moisture dissolves the arsenic and turns it into [7] water. Then it has to be cooked until it dries up. In the same way, the earth needs abundant moisture in winter [8] in order to be increased with it, then plants and fruits grow. The earth is like that. The more it is soaked, [9] the more the fruits get nourished and the plants become good. And it is the same way with our arsenic; the more it is soaked with our moisture, [10] the more its benefit increases.»

She said: «Then tell me about the thing which the sage ordered us to do persistently in the operation.» [11] He said: «It is the cooking in dung-fire.»

She said: «And what is the thing that the sage ordered you [12] to cook in the dung-fire? He said: «It is the elixir. He ordered us to cook it on a gentle fire [13] until the incombustible sulphur solidifies. So ponder over what Maria said [14] about the operation of the elixir and something.»

She said: «What is the elixir and what is this 'something'?» He said: «It is [15] the sour ferment whose fermentation was prolonged, as she said: "Take the water of sulphur and some [16] of a body and put both onto the heat of ashes, so it solidifies at once in the other composition." [17] And also ponder over the statement of God's prophet Moses, peace be upon him, when he mentioned the solidification of [18] the sulphur, saying: "Solidify the water of sulphur on a gentle fire." But here Maria [19] made the truth clear when she said: "Take the plate and mix it with the flower of gold, (fol. 207a) so that it becomes white and becomes red, except that the other white is white in outer appearance [2] but in essence and in its interior it is red." So this work does not need to be pounded [3] by hand,[3] but it needs alum that is put in ~~<waters>~~ a double vessel and waters in order that [4] the poisons do not reach it, otherwise what is in the vessel gets ruined.»

She said: «Then tell me about when he said: "Take [5] Cypriot copper that is our copper, tin that is from our work and the body of [6] magnesia. Then mix them and cook until it is pounded and turns into a stone. Then pound it [7] finely with water of natron, and put it in the casting that we named vapour [8] until it is destroyed, and you should have a vessel with moisture in it."» He said: «This is in fact what you already [9] asked me about, but he has changed the names. Do you not see that he ordered you to use the moisture [10] and to soak it, and that the soaking is only good in the making of the rust?»

She said: «And which rust is [11] that?» He said: «It is the copper that is from our work which they ordered us to cook, to pound [12] with Egyptian vinegar and to dry. Then you will find what you want.»

She said: «Then tell me, O Zosimos, [13] about the statement of Abīsqūs: "Take the honoured body, mix it with mercury of cinnabar, [14] cook it on a gentle fire, and be kind with it during the cooking until the water mixes with the body and [15] both become one water."» He said: «It is what the sages named the other composition, [16] and by this, the first one is transformed by the other composition, and it is this composition [17] which extracts the nature hidden inside the body until [18] it appears. By this dissolving, the water also makes the body lean. [19] So when the body is made lean, it turns into water concealed inside of the other water, and both become (fol. 207b) high-ranking rust. If you want me to make you more certain, then ponder [2] over the statement of the sage in the two books about the making of gold and the making of silver. He started at first [3] with his *Book about the Mercury*. There he said: “Mercury of cinnabar”. Then he said in his *Book* [4] *about the Making of Silver*: “Mercury of arsenic.”»

She said: «Why did Sīūs ask Dīsqūs: “Is [5] mercury ‘other and other’ (*āḫar wa āḫar*)?” And Dīsqūs replied: “Yes, it is ‘other and other’, although it is one.”» [6] He said: «He asked him because of his poor knowledge of the origin.»

She said: «Then tell me about that origin, [7] which ~~<people>~~ Sīūs did not know.» He said: «Do you not understand that the sage ordered us [8] to take the honoured body and to destroy it with the pure water until it turns into [9] one water?»

She said: «Yes.» He said: «Then why do you ask me?»

She said: «In order that you make me more sure.» [10] He said: «Do you not know that the body became mercury with the other mercury?»

She said: [11] «I already knew that.» He said: «This is what Dīsqūs was talking about when he said: “‘Other and other’, so they are [12] two.” When they were united, the two became one mercury composed as one can see, [13] but as for the origin, it is one, and in fact they are two from three.»

[14] She said «As they are ‘other and other’, then why did he not say two?» He said: «And I tell you [15] that they are three. I have previously mentioned to you the three but you always forget. And these three are one, [16] and it has a great power because it creates every thing, and it turns it white. It is [17] what makes the colours of the gold come out in the cooking, and with it the body becomes rotten, [18] and with it the colours appear and fight against the fire and resist it. Before that, it (the body) was neither able [19] to resist the fire nor to fight it, because of its weakness and its tendency to escape. So when it is held, [20] [it holds. And Maria said: (written later by another hand.)]

(fol. 208a) “Solidify that plate in a gentle fire.” And she also said: “Take the water of sulphur, [2] put in it some dye and solidify it quickly in some dung fire.” And she also said: [3] “Take our copper, mix it with gold and put with it a plate that has previously been dissolved [4] at the beginning of the operation, so it is dissolved a second time. Thus the two plates become one plate.”»

[5] She said: «Then tell me about when the sages said: “One should mix with this ferment [6] some of the body which one wants to dye like it; if it is silver, then a plate of silver, [7] and if it is gold, then a plate of gold until it is destroyed and rotten.”» [He said:] «Because in the *Book of Isis*, [8] which is called *The Book of Power*, [Isis said:] “Wheat brings forth wheat, a lion brings forth a lion, [9] and a human being brings forth a human being. This is because the broth is one, making both of them rotten.” And know that if the water of [10] sulphur is mixed in the right way, it becomes good for every thing. And even if you mix the composition [11] in the wrong way, it should show you a good dye because when it is dyed, it dyes. [12] So if you know the truth, do not be afraid of any statement of the sages.»

She said: «Then tell me about [13] these two compositions: are they the other composition?» He said: «No, but the sage [14] named it after all bodies in order to create confusion with it. Ponder over the statement of the sage when he said [15]—as a confirmation of what I told you—that he named the composition after the bodies, saying: “If you want to make use of [16] iron, then soften it first, and if you want to make use of copper, then make it rusty first, and if you want [17] to make use of lead, then remove its air-holes, and if you want to make use of tin, remove its squeaking. In this way, [18] you will not commit an error.”

She said: «And what does it mean, the making rusty of copper, the softening of iron, [19] the removing of the air-holes of lead and the removing of the squeaking of tin?» He said: «A person like you (fol. 208b) should not ignore this, as he named these bodies at the time of the operation of the elixir according to [2] the colours that appeared on it. I will start for you with making the copper rusty, as between the making rusty and the rust there is a difference, [3] because the making rusty is the making white of the elixir, and the rust is its making red.»

She said: «What about her statement: [4] "Put the copper in this broth, leave it for 15 days, and you will find that it has [5] [...] turned white."» He said: «By that she meant the white sulphur, and also [6] Democritus wrote like that and said a great deal. But by his statement he meant the white sulphur.»

[7] She said: «Then they mentioned all the sulphurs.» He said: «All of them are one, because this [8] one sulphur is what makes the copper white in the making rusty. Concerning the rust, (it comes) [9] by this sulphur and its companions which accompany it. Then it is what turned the copper into rust [10] and made it red, because Democritus said about his operation: «Make the copper turn into rust and make it red with colocynth,[11] vitriol (*sūrīn*) and sulphur"» He [Zosimos] continued: «This is the first composition, [12] from which the water of sulphur is extracted.»

She said: «Then tell me about your statement: "All of the dyes can only come into being [13] with the composed water."» He said: «I have already told you that the composed water is what dyes and [14] what makes alumy (white). But as for what the sages mention in their books, such as vinegar, cinnabar [15] and all of the moistures, they meant by that the water composed with the alum. Know that [16] if this water is cooked with its components of the mixture, its components would leave their dyes in it, and they escape into the air. [17] Because of these fugitives, the sages wrote in their books: "The dyeing of the wool [18] with the broth until it turns into a high-ranking purple dye." But by the wool and the broth they meant [19] our elixir, which is the most precious of everything. Then cook the broth with the male, which is the other sulphur, (fol. 209a) and be careful, my lady, that when you cook your dyes, you do not strengthen [2] your fire, otherwise the flowers of the dye will disappear just as when the heat of the sun becomes too strong for the flowers [3] of the plants on earth. It would make them wilt, dry up, burn, and it would remove their glow, splendour and usefulness. [4] So be careful with the fire with regard to your dye.»

She said: «Then tell me about the man who came to you, [5] and he thought that [composed] water alone dyes purple.» He said: «When he came to me with his wool, [6] which he dyed to a purple colour with composed water only, I looked at it attentively, telling him: [7] "O man, this is not a true dye." He said: "Certainly my dye is the right dye which does not vanish." [8] And he was happy with it because its outer appearance seemed good. Then I told him: "O man, [9] you are completely wrong, this is not a (true) dye because if the fire clashes with it, it will disappear and [10] the silver will return to its first state because it did not have any red sulphur in it, [11] and it got dyed only by composed water." So he hurried and tested it with the fire, and [12] its dye disappeared. So he went home, mentally distressed.»

She said: «Then tell me about when you say: [13] «Your lead becomes black, purified, dyes and is dyed, becomes complete and it makes [14] many colours appear from that silvery colour.» He said: «I tell you that this silvery colour is not [15] fixed, but at first it appears to you to be the colour of silver, then black, then yellow, [16] then red, then the colour of blood, and then the *ẖulūfī* colour. So, O Theosebeia, may, whoever [17] ponders over the quest for this work, be blessed, and may his God inspire him with the mixing of these two works [18] until he turns them into one colour.»

She said: «Then tell me about when you say: «The composition of the second work should [19] be the cooked-operated on and (fol. 209b) the moist-operated on together with the dry, and they should be put in its composition.» He said: «Upon the life of your father, O Theosebeia, [2] I have already explained this to you and you should not ask me about it.»

She said: «But [3] I do not ask you because I do not know it, but because I do not want to ignore anything that you wrote to me without [4] asking you, in order to give an enduring basis for those who come after me.» He said: [5] «I tell you that the second work is easy, as it is only that you want to extract the dye from the nature. [6] Therefore Maria warned us when she said: "Whoever is not one of us should not take up [7] our work."»

The 11th Book of the Book of Zosimos is completed
with the help of God, and praise to be God.
[8] The 12th Book follows it.

(fol. 210a) The 12th Book of The Book of Zosimos
About the Other Operation

2 In the name of the merciful, compassionate God.

He said: «I think you have reached 3 your goal in asking me about this secret, which you will not forget any more without 4 bringing it to light.»

She said: «You have already done so and I am grateful, but I still have <names> questions (from the margin).» He said: 5 «What are they?»

She said: «[Tell me about] the other operation alone and its weights.» He said: «Concerning the weight, you have 6 asked me, and I answered you with what the sages said. I tell you that it is different and 7 confusing because they wrote about it in symbols, allusions and examples. And the operation 8 is like this. I gathered for you what the sages dispersed and what they collected. 9 So take what is in this book with gratitude, and you win over misery, whose only cure 10 is by God and His inspiration to whomever of His venerators He wants to give this secret, which the exalted God bestowed upon 11 His best people and His prophets. Woe unto you, O Theosebeia, you have been given mastery over the 12 greatest treasure of God. Do you not see what Democritus said to those (correction from the margin) whose eyes 13 and souls were filled with wealth: "Woe unto those on the day of judgement, 14 if they do not make this work in obedience to God!"»

15 The 12th Picture

16 The Picture of Theosebeia as we described at the beginning of this book, with 17 a crescent moon on her head, coated with water of silver, standing in a green place with plants, between three trees. 18 Hot water in the colour of the sky flows under where she is standing, and in front of her is 19 an upright woman in her image and her position, stretching out her hands towards her. On her breast there is

(fol. 210b) a girdle with three faces of various colours: red, green, the colour of the sky [2] and the water of silver. After this picture comes this dialogue:

Fig. 72: Picture of the 12th Book about the Last Operation, fol. 210b.

(fol. 211a) [… There seems to be a folio missing here] and he said: «When you see that the stone has been destroyed and turned into dust, and some redness has covered it, [2] you should take the rest of the water, which Bidīsus ordered you [3] to divide into two parts, and soak it (the dust) with it several times. At this time, [4] the hidden colours in that body will appear to you. But if you operate on it without knowledge, you will not see [5] anything of these colours. This is because I have seen someone who started this work working [6] with the true natures, but the redness came slowly for him. So when the redness came slowly, he thought that [7] he had committed an error. So he threw away the work he had made, rejecting it. Therefore contemplate how [8] you should mix them. If you mix them as it should be, the redness [9] which you are looking for will appear to you, and it will not come slowly for you.» And he (also) said: «When you see that the stone has turned into dust, [10] then strengthen the fire and soak it (the dust) with the rest of the poison, so the colours will appear to you (pl.). [11] And ponder (sg.) over the power of this water. Indeed, it was dust, capable of fighting the fire, [12] then it (the water) submerged into the body, so it turned it into gold. At the time of the completeness you must test it by the touch. [13] If you find its touch like water that cannot be grasped, then it is good. Otherwise [14] return it to the cooking until it becomes perfect.»

She said: «Then tell me about when the sage said: "Take [15] the copper which we worked upon until it turns into silver, then roast it until it turns into gold."» He said: [16] «It is the stone which I explained to you before, that when it gets cooked, it turns into dust, taking on the redness [17] and the yellowness. The more it gets cooked and soaked, the stronger its redness becomes until it reaches the highest [18] degree, taking on the purple colour which is priceless, and no colour is more precious than it. When [19] you hear the sage saying copper, silver or gold, he means by them the colours (fol. 211b) of the elixir, and he is the one who said: “Return the silver so that it becomes gold, and [return] the gold [2] so that it becomes aqzal-gold, and return it so that it becomes purple gold.” [3] Do not be deluded by these colours which the sages named the bodies, because you do not need [4] anyone of them except the one body which is the master of the bodies, and one water which is [5] the master of the waters. And with regard to this, the sage said: “Only the water turns the copper into [6] rust.” You should limit yourself to it, so do not search for anything else. It is the chrysocolla that is [7] similar to the rust of copper which they ordered to be operated on in the pounding, and to soak with the water [8] seven times.»

She said: «What about your statement, O Zosimos: “Take the gold that you want to increase [9] and to renew, and divide that water into two parts as Bidīsīūs ordered.”» He said: «Yes, because [10] when the copper falls into this water, it (the copper) ferments it (the water). At this time it is called the ferment of gold when [11] it is well operated on. That comes when the two are completely cooked until they are dissolved and become like water. [12] Thus they are solidified and turn into a stone, then they are destroyed and the redness appears. At this time, [13] you should soak it with the rest of the water which is the other part. Soak that [14] seven times until it absorbs all of the water and all the moisture dries up, so that [15] all of it turns into dry dust. It has to be left in the cooking for 40 days until it becomes rotten and brings out [16] its colours. Therefore the sage ordered that one has to take the chrysocolla which is similar to the rust of [17] copper, and it has to be soaked with the urine of calf until its nature thickens because the nature is concealed [18] in its interior.»

She said: «What is this concealed nature?» He said: «It is the spirit of [19] the dyeing body, which it obtained from the eternal, silvery, shining water. And I order you (fol. 212a) to pound it (the copper) and submerge it in that water seven times until it absorbs [2] all the moisture, and gains the power that defeats the fire. At this time, you make the rust lean and rotten [3] until its colour becomes like burnt blood which the fire defeated, until it (the fire) forced it (the rust) to enter [4] inside the nature, so it gave it a colour that does not change. Thus it is the spirit for which [5] the kings and the sages where looking.»

She said: «O Zosimos, do you order me to take the bodies [6] and to put them in the moisture?» He said: «Yes, cook them with it (the moisture) intensively until [7] the blackness of the water comes out of them (the bodies), and they become dust. After that, renew for it (the dust) another sea, and leave it [8] in its vessel to become rotten because that is what Hermes wanted us to realize, although he kept it secret. [9] You have already asked me, O Theosebeia, questions that I answered you, disobeying [10] the sages. And I ignored their oath in obeying you, hating to be in disagreement with you, [11] although God knows that when I answer you, I answer you certainly in a cautious way, out of fear of God that the truth does not become evident, [12] except for those who have firm understanding and are therefore able to know it.»

[13] She said: «I see that you do not want to help me, nor to have a relationship with me.» He said: «Certainly I want that, and by your father, you surely know [14] that the books of the sages are obscure and enigmatic, because they did not name the things by their real names, [15] and they wrote other things with them. Therefore I distinguished for you between what they inserted as invented things and [16] the true ones. I made things clear for you, and I left you on a path with signposts, thanks to which I am not afraid [17] that you will ever go astray.»

She said: «Tell me more and bestow on me a favour.» He said: «I had wished [18] to give you the rest of the operation, but jealousy opposed this, blaming me for revealing things which I answered you [19] and what I wrote to you. Then I remembered the sadness to which you will be exposed if you commit an error.

(fol. 212b) Therefore I thought I should tell you a statement that is the basis of your work.»

She said: «What is it?» He said: «Know, my [2] lady, that if you do not soak all of the things in water at the beginning of the cooking, without pounding until [3] everything turns into water, you will not reach the goal of the work. This work is what Hermes named [4] the sieve, because he said: "If you do not sieve the natures, you will be mistaken because every light, [5] spiritual thing which has been burnt and made lean rises above, while everything heavy falls down [6] to the bottom. But then, what gets sieved becomes sand, so this comes from the pounding of the cooking." Know [7] that they named the things water, sometimes they named them sand and sometimes they named them stone. [8] All of this led to confusion in their operation.»

She said: «Then tell me about the statement of the sage who contemplated [9] the first operation, and did well when he said: "Divide the poison into two parts."» He said: «Yes. He ordered you [10] to burn the body with the first part, and rot it with the second part. And I tell you [11] that the eternal water performs the entire operation, as the sage said: "The thing is one, [12] and with it one attains one's aim." If you do not put in it that thing which you are looking for, [13] it will not have in it the realisation of what you are looking for. But you should pour in that [14] one thing which you are looking for, or something like it, in order to reach what you are looking for.»

She said: [15] «Then tell me about when the sage said: "Take copper, put in it the first part and put it [16] in its vessel, then cook it for 41 days so you will find it as a stone whose moisture has dried up. [17] Then cook it until nothing remains except the sediment. When it reaches that point, wash it with pure water [18] seven times. When the water is used up, then leave it to rot in its vessel until the redness [19] which you want appears."» He said: «Yes, as Sīmās said in brief.

(fol. 213a) The whole work is completed because he ordered us to soak it in sour vinegar seven times and to leave it [2] to rot. But concerning Hermes, he said a great deal about this but was hiding as he said: "Operate on [3] the black alabaster with vinegar and natron." So he named the blackness black alabaster when it became black. [4] Then, after that he said white alabaster, and he ordered it to be operated on with the eternal water. Then, [5] when it became red, he named it red alabaster and ordered it to be operated on with colocynth (*qalqant*) and *šaḥīra* (vitrol?) [6] until it becomes red. But by all of that he meant the seven soakings, [7] and at that time the colours appear. But concerning the work, not many things enter into it, but [8] it is as I told you, that it becomes black, white and red.»

She said: «I have understood, yet tell me more.» [9] He said: «Ask me and I will tell you.»

She said: «Then tell me about when Hermes wanted to mix [10] the natures saying: "Take the stone of gold, mix it, and put it in a vessel on [11] a gentle heat until it dissolves. Leave it until it absorbs all of the water and its parts cling to each [12] other."» He said: «It is what you asked me about, and it is what Agathodaimon told us, [13] namely that after our silver absorbs its moisture we should make the fire stronger [14] than it was at the beginning of the work. When you see it as dust, then know that it is the first beginning of the secret. [15] Then pound it, mix it with the eternal water, and do that many times until [16] its colours appear. So I have told you what you asked me in order to help you, to make you happy and to make you abandon [17] vanities for the truth. Thus make the red black, make it white and make it red.»

She said: [18] «What about when you told me that you had not found any one of the sages who described better than Agathodaimon the pounding, the cooking, [19] the distillation, the soaking and the returning back, and that the whitening (fol. 213b) only comes by intensive cooking because—in spite of the fact that Agathodaimon said much—[2] he said the truth, guiding (the seeker) to do the work promptly—and that if I would cling to his statements, [3] I could do the work quickly.» He said: «I tell you that Democritus and all of the sages [4] had mentioned this pounding, but they did not explain it, nor did they make it as clear as [5] Agathodaimon did when he said: "Pound and cook, and do not be impatient, let the elixir ripen [6] with the water little by little, and pound, make dry, cook, and let it mature with the water little by little." [7] He repeated this statement many times in order that it is better understandable. But as for Democritus, he ordered us [8] to take the rest of the cloud and to cook it with the *šaḥīra* (vitrol?) and the colocynth until [9] the cloud becomes red, and it has to be pounded and submerged in the water several times, so that it will come into being.»

She said: «Then what about the statement of [10] Maria: "Look out, for when you see all of the other water dried up, then leave it (the sediment) [11] down, and it will come into being."» He said: «By that she meant that when you see that [12] all the moisture has turned fine like dust, you should leave it in its vessel on a [13] gentle fire for 40 days until it becomes rust in order that the colours [14] mentioned by the sages change in it. So by this cooking, the bodies put on their spirits, and by that they become [15] spiritual-dyers. So know that I sent it to you the way she ordered you. Then you will obtain [16] from it what fills you with happiness, God willing. My lady, mix [17] your poison as you should, cook and do not be impatient, soak and do not be impatient, and cook until [18] you see that what you have operated on has turned into a spirit that cannot be touched, and until you see that the elixir has dressed in a garment that is only suitable for a king. When you see that purple colour (fol. 214a) you would have obtained what the sages obtained. Know that the sages have dispersed the work [2] in order to confuse people. And I tell you that the work is one, but they kept that secret [3] from the ignorant in order that they should not know it.»

She said: «Then what about when Taūfīl said: "Take one part of the crown of the bodies, [4] one of pyrite, and one of copper, and cast them until they turn into ashes. [5] Then pound them with the colocynth until it becomes red, and soak it with the poison according to what [6] you see, thus it will become gold without shadow."» He said: «I did not think that you would ask me about [7] something like this, since you have asked me about it before. It is the other work. Do you not see [8] that he ordered you to put the colocynth in order that it becomes red because the colocynth is what [9] makes these three red, and it is what solidifies them.»

[10] The 12th Book of the Book of Zosimos is completed,
with praise to God. It is followed by the 13th,
[11] the exalted God willing.

[12] The 13th Book of the Book of Zosimos about Questions [13] about the Other Composition.

[14] In the name of the compassionate, merciful God.

She said: «O Zosimos, [15] tell me also about when Taūfīl said: "Take pure copper from our work [16] and four parts of the round plates which turned into copper, and mix them [17] until the copper turns into water and its colour changes, then cook the two until they thicken."» [18] He said: «This is the other composition. Do you not see that he ordered you to cook it (fol. 214b) until it thickens, and that he told you that, if you want it to become better [2] than it was, cook it till it thickens and pound it with vinegar till [3] the body absorbs the water of the silver of cinnabar[91] and turns into an amalgamated stone. Your cooking [4] it should be with gentle fire, until you see on it the blackness of the murderesses of their husbands. Cook it [5] till all of that blackness disappears, and pound it with the sun till [6] the moisture dries up. Close the mouth of the vessel well, and cook it until it becomes red. When you see [7] the redness, soak it with eternal water and roast it till the silver which [8] has turned into a stone becomes gold. Then continue to cook it and soak it until [9] all of your water is used up. This is the whole secret of the sages. <This is the whole secret of the sages.> [10] Know that the more you soak the composition, the more the water remains with its companions, joins its companions [11] and clings to them. Then wash it with eternal water, however much it absorbs. [12] With this operation, the composition becomes good by washing, cooking and drying. [13] Wash it intensively with the glue of gold, roast it and dry it [14] until all of the moisture is used up. Close the mouth of the vessel well and cook it [15] for 40 days till it becomes rotten by the dry moisture which entered into it [16] till its colour changes, and it becomes softer than ointment, and its colour becomes like [17] burned blood.»

She said: «Then what about when Dīsiqūs said to Sīūs: "If you do not purify [18] the body, change it <~~like burnt blood. She said:~~> and turn it into water, you achieve [19] nothing." He said: «Do you not see that he mentioned the moisture? Know that

[91] Silver of cinnabar (HgS) is mercury.

(folio 215a) this work only becomes right by the moisture that they named herbs.»

She said: «Why did they name it [2] herbs?» He said: «Because in that moisture there are flowers like the flowers of herbs, [3] and the body only takes the flowers from that moisture. This hidden operation [4] destroys those who want to enter into this work, because the truth is in their hands and they see it [5] with their own eyes, but they do not operate on it well. Do you not see that this work only exists or [6] emerges by the moisture?»

She said: «Then tell me about when Maria said: "Roast and cook, so you will find [7] that the copper is destroyed, and that blackness has covered it. Then remove its blackness by cooking, and return it [8] to the cooking till it solidifies and turns into a white stone."» He said: «It is what the sages give birth to [9] every year.»

She said: «What do they call it?» He said: «It has so many names! They call it [10] tin, etesian and lead. If you want to remove the squeaking of [11] what we name tin, take silver and cast it [12] in the vessel the way you know. Then cast it intensively till it changes and becomes like the rust of copper. [13] Then take that copper and cook it with airy water and eternal water. Know that [14] this water is good for the pounding of the rust. Then take the rest of the water and soak with it the rust [15] according to what you see. Know that if it is cooked, matured, and dried after the soaking, [16] you will find that the rust has turned into saffron. So, when you read in the books of the sages: [17] "Take saffron", then it is this. So take that saffron and put it [18] in a vessel and soak it with eternal water. Know that if you soak it and roast it, that will be [19] good for it. Then cook it till its colour satisfies you, and be careful not to soak it before it dries up.

(folio 215b) Whenever it dries up, you soak it until all your water is used up, and leave it in its place [2] for 40 days, so it will come into being.»

She said: «What thing will come into being?» He said: «It will become [3] the perfect poison.»

She said: «What is this poison?» He said: «It is the spiritual dye, which [4] is untouchable and which submerges in the body. When it (the dye) is put on it (the body) it is mixed [5] with it, like the mixing of water with water.»

She said: «Then tell me about what Maria said about making [6] silver.» He said: «These are the things which should enter the making of [7] the silver as she said: "Take one part of silver which is from our work that we prepared for the dyeing, [8] one part of our copper, put some silver on them and it should be [9] four in all. Then put it to cast, put clay on it, set it on fire and you will find that the copper [10] is pounded together with the silver and both are turned into water. Then return it to its vessel, close its [11] mouth, and cook till the blackness of the kohl disappears and the beautiful whiteness appears."» He said: «In this [12] operation, Maria has explained the truth for you because the blackness which appeared over it is [13] from the blackness of the silver. So she ordered you to cook it until it turns into a white stone.»

[14] She said: «And what is this white stone?» He said: «It is the stone that is born from copper and silver. [15] So return it to its vessel and set it on fire again, stronger than before, until [16] the stone breaks into fragments <that is born from copper and silver. So return it to its vessel and set it on fire again, [17] stronger than before until the stone breaks into fragments > and turns into ashes. How beneficial are [18] these ashes, and how honourable is what is extracted from them! Then take the cloud [19] which the sages kept secret, with which the stones are dyed. Then make that fragmented stone mature

(fol. 216a) until it becomes rusty and turns red, then soak it with eternal water as she ordered [2] and close the mouth of the vessel well. This is what turns the bodies into fugitives, and the fugitives into [3] non-fugitives. It is what turns the spirits into bodies and the bodies into spirits [4] until they are united with each other. This union turns the bodies into spirits, [5] and they acquire a dyer-soul because they fecundate each other and hold each [6] other.»

She said: «Then tell me, O Zosimos, about what Maria ordered with regard to the rotting [7] after the soaking of the elixir, and its cooking until it dries up and its moisture disappears.» [8] He said: «You have asked well and contemplated brilliantly.»

She said: «Then tell me about it.» [9] He said: «She ordered the second rotting in order for the coppery body to pick up the flowers [10] of the eternal water, so the copper is dyed with an unchangeable dyeing, better than before. [11] And she ordered that it be made rotten, because if you burn the copper intensively, it absorbs [12] the fiery mercury. Therefore she ordered the copper be made rotten with the cloud which is [13] its relative, in order that it picks up the dye which is in the cloud, in the same way as a garment picks up the dye of [14] the safflower from the water from which it was extracted until it becomes like burnt blood. So this is [15] the remedy for which the sages were looking, but only a sage can know this. Often [16] some people operated on it and fell into error in their operation because they neither knew the mixing nor the operation. [17] But whoever does the mixture by mixing it well with which every dye becomes perfect, will see [18] what he likes. So mix it well with the silver and cook it, until its parts hold each [19] other, and the dye becomes strong and does not decrease in the cooking.»

She said: «Then tell me

(fol. 216b) about what Hermes said with regard to the vessel. What is it?» He said: «It is the lead-copper which was destroyed [2] and pounded. Cook it till it all becomes like burnt copper, and [3] turns into a black-red cluster. Be careful not to soak it with all the tar [4] at one time, but only little by little. But look to see what state it is in [5] every three days, and wipe off what is around the vessel with a clean piece of cloth until water comes down, [6] passing through the tar to the bottom of the vessel. Leave it until it is pounded and cooked, so this is [7] the cooked potash. Then soak that red cluster with tar, half a measure [8] of what it was soaked with first, in order that in this soaking the weight [9] of all the composition becomes six weights. Then soak it every seven days until [10] ten weights are completed.»

She said: «Then tell me about when he said: "Those are the weights of the transformation, [11] which are more clear and evident than anything. If you know properly the spittle of the moon, and you soak [12] the big vessel with it, you will attain the goal of the work."» He said: «The big vessel [13] is the composition. He ordered us to make (it) salty and to put the red one in the furnace, in which are [14] the black sulphur and the red stone that we moistened with the white water in the way [15] the potters wet their clay. So you should cook it until it turns into ashes [16] like the ashes of the bath (*ḥammām*). Then pound it intensively until you make it become lean, and [17] the dye submerges in the depth of the body.»

She said: «Then tell me what you say about the experiment of [18] dissolving of the tar.» He said: «You take a little amount of the water which comes out of cinnabar [19] and put it on the fire. If it escapes quickly, then it is the true one, and if you want (fol. 217a) it not to escape, then put with it a big sheikh, so it will become fixed and will not leave, and it will solidify and become [2] like the flower of salt. And sometimes half of it will be solidified and the other half or some of it remains. If you see it [3] like that, do not be impatient but cook it till all the water becomes pure salt, [4] and the spittle of the moon and its relative turn into a colour like russet. At this time, you should [5] soak it (once) every seven days. And if you want it to absorb the water of thc copper [6] quickly, soak it little by little.»

She said: «Then tell me about the experiment of the chrysocolla, [7] which is the glue of the gold.» He said: «Put it in the vessel. If it clings [8] to the nature quickly, then it is the true one, because there is a relationship between the the two of them by nature, so that it (the glue of gold) clings [9] quickly to the gold. If you want to know its experiment, then put the one you want to glue [10] in the miraculous vinegar, so that it dissolves and becomes like water. Know that if it remains for a long time on [11] the fire, the body and the water will solidify, and then they break into fragments. When they break into fragments [12] it becomes a red cluster. So wash it many times. The more you wash it, [13] the more it becomes pure and good. Know that you should wash it six or [14] seven times, and if you increase it (the washing), it will be better for it, and its dye will be more precious. Then leave it in [15] its vessel until it becomes dry and strong. This is what we named Aqrūnis (see also fol. 85a, 3 f.) and it is the water because [16] at the beginning of its operation it was dissolved and became water. Then when it was cooked, it dried and turned into sand. So this is [17] the one which is dissolved by the one, and the other one dries up in the one.»

She said: «Then tell me [18] about his statement: "One should dry the second in the same way as the first was dried, [19] and the vessel should contain six (parts) of the water."» He said: «Yes, because the first burning is by that water, (fol. 217b) and the second (burning) is (also) by that water, and if you burn it a third time, it multiplies. And I tell you that [2] the more your burn it and return it, the better it becomes, and it is more beneficial for it and soaks it more, [3] because the more the sulphury body absorbs and is burnt, the softer it becomes. And the more [4] you burn the ashes, the more they become gentle and penetrate the bodies more quickly.»

She said: [5] «Then tell me about his statement: "At the beginning of the mixing, divide the nature into three, and dissolve [6] the other nature with it, then you will find the truth."» He said: «If you continue to cook it, it becomes solid [7] like pitch. When you see that blackness like pitch, know that it is [8] the earthly dirt. Continue to cook it until its dirt disappears. Then soak it and cook it until [9] it turns into shining blood. Know that if you soak, cook and dry it, [10] its redness will become stronger. Soak it until it absorbs all the moisture, and cook it for many days [11] after it has absorbed the water till its colour becomes like burnt blood. And know that you should put [12] $^{1}/_{3}$ of the water at the beginning of the second composition. Then, when the sun takes its place in Gemini, you should pour into the sea the [13] $^{2}/_{3}$ of the water that you have preserved. At this time, the snow appears and it seizes [14] the cloud.»

She said: «Then what about when he said: "If you want your work to become perfect, [15] soak it with the rest of the fat till it absorbs it all, and till the two natures burn [16] the biggest nature and what is in the vapour."» He said: «I have already told you that [17] the more intensively you cook and soak it, the first day becoming two days, the third (day) becoming [18] three, the fourth becoming four, the fifth becoming five and the sixth becoming six; and if [19] you increase the soaking, it will increase greatly. In spite of that, when the nature takes its mixture (fol. 218a) and reaches its highest degree, it does not need you because it has become complete, otherwise you would need [2] to increase it (the cooking) and dye it more.»

She said: «Then tell me about this stone [3] which is called pyrite, hollow stone, and a stone with four corners.» He said: «That is [4] the head of the four.»

She said: «Tell me what this stone is, and describe for me the states of its colours, [5] and how it can be operated on in every degree until its colours appear.» He said: [6] «Concerning its true name, it is the stone which is born every year because it has in it [7] the true nature, and by the will of the exalted God it is born every year. And by the moon and its courses it is burnt. [8] In every month it has a habitation in a sign of the Zodiac.»

She said: «Explain that to me.» [9] He said: «The first is the entering of Venus in Libra, because Libra is under the sun, and it (Libra) holds it (the sun). [10] And it becomes another stone in the *Ḥaziza* (?) (another sign of the Zodiac, may be Virgo). Its colour will point it out to you in the plurality of its colours. Once [11] it is seen white, once it is seen in the colour of the moon, once in the colour of the sky, and once in a colour changing towards blackness. [12] When it is dyed and completed, it becomes red and often many colours come out from it. [13] If, my lady, you want this stone to follow you, then soak it and dry it [14] until it turns into a colour like the one that the sage ordered. Thus you will reach its goal, and you will obtain it and [15] the world thanks to your determination.»

She said: «Then tell me about the question of the student of Hermes: [16] "Teach us the rest of the operation of the second work, which is the honoured stone."» He said: [17] «Understand. Concerning the other composition—I do not think that you do not know it—they asked him about the completeness [18] of its operation.»

She said: «Then tell me about what they asked him.» He said: «See what remained [19] of the 2/3 from the eternal water, so I order you to soak the nature with that remaining part, after (fol. 218b) the body is destroyed. Make the heat stronger than in the first operation because the elixir [2] dried up and its parts held each other. Cook it until it absorbs the glue of gold. [3] Then soak it after that with the white water until 2/3 disappear, [4] and the operated earth absorbs all the water. Then the earth has to be left cooking, until [5] its flowers come out and its fruits become ripe. Know that when you leave it—after the absorption—[6] in the cooking for 41 days, that this is the second rotting and the second making lean, [7] and it is the purple stone which I told you that you will find at the head of the river. [8] But concerning the other colour, which is the completion, it is the colour of Aqrūnis (see fol. 217a, 15) looking like burnt blood.»

[9] She said: «Then tell me about a statement which I found in the book of Bidīsīos and the book of [10] the greatest (sage) Ostanes.» He said: «What is it?»

She said: «His statement is: "The pyrite has [11] a close relationship with the copper."» He said: «He is right, because if there were not a relationship between the two, the one could not dissolve [12] the other, nor could it cling to it till it becomes like soft balsam, which is the [13] eternal water.»

She said: «Then what about his statement: "Divide the poison into two parts. Then dissolve the copper in the first part, [14] and preserve the second part for the pounding and the soaking."» He said: «How can [15] you ask me about something that Bidīsīos has already made clear for you!»

She said: «Because I do not know which [16] work this is.» He said: «This is also the soaking of the elixir.»

She said: [17] «Tell me more.» He said: «Leave it on a gentle fire for some days till it turns into water. If you want [18] to be sure whether you are right or not, cool it down and purify it with a piece of cloth. When [19] all of it comes though it (the cloth), know that it is the true one and that you are on the right path, and you have done well. It is (fol. 219a) the greatest remedy. But if it does not come out, return it to the cooking till [2] everything turns into water.»

She said: «Then tell me about when he said: "Pound, dry, return and do not become impatient."» [3] He said: «He gave good advice in what he said, because if that body is not [4] cooked intensively, pounded repeatedly and returned to the fire, it will not dissolve. If you cook it [5] and rcturn it many times, the fire would urge the poison to enter the body. Know that after [6] the poison is dried, it should be soaked with the moisture of the eternal and be dried. And the fire should [7] be stronger than before.»

She said: «Then tell me about the making alumy (= white) because each dye requires [8] a making alumy.» He said: «You are right, and you hit the mark. Ponder over how [9] I describe the operation for you, saying that it is not of the kind with which people are concerned. They (the people) are able to turn [10] the dyer and the dyed into one perfect dye, yet not into this dye of ours. Concerning [11] the first making alumy, I have already described it to you, but the many statements about it confused you, before [12] you reached what you have asked me about here. Therefore do not let anything else enter into what you have asked me [13] about here.»

She said: « I will not.» He said: «Did you not understand the statement of the sage, when [14] he said: "Before the dyeing, make it alumy with the urine of young boys, with the water of the sea or with our pure eternal water."»

[15] She said: «I have understood that, but I did not think that this was for that.» He said: [16] «But the sage ordered you to cook it with a gentle fire until it solidifies and turns into a stone that breaks quickly [17] into fragments. Then he ordered you <~~the sage to cook it~~> to roast it with its moisture until [18] the crimson colour appears, and then the purple. That is because, whenever it becomes dry, you should [19] moisten it with its eternal water. And do that continuously, and do it until the water is used up.

(fol. 219b) This is the other (second) making alumy (white).»

She said: «So which one is the first making alumy?» [2] He said: «It is the rust of the body.»

She said: «And what is the alum?» He said: «It is the broth.» She said: [3] «So is the broth the alum from the beginning?» He said: «No. I told you that it makes alumy (white), [4] a composition, an operation and works stronger than the other one. I did not [5] want to tell you all of this at one time, but I will now complete [6] my statement to you.»

She said: «Then do so.» He said: «Set it on fire until the body absorbs [7] all the water. Do that with it day after day. Then a purple colour will appear, [8] the like of which the people of Syria never dye with.»

She said: «Then what about when you say that it is the mercury which comes out [9] of cinnabar? He said: «It is what you asked me about before, and it is what [10] comes out of the female, and with it the dyeing becomes perfect. And know that although it is white in [11] its outer appearance, it is red in its essence.»

She said: «Then what about your statement that I must make white?» He said: «I did not [12] say that to you in this connection, because it is white in its nature. But I ordered you to do it in the making [13] of the silver, which you would need in order to dye the gold. That is what I ordered you to make white [14] in order for it to solidify and to become a white stone, because it has a relationship with the other copper, and the copper [15] has a relationship with the mercury. And that is why we ordered you to provoke the fighting between them both, [16] because the sage said: "The killer of the copper is the killer of the mercury."»

She said: «Explain this to me.» [17] He said: «Did you not understand the statement when the sage said: "Take mercury of cinnabar, [18] or of kohl that is arsenic and sandarach, then cook it with the male on [19] a gentle fire so they will become mixed, and blackness will cover them. Then return it to the cooking (fol. 220a) until it thickens, and its parts are mixed with each other, because the dry loves the moist [2] and the moist loves the dry. Cook, and be careful that it does not (produce) smoke until the moisture disappears."?»

[3] She said: «Make one aspect clear for me, in order that I might know the mercury by it.» He said: «Put it in a mortar [4] and pound it. When you see that there is some redness in it, know that it is (from) the work. Then return it [5] to its vessel and close its mouth well, in order that its flowers do not disappear, and leave it for [6] 100 days in the cooking. Then you will find the secret complete. Then sweeten it with the dew and the sun.»

She said: [7] «Then tell me what you say about the alabaster.» He said: «It is the lime. When it became a stone, we named it [8] alabaster. <He said> We named it alabaster because of its intense whiteness. As for [9] the lime (we named it like this) because it conceals fire in it, in the same way as the fire is concealed in the lime of ordinary people. [10] As for the head, this is because the dye is concealed in its interior and it hides it (the dye) in its subtle (part), just as [11] the head collects the thoughts, yet people only see the head but cannot see the thoughts in it. In the same way, [12] the white colour is seen on the stone and the dye is concealed in it and cannot be seen.»

She said: [13] «O Zosimos, you described this well. Then tell me more about it.» He said: «Take that stone [14] and destroy it by cooking, then you will like its colour. Then soak it with the vinegar until it absorbs the moisture, [15] and do this seven times daily for 40 days. Sweeten it with the sun and the dew [16] until the secret becomes complete for you, (the secret) that the sages could only explain with symbols and examples.»

She said: [17] «Then tell me more.» He said: «There is more to say about it than can be said in words.»

She said: «In spite [18] of that, tell me!» He said: «The sage said: "It is a stone-not a stone, known-not known, [19] precious-cheap, and it is the only thing that is good for dyeing. This is because (fol. 220b) when the heat of the fire hits this stone, it is destroyed, and it becomes a spirit that is single-unique (*fard*) in its working [2] and there is no other stone which does its work."

She said: «Why is that so?» [3] He said: «Because it is what makes the copper white, what makes it red and what [4] turns it into a spirit.»

She said: «Is it single-unique from the beginning?» He said: «When it reaches [5] this stage that you asked me about concerning its names, it is single-unique (*fard*) with regard to the name because [6] everything is collected in it. However, before that, it was not single but it was composed. Then [7] the dyes were collected in it, therefore it became one, like a human being which contains [8] various things.»

She said: «Then tell me about the power of the vitriol (*šaḥīra*) when it is cooked with the fat, [9] which is the power of the female.» He said: «The vitriol is not vitriol, but it is the male, [10] and the female is then the moisture.»

She said: «Does it have an aspect that I can know when the two are mixed and turn into [11] one thing?» He said. «Yes. When the body is mixed with the moisture and then cooked, [12] all of the body and the moisture turn into water, covered by blackness. If you want to know [13] whether all of it has been dissolved, take a piece of tightly woven cloth, put that moisture [14] in it, and wring it until all that water comes out. If everything comes out, [15] then you have done the cooking well. But if something of the body remains in the piece of cloth, then return it [16] to the cooking, so everything will turn into water.»

She said: «Then what?» He said: «Cook it [17] until it thickens, and return it < until it thickens, and return it > until their blackness comes out, and they solidify [18] and become white. Know that if they do not become white, they will not become red.»

She said: «What is it that makes it white?» [19] He said: «It is the eternal water alone, with it the stone becomes white, and with it the body becomes red.»

(fol. 221a) She said: «I see that all the work has to be made with this eternal water that makes white.» He said: «Yes, it is [2] the head of the work, and it is that about which the sage said: "With that one, everything comes into existence [3] and if everything is not with that one, nothing can exist."»

She said: «You spoke well.» [4] He said: «On the contrary, I spoke badly.»

She said: «Why?» He said: «Because I did not keep the oath of the sages, when [5] I revealed their secret, and I have said a terrible thing. "O my God, You are its (the work's) protector, so hide it from whomever You want, [6] and forgive me for what I revealed of this secret." <He said:> And I tell you that [7] when the components of the mixture of the elixir are united, in every level it acquires a colour by which we name it. [8] And I will tell you also that the operation of that elixir is not easy, and it does not come out [9] for you in a few days. But you should operate on it with gentleness, patience, [10] without boredom, good contemplation and begging the exalted God that He completes for you [11] what you are looking for. And beware that stupidity does not make you throw away what is in your hands, otherwise you would regret it. [12] Beware of annoyance and know that the more you cook gently and well, the more the elixir [13] becomes married, more dyed and more perfect in its action. Beware of annoyance and [14] be cautious with the fire.»

She said «How can I be cautious with the fire?» He said: «Make it [15] moderate, not hot, ~~<and not cold>~~ otherwise the flowers will be destroyed and nothing would be dyed, nor cold; [16] otherwise the elixir will not become mature, and if it does not become mature, its colours will not appear, and it will not be able to dye. [17] So your fire must be moderate. Know that nature will teach you the measures of [18] its fire if you are intelligent, because a moderate fire is suitable for every [19] operation, every degree and every dye until the exalted God completes what you want.»

She said: «Then what about when Maria (correction)

(fol. 221b) said: "Take the androdamus, pound and cook it until it becomes white. [2] If you want to turn it red, put some water of sulphur on it."» [3] He said: «Here she also named the other composition androdamus, [4] so when it was cooked, it turned white. Then she ordered it to be cooked and soaked in the water of sulphur, and to be cooked (again).»

[5] She said: «Then what about her statement: "Take pure gold and amalgamate it with the operated on poison."?» [6] He said: «This comes in the other composition. And I order you to cook it until [7] it is made lean. Know that when it is made lean, then you will find it to be black water. Then cook it until [8] its blackness disappears and is solidified, and its colour appears. Then soak it with some of the poison and cook it until [9] its colour satisfies you.»

She said: «Then what about when she said: "Take mercury."?» He said. «She meant the mercury [10] of cinnabar. So do not operate with anything else.»

She said: «And what about when she said: "Take the Cypriot mercury,"?» [11] He said: «This is our copper which we burnt, and from it we extracted its flowers. [12] And know that the copper is not burnt at one time but little by little, and whenever [13] some of it is burnt, the subtle part of the burnt one is concealed in our moisture [14] until all of it is burnt and rotten, and falls down destroyed. Know that every nature, [15] when it is cooked with sulphur and it contains some sulphur, dissolves [16] and the sulphur extracts its spirit.»

She said: «And which sulphur is this?» He said: [17] «It is our silver which we made. Everything that is cooked has to be cooked [18] gently until it has learnt to fight the fire, and to be firm against it. So be careful with the burning, [19] and know that the more the body is cooked with its mercury, the more it becomes dyed. So be careful (fol. 222a) only to cook it in the suspended furnace.» She said: Then tell me about when you said that you saw [2] people who, when they attained the rust, thought that their work was completed, but they were [3] wrong in that.» He said: «Concerning those people, if they had read the books with intelligence, they would have known the statement of [4] Democritus, who said: "Return the gold so it will become more dyed that it was before."»

She said: [5] «I do not understand what he said.» He said: «He meant that one should treat it after the reddening in order that [6] the superior redness increases. I have seen some sages who say that there is [7] nothing more beneficial for the operation than the pounding.»

She said: «Is it the pounding by hand?» He said: «No. But it is the cooking [8] because the pounding should be by intensive cooking. At this time, the many colours appear.»

She said: [9] «Then who cooked for a long time?» He said: «Truly, they are the students of Agathodaimon, because all of his statements [10] are about the cooking and the pounding, and the sages do like that. If you want to know the power [11] of that poison, then take a vessel of silver and render it into the thickness of a fingernail. Then splash [12] half of the vessel with some of that poison and roast it gently, thus [13] the splashed part becomes gold and what is not splashed remains silver.»

She said: «Then what about your statement that the sages do not like [14] to burn their natures strongly at the beginning?» He said: «That is because they are afraid [15] to destroy the dyer-spirit. I have warned you many times about the fire with regard to its burning, [16] composition and operation.»

She said: «Then give me a limit for it (the burning) that I can rely on.» He said: [17] «You have to burn with utmost gentleness, because from the very beginning of this work you burn it [18] little by little, and you continue to burn when it is magnesia, and it has to be burnt in the making white, [19] and it has to be burnt in the pounding and at the time of returning it. Also when they wanted to (fol. 222b) turn it rusty, they burnt it. They therefore avoided the intense burning in [2] making the rust. But at the beginning when you should mix the things, only mix them [3] on hot ashes in order that the bodies of magnesia remain alive, neither burnt [4] nor dead, because if they are alive, the mercury mixes with them quickly. If you [5] burn them intensely, the mercury will reject them, and you could mix them only after [6] long suffering. I will write about these things for you in their proper place. But now [7] I am concerned with the body of magnesia, and I will make you more certain by telling you [8] that all the sages had no other intention or quest except for these ashes. [9] Therefore they praised them and they told us that the entire secret is in them. They said the blackness, then the whiteness, [10] and after that comes the redness. So operate on these precious ashes and do not [11] look for anything else, because about these Democritus said: "Why you are looking for the many things [12] while the nature is one, and from it, the work comes into existence." And Abālīnūs also said: [13] "Take the stone of gold which we named the male and make it marry the stone of [14] the female, because her drops dissolve the earth of Ethiopia. " Bālīnūs also said: [15] "When the moist, pure, black spirit is mixed with the body, which is its relative, it will cling [16] and be clung to, and it will solidify, and be solidified." With all of this, I only repeated my statement to you, giving some of the testimonies of [17] the sages to assure you more that the thing is one. But with what that [18] one is operated on until it becomes one dye, is another thing. Do you not remember the word of Maria [19] in 1000 places: "Lead-copper." So she named them two. Then she said after that:

(fol. 223a) "Honoured stone." Thus she made the name of the two one. She said that the thing is one, and what [2] operates on it is one. Thus do not be deluded by the many things, and often beg [3] the exalted God to inspire you with what improves both in the composition.»

She said: [4] «Then tell me about the statement of the sage: "Take one weight of pure Cypriot copper, [5] and two weights of round alum, and one of pure white tar. [6] Then put them in a vessel, close its mouth well and put it on gentle fire for [7] seven days, so you will find that the lead has turned white. Then the magnesia becomes [8] a magnetic stone.» He said: «This is the other composition. Know that when it reaches this [9] point and turns into a stone, the four that have been made red cling together. Then put them in a vessel, [10] put some of the broth on them, close the mouth of the vessel well and cook it until [11] its moisture dries up, God willing. And there is no power and no strength save in the exalted and great God.»

[12] The 13th Book of the Book of Zosimos, which [13] he wrote for Theosebeia is completed, praise be to the exalted God, and by His help [14] the entire Book is completed. May God greatly bless the best of His prophets [15] our master Muḥammad and his people and his companions granting them salvation. [16] Its writing is finished on the blessed day 18th gummadah [17] the second, of the year 668 after the hiğra (1270 AD), [18] corresponding to the 19th of amšīr (Coptic month), year 289 (written on the margin) [19] during the reign of King Ṭiqlādīānūs (Diocletian).
Praise be to the grateful ones to God.

Part IV

Apparatus

1. Bibliography and Further Reading

Alchemical treatises in Greek

BERTHELOT, Marcellin: *Collection des Anciens Alchimistes Grecs*, avec la collaboration de Ch.-Em. Ruelle, Vol. I-III, Paris 1887/88; reprint Osnabrück 1967.

MERTENS, Michèle: „Zosime de Panopolis - Mémoires authentiques“ in: *Les Alchimistes Grecs* Vol. IV. 1, Collection des Universités de France.

Alchemical treatises as translations from Greek to Syriac

BERTHELOT, Marcellin: *La Chimie au moyen âge* II: L'Alchimie Syriaque. Comprenant une introduction historique et plusieurs traitées d'alchimie Syriaques et Arabes d'après les manuscripts du British Museum et de Cambridge, Texte et traduction avec la collaboration de M. RUBENS Duval, Paris 1893; reprint Osnabrück 1967.

Alchemical treatises as translations from Greek to Arabic

ZOSIMOS OF PANOPOLIS: *Kitāb aṣ-ṣuwar* (The Book of Pictures by the sage Zosimos and it is named the Book of the Epistles from the sage Zosimos to the Queen Theosebeia, Daughter of Maria the Copt), Ms. Cairo, Dār al-kutub, kīmiyāʾ 23 M. Publication in Arabic of a part with English translation in: Benjamin C. HALLUM, *The Reception of Zosimos of Panopolis in the Arabic/Islamic World*, PhD Thesis, Warburg Institute, London 2008.

–*Nusḫat Kitāb Rīsamūs al-ḥakīm* [*al-kabārīt*] (Copy of the book of Zosimos the sage [The Sulphurs]), Book I-VI, Raza Library, Rampur, Ms kīmiyāʾ 12, 55a-76a.

Alchemical treatises that are probable translations from Greek to Arabic

ZOSIMOS OF PANOPOLIS: "Kitāb Qirāṭīs al-Ḥakīm" (Book of Krates), in: M. Berthelot, *La chimie au moyen âge* III (Arabic text with French translation), Paris 1893; 1st reprint Osnabrück 1967; 2nd reprint Frankfurt 2002 (Natural Sciences in Islam 64). For the authorship of most of this text see introduction of Th. ABT to Vol. II.1 of the Corpus Alchemicum Arabicum series (CALA II.1), ed. by Th. ABT and W. MADELUNG, Zürich 2007, p. 51 (reprinted in this volume as Part I).

– "Kitāb al-Ḥabīb" (Book of the Lover), in: M. Berthelot, *La chimie au moyen âge* III (Arabic text with French translation). Paris 1893; 1st reprint Osnabrück 1967; 2nd reprint Frankfurt 2002 (Natural Sciences in

Islam 64). For the authorship of most of the text see the introduction of Th. Abt to Vol. II.1 of the Corpus Alchemicum Arabicum series (CALA II.1), ed. by Th. Abt and W. Madelung, Zürich 2007, p. 49 (reprinted in this volume as Part I).
– *Kitāb mafātīḥ aṣ-ṣanᶜa* (The Book of the Keys to the Art). Ms. Cairo Dār al-kutub, 395 kīmiyāᵓ 23 M; (to be published in the CALA Series).
– *Muṣḥaf aṣ-ṣuwar* (The Book of Pictures), Facsimile with an introduction by Th. Abt as Vol. II.1 of the Corpus Alchemicum Arabicum (CALA II.1). Ed. by Th. Abt and W. Madelung, Zürich 2007.

Alchemical treatises in Arabic

ABŪ AL-QĀSIM MUSSAMMAD IBN ASSMAD AL-ᶜIRĀQĪ: *Kitāb al-Aqālīm as-sabaᶜa fī al-ᶜilm al-mausūm bi aṣ-ṣanᶜa* (Book of the Seven Climes on the Science called the Art). British Library, London 1517,1 (= Add. 25724), and Chester Beatty Library 5433, Dublin (M. Ullmann points in his *Die Nautr- und Geheimwissenschaften im Islam* to a second Ms of this text in the same library).
– *Kitāb al-ᶜIlm al-muktasab fī zirāᶜat aḏ-ḏahab* (Book of Knowledge Acquired Concerning the Cultivation of Gold). Arabic text with translation and introduction. E. J. Holmyard, Paris 1923.
ANONYMOUS: “Risāla Qabas al-qābis fī tadbīr Harmis al-Harāmis” (The treatise on the light about the operation of Hermes of the Hermeses). Ms. Cairo, private library of Nūr ad-Dīn Muṣṭafa. Arabic text with German translation and introduction by A. Siggel, “Das Licht über das Verfahren des Hermes des Hermesse dem, der es begehrt”, in: *Der Islam*, 24 (1937); reprint in F. Sezgin et al. *Natural Sciences in Islam, Chemistry and Alchemy* VII, Frankfurt 2001.
APPOLONIUS OF TYANA; (see Alchemical treatises in Arabic: Balīnās).
IBN ARFᶜA RAᵓS: *Šuḏūr aḏ-ḏahab* (The Filings of Gold), Ms Berlin 4180.
ARŠILĀWUS AL-FIṮĀĠŪRĪ (Pythagoras’ Archelaos): *Muṣḥaf al-ǧamāᶜa* (The Book of the Reunion, generally known as *Turba philosophorum*). Fragments of the Arabic text and German translation and extensive commentary on the history and German translation of the Arabic parts and the Latin text by J. RUSKA; (see General Literature: RUSKA, Julius).
BALĪNĀS (APOLLONIUS OF TYANA): *Kitāb Sirr al-ḫalīqa* (The Book of the Secret of Creation). Ed. and German transl. by U. WEISSER, Berlin 1980.
BERTHELOT, Marcellin: *La Chimie au moyen âge* III: L’Alchimie Arabe. Comprenant une introduction historique et les traités de Cratès, d’al-Ḥabīb, d’Ostanes et de Djàber tirés des manuscrits de Paris et de Leyde. Texte et traduction par Octave Houdas, Paris 1893; 1st reprint

Osnabrück 1967; 2nd reprint ed. F. Sezgin et al. in: Natural Sciences in Islam 64, Frankfurt 2002 .

CLEOPATRA: *Risāla Qalūbatra malikat Samannūd* (Treatise of Cleopatra, the Queen of Semennud = Sebennyos). Arabic text and German translation by M. Ullmann; (see General Literature: ULLMANN, Manfred, "Kleopatra in einer arabischen Disputation").

ĞAᶜFAR AṢ-ṢĀDIQ: *Risāla fī ᶜilm aṣ-ṣanāᶜa wa al-ḥağar al-mukarram* (Treatise of the Science of the Art und the Precious Stone). Edition of Arabic text and German translation by J. Ruska; (see General Literature: RUSKA, Julius).

HARMIS, HIRMIS or HURMUS (see HERMES and ANONYMOUS).

HERMES BUDASHIR: *Risāla as-Sirr* (Treatise of the Secret). Edition of Arabic text and German translation by I. VERENO; (see General Literature: VERENO, Ingolf).

HERMES: *Kitāb al-Lauḥ az-zumurrudī* (Book of the Emerald Tablet that is generally known as *Tabula Smaragdina*). Edition of Arabic text and German translation with an extensive commentary on the history of the text by J. RUSKA; (see General Literature: RUSKA, Julius).

HERMES OF DENDERA: *Risāla al-Fakīyāt al-kubrā* (Great Epistle of the Spheres). Edition of Arabic text and German translation by I. VERENO; (see General Literature: VERENO, Ingolf).

IBN UMAIL, Muḥammad: *Kitāb Ḥall ar-rumūz* (Book of the Explanation of the Symbols). Edited by Th. Abt, W. Madelung and Th. Hofmeier, translation by S. Fuad and Th. Abt, Corpus Alchemicum Arabicum I (CALA I), Zürich 2003.

– *Ad-Durra an-naqīya* (The Pure Pearl). Ms. Āṣafīya Library 1410, Hyderabad (Dekkan) and others; (to be published in the CALA series).

– *Al-Māᵓ al waraqī wa-l-arḍ an-nağmīya.* Topkapı Sarayı Ahmet III (Istanbul) 2075, and Beşir Ağa (Istanbul) 505; (see also IBN UMAIL, Muḥammad, *Three Arabic Treatises*).

– *Al-Qaṣīda al-mīmīya* (Poem rhyming on the Letter Mīm), with a commentary also written by Ibn Umail. Ms. Beşir Ağa (Istanbul) 505; (to be published in the CALA series, together with *ad-Durra an-naqīya*).

– *Al-Qaṣīda an-nūnīya*; (Poem rhyming on the Letter Nūn), with a commentary written by Ibn Umail. For the poem alone: see *Three Arabic Treatises on Alchemy by Muḥammad ibn Umail.* The commentary, however without the described pictures from a Pharaonic temple, is in the Ms Beşir Ağa (Istanbul) 505; (to be published in the CALA series).

– *Three Arabic Treatises on Alchemy by Muḥammad ibn Umail* (10th century). Edition of the texts by M. TURĀB ᶜALĪ, Excursus on the Writings and Date of Ibn Umail with Edition of the Latin Rendering of the *Māᵓ al-waraqī*, H. E. STAPLETON and M. HIDĀYAT ḤUSAIN, *Memoirs of the Asiatic Society of Bengal*, Calcutta, Vol. XII (1933) No. 1, p. 117 f.; Reprint in: Ibn Umayl Abū ᶜAbdallāh Muḥammad, Texts and Studies. Collected and reprinted by Fuat Sezgin et al. Natural Sciences in Islam 75, Frankfurt 2002.

IBN AL-MUHTĀR, Abū ᶜAbd Allāh Muḥammad: *Kitāb Miraᵓāt al-ᶜağāᵓib* (Mirror of Wonders). Lucknow manuscript, legacy H. E. Stapleton, Museum of the History of Science, Oxford, and Bodleian Library, University of Oxford, Ms Greaves 14.

IBN NADĪM, Muḥammad Abī Yaᶜūb: *Kitāb al-fihrist*, ed. Gustav Flügel, Leipzig 1871-72. Reprint Frankfurt 2005.

AL-MAĞRĪṬĪ, Abū Maslama ibn Aḥmad: *Rutbat al-ḥakīm wa-mudḫal at-taᶜlīm* (Rank of the Sage and Introduction to the Teaching). Raza Library, Rampur (North India) Ms Nr. LXXVII.

MAQBŪL, Aḥmad: "A Persian Translation of the 11th Century Arabic Alchemical Treatise *ᶜAin aṣ-ṣanᶜah wa ᶜaūn aṣ-ṣināᶜah* (The eye of the Art and the eyes of the Adept)". In: *Memoirs of the Asiatic Society of Bengal*, Vol. VIII (1929), no. 7, p. 419-460.

MARIA THE JEWESS: *Risāla*. Āṣafīya Library, Hyderabad, India, Mss. 885 and 941.

MARIA THE COPT: *Risāla at-Tāğ wa-ḫilqat al-maulūd* (The Crown and the Creation of the Child). Arabic text and English translation (see General Literature: HOLMYARD, Eric John).

AL-MARRĀKUŠĪ, Abū Abdullah Muḥammad: *Muṣaḥḥaḥāt Aflāṭūn*. Ms 562, 35b-43b, Manuscript Collection of the al-Biruni Institute of Oriental Studies, Tashkent.

MARIYĀNUS AR-RĀHIB: *Risāla Mariyānus ar-Rāhib al-ḥakīm li-l-amīr Ḫālid ibn Yazīd* (Epistle of Mariyānus the wise monk to the Prince Ḫālid ibn Yazīd). Ms. Fatih (Istanbul) 3227.

PSEUDO-ARISTOTELES: *Kitāb al-Aḥğār* (The Book of the Stones). Arabic text and German transl. by J. RUSKA; (see General Lit.: RUSKA, Julius).

PSEUDO-MAĞRĪṬĪ: *Ġāyat al-ḥakīm wa aḥaqq al-natīğatain bi-'l-tawdīm* (The Goal of the Wise and the true two Results that are to be most Preferred), translated in Latin as *Picatrix, Das Ziel des Weisen*. Translated into German from the Arabic by Helmut RITTER and Martin PLESSNER, Studies of the Warburg Institute, Vol. 27, London 1962; Arabic Text: Vol. XII, London 1933.

AR-RĀZĪ, Muḥammad ibn Zakarīyāᵓ: *Al-qaul fī al-milḥ* (The Book on Salt). Ed. of text and German translation by J. Ruska; (see General Literature: RUSKA, Julius).

AR-RĀZĪ, Abū Bakr Muḥammad ibn Zakarīyāᵓ: *Kitāb aš-Šawāhid* [*wa-nuqat ar-rumūz*] (Book of Evidences and the Points on the Symbols).

Ms. Rampur, kīmiyāʾ 16.11. Edited by H. E. STAPLETON and R. F. AZO in: *Memoirs of the Asiatic Society of Bengal*, Calcutta, 3, 1910; (see General Literature, STAPLETON, Harry E.).

Alchemical treatises in Latin

Artis auriferae quam chemiam vocant, Basle 1610 (first printed 1593).
– Rosinus (Zosimos) ad Euthiciam, I, p. 165f.
– Morienus Romanus. Sermo de transmutatione metallorum, I, p. 311f.
– Merlini allegoria profundissimum philosophici lapidis Arcanum, I, p. 392-396.
AQUINAS, Thomas: *Aurora Consurgens*. Codex Rhenovensis 172, Zentralbibliothek Zürich 1420/30, translated by M.-L. von FRANZ. (See General Literature: M.-L. von FRANZ).
BARCHUSEN, J. C.: *Elementa chemicae*, Leiden 1718.
DORNEUS (DORN), Gerhard; PARACELSUS, Phillipp Aureol Theophrastus Bombastus von Hohenheim: *Aurora Thesaurusque Philosophorum, Theophrasti Paracelsi.* Basel 1577.
MAIER, Michael: *Atalanta fugiens. Hoc est emblemata nova de secretis naturae chymica.* Oppenheim 1618; Facsimile edition by L. H. WÜTHERICH, Kassel 1964; Introduction, text, emblems and commentary by H. M. E. JONG, New York, Maine 2002.
MAIER, Michael: *Symbola aureae mensae duodecim nationum.* Frankfurt am Main 1617; reprint with a German introduction by K. R. H. FRICK, Graz 1972.
MANGETUS, Johannes Jacobus: *Bibliotheca chemica curiosa.* Two volumes, Geneva 1702; reprint Naples 1976.
– Mutus Liber, Vol. I, after p. 938 (First printed: La Rochelle, 1678)
– Petrus Bonus, "Pretiosa margarita novella", Vol. II, p. 1 f.
– Senioris antiquissimi libellus (de chemia), Vol. II, p. 216 f.
MORIENUS, Romanus: "Sermo de transmutatione metallorum" (see Alchemical treatises in Latin: *Artis Auriferae*, and Alchemical treatises in Arabic: MARIYĀNUS AR-RĀHIB).
Musaeum Hermeticum, Frankfurt am Main 1678; reprint with a German introduction by K. R. H. FRICK, Graz 1970.
- LAMBSPRINCK, Abraham: *De lapide philosophico*. p. 337f.
- VALENTINUS, Basilius: "De Lapide Sapientum", p. 393-423.
Pistis Sophia, ed. C. SCHMIDT, translated by V. MACDERMOT, in: Nag Hammadi studies; Vol. 9., LEIDEN 1978.
RULANDUS, Martin: *Lexicon alchymicae*, Frankfurt 1612.
Rosarium philosophorum, Vadiana library, Ms 394a, St. Gallen.

STOLZIUS VON STOLZENBERG: *Chymisches Lustgärtlein*, Frankfurt 1624. Reprint with a German Introduction by F. WEINHANDL, Darmstadt 1964.
Tabula Smaragdina; (see General Literature: Julius RUSKA, and Alchemical treatises in Arabic: HERMES, *Kitāb al-Lauḥ az-zumurrudī*).
Theatrum Chemicum, edited by L. ZETZNER, Argentorati (Strasbourg) 1659-1661; reprint of the six volumes, Turin 1981.
– Artificium supernaturale, Vol. I 1659, p. 277-325.
– Davidis Langnei, Harmonia Chemica, Vol. IV 1659, p. 719-804.
– Senioris Zadith, filii Hamuelis tabula chimica (De Chemia), V, p. 191 f.
Turba philosophorum; (see General Literature: J. RUSKA, and Alchemical treatises in Arabic: ARŠILĀWUS AL-FIṮĀĠŪRĪ, *Muṣḥaf al-ǧamaᶜa*).

General Literature

ABT, Theodor: *Psychological Commentary of the Book of the Explanation of the Symbols* (Kitāb Ḥall ar-rumūz) by Mohammad Ibn Umail, Corpus Alchemicum Arabicum I B (CALA I B), Zurich 2009.
– *Introduction to Picture Interpretation according to C. G. Jung*. Zurich 2005.
– *The Egyptian Amduat*; (see General Literature: E. HORNUNG and Th. ABT).
ABT, Theodor and HORNUNG, Erik: *Knowledge for the Afterlife, The Egyptian Amduat – A Quest for Immortality*. Zurich 2003.
ABŪ AL-QĀSIM; (see Alchemical treatises in Arabic).
Acts of Thomas; (see General Literature: M.R. JAMES: *Translation of "The Apocryphal New Testament*")
ALFONSO-GOLDFARB, Ana Maria and JUBRAN, Safa Abu Chahla: "Listening to the whispers of Matter Through Arabic Hermeticism - New Studies on the Book of the Treasure of Alexander" in: *AMBIX* 55/2 (2008).
ARNOLD Dieter, *Die Tempel Ägyptens,* Zürich 1992.

Bible, *The New Jerusalem Bible*. Reader's edition. New York 1990.
BERLEKAMP, Persis: "Painting as Persuasion: A Visual Defence of Alchemy in an Islamic Manuscript of the Mongol Period", *Maqarnas* 20 (2003), p. 35-59.
BERTHELOT, Marcellin: *Collection des anciens alchimistes grecs*. Tome I-III, Paris 1887/88; reprint Osnabrück 1967.
– *La Chimie au moyen âge*. Tome I-III, Paris 1893; 1st reprint Osnabrück 1967; 2nd reprint of Tome III: F. SEZGIN et al., Natural Sciences in Islam 64, Frankfurt 2002.
BLADEL, Kevin van: *Arabic Hermes - From Pagan Sage to Prophet of Science*, Oxford 2009.

BROADHURST, R. J. C.: *The Travels of Ibn Jubayr,* transl. from the original Arabic, London 1951.

BRUNNER-TRAUT, Emma: „Aspective“ in: H. SCHÄFER, *Principles of Eyptian Art*, ND Oxford 2002.

BOAS, G; (see General Literature: HORAPOLLO).

Book of Krates, in: M. Berthelot, *La Chimie au moyen âge* III: *Le Traité de Crates.*

Book of the Lover, in: M. Berthelot, *La Chimie au moyen âge* III: *Le Traité de al Habib.*

Corpus Alchemicum Arabicum (CALA), ed. by. Th. ABT and W. MADELUNG, Zurich, since 2003:

CALA I; (see Arabic Literature, IBN UMAIL, Muḥammad: *Kitāb Ḥall ar-rumūz*).

CALA I A; (see General Literature: VON FRANZ, M.-L.: *Psychological Commentary of the Book of the Explanation of the Symbols*).

CALA I B; (see General Literature: ABT, Th., *Psychological Commentary of the Book of the Explanation of the Symbols*).

CALA II.1; (see Alchemical treatises that are probable translations from Greek to Arabic: ZOSIMOS, *Mushaf as-suwar*).

Corpus Hermeticum; (see General Literature: COPENHAVER, B. P. and SCOTT, W.).

CONTADINI, Anna (ed.): *Arab Painting. Text and Image in Illustrated Arabic Manuscript.* Leiden, Boston 2007.

COPENHAVER, Brian P.: *Hermetica, The Greek Corpus Hermeticum* and the Latin Asclepius in a new English translation. Cambridge 1992.

DORNEUS: *Aurora Thesaurusque Philosophorum.* (See Alchemical treatises in Latin).

DERCHAIN, Philippe: "L'authencité de l'inspiration Egyptienne dans le Corpus Hermeticum", *Revue de l'Histoire des Religions,* 161 (1962).

DERCHAIN-URTEL, M. T.: "Thot at Akhmim", in *Hommages à François Daumas*, Montpellier 1986.

Encyclopedia of Ancient Egypt. (See *Oxford Encyclopedia of Ancient Egypt*).

Encyclopedia Britannica, Chicago, London, Toronto 1960.

Encyclopedia of Islam, New Edition, Leiden 1986.

ETTINGHAUSEN, Richard: *Arab Painting,* Geneva 1962 and 1977.

FIHRIST; (see Alchemical Treatises in Arabic: IBN NADĪM and FÜCK, J.W.).

FOWDEN, Garth: *The Egyptian Hermes; A Historical Aproach to the Late Pagan Mind,* Princeton 1993[2].

FRANZ VON, Marie-Louise: *Psychological Commentary on the Book of the Explanation of the Symbols* (*Kitāb Ḥall ar-rumūz* by Muḥammad ibn Umail). Corpus Alchemicum Arabicum (CALA) I A, Zürich 2006.

FERARIO, Gabriele: "An Arabic Dictionary of Technical Alchemical Terms: Ms Sprenger 1908 of the Staatsbibliothek zu Berlin (fols. 3r-6r)", *AMBIX* 56/2 (2009), p. 36-48.

FÜCK, Johann W.: "The Arabic Literature on Alchemy According to An-Nadīm (A.D. 987). A translation of the Tenth Discourse of the Book of the Catalogue (Al-Fihrist) with Introduction and Commentary", *AMBIX* 3/4 (1951), p. 81-144. Reprint in: *Chemistry and Alchemy,* Vol. I, Frankfurt (2002), pp. 303-366.

"Gospel of Thomas", in: J. M. ROBINSON, *Nag Hammadi Library*, p. 124-138.

HALDANE, Duncan: *Mamluk Painting.* Warminster, 1978.

HALLUM, Benjamin Charles: *The Reception of Zosimos of Panopolis in the Arabic/Islamic World.* PhD Thesis, Warburg Institute, unpublished, London 2008.

– "Tomb of Images: an Arabic Compilation of Texts by Zosimos of Panapolis and a Source of the Turba philosophorum", in: *AMBIX* 56/1 (2009), p. 76-88. Vol. 56, No. 2 (March 2009), p. 76-88.

HAARMANN, U.W.: "Islam and Ancient Egypt", in: *Oxford Encyclopedia of Ancient Egypt*, Vol. II, Oxford 2001.

HERTZ, Wilhelm: *Die Sage vom Giftmädchen.* München 1893 (without English tranlsation).

HORNUNG, Erik: *The Books of the Afterlife.* Translated by D. LORTON, Ithaca, 1999.

HORNUNG, Erik and ABT, Theodor (eds.): *The Egyptian Amduat, The Book of the Hidden Chamber*, Zurich 2007.

– *Knowledge for the Afterlife;* (see General Lit. Th. ABT and E. Hornung).

IBN NADIM; (see Alchemical treatises in Arabic).

IBN UMAIL, Muḥammad; (see Alchemical treatises in Arabic).

JAMES, M.R.: *Translation of the «The Apocryphal New Testament»* with notes, Oxford 1924.

JASNOW, Richard and ZAUZICH, Karl-Theodor (eds.): *The Ancient Egyptian Book of Thoth, a Demotic Discourse on Knowledge and Pendent to the Classical Hermetica*, Wiesbaden 2005.

JUBRAN, Safa Abu Chahla: “Listening to the whispers of Matter Through Arabic Hermeticism” (see General Literature: ALFONSO-GOLDFARB).
JUNG, Carl Gustav: *Psychology and Alchemy*. Collected Works 12, Princeton 1968.
– *Alchemical Studies*. Collected. Works 13, Princeton 1967.
– *Mysterium Coniunctionis*. Collected Works 14, Princeton 1974.
– *The Practice of Psychotherapy*. Collected Works 16, Princeton 1970.
– *Man and his Symbols,* in Collected Works 18/1, Princeton 1970.

KARBSTEIN, Andreas: *Die Namen der Heilmittel nach Buchstaben. Edition eines arabisch-romanischen Glossars aus dem frühen 17. Jahrhundert*, Kölner Romanistische Arbeiten. Neue Folge, Heft 81, herausgegeben vom Romanischen Seminar der Universität Köln, Genève 2002.
KHALIDI, Tarif: *The Muslim Jesus. Sayings and Stories in Islamic Literature*, edited and translated by Jarif KHALIDI, Cambridge, Massachusetts, London 2001.
Koran, see *Qurʾān*.

LANE, Edward William: *Arabic-English Lexicon*. London 1863-93, reprint Cambridge 1984.
LINDSAY, Jack: *The Origins of Alchmey,* London 1970.

MANGETUS, Johannes Jacobus; (see Alchemical treatises in Latin).
MARTELLI, Matteo: “Divine Water’ in the Alchemical Writings of Pseudo-Democritus”, *AMBIX* 56/1 (2009), p. 5-22.

Nag Hammadi Library (see, ROBINSON, James M).
NASR, Seyyed Hossein: *An Introduction to Islamic Cosmological Doctrines*. Cambridge, Massachusetts 1964.
NORDEN, Frédéric-Louis, *Voyage d’Égypte et de Nubie*, Tome Second, Paris 1785.
Oxford Encyclopedia of Ancient Egypt, 3 Vols, Oxford 2001.
OBRIST, Barbara: “Visualisation in Medieval Alchemy” in: *Hyle-International Journal for Philosophy of Chemistry* 9/2 (2003), p. 131-170.
– *Les débuts de l’imagerie alchimique (XIVe-XVe siècle)*, Paris 1982.

PAGELS, Eliane: *The Origin of Satan,* New York 1996.
Picatrix; (see Alchemical treatises in Arabic: PSEUDO-MAĞRĪṬĪ).
Pistis Sophia; (see General Literature: SCHMIDT, C.).
PLATO: *Politea*, Text ed. by Emile Chamby, Paris 1965.

PLESSNER, Martin: *Vorsokratische Philosophie und griechische Alchemie in arabisch-lateinischer Überlieferung*, Studien zu Text und Inhalt der Turba Philosophorum, Wiesbaden 1975.

– "Neue Materialien zur Geschichte der Tabula Smaragdina", *Islam* 16, 1-2 (1927), p. 77-114.

AL-QĀSIM, Abū; (see Alchemical treatises in Arabic).

AL-QURṬUBĪ, Abū ᶜAbdullāh: *Tafsīr* (Qurᵓān exegesis), ed. Mohammed Ibrahīm el-Hifnāvī ve Mahmūd Hāmid Osman, I-XXII, Kahire 1414/1994.

Qurᵓān, The Holy: English translation of the Meanings and Commentary. Revised and Edited by THE PRESIDENCY OF ISLAMIC RESEARCHES (IFTA), Riyad, 1410 H.

RATZINGER, Joseph Cardinal: *Spirit of Liturgy*. Translated by John Saward, San Francisco 2000.

ROBERTS, Alison: *Golden Shrine, Goddess Queen, Egypt's Anointing Mysteries*, Rottingdean 2008.

ROBINSON, James M.: *The Nag Hammadi Library*. Third revised edition, Leiden 1988.

RAY, John David: *The Archive of Hor*. Texts from Excavations (2), London 1976.

RICHTER, Tonio Sebastian: "The master spoke: «Take one of 'the sun' and one unit of almulgam»", Hitherto unnoticed Coptic papyrological evidence for early Arabic alchemy, Leipzig 2000. Publ. in: Petra SIJPESTEIJN et al. (eds.), *Documents and the History of the Early Islamic World*. Acts of the 3rd Conference of the International Society for Arabic Papyrology, Alexandria, 23-26 March 2006, Leiden 2010.

– "What kind of Alchemy is Attested by Tenth Century Coptic Manuscripts?", *AMBIX* 56/1 (2009), p. 23-35.

– "Naturoffenbarung und Erkenntnisritual. Diskurs und Praxis spätantiker Naturwissenschaft am Beispiel der Alchemie", in: Hermann KNUF, Christian LEITZ & Daniel von RECKLINGHAUSEN (eds.), *Honi soit qui mal y pense. Studien zum pharaonischen, griechisch-römischen und spätantiken Ägypten zu Ehren von Heinz-Josef Thissen*. Leuven, Paris – Walpole, 2010, p. 585-605.

RUDOLPH, Ulrich: "Christliche Theologie und Vorsorkatische Lehren in der Turba Philosophorum", *Oriens* 32 (1990), p. 97-123.

RUSKA, Julius: *Arabische Alchemisten*. 2 Vols., Heidelberg 1924; (see also Alchemical treatises in Arabic: ARŠILĀWUS AL-FIṮĀĠŪRĪ).

– *Tabula Smaragdina*. Heidelberg 1926; reprint together with articles concerning this text by E. J. HOLMYARD and M. PLESSNER, ed. by F. SEZGIN, Natural Sciences in Islam Vol. 57, Frankfurt am Main 2002;

(see also Alchemical treatises in Arabic: HERMES).
– *Turba Philosophorum.* Berlin 1931; reprint ed. F. SEZGIN, Natural Sciences in Islam Vol. 65, Frankfurt am Main 2002; (see also Alchemical treatises in Arabic: ARŠILĀWUS AL-FIṮĀĠŪRĪ).

SCHÄFER, Heinrich: *Principles of Eyptian Art*, ND Oxford 2002.
SCHMIDT, Carl (text ed.): *Pistis Sophia*, translation and notes by Violet Macdermot, Nag Hammadi Studies IX, Leiden 1978.
SCOTT, Walter and FERGUSON, Alexander Stewart (ed.): *The Ancient Greek and Latin Writings Which Contain Religious or Philosophic Teachings Ascribed to Hermes Trismegistus*, 4 Vols. Ed. with English translation and notes by W. SCOTT. Oxford 1924-36.
SEZGIN, Fuat: *Geschichte des arabischen Schrifttums*, Vol. IV. Leiden 1971.
SEZGIN, Fuat et al. (eds): *Ibn Umayl Abū ᶜAbdallāh Muḥammad. Texts and Studies.* Collected and reprinted by Fuat SEZGIN et al., Natural Sciences in Islam, Vol. 75, Frankfurt 2002.
SIGGEL, Alfred: *Arabisch-Deutsches Wörterbuch der Stoffe aus den drei Naturreichen, die in arabischen alchemistischen Handschriften vorkommen*. Berlin 1950.
– *Decknamen der arabischen alchemistischen Literatur*. Berlin 1951.
Suda, Byzantine Lexicon, 10th century. (see: Suda On Line: Byzantine Lexicography).
STAPLETON, Harry Ernest: "Alchemical Equipment in the Eleventh Century". In: *Memoirs of the Asiatic Society of Bengal*, Calcutta, Vol. I (1905), No. l, p. 47 ff.
STAPLETON, Harry Ernest and AZO, Rizkallah F: "An Alchemical Compilation of the Thirteenth Century", in: *Memoirs of the Asiatic Society of Bengal*, Calcutta, Vol. 3 (1910), No.2 .
STAPLETON, Harry Ernest, and HIDĀYAT HUSAIN, Muḥammad: "Three Arabic Treatises on Alchemy by Muhammad ibn Umail (l0th Century AD)". Edition of the Texts by M. TURĀB ᶜALĪ, in: *Memoirs of the Asiatic Society of Bengal*, Calcutta, Vol. XII (1933), No. l, p. 117 f.; reprint in: "Ibn Umayl Abū ᶜAbdallāh Muḥammad. Texts and Studies". Collected and reprinted by Fuat SEZGIN et al. *Natural Sciences in Islam*, Vol. 75, Frankfurt 2002.
STAPLETON, Harry Ernest, G. L. LEWIS and F. SHERWOOD Taylor: "The Sayings of Hermes quoted in al-Māᵓ al-waraqī of Ibn Umail". In: *AMBIX* Vol. 3.3-4 (1949), p. 69-90.

Turba Philosophorum; (see General Literature: RUSKA, J, and Alchemical Treatises in Arabic, ARŠILĀWUS AL-FIṮĀĠŪRĪ, *Muṣḥaf al-ǧamaᶜa*).

ULLMANN, Manfred: "Kleopatra in einer arabischen Disputation". In: *Wiener Zeitschrift für die Kunde des Morgenlandes*, Wien, Vol. 63/64 (1972), p. 158-175; (see also Alchemical treatises in Arabic: CLEOPATRA).
– *Die Natur- und Geheimwissenschaften im Islam*. Handbuch der Orientalistik I, VI.2, Leiden 1972.

VERENO, Ingolf: *Studien zum ältesten alchemistischen Schrifttum. Auf der Grundlage zweier erstmals edierter arabischer Hermetica*. Islamkundliche Untersuchungen Band 155, Berlin 1992; (see also Alchemical treatises in Arabic: HERMES).

WEHR, Hans: *A Dictionary of Modern Written Arabic*. Wiesbaden 1961, 1994.
WEISSER, URSULA: *Kitāb Sirr al-ḫalīqa* (The Secret of Creation). Edition and German translation by U. WEISSER, Berlin 1980 (see also Alchemical treatises in Arabic: BALĪNĀS (APOLLONIUS OF TYANA).
Wörterbuch der Symbolik, Unter Mitarbeit zahlreicher Fachwissenschaftler herausgegeben von Manfred LURKER, Stuttgart 1979.

ZAUZICH, Karl-Theodor; (see General Literature: R. JASNOW and K.-Th. ZAUZICH).

List of Illustrations

Part I

Fig. 1: fol. 38a, Zosimos, *Muṣḥaf aṣ-ṣuwar.* 30
Fig. 2: fol. 99a, Zosimos, *Muṣḥaf aṣ-ṣuwar.* 34
Fig. 3: fol. 171b and 172a, Zosimos, *Muṣḥaf aṣ-ṣuwar.* 38
Fig. 4: fol. 157a, Zosimos, *Muṣḥaf aṣ-ṣuwar.* 42
Fig. 5: fol. 210b, Zosimos, *Muṣḥaf aṣ-ṣuwar.* 43
Fig. 6: Conjunction of dragon and the murderess of her husband. M. Maier, *Atalanta fugiens* (1618), emblem 50. 57
Fig. 7: King and Queen on sun and moon, *Rosarium cum figurius,* fol. XX, Vadiana Library, St. Gallen, Ms 394a. 60
Fig. 8: Mercurius with Sun-king and Moon-queen in a retort. *Mutus Liber,* Pierre Savouret (ed.), La Rochelle, 1677[1], 2nd plate. 65
Fig. 9: Zosimos and Theosebeia with alchemical oven, fol. 153a, Zosimos, *Muṣḥaf aṣ-ṣuwar.* 66
Fig. 10: Oven, woman with moon and man with sun on the head. *Mutus Liber,* Pierre Savouret (ed.), La Rochelle, 1677[1], plate 13. 67
Fig. 11: The alchemical oven. Theophrastus Paracelsus and Gerhardus Dorneus, *Aurora Thesaurusque Philosophorum* (1577), p. 137. Libr. of the Basle Univ. 67

Part II

Fig. 12 Overview of the 42 pict. of *Muṣḥaf aṣ-ṣuwar.* 75
Fig. 13 First series of pictures of *Muṣḥaf aṣ-ṣuwar.* 76-7
Fig. 14: Second picture series of *Muṣḥaf aṣ-ṣuwar.* 82-3
Fig. 15-16: Third picture series of *Muṣḥaf aṣ-ṣuwar.* 86-9

Fig. 17: fol. 38a, Zosimos, *Muṣḥaf aṣ-ṣuwar.* 100
Fig. 18: Three-headed Hermes. Muḥammad Abū al-Qāsim, *Kitāb al-Aqālīm as-sabaᶜa*, Ms Add 25724 fol. 17b. © British Library, London. 101
Fig. 19: fol. 102b, Zosimos, *Muṣḥaf aṣ-ṣuwar.* 102
Fig. 20: Two human beings, holding each other. Muḥammad Abū al-Qāsim, *Kitāb al-Aqālīm as-sabaᶜa*, Ms Add 25724 fol. 12b. © British Library, London. 103

Fig. 21: fol. 196a, Zosimos, *Muṣḥaf aṣ-ṣuwar*. 104
Fig. 22: Three winged humanlike beings carrying a lying body. Muḥammad Abū al-Qāsim, *Kitāb al-Aqālīm as-sabaᶜa*, Ms Add 25724 fol. 18a., © British Library, London. 105
Fig. 23: fol. 205a, Zosimos, *Muṣḥaf aṣ-ṣuwar*. 106
Fig. 24: Zosimos and Theosebeia holding six human beings together. Muḥammad Abū al-Qāsim, *Kitāb al-Aqālīm as-sabaᶜa*, Ms Add 25724, fol. 18b. © British Library, London. 107
Fig. 25: Left: Examples of eyes in the aspective way. Hathor giving ankh-sign to Pharaoh Thutmosis IV, © Th. Abt.
Right, above: Aspective view of Zosimos' eye. Detail of Zosimos, *Muṣḥaf aṣ-ṣuwar* fol. 99a.
Right below, Detail of *Kitāb ad-Diryāq* of Pseudo-Galen, Paris Bibliothèque Nationale, Ms Arabe 2964, p. 22 in: R. Ettinghausen, *Arabic Painting*, p. 84. 108
Fig. 26: Left: *The Egyptian Amduat*, ed. by E. Hornung and Th. Abt, Zurich 2007, p. 200.
Right: Detail of *Muṣḥaf aṣ-ṣuwar* fol. 196a. 109
Fig. 27: Great Vision of M. Ibn Umail. *Al-Māʾ al waraqī wa-l-arḍ an-naǧmīya.* Topkapı Sarayı Ahmet III (Istanbul) 2075. 110
Fig. 28: Acacia tree. © George Castel. 131
Fig. 29: Representation of the alembic. Left: Codex Parisinus Graecus fol. 81v; Right: *Muṣḥaf aṣ-ṣuwar,* fol. 153a. 134

Part III

Figures 30-72 represent the 41 Pictures of the *Muṣḥaf aṣ-ṣuwar*. Only the corresponding book within the *Muṣḥaf aṣ-ṣuwar* and the folio-numbers are given.

Fig. 30:	fol. 38a	(Picture of the 2nd Book, 1st picture)	211
Fig. 31:	fol. 64b	(Picture of the 3rd Book, 2nd picture)	264
Fig. 32:	fol. 86b-87a	(5th Book, 1st picture)	308-9
Fig. 33:	fol. 89b	(5th Book, 2nd picture)	314
Fig. 34:	fol. 97b	(5th Book, 3rd picture)	330
Fig. 35:	fol. 99a	(5th Book, 4th picture)	333
Fig. 36:	fol. 100a	(5th Book, 5th picture)	335
Fig. 37:	fol. 101b	(5th Book, 6th picture)	338
Fig. 38:	fol. 102b	(5th Book, 7th picture)	340
Fig. 39:	fol. 103a	(5th Book, 8th picture)	341
Fig. 40:	fol. 104a	(5th Book, 9th picture)	343

Fig. 41:	fol. 105b	(5th Book, 10th picture)	346
Fig. 42:	fol. 106b	(5th Book, 11th picture)	348
Fig. 43:	fol. 128b	(6th Book, 1st picture)	392
Fig. 44:	fol. 134b	(7th Book, 2nd picture)	404
Fig. 45:	fol. 136b-137a	(7th Book, 3rd picture)	408-9
Fig. 46:	fol. 138b, 139a	(7th Book, 4th picture)	412-3
Fig. 47:	fol. 140a	(7th Book, 5th picture)	415
Fig. 48:	fol. 141a	(7th Book, 6th picture)	417
Fig. 49:	fol. 142a	(7th Book, 7th picture)	419
Fig. 50:	fol. 143b-144a	(7th Book, 8th picture)	422-3
Fig. 51:	fol. 145a	(7th Book, 9th picture)	425
Fig. 52:	fol. 145b	(7th Book, 10th picture)	426
Fig. 53:	fol. 146b	(7th Book, 11th picture)	428
Fig. 54:	fol. 147a	(7th Book, 12th picture)	429
Fig. 55:	fol. 147b	(is to be deleted)	430
Fig. 56:	fol. 148a	(7th Book, 13th picture)	431
Fig. 57:	fol. 149a	(7th Book, 14th picture)	433
Fig. 58:	fol. 149b	(is to be deleted)	434
Fig. 59:	fol. 150a	(7th Book, 15th picture)	435
Fig. 60:	fol. 151a	(7th Book, 16th picture)	437
Fig. 61:	fol. 151b	(7th Book, 17th picture)	438
Fig. 62:	fol. 152a	(7th Book, 18th picture)	439
Fig. 63:	fol. 153a	(7th Book, 19th picture)	441
Fig. 64:	fol. 154a	(7th Book, 20th picture)	443
Fig. 65:	fol. 154b-155a	(7th Book, 21st picture)	444-6
Fig. 66:	fol. 157a	(7th Book, 22nd picture)	449
Fig. 67:	fol. 171b-172a	(Picture of the 8th Book)	478-9
Fig. 68:	fol. 191b	(Picture of the 9th Book)	518
Fig. 70:	fol. 196a	(Picture of the 10th Book)	527
Fig. 71:	fol. 205a	(Picture of the 11th Book)	545
Fig. 72:	fol. 210b	(Picture of the 12th Book)	556

3. General Index

As the content of the book is rather obscure and difficult to understand, the index is intentionally very detailed. Thus words that may seem unimportant were also listed, the aim being to help readers with different interests and backgrounds who might wish to look up a quote or search for a certain subject.

The indicated word may either appear within the text and/ or in the footnotes.
– (n) indicates a noun
– (vb) indicates a verb

The letters of Arabic transcripts are integrated into the English alphabetical order

–A–

Ābālīnūs 580
abarakānūn 475
Abdera, Democritus of 27
Abīsiqūs 549
above; *see also rise; ascend; go up* 79, 122
– and below 122, 163-4, 198, 246, 287
–, the 163, 198, 291
absorb/ absorption 144, 152, 268, 278, 367, 486, 500, 564, 570, 572
–, abšimīt/ pure water/ glue/ kohl 287, 395, 353, 384, 395, 420
–, body absorbs 249, 531, 564, 574
–, copper ...s fiery mercury 567
–, fire ..s remedy 486
– glue of gold 572
– gum 491, 321, 525
–, mix … and mercury of cinnabar 235
– moisture 529, 531, 559, 561, 570, 575
–, red 248
– water 249, 278, 485, 489, 558, 531, 561, 570, 572, 574
– water of copper 569
–, white/ make white 541, 548
–, vapour of 247
–, yellowness of 527
Abt, Theodor 8, 14, 19, 31, 39-40, 59, 80, 85, 109-10, 116-7, 127
Abū al-Qāsim al–Iraqi 92-5, 99, 101, 103, 105, 107, 126, 138-5
Ābullūn (Apollonius) 229, 247, 390, 402, 462-3, 473-4
–, book of 320
–, statement of 229, 402
abundance/ abundant 144, 167, 293, 345, 367, 507, 537, 548
Abydos 9
acacia/ ascunia/ ašqunīa 36, 55, 125-6, 130, 151, 172, 213, 231, 258, 293, 317, 374, 378, 389, 394-5, 425, 470-1, 540
– and/ as sulphur 447, 470
–, acacian stone 231
–, gum of 128-31, 172-3, 213, 242, 302, 468
–, thorns of 55, 126, 128, 134, 172
– tree 131, 128
accept 154, 156, 181, 192, 217, 231, 233, 252-3, 268, 287, 319, 321, 466, 492, 498, 504, 535, 541, 548
– statement 328, 332, 334
accompany 98, 552
accord/ accordance 323, 401, 439, 520
– (not) in 152, 299, 313, 320, 323, 455, 457, 520
– with nature 446, 474
– with lead/ sulphur 299
accumulate 157-8
accuse 257, 339, 350, 432
achieve (vb); *see also attain*
– aim/ goal 278, 317, 494
–, beginning as achievement 65, 202
– knowledge 477
– making of poison 286B
– nothing 214, 564
– work/ success 85, 152, 171-2, 241, 450, 490, 516
act(s)/ acted 188, 249
– badly/ corruptly 215, 217
–s of Thomas (n) 90

action(s) 122, 176, 193, 243, 462, 458, 498, 577
Adam 92, 122, 203
– and Eve 359
–, son of 145
adapt (vb) 119
–, adapter 26
–, adaptation(s) 26, 68, 99, 118-9, 136
address/ addressee 20-1
adept 39, 44-5, 59, 63-5, 67-8, 81, 90, 95, 130, 135, 138
– and soror mystica 59, 64-5, 67
–, death of 84
adhere 160, 395, 485
adoration 432-3
adulteration 146
advice/ advise 98, 146, 219, 286, 365, 465
afflict (vb)/ afflictions 336, 340, 406, 439, 447-8, 495
afraid 150, 219, 257, 289-90, 312, 370, 433, 447, 454, 474, 495, 522, 525, 579
– of fire/ burning/ water 209, 320, 474, 510, 520
– of God 297
–, not ... of 260, 283, 297, 312, 510, 551, 559
Afrāsus 312
Africanus 194, 204, 228, 231
afterlife 20, 40, 110
–, Books for the Afterlife; *see also Amduat* 80, 109-10, 113, 123, 127, 136
again and again; *see also repeatedly* 173, 364
Agathodaimon 12, 23-4, 37, 149, 190, 195, 204, 207, 216, 246, 253, 255, 265-67, 275, 286, 288, 303, 344, 349, 355, 377, 379, 380, 462, 530-2, 561-2, 579
–, books of 399, 465
–, student of 531, 579
agreement 390, 485
– agree 267, 396, 483, 539
– disagreement 63, 418
–, in 173, 188, 310, 312, 356, 418, 457
–, in … with composition 427
aim; *see also goal* 384, 477, 560
– of alchemy/ of work 24, 28-9, 45, 192, 494
– of pounding 501
–, single body as 193
air 24, 166, 218, 223, 481, 552
– and smoke 228
–, earth enters into 228
–, escape/ up into 298, 461, 436, 505, 514
–, fire and 228, 370-1, 520-1
–, fire, water, … and earth 222, 359, 515
–, heat of 236
– -holes 551
–, imprison earth in 228
–, inhale soul from 521
–, mix (vb)/ mixture of 63, 221, 524
–, mix … with dry and moist 218
–, nourishment for 218, 223
–, part of 154
–, rise/ up into 31, 48, 218, 509
–, unite with 334
–, warmth of 524
–, water becomes/ into 370-1, 520
–, water of/ water-air 382, 464, 489
airy 160, 164, 298, 436, 489, 502, 505, 509
– and moist water 161
–, put … into sea 382
– spirit 362
– water 291, 292, 382, 538, 565
Akhmīm 9-10, 121
alabaster 24, 40
– and body 173
– as lime 41, 575
–, black … as blackness 561
–, like 48, 244
–, red 561
–, rock like 300
–, symbols of 117
–, white 561
Al-āsārdus 28, 523
al-Azharī, Muḥammad ibn Mūsā 20
alchemical
– book/ texts/ manuscripts/ documents/ literature 7, 12, 17, 22, 24, 30, 58, 60, 90-1, 94, 97-9, 113, 116, 118, 125, 137-8
– images/pictures 12, 65, 74, 85, 94-5
– process 24, 41, 74, 80, 90-1, 98, 101, 113, 117
– symbols/ symbolism 33, 92-5
– teachings 81, 137
– tradition 28, 68, 97
– work 22, 26, 28-9, 35, 39, 44-5, 54, 63-4, 80-1, 84, 134, 137-8
alchemist(s) 11, 22, 40, 47, 54, 61, 64, 67, 81, 92, 94, 112, 120, 122, 135

– and soror mystica 20, 59, 64, 137
–, Arab/ Muslim 26, 68, 119-20, 138
–, Egyptian 9, 136
–, Greek; *for Les Alchimistes Grecs see book(s)* 45, 49, 96
–, Latin 12, 31, 59, 95
alchemy; *see also art; work* 5, 12, 25, 44, 65, 80, 84, 93-5, 99, 122-3, 126, 128, 136, 138
–, aim of 39
– and Pharaonic culture/ knowledge 11, 29, 54, 80, 99, 108-10, 113, 123, 127, 136
–, Arabic 5, 9-11, 13, 17-8, 25, 39, 59, 69, 95, 121, 136
–, Greek 9, 17, 109, 122
–, Greek and Arabic 6, 59
–, guide of 31
–, historians of 36, 55, 60, 138
–, knowledge of; *see also knowledge* 11, 22
–, Latin 33-4, 41, 59, 61, 68, 81, 130, 136
–, manuscripts on; *see also texts* 20
–, master of 133
–, opus alchemicum 10, 44-5, 64
–, practice 10
–, religious-symbolic 26, 35, 68-9, 80, 95
–, symbolic 12, 68, 122
–, text on 17
alembic(s) 134, 440, 496
Alexandria(n) 10, 20, 90, 96, 123, 136, 269, 509
alien 167, 534-5
alive 29, 32, 36, 182, 285, 288, 342, 374, 536, 580
all
– and one; *see also one and many* 224, 266, 269, 324, 326, 373
– things 324
Allah; *see also god(s)* 44
allegory/ allegories; *see also allude; analogy; symbol* 90-5, 97
–, allegorical 85
– Merlini 90-1
allusion(s)/ allude; *see also allegory; analogy; symbol; veil* 91, 93, 140, 148-49, 203, 227, 273, 303, 310, 315, 327, 358, 474, 556
Almighty; *see also God* 480
almond, gum of 401
alter (vb) 261
alum 147, 288, 375, 389, 468, 490, 501, 540, 549
– and gum 321, 470
– and tin 250
– and wool 271, 317, 324, 510
– as broth 574
–, copper, sulphur, salt and 497
–, cracked 368
–, Egyptian alum 489
– extracts moisture 297
–, herb, water and 475
–, flour of barley, … and water 504
– from beginning 574
–, glue, natron, … and blood 382
– leaves glue not 475
–, mercury, … and dye 452
–, mix dye with … and water 452
–, mixed 475
–, moist 321
–, rounded 581
–, salt, …, natron, lime and makrasīūn 325
–, salt, …, white lead, polished earth and living water 395
–, solidify 475
–, treat (not) (with) 317-8, 321, 323-24, 389
–, urine, (natron), … and water (of lime) 323-24
–, vinegar, sea shell and 299
–, wash with water of alum 507
–, water composed with 552
–, water of 284, 507
–, white sulphur, … and broth 497
– with mercury 378
alumy 453, 542, 573
–, first/ second making 573-4
–, making 294, 389, 451-53, 541, 573-4
–, purple 473
–, water makes 170, 552
Amail/ Amṯiāīl 358
amalgamate/ amalgamation 155, 248, 325, 578
– stone 564
AMBIX (journal) 10, 18, 73, 91, 94, 121, 133
Amduat; *see also Afterlife* 19, 39-40, 80, 109
ameliorate/ amelioration 6, 13, 162, 178, 197, 290, 470, 540

amount 49, 68, 248, 323, 406, 458, 471, 503, 512, 568
–, balanced 158
–, equal 265, 442, 468
– of sulphur 407
– of wisdom 142
amplification 13, 92, 94, 138, 463
–, amplify 95, 117
Amṯiāīl/ Amail 358
amulets 370
analogize 359, 436
analogy/ analogies; *see also allude, disguising, similes, names, veiling,* 29, 33, 39, 46-7, 61, 63-4, 85, 90, 147, 158, 177, 182, 194, 202, 212, 221, 241, 273, 290, 327, 361, 374, 387, 502, 520, 537, 539
– for (4) four natures/ periods of time 222, 522
– about operation 387
– and secret 320
– and truth 147, 165
–, description/ every thing/ things as 153 281, 370
– for composition 64, 221
– for dye 406, 503
– for operation 166, 524, 537
– for/ of/ to work 153, 161, 174-75, 228, 318, 370, 438, 463, 480, 508
– of (similar) things 178, 281
–, ponder over 387
–, truth of 174
analyse/ analysis 59, 81, 110, 351
anāgālīs 187
anchorites 11
androdamus 129, 199, 377, 386, 451, 456, 483, 578
–, operation of 248
–, turn white/ red 578
–, water of 208
androgynous 130
angel(s) 92, 217, 462
– and daughters 22
–, names of 462
anger 154, 216, 315, 327, 329
– angry 56, 197, 242, 315, 327, 329
angles, (stone with) three 74, 81, 223, 507
Anīlūtis 234
anima; *see also archetype of female principle; side, feminine* 39
animal(s); *see also lower; body; name of animals: bird; bitch; bull; cow; dog; donkey; fish; mare; scarab; serpent; snake; snail; wolf* 64, 130, 208, 283, 356, 359
– eight-legged 290
–, froth of every 418
– -humans 31
– of the sea 218
– -shape 32
– tail and paws 31
Ankara 6, 8, 13
ankh-sign 108
annoyance 577
– annoyed 155, 275, 406, 455, 508, 511
answer (vb/ n); *see also ask; question; statement*
–, clear/ good 176, 262, 328
–, differentiated 115
– not! 154-5, 160, 165, 224, 242, 310, 327, 365
–, question-and-answer (dialogue) 18, 51, 58, 62, 97, 111, 115, 117, 119-20
–, symbolic(ally) 19, 53, 484
Anṭalīnūs (sages of) 471
anthology 47, 99, 315
anthropos 31-2, 39-40
antimony 272, 287, 367
– and magnesia are one 272
–, cast … and etesian 376
– etesian and copper 376
–, talqine 395
Antiquity 18, 69
Ānṭiqūs 486
Antonius, St. … Eremita 11
ants 147, 509
Apep/ Apophis 48, 127
Aphrodite 305, 312
Apollo; *see also Ābullūn* 113, 320, 390
Apollonius; *see Ābullūn*
Apophis; *see Apep*
apparatus; *see also illustration* 64, 67, 99, 134
appear; *see also essence, in* 5-7, 17-8, 57, 80, 90, 110, 114, 118-9, 142, 155, 157, 162, 167, 169, 208, 216, 256, 268, 279, 322, 532, 549, 557
–, blackness 144, 248, 446, 469, 508-9, 566, 576

–, blood 161
–, colour(s) 33, 37, 176, 190, 199-200, 246, 253, 270, 275, 294, 297, 315, 326, 331, 342, 372, 452, 499, 519, 528, 550, 552, 554, 557, 561, 571, 573, 577-9
–, copper 547
– dead 480
–, disappear; *see disappear*
–, dye 302
–, error 181
–, flower(s) 286, 492, 525
–, light 295, 305
–, man 216
–, moon-light 279
–, pearls 167, 492
–, pregnancy 530
–, problems 516
–, purple 167
–, redness 277, 491, 558, 560
–, sand 529
–, science 25, 155
–, secret 57, 157, 166, 373, 475
–, shadow...s (not); *see also disappear, shadow* 369, 374
–, snow 570
–, spirit 33, 35, 332, 336
–, truth 148
–, whiteness 499, 542, 566
–, work …(to people) 164, 176, 219
– yellow 499
appearance(s) 31, 192, 276, 282, 489, 475, 493
–, (1) one in/ is (1) one 439, 457
–, cast 376
–, different appearances 31
–, gold 376
–, lunar 160
–, outer 151, 169, 192, 222, 373, 397, 462, 475, 554, 574
–, red 373
–, weak in 169
–, white in (outer) 151, 370, 373, 458, 549
apple(s) 249
appropriate 33, 331-2, 336, 440
april 366
Aqrūnis/ aqrūnis 305, 569, 572
–, and Ars 305
Aquarius 494
Āquasṭus/ āqusṭus 473, 320
aqzāl (higher quality of gold) 209, 280, 295, 373, 410, 490
– and spittle of moon 321
– as redness 493
– -gold 245, 246, 261, 266, 280, 373, 410, 538, 548
–, gold into aqzal-gold 528, 538, 558
– -gold, spittle and mercury 500
– -gold, return 528
– -gold, turn into 245, 363-4
– into purple gold 528
–, melted 493
–, solid 493
–, spittle of moon and mercury 472
Arabic; *for Arabic Zosimos see Zosimos Arabus* 7, 12-3, 17-8, 20-1, 24-7, 47, 54, 59, 61, 93-4, 98-9, 110-1, 113, 117, 132, 135-6, 140
– alchemy 6, 9-11, 13, 17-8, 25, 39, 59, 69, 95, 121, 136
– compilation 25, 73, 114
– early Arabic alchemy 10, 121
–, (from) Greek and/ translated into Arabic 25, 59, 68, 96
–, Greek, Syriac and … alchemy 6
–, Hermetica 10
– literature 18-19, 26
–, manuscripts 11, 58, 133, 137
– origin 54, 58
– text 6, 10, 17, 21, 24, 61, 132
– translation 8, 27, 68
arcane substance 130
archetype(s); *see also anima; moon; self; sun* 32, 59
–, archetypal 39, 54, 59, 64-5, 67, 92, 112, 118
–, integrate 32
– of divine/ demonic 32
– of female/ male principle 32, 93
– of self 44, 92-3
– of sun/ moon 37, 39
–, possession by 32, 39
– projection of 44
Ares; *see Aries*
argument(s) 7, 21, 25, 54, 58, 59, 74, 96-8 113-5, 118-9, 120, 124-5, 131, 133, 135-6
–, key 125, 131
Aries/ Ares/ Ars/ Mars 58-9, 281, 292, 305, 311-3, 450

–, and Aqrunis 305
Aristotle 195
Arkeoloji Müzesi 13
Armenian 503
Arnold, Dieter 130
Ars; *see Aries*
arsenic 141, 183, 235, 283, 468, 500-501, 574
– and female 233
– arsenic, sandarach (and body of magnesia / sulphur/ sulphury bodies/ kohl) 325, 411, 418, 468, 505
–, arsenics 349
– as sulphurs 467
–, cloud of 288
–, dissolve 548
–, flower of 289
–, golden 190, 191
– has no body 190
– is male 235
–, mercury from/ of 226, 416, 421, 550
–, mercury from/ of … and sandarach 353, 416, 421
art (= alchemy); *see work; see also Book of the Keys of the Art; Book of the Seven Climes ... called the Art* 11, 62, 97, 133
– of picture interpretation 12, 31
–, teaching of; *see also teaching of Zosimos* 74, 543
Artis auriferae 59, 61, 68, 90
ascends, water 492
ascetic 29
ascoria/ ascunia/ ašqunīa; *see acacia*
Asfīḫās/ Asfīḫānus; *see also Africanus* 166, 228, 231
ash; *see also ashes* 483, 506
– and salt 385
–, despise not 487
–, dry 493
–, extract from 483, 504
– first, separate moisture from 511
–, flowers of gold, …, glassy natron, Egyptian vinegar 504
– of firewood 515
– of natures 515
– of sea 509
– of sulphur 501
– of sun 509
–, pyrite into 486
–, return 504
–, soak … in moisture 480
–, turn (body/ natures) into 480-81, 483, 486, 496, 521
–, water of … of firewood 507
–, white 515
ashes 36, 49, 167, 198, 254, 339, 459, 461, 474, 480, 511, 539, 566
–, (2) two 254
– and gum 388
– and poison 168
– become mature 489
–, burn 570
–, colour(s) of 316, 471, 499
–, come out from 511
– conceal spirits 511
–, dry, dead, soulless 283
– extract dye by 515
–, extract waters/ moisture/ everything from 168, 232, 253, 461, 511, 566
–, extracted from ashes 533
–, heat of/ hot 189, 323, 548
–, (heat) turns into 36, 56, 127, 157
– incombustble 515
–, mixed 173, 168
– of the bath 568
–, pure 4, 300
–, purify water of its 509
–, red 282
–, rust from 283
–, searched-for secret 580
–, soaked in moisture 480
–, turn bodies/ thick part/ male/ natures into 235, 336, 339, 476, 515, 534-35, 563, 566, 568
–, water of 284
Asīdā; *see also Isis* 404
ask (vb) 111, 121
– about work 351
– Disqīus 151
– me! 29, 33, 37
– me not! 36, 331, 336, 339, 341, 358
– questions 33, 37, 142, 331, 342, 482, 484
–, spirit asks spirit 33, 331-2
asparagus 201, 374
aspect 98, 108, 134, 171, 179, 521, 575-6
–, divine 31, 33, 67

–, female 41
–, hideous 32
–, material/ spiritual 33, 44
– of body of magnesia 368
– of iron 234
– of it, explain/give me an 128, 180, 206, 237-8, 368, 403, 405, 465, 494, 510, 519
– of measures (of fire) 516, 519, 525
– of mercuries 403
– of psychological process 30
– of second work 526
– of stone 128, 172, 237
– of truth 405
–, projected 33
aspective 108
ašqunīā; *see acacia*
assimilated 28
association(s) 10, 521
–, historical 126
–, necessary 93, 95, 126, 131
assumption 54, 58, 85, 111, 135
asṭām 361
astral 454
– soil 395
attach 11, 57, 127
attack (vb) 47, 130
attain; *see also achieve* 178, 212, 214-215, 260, 317, 477, 522, 523, 560, 579
– science 293
attention 12, 213, 299
–, pay 23, 143, 182, 242
–, pay not 192, 198, 206, 209, 294, 542
attitude 28-9, 31, 44
–, conscious 29
–, magic 21
–, materialistic 21
–, new 134
–, right , 149
attract (vb) 385
–, attraction 118, 137
–, attraction of iron 290
– flowers of gold and vinegar 504
– nature by nature 291
Atum 80
Aurora 67
authentic 21, 91, 97, 110-1, 113, 115-6, 133, 137
–, authenticity 19, 21, 73, 133, 137
– Greek texts 24
– works/ letter/ book/ text of Zosimos 9, 17, 20, 24, 73
author(s)/ authorship 9, 11-2, 18, 52, 59, 67-9, 93, 95, 115-6, 118, 138
–, anonymous/ unknown 117, 135
–, Arabc/ Islamic 96, 113, 132-3, 136
–, authorities; *see also Democritus; Maria; Agathodaimon* 9, 24, 27, 95
–, authorship 24
–, Muslim author(ship) 119-21, 124
– of Mushaf as-suwar/ book/ text/ 73, 112-3, 135, 137
– pre-Islamic 113
autumn 236
available 345, 358
awake 48, 55, 331
axe(s) 216, 458
al-Azhari, Y…suf ibn Mu®ammadibn M…s¡ (copyist) 20

–B–

baby 387
back (n); *for verb see hold back; keep back; put back; return back; throw back; life, come back to* 109, 141, 433
–, bring back to start of work 180
– of viper 78
Badīsios; *see* Butīṭus
badly 528
badness 240
Baghdad 18, 133
bag(s) 473, 488
–, threefolded 472
–, triangular 470, 472-3
balance 112, 230, 263-264, 276
– out (vb) 26, 78-9
–, balanced 158, 229, 276
–, balances 79
Balgus 52
ball 389
Bālīnūs 580
bank 47
balsam 572
barley 358

–, flower of 475, 504, 512
barn 122
Barmaq 495
base/ basis 17, 44, 58, 74, 251, 262, 357, 390, 395, 488
–, enduring 555
–, first burning as 497
– of all 27, 166
– of operations 521
– of the matter 525
– of translations 27
– of work 22, 237, 390, 395, 414, 497, 503, 511, 560
bath 157, 318, 356, 387, 486, 568
bathhouse 507
beans 512
bear 492
beast(s) 196, 322
beat with iron 458
beautiful 178, 223, 228, 233, 256, 310, 369, 385, 389, 390, 451, 512, 566
beauty 55, 240, 270, 305, 310, 318, 362, 471, 492
bed 306, 313
bee, honey 154
beetroot 492
beginning; *see also origin* 41, 61, 141, 144, 158, 177, 202 210, 224, 231, 236, 239, 253, 258, 296, 349, 354, 360, 459, 523, 561, 576
– of (1st) first book 19
– of (1st) first millenium 17
– of (2nd) second book 29
– of book(s)/ 3rd/ 4th/ ....12th book 29, 37, 75, 79-81, 93, 119, 212, 264, 276, 306, 341-342, 349, 402, 414, 477, 544, 546, 556
–, alum from the 574
– and end 187, 537
– as achievement 202
– begin 224, 491
–, degree of burning at 579
– of 8, 54, 109, 116
– of (alchemical/ this) work 32, 84, 128, 171, 181, 183, 187, 189, 192, 213, 229, 250, 287-8, 316, 361, 368, 372, 424, 458, 462, 487, 541, 579, 456, 490, 540, 561
– of burning 523
– of chapter 61, 526, 543
– of composition 170, 240, 271, 304, 452
– of cooking 220, 282, 560
– of dye 490
– of matter 238, 534
– of mixing 23, 149, 289, 537, 570
– of mixture 178, 522
– of operation 173, 194, 249, 284, 486-487, 551, 569
– of second book 29
– of second composition 570
– of secret 561
– of soul's separation from body 322
– of statement 301, 325, 361
– of talk 344
– of way 531
–, picture at 75
being 184, 552, 566
–, (3) three branches as one living 84
–, (3) three-headed 30
–, come into; *see existence, come into*
– human 33, 44, 46, 59, 67
– large 30
belief, disbelief 345
believe 184, 248, 431
–, cease to ... (in work) 522
– disbelieve 237, 242
– unbeliever 336
belly 56, 177, 477
–, enter 305
–, green 141
beloved 29, 39, 55, 117, 537, 143
below 376
– and/ to above 122, 163, 198, 246, 287
beneficial 63, 129, 175, 177, 222, 240, 303, 340, 344, 456, 469, 498, 537, 566, 570, 579
–, beneficience 327, 339, 416
– dye 459
–, red copper is not 499
benefit(s) 19, 57, 62, 143, 148, 155, 163, 169, 179, 190, 198, 207-208, 215, 221, 231, 237, 239-40, 268, 279, 303, 313, 315, 321, 323-4, 341, 365, 368, 387, 390, 394-396, 432, 446, 450, 498, 499, 502, 504, 523, 554
– increases 502, 548
– of knowing 22, 393
–, threefold with 351, 360, 373, 461, 464, 473, 475

– with many names 148, 170, 173, 187, 410, 451, 482
Berlecamp, Persis 110
Bersīūs 195
Bernett, Charles 8
Berthelot, Marcellin 9, 17-8, 21-2, 27, 58, 66, 93-4, 96-7, 123-4, 133
betrayal 334, 339
beyond (n); see also unconscious, Nun 91, 94-5, 130-1, 136
Bible 10
Bidīsīos 427, 432, 557-578, 572
big; *see also dream, big; Theosebeia, huge* 31, 47, 64, 79, 149, 180, 192, 295, 300, 367, 406, 492, 522
– quantity 171
– vessel/ furnace 267, 269, 406, 568
biggest 180, 476
– nature 570
bile(s) 47, 317
Bilbis/ Bīlīs/ Bīlis; *see also Neilos* 21, 143, 217, 336
bind (vb)/ binding 141f, 526
–, fugitive spirit 46
–, unbind 222, 224
bird(s) 51, 64, 79, 109, 256, 369, 372, 513
–, (2) two 263, 517
–, (3) three 79, 263
–, eggs of 370
–, green/ red/ yellow/ yellow-green 263, 517
–, serpent- 73, 109
birth 54, 173, 305, 311, 359
–, birthplace 514
–, first 252
–, give (to) 55, 166, 168, 176, 232, 252, 565
– of thoughts 305
– of work 356
Bīr Zaibaq 129, 447, 451, 495
bitch 192
bitter 237, 381
–, bitters/ bitterness 239, 254-5
Bīūn 461
black 31, 36-7, 164, 215, 228, 259, 270, 282, 303, 316, 318, 323, 339, 344, 355, 383, 401, 436, 451, 459, 554, 580
– alabaster as blackness 561
– and white 296, 506
– and yellow 166
–, (āsqūnīa makes) body 447, 470
–, blacker 510
– burning 350
– copper 447
– cow 400
– dye 248, 316, 455, 495, 510
– earth 237, 386, 580
– filings (of copper) 440, 508
–, get 456
–, head 339
– Indian 471
– inside 247
– intensity of making 456
– lead 144, 156, 216, 289, 326, 350, 353, 366, 377-379, 381, 523, 554
– lead and/ as (body of) magnesia 376-377
– lead, purified, dyes, is dyed, becomes complete 554
–, make copper 216, 315, 355, 440, 470
–, make silver 283, 466-467
–, make the red 561
–, make/ turn/ become 144, 170, 195, 233, 248, 291-2, 297, 317-8, 321-3, 354, 357, 364, 376, 456, 509-10
– mercury 458
–, purply-black 512
– -red 31, 568
– (to) silver 144, 205, 350
– spirit 402
– stone 367
– sulphur 568
–, sulphur makes 396, 446
–, the ... whose inside is 342
– thing(s) 317, 522
– turbidity 520
–, turn chrysocolla 530
– water 145, 493, 578
blacken 183
– body 509
blackness 129, 144, 175, 205, 216, 282, 364, 456, 470, 537, 570, 580
– (dis)appears 129, 248, 292-293, 357, 454, 482, 508, 531, 535, 538, 564, 566, 576, 578
–, appeared 469
– as black alabaster 561
– as litharge 446
–, colours changes to 571

– conceals whiteness 509
– covers 282-283, 356, 360, 363, 368, 507, 523, 565, 576
–, extract (redness/ whiteness by/ from) 446, 480, 509
– extracts redness 469
–, first 446, 469
– from nature of litharge 509
–, hidden 229
– leave 317
– makes peace 470
–, mixing of 236
– of copper 167, 216
– of kohl 283, 566
– of murderess(es) of husband(s) 129, 564
– of silver 216, 282, 461, 566
– of sun 482
– of the water/ water of 206, 559
–, purification of 167
– reconciles 509
–, remove 168, 283, 565
Bladel, Kevin van 99
blame (vb) 143, 155, 158, 194, 227, 236, 242, 282, 289, 336, 355, 370, 386, 410, 420, 524, 528, 559
blaze of fire 250
bleach (vb) 385, 394, 387, 397, 504
–, bleacher 387
– of lead-copper 22
–, wash, … and purify 503, 511
bless 142, 351
–, blessed water 28
blessing(s) 20, 55, 157, 165, 212, 215, 266, 273, 344, 353, 406
–, Muslim 20
–s of world 484
blind 208
–, blinded 400
–, blindness 154, 196, 257, 358
blond 356-358
blood 47, 57, 127, 157, 160, 180, 216, 290-291, 302, 305, 322, 352, 375, 387, 436, 460, 481, 485, 520, 554
– appears 161
– become 48, 300
–, burnt (vb) 559, 564, 567, 570, 572
–, canals of 173
–, colour of 387
– decomposes/ feeds sperm 174
– dries up 57, 127, 157
– gets cooked 173
–, glue, natron, alum and 382
– meets blood 387, 485
–, mix with sperm 387
–, moisture of 539
– of male 485
– of womb 485
–, origin is 173, 485
– rejoices in sperm 387
– shining 367, 570
–, turn dyed like 491
–, turn into whales 302-3
bloom 166
blossom 210, 216, 220, 223, 255, 393
–, colours 258
blow (at (vb)) 48, 278, 292, 469
–s, spirit 278
blue 141, 306
– herb 471
– water 79
bodies 50-51, 129142, 175, 179, 190-191, 193, 195, 200, 222-3, 246, 252, 273-275, 279, 281, 286, 290, 292, 301, 303, 378, 393, 397, 421, 454, 456, 460-461, 471, 481, 514, 530, 543, 551
–, (1) one body and all 410
–, (2) two 195, 274
–, (3) three 265, 274
–, (4) four 184-185, 195, 200, 225, 269, 273-4, 298, 369, 386, 410
– all bodies 207
–, alive 288
–, all 301
– and blackness of water 559
– and fugitive(s) (natures) 277, 539
– and natures 192, 277
– and no body/ non-bodies/ not body 162, 249, 254, 258, 393, 483-4, 513, 533
– and water 362
– are from the earth 175
– become spirits 539
–, burn 50-1, 286, 480, 496, 515
–, burning of 52, 170, 288, 515
–, cast 261
–, change 482
–, cling 285

–, conceal in 303, 477
–, copper, iron, tin, lead 398, 468
–, crown of 563
–, dead 130, 229
–, destroy 498
–, dissolve/ dissolving of 228, 237, 462
–, dye/ dye of 181, 200, 302, 538, 294
–, dyed by tin 460
–, dyes/ spirits and flowers of hard 513
– enter composition 303
–, escape/ leave not 467
–, extract dye from 514
–, extract from 49, 305, 476
–, extract mercury from 261, 542
–, extract silver from 410
–, extract spirits from 190, 496
–, flowers as spirits of bodies 513
–, flowers of 283, 301
–, fragmented 288
– get burnt 288
–, hard 226, 369, 514, 522
–, head of 483
–, hurt 352
– into dust 559
– into mercuries 427
– into non-bodies 477
– into spirits 521
–, joint 521
–, knowledge of 461
–, many 201
–, master of 529, 558
–, mercuries of 430, 543
–, mercury coagulates with hard 287
–, mercury extract from 543
–, mix with 181, 398
–, mix not stone with 237
–, name 267, 551-552, 558
–, natures of 201
– of magnesia, mix ... with mercury 580
–, other 193
–, part of 166
–, penetrate 570
–, preserve 190
–, put … in moisture 559
–, rejected 514
–, relax 318
–, remain 398
–, separate … and earth 394, 395
–, separate spirits of 476
–, souls come out of 515
–, submerge into/ into 538, 546
–, sulphury 468
– take on spirits 562
–, (turn into) non–bodies 162, 254, 258, 393, 398, 533
–, take dyeing spirits from 521
–, thick/ subtle part of (hard) 395, 514
–, torturer enters 192
–, turn ... burnt 282
–, turn … into ash 496
–, turn … into fugitives 567
–, turn … into mercuries 427
–, turn … into non-bodies 172, 253-4
–, turn … into spirits 567
–, turn spiritual … into fire 482
–, unite(d) 52, 424
–, various 166
–, wash 247
–, whiten, soften 301
–, with/ without 181, 398
– without natures 397
–, work on 543
bodily 24, 29, 31-2, 35, 66, 81, 91-2
body 31-2, 50, 154, 184, 217, 227, 235, 246, 249, 267, 288, 302, 323, 350-351, 355, 357, 364-365, 369, 371, 378, 396, 402, 410, 420-421, 477, 524, 530, 537, 548-9
–, (1) one … (with three faces) 184-185, 150, 195, 207, 225, 266, 410, 418
–, (3) three in one 407, 414, 416, 426, 428-429, 431, 435, 436
– absorbs (moisture/ water) 249, 531, 564, 574
–, all bodies 410
–, ameliorate 540
– and alabaster 173
– and chrysocolla 254
– and dissolved 156
– and fire 152
– and mercury 363
– and moisture 166, 279, 280, 397, 537, 539, 548
– and nature(s) 152, 249, 393, 549
– and non-body 254, 279, 366, 393, 483, 520
– and poison falls on 265, 520

– and (white) poison/ poisonous 151-152, 232, 245, 281, 533
– and soul 51-2, 322, 372, 290, 322, 370, 436, 514, 539
– and spirit 33, 170, 233, 235, 246, 296, 322-323, 491, 547, 558
– and spiritual part of work 436
– and sulphurs 398
– and water(s) 263, 265, 362, 539, 549, 557, 569
–, another 178
–, appear in body 279
– as changer 362
– as composed 546
– as decomposed male 362
– as fired clay 490
–, āsqūnīa makes … black 470
–, beloved 143
–, blacken 509
–, body-less 162
–, break … into fragments 540
–, burn 129, 477, 481, 560
–, ceases to be 530
–, change/ changer of 128, 242, 564
–, coagulate … and mercury 363
– coagulates water 265
–, cold/ fire destroys 152
–, colours hidden in 557
–, composed 226, 351, 546
–, conceal 231, 259
–, conceal shadow in 172
–, cook 485, 505, 530, 573, 578
–, copper with ... and spirit 481
–, copper, tin and … of magnesia 549
– copper(y)/ of copper; *see also copper–man* 23-4, 145, 149, 267, 279, 567
–, core of 505
–, corners of 48, 300
–, cut 56, 157
–, dead 38, 127, 289-90
–, definition of 222
–, depth of the 568
– desires 159
–, destroy/ destroyed/ destruction of 129, 150, 152, 190, 214, 225-6, 550
– dies 514
–, dissolve 128, 150-151, 155, 159, 171-2, 192, 244, 321, 364, 482, 529, 531, 535
– disappears 537
–, dough of 245
– dries up moisture 534
–, dry (out) 157, 290, 528
–, dye 154, 178, 266, 279, 380, 410, 452, 454, 529-30
–, dye submerges in 255
–, dye thrown on 566
– dyed by spirit/ dyes spirit 178, 233
– dyeing 558
–, egg has 227
–, enter 354, 488, 537, 573, 520
–, escape with 483
–, eternal 231, 280
–, every 165, 173, 185-186, 189, 206-207, 245-246, 255, 261-262, 266, 301, 410, 454, 529-530
–, extract (from) 227, 245, 402, 482, 468, 488, 493, 520
–, feed 157
–, female 56, 127, 157, 231
–, hard 185, 396
–, heart of 436
–, hold other 259
–, honoured 529, 549, 550
– human 67-8
–, increase 177
–, inside 165, 509
– into soul 53
– is put on fire without vinegar 524
–, kill/ killed 157, 158, 259, 296, 289
–, make black/ white 447, 226
–, male 362, 530
–, mercury, … and poison 151
– mixed 248
–, mix … with (spirit/ poison/ magnesia/ pyrite/ water/ chrysocolla/ ferment/ natures/ moistures) 154, 253, 361, 365, 368, 379, 551, 576, 580
–, moist 520
–, name (of a) 175, 265-7, 410, 532
– named with all the bodies 151
–, no/ non-body 190, 225, 253, 483
–, nourished 190
–, obtain from 529
– of arsenic 190
– of chrysocolla 253
– of egg 51, 372

– of gold 37, 293, 345
– of gum 547
– of human(s) 161, 214, 226, 286
– of (ingot of) glass 318-9
– of king 91
– of magnesia 37, 172, 183, 251-2, 254, 256, 261, 282, 285, 287, 289, 313, 321, 328, 331, 344-345, 349-353, 360-366, 368-369, 361, 365, 376-379, 372-373, 378-379, 381-4, 386, 399, 424, 442, 475, 497, 530-531, 549, 580
– of magnesia and black lead 376-7
– of mercury 183, 278
– of non-fugitive 489
– of silver 178
– of Theosebeia 141, 336
– of things 375
– of Venus 279
– of youth 53, 485
– of Zosimos; *see also Zosimos, body/ corps of* 31, 141, 339
–, operate on 214
–, other 163, 189, 296
–, part(s) of/ from 265, 268, 275, 282, 369, 399, 502, 510
–, pound (with) 164, 214, 491
–, pure/ purify 146, 477, 564
–, red/ reddish 363, 370, 379, 576
– rejoices 235
– remains (of)/ rest of 217, 369, 502, 576
– resists fire 398
–, return … to cooking/ heat/ moisture 440, 508
–, return soul/ spirits to 487-8
–, rot/ rotten 190, 255, 550
–, rust of the 574
–, silvery 471
–, single 193
–, soak 248, 557
–, soft 145
–, solidify … and water/ solidify in body 344, 383, 569
–, soul leaves/ separates from 322-323, 332, 370, 436, 438
–, soul, spirit and body 520
–, spirit (concealed) in 150, 214, 233, 322
–, spirit separates from 29, 33, 35-6, 322, 370, 439
–, strong 172
–, submerge in/ into 222, 245, 265, 470, 566
–, substance of 223
–, subtle (part of hard) 369, 502
– sucks 161
–, suitable for 157
–, sulphury 570
– takes flowers from moisture 565
– takes spirit quickly 235
–, thick (earthly)/ thickness of 178, 225-6, 233, 362
–, torture (soul with)/ torturer in 190, 233, 235
–, touchable 258
–, turn … into non-body 254
–, turn … into ash 481
–, turn … into black lead 155
, turn … into metal/ mineral 177, 192, 547
–, turn … into non-body 253
–, turn … into soul 146
–, turn … into spirit 164, 170, 179, 259, 296, 369, 468, 491, 547
–, turn … into sulphur 258
–, turn … into water 146, 156, 159, 482, 549, 564
–, turn no body/ non-body/ sperm into 353, 378, 481
–, unburnt 265
–, vapour of 292
–, visible 502
– which moves not 296
–, white/ whiten/ whitened 152, 166, 216, 368, 468, 554
–, winged 407, 411, 414, 416, 418, 421, 426, 428-429, 431, 435, 436
– with nature 289
–, without body 258
– without moisture 528
boil
– over 475
– wool 509
bone(s) 23-4, 149, 319, 505
–, dissolve 249
–, ivory 461, 474
–, male/ female 474
–, white 474
book(s); *see also epistle; kitāb; letter; poem; risāla; treatises* 22-3, 25, 45-7, 54, 58-

9, 61, 64, 68, 75, 78, 84-5, 96, 98-9, 103, 108, 110, 113-4, 116, 119, 121, 123, 136, 138
–, (1st) first 75, 78-9, 81, 114
–, (1st) first book of the Learning 79
–, (2nd) second 75, 78-9, 95, 114
–, (3rd) third 75, 78-80, 93, 112
–, (4th) fourth 75, 79
–, (5th) fifth 79, 81, 84, 120
–, (6th) sixth 79
–, (7) seven Climes; Book of the 99
–, (7th) seventh 75, 79, 84
–, (7th) seventh letter 414
–, (8th) eighth 80
–, (9) nine letters 450
–, (9th) Ninth letter 407, 414, 432, 442, 457
–, (10th) tenth 80
–, (10th) Tenth Key, Book about the 529
–, (11th) eleventh 80
–, (12th) twelvth 79-80
–, (13th) thirteenth 75, 119
–, (24) twentyfour …s (of sages) 22, 393
–, (28) twenty-eight 20
–, (70) seventy Epistles 18
– ascribed to Zosimos 20, 22
–, authentic book (of Zosimos) 73
–, Bibliotheca curiosa 64
–, Book about Questions about the Other Composition 563
–, Book about the Broth 272
–, Book about the Composition 79, 275
–, Book about the Fire (treatise) 96-7, 491, 516
–, Book about the First Composition 19
–, Book about the Glass 385
–, Book about the last Operation only and its Weights 80
–, Book about (the) Magnesia/ Book of (Examples about) Magnesia 19, 33, 81, 120, 274, 306
–, Book about the Making of Gold 550
–, Book about the Making of Silver 550
–, Book about the Measures of the Fire 22, 79, 96, 516
–, Book about the Mercuries 19, 21, 31, 79, 84
–, Book about the Mercury 550
–, Book about the Nature 22, 79, 389
–, Book about the Operation 80, 476
–, Book about the Other composition 543
–, Book about the Questions concerning the last Composition 75
–, Book about the Second Work 525
–, Book about the Weights 19, 78-9, 112
–, Book of Action 123
–, Book for the Afterlife; *see also Afterlife; Amduat* 19, 80, 39, 54, 109-10, 113, 123, 127, 136
–, Book of Chrysocolla 529
–, Book of Friend/ Lover 24-5, 49, 123-4
–, Book of Gold 457
–, Book of Imuth 21-22, 385, 389-90, 393, 467, 471
–, Book of Isis (Asida) 404, 551
–, Book of Keys; *see Book of the Keys*
–, Book of Krates 25, 51, 68
–, Book of Learning 81, 141-2
–, Book of Pictures 5-7, 11-3, 18-29, 36, 39-41, 44-8, 51, 55, 57-9, 61, 63-4, 66-9, 73-5, 80-5, 91-2, 95-100, 102-7, 109-11, 113-5, 117-21, 123-6, 131-8, 142
–, Book of Power 551
–, Book of the Angels 22
–, Book of the Elements 18
–, Book of the Epistles 73
–, Book of the Explanation of Symbols 5, 81, 93
–, Book of the Key (by Hermes) 292, 487
–, Book of the Key(s)/ the Tenth Key/ The Keys; 18, 46, 116, 129, 315, 404, 411, 414
–, Book of the Keys of the Art 18, 45, 116, 132-3, 137
–, Book of the Names 29-30, 61, 63, 68, 78, 95, 212, 262
–, Book of the Operation 516
–, Book of the Seven Climes on the Science called the Art 99
–, Book of (the) Truth 19, 23, 78, 141
–, Book of the Vessels 460
–, Book of the Weights 93, 262, 275
–, Book of Thoth 123
–, Book of Wisdom 215
–, Cheirokmeta (Manual Skills) 20
–, Chemeu 22
–, Corpus Alchemicum Arabicum, *see Corpus*
–, Corpus Hermeticum 123

–, De Lapide Sapientum 81
–, Fihrist 133
–, golden; *see also Book of Gold* 229
–, how to read 194, 256
–, Hymn of the Pearl 90
–, La Chimie au Moyen Age 9, 11, 17-8, 21-2, 25, 27, 58, 94, 123-4, 371
–, Laila and Maǧnūn 39
–, last 46
–, Les Alchimistes Grecs 9, 17, 93-4, 96-7, 123, 133
–, list of 18
–, Manual Skills 20
–, market 133
–, Mémoires Authentiques 9, 17-8, 21-2, 32, 40, 92, 126, 134
–, obtain 22
– of Abullun (Apollonius, Ābullūn) 320, 402
– of Agathodaimon 246, 399, 465
– of Bidīsos 432, 572
– of C. G. Jung 31-2, 39, 40, 45, 59, 90, 93, 98, 130, 133, 138
– of Democritus; *see also four treatises; Keys; Sartamita* 199, 256, 273-4, 287, 299, 345, 377-8, 389, 404, 453, 498
– of gold (golden book) 337, 427
– of greatest experiment 389
– of Hermes 118, 146, 215, 299, 464-465, 544
– of Maria 274, 375, 377, 385, 465, 542
– of Mercuries 402
– of Ostanes 202, 572
– of Theodorus 152
– of the people 176
– of Zosimos for Theosebeia 97, 133, 170-171, 204, 216, 242, 274, 315, 318, 375, 414, 544, 581
–, On the Fire 491
–, On the Letter Omega (letter) 32, 91
–, Pistis Sophia 121, 124
–, Poem rhyming on the letter Mīm 116
–, Poem rhyming on the letter Nūn 99
–, ponder over; *see ponder*
–, read/ study/ written/ said in the 145, 147-148, 154, 158, 160, 165, 168, 173, 194-196, 202-203, 209, 219, 221, 256, 272, 281, 285, 289, 295, 317, 350, 358, 366-367, 381, 388, 393-394, 398, 405-406, 410, 418, 427, 430, 457, 462, 466, 477, 526, 565, 579
–, Rosarium philosophorum 59-64, 68, 136
–, Royal Books (for Afterlife); *see book(s) for Afterlife, Amduat*) 54, 80
–, Sartamita/ Sarṭamīṭā/ Sarṭiṭa 46, 111, 315, 249, 261, 315, 411, 414, 442, 540
–, similar/ comparison of 52
–, spread in the ...s 399
–, summary of 261
–, that does not vanish 473
–, The Pure Pearl 116
–, The Sulphurs (book) 116-7, 132
–, Treatise of the Idol 497
–, Turba Philosophorum 124
–, write; *see also Zosimos writes books* 22, 111
bone(s) 23, 149, 249, 319, 461, 474, 505
boredom 503, 577
– bored 508
born 32, 46, 91, 143, 209, 212, 252, 367, 368, 486, 535
– from the (2) two 156
– every year 325, 481, 507, 571
– in fire 284
– in sea 500
–, stone … from copper and silver 566
–, thoughts are 305
bottle 283, 462, 522
bottom 291, 560
– of the vessel 145, 167, 285, 540, 568
– of pot 487
bough 227
bowl 394
boy 53, 391, 485-7
–, urine of (young) 156, 573
branch 448, 495
–, (colours of) (3) three ...es 84, 447-8, 495
–, of alchmey, religious-symbolic 68
bread 189
–, ferment of 303
break; *see also disguise; cut; scatter; veil* 288, 364, 374, 378, 400, 474, 533
– into fragments/ pieces 366, 569, 369, 460-461, 474, 487, 490, 499, 536, 566
– lead (n) 353
– gold 418
–, stone ...s quickly 573

breast 433, 556
breath/ breathe 48
– hole 402
–, breathing 481
brick(s) 161, 395
–, mud- 161
bridal money 55, 157
bridge 69
brightness 297
brilliance 37, 342, 352, 394, 440
–, brilliant 403
–, fix 385
bring
– back to start of work 180
– forth 551
– it to light 556
– out natures 147
– together 160, 164, 185, 310
Brisius 204
Broadhurst, R. J. C 10
broth 160, 186, 192, 245-6, 292, 317, 395, 470-1, 497-8, 552, 581
– is (1) one 551
– and wool 552
– as alum 574
– as water 384
–, cook … and male 552
–, dye with 452
–, making of 247
–, mix … with nature gold 245, 489
– rots composition 541
–, strengthen 490
–, turn ... into 398, 452
–, white 434
–, white sulphur, alum and 497
brother(s) 94, 121, 240, 311, 447, 464, 495
–, brotherhood 311
Brunner-Traut 108
Buber, Martin 11
build 217
–, building 85, 161
Būlīs 319
bull(s) 35, 64, 271, 307, 313, 332
– -energy 35
–, gallbladder of 547
–, glue of 401
–, white/ green-white 34
burdensome 489
buried 39, 56, 181
burn (vb) 129, 151, 157-8, 175, 180, 184, 190, 192, 201, 228, 251, 255, 282, 285-6, 288, 325, 354-5, 374, 378, 385, 394, 400, 455, 461, 465, 495, 497-8, 522, 536, 554, 560, 570-1
– and kill 533
– ashes 570
–, (not …t) in origin 167
–, burnt blood 559, 564, 570, 572
–, burnt copper 220, 377, 379, 380, 481, 531, 535-6, 568, 578
–, burnt by water 569-70
–, burnt gum 501
–, burnt little 496
–, burnt marble 506
–, burnt part 578
–, burnt shells 474
–, burnt, sulphur which gets not 407
– bodies 190, 480, 288, 496
– bodies with sulphur 286
– body 477, 560
– burnable 283
– burnt blood 567
– completely 196
– copper (with (soft) sulphur/ salt and alum/ oleander leaves/ water and flowers) 251, 288, 296-7, 350, 365, 376, 480, 487, 496-8, 506, 513, 535, 567
– copper and sulphur 288, 350
– dyes … not up 494
– egg 487
– flowers 255, 522-3
– gentle 579
–, get burnt 183, 213, 299, 381, 508, 524, 537
–, get not burnt 284-5, 362, 451, 508, 513
–, heat/ fire burns 239, 397, 523, 540
– in making white 579
– in pounding 579
– in vessel 288
– iron and magnesia 288
– lead 168, 289
– linen 394
– magnesia with iron 350
– mixture 523
– more than fire 355
– natures 480, 515, 579
–, non-burnable/ unburnt 186, 265

– not 196, 440, 493, 501
– second elixir 505-6
– spirits 379
– sulphur 284
–, sulphur gets not burnt/ does not burn 267, 362-3, 493, 513
–, sulphurs …s copper 501, 506
– things 496
– tongue 512
– with milk 400
– wool 510, 524
burning 143, 151, 180, 199, 228, 297, 321, 402, 436, 456, 487, 498, 505, 509, 578
– as head of work 288
– as making red 288
– as whiteness/ of whitening 288, 523
–, beginning of 523
– be not afraid of 510
–, black 350
–, composition and operation 579
–, destructive 288, 350
– fire 36, 342, 436
– first/ second 23, 288, 497, 569-70
–, intense 403
– of (all) bodies 50-1, 170, 288, 515
– of copper 365
– of natures 172
– of reddening 523
– of sages 286, 350
–, white 350
Burnett, Charles 8
bury 216-7
Būtīṭus/ Būtiṭos/ Badīsios 58, 311-2, 368
buy 171
Byzantine 10, 19, 51

–C–

Cairo 7-8, 12-3, 18, 21
CALA; *see also Corpus Alchemicum Arabicum* 13
–, I 12
–, IA 5, 12
–, IB 5, 12, 40, 81, 92, 99, 110, 117, 128
–, II.1 5-7, 12, 73, 96
–, II.2 7, 12
calendar 54
C.G. Jung-Institute 12
Caliph Umar 26
calcify (vb) 323
calculation 305
calf, urine of 547, 558
camomilla 395
canals of blood; *see also veins* 173
cancer 367
Cancer (sign of Zodiac) 494
capture (vb) 293, 488
carafe 504
care 300
–, careful 5, 13, 44, 48, 53, 126, 155, 173, 182, 304, 321, 344, 355, 436, 487, 492, 502-3, 523
–, carefully 17-8
–, careless(ly) 403, 509
carpenter 151
carry 23, 43, 391
case material 98
cast 189, 258, 270, 283, 375, 386, 388, 395, 403, 454, 467-8, 469, 472, 500, 563, 566
– antimony and etesian 376
– appearance 376
–, casting(s) 283, 293, 324, 364, 454, 489, 494, 549
– cast off 502
– copper 385
–, decreases in casting 173
– silver 292, 456, 565
–, soften casting 376
– thing 304
– tin 394
castor-oil 158, 288
catch 320
cautious; *see also careful* 118, 289, 536, 544, 559
– with the fire 525, 577
cave 90
cease to believe (in work) 522
central (thing) 26, 45, 84, 91, 157
– topic 61
centre 31, 39, 44
–, inner 39
–, Research and Training Centre for Depth Psychology, Zurich 5, 8, 12-3
century
–, (2nd) second 122, 124

–, (3rd) third 122
–, (3rd/ 4th) third/ fourth 78, 113
–, (4th) fourth 113, 136
–, (4th/ 5th) fourth/ fifth 98, 123, 136
–, (5th/ 6th) fifth/ sixth 93, 96, 97, 123, 136
–, (10th) tenth 94, 125, 133
–, (11th) eleventh 94
–, (12th) twelvth 108
–, (13th) thirteenth 92, 110, 138
–, (15th) fifteenth 81
–, (16th) sixteenth 119
–, (18th) eighteenth 99
chaff 303, 474, 503
chain; *see also rope* 477
chair 307
chalcedonian; *see also stone* 209
change (vb, n) 25, 78, 96, 166, 146, 179, 222, 246, 261, 298, 318, 347, 356, 387, 397, 407, 456, 465-6, 472, 486, 521, 532, 565
– (1) one 214
– and precious/ expensive 170, 225
–, beginning of 526, 543
– bodies 482
– body 564
–, body and changer/changer of body 128, 242, 362
–, changeable 470
–, changer and changed 361
–, changer(s) 470, 472
–, changing one 210, 455
–, Chapter on the Operation 476
–, characteristics 416
–, cheaper 176
–, cheaply 171, 214, 231
– colour(s) 19, 46, 199, 200, 212, 277, 322-3, 353, 360-2, 387, 397, 436, 442, 456, 459, 464, 562-4, 571
–, colours of … ones 455
– composition 212
–, dissolve before 472
–, dye changes not 468
–, inner 161
– name(s) 51, 199, 277, 365, 372, 500, 511, 540, 549
– natures 218, 301-2, 493, 509
– nature of copper 200
– not colours 153, 396, 559
– not herbs 389
– of book 540
– of Book of Zosimos 516
– of relative 334, 339
– of silver 461, 466
– old into young 53, 485
– operation 397
– silver (into colour) 205, 292-3, 454-6, 467
– statements 268
– states 340, 530
– stones 456
– subject 114
– sulphur 456
– tail to water 50
–, time of 156
–, unchangeable 233, 509
channels 290
character 178, 360
chaste 320
cheap 29, 41, 162, 170, 213, 237, 345, 455
chemical
– process 39
– symbols 33, 39, 44
chemistry 33, 123
Chepri 80, 109
chest 31, 477
child/ children 10, 55, 58, 122, 157, 177, 182, 311, 357, 486
–, child-bearer 197
–, divine 44
Chimie au Moyen Age; *see book(s), La Chimie…*
choice 212
Christ; *see also Jesus* 28, 31, 120, 123-4, 219-20, 523
– as a teacher 28
–, Gnostic or Muslim 121-23, 136
Christian(s) 10, 28, 37, 110
– writers; *see also author* 19
–, Christianity 11, 29, 113
–, Christian-Gnostic 99, 118, 120
chrysocolla 24, 128, 191, 242-3, 246, 253-4, 266, 350, 377, 468, 529
– and body 254
– and cloud 462
– and rust of copper 558
– as stone 462
–, body of magnesia and eternal water 265-6
–, Book of Chrysocolla 529

–, coppery 462
–, dissolved … into lead 530
– escapes not 253
–, experiment of 569
– gets destroyed 530
–, mercury from 269
–, mix … with body 253
–, roast 529
–, spirit of 253
–, turn ... into rust 529-30
cinnabar 48, 141, 156, 197, 199, 226, 232, 237, 246, 251, 281, 352-3, 425, 457
– and cloud 189, 285, 462
– and sparkling 281
– as body of magnesia 373
–, colour of 546
–, copper becomes 156
–, extract from 420, 490, 424, 535
–, fiery (sulphur) of 542
–, holds dye of mercury 490
–, mercury from/ (out) of 151, 213, 226, 235, 244, 261, 277, 278, 280, 325, 352-3, 373, 420, 424-5, 472, 549, 550, 567, 574, 578
–, mercury of tin clings to 403
–, operation of the mercury of 500
– rarely found 213
–, red 535
–, second 484
–, smoke into 483, 254
–, spirit of 484
–, subtle part of 505
–, vapour, … and cloud 246
–, vinegar, … and all moistures 552
–, water of (silver of) 568, 564
circles (n) 110, 123
–, circle around symbol 95
–, circulate, fire 166, 513
city 125
claim 7, 110, 161, 344
clanking 271
clarification 302
–, clarify 19, 213, 292, 385, 460
–, clarity , 262, 270
claudianus 191, 243, 377, 388, 451, 483, 546
– and lead 399
– -stone 399
clay 482, 488, 492, 511, 566
–, coat in 522
–, fired 490
–, layer of 525
–, wet 568
clean 367, 492, 568
clear 21, 27-9, 41, 44, 55, 64, 66, 95, 109, 140, 161, 164, 167, 180, 182, 194, 196, 216, 221, 233, 242, 259, 263, 270, 274, 276, 277, 281, 287, 291, 295, 297, 301-2, 304-5, 315, 322, 328, 345, 347, 349, 358-9, 363, 385, 398, 455, 460, 467, 499, 502, 504, 509, 511, 519, 525-6, 529, 532, 537, 548, 562, 568, 572, 575
–, clear up 237
–, clearly 22, 152, 155, 185, 202, 257, 280, 296, 347, 349, 366, 394, 416, 467, 516, 559
– color 436
– not 148
–, pure and 159, 502
– water 489
climax 304
cling (vb) 56, 127, 151, 157, 160, 168, 183, 192-3, 197, 232, 238, 261, 277, 284-5, 299, 322-3, 326, 360, 366, 393-4, 396, 402, 407, 469,430, 438, 463, 472, 480, 530, 537, 540, 543, 561-2, 564, 569, 580-1
–, clinger stone 238
–, cloud clings to coppery chrysocolla 462
–, clung one 446
–, fighter, clung-to and lime 446
–, mercury clings 466
–, mercury of tin clings to cinnabar 403
–, mix fugitive with clinger 172
–, nature clings to nature 168, 280, 301, 401, 488, 569
–, seeker clings to fugitive/ sought 197, 384
–, spirit clings to body 322
–, sulphur clings 232
– to bodies 285
– to each other/ together 197, 218-9, 277, 298, 301, 360, 385, 487, 494, 534, 581
clod
– of earth 161, 506
–, turn … into stone 161
–, turn tin into 158
close (vb) 203, 277, 283, 290, 300, 311, 336, 355, 436, 458, 463, 465, 485, 505, 531,

537, 547, 567, 572, 576
–, closed stone 166
–, closeness 197, 334, 462
– holes 516, 524
– mouth of vessel 564, 566, 575, 581
– one 142, 168-9, 192, 201, 232, 258, 334, 340
– one and nature 232, 258
– top of vessel 317
– to work 219
– well! 235, 547
cloth 216, 394, 576
–, piece of 215, 394, 473, 568, 572, 576
clothes 141, 179, 204, 264, 276, 341, 421, 474
–, dye 204, 472, 512, 453
–, dyeing 406
–, green 391
– of dyers 504
– of gold 36, 341
– of king(s) 167-8, 495-6
–, purple-coloured 167
–, red 391
cloud 162, 164, 215, 225, 244, 245, 247, 251, 267, 285, 298, 305, 315, 360, 378, 383, 418, 566
– and castor-oil 288
– and chrysocolla 462
– and cinnabar 189, 285, 462
– and lead-copper 464
– and mercury 164
– and rising of water 164, 272, 359, 400
– and saffron 498
– and water (of sulphur) 189, 197, 288
– and work 489
– as relative and dye 567
–, ascend/ rise cloud(s) 164, 198, 513
– clings to coppery chrysocylla/ copper 462
–, clouds 169, 292, 360
–, cloud and broth 245
–, clouds as soul/ spirit 215
–, coagulate(s) 251-2
–, concealed inside 489
–, cook with 532, 562
–, dryness, moisture, spirit and 360
– escapes 197
– extract 489
–, ferment and cultivation of gold 245
– holds relative 360
– makes composition 489
– makes red 247
–, mix … with gold 245
–, mix … with water of sulphur 189
– of arsenic 288
– of mercury and sulphur 374
– preserves its relative 278
–, rest of 562
–, rub with 539
–, sea of 292
–, snow seizes 570
–, sulphur is 384
– turns red 562
–, turn white 374
–, vapour, cinnabar and 246
clung, fighter, … and lime 396
cluster 277, 451, 489, 568
– fermented 373, 475
–, red 461, 569
–, white 366, 367, 382
coagulate 59, 151, 168, 197, 220, 287, 360, 362-3, 481, 490, 498, 547
–, cloud coagulates/ coagulate cloud 251-2
–, coagulation 44, 196
–, first and second coagulation 287
– mercury 287, 361
– moisture 166
–, solve et coagula 41
– stone with water and gum 447, 495
– water 265
coal 385
– of the mountain 237
coat 144, 500, 525
– in clay 522
codename(s) 91, 93-5, 125
– and symbol(s) 126, 131
codex 20
– Codex Marcianus 94
– Codex Parisinus gr. 64, 134
coherence/ coherent 7, 111
– of book 135
– of pictures series 80, 84
cold (adj, n) 78, 157, 175, 169, 209, 275, 292, 460, 541, 577
– and dry 169, 228
– and hot 63, 142-3, 169, 222, 227, 487
– as winter 152
–, cold, hot, dry and moist 142, 169, 175

–, coldness (n) 173, 175, 209, 228, 286, 474
– dyeing of purple 453
–, dye purple with 541
–, moist, weak and 174-5
– one 142, 152, 541
– water 447, 495
– wind 127, 159
collation 20
collect (vb) 13, 45-6, 48, 95, 130-1, 168, 196, 216, 223, 367
–, collection 9, 11, 17-8
–, collection of flowers 47
–, collector of dispersed 9
– everything 41, 576
–, moisture collects 161
–, projection and recollection 39
–, sages dispersed and collected 555
– teachings 11
collective 41, 45, 69
– unconscious 40, 44
colocynth 250, 299, 317, 349, 375, 502, 510, 552, 561
–, and sulphur 552
–, cook with cloud 562
–, makes red 563
– of Cyprus 321
–, operate with 561
–, pound with 563
colophon 20, 120
colour(s) (n, vb) 35, 46, 78, 99, 103, 107, 161, 166, 168-9, 177, 187, 192, 199, 208, 226-7, 231-2, 237-8, 245-6, 248, 252-3, 268, 270, 286, 295-7, 311, 318-19, 322, 336, 353, 357, 363, 401, 403-4, 406, 464, 466, 471-2, 475, 498, 506, 512, 517, 527, 532, 538, 554, 559, 565, 570-1, 557, 577
–, (1) one 162, 205, 361, 406, 532
–, (1) one/ good ..., become 162, 256
–, (1) one ..., work into 405
–, (2) two 161, 270, 296, 506
– of (2) two 270
–, (3) three 401
–, (4) four 229
– appear/ come(s) into existence 33, 200, 246, 275, 297, 315, 318, 326, 331, 372-3, 396, 452, 519, 550, 552, 557, 561, 571, 574, 577-8
– as soul 190
–, beautiful/ beauty of 240, 369, 385
–, black 31, 36, 554
–, blue 19
– blossom 258
–, bring/ come (not) out 515, 558
–, change/ change of 19, 46, 199-200, 212, 277, 322-3, 353, 360-1, 387, 397, 436, 442, 446, 456, 459, 480, 562-4, 571
– change not 396, 559
–, change silver into 454
–, clear 436
–, coloured/ uncoloured 31, 481
–, colourful 512
–, colouring of silver 466
–, coloured illustrations/ colouring of pictures 19, 26
– come out in cooking 550
–, cover 201
–, crimson 573
–, different/ difference of 256, 447, 458, 495, 519
– disappear not 318, 396, 577
– do not escape 369
–, dyeing 178, 481
–, every 275
–, exalted 315
–, external 505
–, extract 179, 260, 316, 323, 396, 404, 406, 446, 450, 511, 529
–, fix 385, 454
–, flowers of 279
–, gold 295
–, green 19, 35
–, grey 48
–, hide/ hidden in body 318, 557
–, hot 279
–, imagined 33, 331
–, improve 279
– in summer 511
–, known 318
–, looked-for 511
–, lowest of 36, 339
–, luminous 512
–, lunar 258
–, magnesia changes colour 362
–, many 162, 166, 179, 279, 290, 294, 393, 457, 571, 579

–, missing 19
–, names of/ name with 226, 246, 558
– of apple 259
– of aqrūnis 572
– of ashes 316, 499, 471
– of black lead 523
– of blood 387, 554
– of branches 447, 495
– of changing ones 455
– of cinnabar 48, 546
– of citron 259
– of composition 480
– of copper 252, 499, 528
– of diamond/ pyrite/ potash 47-48
– of dye 575
– of egg 50, 370, 372
– of elixir, metals as 557
– of etesian 521
– of froth 388
– of gold 253, 257, 278, 349, 463, 550
– of India/ shining Indian 316, 499
– of metals 166-7
– of mixture 257
– of moon 571
– of pounded saffron 538
– of purple 554, 557
– of rainbow 37, 342
– of Saturn 253
– of seven stars 450
– of silver 252, 257, 386, 473, 404
– of sky 141, 276, 391, 477, 556-7, 571
– of stones/ litharge 521
– of tin 252
– of (water of) gold/ silver 78
– of woman/ man 475
– of work 176, 177
–, perfect 280
–, plurality of 571
–, pure 502
–, purple 36, 231, 341, 347, 447, 470, 562, 574
–, red 31, 47, 554
–, reddish 349, 383
– return 480, 524
–, russet 569
–, satisfies 578
–, series of 47
–, seven 465
–, shadow as 528
–, silver(y) 467, 554
–, smoke with splendour, dye and 505
–, states of 571
–, strong 297
–, sulphur gives 504
–, take up 508
–, ten as 326
–, turn (to) 153, 179, 256
–, unchangeable/ permanent/ remain 153, 232-3
– vanish (not) 323, 454
–, various 557
–, visible 436
–, white 35, 575
–, yellow 34-5, 43, 48, 554
columns
–, (2) two green 306
–, (4) four 517
–, (6) six 276
combination 166, 365
–, combinations 221, 519, 526
–, of natures 168
combine (vb) 195, 394
– bodies 292
come
– down 568
– into being; *see also existence* 62, 122, 144, 151, 152, 177, 193, 221, 223, 249, 253, 262, 303, 577, 580
– out (e.g. extracted, newborn, ...) 160, 163, 177, 186, 195, 236, 260, 290, 322, 364, 379, 385, 457, 471, 473, 481, 512, 515, 522, 524, 528, 530-1, 537, 550, 571-4, 577
– together 180, 298, 546
–, they who … after me 221, 237
comfort 286
commentary/ comment on 10, 18, 22, 28, 45, 61
–, psychological 5-6, 12, 92
community of sages 28, 120, 219, 523
companion(s) 142, 238, 312, 358, 389, 416, 432, 457, 581
–, cook water with … of mixture 552
–, escape with 51, 372
–, flavour of 191
–, its 142, 187, 192, 238, 320, 399, 497
–, join 564
–, long for 462
–, mix with 411

– of mercury 430
– of sulphur 552
– of water 480
– of iron 374
–, push heat of fire away from 473
–, separate from 500, 508
–, taste of its 497
–, teach 362
–, ten 273
compare 158, 223, 271, 322, 469
–, comparison(s) 24, 26, 48, 50, 63, 99, 111, 115, 371, 350
–, understanding by comparing 158
compassion 143, 312, 477
compilation(s)/ compile (vb) 7, 19, 24-5, 48-9, 61, 73, 96, 111, 113-4, 122, 124, 133, 135-6
compiler 114
complain 20, 33, 332
complete 20, 38, 55, 63, 98, 144, 152, 156, 159, 161, 164, 166, 173, 177, 181, 185, 187-8, 194, 203, 206, 212, 223-4, 226, 229, 232, 234-5, 248, 252, 255, 257, 262, 288, 291, 327-8, 354, 357-8, 364, 382, 402, 414, 486, 526, 536, 554-5, 563, 568, 574, 577, 581
–, completeness 161-2, 165, 174, 178, 197, 224, 227, 328, 352, 354, 370, 453, 464, 476, 530, 557, 571
–, completely 15, 134, 158, 196, 360, 381, 394, 403, 456, 506, 535, 547, 554, 558
– composition 260
– desire 143
– dye/ dyeing 248, 357, 546
–, incomplete 185, 291
– matter 522
– mixing 373
– secret 575
– with nature 393
–, work 120, 494
– your favours 29, 45
completeness 165, 178, 224, 227, 328, 352, 354, 370, 453, 464, 530, 557
– and moisture 162
– of days 174
– of operation 571
– of statement 451
– of work 476
completion; *see also complete* 166, 178, 257, 260, 262, 273, 278-9, 349, 379, 486, 572
– of dyeing 120, 219
– of month 305
– of number 273
– of reddening 189
– of sought 261
– of whitening 189
– of work 259, 296, 497, 508
components 162, 170, 197, 252, 283, 350, 359, 368, 486
–, mix with 531
– of magnesia 310, 313
– of mixture 462; 201, 205, 321, 366, 376, 382, 399, 425, 461, 465, 472, 492, 577
–, pound 501
–, second 252
compose 142, 169, 183, 195-6, 198, 208, 247, 253, 277, 322, 405, 458, 499
– copper and salt 442
– gum 401
– operate and cook 205
– pyrit with iron 472
– sulphur with copper 501
– the remedies 169, 542
– water with alum 552
composed 44, 68, 164, 205, 226, 244, 256, 277, 284, 297, 315, 318, 521, 576
–, (1) one and composed 161
– body/ body as 226, 267, 351, 546
– gum 402
– lead 326
– magnesia 327
– mercury 353, 459
– nature(s) 195, 355, 450, 459, 393, 326
– not 195, 459, 516
– one/ one is composed 171, 176, 263, 268, 285, 288, 546
– poison 492
–, power of 354
– sulphur 296, 384, 442
– water 541, 552-4
–, water not 516
composition(s) 46-7, 64, 129, 155, 159, 183-6, 191, 219, 212, 225, 228-9, 232, 244, 252, 259, 265-7, 273-4, 277-9, 283, 321-2, 326, 328, 357, 359, 369, 376,

383, 394, 405, 407, 410, 439, 463, 465, 491, 543, 547, 551, 555, 563, 574, 578, 581
– (1)one, ... is 377
–, (1) one… of poison 294
–, (1) one thing of … and whole 373
–, (1st) first 187, 243-4, 273, 276-7, 287, 405, 463, 524, 533, 537-8, 552
–, (2) two compositions 212, 192, 272, 360, 551
–, (2nd) second/ other 179, 224, 244, 248, 253, 258, 265, 268, 272-3, 277, 282-3, 285, 287, 384, 393, 410, 424, 476, 491, 524, 538, 548-9, 551, 563, 571, 578, 581
– of (2nd) second work 554
–, (2nd) second ..., beginning of 170, 271, 304, 452, 570
– (4) four weights, ...is based on 267
–, About the Other Composition 543
–, all (of) the 161, 185, 207, 244-5, 247, 252, 289, 376, 489, 568
–, analogy for 64, 221
– and talismen 463
– and weights 531
–, beginning of 240
–, bodies enter 303
–, Book about the Composition 19, 275, 563
–, broth rots 541
–, burning, the …. and the operation 579
–, cloud makes 489
–, colour, ripeness 480
–, combinations, colours, … and operations 526
–, complete 260
–, cook 248, 457, 520
–, cook/ pound 198
–, copper is whole 251
–, date (of) 25
–, end of 224
–, enter 397
– extracts nature 549
–, fire ruins 490
–, first… as making rusty 493
–, good 564
–, hard 324
–, hidden 182, 376
–, in agreement with 427
–, irrigate 248
–, know 221
–, make clear 296
–, many 162
–, mix … with gold 493
–, mix sulphur with 541
–, name/ name with/ name of their 287, 394-5, 551
– named body of magnesia 289
– of alchemists/ of body 45-6, 63
– of body 129
– of cloud and raising water 164
– of fat 196
– of lead 456
– of lead and copper 245
– of lead-copper 472
– of magnesia 351, 365
– of Mushaf as-suwar 115
– of natures 326
– of other one 269
– of red copper, lead and silver 468
– of stones 456
– of sulphur 320, 385, 456
– of the sages 174
– of vapours 46
– of water 268
– of white 296
– of work 215, 265
– of Zosimos 113
–, operation of 507
–, poison and its 522
–, put into vessel 288
–, red 284
–, rest of 184
–, rot 520
–, secret of 279
–, soak 268, 369, 480, 539, 564
–, strength of fire in 523
–, surface of 368
–, things of 161
–, true 246, 270, 500, 506
–, vessel as 568
–, wash 507
–, weight of 568
–, white/ red 212, 326
–, whole 224, 373
–, whole … as gum 384-5
comprehend/ comprehension 406, 464

conceal (vb); *see also reconcile* 44, 93, 150, 162, 165, 220, 239, 246, 282, 369, 371, 374, 382, 424, 457, 463, 477, 489, 532, 549
– dye 229, 515, 575
– fire in air 228
– fire, concealed in lime 41, 575
– gold in bodies 303
– (in) body 231, 259, 296
– in mercury 514
– in moisture 578
– inside 183, 302, 382, 509, 549
– nature 302, 394, 558
– redness 493, 533
– redness in whiteness 183, 541-2
– shadow in body 172
– shadow of copper in whiteness 373-4
– smoke 192
– spirit(s) 198, 214, 322, 511, 533, 537
– spirit in spirit 33, 332
– sun in dark night 305
– whiteness 509
conclusion 26, 64, 111, 125-6, 131, 135
condensed way 380
confirm (vb) 319, 334, 365, 390
confirmation 23, 27, 129, 188, 200, 250, 298, 360, 374, 401, 528, 551
conflicting 169
confuse (vb) 9, 47, 128, 147, 165, 180, 205-6, 208, 217, 221, 232, 237, 260, 262, 277, 304, 315, 344, 349, 353, 370, 383-4, 452, 466, 487, 517, 542, 551, 556, 563, 573
– mind 150, 172, 214, 263, 537
– not 406
confusion 94-5, 138, 263, 304, 494, 560
coniunction 32, 59, 166, 485
– mysterium coniunctionis 40, 45
– of male and female 58
connect/ connection(s) 10-1, 21, 31, 39, 41, 44, 49, 59, 68, 91, 117, 119, 125-7, 129, 133-4, 137-8, 174, 468, 574
–, connect cultures 68-9
–, connect pictures 59, 61, 78-9
–, reconnect/ reconnection 69
– to Egyptian/Greek knowledge/ myth 39, 78-80, 109, 113, 117, 123
conquer 169, 224, 287, 296, 393
–, Islamic conquest 113
– nature …s nature 344
–, magnesia conquers shadow of copper 374
–, weak .. the strong 169
–, with whiteness 374
conscious 29, 32-3, 40, 91, 94
– attitude 29
– to become 80, 90
consciousness 18, 32, 35, 41, 44, 91
– and unconscious 32, 39, 91-2
consider/ consideration 158, 191, 242, 355
consistent (book, teaching) 23, 45, 51, 85, 111, 135
constitutents 261
consume 240, 398, 465
–, fire ….s the dye 524
Constantine 11
contain (be contained) 5, 18, 22, 33, 35, 39, 44, 62-5, 81, 96, 118, 124, 128, 136, 153, 172, 217, 220-1, 230, 234, 236, 351, 365, 402, 450, 511, 569
–, containment 137
– dyes 184, 236
– everything 386
– fire 118, 137
–, hard ones 284, 285
– male 235
– sulphur 513
– truth 474
– wanted 514
contemplate; *see also ponder* 146, 151, 196, 212, 215, 359, 402-3, 405, 463, 465, 557, 560, 567
contemplation 359, 577
content(s) (adj, n) 26, 45, 51, 64, 75, 90, 115, 133-4, 155, 158, 165, 174, 244, 287, 354, 376, 400, 451
–, psychic 33
–, symbolic 113
contextualise 138
continuation 438
–, continue (vb) 295
–, continuity of culture/ civilization 59, 69, 113
–, continuously 573
contract 91, 436
contradict/ contradiction/ contradictory 116, 161, 184, 242, 257, 268
controlling 278

conviction 194
convince (vb) 47, 111, 250, 265, 282, 291, 315, 377, 395, 454, 532
cook (it) 47, 63, 144, 155-6, 158, 165, 168, 173, 183, 188-9, 195, 197, 199, 205, 212, 220, 222, 234-5, 247-9, 266, 268, 277-8, 282-4, 286, 297, 301, 317, 319, 321, 325, 352, 355-7, 364-7, 371, 376, 379, 383, 388, 405, 410-11, 430, 436, 456, 458-9, 460, 463, 470-1, 473-4, 481, 483-4, 486-7, 489-90, 493, 496-7, 500-4, 508, 510, 512, 515, 519, 521, 523-4, 528-31, 534-6, 539, 542, 546-9, 547, 549, 554, 557-8, 560, 562-3, 566-70, 572-4, 576-9, 581
– and operate 205, 405
– and pound 149, 562
– androdamus 386, 578
– black filings 440
– blood 173
– body 505, 573
– body of magnesia 530
– cloud with šaḥīra and colocynth 562
–, compose, operate and 205
– composition 248, 457, 520
– continuously 484
– cooked gold 363
–, cooking makes blacker 510
–, cooks cover pots 505
– copper 487, 521, 532
– copper and zandarīḥ 536
–, dissolve, pound and 532
– dyes 491, 523, 554
–ed 152, 282, 436
–ed, gold 364
–ed hot dyeing 453
–ed multiplies 376
– elixir 548
– female and male 552
– flowers 255
– food 48, 300
– for days 368, 370-1, 560, 564
– fruits 236, 524
– gently 255, 275, 465, 505, 509, 578,
– gum 291
– herb with water and alum 475
– in body 485
– in fire 364
– in sea 216
– in water 453
– in wine 453
– in womb 173
– long/ long time 317, 508, 510, 512
– magnesia 458
– male 233
– many days 505
– marriage 487
– mercury 283,363
– moisture 283
– much 579
– nature 515
– on fire 458
– our silver 493
– plant/ dye in water 502
–, plates 498
– poison 255
– poison, water of sulphur and arsenic 283
–, pound and 23, 578
– pyrite 538
– raw 376
– repeatedly 480, 484
–, roast and 565
– rust of copper 565
– semen/ sperm 481, 174
– spirit 243
– stone gently 367
– sulphur 418, 493
– things 491
– till it thickens 564
–, uncooked 513
– water 49, 460, 514, 552
– well 512
– white stone in sun 490
– with cloud and water of sulphur 288
– with eternal water 295
– with fire (of dung) 153, 218, 262
– with milk/ honey/ rainwater 453
– with moist/ moisture 481, 511, 559
– with sulphur 578
– with urine 511
– with vinegar 453, 507
– with water, vinegar and rainwater 511
– wool 542
cooking 23, 63, 129, 143, 144-6, 149, 173-4, 189-90, 235-6, 243-4, 246, 254-5, 275, 282, 284, 288, 360, 363, 370, 399, 406,

456, 473, 480-2, 484, 486-7, 499-500, 531, 538, 548-9, 562, 564-5, 567, 572-5
–, (2) two ...s 508
–, ($1^{st}/2^{nd}$) first/ second 144, 282, 508, 542
– (2nd) second 508
–, (7) seven 505
–, (7th) seventh 436
– and/ by/ of/ is pounding 145-6, 198, 254, 399, 560-1, 532, 579
–, appear by 531
–, beginning of 220, 282, 560
–, burn by 535
–, by pounding 532
–, clarify by 460
–, coagulate by 363
–, colours come out in the 550
–, destroy by 575
– difference in … with fire 507
–, enter 277
–, gentle 521
–, intensive/ intense 63, 164, 222, 254, 364, 370, 486, 531, 562, 579
–, leave in 489, 558
– of natures 461
– of vinegar 151
– operation in the 174
–, raise by 461, 502
–, refine by 480
–, remove blackness by 565
–, return body to …/ moisture 440
–, return to 145, 503, 512, 557
–, rotting, …, soaking and roasting 481
–, sieving as pounding of 145
–, stone in 515
–, taste of 505
–, well 576
– with fire 129, 406, 507, 548, 564
–, written frequently about 149
cool 502
– it down 572
– natures 381
Copenhaver, B.P. 19
copper 145, 158, 164, 183-4, 187, 189, 191, 195, 200-1, 209, 244, 247-8, 250-1, 257, 261, 263, 266, 268-9, 270, 273-4, 283, 286, 288, 353, 397-8, 411, 460, 463, 469, 499, 536, 552, 559, 563
–, abundant 167
– and dirt 165
– and eternal water 160, 528
– and fiery stone 201-2, 398
– and fire 221
– and gum 171
– and iron 298
– and lead 535
– and mercury 225, 353
– and moisture 156, 513
– and moon 484
– and natures 498
– and pyrite 572
– and salt 442
– and sandarach 536
– and silver 220, 566
– and silver become water 283
– and stone 275
– and subtle parts of dye 498
– and sulphur(s) 296, 350, 501
– and tin 430
–, antimony, etesian and … burnt with sulphur 376
– appears 547
– as/ and human being 46, 293, 302, 520
–, as burnt iron 374
– as mercuries 414
– becomes cinnabar 156
– becomes silver 220
–, black filings of 508
–, blackness of 167, 216
–, body of 226
– -body; *see also copper–man* 24, 149, 267
–, born from … and silver 566
–, burn 251, 296-7, 480, 496, 513, 535, 567
–, burning of/ burnt 158, 220, 277, 365, 377, 379-80, 481, 487, 531, 535-6, 568 578
–, burn … with oleander leaves 497
–, burn … with (soft) sulphur 288, 497-8, 506
–, burn … with sulphur and body/ natron/ salt (and alum) 497
–, burn … with water and flowers 497
–, burn not 501
–, casted 385
– chrysocolla (saffron and eternal water) 266, 462
–, cloud clings to/ improves 462
–, colour of 252, 499, 528

–, compose sulphur with 501
–, cook 532
– copper, kohl and magnesia 463
–, copper, lead and honoured stone 265-7
–, Cypriot 220, 378, 382, 549, 581
–, destroy/ destroyed 225, 283, 565
–, dissolve lead, … (and honoured stone) equally 273-4, 282, 298
–, dissolve/ dissolving of 244, 572
–, dyes (of) 447, 501, 503
– dyes (not) 368-9
–, Egyptian 442
–, extract from (lead-) 245, 280, 450
–, fiery 375
–, filings of 244, 440
–, flower(s) of 364, 368, 461, 516, 527, 538
–, fragment 508
– from our work 549
–, get destroyed; *see works, stone,...* 497
–, glue of 469
–, gold, silver and 161, 388, 465
–, gum and fat 487
– has body and spirit 481
– has many names 521
–, heat of …, lead and tin 403
–, Indian 316, 499
–, ingot of 129, 243
– inhales spirit from moisture 481
– into silver 372
– into silvery water 379
– into water 558, 563
–, iron, lead, … and tin 287, 293, 301
–, iron named 273
– is whole composition 251
–, juice of 469
–, killer of 574
–, lead 275, 245, 381, 410, 447
–, lead-copper 22, 24, 44, 85, 195, 204-5, 246, 248, 256, 261, 270, 280, 289, 294, 299, 319, 325, 375-6, 379, 386, 425, 448, 450, 452, 459, 463, 470, 472, 474, 495, 498, 502, 568, 580
–, lead-copper and cloud 464
–, lead-copper and tin 325
–, lead-copper as magnesia 381
–, lead, etesian and 378
–, lead obtains power from 535
– leaves not 468
–, looked-for comes from 521
–, magnesia and shadow of copper 374
–, magnesia as 381
–, make … black/ rusty 216, 379, 355, 447, 470, 315, 440
–, make ... rotten with cloud 567
–, make shadow of … disappear; see also copper without shadow 420, 528
–, make/ turn ... red 41, 183, 373, 420, 576
–, make/ turn … rusty/ into rust 303, 493, 551-2
–, make/ turn … white 41, 232, 244, 250-1, 261, 353, 397, 420, 576
– -man 23-4, 40
–, melts 493-4
–, mercury fights 372
–, mercury from (flowers of) 426, 513
–, mercury with alum, lead-copper and lime 378
–, mix/ mixed/ mixing/ mixture of 275, 372, 388, 469, 546
–, mix …, lead and honoured stone 375, 546
–, mix …, tar and silver 499
–, mix … with female 536
–, mix … with ferment of gold 411
–, mix ... with gold and silver 297
–, mix … with gum 473
–, mix ... with Indian 316
–, mix ... with sulphurs 200
–, mix … with water 248
–, mix silver and 469
– mixed with cloud 197
– mixed with taste 191
–, name 513, 530
–, nature burns 535
–, nature of 200
– not beneficial 499
–, nourishment of 486
– of people 467, 462
– of truth 278
–, operate on/ operation for/ of 207, 398, 481, 528
–, operation of lead- 299, 377
–, our 151, 157, 160, 191, 285, 296, 353, 362, 455, 528, 551, 578
–, our …, tin and body of magnesia 549
–, part of 298
–, peeled 156

–, plates into 563
–, plate(s) of 245,489, 536
–, pound/ not pounded 399, 508, 566
–, power of 512
–, pure 563
–, red 225, 245, 282, 466, 499
–, red …, lead and silver 468
–, red …, turned white 466
–, relationship with white stone and mercury 574
– remains 297, 501, 508, 496-7
–, remove shadow of copper 506
–, return 156
– rots 487
–, rubb 385
–, rust as 549
–, rust of 129, 141, 286, 529, 531, 558
–, rusty 195, 364
–, sages/ their 247, 467
–, shadow of 173, 187, 206, 247, 282, 369, 374, 410-1, 528
–, shadow of … concealed in whiteness 373-4
–, silver and gold 411, 497
–, silver into rust of 565
–, single 499
– solidifes water 248
–, soul of 226
–, sour water and moisture 493
– spirit of 200
–, spiritual 506
–, stone made from … and silver 539
–, stone of 483
– suffers 373
–, sulphurs burn 501, 506
–, sulphur separates from 501
–, taste of 200
–, tin, mercury and 455, 472
–, treatment of lead-copper 385
–, turn ... black, red, into rust, white; *see make copper black/ red/ rusty/ white*
–, turn … into (dyed) silver 183, 156, 231, 364, 473, 493
–, turn … into flowers 366
–, turn …. into gold 498
–, turn … into magnesia 183, 497
–, turn … into mercury 183
–, turn … into spirit 41, 536, 576
–, turn mercury into … without shadow 379
–, vapour of 244
–, wash 165
–, water mixed with 528
–, water of 426, 569
–, water turns … into rust 558
–, weight of 191, 274
–, white 232, 244, 316, 363, 473, 494, 499
–, whiten 191, 220, 379, 498
–, white red copper 468
– with body and spirit 481
– without rust 183
– without shadow 24, 197, 201, 220, 381, 379, 386, 410, 497, 499, 536
–, work upon 557
coppery
–, (3) three mercuries as … water 414
– body 279, 567
kohl 463
– stone 493
– water 129, 414
Coptic 9-10
copy 5-6, 12, 51, 68
copyist 20, 25
core 41, 345
– of body 505
– of burned 506
–, red 533
corner(s)
–, (4) four 223, 571
– of body 48, 300
–, stone with 571
corpse/ corpus; *see also body* 24, 38, 40, 48, 105, 107, 109, 132, 149, 277, 480
–, Corpus Alchemicum Arabicum (CALA); *see also CALA* 5, 7, 73
–, Corpus Alchemicum Graecorum 17
–, Corpus Hermeticum 123
–, embalming 41
– of Osiris 41
correct 44, 140, 397, 439
–, corrections 6, 20
correspond 151, 511
–, correspondence 69
corrupt 175, 259, 296, 323, 480, 538
–, corrupted 255, 394, 459
–, corruption 168, 225, 289
–, mercury 394
–, mixed with things 159

– spirits 281
– the world; *see also world* 23, 145, 149, 215, 217, 236
– tin with lead 394
– work 159
counter-hypothesis 73-4, 96, 113-4, 133, 135
countries 58, 311
– country, every 488
couple(s) 7, 31
–, alchemical 137
courage 327
course of moon 291
courtesy 322
cover; *see also disguise; hide; keep secret; protect; scatter; trickery; ruse; veil;* 151, 255, 336, 360, 384, 436, 460, 492, 503, 510, 541, 543, 574
–, blackness ...s 282, 363, 368, 507, 565, 576
–, cover-name 36, 55
– of pot 503, 512
–, operation ...s 201
– surface of water 283
– up 69
– vessel 492
– wool with moisture 510
cow
–, black 400
–, glue of ...s 475
crack 501, 506-7
–, cracking 301
–ed alum 368
–ed stone 317
crafts 151, 390
create 29, 56, 84, 174, 176, 204, 218, 255, 359, 440
–, creation 40, 44, 58, 118, 485, 223
–, creation of the stone 44, 117
–, creativity 480
–, creator 53-4, 59-60, 142, 305, 485
–, creature 214, 260, 334, 470
–, creatures 142, 145, 181, 358, 521
crimson 316, 542
– and urine 512
– colour 573
–, dye wool 541
–, power of 503, 512
crocodile, egg of 47-8, 300
cross out 439
crown(s) 27, 197, 347, 526, 547
– of all things 367
– of bodies 563
– of favour 159
– of sages; *see also Zosimos* 9
– of the dyeing 547
– of victory 487
– of work 251
–, magnesia as … of every thing 381
crystal(s); *see also stone* 256, 318, 471
– and gum 319
– and lead-copper 210
– dissolve 210, 318
cubits 47-8, 300
cultivate 293
– gold in earth 515
cultivation 245, 401
– of dragon 426, 458
– of gold 280, 299, 538
culture 69
–, Arabic-Islamic 69
–, continuity of 60
– Pharaonic 29, 80
– Western 13, 59, 69
cuncal (k-nk-l) 502
cunning 360
cup 459
cupola(s) 167-8, 200, 251, 306, 492, 526
–s, pearls of 492
cupping glass 292, 440
cure (vb), *see also disease; doctor; illness; medical; remedy* 142, 169, 194, 319, 351, 390, 400, 402, 529, 556
– soul 169, 536
cut; *see also break; scatter; veil* 47, 84, 113, 127, 157, 400, 458
– body (up into pieces/ parts) 23-4, 56, 149
–, cutting and pounding 24
– dragon 47, 56
– head (off) 48-9, 216, 300
– into fragments 24, 149
– into pieces 23
–, recutting 119
Cypriot 269, 317, 395, 578
– copper 220, 382, 378, 549, 581
– mercury 578
– soil 395
Cyprus, colocynth of 321

–D–

daemonic 32
damage; *see also benefit; destroy; harm* 240, 323
dampen/ dampness 500, 505
Danliṣṭūs 386
Daphne 113, 320
Dār al-kutub 18, 21, 73, 111
daring 202
dark 28, 31-2, 37, 53, 485
– and light 44
–, darker 473
– face 37
– side 31-2
– sulphur 400
darkness 357
– and light 121
– of night 305
– of womb 174
date (n,vb) 9, 17, 20, 25, 27, 31, 58, 73, 96, 131, 135
–, dating of Turba 54, 58, 125, 131
– of life 9
day/ days 53, 57, 180, 367, 504, 581
–, (1) one 379, 459
– after day 574
–, daylight 203
–, day–world 44, 79
– of Judgement 155, 556
–, twice a 506
days 112, 248, 320, 358, 368, 371, 471, 481, 485, 490, 494, 507, 521, 530, 538, 547, 552, 558, 560, 562, 570, 572, 575
–, (1st) first 489
–, (2) two 470, 519, 570
–, (3) three 188, 475, 519, 568
–, (4) four 293, 320, 506
–, (5) five 507
–, (6) six 488
–, (7) seven 156, 234, 283, 367, 488, 503, 531, 568-9, 581
–, (10) ten 531
–, (15) fiften 552
–, (40) fourty 255, 368, 485, 531, 538, 547, 558, 562, 564, 566, 575
–, (41) fourty-one 485-6, 489, 572
–, (80) eighty 370-1
–, (90) ninety 490
–, (100) hundred 575
–, (150) hundred and fifty 233-5
–, (180) hundred and eighty 53-4, 485
–, (360) three hundred and sixty 54
– ago 209
–, are not days 488
–, completeness of 174
–, cook for 564
–, few 367, 496, 577
–, for 255, 381, 400
–, many 57, 127, 157, 207, 248, 261, 297, 320, 356, 475, 501-2, 504-5, 510, 512, 519, 523, 529, 570
–, number of 345, 501, 546
–, single 155
–, some 144, 235, 380
dead; *see also decease* 36, 38, 40, 54, 80-1, 84, 90, 105, 109, 190, 198, 238, 283, 341, 389, 439, 480, 539, 580
– bodies 130
– body 38, 289-90
–, deadly 181
–, dry-dead 243
– earthiness 167
– human being 290
– Zosimos 37, 477
deal equally 166
death 9, 36-7, 40, 48, 56-7, 81, 122, 155, 235, 253, 328, 342, 344, 360, 476
–, after 39
– and resurrection 37, 39-40, 53, 81, 91, 110, 135, 138, 485
– of the adept 84
– of the natures 176
– of Zosimos 36, 342
–, life and/ life after 121, 123, 480, 521
–, put to …. the natures 521
–, symbolic 39, 81
debate 7, 58, 74, 96, 135
decay (vb) 24, 48, 149
– of tin 487
decease; *see also dead* (vb) 39, 109, 127
deceive 327
–, deceiver 432
–, deception 529
decision 341
declare (vb) 31, 44, 93, 150, 153, 189-90,

207, 239, 244, 249, 256, 266, 310, 316, 339, 355, 357, 362, 390, 395, 400, 444, 454, 462-3, 475, 483, 543
decline 313
decompose (vb) 152, 156, 160, 174, 177, 181, 234, 387, 480
–, blood … sperm 174
–, decomposing 174
–, decomposition 362
–d male, body as 362
–, thick 371
decrease 263, 265, 269, 272, 279, 406, 453, 567
– in casting 173
– stone 166, 173
– weight 189
decree 357, 480, 521
dedicate 46 315
deeds 26, 142
defeat (vb) 47, 201, 216, 363, 374, 393, 398
– fire 559
– natures 151, 490
definition 222
degree 117, 571, 577
– every 275
– first … of work 205
–, highest 512, 557, 571
delicious 291, 436, 488
delight 376
– soul 157
delivery 181-2, 356, 390
delude (vb)/ delusions 162, 173, 353, 359, 378, 558, 581
Democritus 24, 27-8, 45, 51, 85, 125-6, 147, 152, 162, 184, 186, 188, 191-2, 194-5, 197-9, 201-2, 204, 208, 210, 213, 216, 244-5, 247-8, 250-1, 254-5, 258, 261, 265, 269, 271-3, 287-9, 294, 296-7, 302-3, 328, 344-5, 347, 351, 355, 372, 374, 376, 378, 380, 383, 386, 389, 393-4, 397, 399-401, 403, 411, 418, 420, 424, 452, 454, 457, 460, 463, 498, 515, 529, 532, 540, 552, 556, 562, 580
– and Ostanes 347
– as best of sages 347
–, book of Democritus 273, 274, 287, 345, 377, 378, 389, 404, 453, 498
–, books of (Sartamita); *see also books* 261, 299
–, Book of Ten Keys; *see Book of Keys*
– of Abdera 27
–, operation of 552
–, role of 45
–, statement of 168-9, 189, 199, 195, 201, 213, 216, 231-3, 247, 250-1, 255, 266, 268, 285, 291, 296, 349, 359, 395, 400, 453, 475, 532, 541, 579
–, words of/ quotes from 37, 344-5
– writes 249, 256, 298
–, Zosimos as student of 347
demonic 32, 249
–, demons 11
demotize 127
denial 327
–, deny 144
depict 262
–, depictions 29
depth 129, 451
– of the body 568
Derchain-Urtel, M.T. 10
descend
–, descending 357, 571
– in water 512
–, sun, ...s 281, 367, 570
describe (vb) 25, 36, 52, 63, 90-1, 93, 149, 155-6, 170, 182, 196, 208-9, 213, 231, 237, 239, 280-1, 306, 310, 315, 321, 340, 342, 358, 370-1, 377, 403, 406-7, 414, 465, 471, 477, 483, 487, 510, 512, 527, 537, 571, 573
–, as described 79-80, 263-4, 276, 329, 411, 414, 416, 421, 425, 428-9, 439, 442, 445, 477, 517, 544, 556
– by/ as analogy 153, 174, 281
–, describable 93
– mercuries 416
– work with allusions 474
description(s) (of an illustration) 10, 18-9, 29, 36-7, 68, 75, 78-9, 84, 93, 103, 109, 137-8, 142, 144, 148, 154, 182, 194, 200, 210, 215, 251, 414, 434, 451, 453
– and illustration 81
– of Africanus 231
– of alchemical work 81
– of innerpsychic process 44
– of Jesus 121, 124
– of transformation 33
– true/ false 259

–, manifold 455
–, subtle 153
desert 130-1
deserve 260, 281
desire (n, vb) 19, 22-3, 25-7, 57, 119, 149, 155, 178, 180, 214-5, 217, 274, 281, 304, 311, 322-3, 347, 406, 458, 481, 516
– desirable 128, 172, 310
– desirousness 56, 118
– for magnesia 402
– my 143
– of body 159
– of dragon 56, 127, 157
– work 23
despair 26, 31, 26, 90, 116, 155
despise 144, 149, 174, 182-3, 228-9, 539
– body 322
– despicable 210, 214
–, despised 28, 162, 196, 322, 345, 356, 454
–, despised-exalted 214, 225
–, despised-honoured/ honourable- 128, 172, 236
– metals 166
– not ash 487
– thing 144
–, Zosimos books 329
destroy (vb); *see also harm; damage; scatter* 9-10, 36, 41, 63, 129, 152, 155, 157, 159, 162, 168, 222, 226-7, 234, 246, 249, 280, 283, 312, 354, 339-40, 358, 362-3, 368, 387, 457, 467, 474, 524, 539, 549, 551, 557, 565, 568, 575-6, 578
– bodies 303, 498
– body 152, 190, 214, 225, 322, 537, 572
– body with pure water 550
–, chrysocolla gets destroyed 530
–, cold/ fire …s body 152
– copper 283, 225, 497, 513, 565
– copper and silver 566
– dyer-spirit 579
– dyes 379
– exalted nature 172
– fighter 396
–, fire …s work 171
– flower(s) 275, 494, 522-3, 577
–, get destroyed; *see works; stone* 253, 436, 558
– in fire 191
– itself 512
– mercury 321
–, mix with what 169
–, nature …s fighter 446
– stone 156, 173, 491, 524-5
–, sulphur destroys 323
– thick part/ thickness 233, 521
– things 249
– wealth 352
– with sulphurs 284
– work 522
– world; *see also corrupt world* 259
– Zosimos; *see also Zosimos, dead/ killed* 36, 339-40
destruction 57, 127, 129, 157, 160, 225, 228, 259, 262, 286, 312, 351, 362, 522, 533
–, destructive burning 350
detail 349
deter from science 23, 149
determination 571
development 80, 123
– of consciousness 18
– of this science 24
– of Zosimos' teaching 81, 112, 116
–, psychological/ psychic 45, 137
devil(s); *see also dark; evil; luna; the other; satan* 32, 219
–, devilish 29, 44
–, envious 519
devote/ devoted 17, 138, 450, 464, 477
devotion 7, 13
dew 53, 127, 159, 231, 247, 286-7, 426, 485, 530, 575
– and sun 481, 528, 575
– as nourishment 231
– from sea 291
– prevents escaping of moisture 539
–, water of 540
dialogue(s) 5-6, 18-9, 33, 35, 37, 46, 51, 55, 61, 68, 81, 90, 98, 112, 114-6, 123-4, 135-7, 544, 557
– and illustrations; *see also text and picture/ image* 111
–, dialectic 45
– form 45, 51, 97, 111, 113-5, 117, 132-3
–, Greek 97, 115, 135

diamond 47
die 53, 98, 162, 181-2, 253, 336, 357, 360-1, 365, 485
– not of thirst 291
differ 153, 177, 199, 305, 401, 519, 521
– about names, dyeing of stone and work 294
– over weight 269
–, see different 519
difference 44, 198, 323, 552
– in cooking 507
– in name 161
– of colours 519
different; *see answer; languages; fruit; flowers; kind; thing; tastes* 119, 162-3, 205, 229, 241, 354, 489, 514, 520, 556
– appearances 31
– aspects 355
–, become 174
– colour(s) 46, 495, 212, 256, 279, 447, 458
–, differentiate 154
– fires 519
– meaning 289
– mercuries 352
– mixtures 519
– moistures 199, 284
– name(s) 257, 401
– nature 162-3, 298
– opinions 153
– ovens 496
– pictures 33, 331
– power 326
– questions 452
– statement(s) 145, 217, 294, 297
– tastes 166
– things 143, 188, 223, 224, 322, 350, 386, 511
– weights 271, 276
–, Zosimos not 305
difficult(y/ ies) 112, 273, 277-8, 326, 344-5
dig (vb) 56, 127, 157
–, digger 292
dignity 334
Dīlsiqūs; *see Disqīus*
dilute with wisdom 488
diminish (vb) 246, 456, 458, 484
Diocletian 20, 581
direction, eastern 120
dirt 165, 388, 394, 440, 509, 570
– and copper 165
– disappears 394, 570
–, greasy 167
–, remove 508
disagreement 63, 177, 194, 221, 293, 559
–, disagree 380
– of sages 219
disappear 240, 301, 357, 362, 572
– blackness 129, 282, 292-3, 454, 535, 564
–, body ....s 537
–, colours 315, 318, 396
–, dirt ....s 394
–, dye …(not) 468, 554
–, dye (of flowers) ....s 508
–, earth … not 371
–, earthiness ....s 164
–, earthly thickness ....s 369
–, everything in composition ....s 191
– flower(s) 289, 554, 575
– from rest 191
– in operation 504
–, kohl ....s 566
– let not … from thinking 192
– mixture 397
– moisture 356
–, moisture ....s 235, 395, 475, 510, 528, 531, 536, 542, 547, 567, 575
–, moisture …s from litharge 326
– passion 458
–, poison and mixture 293, 454
–, salt ....s 487
–, shadow ....s 173, 201, 373, 386, 410-1, 420, 498
–, shadow of copper ....s 200, 247, 410, 420, 528
–, silver ....s 554
–, soul ....s 190
–, spirits 505
–, splendour ....s 56, 157, 336
–, squeaking ....s 234
– sulphur 296
–, thick part ....s 190
–, tin ....s 190
–, vinegar ....s 233-5
disasters 118
disbelieve (vb) 25, 118, 155, 169, 194
discover/ discovery 97, 131, 138
– of the unconscious 93
diseases; *see also cure; doctor; illness;*

medical; remedy 169
disguise (vb); *see also analogy; cheat; cover; names; similes; trickery; ruse; veiling* 24, 93, 128, 145, 147, 149-51, 155, 159, 171, 178, 184, 194, 199, 202-4, 206, 219, 221, 228, 24-6, 257, 259-60, 267, 297, 312, 315, 321, 327, 383-4, 488, 516
–, disguised and truth 315
– statement 350
– work 349
disidentification/ disidentify 39-40
Dīsīus 361
Disqīus/ Dīlsiqūs 150-1
– and Sīūs 550, 564
disobey (vb) 217, 242, 315, 559
disperse (vb) 9, 23, 97, 149, 202, 263, 563
–, sages dispersed and collected 555
disposition 53, 174, 360
dissimlilarity 455
dissolution 258, 451
– of other composition 258
dissolve (vb) 145-6, 155, 158-60, 167, 175, 187, 195, 197, 201, 210, 223, 256, 261, 266, 268, 277-8, 298, 304, 323-4, 353-6, 360, 362-3, 376, 380, 387, 396, 484, 489, 492, 500, 505, 507, 522, 530, 558, 561, 569-70, 572-3, 576, 578
–, (1) one dissolved by the one 569
– (2nd) second time 551
– (3rd) third elixir 505-6
– and solidified/ solidify 156, 256
– aqzal and spittle of moon 321
– arsenic 548
–, before changing 472
– bodies 237
– body 128, 150-1, 155-6, 159, 172, 192, 244, 321, 354, 364, 529, 531, 535
–, body dissolves water 482
– by milk-like kohl-stone 472
– copper 572
– crystal 210, 318
–, dissolved, plates, moisture 548
– each other 572
– egg 487
– equally 263, 273-4, 282, 298, 376, 398, 546
– every body 261
– everything 173, 507
– garlic 512
– glass 319
– gold 293, 320
– gum 388
– hard body with waters 396
– heat 492
– immediately 472, 474
– in fire 492, 525
– iron 485
– lead-copper 210
– lead(-copper), copper, (honoured stone) equally 273-4, 282, 298, 398, 376, 546
– lime 510
– magnesia 366, 372
–, mercury of arsenic and sandarach 353
–, moisture …s body 548
–, name the 146
– nature 201, 270, 302, 396, 489
– not 146
– other 570, 572
– plate(s) 243, 489, 529, 551
–, pound and cook 532
– relatives with natures 399
– silver 410, 418, 442, 455-6, 472
–, solidify after first dissolving 353, 484
– stone 210, 249
– sulphur and magnet 321
– the …d 146
– things 414
– to water 569
–, water dissolves everything 501
–, water is dissolved 159
– well 156
– with dissolved 366
dissolving 50, 146, 159, 197, 294, 354, 366, 372, 393, 451, 456, 482, 501, 540, 549
–, (1) one 294
– and solidifying 484
– female 304
–, greatest 535
–, last 535
– of bodies 228, 462
– of body of gold 293
– of bones/ ivory 249
– of copper 244
– of gum 452
– of idol 287

– of tar 568
–, work is not possible without 128, 159
distillation; *see also pondering* 5, 41, 66-7, 134, 561, 575
– apparatus 64
distinction 95, 126, 315
distinguish 205, 221, 240, 280, 453, 467, 517
distort (vb) 61, 275, 394
– operations 349
distress 317, 331, 345, 491
divide (vb, adj) 24, 64, 74, 114, 149, 167, 210, 229, 368, 557, 560
– into (4) four parts 50, 371
–, division 166, 525
– dye 473
– egg 50
– equally 48, 166, 300
– fire 491, 525
– nature 570
– nine 269
– poison 560, 572
– treasures 450
– water 558
– work 153
divine 31-3, 35, 37-9, 59, 64, 78, 80, 124
– and human 40-1
– art 97
–, aspect 33, 67
–, child 44
– core 40
–, divinities 108, 112
– figures 25
– nature 32
– water 19, 24, 38, 44, 91
– Zosimos 9
doctor(s) 98
–, medical 67, 90
document; *see also book; epistle; letter; poem; text* 33, 36, 40, 74, 96, 98, 111, 117, 132-3, 135 137-8
dog 84, 216, 290, 439, 501
– and wolf 289, 498
–, dogs 59, 64, 347, 450
–, green 439
– of the water 517
– rises 494
donkey/ she-donkey 192, 401
– and horse 498
door 53, 203, 215, 396
–, open 323, 446
Dorneus, Gerhard 67
doubt 143-4, 158, 189, 194-5, 219, 260, 285, 321, 327, 357-9, 362, 370, 475, 500, 504, 526, 529, 539
–, doubtful 180, 418, 483
–, no 170, 267
– operation 148
– relieve 217
– Zosimos 148
dough 245
– is fermented 165
down, go 145
dragon; *see also serpent; Ouroboros* 47-8, 56-7, 127-30, 366, 458, 514
– and its wife 47
– and water 48
– and woman 56, 127, 157
– and young man 51
–, cultivation of 426
–, defeat 47
–, desire of 56, 127, 157
– eating its tail; *see also serpent; tail* 50, 263, 318, 371
– egg and water 159
–, egg of 48
–, extract egg 300
–, eye(s) of 47
–, fight 47, 300
–, gallbladder of 458
–, head of 48, 300
– is yolk 159
–, kill(ed) 48¸ 56, 127, 157, 300
–, sperm of 426
–, tomb for 56, 127, 157
–, water of 426, 474
draw
–, cloud …s water/ dye 162
dream(s) 5, 23-4, 93, 98, 112, 132, 137, 143, 331
–, (3) three dreams 23
–, big/ great dream(s) 23, 40-1, 47, 132-33, 137, 149, 217, 300, 514
–, -life of Zosimos 23
– of dragon fight 47-8, 51, 300
– of killed, cut man 149, 216-17
– of Zosimos 6, 20, 24, 47-8

– -world 7, 41, 137
dregs 204
dress (n/ vb) 36, 141, 156, 339, 391, 562
drink (vb) 90, 161
– from resurrecting water 53, 485
– salty sea 292
drives 250
–, drivenness 35
drop (vb, n) 387, 512
drops 469, 580
– dissolve earth 580
– of gold 538
dry 161, 169, 175, 181, 205, 218, 223, 235, 237, 243, 248, 268, 280, 283, 295, 297, 302, 304, 321, 362, 364, 389, 399, 402, 405, 453, 473-4, 489-90, 495, 497, 500, 504, 506-7, 529, 536-8, 543, 547, 549, 555, 562, 565, 569-71, 573
– and cold 228
– and (the) moist 63, 143, 152-3, 217-8, 222, 243, 370, 487
– ash/ sediment 493
–, become 277, 321, 362, 569, 573
– body 290
–, cold, hot, … and moist 142, 169, 175
– -dead 243
–, drying 564
–, dryness 63, 173, 175, 215, 240, 547
–, dryness, moisture, spirit and cloud 360
–, every … thing 362
– first/ second 569
– gum 277, 491
–, heat dries 161
– iron 442
– loves moist 575
– magnesia 524
–, make moist dry 176
–, mix … and moist 217-18, 487
–, names for/ of 405, 453
– one 142, 326, 511
– out body 157
–, plates dry up moisture 529
– poison 573
–, power of 326
– silver 206
–, spirit dries soul 218
– stone 531
–, strong, powerful, … and hot 174
– sulphur 198
–, sun dries 501
– thing 167, 297, 304
–, uncooked 405
– up 173, 229, 471, 519, 523, 529, 547-8, 554, 565-7, 569
– up blood 57, 127, 157
– up elixir 572
– (up) moisture 30, 129, 529, 534, 558, 560, 563-4, 581
– up water 562
– vapour 198
dung 303, 474, 507
–, dog 501
–, dunghills 231
– -fire/ fire of 188-9, 262, 268, 280, 548, 551
–, human 501
–, leave in 508
– of the moon 128, 172, 237
dupe (vb) 149
durable relationship 39, 44
ad–Durra an-naqīya 5, 10
dust 24, 53, 153, 167, 176, 207, 210, 218, 234, 256, 298, 302, 480, 482, 548, 561
– and gum 454
– and marble 284
– and/ into water 192, 529
–, become 145, 258, 320
–, bodies into 386, 559
–, cover … with water 531
–, dry 558
–, dusty 395
–, fine 23-4, 227, 286, 530, 537
–, fine like 149, 196, 234, 482, 562
–, fine-spiritual 145
–, gather 161
–, golden 271, 317
– is extracted 167
–, lower than 176
–, moisture into 156, 537
–, nature into 154
–, pyrite into 234
–, red 278, 295, 363
–, soak 557
–, sulphur turns into 528
–, turn into 146, 154, 227, 295, 350, 480, 482, 531, 536, 547, 557-8
– water and herbs 286

–, white 284
dusts 194, 208, 215, 252, 349, 375
– as sulpur 289
–, dusts, herbs and milks 454
– escape 190
–, names of 375
Duval, Rubens 11, 17, 22, 27
dwelling 166, 356
dye (vb, n) 56, 63, 163, 165-7, 170-1, 179, 185-6, 190, 195, 200, 207-10, 220, 222, 227, 235-6, 247-51, 259, 261-2, 267-8, 271, 275, 279-80, 283, 285-7, 291, 299, 302-4, 317-8, 324-6, 347, 364, 370-1, 375-6, 380, 388, 407, 411, 431, 447-8, 468, 470, 473, 495-6, 498, 502-3, 512, 536, 540, 542, 544, 551, 554, 566, 569, 573-5, 571, 577
–, (1) one 184, 205, 304, 405, 580
– (1) one, ... is 205, 251, 302, 461
– (3) three times 473
–, accept 504, 541
– and dye not/ not dyed 369, 509
– and dyed 551
– and dyer 248
– and fire 554
– and sulphur 247
–, aquire 484
–, become dye(d) 248, 578-9
–, beginning of 490
–, beneficial 240, 459
– black 248, 316, 455, 495, 510
–, black and gum 316
– bodies 181, 369, 538
– bodies by tin 460
– bodies into gold 294
– body 154, 178, 279, 452, 551
– body of magnesia 380
– by earth 304
– changes composition 212
–, cinnabar holds … of mercury 490
–, clings 256
–, cloud as 567
–, cloud draws 162
– clothes 204, 472
–, cold 471
– colours 481
– comes out 512
–, complete 120, 248, 357, 546
– concealed (in head) 515, 575
–, cook … in water 502
– copper 501, 503
–, copper turns into died 364
– core of metals 204
–, crystal accepts 319
– disappears 508, 554
–, divide 473
–, dyed by bodies 302
–, dyed dyes 251, 369
–, dyed one 270, 320, 474
–, dyeing/ dyer/ dyes; *see dyes; dyer; dyeing*
– elixir 275
– every 275, 400
– every body/ everybody 164, 189, 206, 261, 266, 380, 386, 410, 454, 468, 529-30
–, exalted 172, 271, 432
–, extract … from gold 447
–, extract … from nature(s) 387, 405, 555
–, extract colour of dye 511
–, extract dye from bodies/ sulphurs 49, 514-5
–, ferment of gold …s every body 189
–, (fire) consumes 524
– fixed 205
–, flowers of dye/ dye as flowers 508, 554
–, fugitives' true dyeing 453
–, get dyed 541
– glass 350
– gold 165, 204, 226, 277, 361, 490, 493-4, 538, 540, 574
– gold dyes silver 183
– gold with gold 280
–, good 235
– gum and honoured stone 492
– herbs 226
–, hide 452
–, hold 277, 489
–, hot dyeing 453
–, improve 497
– is concealed 229, 575
– is smoke 505
–, key of dyeing 316
– leathers 204
–, luminous 269
– many things 481
–, mercury, alum and 452
–, mix 255, 319, 466, 452, 456, 471-2, 512
– nature(s) 291, 246, 326, 488

– not quickly 504
– of bodies 200
– of dyers 504
– of fugitives 524
– of gold 463
– of man 540
–, operation of 503
–, our 210
–, penetrating 510
–, perfect 295, 567
–, pound before you 389
–, preparation of 490
–, purple 248, 316-7, 319, 321, 446, 495, 540, 552
–, put… in its water 511
– red 420
–, rest in 495
–, right 554
– rust 250
–, sea dyes 255
– silver 349, 375, 455
– silver into gold 235
–, smoke with splendour, … and colour 505
–, soak with 547
– solid with solid 369
–, soul is/ dye soul 370, 539
– spirit/ dyeing 129, 178, 247, 520, 543
–, spiritual 566
–, spirit dyes body 233
– stone(s) 204, 294, 319, 375, 496, 566
–, strong 567
– submerges 255, 568
–, subtle 510
– subtle part of 498
– sulphur(s) 416, 461
–, sulphur …s every body 251
–, sulphurs get dyed 475
–, sun into incombustible 522
– that does not vanish 370
– the dye 251
– the purple 168, 541
–, thing dyes 195
–, thing good for dyeing 41, 575
–, throw … on body 566
–, tin dyes 460, 546
–, true 496, 554
– turn dyed like blood 491
–, turn into 488
– untouchable 482
– vanishes 539
– wanted 510
– water 209, 248
– water and stones 464
– waters remain from 302
– well 168
– white/ red 205, 420, 541
– with broth 452
– with glue 474
– with spirit 214
– with unchangeable dye 567
– wool 204, 539, 541, 552
dyeing 23, 149, 177, 179, 199, 396
– as perfection of things 461
– as treating with alum 324
–, cold ... of purple 453
colour 178
–, completion of 120, 219
–, crown of 547
–, first 520
–, good 547
–, ivory, horns, bones 319
– mercury 425
– nature(s) 196, 229, 524
– of clothes/ wool 271, 406, 453
– of gold 453
– of magnesia 380
– of purple 323
– of stone 256
– poison 287, 301
– soul 225
– spirit disappears 505
– spirit(s) 129, 200, 223, 225-7, 521, 524
–, spiritual-dyers 562
–, unchangeable 567
dyer 188, 470, 502, 573
– and dyed 165, 184, 188, 247-8, 262, 304, 369, 573
– and dyeing 207
– and torturer 447
– as analogy for work 463
–, become 369
– does not get burnt 284
–, female sulphur 509
– from earth 153
– -soul 567
– spirit 255

– water 304
dyers 452-3, 472, 508, 510
– cook dyes 491
–, dye of/ dyes of 502, 504
–, dyer-spirit 579
–, fire of 492, 525
– should guide seekers 452
dyes 141, 172, 179, 184, 192, 204, 225, 261-2, 287, 380, 403, 464, 503, 525, 527, 536, 542, 544
–, (2) two 464
–, all 259
– and composed water 552
– as flowers 508, 513
–, collected 44, 576
– comes from waters 473
– come up to air 461
–, companions leave 552
–, cook 523, 554
–, destroy 379
– dye/ dyed 251, 369
–, dyers cook 491
–, extract 470
– extract … by ashes 206, 515
–, fire turn sulphur into 494
–, fix 401-2
–, flowers of 452
– have nature 406
–, hold 229
–, improve 490
–, let not escape 369
–, natures contain 236
– of copper 447
– of dyers 502
– of making clothes purple/ alumy 452
–, permanent 212
– remain 461
–, turn … non-fugitives 300

–E–

ear(s) 303, 455
earth 41-2, 78-9, 109, 179, 181, 198, 201, 215, 223, 256, 258-60, 278, 295, 304, 310, 312, 362, 366, 374, 388, 447, 458, 507, 554, 572
– accepts rain 548
– and water 304, 520
– as dyed one 304
– as gum 293
– becomes hot 218
–, black 237-8, 386, 580
–, bodies are from 175
–, clod of 161, 506
– cracks 507
–, cultivate gold in earth 515
–, dead earthiness 167
–, dissolve... by drops 580
–, earthiness disappears 164
–, earthly 41, 134, 240, 362, 369, 570
–, earthy 163, 227, 493
– enters air 228
– extracts moisture 297
–, fire, water, air and 222, 515
–, heat cracks 501
–, hide 259-60
–, imprison … in air 228
– of Ethiopia 580
– of/ from things 153
– of Nile 501
– of Sudan 209
–, operated (vb) 572
– operates on magnesia 369
–, plants of the 523
–, polished 250, 397
–, return to 218
–, rot … with water 303
–, salt, alum, white lead, polished … and living water 395
–, separate from 238, 507
– -smoke/ smoke of 218
–, snowy 151, 297, 395
–, starry 151, 250, 297, 410
–, sudanian 209
–, thirsty 402
–, turn ... into gold 386
–, tun ... into water 228, 370-1, 548
–, water, air and fire 359
–, water, …, wind and light 122
–, white 126, 293
–, wisdom of 67
East 58, 286, 310-12, 494
– bank 9
–, Eastern 120, 278, 450
easy 144, 405, 496, 555

–, not 577
eat (vb) 50, 52-3, 130, 161, 239, 318, 324-5, 484, 498, 522
–, dragon/serpent eats tail 50, 263, 371
–, edible 156
–, fire eats blackness 167
– fruits 504
eclipse 281
Eden 209, 231
edited 17, 51
–, edition 17, 20, 51
–, facsimile edtion 6-7
– texts 18
educate 298
–, education 29, 212, 221
effect 401, 454
efficiency 238
effort; *see also achieve; aim; goal; hardship; harm; disease; suffer* 12, 127, 178, 203, 205, 257, 485, 515
egg(s) 50, 159, 204, 227, 369, 371, 374, 520
–, burn 487
–, colours of 50, 370, 372
–, dissolve 487
–, dragon, … and water 159
– of a crocodile/ dragon 47-8, 300
– of birds 370
– of hen 50, 371-2
– of sages 51, 369, 372
–, shell is 159
ego 32, 40, 44
Egypt 5, 9, 11, 20-1, 25, 29, 58, 109-11, 113, 118, 123, 249, 280, 451
–, Ancient 8, 17, 19, 35, 39-40, 52, 54-5, 80, 108, 113, 123, 127, 130, 136
–, Egyptian(s) 10, 54, 50, 78, 80, 90
–, Egyptian alchemist 9
–, Egyptian vinegar 549
–, Islamic/ pre-Islamic 113, 136
–, mountains of 367
–, people of 352
–, sage in 471
–, Upper 7, 28, 121, 124, 130-1
eight (8) 268, 516
–, (8) eight-legged 290
–, ($8^1/_2$) eight and a half ounces 320
–, (8500) eight thousand five hundred 327
eighteenth (18th)
–, (18th) eighteenth century 99
–, (18th) eighteenth picture 84, 439
eighth (8th) 80-1, 341, 421, 476
–, (1/8) one eighth 267
eighty (80) days 370-1
element(s) 344, 393
–, (4) four 92, 122, 256
elevate 493
–, elevated nature 170, 393
–, elevation 393
eleventh (11th) 17, 80-1, 84, 347, 427-9, 543-5, 554
– century 94
Elias*; see Elinus*
eliciting 114, 116
Elinus (Elias?) 215
elixir 66-7, 165, 206, 233, 235, 257, 456, 465, 506, 538-9, 548, 552, 562, 577
–, (1st) first ... mixes 505-6
–, (1st) first/ (2nd) second/ (3rd) third 319
–, (2nd) second … burns 505-6
–, (3rd) third … dissolves 505-6
–, all 506
–, and something 548
– and splitting 206
–, become mature 577
–, colour/ s of 245, 558
–, components of 577
– dries up 572
–, extract subtle part of 506
–, making white of 552
–, marriage of 275
–, name bodies 552
–, operation of 577, 548
–, perfect 533, 534
–, red 567
–, ripen with water 562
–, soaking of 567, 572
–, turn into 431
–, water as 248
emaciate/ emaciation 481, 492, 502
embalming 39-40
embark 400
embrace/ embracing 56, 127, 157, 225, 264, 276, 360, 391
embryo 174, 486
emendation 48, 56, 27, 140-1, 147, 156-7, 162, 164, 169, 172, 193, 253, 288, 300,

320, 327, 369
emerald; *see also stone* 176, 256, 347
–, green 450
emerge/ emergence; *see also existence, come into* 39, 235, 300, 364, 477
emit 436
enclosing 322
Encyclopedia 9-10, 113, 130
end (vb, n); *see also final; last* 20, 37, 41, 48-9, 63, 66, 84, 98, 113, 120, 146, 184, 210, 239, 253, 303, 313, 350, 361, 420, 490-1, 544, 567
– and beginning 537
–, fight the 336
– of book/ of sages' book 266, 268, 274, 324
– of Book about the Broth 272
– of composition 224
– of life 170
– of statement 254, 363
– of time 25, 119, 154-5
– of whitening 216, 355
– of work 33, 128, 158, 163, 171, 187, 213, 229, 241, 247, 328, 331, 349
–, replaces beginning 349
enemy 28, 35-6, 48, 121, 127, 192, 232, 289, 300, 305, 336-7, 379, 418, 457
–, harmful 521
– of water 28, 120, 219, 523
– of work 491
energy, archetypal 118
enigma/ enigmatic/ al 9, 27, 74, 79, 81, 84, 91, 111, 116, 128, 137-8, 140, 143, 148, 170, 178, 180, 194, 203, 220, 236, 292, 297, 344, 347, 358, 370, 402, 410, 450, 452, 462, 488, 516, 532, 541, 559
enjoy/ enjoyment 56, 127, 157, 258
– nature …s nature 291, 352
enlighten/ enlightenment 137, 148, 494
enmity 168
enter into (vb) 33, 47, 50, 143, 146, 150, 153, 159, 178-9, 203, 215, 223, 228, 241, 273, 292, 301, 332, 357, 371, 383, 434, 456, 482, 534, 573
– art 62
– bath 318
– belly 305
– bodies 192
–, bodies … composition 303
– body 354, 488, 520, 537, 573
composition 129, 192, 397
– consciousness 35
– cooking 277
–, copper enters making rusty 373
– fire 152, 304, 521
–, fire … silver 246
–, foreign 143
– in form 341
– lead-copper 500
–, let glass 512
–, let male 304
–, let not 167
– making of silver 566
–, mercury …s lead-copper 472
–, moisture enters vessel 564
– nature 390, 480
– operation 207
–, poison enters 287
–, rust enters nature 559
– science 385, 454
–, sperm 387
–, spirit … body 235
–, spirit …s soul/ soul …s spirit 154
– work 28, 37, 62, 150-3, 166, 169, 188, 190, 194, 203, 207-8, 219, 221, 223, 229, 278, 280, 284, 315, 345, 359, 365, 368, 370, 389, 397-8, 434, 451, 454-5, 459, 487, 491, 499, 524, 537, 561, 565
enthusiasm 5, 26, 119, 155
Epimetheus 92
epistle(s); *see also book; kitāb; letter; poem; risāla; treatise* 18, 73, 111-2, 114-6
–, (3rd) Third ... of Zosimos 111, 114-5, 125
–, (4th) Fourth ... about the Weights 112
–, (7) seven 73, 112, 114, 132
–, (25th) twenty-fifth 132
–, (29th) twenty-ninth 132
–, (70) seventy, The 18
–, Book of the 73
–, Epistle about the Dissolving of the Idol 287
–, epistolary 112, 114
– of Lead-Copper, Sulphur, and the Rest of the Things 299
– of Maria 287, 462
– of the Teaching 462
– of Zosimos 46, 315
–, Saramīṭā; *see Sartamita*

–, special ... for Theosebeia 46, 315
–, The great Epistle of the Spheres 95
–, The Letters 407, 411, 434
–, The Sulphurs 43, 116-7, 132
epitome 68
equal 265, 269, 271-2, 274, 468
– amounts 442
–, balance is 263, 264, 276
–, measures 500
– things 440
– to God 148
–, to man 390
– weight(s) 275, 298
– with equal 365
equally 158, 166, 265, 273-4, 275, 284, 340, 365, 398
–, dissolve 263, 376
–, dissolve lead, copper (and honoured stone) 273-4, 282, 298
–, divide 48, 300
–, mix 546
equivalent(s) 178, 291
erotapokriseis 18
error(s) 140, 180, 184, 197, 206, 284, 289, 299, 304, 405-6, 456, 486, 489, 491, 496, 508, 522, 540, 551, 557, 559, 567
–, fall into 146, 148, 208, 257, 305, 312, 317, 349, 354, 370, 405, 454, 462, 467, 491, 523
– from fire 524
– from natures 379
–, no 267
–, pains of 180
escape (vb); *see also flee* 190, 194, 197, 232-3, 253, 268, 277, 281, 324, 360, 372, 378, 402, 416, 488, 497, 538, 540, 552
–, (1) one is ...ing/ escaping and what does not escape is (1) one 165, 439
–, bodies that … not 378
– chrysocolla ... not 253
–, colours do not 369
–, dyed sulphur escapes 461
–, earth …s not 371
–, escaping 165, 232, 339, 360, 371, 439, 488
–, escaping block 281
– fire/ not fire 63, 172, 398, 514
– from body 539
– from fire 151, 191-2, 198, 222, 284, 301, 399
– let dyes not 369
– magnesia lets not … spirit 372
–, male and spirit 304
–, mercury ...s 321
–, moisture ...ing from fire 396
– not! 49, 169, 192-3, 253, 268, 305, 323-4, 360, 363, 371, 396, 400, 446, 453, 467, 468, 470, 569
– of fugitive 540
–, prevent ...ing 164, 197, 200, 285, 465, 483
–, prevent from ...ing 396, 372, 541
–, stop/ stops ...ing 166, 362, 465-6
– quickly/ not quickly 153, 467, 568
–, spirit …s not 253
–, tendency to 550
– to air 505
–, water ...s 436
– with body 483
essence 134, 174, 222, 238, 284, 373, 376, 397, 462, 533
–, essential 476-7
– of mercury 458
– of nature 444
– of teaching 11, 134
–, red in 151, 352, 373, 475, 483, 493, 549, 574
–, strong in 169
–, yellow in 499
eternal 39-40, 90, 228, 231, 364, 488, 531-2, 573
– body 231, 280
–, chrysocolla, body of magnesia and … water 266
–, flowers of … water 567
–, gold with … water 548
–, operate with … water 561
–, pure … water 573
–, second work made water eternal 491
– stone 238
– water 160, 171, 213, 266, 277-8, 295, 319, 355, 363-4, 480, 482, 490-1, 528-9, 537-8, 558, 560-1, 564-5, 567, 571-2, 576-7
– water and honoured body 529
– water and lead 546
–, wash with … water 564
etesian 46-47, 227, 368, 565
–, antimony, … and copper burnt with

sulphur 376
– as benefit with many names 451
–, cast antimony and 376
–, lead, … and copper 378
–, making of 465
– stone 24, 46-7, 212, 252, 282, 304, 325, 464-5, 507, 515, 521
Ethiopia 580
Ettinghausen, Richard 99
Europe 59
evaporate 218
Eve, Adam and 359
every
– body 165, 173, 185, 186, 189, 206-7, 235, 245, 246, 255, 261, 262, 266, 301, 454, 455, 460, 468, 529-30
– day 166, 519
– dry 362
– everyone 177, 507
– moist 362
–, operate 146
– soil 395
everything 41, 62-3, 142, 151, 162, 165, 170, 172-3, 178-9, 187, 191, 195, 197-8, 210, 220, 222-4, 227, 239, 251, 254-5, 258, 261, 272, 282, 284-5, 292, 294, 296, 305, 319, 325, 355, 359, 360, 362, 370, 372, 374-5, 380-2, 393, 418, 458, 465, 471, 475, 477, 480-2, 489, 497, 501, 511, 521, 530, 547, 552, 560, 576-7
–, (1) one, ... is 514
– as analogy 370
– becomes water 147
– comes from it (nature) 162
–, contain 386
–, creates everything 550
–, crown of 197
–, dissolve 507
–, extract 504
–, good for 210, 551
–, head of 197
– in nature 384
– is by it and from it (nature) 162
–, name of 256
–, nature is in 162
–, pound 249
–, turn ... into dust 145
– turns into water 573
– vanishes 191
evidence 9, 49, 58, 68, 75, 81, 96-7, 111, 115-7, 124, 136, 387
– evident 31, 54, 81, 156, 242, 559, 568
evil; *see also devil* 28, 31, 36, 122, 336
exalted 26, 28, 33, 119-20, 152, 154-5, 169, 173, 176, 204, 216, 219, 221, 227, 237, 241, 243, 251, 277-8, 283, 285, 293, 296, 299, 303, 310, 315, 317, 323, 332, 355, 357, 359, 363, 365, 367-8, 387, 393, 402, 420, 451, 455-6, 464, 476, 486, 489, 497, 517, 535, 543, 556, 563, 571, 577, 581
– (1) one 214
– colour 168
– -despised 225
– dye 172, 432
– God 148, 150
– -inferior 214
– mixture 128, 243
– nature 170
– work 539
examination of mercury 394
example(s) 23, 27, 45-7, 51, 58, 92, 98-9, 111, 113, 117, 130, 140, 145, 147-8, 160, 177, 203, 306, 310, 315, 327, 450, 474, 477, 556, 575
– about nature 387
– as help 328
– of secret 473
excerpts 114
exhaust (vb) 129, 217, 451
exist/ existence 53, 62, 98, 161, 231, 226, 228, 235, 290, 305, 440, 484, 497
–, come into being/ existence; *see also emerge* 62, 122, 144, 151-2, 177, 214, 221, 223, 249, 254, 256, 262, 281-2, 303, 357, 475, 513, 532, 577, 580
–, dye ...s 262, 552, 544
–, needs opposite 214
–, -non-existing 214
–, not without eternal water/ nothing comes into existence without (eternal/ composed) water/ moisture 285, 298, 552, 577
–, not without/ only with; *see also exist, without which nothing* 162, 219, 298, 373, 491, 516, 544, 546, 552, 577

–, without lead nothing could/ can/ would exist 144, 152-3, 162, 165, 192, 236, 376, 546
–, without which nothing could be/ comes into existence (being)/ would be; *see also exist not without* 144, 152-3, 162, 165, 170, 192, 236, 285, 293, 298, 351, 483, 513, 577
expense/ expensive 162, 214, 222, 345
– -cheap 214, 225
–, expenses 219
experience(s) 11, 32, 39, 44, 59, 93, 98, 118, 130, 133, 138, 169, 179, 201
– of love 135
–, people of 159
–, work 497
experiment(s) (vb, n) 10, 210, 285, 317, 405, 407, 434, 476, 494, 506, 519 540
– about mercury 434
–, experimental alchemy 11
–, greatest 389
– guides you/ will show you 405, 472, 500, 507
–, know 404-5, 569
–, make 519
– of chrysocolla 569
– of dissolving 568
explain (vb) 22-5, 33, 35-6, 39, 45, 54, 62, 79, 84-5, 92, 94-5, 97-8, 115, 117, 128, 138, 149-50, 154-5, 161-2, 164, 171-2, 202, 221, 227, 250, 257, 259, 263, 273, 280-1, 296, 303, 325, 344, 358, 407, 420, 447, 453-4, 465, 485, 490, 498, 537, 540, 547, 555, 557, 562, 566, 571, 575
– in book(s)/ book(s) 154, 452
– in pictures 39
– mixing 385
– work/ art 73. 97
explanation(s) 11, 39, 62, 64, 85, 111, 113, 117, 119, 144, 151, 153, 271, 288, 301, 327, 382, 411, 434, 508
–, Book of the Explanation of Symbols 6
–, complete 53, 484
– of magnesia 329
– of stone 471
expose 150, 169, 559
extend 389
external 505
extinguish (vb) 118, 175, 279
– colour(s)/ light 37, 342, 344, 507
extract (vb) 45, 52, 127, 159, 162, 164, 166, 179, 194, 416, 451, 469, 502, 519
– (1) one colour 406
– (2) two waters from stone and Cypriot copper 382
– (3) three froth, ...from 446
– all dyes 206
– blackness 480
– bodies from mercury 261
– body 482
– by cloud 489
– by contemplation 359
– colours 179, 260, 316, 323, 396, 404, 446, 450, 483, 529
– concealed nature with fire 302
– dust 167
– dye 49, 200, 370, 387-8, 405, 514, 555
– dyeing spirits 521
– dyes 447, 470, 515
– egg from dragon 300
– everthing from/ in ash(es) 504, 511
– extraction 426, 458
– ferment 245, 503
– flour 303
– flowers 256, 578
– from ash(es) 232, 253, 504, 566
– from bodies/ bodily reality 24, 476, 524
– from cinnabar 420, 424, 535
– from earthy body 493
– from elixir 506
– from first work 386
– from lead-copper 245, 256
– from metals 238
– from mineral 488
– from non-fugitive 514
– from operation seven colours 465
– from sediments 503
– from spirit 214
– from sulphur 420
– from things 128, 159
– from treasure house 389
– from water 567
– froth 323, 396
– fugitives 183
– gentle part 369
– gold 303

– grain of wheat from ear 303
– mercuries 402, 476
– mercury 280, 352, 402, 424, 490, 542-3
– moisture 283, 297, 493, 515
– nature 549
– not dye 515
– poison 232, 440, 533, 535
– power of copper 512
– power of crimson 512
– pure water of sulphur 516
– purple 508
– redness 491, 446
– red stone 488
– silver from bodies 410
– soul/ souls 51, 190, 225, 227, 480
– soul from body/ bodies 163, 477, 488, 514
– spirit 150, 179, 198, 243-4, 246, 255, 323, 371, 488, 513, 520
– spirit from body 215, 369, 477, 488, 520
– spirits 167
– spirits from bodies 190, 496, 305
– stone from metal 209
– subtle (parts) 164, 218, 303, 461, 498
– sulphur 185, 493
– mercury from bodies 261
– moisture 167
–, nature from names 539
–, redness by blackness 509
– things from magnesia 156
– true mercury 457
– vapour 190, 244, 386, 503
–, vapour extracts spirit 533
– water of gold/ silver 243, 457
– water of sulfur 185, 489, 552
– water from vapour 493
– waters from ashes 461
– what is inside 150
– white 284, 468
– whiteness from blackness 509, 542
– wisdom 469
– with mercury 567
extremes 158
extroverted 132
eye(s) 29, 31, 33, 108, 148, 150, 174, 182, 200, 208, 214, 217, 229, 240, 242, 270, 285, 289, 323, 352, 310-11, 318, 322, 331-2, 336, 397, 406, 455-6, 462, 464, 502, 505, 556, 565
–, eyesight 331, 424, 550, 563
– of the dragon 47
–, pupil of 237
–, see (with own) 328, 331

–F–

face(s) 38, 41, 48, 108, 208, 216, 286, 300, 311, 421, 428, 450
–, (3) three faces 418, 557
– dark 37
–, golden 429, 431, 435, 436, 442, 445
–, no 34-5, 37-8, 41
– of lion 473
–, sun/ moon with 34, 37, 41, 43
facsimile edition 5-7, 11-13, 73, 80, 84, 118, 135, 140
faint 356
fairy tale 59
faith 122
–, faithful/ faithfulness 361
–, faithlessness 388
fall (vb) 32, 212, 218, 220, 284, 362, 387, 520, 558
– down 208, 220, 300, 560, 578
– down in fire 397
– in body 360
– into cooking 481
– into doubt 539
– into error; *see error*
– into water 146, 482
– poison …s on body 520
false 202, 259, 359, 385
– names 212, 221
– natures 467
– parts 147
fan 313
far and near 180
farmer 201
fat 196, 199, 233, 288, 294, 321, 576
– and body of magnesia 381
–, accumulates 157
–, copper, gum and 487
–, every 247
–, fatness 158, 509
–, fats 349
–, gold, vinegar and 457

–, lime, vinegar and 457
–, marble water, lime, sediment and 381
–, rest of the 570
–, thick 521
–, vinegar and honey 199
father 25, 53, 155, 177, 182, 259, 262, 290, 296, 360, 398, 455, 501, 526, 555, 559
– and child 177
– and son 37, 182, 342
–, turn ... into sun 53, 485
fault, small 328
favour(s) 29, 45, 150, 156, 181, 212, 237, 328, 432, 463, 491, 499, 526, 540, 559
–, crown of 159
fear 25, 47, 148, 154, 178, 219, 236, 242, 310, 329, 334, 382, 383, 390, 405, 427, 540, 559
– not fire 490
– of Master 155
fecundate(s) 128, 155, 242, 278, 382, 480, 567
– and fecundated 278
–, fecundation 55, 157, 326, 359, 480
feeble/ feebleness; *see also mind, weak-minded 18, 63, 327,* 329, 400, 533
feed 177
– body 157
–, feeding 158, 161, 290
feedback 175, 195, 271
feeling(s) 11, 18, 39, 132
feet 307, 426, 436, 442, 445, 477
female(s); *see also body; earth* 41, 56, 122, 135, 164, 177, 181, 197, 238, 249, 292, 310, 313, 320, 372, 396, 474, 530, 533
– and arsenic 233
– and male(s) 29, 32, 44, 53, 58, 116, 122, 129, 134, 136-7, 164, 174-5, 182, 225, 233-5, 249, 258, 278, 296, 310-1, 363, 366, 474, 485, 534, 546, 580
– body; *see body, female*
–, dissolve 304
–, female-male relationship 136-7
– found male/ unites with male 175, 177, 465-6
– is magnesia 530
–, mix copper with 536
–, moisture of 536
–, non- 129
–, out of 574
–, power of 576
– principle 32, 93, 127
–, pure white 388
– rejoices 233, 304
– spirit 360
– statue 270
– turns copper into spirit 536
feminine 285, 344
– power 126, 131
– principle 55
– sulphur 373, 467
ferment 62, 245, 410, 490
– and mercury 380
–, cloud, … and cultivation of gold 245
–, extract 503
–, fermentation 548
–, fermented 373, 475 , 489
–, fermenting the elixir 165
–, lead, …, eternal water and sour vinegar 355
–, mix copper with … of gold 411
–, mix … with body 551
– of bread 303
– of dough 165
– of gold 156, 165, 170, 189, 245-6, 248, 253, 266, 268-9, 272-3, 280, 285, 301-3, 386, 410-1, 457, 538, 558
– of purple 503
– of silver 302, 457
–, soak with 547
–, sour 548
– water 180
–, water ferments copper 558
–, water of 503
–, whiten by 502
Ferrario, Gabriele 94
ferrous stone 500
field of wheat 293
fiery/ fieryness 172, 320, 533
– copper 375
– mercury 368, 567
– nature 474
– of cinnabar 542
– one 377
–, operation of 377-8
– poison 226-7, 254
– stone 201, 380, 399
– stone and copper 201-2

– sulphurs 397
– sun 218
– sword 358
– water 482
fifteen (15)
– (15th) fifteenth century 59, 81
fifth (5th) 334, , 389, 414, 570
–, (1/5) one fifth 189
–, becoming (5) five 570
– book 19, 33, 306
– century 93, 96-8, 123, 136
fig 261
fight (vb) 166, 216, 225, 287, 574
– against fire 258, 350, 352, 520, 550
– dragon 47, 300
– enemies 35, 336
– fire; see fire
–, moisture …s fire away 397
– nature …s not the fire 398
– sandarach 376
fighter 305, 323, 357, 396
– and fugitive 446
–, and Saturn 305
– clung and lime 396, 446
–, destroyed 396
–, extract colours from 446
–, fugitive and 470
–, nature destroyed/ tortures 446
–, (nature) turns … into spirit 396; 446
– of fire 232
–, spirit of 396, 446
–, sulpur turns … into fugitive 446
figures 31, 61, 212, 276
–, (2) two 276
–, divine/ demonic 25
–, figurative 92
Fihrist; *see also book(s), Fihrist* 18, 24, 45, 68, 133
Fīlbis/ Filbus 21, 143
filings 283
– black ... of copper 508
–, cook black 440
–, iron, magnesia and … of silver 472
– of copper 244, 440, 508
– of gold 278, 528
– of silver 500
– of tin 278
– take up sediment 508
filter 473, 487, 502, 504, 511
filth 492
find 52, 209, 232, 410, 484
–, all over/ everywhere 176
– rarely 151, 213
fine 24, 234, 530, 562
– (like) dust 23-4, 149, 196, 227, 234, 286, 530, 537, 562
–, make 452
finger 141
–, fingernail 579
–, fingers 23-4, 149, 264
finish 56, 224, 300, 331, 336, 397, 460, 506, 526, 529, 581
– not 176
– operation/ finished operation 382, 389
– rotting 440
– whitening 269
fire 28, 44, 55, 63, 97, 129, 153, 168-9, 176, 188, 190, 196, 202, 220, 239, 243, 259, 281, 283, 287, 294, 304, 320, 325, 337, 365, 367, 380, 383, 403, 405-6, 440, 473, 484, 516, 521, 523-5, 539, 566, 568-9, 577, 579
– absorbs 486
–, afraid of 520
–, air into 370-1, 520
– and air 228, 521
– and body 396, 370, 398, 524
– and copper 221
– and dye 554
– and lime 41, 575
– and moist 405
– and moisture destroy stone 280
– and natures 488
– and spirit 192
– and sun 192, 494
– and water 28-9, 120, 137, 219, 523
– as āqusṭus 473
– as enemy of work 491, 521
– as summer 152
–, benefits of 240
–, blaze of 250
–, Book/ Treatise On/ About (the Measures of) the Fire; *see also book; treatise* 491, 516
–, born in 252, 284
– brings death and life 176
–, burn(s)/ burning of 36, 284, 342, 355, 397,

436, 540
– causes error 524
–, cautious with ...(s) 525, 577
– circulates in vessel 166, 513
– clashes 554
–, controls/ reins 278
–, cook in/ with 153, 218, 364, 458
–, copper remains in 497
–, defeat 559
–, destroy in 191
–, destroys work 171
–, difference in cooking with 507
–, different ...s 519
–, dissolve in 492, 525
–, divide 491, 525
–, dung fire 268, 280, 548, 551
–, dust and water turn into 298
–, dye vanishes not in 370
–, earth, water, air and 359
– eats blackness 167
–, enter 152, 521
–, escape (not) from 63, 151, 172, 191-2, 198, 222, 284, 301, 399, 514
– extracts colours 529
–, extract soul by 480
–, extract spirit with 520
–, fall into 197
–, fear not 490
–, fight 178, 192, 215, 258, 284, 287, 350, 352, 393, 396, 398, 491, 520, 528, 533, 535, 541, 550, 557, 578
–, fighter of 232
–, fired clay 490
–, fireplace(s) 519, 525
–, flee 166, 514
–, fugitive from 232
–, gain by 494
–, gentle 129, 180, 189, 247, 249, 277, 297, 302-3, 318, 325, 354-5, 360, 462, 474, 487, 491-2, 494, 499-500, 508, 512-3, 516, 519-25, 528-9, 531, 534, 537, 548-9, 551, 562, 564, 572-4, 581
–, gentle/ moderate/ strong 380
–, gently 244
–, heat of 41, 246, 289, 291, 320, 359-60, 397, 473, 482, 490, 499, 513, 531, 576
–, increase 249
– in operation 28, 120, 219
–, in the 147, 169, 350
– is without body 398
–, intense/ intensive 379, 516
–, intensity of 436
–, important for work 491
–, importance of 97
–, kindle 156
– lets whiteness disappear 56, 127, 157
–, maintain 505
– makes gum strong 173
–, male enters 304
–, matters of 516
–, measures/ measurement of 79, 96143, 192, 253, 275, 289, 345, 350, 379, 396, 405-7, 444, 453, 491-2, 511, 516, 519, 521-5, 577
–, meats the fire 239
–, moderate 519, 577
–, moist 167
–, moisture fights … away 397
–, nature fights/ resists not 398
–, nature resists not 398
– neither burns nor consumes 465
– nourishes 252
–, nourishment for 223
–, on 155
– of attraction/desirousness 118, 137
– of dung 188, 189, 262
– of dyers 492, 525
– of gum 492
–, operate on and soften 494
–, operate with 254, 532
–, operation of the 519
–, overcome not 490
–, part of 153-4
– perfects work, 243
–, pound with/ pounds 513, 533
–, power by 239
–, prevent .. from ruining composition 490
–, prevent moisture from escaping 396
–, protect from 535
–, push heat of … away from companions 473
–, remain in 192, 398, 496
–, remedies of 354
–, resist (to)/ resistance 151, 178, 186, 188, 192, 202, 213, 226, 248, 362, 403, 528, 533

–, return to 482, 573
–, set on 233, 286, 566, 574
–, son of the 252
– solidified mercury 372
–, strength of the 249, 323, 355, 491, 523
–, strengthen/ make stronger 221, 234, 323, 355, 486, 491-2, 499, 519, 523, 525, 547, 553, 557, 561
–, strong/ make ... strong 28, 233, 239, 255, 357, 364, 380, 481, 491, 492, 499, 505, 508, 522-5, 529, 537, 552, 566
–, stronger/ stronger than/ strong against 160, 202, 239, 254, 481, 486, 491, 499, 522, 525, 561, 573
–, sword of 370
–, third 492
–, torture of 171
–, turn bodies spiritual in 482
–, turn into airy 298
– vessel on 469
–, water, air and earth 222, 515
–, water and 28, 120, 122-4, 220
–, water becomes 228
– weak 522
–, wind of 489
–, without 249, 389, 491, 494
–, work by 152
–, work cannot be completed/ exists not without 491, 494
–, work of the 254, 397
fires
–, be cautious with 525
–, different 519
firewood 254, 320
–, ash of 507, 515
– of oleander 320, 385
– of white sulphur 507
– of willow/ osier (Salix aegiptica) 385
–, white 459
firm 169, 176, 218, 226, 277, 362, 559, 578
–, firmness 166
first (1st) 227, 233
–, (2) two, ... day becoming 570
– birth 252
– blackness 446, 469
– body 362
– book; *see book(s)*
– burning 288, 569
– coagulation 287
– composition 187, 243-4, 273, 276-7, 405, 463, 493, 524, 533, 537-8, 552
– cooking 282, 508
– dyeing 520
– elixir 319, 505-6
– making alumy 573-4
– measure 406
– mercury 261
– nature(s) 301, 387, 396-7
– one 166, 215, 249, 252, 383, 549
– (other) operation 183, 252, 255, 560, 572
– part 473, 560, 572
– picture 141, 306, 402
– sages 22, 255, 393-4, 401, 469, 530
– solidification 325
– sulphur 284, 295, 301
– teaching 526
– time 212, 505
– whitening/ reddening 167, 532
– work 192, 205, 241, 253, 301, 361, 386, 405, 526, 536
fish 494, 502, 517, 525
five (5) 273, 324
–, (3) three, turn .... into 273
– days 507
– times 504, 511
– weights 269
fix (vb) 142, 152, 223, 249, 260, 292, 297, 361, 554
–, become fixed 569
– brilliance 385
– colour (not)/ fixed colour 201, 385, 454
– dye(s) 205, 401-2
–, fixed nature 201
–, fixed poison 153
–, fixed sulphur 504
–, fixing of nine spirits 80
– fugitive 176
– gold 279
–, spirits 80, 172
– water 480
flame 9
flattery 302
flee (vb) 49, 55, 63, 156, 497-8, 509
– fire (not) 166, 514
flesh 157, 160-1, 352, 387
float 282-3

flood 259, 278
florilegium 47, 60, 315
flour 303
–, extract 303
– of barley, alum and water 504
flow (vb) 91, 175, 228, 244, 291, 440, 458, 512, 543, 556
– like tears 401
–, moisture …s over wool 542
–, water flows 325
flower 156, 210, 275, 289
–, appear 286
–, disappear 289
– extract subtle part 303
–, improve 366
– of arsenic 289
– of barley 475, 512
– of copper 364, 461
– of gold 246, 253, 268, 285, 289, 364, 399, 410, 457, 548
– of ẖāmūm (camomilla?) 395
– of sea 231
– of the salt 569
flowers 166, 170, 236, 259, 279, 364, 389, 522, 524, 572
–, airy 502
– appear 492, 525, 547
–, burn 255, 497, 522-3
–, collection of flowers 47
–, cook 255
–, destroy 494, 522, 577
– disappear not 575
–, dyes as 508
–, extract 256, 578
– fire eats … of brothers 240
–, flowery water 538
– from moisture 565
–, grow 494
–, herbs as 286
– of bodies 283, 301
– of copper 368, 513, 516, 527, 538
– of dye 523, 554
– of eternal water 567
– of gold 355, 504, 511, 538
– of hard bodies as dyes/ spirits 513
– of herbs 291
– of plants 554
– of trees 154
– of vinegar 504
–, pure 510
– put back 497
–, turn copper into 366
flying (vb) 339
foamy 506
foetus 55, 182
follower(s) (those, who come after); *see also offspring* 68, 73, 113, 135, 142, 490, 502
food 47, 53, 161, 218, 366, 436, 469, 505, 530
– changes in stomach 521
–, cooked 48, 300
forbidden 316
force 32, 79, 174, 177-8, 416
foreign 143, 159
forelock 391
forgiveness 166
form(s) 32, 36, 40, 59, 67, 68, 80, 90, 98, 135, 142, 154, 174, 341, 395, 462
forty (40)
– days 368, 485, 486
– nights 160
forty-one (42) days 489
forty-two (42) pictures 75
found rarely 128, 242
fountain of mercury; *see also well* 129, 451
– Fountain of Mercury (book) 447
four (4) 50, 175, 185, 191, 243, 265, 271-2, 360
– and (1) one 184-5, 195, 273, 379
– and (from/ into) (3) three 224, 269, 370, 379, 513
– as (1) one of (3) three 325
– bodies 184-5, 192, 195, 200, 225, 269, 273-4, 298, 369, 386, 410
– books 18, 400
– colours 229
– columns 517
– corners 223
– days 293, 320, 506
– elements 92, 122, 256
– four-fold 92
– hours 316
– kinds 524
– knots 263
– made red 581

– measures 489
– mixtures 301
– natures 45, 47, 50, 153, 166, 218, 222, 228, 236, 298, 301, 359, 371, 521
– ounces 271-2, 274, 319, 506
– parts 48, 50, 267, 270-1, 275, 279, 282, 298, 300, 368, 371, 491, 525, 547, 563, 566
– seasons 236, 299, 522
– single natures 165
– spirits 546
– times 471, 504, 511
– treatises 199, 256
– weight(s) 267, 269
–, weight is … parts 267
fourth (4th) 44, 58
– (1/4) one fourth 265, 374, 486
–, (3) three/ three-fold and (1/4) fourth 224
–, book 19
–, century 9, 18, 27, 78, 98, 113, 123, 136
–, head of 571
–, letter 260
–, part 492
–, season 522
–, weights of 275
Fowden, Garth 11
fragment/ ed 21, 234, 321, 474, 496, 512
–, fragmented clod of earth 506
–, fragmented copper 508
–, fragmented stone 566
fragment(s) 20-1, 117, 190, 277, 353, 364, 374, 378, 400, 418
–, break in(to) 234, 288, 366, 369, 460-1, 474, 490, 499, 533, 536, 540, 566, 569, 573
Frankfurt 5, 11, 13
Franz, Marie-Louise von Franz Foundation 8, 13
free 293, 320, 360, 416, 474
friends 202
friendship 111, 123, 168
frighten 336, 524
frog-stone 361-2
from it, by it and for it! 162, 178
froth
–, colour of 388
–, extract 396
– non-escaping 396
– of every animal/ moist 418
– of mooon 350, 388, 418, 426
– of natron 389
– of the sea 442
– that does not escape 323
–, white 173, 387, 485
fruit(s) 13, 52-3, 156, 447, 484, 495, 524, 548
–, cook 524
– eating … stills hunger 504
– of work 504
–, pick 524
– ripe/ ripen 236, 278, 572
frustrate(d) 154, 501
Fuad, Salwa 5-7, 12
Fück, Johann W. 18
fugitive(s) 49, 167, 169, 176, 178, 227, 231, 238, 251, 253, 301, 323, 360, 364, 371, 466-7, 488, 490, 533, 541, 546, 552
–, dye (1) one 324
–, alum prevents escaping of 540
– and bodies 277
– and fighter 446, 470
– and fugitives 446
– and seeker 232, 278
– as composed 546
– as magnesia 51, 372
– as mercury 468
– come to life 524
–, dye of 524
– dye true dyeing 453
–, extract 183
–, fix 176
–, flying 50, 372
– from fire 232
–, gum clings to 299
–, marry soul of 489
– meets seeker 465, 468
– mercury 416
– mixed with clinger 172
–, mix seeker with 152, 468
–, moisture as 546
– natures and spirits 539
–, non-fugitive/ not 248, 284, 300, 397-8, 418, 446, 466, 489, 513-4, 533, 546, 567
–, seeker cling to 384
–, six 324

–, soul as 487
– spirit(s) 46, 229, 231, 488, 503
– sulphur/ sulphur as 365, 475
–, sulphur turns fighter into 446
– taken by seeker 166
–, turn dyes non-fugitives 300
– turns into ashes 364
–, turn (thing/ fugitive) into fugitive(s) 240, 238, 396, 446, 567
–, turn ... into non-fugitives 397, 567
–, turn non-escaping into 396
– unites with seeker 466
fundament, moisture as 476
furnace 64, 134, 156, 195, 382, 388, 403, 440, 496, 499, 568
–, furnaces 269, 519
–, key to 299
– raise in 380
–, suspended 579
fury 216
fusion of tin and mercury; *see also coniunction; union; reconcile* 21
futile 361

–G–

Ǧābir ibn Ḥaiyān 13, 59
gain 494
gallbladder(s)
– of bull 271, 547
– of dragon 458
– of every thing 418
gallnuts 318, 321
galls 515
game of boy 487
garlic 503, 512
garment 316, 567
– of king 562
–, mix … with urine and dye 512
gates 165, 235, 237
gather (vb) 47-8 141, 161, 202, 216, 229, 271, 300, 310, 315, 347, 439, 489, 556
– colours/ elements 256
– mercuries 432
– things 152
– truth 473
gaze 311
Gemini 570
generate stone 539
gentle 129, 180, 188, 208, 220, 247, 277, 289, 302, 318, 322, 325, 354-5, 360, 369, 473-4, 481-2, 487, 491-2, 494, 499-500, 508, 512,-3, 515-6, 519-25, 528-9, 531, 534, 537, 539, 548-9, 551, 561-2, 564, 570, 572 4, 581
–, cook gently 578
– fire 168, 249, 297, 303, 380, 462
–, gentleness 45, 56, 127, 143, 156, 157, 159, 162, 201, 360, 486, 520, 524, 577, 579
–, gentlest 515
–, gently 214, 255, 281, 321, 436, 465, 470, 473, 505, 509
–, treat gently 486, 512
– water 368

germinate 181
get black 456
gift 22, 203, 219, 345, 483
– of God 128, 172
Giftmädchen (poison girl) 36, 54, 125, 131
gilded 141, 164, 191
girdle 557
give
– birth 166, 168, 176, 232, 252, 292, 565
– preference 393
glass 187, 205, 319, 502, 512
– and mercury 403
– as magnesia 385
–, body of 318
–, cupping 292, 440
–, dye 350
–, glassmakers 480
–, glass-making 145
–, ingot of 319
– into sea 513
–, let enter 512
– making (of) 145, 471, 517
–, mercury makes glass sick 318
–, mix 318, 385
–, plate of 319
– purify 513
–, shape 480
–, three-fold 319
– vessel/ vessel of 234, 286, 427, 462, 492, 525, 539

–, water becomes like 317
–, water of 418
glassy 317, 321
– natron 504
gloomy 167, 175
glorification/ glorify 153
glow 554
glue 334, 474
–, absorb 572
– and ivory 474
– mercury of arsenic and sandarach 384
– mercury on body of magnesia 384
–, natron, alum and blood 382
–, nature of 475
– of copper 469
– of bull 401
– of cows 475
– of gold 253, 362, 484, 535, 564, 569, 572
– of stones 401
– of whales 401, 474-5
– of wisdom 474
–, power of 474
–, turn into 469, 532
Gnostic 11, 99, 110
–, Christian- 118, 120
–, Gnosticism 123
– thoughts and Zosimos' teaching 122-3, 145
goal; *see also aim* 41, 44, 80, 84, 317, 556
– of work 44, 84, 137, 278, 560, 568
–, reach 370, 571
God/ gods 9-11, 28, 32, 39-40, 53, 55, 58, 97, 109, 120-2, 128, 141-3, 145, 147, 150-1, 153-5, 157-8, 160, 165, 171, 174, 176, 181-2, 184, 186, 191, 195-6, 202-3, 207, 209, 212-3, 217-20, 222, 228, 236-7, 240-3, 251, 255, 257, 260, 262-3, 266, 275-7, 279, 281, 291, 293, 295, 297, 299, 301, 305-6, 310-12, 323, 328-9, 340-1, 344-5, 349-51, 354-6, 358-60, 363, 366-7, 370, 372, 380, 384, 387, 389-90, 393, 398, 400, 402, 416, 418, 420, 424, 431-3, 440, 448, 450-2, 463-4, 472, 476-7, 480-1, 484-6, 494-5, 497, 508, 513, 516-7, 521-3, 525-6, 531, 540, 543, 548, 554-6, 559, 562-3, 577, 581
– is (1) one 148
–, deus absconditus 24
–, equal/ similar to 148
–, exalted 26, 28, 33, 119, 145, 148, 151, 154-5, 169, 173, 176, 204, 221, 227, 241, 278, 285, 293, 299, 310, 332, 357, 359, 363, 365, 367-8, 387, 393, 402, 420, 432, 451, 455-6, 464, 476, 486, 535, 543, 556, 563, 571, 577, 581
–, gift of 128, 172
– image 39
– inside 11
–, inspiration of 153, 480
– knows best! 169, 191, 256, 362
– makes 56, 186, 299
– -man 11, 23, 40, 44
– of Goodness and Justice 11
–, name of 169
–, obedience to 556
–, treasure of 180
–, union with 40
–, will of 215
goddess(es) 10, 32, 39, 54, 108
godliness 450
gold 29, 36-7, 62, 91-2, 129, 142, 148, 150, 161, 164, 171, 185, 216, 220, 222, 229, 245, 257-8, 270, 277-8, 280, 282, 287, 294-5, 302, 313, 339, 341-2, 347, 352, 376, 403, 411, 421, 442, 455, 469, 515, 526, 535-6, 558, 579
– and mercury 277
– and silver 165, 257, 260, 277, 319, 398, 470, 488, 498-9
– and sun 463
–, aqzal(-gold) 245, 246, 295, 363, 364, 373, 410, 500, 538, 548, 261, 266, 280, 490
–, aqzal-gold into purple 538 , 558
– as copper without shadow 498
–, become 184, 293, 349, 579
–, body of 37, 293, 345
–, book of/ Book of Gold 337, 427, 457
–, break 418
–, cling to 569
–, clothes of 36, 341
–, cloud, ferment and cultivation of 245
–, colour(s) (of) 253, 278, 295, 349, 463, 550
–, conceal … in bodies 303
–, cooked 363-4
–, copper, … and/ or silver 161, 297, 388, 411, 497, 557, 465
–, cultivate/ cultivation of 280, 299, 515, 538

–, dissolve 293, 320
–, drops of 538
–, dye 165, 204, 226, 277, 361, 453, 490, 493, 494, 538, 540, 574
–, dye bodies into 294
–, dye gold with 280
–, dye of 463
–, dye silver into 183, 235
–, earth into 386
–, extract 303
–, ferment and flower of … and gum 285
–, ferment of 156, 165, 170, 189, 245-6, 248, 253, 266, 268, 269, 272, 273, 280, 285, 302, 303, 386, 410, 411, 457, 538, 558
–, ferment of ... for (/and) everybody 189, 301
–, filings of 278, 528
–, fix 279
–, flower of 246, 253, 268, 285, 289, 364, 399, 410, 457, 548
–, flowers of 355, 538
–, flowers of … and vinegar 504
–, flowers of …, (ash), glassy natron, (Egyptian) vinegar 504, 511
– from gold 451
– gets not burnt 362
–, glue of 253, 362, 484, 564, 535, 569, 572
–, grow 494
–, gum of 453
–, harvest 358
– in appearance 376
–, increase 494
–, incombustible sulphur as ferment of 386
–, lime and fat 457
–, little 171
–, make 233, 352, 377
–, make equal with gold 267
–, making of 176, 207, 280, 349, 352, 400, 550
–, making of/ make … and silver 166, 357, 447
–, mercury into (aqzal) 411
–, mercury of 427
–, mix … with broth/ cloud 245
–, mix … with silver 315, 442, 538, 547-8
–, mix composition with 493
–, mix copper with (silver and) 315, 551
–, mix copper with ferment of 411
–, mix with 260
–, multiply 293, 499
–, name 530
–, our 277, 386, 497
–, plate(s) of 391, 427, 551
–, pure 578
–, purple 246, 261, 268, 295, 363, 364, 528, 548
–, return 528, 558, 579
–, river of running 147
–, roast 461, 546
–, rusty 225
– silver, ..., iron and copper 167
– sprouts and grows 522
–, stone of 561
–, sea of 461
–, seed of 253
–, stone of 483, 580
–, their 467
–, tin, ... and mercury 278
–, turn body into 557
–, turn copper into 498
– turn ... into aqzal-gold 528, 538, 558
–, turn ... into/ put ... into 37, 221
–, turn … into silver 37, 239, 349, 344
–, turn into 62, 178, 181, 206, 221, 248, 363, 557
–, turn into aqzal 245
–, turn mercury, sulphur and … into dyeing poison 287
–, turn silver into 528, 558, 564
–, vinegar and fat 457
–, water of 78, 428-9, 457, 482, 526-7, 544
–, weave with 474
– with eternal water 548
– without shadow 497, 563
– with silver 206
–, work of 462-3
golden 36, 81, 208, 210, 234, 305, 307, 317, 319, 339, 341, 344, 389, 403, 421, 425-6, 428, 477
– arsenic 190
– book 229
– dust 271
– face 429, 431, 435-6, 442, 445
–, gold-silver 195
–, goldsmiths 304
– green 451
– man 36, 341

– names 429
– roots 249
– stone 22, 375, 388, 471, 515
– water 141, 164
–, white 451
– Zosimos 37, 345
Goethe, Johann W. 13
good 214
– and evil; *see also devil* 122
– composition 564
– for everything 210, 551
–, goodness 29
– in nature 147
–, make it 168
– with the good 31
gospel
– of Muslim 121
– of Philip 121-3
– of Thomas 122
Graeco-Roman literature 131
grapes, green 498
grass 154
grateful 7, 150, 217, 526, 556, 581
–, gratefulness 432
gratitude 432
gravedigger 292
Greek 9, 17-8, 20-1, 24-5, 26-7, 45, 47, 49, 52, 58-9, 68, 90-1, 94, 109, 112, 117, 125, 127, 134, 136
– alchemy; *for Les Alchimistes Grecs see book(s)* 9, 17, 122
– compilation 96
–, dialogue 97, 115, 135
–, Graeco-Roman 54, 131
– manuscripts 17, 134
– origin/ original 26, 68, 113, 119, 123, 135, 137
– philosophers 58
– text(s)/ manuscript/ works 21, 23-5, 64, 96-7, 113, 117-8, 122, 124, 126, 132-4, 137
–, translated/ translation from/ into Arabic 96, 133
– treatise 40
green 19, 34-5, 130, 141, 276, 306-7, 347, 421, 451, 477, 498, 556-7
– bird 263
– clothes 391
– dog 439
– emerald 450
– flowers 259
–, golden 451
– stone 207
– -white bull 34
–, yellow-green 517
Gregorius 51
grief 37, 342, 361, 522, 541
grind 303
grip (vb, n) 29, 31-2, 40, 78, 157
ground (n, vb) 36, 78, 81, 84, 246, 341, 432-3, 439, 455, 544
group(s) 80, 132-3, 137
grow (vb) 12, 41-3, 122, 130, 143, 161, 216, 252, 374, 447, 481, 495, 522, 548
– flowers 494
–, fruit ...s on tree 156
– gold 494
–, growth 53, 84
guard 290, 439, 450
–, guardian 289
guide(d) (vb, n); *see also guru* 47, 59, 194, 260, 274, 310, 361, 387, 436, 494, 507, 536-7
–, dyers should 452
–, innerpsychic 39
– of alchemy 31
– to truth 285
– to work 84
gum 22, 47, 125-6, 128-31, 172, 174, 182, 186, 213-4, 231-2, 247, 251, 255-6, 261, 267, 277, 285, 393, 401, 480, 486, 489, 492
– with (3) three colours 401
–, absorb (all of) 491, 525
– and (moist) alum 321, 470
– and ashes 388
– and black dye 316
– and copper 171, 174
– and crystal 319
– and ferment and flower of gold 285
– and moisture 186
– and rainwater 320
– and spittle of moon 256, 454
– and tar 277
– and/ as water 286, 384
– as murderous to husband 126, 128-31, 182
– as nature 209

– as spirit 172
– as whole composition 384, 385
–, become dry 277
–, body of the 547
–, book about the 171
–, burnt 501
– clings to fugitives 299
–, coagulate stone with water and 447
–, composed 401
–, cook 291
–, copper, … and fat 487
–, dissolve/ dissolving 388, 452
–, dry 491
–, dust and 454
–, dye … and honoured stone 492
–, earth as 293
–, every dye from 400
–, fire makes … strong 173
–, fire of 492
–, gummi arabicum 128
–, gums 349
–, hide 453
–, improve … with similar gum 47
– is gums 366
–, lives and dies 480
–, living water as composed 402
–, making of 464
–, mercury, ... and sulphur 407
–, mercuries, water of sulphur, … , saffron 430
–, milk of 418
–, mix copper/ silver with (water of) 472-3
–, mix … with moisture 255
–, names (examples) of 401
– of acacia/ ašqunīa/ ašqūnīa 128, 173, 213, 242, 302, 468
– of all things 401
– of almond 401
– of gold 453
– of herb 293
– of sages 285
– of Skythia 125
– of thorns 401
– of tree 402
– part of 208
–, power of this 171
–, rest of 321
–, solidify stone with 447, 495
–, stone absorbs 321
–, stone with water and 495
–, sulphur, … and herb 186
– turn into 173, 255, 302
–, water of 456
–, white 547
guru, inner; *see also guide; teacher* 27

–H–

Haarmann, U. W. 113
habitation 571
hadith; *see also literature* 26, 119
hair of Isis 290
half 32, 43, 205, 321, 456, 569
–, (1) one .. part(s)/ (2) two and a .... part(s) 500, 510
a measure 568
–, halves of symbol 91
– of moisture 512
– of sulphur 374
– of vessel 579
– of work 440
Ḥall ar–rumūz; *see also book(s)* 5, 40
Hallaj 44
Hallum, Benjamin Charles 8, 73,-4, 85, 92, 95-9, 110-1, 113-7, 119, 125-6, 131-3, 135-6
halo of sun 43, 66, 429
2alqadūnī 209
2alqṭārāt 414
hand 41-2, 141, 239, 342, 407, 433, 439, 477, 516, 536, 549
–, left 391
– of Theosebeia 544
– of Zosimos 141, 307, 329, 544
– put your … in the work 525
–, pound with/ pounding by 145, 447, 495, 579
–, right 263, 391
–, rub with 459
hands 24, 29, 31-2, 62, 196, 206, 213, 221, 227, 276, 292, 370, 433, 458, 466-7, 526, 536, 556, 565, 577
–, (2) two 23, 149
–, pure 367
–, red 339
handsome 216
hang from (vb) 345

–, hanging sulphur 418
happiness 219, 286, 355, 562
– happy 295, 336, 358, 382, 432
hard 219, 227, 237, 247, 405, 489
– and moisture 185, 187
– bodies 226, 287, 369, 513-4, 522
– body 185, 396
– composition 324
–, hardness 205
–, hardship; *see also effort; harm; disease; suffer* 180, 298, 535
– one(s) 185, 215, 285, 396, 456
harm; *see also damage; destroy* 169, 207, 265, 357, 365, 368, 396, 446, 504
– from work 169
–, harmful 215, 240
–, harmful enemy 521
–, Harmful One 181
harmonious 169, 188, 249, 277
–, and suitable 162
–, harmonize 293
–, harmony 63, 123, 173, 201, 221, 273, 277, 322-3, 355, 390, 439, 457-8
harvest 122, 358
hatching 520
– as pounding 554
–, of birds 513
–, of egg 51, 372
hate (vb) 438-9
– body/ spirit hates body 322-3
–, hatred 28, 36, 219, 337
Hathor 54, 108
Ḥazizah 571
head 31, 41, 43, 66, 105, 109, 162, 217, 277, 307, 313, 354, 358, 391, 426, 544, 565
–, (2) two heads/ (3) three-headed 30-1, 109
–, above 292
–, black 339
– collects thought 575
–, cut off 544
–, dye concealed in 575
–, hold heads 276
–, nature is/ completes 162
– of bird 109
– of bodies 483
– of dragon; *see also head of serpent* 48, 300
– of everything 197
– of four 571
– of gold 216
– of human being 292
– of metals 529
– of philosophers 9
– of river 572
– of sages 45, 58, 311-2
– of seers 319
– of serpent 109
– of Theosebeia 134, 444
– of vessel 519
– of wisdom 242
– of work 189, 251, 288, 317, 395, 444, 577
– of world 236, 295, 546-7
– of Zosimos 444
–, operation of 162
– yellow 279-80
– with moon/ sun 30-2, 34-5, 37, 64, 78-80, 84, 92, 108-10, 141, 391, 421, 439, 444, 477, 526, 391, 556
healing 90, 138, 331
heart 179-81, 239-40, 331, 452
–, hearts 208, 237, 400
– of body 436
– of sun 238
–, pure 367
–, queen of 20
heat 63, 130, 168, 218, 236, 239, 255, 321, 356, 485, 505, 572
– turns (9) nine into (3) three 160
– and moisture 161, 173, 481, 486, 508
–, completion 486
– cracks earth 501
– dissolves 492
– dries 161
– exact heat 486
–, gentle 208, 561
–, heater 440
–, heating 23, 149, 397, 494
–, limit of 486
–, measures of 157
– of air 236
– of ashes 548
– of copper 403
– of fire 41, 246, 289, 291, 320, 359-60, 397, 473, 482, 490, 499, 513, 531, 576
– of summer 524
– of sun 360, 494, 522-3, 530, 554
– of male 175

– of stomach 174
–, power of 281
–, strong 522
– turns into ashes 56, 127, 157
heavenly 92, 134, 162, 498
– nature 151, 225, 291
– natures 177, 326
heavy 145, 227, 483, 534, 560
– stone 166
height 58, 281, 311
hell 121
Hellenistic 29, 80, 109, 113
– origin 58
– -Hermetic 113
help 47-8, 91, 95, 112, 114, 127, 140, 143, 213, 241, 263, 300, 327-8, 331, 402, 464, 476-7, 515, 519, 543, 555, 559, 561, 581
hen 50, 298, 371-2, 383
herb 187, 207, 418, 470, 472
– al abarakānūn 475
–, blue 471
–, gum of 293
–, sulphur, gum and 186
herbs 179, 190, 192, 194, 225-6, 246, 284, 286, 349, 541-2
–, (2) two 389
– as flowers 286
–, change not 389
–, dust, water/ milks and 286, 454
–, flowers of 255, 291, 565
–, name moisture 565
– solid, moist and 225
heritage 129, 138, 243
–, cultural/ human 7, 138
– of Maria 148
Hermes 12, 19, 31-2, 36, 40, 48, 99, 101, 109, 118, 145, 148, 150, 152, 167, 173, 191-2, 194, 198, 201, 204, 207, 215, 247, 249, 252, 259, 265, 267, 289, 292, 329, 337, 351, 360, 366, 373, 375, 380-2, 386, 398, 461, 464, 473, 475, 480, 482, 494, 515, 520, 522, 534-5, 543-4, 559-61, 568, 571
–, (3) three-fold with benefit; *see threefold with benefit*
–, Arabic 99
–, book(s) of 146, 152, 215, 299, 464-5
–, heads of 78
–, Hermetic/ hermetica 10-11
– Mercurius 31-2, 78
– most entitled 380
–, Quṣṭūs to 486
–, secret of 49
–, statement of 146, 158, 250, 267, 277-8, 360, 475, 544
–, students of 146
–, ter unus 78, 99
– Trismegistus 10, 19
hero, sun 92
Hertz, Wilhelm 54
hide/ hidden (truth, secret, knowledge, experience); *see also cover; keep seret; protect; veil* 27, 91, 93-4, 98, 118, 123, 143, 145, 150, 153, 162-3, 171, 178-80, 188, 192-3, 229, 237, 241, 267, 279, 315, 328, 347, 357, 370, 383, 394, 398, 400, 420, 453, 507
– blackness/ black lead/ black silver 144
– body of mangesia 378
– body with bodies 194
– colours 318, 557
– composition 182, 365, 376
– dye 452
– earth 259-60
– gold 204, 427
– gum 453
– matters 142
– meaning/ hidden meaning 91, 93
– mercury/ hidden in mercury 236, 418, 427
– name/ (true) nature 291, 388, 483, 549
–, obscurely 416
– operation 565
– poison 213
– science 454
– secret(s) 150, 152, 162, 166-7, 214, 304, 312, 345, 367, 382-3, 399, 530
– soul 225
– spirit 214
– stone 259
– thing 170, 359
– truth 27, 347, 410, 561
– weight 265, 267, 268
– wind 57
– with answers 327
– work(s) 203, 365, 368, 383, 420, 577

hieroglyphs 113, 136
hierosgamos 32
high
–, high(er) and low(er) 29, 487
–, higher water 487
– ranking 241, 345, 354
highest 379, 456
– degree 512, 557, 571
– to the lowest 167
Hindu 32
hiss in face 48, 300
historians of alchemy 36, 55, 60, 138
history 12
– of Arabic and Islamic science 13
hit natures 444
hold (vb) 31-2, 34-5, 37-8, 79, 93, 99, 141, 197, 199, 200, 222-3, 225, 227, 232-3, 243, 262-3, 276, 296, 302, 313, 325, 329, 342, 345, 366, 393, 458, 536, 543, 550, 567, 571
– back 24, 36, 149, 342, 360
– balance(s) 264
–, cinnabar ...s dye of mercury 490
–, cloud …s relative 360
– dye 229, 277, 489
– each other 249
– hard ones 285
– heads 276
–, holder 63, 165, 222, 238, 243, 483
– moisture 532
– nature 258, 259, 291
– nature ...s nature(s) 162, 296
–, nature ...s relative 284
–, on to things 490
– other body 259
– relative 284
– spirits 483
–, spirit …s body/ soul 218, 296
– sulphur(s) 325, 465, 515, 532
–, sulphurs ...s fugitives 475
–, sulphurs ...s mercury 416
–, take 292
– together 31, 37, 345
– touchable element 258
hole(s)
–, (7) seven 440
–, air-holes 551
–, breath 402
–, close/ open 516, 524
Holmyard, E.J. 17-8
Homer 112
hollow 209, 571
– stone 176, 204, 231, 388, 395, 571
holy 120, 130, 186, 197
honest-protective 289
honey 129, 154, 199, 233, 247, 293-4, 320, 418, 442, 453, 456, 531, 541
–, bee 154
–, cook in 453
–, fat, vinegar and 199
–, mix water and 520, 534
–, poison/ taste of 49, 514
honour (vb) 162, 171, 229, 261, 367, 394, 420, 497
–, copper, lead, …ed stone; *see under copper*
–, despised-...ed/ honourable-despised 128, 172, 236
– honourable 197, 566
–, honoured blond 356
–, honoured body 529, 549-50
–, honoured nature 214
–, honoured one 144, 214, 547
–, honoured stone 171, 263, 265-7, 270, 274, 282, 364, 375-6, 483, 492, 546, 571, 581
– moisture 229, 476
– nature 356
hope (vb) 122, 144, 158, 240, 260, 263, 290, 303, 327, 351, 448, 491, 495, 525
–, hopelessness 119, 155
horns 319, 505
Hornung, Erik 8, 13, 19, 39, 80, 109, 127
horse and donkey 498
hot 92, 157, 169, 175, 239, 275, 318, 389, 453, 494, 506-7, 577, 580
– and cold/ with cold 63, 142-3, 222, 227, 487
– and moist 228
– ashes 189, 323, 580
–, become 218
–, cold/ strong, dry (, and) hot 142, 169, 174
– colour 279
– dyeing 453
–, hotness 236, 474
–, not 321, 577
– one 143
– sun 547
– water 286, 556

Houdas, Octave 17
hour(s) 316
–, (1) one 495
–, (6) six/ (6th) sixth 109, 473
–, (12) twelve 80
house 53, 58, 209, 217, 292, 311, 313, 485
–, desert ...s 231
–, make ripe 469
– of king 58, 311
–, treasure ...(s) 203, 389
hug 391
2ul…f(553
human 18, 24, 31-3, 35, 39-40, 59
– and divine 40-41
–, animal- 31
–, archetypes entered … realm 39
– being and body, spirit, soul 351
– being and copper 46, 293, 520
– being and tin 235
– being, head of 292
– being(s) 31, 33, 40, 44, 59, 67, 78-81, 84, 101, 108, 120-21, 176, 214-5, 226, 270, 290, 297, 302, 350, 356, 359, 361, 469, 481, 521, 576
– body 67, 161, 286
–, brings forth a ... being 551
–, dead … being 290
– dung 501
–, existence 31
–, greater 32
–, heritage 138
–, inner 32
– level 64
–, lower- 35
–, spiritual- 31
–, super-human 39, 41
humidity 215
hundred (100); *see also days, measures, rutls; years* 67, 269, 485, 509, 575
–, (110) hundred and ten years 10
–, (140) hundred and forty years 25
–, (150) hundred and fifty 233-5
–, (160) hundred and sixty years 25, 155
–, (180) hundred and eighty 53-4, 485
–, (365) three hundred and sixty-five stones 208
–, (660) six hundred and sixty 27, 347
– (900) nine hundred 54, 58, 78, 96, 131, 135-6
– years 53, 485
hungry 52, 484, 504
hurry 227, 471, 537
hurt
– bodies 352
– soul 157
husband(s) 55, 94, 125, 157, 304, 360
– dies 129, 243
–, kill 129, 181-2, 213
–, meet her 164
–, murderer/ murderess(es) of her/ their 36, 57, 125-9, 131, 159, 242, 451, 564
–, no 530
– torturer of her 128, 172, 233, 277, 354, 363, 427, 509
Hyderabad 10, 116
Hymn of the Pearl 90
hypothesis 73-4, 96, 110, 112-4, 116-7, 125, 134-8
– counter- 73-4, 96, 113-4, 133, 135

–I–

ibn Arfaʿ Raʾs 9, 311-3
ibn Ǧubair 10
ibn Mūsā al-Azharī 20, 142
ibn Nadīm 18, 45, 68, 133
ibn Umail, Muḥammad 5, 10, 12, 39-40, 59, 68, 81, 92-3, 95, 99, 110, 116, 136
Ibrahim, sons of 25, 155
iconography 99, 108, 136
idea(s) 29, 63, 68, 130-1
identical 22, 131
identification 41, 44
–, identify, disidentify 39
idol 296, 506
–, dissolving of 287
–, idols 270, 316, 499
ignorance 63, 115, 169, 178, 196, 221, 242, 257, 322, 327, 345, 354, 357-8, 368, 379, 447, 464, 491, 495
–, ignorant (adj, n) 33, 93, 118, 127, 144, 159, 170, 182, 184, 188, 204, 213, 229, 237, 257, 288,290, 292, 294, 326-7, 332, 345, 350, 357, 370, 385, 390, 454, 467, 482, 495-6, 519, 563

–, ignore 325, 327, 361, 522, 559
illness (also cure, disease, doctor, medical, remedy) 169, 350
– of soul 536
illuminate 32, 37, 203, 240, 327, 342, 347, 358, 371, 400
–, illuminating 27, 327, 347, 450, 451, 452
–, illumination(s) 347
–, illumine 217
– stone 471
illustrate (vb) 33, 59, 64, 73-5, 85, 96, 98-9, 110-1, 115, 118, 331, 544
–, illustration(s) 26, 48, 75, 91, 108
– manuscript 99
–, illustrations of alchemical work 81
image(s); *see also pictures, illustration* 10, 19, 30, 35-6, 39, 66-7, 81, 84, 90-1, 94-5, 99, 112, 122, 134, 290, 292, 477, 526, 556
–, (2) two 434
–, alchemical (series of) 74, 94-5
–, allegorical 85
– and word/ text 19, 29, 111, 136
– as guideline for Zosimos' teaching 74
–, inner/ outer 161
– of Christ 28
– of God/ God-image 41, 160
– of golden man 544
– of man 36, 339, 341, 433
– of unconscious 94
– of weights 276
– of winged man 307, 329, 334
– of Zosimos and/ or Theosebeia 35, 263-4, 276, 306, 313, 329, 332, 337, 342, 345, 391, 404, 407, 411, 414, 416, 418, 421, 425-6, 428-9, 431, 434-6, 439-40, 442, 444-5, 448, 477, 526, 544
–, Pharaonic 10
– shadowy 90
–, symbolic 10, 19, 58, 112
imagination 328, 480
–, imaginatio vera 33
–, imagine 33, 331-2
Imhotep; *see also Imuth* 22
immortal 40, 44, 57, 130
–, immortality 69
–, quest for immortality 138
impatience 18, 242, 297, 503
–, be not impatient 23, 149, 219, 366, 486, 496, 515, 529, 535, 562, 569
– impatient 24, 36, 85, 149, 167, 261, 283, 341, 464, 487, 510, 573
impermanent 147
importance 138, 228, 232
imprison 142, 218, 225, 227-8, 360, 436, 489
improve 175, 177, 203, 241, 252, 279, 290, 375, 385, 394, 459, 462, 469, 540, 543
– both 581
– copper 486
– dye(s) 490, 497
– each other 219
– flower 366
– soul 539
– themselves 396
impure 293, 394
–, impurity 168, 492, 504
– mercury 458
Imuth; *see also Book of Imuth* 21-2, 385, 389-90, 393, 467
inaccessible 23, 149
incombustible 258, 301, 528
– ashes 515
– dyes, sulphurs into 522
– sulphur 235, 248, 250, 258, 363, 386, 393, 548
– sulphur as cinnabar 373
– sulphur as dry body 528
– sulphur as ferment of gold 386
increase (vb) 26, 37, 62, 117-8, 155-7, 194, 221, 228, 240, 263, 265, 269-70, 272, 278-9, 281, 289, 331, 342, 358, 365, 383, 393, 411, 447, 453, 462, 471, 505, 537, 547-8, 558, 571
– (9) nine 223
– benefit 502, 548
– body 177
– by impregnation, operation, imagination and sagacity 480
– fire 249, 294
– gold 494
– redness 579
– soaking 570
– stone 166
– washing 569
– water 542
increment 53

India 27, 54, 125, 249, 316
–, black Indian 471
–, land of 93
–, Indian 99, 316, 361, 388, 502
–, Indian copper 499
–, Indian iron 378
–, Indian libraries 11
–, mix Indian with copper 316
individual 32, 39-40, 44, 67, 81, 118, 127, 138, 152, 384
– relationship 59, 64
individuation/ principium individuationis 32, 44, 59
infatuate 207
inferior 29, 176, 214, 317, 354, 407, 455, 537
influence 136
ingot 363
ingredient 91, 130
injustice, turn into 327
inner; *see essence; introverted* 27, 33, 39-40, 44-5, 67, 109, 118, 136-7, 222, 289
– character 161
– coherence 80, 84
– God/ God-man 11, 23
– human 32
–, inner-psychic 137-8
– nature 322-3
– process 37, 98
– structure 85
– world 91
inseminate itself 176
inside 44, 47, 56, 127, 157, 162, 169-70, 183, 186, 192, 209, 215, 218, 223, 228-9, 233, 246, 261, 311, 318, 344, 355, 374, 387, 397, 424, 463, 513, 537
– and outside 122
–, black 37, 247
– cloud, concealed 489
–, concealed 150, 382, 493, 509, 549
–, enter its 154
–, extract what is 150
– nature 302, 559
– of body 165, 509
–, the one whose ... is black 342
insight(s) 17, 27, 94, 135
insignificant thing 144
insist (vb) 152, 154, 156, 237, 315, 533, 536
inspiration 27, 58-9, 63, 153, 171, 196, 221, 293, 387, 556
–, inspire (vb) 352, 554, 581
–, Inspirer of benefits 450
instincts/ instinctual 32, 59
Institute 7-8, 12-3, 73
–, Swiss Institute for Archeological and Architectural Research for Ancient Egypt, Cairo 8, 13
– C.G. Jung-Institute, Zurich 12
instruction(s) 92, 432
instruments 496
intelligence 188, 202, 229, 242, 275, 310, 312, 496, 519, 579
– intelligent (vb) 144, 160, 236, 262, 304, 416, 501, 519-20, 577
intellectuals 215, 219
intense 134 234, 239, 255, 310-1, 370, 482, 516, 531, 535, 580
– burning 403, 580
– light 63, 222
–, intensity 291
–, intensity of fire 436
–, intensity of making black 456
–, intensive 63, 164, 203, 209, 222, 254, 282, 364, 579
–, intensive cooking 562
–, intensive reading 158
– whiteness 41, 575
intention 11, 172, 190, 262, 532, 580
– of Zosimos 143-4, 158-9, 242, 257, 559
–, sincere 367
intercourse, sexual 55-56, 127, 157, 181-2, 192, 304, 481, 536
interest (vb, n) 191, 296, 536
interior 169, 208, 256, 286, 292, 369-70, 457, 543, 549, 465
–, conceal in 558, 575
interlocutor 114, 116
interpolation(s) 26, 68, 96, 119-20
interpretation 5-6, 31, 80, 93, 129, 457
–, alchemical 10
– of picture(s) 12, 31, 79
– of sun 473
–, psycholocial 90
intimacy/ intimacies 97-8, 111
introduction 13, 35-6, 46, 61, 68, 73, 79-80, 84, 116, 119, 131, 133, 135, 279
introverted 132, 137

intuition 232
inundation 91, 357
invent (vb) 388
– mixtures 404
– names 177, 158, 206, 237, 259, 262, 266, 384, 397, 442, 467-8, 472, 530
– things 206, 559
invisible 177, 200-1
invoke 463
al–Iraqi, Abū al-Qāsim; *see also as–Simawi* 92-3, 99, 101, 103, 105, 107
iron 47, 119, 179, 184, 233-4, 250-1, 257-8, 271, 273-4, 298, 321, 353, 374, 398, 458, 460
– absorbs water 485
– and copper 298
– and lead 155
– and magnesia 350, 385
– and magnet 160, 290, 384, 442, 463
– and operation of silver 377
– and water 233
–, as lead-copper 386
–, as our gold 386
–, asqunian 258
–, attraction of 290
–, beat with 458
–, burn with magnesia 288
– copper, …, tin and lead 287, 293, 301
– dissolves 485
–, drops of 469
–, dry 442
– from black earth 386
– from lead 269
–, gold, silver, … and copper 167
–, Indian 378, 388
– leaves not 468
–, magnesia and filings of silver 472
–, magnet attracts 387
–, mercury from 425
–, mercury, vinegar and salt 320
– mix lead, … and wax 155
– named copper 273
– of sages and of people 462
– operate on/ operation of 320, 463
–, plates of … and dissolved silver 442
–, purified 191
–, pyrit composed with 472
–, roasted gold as 461
–, rust of 316, 461, 510
– rusts with moisture 53, 485
–, silver from 385
–, soften 251, 551
– solidifies 485
– stone 425
–, sulphuric 288
–, turn … into copper 442
–, turn … into plates 485
–, turn … into water 386
–, two-pointed 48, 300
irrigate 248
irritate 406
Isenberg, Wesley W. 122
isṭafar 250
Isis 272, 290, 357-8, 404, 450, 462, 532, 551
– and Osiris 37, 94
–, Book of Isis; *see book(s)*
–, statement of 356
Islamic 79, 110, 113, 121, 124, 136
–, pre- 25, 98, 110, 113, 123-4, 131, 136
– times 9, 24, 113
Ismāʿīl/ Ismail, sons of 25, 118-20, 155
Israel, people of 363
Istanbul 12-3, 116
ivory; *see also stone* 197, 319, 475
– and glue 474
– bone(s) 461, 474
–, dissolve 249
–, soak 504
–, splash 475

–J–

Jaffé, Aniela 32
Jasnow, Richard 123
jealous/ jealousy 22-23, 149, 159, 203, 214, 241, 257, 260, 262, 270, 316, 329, 331, 374, 378, 383, 390, 394, 467, 501, 516, 519, 526, 559
Jesus (Christ, Messiah); see also Christ 28, 31, 37, 120-24
–, Gnostic/ Muslim 136
Jews 25, 110, 155, 451
join (vb) 23, 56, 180, 214, 241, 249, 301, 336, 395, 403
– companions (and water) 480, 564

–, joining one 164
–, join together 159
–, spirit with spiritual one 439
joint (n, adj) 149
– bodies 521
– by joint 24
–, joints 161, 520
journey 40, 112
– of the Sungod 39, 54, 80, 109
joy 37, 203, 240, 313, 342, 492
Jubayr, Ibn 10
judge 155, 358
–, Day of Judgment 155, 556
–, judgment 302
jug 141
juice 192, 323, 469, 492
– of sages 321, 474
–, pure 502
Julius Africanus 9
Jung, Carl Gustav 12, 32-3, 39-40, 44-5, 59, 69, 90, 93, 98, 130, 133, 137-8
Jupiter 252, 279, 311
justice 11

–K–

Ka 35
keep
–, away from people/ hide 203
– back (not) 37, 148, 342, 447, 495
– secret (the science) 145, 161, 171, 177, 193, 213, 215, 260, 278, 297, 359, 390, 394, 414, 453, 487, 501, 563, 566
– subtle 286
kernel 303
key 22, 24, 54, 58, 68, 93-4, 131, 136, 138, 165, 215, 236, 262, 278, 292, 390
– argument 125, 131
–, Book of (Ten) Keys 28, 129, 532
–, Book of the Keys of the Art 116, 132, 133, 137
– of dyeing 316
– of/ to science 259, 414
– of truth 358
– symbol 126
– text 5, 68
–, The Key(s) (book, letter) 404, 411, 487
– to furnace 299
– to work 414, 521
Khalidi, Tarif 121
kill (vb, noun); *see also murder* 24, 36, 47, 54, 125, 151, 156, 312, 342, 357, 480, 536
– body 157-8, 259, 289, 296
–, burn and 533
– dragon 48, 56, 127, 157, 300
– husband 129, 181-2, 213
–, husband ...s torturer 172
–, killed man 24, 149, 216
– lover 54
– Zosimos 80
killer
–, merciful 305
– of copper 574
– of mercury 574
– of soul 216
kind, be 331, 436, 452, 472, 537, 549
–, kindness 148, 150, 202, 212, 302, 526, 543
–, same 163
kindle 277, 534
– fire 156
king 352, 471, 581
– and queen 39, 59-61, 65
–, body of 91
–, clothes of kings 36, 167-8, 341, 495-6, 562
–, healing of 90-1
–, house of the 58, 311
–, kingdom 122
–, kings 142, 203, 269, 494, 559
–, New Kingdom 109
kinship 151, 258-9, 311
k-nk-l 502
Kitāb (book); *see also risāla (epistle)*
– al-Aqālīm as-sabaʾa fī al-ʾilm al-mausūm bi aṣ-ṣanʾa (Book of the Seven Climes on the Science called the Art) 94, 99, 101, 103, 105, 107
– al-ʾanāṣir (Book of the Elements) 18
– ad-Durra an-naqīya (The Pure Pearl) 116
– al-Fihrist (Fihrist) 18, 24, 45, 68, 133
– al-Ḥabīb (Book of the Friend/ Lover) 24-25, 49, 123-4
– al-Ḥabīb and Muṣḥaf aṣ-ṣuwar (Book of the Friend/ Lover and Book of Pictures) 46-47, 49-50, 68
– Ḥall ar-rumūz (Book of the Explanation of

the Symbols) 81, 93
– ilā ğamī1 al-ḥukamā^c fī as-saba^ɔa (Book of all the Sages on the Art) 18
– al-ɔIlm al-muktasab fī zirāɔat aḏ-ḏahab 93
– al-Mafātīḥ (fī aṣ-ṣanɔa) (The Book of the Keys to the Art) 18, 20-1, 23-4, 28, 45-7, 51, 68, 116, 132-3, 137, 529
– al-Mafātīḥ aṣ-ṣanɔa and Muṣḥaf aṣ-ṣuwar 116, 132-3, 137
– al-Māc al-waraqī 93, 110
– Muṣḥaf aṣ–ṣuwar (Book of Pictures) 5-7, 11-13, 18-29, 36, 39-41, 44-8, 51, 55, 57-9, 61, 63-4, 66-9, 73-5, 80-5, 91-2, 95-100, 102-7, 109-11, 113-5, 117-21, 123-6, 131-8, 134
– al-Qasīda al-mimīya (Poem Rhyming on the Letter Mīm) 116
– al-Qasīda an-nunīya (Poem Rhyming on the Letter Nūn) 99
– Qiratis al–hakim (Book of Krates) 25, 51
– Qiratis and Kitab al-mafātīḥ (Book of Krates and Book of the Keys of the Art) 68
– Qiratis and Muṣḥaf aṣ-ṣuwar (Book of Krates and Book of Pictures) 49
knead 165, 400
knee(s) 64-5
knot(s) 78, 222, 224
–, (2) two 141, 263
–, (4) four 263
know 116, 146, 152, 154, 168, 171, 213, 217, 252, 269-70, 279, 285, 298, 344, 355, 382, 402-3, 406, 416, 420, 452, 496-7, 516, 531, 562, 564, 567
– all written 166
– body of magnesia 384
– combinations/ mixtures 168
– dyer 188
– experiment 569
– gum 171
– it! 144, 237, 239, 243, 248, 257, 345, 401, 410, 469, 525, 559
– measures of fire 491, 523
– natures 142, 169, 221, 223, 228, 298, 326, 359, 491, 519, 540
– needed things 227-8
–, need to 29, 212, 543
– not cloud/ cinnabar 285
– not measures of fire 523-4
– not truth 278
– operation 375, 491
– our silver 467
– our work 467
–, prevent knowing 540
– sages by their science 28, 120, 220, 523
– that! 29, 51, 143-4, 146, 151, 165, 170-1, 174-5, 177, 181-2, 191-2, 194, 196, 199-201, 205-7, 210, 226-7, 235, 239, 242, 244, 257, 259, 261, 263, 266, 279, 285-6, 288, 291, 295, 297, 304-5, 310, 312, 317, 324-5, 327-8, 356, 358-60, 366, 369, 371-2, 375-6, 382, 386, 389, 394-5, 399, 403, 433, 436, 447, 450-5, 457-60, 462, 464-5, 469, 471, 473-5, 484, 486, 491-2, 498, 509, 512, 515, 522-5, 531-4, 537, 546, 550, 559, 561, 565, 570, 572, 574-5, 577-8
– the one close to you 334
– (these) things 169, 397
– thing/ natures 228
– thoroughly 173
– tree 448, 495
– truth 154, 410
–, unknown 215
– water 501
– weights 274
– what resists the fire 188
– work 260, 454
knowledge 6, 19, 27-9, 39, 45, 54, 68, 113, 122, 133, 136-7, 143, 145, 150, 154, 165, 169, 202-3, 212, 215, 222, 300, 304, 328, 345, 347, 350-1, 432, 468, 477, 495, 516, 523, 526, 540, 557
– about origin 550
– colours 318
–, disperse 97
–, how to aquire 154, 156, 158, 196
–, knowledgeable 35, 203, 319, 336
– of alchemy 11, 22
– of bodies 461
– of dialogue 97
– of hieroglyphs 10
– of measures 522
– of Mushaf as–suwar 52
– of teacher 19
– of things 477
– of water 501

–, Pharaonic 127
–, reach 151
–, temple 21, 123
–, thorough 152
known 23-4, 26-7, 50, 54, 56, 63, 67-8, 80, 85, 90-2, 9-5, 99, 113, 117-8, 126-7, 130, 133, 137, 141, 149, 160, 239, 242, 266, 275, 320, 322, 347, 356, 359, 371, 389-90, 399, 450, 529, 579
–, known-unknown/ known-not known 41, 128, 172, 225, 575
– name(s) 50, 488
–, not longer 136
kohl 233, 350, 468, 574
–, arsenic/ mercury, sandarach and 436, 505
–, blackness of 566
–, copper, magnesia and 463
–, coppery 350, 463
–, magnesia, … and spittle of moon 324
– stone 472, 500
komaris 125-6

–L–

ladder 208
lady, my 21, 24, 27, 149, 200, 347, 562
Laila and Mağnūn 39
lake 79, 517
– with water 391
lamp 112, 209, 256
lance 47
land 125, 447, 495
–, arable 130
–, lands 215
l– of dead 54
– of India 249
anguage 5, 68, 91-2, 95
–, alchemical 40
–, symbolic 112, 500
lapis lazuli 141
–, colour of 527
large(r) 30, 41, 43, 49, 78-9, 305
last 289
– book 46
– dissolving 535
– mixture 167
– picture 80
lasting way 293
Latin 61
– alchemists 59
– alchemy 33-4, 41, 59, 61, 68, 81, 130, 136
– text(s) 125
laugh 304, 469
–, laughed 300
laurel 320
laziness 227
lead (n) 34, 90, 94, 119, 158, 183-4, 189, 195, 234, 251, 260, 263, 272-3, 282, 289, 297-9, 344, 374, 376, 378, 395, 397-8, 410, 418, 464, 469, 495, 513, 528
– and claudianus 399
– and/ as copper 245, 535
– and eternal water 546
– and ferment, eternal water and sour vinegar 355
– and iron 155
– and magnesia 220, 288
– and male 233
– and mercury 395
– and mother-of-pearl 297
– and tin 260, 273, 287, 293, 298, 301, 394, 403, 461
– asṭām 361
– as pyrite 234
–, black 144, 155-6, 216, 289, 350, 366, 376-9, 381, 523
–, black ... and body of magnesia 376-7
–, black and white 326
–, break (vb) 190, 353
–, burn the 168
–, composed/ composition of 326, 456
–, copper, …, (and honoured stone) (dissolve equally/ mix) 265-7, 273-4, 282, 298, 376, 398, 546
–, copper, iron, tin and 287, 293, 301
–, enter lead-copper 500
–, etesian and copper 378
–, extract moisture from 297
–, heat of copper, … and tin 403
–, iron from 269
–, iron and; *see lead, copper*
–, lead, white ... and tin 260
–, leaden/ leady 375, 461
– leaves not 468

–, magnesia as lead-copper and black 379
–, moisture of 51
–, name 530
–, nature of 326
– of one body 355
–, of people/ sages (our) 183, 220, 288, 354-5, 462
–, operation of 399
–, pound 395
–, power of red 326
–, purified 355
–, red 297, 326, 527, 546
–, red copper, … and silver 468
–, remove air-holes of 551
–, rub 397
–, salt, alum, white …, polished earth and living water 395
–, single 289
–, tin corrupted with 394
–, tin named 273
–, turn body into black 155
–, turn dissolved chrysocolla into 530
–, turn into 324
– turns black 144, 353
– turns white 581
– without moisture 397
–, water of 418, 425
–, weight of 274
–, white 183, 272, 350, 475, 535, 541
–, white … and litharge 272
–, white … as subtle tin 461
–, whose mixture disappeared 397
lead-copper 22, 24, 44, 85, 195, 204-5, 210, 245-6, 248, 251, 256, 261, 270, 275, 280, 289, 294, 299, 319, 325, 364, 375-6, 379, 381, 386, 410, 425, 447-8, 450, 459, 463, 470, 472, 474, 495, 498, 502, 568, 580
– and cloud 464
– and crystal 210
– and tin 325
– as magnesia 381
–, composition of 472
– dissolve; *see also lead, copper* 210
–, extract colours from 450
–, extract from …-copper 245
–, magnesia as … and black lead 379
–, mercury with alum, … and lime 378
–, operation of 299, 377, 452
–, treatment of 385
lean 255, 279, 357, 480, 536, 559
–, make 174, 227, 289, 440, 482, 531, 560, 568, 578
–, make body 370, 549
–, make salt 456
–, rotting and making 440
–, second making 572
leap 48, 300
learning
–, Book of Learning 141-2
–, learn 299, 485
–, limit of 142
– of the truth 144
leathers 204
leave (vb) 37, 53, 57, 127, 152-3, 157, 190, 192, 194, 203, 205, 207, 215, 234, 240, 257, 283, 291, 293, 320, 323, 328, 342, 350, 382, 366, 390, 396, 400, 459, 467-8, 484, 488-9, 495-6, 501-2, 505-7, 512, 520, 529, 531, 542-4, 547, 555-6, 559-62, 566, 568-9, 572
– aside 148, 188, 232, 261, 288, 502
– away 159, 542
– blackness in things 317
– dyes 552
– for days 488, 520, 531, 547, 552, 575
– for long time 542
– glue 475
– impurity 504
– in cooking 489, 507, 531, 558, 562, 575
– in dung 508
– in its place/ in their house 485, 566
– in its vessel 529, 559-60, 562, 569
– in sun; *see also dry* 57, 157, 127, 489, 500, 531
–, left-over 223
– not 160, 177, 283, 342, 350, 467-8, 475, 485, 505, 569
– out 158, 164, 188, 191, 210, 283, 294, 397, 485
– sediment 509
–, soul leaves body 436
– sulphurs 543
– to rot 560-1
– wool 495
– you 143, 334

leaves (of a plant) 447, 495
– of acaia tree 130
– of apples 249
– of oleander 320, 473, 497, 541
– of pomegranate 316
–, white, red, purple 448
left; *see also leave*
– and right 121
– hand 31-2, 142, 263, 391
leg(s) 31, 142, 307, 339, 345, 391, 477, 526, 544
–, (3) three 440
–, (8) eight-legged 290
– of Zosimos 78, 141
legend 125
leprosy 336
lesson 202, 274, 502
letter(s); *see also book; epistle; poem; Satarmīta; Treatise of Magnesia* 111, 242, 373, 375, 388, 407, 414, 464, 475
–, (2) two (alphabetical) 279
–, (4th) fourth 260
–, (4) four 92
–, (7th) Seventh 414
–, (9) nine 450
–, (9th) Ninth 407, 414, 432, 442, 457
– (10) ten (alphabetical) 224
– (70) seventy epistles 18
–, authentic 20, 111
– in (Book of) the Sartamita 414, 442
– of alphabet 23, 92, 224, 279, 373
– of Zosimos for/ to Theosebeia 111, 114-5, 171, 375, 388, 407, 414, 434
–, On the letter Omega (by Zosimos) 32, 91
–, The Keys 411
–, The Letters 407, 411, 434, 475
–, three-fold with 475
level (of alchemical process); *see also register; sphere* 35, 59, 64, 238, 240-1, 253
– of archetypes/ divinites 112
– of operation 46, 212
– of work 33, 331
lexica/ lexicon 10, 94-5
Libra 494, 571
library/ libraries 9-11, 13, 20, 60, 99, 110, 116-7
–, Asafiya (Hyderabad) 10, 116
–, Nag Hammadi 9, 121-2
lie (vb, n) 36, 81, 84, 109, 209, 232, 341, 350, 439, 544
–, liar(s) 257
life 20, 53, 98, 108, 130, 161, 164, 170, 182, 198, 213, 238, 242-3, 259, 262, 292, 296, 299, 322, 339, 350, 359, 363, 400, 436, 455, 481, 485, 508, 521, 530, 555
– and/ after death 121, 123, 480, 521
– as water/ water of life 53-4, 485
–, colour of 35
–, come to 36, 44, 48, 53, 340, 485, 524
–, lifetime 20, 39, 98, 108, 130, 176, 213, 547
– of natures 176
– of sperm 486
– of Zosimos (dating) 9, 27
–, -providing 35
–, rest of 143
–, return to 48
–, -span 10
–, spend 147
–, tree of 41-2
–, upon my 162
light 28, 31, 35, 37, 54-5, 58, 63, 94, 112, 209, 222, 224, 258, 279, 312, 319, 342, 344, 383, 560
– and dark/ darkness 44, 121
–, bring it to 556
–, extinguish 507
– from/ of sun 295, 305
–, intense 63, 222
–, make appear 305
– of moon/ moon- 279, 281, 507
– of Zosimos 37
–, preserve 507
–, water earth, wind and 122
like with like; see also similar/ simile 46
limbs 57, 216
lime 185, 227-8, 284, 323-4, 349, 389, 396, 501, 510
–, alum, urine and water of 324
– and fire 41, 575
– and sulphur 460
– as alabaster 41, 575
–, ašqunīān 317
– as symbol 457
– dissolves and transforms 510
–, fighter, clung(-to) and 396, 446

–, gold and fat 457
–, marble water, …, sediment and fat 381
–, marinal 505
–, mercury with alum, lead-copper and 378
–, mix with 457
– of ordinary people 41, 575
–, salt, alum, natron, ... and makras(…n 325
–, zinc 436
limit 142-3, 207, 236, 238, 331, 356, 558
– for heat 486
–, limits 178
line 361
– up 407, 411, 425, 428-9, 435-6, 442, 445
linguistic 138
linen 303
–, piece of 394, 459
link
–, together 544
–, missing 136
Lindsay, J. 11
linseed 503
lion 367
– brings forth a lion 551
–, face of 473
Lippmann, E. von 28
liquid 418
–, liquified mercury 513
listen 519
literature 36, 54, 94-5, 121, 125, 136
–, alchemical
–, Arabic 26
–, Graco-Roman 131
–, hadith 26
–, Islamic 121
– of Ancient Egypt 136
–, Syriac 19
litharge 247, 270, 272, 287, 317, 326, 350, 470, 510
– and magnesia 270
– and similar to stone 464
– and white lead 272
– as blackness 446
–, blackness from nature of 509
–, colour of 521
– make from tin 261
–, nature of 446, 469
–, operation of 377
–, power of 326
–, silver mixed with 520
–, white 395, 541
little 35, 62, 140, 156, 171, 196, 205, 210, 213, 221, 271-2, 274, 351, 365, 367, 406, 481, 536-7, 568
– amount 248
– by little 156, 177, 220-1, 249, 252, 278, 293, 454, 462, 486-7, 489, 496, 537, 562, 568-9, 578-9
–, much comes from 62
– understanding 228
live (vb)
–, living being
–, living ones 389
–, living water 395, 400-2
– together 28, 523
liver 173
locks of sages 154
long for 310, 334, 322, 344, 382, 387, 438, 455, 462, 485, 536
–, longing 241, 439, 201
look 311
look at (pictures; vb) 29, 59, 61, 85, 90, 92, 95, 119, 195, 312, 402-3, 420, 457
look for (vb) 69, 121, 129, 143, 148, 158, 162, 178, 190, 197, 208, 226, 253, 257, 273, 310, 357-9, 387, 403, 427, 451, 453, 467, 474, 504, 511, 513-4, 519-21, 523, 542, 557, 560, 577, 580
– our work 299
–, pour in looked-for 560
– stone 464, 465
loose 490
–, loosen silver 540
–, loosen up 548
loss 219, 282
–, get lost 401
–, lost way 349, 381, 458
lot /a lot 210, 213, 375, 406, 530
love (vb, n) 18, 29, 32, 55, 58, 63, 111, 122, 132, 135, 137, 164, 180, 222-3, 273, 290, 310-1, 320, 334, 357, 366, 385, 390, 474, 536-7, 575
– each other 168
–, lovers 36, 49, 54, 59, 156
– of virgin 473
–, tin loves slave girl 458
– truth 155

lower 38, 59, 64-5, 78, 176, 406
– and higher/ upper 121, 487
– dark-evil 28
–, highest to the lowest 167
–, lowest 167, 349
–, lowest of colours 36, 339
– part of human being/ (human) realm 31, 34-5
– register 34
–, turns black lowest 167
– water 487
Lucifer–Prometheus 32
luminaries 59, 78-9, 92
luminous 160, 175, 512
– dye 269
lunar
– appearance 160
– colours 258
– quality 222, 224
lustre 523
Luxor 9

–M–

Madelung, Wilferd 7, 13, 26, 97, 118
Mīdunah 196
maġnīs 456
magic 21
– attraction 118, 137
– power 25
– words 203
magnesia 24, 37, 79, 81, 84, 159, 164, 200, 226, 251, 254, 306, 310, 326, 328, 331, 344-5, 350, 352, 356, 361, 364-6, 375, 381, 383-4, 388, 390, 402, 500, 523
–, (1/6) a sixth of 486
– all of work is in 156
– and antimony are (1) one 272
– and iron 350, 385
– and lead 220
– and litharge 270
– and mercury 361
– and sulphur 325
– as black lead/ lead-copper 377, 379, 381
– as copper 381
– as crown of every thing 381
– as escaping 51, 372
– as glass 385
– as moist and dry 297
– becomes magnetic stone 581
–, all things come together in 351
–, as composition named copper, iron, tin and lead 287
–, body of 37, 183, 251-2, 254, 282, 285, 287, 289, 313, 321, 345, 352-3, 360-4, 366, 369, 373, 375 6, 378-9, 381-2, 386, 399, 424, 475, 530-1, 580
–, body of …, and black lead 376-7
–, body of …, and magnet 384, 442
–, body of …, and/ as mercury (of cinnabar) 349, 350, 352, 378, 384, 402
–, body of …, as arsenic/ sandarach 353
–, body of ..., as mixed magnesias 381
–, body of …, as unit of escaping and non-escaping 378
–, body of ..., burn copper with sulphur and 497
–, body of …, chrysocolla, ... and eternal water 265
–, body of ..., cinnabar as 373
–, body of ..., cook 530
–, body of ..., copper, tin and 549
–, body of ..., dye 380
–, body of ..., fat and 381
–, body of ..., glue mercury on 384
–, body of ..., mixed with mercury and 164
–, body of ..., mix natures to 379
–, body of ..., naming of 378
–, body of ..., of ordinary people 361
–, body of ..., operation of 382
–, body of ..., red 379
–, body of ..., silvery 471
–, body of ..., solidify mercury in/ with 351, 353, 372-3, 376-7, 383
–, body of ..., unite components and 376
–, body of ..., weight of 382
–, body of ..., whitened 368
–, burn as 579
–, burn iron with 288
– changes colour 362
– composed 327, 351
– conquers shadow of copper 374
–, components of (fire of) 313, 350
–, composition of 351
–, cook 458
–, copper tuns into 497

–, copper, … and shadow of copper 374
–, destruction of bodies with mercury and 533
–, dissolve 366
–, dry 524
–, dyeing of 380
–, earth operates on 369
–, explanation of 329
–, extract things from 156
–, female 372, 530
–, iron, … and filings of silver 472
–, kohl and spittle of moon 324
–, kohl, copper and 463
–, lead as/ from 288, 425
– lets not escape spirit 372
–, making of 377
– marry … and components of mixture 382
–, meaning of 81
–, mercury from/ into 372, 425
–, mix honoured stone and 270
– mix …. with white nature 367
– mix body with 368
– of people 350
– of sages (about) 183, 350
–, only with … colour secret comes into 373
– operated 164
–, operation for/ of 207, 377
–, origin of 378
– our 220
–, secret 463
– transformation of 81
–, true 324
–, turn copper into 183
–, turn into 360, 403
– unite sulphury bodies with 468
–, wash with sweet water 531
–, white/ whiten/ whiteness of 367, 369, 372, 374
magnet 244, 384, 418
– and iron 160, 290, 384, 442, 463
– and sulphur 321
– as body of magnesia 442
– attracts iron 387
– of people 442
maiden, poison (Giftmädchen) 36, 54, 125
Maier, Michael 57
make/ making of
– (2nd) second work 405
– (3) three as (1) one 550
– alumy 170, 294, 389, 451-3, 541-2, 552, 573-4
– black 170, 195, 292, 321, 354, 447, 456, 561
– black of silver 466
– body lean 370
– body of magnesia 382
– body white 399
– broth 247
– clear 155, 185, 202, 257, 349, 516; 559
– copper black 216, 355
– copper rusty 195, 216, 303, 355, 552
– dry 165
– equal with gold 267
– etesian 465
– experiments 519
– ferment of gold 248
– fine 452
– glass 471
– gold 176, 207, 233, 349, 352, 377, 447, 550
– gold and silver 166, 280, 357, 400
– gum 464
– ingot 363
– ivory, horns, bones 319
– lead-copper 85, 204, 425, 474
– lean 227, 289, 549, 560, 568, 578
– litharge 261
– magnesia 377
– mercuries 414
– mercury 283
– pearls 492
– poison 144, 255, 286
– pure 190
– purple 323, 509
– red 143, 164-5, 170, 184-5, 197, 207, 212, 236, 245-7, 249-50, 252, 267, 288, 295, 321, 373, 377, 397, 411, 421, 460-1, 468, 498, 525, 532-3, 549, 552, 561
– red black 561
– rust 549
– rusty 250, 360, 373, 411, 489, 532, 552
– salt made lean 456
– salty 568
– silver 260, 349, 377, 379, 420-1, 447, 550, 566, 574
– silver black 283
– solid 150
– thin 294

– use of 258, 359, 390, 453, 522, 542
– well 166
– white 143, 165, 170, 183, 185, 187, 195, 197, 199, 212, 236, 246-7, 251-2, 254, 267, 283, 288, 292, 294-5, 297, 354, 362, 373, 377, 379, 384-5, 397, 402, 444, 460-1, 465, 494, 498, 533, 561, 574, 577
– white lead 260
– white sulphur 192
– white themselves 396, 444
– wool (not) alumy 453
– work 469
makrasīūn, salt, alum, natron, lime and 325
male(s); *see also man* 44, 164, 177, 181, 220, 222, 225, 238, 247, 249, 254, 270, 272, 280, 292, 295, 313, 362, 363, 372, 474, 481, 530, 533, 546, 574
– and female(s); *see also male-female relationship; male unites with female* 29, 32, 53, 58, 116, 122, 129, 134, 136-7, 164, 174-5, 182, 225, 233-5, 249, 258, 278, 296, 310-1, 363, 366, 474, 485, 534, 546, 580
– and moisture 576
– and sparkling 281
– and spirit 304
– and water 363
–, arsenic is 235
–, blood of 485
– body 362, 530
– contained in tin 235
–, cook 233
–, cook broth and 552
–, -female relationship 137-8
– found female 465
–, heat of the 175
– is in lead 233
–, let … enter 304
–, mix … with vapour 490
–, mix mercury with 368
–, natural 296
–, non-males 129
–, one part from 265
–, plates of 529
– principle 32, 93
–, red 295
– sea 231
– sulphur 247
–, turn … into ashes 235
– unites with female 175, 466
–, water of 529
–, whiten 231
Maltese 503
Mamluk 98-9, 108, 110
man 11, 92, 174, 256, 310, 387, 391, 433, 447-8
– and woman 310-1, 320, 326
–, colour of man 475
–, copper- ; *see also copper-body, kalkanthropos* 24
–, dye of 540
–, equal to 390
– fighting dragon 47
–, gold(en)/ man of gold 40, 339, 526, 544
–, great 59
–, killed 149, 216
– of wool 539
–, old 53-4 464-5, 485
–, outstanding 390
– skilful in the science 154-5
–, winged 35, 307, 332, 342, 477
– -woman relationship 136-8
–, young; *see also youth* 47, 53-4, 300
Mangetus, Johannes Jacobus 64
manifestation 432
manifold; *see also various* 62, 173, 207, 221, 400, 455
manuscript(s); see also text(s) 5, 11-3, 17, 19, 21-2, 69, 73-4, 78, 84-5, 99, 118-9, 123, 131-4, 136-8, 140
–, Arabic 58, 137
–, complete 20
– of Muṣḥaf aṣ-ṣuwar 6-7
– of Zosimos 54
– on alchemy 20
many; see also *various, manifold*
– and (1) one 148, 150-1, 162, 187, 170, 173, 201, 205, 291, 294, 301, 305, 351, 359, 368, 382, 394, 418, 424, 432, 439, 458, 481, 484, 537, 542, 550, 581
– colours 162, 166, 179, 279, 290, 294, 393, 457, 554, 571, 579
– days 57, 127, 157, 207, 248, 261, 297, 320, 356, 475, 501-2, 504-5, 510, 512, 519, 523, 529, 570

– months 504
– names 50, 206, 208, 226, 252, 259, 266, 273, 290, 302, 349, 371, 375, 453, 483, 488, 502, 511, 521, 540, 565
– things 148, 151, 205, 252, 273, 294, 296, 394, 452, 484, 580-1
– times 23, 149, 170, 243, 251, 280, 384, 487, 528, 573
marble 234, 251, 284, 319, 350, 380, 395, 487, 504, 511, 532
–, and dust 284
–, burnt 506
– water 381
mare 192
margin 23, 58, 119, 129, 151, 154, 179, 191, 193, 195, 197, 219, 227-8, 234, 250, 252, 256, 261, 311, 354, 360, 362, 390, 427, 436, 440, 442, 466, 473, 476, 505, 513, 515-6, 528, 548, 554-5, 567, 579, 581
Maria 12, 24-5, 27, 128, 143-4, 148, 154, 184, 186, 189-90, 192, 197, 201, 204, 209, 221, 243, 248-9, 251, 253-4, 263, 265-8, 270, 272, 274-5, 285, 347, 363-5, 372, 374, 376, 378-9, 398-401, 405-6, 453, 456, 462-3, 472, 481, 483, 487, 497, 511, 513-4, 528, 531, 536, 546, 548, 550, 555, 565-7, 577
– and Jesus/ dead son 37, 94
–, books of 221, 274, 375, 377, 385, 389, 465, 542
–, epistle of 287
–, statement of 25, 154-5, 190, 192, 220, 244, 247, 261, 263, 273, 282, 288, 298, 416, 461-2, 481, 552, 562, 578, 580
–, the Copt 73
marinal 436, 489
– lime 505
marine 319, 401, 507
–, reddish 383
market(s) 231
–, book 133
Marocco 458
marry 164, 177, 188, 195, 200, 213, 222, 224-5, 277, 280, 311-2, 356, 375, 390, 486-7, 534, 539, 580
– magnesia and components of mixture 382
–, marriage 118, 249, 256, 273, 275, 313, 359, 375, 390, 405, 533-4, 487
–, married, elixir is 577
–, married, single into 397
–, married, things … in sea 380
–, marrying; *see also marriage, coniunctio* 159, 200, 277, 279, 352
– natures 535, 537
– soul of fugitive and body of non-fugitive 489
Mars; *see Aries*
Martelli, M. 91, 95
masculine 344
master(s) 19, 91, 95, 117, 142, 262, 275, 292, 352, 357, 359, 389, 432, 581
– and student 78, 118
–, fear of Master 155
–, mastery 556
– of natures 228
– of science , 540
– of the art 133
– of the bodies 529, 558
– of waters 558
–, question 486
material 37, 44, 47, 49, 96, 114-5, 118, 130, 132-3
–, case 98
–, from teacher 19
–, materialistic 21
–, source 114, 137
–, side 126
matter; *see also material* 28, 44, 48, 101
māṭīṭus 388
mature 174, 275, 386, 565-6
– elixir 577
–, let it 562
meaning(s) 12, 23, 27, 29, 40, 69, 84-5, 91, 93, 111, 123, 135, 137, 203, 236, 253, 317-8, 363, 546
– of (3) three mercuries 84
–, grasp 546
–, inner/ spiritual 94, 289
– of images 19
– of magnesia 81, 84
– of symbol/ symbolic 45, 93, 95, 126, 138
– of symbolic alchemy/ alchemical symbolism 12, 33
– of teachings 19

– of transformation of arcane substance 84
–, true 154
–, understand 291, 300
means 93, 207, 427, 489, 513
– of living 143
measure(s); *see numbers; parts; rutls; weights* 248, 321, 354, 509
–, Book of the Measures of the Fire 516
–, equal 271-2, 500
–, first 406
–, four 489
–, half a 568
–, knowledge of 522
–, moderate 275, 577
– of eye 456
– of fire 22, 79, 96, 143, 192, 253, 275, 289, 345, 350, 365, 396, 379, 405-6, 444, 453, 491-2, 511, 516, 519, 521 5, 577
– of fire and success/ key of work 492, 521
– of heat 157
–, right 396, 403, 507
–, suitable 157
–, ten 502
–, understand 519
–, weight 158
mediating 11
medical doctor; see also cure; disease; illness; doctor; remedy 90, 169
medicine 166, 195
meet 299, 382
– blood 485
– close one 201
– her husband 164
– nature of its own 296
meeting (n)
– of philosophers/ Zosimos and Theosebeia 68, 327
– with its own nature 259, 296
melt (vb) 249, 318, 324, 394, 493
–, copper melts 494
–, melting 294
memorize 285
Memphis 48, 300
men 310, 347, 407, 458
–, (2) two 79, 141, 391
–, (3) three 411, 414, 416, 421, 426, 544
–, winged 141, 544
menstruation 387
mercury/mercuries 21, 94, 128, 183, 187, 196, 210, 220, 242, 244-5, 261, 272, 280, 282, 289, 302, 321, 352, 356, 361, 365, 395, 399, 403, 411, 416, 420, 429, 431-2, 458, 462, 465, 468, 476, 482, 543
–, (1) one 352, 403, 414, 416, 420, 424, 432, 458, 550
–, (1) one, turn mercuries into 403
– is (1) one in appearance/ name 457
–, action of mercury 458
–, alum, ... and dye 452
– and/ as body of magnesia 349, 361, 378, 383-4
– and cloud 164
– and copper 225, 353, 411
– and ferment 380
– and glass 403
– and gold 277
– and lead 395
– and magnesia 361
– and mercuries of bodies 543
– and poison 457
– and pure water of sulphur 434
– and sandarach 416
– and spittle of the moon 226
– and sulphur(s) 260, 287, 416
– and tin 21, 226, 399, 426, 466
– and vinegar 394
– and body of magnesia 361
–, aqzal, spittle (of moon) and 472, 500
– as crown of dyeing 547
– as silver 566
–, black impure 458
–, body into/ of 151, 183, 278, 550
–, Book about the Mercury 550
– born every year 507
–, cinnabar holds dye of 490
– clings to (companion) 430, 466
–, cloud of … and sulphur turn white 374
– coagulates with hard bodies 287
–, companions of 430
–, composed 353
–, conceal in 514
–, cook (with) 283 578

–, copper absorbs fiery 567
–, corrupted 394
–, Cypriot 578
–, destroy 321
–, destruction of bodies with 533
–, different 550
–, dissolve with 151
–, dyeing of/ dye of 425, 490
–, Eastern 93
– enters lead-copper 472
– escapes 321
–, examination of 394
–, experiments of 434
–, extract … from (bodies) 280, 457, 542-3
–, extract with 567
–, fiery 368
– fights copper 372
–, fire solidified 372
–, first 261
–, fountain of 129
– from arsenic and sandarach (and pure water) 287, 353, 421
– from arsenic, sadarach, abšimīt and rest 420
– from ašqunīa nature 395
– from chrysocolla 269
– from cinnabar 151, 325, 352, 420
– from copper 426
– from flowers of copper 513
– from iron 425
– from lead 425
– from magnesia 425
– from silver 425
–, fugitive 416, 468
–, glue 384
–, gold, tin and 278
–, gum, …, and sulphur 407
–, hide/ hidden in 236, 418
–, iron, …, vinegar and salt 320
–, liquified 513
– in operation 483
– in water 459
–, killer of 574
–, know 575
–, magnesia mixed with … and body 164
–, make 283
– makes disappear shadow 528
– makes glass sick 318
– makes work 425
–, mix arsenic and … of cinnabar 235
–, mix bodies with 398
–, mix glass with 385
–, mix ... with 410, 376, 385, 547
–, mix … with male 368
–, mix sulphur with 377
–, mixing, power, action, extraction and essence of 458
– mixes with bodies of magnesia 580
–, names of 425
–, nature of 277
–, nature turned thick part into 514
– of arsenic 226, 416, 550
– of body of magnesia 362
– of/ from/ out of cinnabar 213, 226, 235, 244, 261, 277-8, 280, 352-3, 373, 420, 424, 425, 472, 500, 550, 567, 574, 578
– of cinnabar and honoured body 549
– of cinnabar from body of magnesia 352
– of gold 427
– of reddening 420
– of sages 229
– of the people 95, 433, 458
– of tin clings to cinnabar 403
– of truth 403, 424, 427
– of whitening 420
– of work and … of people 425
–, operate on … with white sulphur 379
–, operation of 151, 432 , 500
–, other 261, 420, 514, 550
–, prevent … from escaping 372
– raises 455
– rarely found 242
–, red 256, 430
–, relationship of ... with copper 574
–, sandarach, ..., and kohl 436
–, solid 172
–, solidification of/ solidify/ solid 172, 251, 256, 268, 344, 351, 353, 278, 363, 372-3, 416, 424, 430, 457, 513
–, solidify … in/ with body of magnesia 372, 376-7, 383
–, spirit of 490
– spirits 109
–, take 578
–, test 459
–, tin becomes 541, 546

–, tin, … and copper 455, 472
–, true 457
–, turn … into stone 356
–, turn …, sulphur and gold into dyeing poison 287
–, turn copper into 183
–, turn into 395
–, turn ... into magnesia 372
– turns body into non-bodies 477
– turns sulphur into rust 250
–, well of 451, 447, 495
–, white (pure) 352-3, 362, 459, 528
–, white lead, ..., and sulphur 260
– with alum, lead-copper and lime 378
– without body 398
Mercurius 65, 78
–, androgynous 130
–, Hermes-Mercurius 31
mercy 32, 125, 181, 196, 213, 257, 352, 477, 516
merit 13, 69, 135, 142, 144, 154, 162, 170, 175, 355
Meritamun 10
Merlin 90-1
Mertens, Michèle 9, 17-8, 21-2, 24, 27, 40, 64, 92, 126, 133, 134
message, written 217
metal(s) 78, 94, 177, 193, 207, 226, 289, 304, 464-5, 488
–, extract stone from 209
–, perfection of 461
–, purple 451
metallic 195, 410-1
metals 143, 148, 256, 274, 287, 289, 457, 468, 488
– as colours of elixir 557
–, colours of 167
–, despise 166
–, dry 198
–, dye core of 204
–, extract from 238
–, head of 529
–, rot 302
–, vapour of 223
metaphor(s) 90-1, 97, 203
method 129, 138, 451
m-ġ-r (muġrāt/ muġra, reddish/russet colour) 349, 406, 454
microcosm 64
middle 58, 157, 311-3, 450, 506, 517
– Ages 10
– of work 213
Mīdunah 196
mild 180
–, mildness 236
milk(s) 247, 261, 349, 400-1, 474, 486
– and water 400
–, burning with 400
–, cook in 453
–, dusts, herbs and 454
– -like 472
– of gum 418
– of moon 484
– of roses 261
– of she-donkeys 401
millenium, first 17
minaret(s) 120, 293
mind 128, 158, 172, 176, 178-9, 214, 229, 328, 331, 344-5, 351, 365, 367, 386-7, 402, 455, 485
– becomes clear 154
–, confuse/ ... is confused 150, 263, 537
–, feeble; *see mind, weak-minded*
–, grasp (work/ secret) 152
–, keep in 146
– not able to understand 336
– of woman 150, 315
–, weak/ weak-minded/ feeble 176, 179, 315, 329, 400
mineral; *see also alabaster, alum, androdamus, arsenic, chrysocolla, cinnabar, claudianus,* clay, *coal,* crystal, *emerald, etesian, glass, kohl, lime, litharge, magnesia, magnet, marble, pearl, pitch, potash, pyrite, ruby, salt, sand, sapphire, sulphur, talc, tar, vitriol; see also metal*
–, body turns into 192, 396
–, extract dye from 179
–, mercuries of minerals 430, 489
–, minerals 166, 179, 194, 397, 430, 488
– natures 515
mingle (vb) 276, 229, 318, 398
–, mingling 142, 534
miracles 33, 176-7, 332

mirror 11, 260, 270, 385
–, polish/ treat 385
misery 556
misfortune 289, 312
misled 350
misqals 278
miss (not) 183, 174, 177
– (2) two natures, ... not 249
–, missing; *see also picture; page; part; question; text* 141, 210, 263, 297, 402, 450, 512
–, missing link 136
– out 359
mistake 282, 294, 434
– at beginning 192
–, mistaken (not) 281, 523, 560
–, mistakes 289
mistress 249, 292
misunderstand(ings) 5, 18, 137, 541
mix/ mixing 22, 50, 57, 63, 128-9, 143, 206, 298
–, beginning of mixing 23, 289
– honey with water 49, 514
– like with like 46
–, mixing of air 63
– with black inside 37
– water with bodies 49
mixture(s) 128, 151, 197, 205, 222, 243, 252, 271, 273, 277, 283, 287, 344, 352, 375-7, 459, 468, 503, 506, 515, 542, 567, 570, 531
–, (1) one 270, 301
–, (2) two, ... of 324
–, (4) four ....s 301
–, (9th) ninth 414
– and poison disappear 293
– becomes dry 321
–, beginning of 178, 522
–, burn 523
–, colours of 257
–, companions of 552
–, completed 475
–, components of 201, 205, 321, 366, 376, 382, 399, 425, 461-2, 465, 472, 492, 577
–, different ...s/ ... differ 519
– disappear(s/ ed) 397, 454
–, first 289
–, invented ...s 404
–, last 167
–, mixtures of natures 168
–, moisture in 397
–, natures of … into ash 486
– of air 524
– of copper 388
– of poison 522
– of sages 401, 499
–, other 247
–, pounding 407
–, reach 223
–, second 253
mock (vb) 37, 342
moderate 26, 157, 275, 278
– fire 275, 380, 519, 577
modesty 155, 433
Mohammed; *see Muḥammad*
moist (adj, n) 63, 161,167, 169, 175, 185, 205, 222, 225, 227, 247, 297, 304, 362, 370, 387, 399, 405, 473, 481, 489, 539, 543
–, about the moist 397
– alum (n) 321
– and airy water 161
– and dry/ mix dry and 48, 63, 142-3, 152-3, 169, 217-8, 222, 243, 370
– and fire 405
– and hot 142, 228, 169
– body 520
–, cold, hot, dry and 142, 169
–, cook and operate on 405
–, every (thing) 247, 362, 497
– fire 167
–, froth of every 418
– loves the dry 575
–, moisten (vb) 290, 389, 568, 573
– names for ... one 511
– nature 166
– one 63, 142-3, 153, 166, 185, 217-8, 222, 405, 498, 511
–, -operated 555
–, solid, … and herbs 225
– spirit 186, 198, 215, 247, 290, 402, 520, 521, 580
– thing 304
–, turn 176, 198
– water 198

–, weak,..., and cold 174
moisture(s) 48, 91, 147, 156, 160, 167, 174-5, 185-6, 192, 194, 198-9, 205, 216, 218, 220, 223, 226, 229, 236, 247-8, 255, 272, 278, 286, 289-90, 294, 298, 302, 317-8, 357, 360, 387, 396-7, 402, 406, 434, 480, 486, 490, 500, 504, 549, 564
–, (2) two ...s 173
–, (3) three parts from 265
–, absorb 559, 570, 575
–, abundant 507, 548
– and body 166, 279-80
– and completeness 161-2
– and copper 156, 513
– and fire destroy stone 280
– and gum 186
– and hard 185
– and heat 161, 173, 481, 485-6, 508
– and male 576
– and plate(s) 255, 529
– and sediment 167
– and sperm 173
– and sun 318
– as fugitive 546
– as fundament 476
– as sulphur 515
– as water 288
–, body takes flowers from 565
–, (body) turns … into dust 156, 537
–, coagulate 166
– collects 161
–, conceal in 578
– conceals smoke 192
–, cook (with) 283, 481, 559
–, copper inhales spirit from 481
–, copper, sour water and 493
–, cover wool with 510
–, different in water 284
–, disappear 531
–, dry/ dry up 129, 534, 564, 558
–, dryness, …, spirit and cloud 360
– disappear(s) 235, 301, 356, 395, 510, 512, 528, 542, 547, 567, 575
– dissolves plates 548
– dries up 560, 564, 581
– escapes from body 539
–, exist not without/ only by 298, 565
–, extract 167, 283, 493
–, extract colours by 316
– extracts dye from bodies 49, 514
–, extract … from ashes/ lead/ nature 168, 297, 515
– fights fire away 397
– flows over wool 542
–, half of 512
– holds moisture(s) 199, 227, 232, 532
–, honour 162, 476
– in mixture 397
–, iron rusts with 53, 485
–, lead without 397
–, measure of fire for 453
–, measure of … in summer and winter 511
–, mix 247, 490
–, mix bodies/ body and 181, 537, 576
–, mix gum with 255
–, names of 255, 453, 565
– of blood 539
– of female 536
– of glue disappears 475
– of lead 251
– of lead-copper 498
– of truth 357
– of vinegar 531
– of water 539
– of water of sulphur 521
– of winter 524, 548
–, plates absorb/ dry up 529
–, preserve 539
–, prevent … from escaping fire 396
–, put bodies/ plates in 548, 559
–, remove 498
–, return (to) 283, 440
–, roast 573
–, separate from 357, 511
–, silver absorbs 561
–, soak ash in 480, 573
–, solidify/ solidifies ... 213, 366, 537
–, turn ... fine like dust/ into sand 145, 562
–, turn ... into water 576
–, use up 542, 564
–, vapour of 198
–, vessel with 549
–, water is 159
–, without which nothing can be done 294
–, yolk and shell 159

moment 304, 362
money 143, 180, 214, 237, 262
–, bridal 55, 157
month(s) 46, 152, 212, 366, 496
–, (2) two ...s 160
–, (6) six ...s 53, 485
–, completion of 305
–, every 46, 571
–, many ...s 504
moon 34, 38-9, 41, 59-60, 63, 65, 79, 92-3, 222, 229, 252, 258, 277, 281, 291, 295, 494, 571
– and copper 484
– and silver 463
– and stars 291
– and sun 59, 535
–, archetype 39
–, colour of the 571
–, crescent 141, 391, 556
–, dung of 128, 172, 237
–, froth of 350, 388, 418, 426
–, full 507
– -light 279, 281, 507
–, Luna 32, 40
–, magnesia, kohl and spittle of 324
–, milk of 484
–, moon in feminine form 292, 484
–, moony 222
–, nature of 535
–, newmoon/ crescent 43
– on head 30-2, 35, 37-8, 41, 43, 64, 67, 78, 80, 92, 108, 141, 391, 444, 556
–, -queen 39, 61
–, spittle of 128, 170, 172, 210, 226, 231, 242, 256, 324, 350, 418, 500, 568-9
–, spittle of … and aqzal (and mercury) 321, 472
–, spittle of … and gum 256, 454
–, sun, … and stars 175
–, waning 321
Morienus, Romanus 12
mornings 231
mortal 44
mortar(s) 167, 210, 406, 500, 503, 506, 575
–, (3) three 454, 511
– of tin 395
–, pound 501
mortification 228
Moses 119-20, 129, 207, 209, 243, 277, 365
–, prophet 363, 451, 497, 548
mosque(s) 120, 293
mother 154, 177, 182
– and son 142
–, Mother Nature 166
– -of-pearl 280, 297, 324
motif(s) 78, 81, 84, 90, 93, 109, 110
– of birds 79
– of dragon 127
motion 283
mountain(s) 48, 127, 147, 159, 215, 300, 464
–, coal of 237
–, mountainous 388
– of Egypt 367
mouth 24
–, close 566, 575, 581
– of the vessel 277, 355, 436, 505, 507, 531, 547, 564, 566-7, 575, 581
–, tail in; *see also dragon eating tail; see uroboros; tail*
move 47, 259, 296, 512
much and little (amount of s.th) 271-2, 274
mud 504
–, -brick 161
–, turn into 303
muġrā(t); see also russet colour 187, 349, 454, 506, 511
Muḥammad; *see also Ibn Umai; al-Azhari*
–, master 142, 389, 581
multiplicatio(n)(s) 67, 171, 195, 315-6, 325 379-80, 498
–, multiplicity 442, 455
–, multiply (vb) 55, 223, 278, 359, 376, 481, 570
– of gold/ silver/ multiply gold (and silver) 293, 316, 498
mummification 113, 130
murderer; *see also kill* 216, 337
–, murder(ing) 536
–, of her husband, murderess(es) of/murderous to her/ their husband(s) 36, 55-7, 125-9, 131, 157, 159, 242, 451, 564
– of red arsenic 248
– of sandarach 248
Musaeum Hermeticum 81
Muṣḥaf aṣ-ṣuwar see under books, Kitāb

– and Kitāb mafātīḥ aṣ-ṣanᶜa 68
– and Mutus liber 64, 136
– and Rosarium philosophorum 59, 61-2, 63, 136
– and Turba philosophroum 52-3, 55-8, 68
–, comparison with Kitāb al-Ḥabīb 49-50, 68, 123
–, comparison with Kitāb mafātīḥ aṣ-ṣanᶜa 46-7
–, comparison with Kitāb Qirāṭīs al-Ḥakīm 49
–, fragments and complete text of 20
–, knowledge of 52
–, origin of 21
Muslim; *see also author; Jesus* 20, 99, 118-21, 124, 136
– elements 136
mustard seeds 401
mutual 28, 41, 120, 219, 485
Mutus liber 31, 59, 65, 67, 68
– and Muṣḥaf aṣ-ṣuwar 64, 136
my lady; *see also addressee* 11, 45, 51 152, 157, 178, 180, 203, 206, 213-4, 244, 255, 260, 265, 276, 295, 304, 315, 344, 354, 359, 387, 442, 450, 454, 461, 466, 473, 480, 499, 554, 560, 571
myrtle 249
mysterium coniunctionis; *see also coniunction; fusion;, reconcile; union* 40, 138
mystic 44
–, mystical 27
–, soror mystica 20
myth 22, 113
–, alchemical 98
–, mythology 32

–N–

Nag Hammadi library 121-2, 124
naked 84, 122, 439, 458
name (vb, n); *see also analogy;* names; *similes; veiling* 22, 36, 49, 85, 128, 165, 176, 184-6, 195, 198, 206, 212-3, 215, 226, 231, 234, 241-2, 245-6, 251-2, 257, 259-61, 269, 273, 284, 289, 297-8, 302, 304, 316, 323, 326, 337, 349, 351, 357, 362-3, 368, 370, 373, 375, 385, 390, 393, 394-5, 397, 400-1, 410, 424, 429, 442, 461, 466-7, 471, 482-3, 488, 490, 514, 539, 559, 578, 580
– (1) one (in name)/ name is one/ all things are one 81, 224, 244, 261, 351, 382, 386, 418, 439, 457
– and truth 150
– bodies elixir 552
– body 151, 175
– by/ of colour 226, 577
–, change; *see also names, change* 51, 199, 372, 540
– chrysocolla lead/ copper/ tin/ silver/ gold/ rust/ poison 530
– composition 287, 551
– copper 513
– differs/ different 161, 257
– dissolved 146
–, every 248
– for nature 22
–, hide 388
– in the name of 141
–, invent(ed) 85, 177, 246, 397, 245, 253, 255, 257, 388, 472
– looked-for 514
– magnesia 399
– mercury 418
– moisture everything 255, 565
– natures 177
– of a body 265, 532
– of every body 189, 530
– of everything 256
– of fugitive 50, 371
– of God 169
– of operation 152
– of sediment 167
– of things 194, 304
– of Zosimos 51
– part with name of body 266-7
– salt, copper 294
– same 9
– things water 560
–, named (it to you) 170, 350, 368, 377, 460
–, naming of body of magnesia 378
–, proper 127, 159
–, real 257, 384
– silver, lead-copper, copper, salt 294
–, single 170, 241, 244, 576

–, symbolic 22, 365
–, true 170, 212, 237, 269, 349, 368, 422, 424, 571
names; *see also analogy; disguising; name; similes; veiling* 25, 29, 41, 61-2, 93-5, 118, 129, 145, 166, 204, 208, 219, 232, 246, 250-1, 266, 272-4, 284, 294, 328, 369, 395, 401, 410, 418, 452, 461, 466, 483-4, 530, 539, 560, 576
–, (3) three 266, 462
–, (1.000) thousand 128
–, alchemical 93-5
– and truth 147, 165
– as colours 246
–, benefit having many 148, 170, 173, 187, 451, 482
–, Book of the Names 29-30, 212
–, change; *see also name, change* 277, 365, 500, 511, 549
– code- 91, 93-95, 125-6, 131
–, differ/ different 138, 294, 401
–, equivalent ... to water of sulphur 247
–, false 212, 221
– for moist one 511
– for/ of dry one 405, 453, 511
– for white stone 565
– insufficient 261
–, invented 177, 206, 237, 241, 259, 262, 266, 384, 442, 467-8, 530
– know/ known (not) 24, 149, 488
–, many 50, 161-2, 94, 128, 167, 170, 175, 179, 192, 195, 198, 206, 208, 226, 236, 242, 252, 259, 266, 273, 290, 302, 349, 362, 371, 375, 405, 410, 418, 453, 483, 488, 502, 511, 521, 540, 565
–, new 51
– not similar 349
– of dusts 375
– of every body 245
– of every stone 256
– of first/ their/ with composition(s) 394-5, 463
– of first work 526
– of golden 429
– of gum (examples) 401
– of males/ females/ non-males / non-females 129
– of mercury 425
– of moist things 198
– of moisture 453
– of stone 128, 172, 259, 375
– of visible nature 206
– of white sulphur 250
–, other 29, 237, 516
–, proper 159
–, real 559
–, similar 285
–, sorts of 176
–, statement about 161
–, title-names 269
–, true 29, 221, 269, 418
–, various 249, 539
nation 25, 155
natron 379, 468, 503
–, burn copper with sulphur and 497
–, flowers of gold, (ash), glassy … and (Egyptian) vinegar 504, 511
–, froth of 389
–, glue, …, alum and blood 382
–, natruny 396
–, operate with vinegar and 561
–, pound with 381
–, roasted 501
–, salt, alum, …, lime and makrasīūn 325
–, spirit, … and oil 465
–, urin, …, alum and water 323
–, water of 233, 284, 293, 535, 549
nature; *see also natures* 127-9, 143, 145, 152, 159, 177, 182, 191-2, 204, 209, 213-4, 216, 224-6, 231, 243, 253, 260, 279, 286, 290, 295, 320-2, 326, 344, 354-5, 357, 360, 373, 383, 386, 393, 396-9, 407, 418, 436, 457, 459, 481, 486, 492, 498, 580
–, (1) one .... / ... is one 148, 150, 162, 164, 174, 195, 208, 223, 258, 285, 291, 344, 351, 355, 384, 394, 459, 535, 580
–, (1) one and composed 161
–, (1) one nature and ...s, mix 535
– (1) one truth, ... of 162, 168
–, and body 289, 393
– and close one 232
–, ash of 515
–, attract nature by 291
–, biggest 570
–, bodily 31
–, Book of the Nature 22, 389, 390

– burns copper 535
– called tree 52, 484
–, change 200
–, clings to 168, 280, 401, 488, 569
–, complete with 393
–, composed 195, 285, 355, 450, 459
–, conceal(ed) 302, 394, 532, 558
– conquers nature 344
–, cook 515
–, defeat 393
–, despicable ..., sold cheapley 214
– destroys fighter 396, 446
–, destroy exalted 172
–, dissolve 396, 489, 570
–, divide 570
–, divine 32
–, dyeing 196, 229, 246
–, dyes have 406
–, elevated 393
– enjoys nature 192, 291, 352
–, enter 390
–, everything (is) in 162, 384
–, exalted 170, 172
–, examples about 387
– exists not without 162
–, extract dye from 405, 555
–, extract hidden 549
–, false/ true 291
–, fiery 474
– fights not fire 398
–, first 387, 396-7
–, good in 147
–, heavenly 151, 162, 163, 225, 291
– hidden inside body 549
–, hide 388
– holds nature 162, 228, 242, 258-9, 291, 296
– holds relative 284
–, honoured 214
–, in accordance (with) 446, 474
–, inner 322-3
– into sea, put 530
–, is/ completes head 162
–, kept its … secret 175
–, living 192
– meets own nature 259
–, mercury from ašqunīa nature 395
– mix white … with magnesia 367
–, mix with/ mixed 223, 446
– mix with poison 298
–, moist 166
–, moisture enters 480
–, Mother Nature 166
–, multiplies nature 168
–, name for 22
–, needed 387
–, noble 128, 172
–, non–fugitive 513
– not changeable 470
– not vanishing 470
– of acacia 389
– of bodies 49
– of copper 200-1
– of glue 475
– of litharge 446, 469, 509
– of mercury 277
– of moon 535
– of sulphur 397
– of sun 494, 522, 535
– of symbols 90, 111, 135
– of work 154
– operates 168
– operation of (greatest) 366, 512
–, overcome 258, 291
–, own 195, 296
–, pound 145, 501
–, pound with 447, 495
–, power of 354, 355
– rejoices in close one 258
– rejoices in nature(s) 162, 241, 201-2, 228, 242, 258-9, 296, 529
–, remaining; *see also copper* 191
– resists not fire 398
–, return to its original 502
–, rust enters 559
–, science (of alch.) is 143
–, separate from 258
–, similar one to 513
–, single 22, 390
–, soak the 571
–, spirit as/ of 396, 446, 533
– supports work 390
–, symbolic 85, 95, 129, 132, 138
– takes mixture 570
– teaches (measures) 275, 577
– thickens 558
– tortures fighter 446

–, transform 277
–, true 162, 223, 355, 557, 571
– turned thick part into mercury 514
–, turn … into unchangeable 509
–, turn … into spirit 356
– turns fighter into spirit 446
–, turn over 150
–, unchangeable 446
–, veiled 127, 159
– which 162
–, white 353, 363, 372, 574
–, wins 296
– wins over nature(s) 162, 195, 228, 241, 258-9, 285, 296, 326
–, with sulphur 578
–, work comes from 356
–, work upon 170
– works with nature 356
natures 53, 165, 168-9, 178-9, 277, 279, 355, 358-9, 395, 397-8, 447, 485
–, (1st) first 301
–, (1) one nature, make ...s into 214
–, (2) two 160, 174, 214, 236, 249, 534, 570
–, (2) two, destruction of 160
–, (4) four 45, 47, 50, 153, 166, 222, 228, 236, 298, 301, 359, 371, 521
–, (4) four (single) … and work 165, 218
–, (6) six 450
– and copper 498
– and fire 488
– and nature 535
–, ants bring out 147
– as bodies/ bodies without 192, 249, 397
– become spirits 539
–, burn 172, 480, 515, 579
–, change/ changing 301, 493
– change each other 218
–, cling 301
–, come together 485
–, composed/ composition of 326
–, contain dyes 236
–, cooking of 461
–, cool … and mix with rest of things 381
–, death of 176
–, defeat 490, 151
–, dew accepts 287
–, different 162, 298
–, dissolve 201, 302
–, divide not 210
–, dye 291, 326
–, dyeing 488, 524
–, elevated 170
–, error from 379
–, essence of 444
–, extract colours from 260
–, extract dye from 387
–, fugitive … and spirits 539
–, give birth to 166
–, harmonize 293
–, heavenly 177, 326, 354
–, hit 444
–, know 142, 169, 221, 223, 298, 326, 359, 491, 519
–, know …, combinations and weights 519
–, make red 147
–, married and clung 487
–, marry 535, 537
–, master of 228
–, meet their 168
–, mix 152, 168, 214, 361, 399, 452, 537, 561
–, mix broth with 489
–, mix … to body of magnesia 379
–, mix not 535
–, mix, operate and unite … 454
–, mixture is 375
–, name 177, 302
–, natures, whiteners, galls, urines, virtous mineral 515
–, no 200
–, non-separable 251
–, obscure s.th. with 457
–, obtain 395
–, operate on 223
–, operation of 454, 524
– of bodies 201
– of dyeing 177
– of lead 326
– of mixture 486
– of secret 328
–, pound 192
–, pure, clear 159
–, put … in the vessel 145
–, put to death/ revive 521
– rejoices in nature 280
–, search for 147

–, separate 168
–, sieve (made of) 488, 560
–, similar 355
–, single out 457
–, splashing 397
–, subtle (part of) 286-7, 298
–, take 509
–, thick parts of 520
–, torturing 470
–, transform 177, 298
–, true/ (false) 206, 215, 352, 467
–, turn … into ashes 480, 515, 534
–, turn … into plates 381
–, turn … uncracked 300
–, turn over 172
–, union of 454
–, unite/ operate on 328, 387
–, various 166
–, virtous mineral 515
–, virtue of 354
–, visible 206
– win over/ overcome 229, 354, 483
–, without 214
–, work transforms 299
near and far 180
neck 84, 141, 263, 307, 313, 329, 477, 494, 544
–, necks 347, 526
need(s) (vb, n) 29, 35, 37, 46-7, 64, 90, 93, 96, 142, 147, 178, 184, 190, 192, 199, 201, 208, 217, 220, 238, 255, 258, 277, 280-1, 296, 299, 315, 318, 342, 395, 414, 444, 453, 461, 471, 485, 494, 508-9, 514-5, 519, 526, 542-3, 549, 558, 571, 574
–, in need of 144, 453
–, needed nature 387
– not 25, 148, 155, 191, 215, 395
– of learning 268
– of the one 148
– to know/ knowledge 23, 212, 432, 543
Neilos/ Nilus (Fīlbis; Bīlis; the priest) 21, 132, 137, 143, 217, 327, 336
nerve of Osiris 290
Netherworld 24
Newton, Isaak 98
night(s) 63, 80, 127, 147, 180, 209-10, 222, 305, 367
–, (3) three 188
–, (40) fourty 160
–, night–journey 54, 109
–, night–world 44, 54, 78-9
Nikosios 497
Nile 9, 47, 93, 130278
–, earth of 501
–, Nilotic 538
–, water of 418, 489
nine (9) , 160, 223-4, 269, 317
–, (9th) Ninth Letters/ (9) Nine Letters 450, 457
–, divided 269
– letters 279
– operations 323
– ounces 474, 505
– rutls 503
– spirits 80
– spiritual 269
–, three-folded 280
–, weight is nine 269
– weights 279
– winged statues 517
nine hundred (900) 54, 58
nineteenth (19th) 440
ninety (90) days 490
ninth (9th) 22, 342, 407, 414, 425, 432, 442, 516, 525
–, (9th) ninth book/ chapter 516
Niẓāmī/ Nizami 39
noble 320, 356
– nobler 317
Nofil; *see Theophilius* 54-5
non-body; *see body*
Norden, Frédéric-Louis 130
north, wind from/ North wind 127, 159, 278, 292
nothing 176
–, from ... comes something 168
–, without lead/ which ... could/ can/ would exist/ comes into existence/ could be; *see existence*
–, without moisture ... can be done 294
nourish (vb) 23, 44, 53, 91, 122, 157, 168, 234, 252, 357, 394, 406, 486, 548, 579

– body 190
– by sea 500
– stone 252
– sun 512
– themselves 396
nourishment 53, 161, 359, 363, 366, 484
–, due becomes 231
– for air 218, 223
– for fire 223
– for sun 218
–, heat and moisture as 486
– of copper 486
–, silvery 489
Nubia 316, 499
number; *for the several numbers see there: one (1), two (2), three (3),.... sixteen (16), nineteen (19), twenty (20), ...twentyfour (24), twentyfive (25), fourty, (40), fourty-two (42), three hundred and sixty (360), hundred and forty (140), hundred and fifty (150), hundred and eighty (180), three hundred and fifty (350), three hundred and sixty-five (365), thousand (1.000), thousand eight hundred (1.800),six thousand and six hundred (6.600),* eight thousand and five hundred (8.500), *ten thousand (10.000); see also chapter, picture, days, years, measures, ounces, parts, rutls, weights* 53, 108, 188, 202, 206, 243, 273, 325, 326, 354, 359, 384
–, completion of 273
–, numerous 194
– of books 150
– of days 345, 501, 546
– of seekers 26, 118, 155
–, uneven 223
numinous 93
Nun 40, 54
nurture 436
–, nutrient 291
–, nutrition 469, 530

–O–

oath(s) 202, 213, 529, 559
– of sages 577
obey
–, disobedience 196
–, disobey 217, 242
–, obedience 345, 464, 519, 556
object (n) 95, 108
obscure 93, 95, 148, 162, 179-80, 194, 212, 259, 315, 332, 344-5, 452, 469, 487
–, obscurity/ obscurities 142, 148, 155, 194, 203, 208, 215, 217, 327, 539
– science 206
– statements 349
obtain; *see also achieve*
– from sediment 512
– work 85, 217, 241, 499, 536
october 366
Odysseus 112
oil 239, 379, 400
–, castor- 158, 288
–, spirit, natron and 465
ointment 480, 564
old 47, 514
– man 53-4 464-5, 485
–, oldest 26, 117, 138
– woman 168, 216
oleander
–, firewood of 320, 385
– leaves; *see leaves, oleander*
–, leaves as white sulphur 497
olives 290
Olympiodor(from Alexandria) 22, 93, 96-7, 123-4, 136
Omega; *see book(s), On the letter Omega*
omit (vb) 52, 161, 298, 365, 489
omnipotence 29, 455
one (1) 9, 11, 47, 90, 146, 165, 177, 191, 226, 243, 244-5, 247, 272, 278, 307, 311-2, 317, 371-2, 469, 495
–, (1/2) half part, ... and 510
–, (1/3) one third 547, 570
–, (1/4) one fourth 265, 374, 486
–, (1/5) one fifth 189
–, (1/6) one sixth 486
–, (1/8) one eighth 267
–, (2/3) two third 572
–, (6/6) six of six 268
–, ($1^1/_2$) one and half 191, 319
– (1) one, (2) two, (1) one 85, 513
–, (1st) first 252, 402, 489, 491

–, turn (2) two into 210, 268
–, (2) two-oneness 44
–, (2) two, ...and/ from 156, 158-61, 174, 178, 184-5, 192, 207, 210, 269, 275, 325, 370, 420, 446, 470, 482, 489, 491, 509, 534, 547, 550-1, 554, 581
– (3) three, ... and/ of/ becomes 160, 266, 325, 424, 439, 473, 508, 513, 547
–, (3) three become/ turn into 265, 273, 416, 452, 516
–, (3) three in … body 411, 414, 426, 428-9, 431, 435-6
–, (3) three names for … thing 266
–, (3) three to ..., mix 367
–, (4) four and/ become 273, 379
–, (4) four, ... and 184-5, 195
– , (9) nine/ (10) ten, and/ ... becomes 224
–, all things are/ turn into 16, 240
– and all 227, 244, 266, 269, 373
– and asked 368
– and composed nature 161
– and many 128, 148, 150-1, 162, 170, 173, 187, 201, 242, 266, 291, 294, 301, 305, 351, 359, 368, 382, 394, 418, 424, 432, 439, 458, 481, 484, 537, 542, 550, 581
–, become; *see also unity; unify; unique; many* 44, 158, 223, 304, 362, 379, 576
– bird 263
– body 150, 207, 225, 266, 275, 418
– body and soul are 92
–, broth is 551
– casting 454
– close 258
– colour 162, 205, 256, 361, 405-6, 532, 554
– composed 285, 288
– composition 377
– day 459, 504
–, dissolved by and dried in the 569
– dissolving 294
– dye 205, 251, 302, 304-5, 461, 580
–, dye and dyer are 165, 248
–, everything is 514
–, God is 148
– in name/ appearance 351, 457
– measure 511
– mercury 424
– mixture 270, 301
–, name 261, 386
– nature/ nature is 148, 150, 162, 164, 174, 195-6, 208, 214, 223, 258, 285, 291, 296, 326, 344, 351, 355, 384, 394, 459, 535, 580
–, need of 148
–, once 512, 569
– opening 380
– operation/ operation is 45, 288, 355
– opposites are .../ actor and being acted on is 214
– origin 359
–, Other-One 40, 42-3
– ounce(s) 233, 274, 319, 501, 506
– part 91, 208, 265-6, 268, 270-2, 275, 277, 282, 285, 287, 298, 368, 376, 388, 436, 460, 492, 500, 503-5, 510-11, 547, 563, 566
place 325
– pounding 294
– puffs 459
–, rotting and making lean is 301, 440
– rutl 501
– sage 511
– side 238
–, soul and body are 92
– spiritual soul 322
– stone 267, 305, 534
– sulphur 301
– testimony 355
–, the ... whose inside is black 37, 342
– thing 50, 62, 81, 159-60, 162, 170, 174, 187, 189, 194-5, 206-7, 221, 224, 227, 248, 251, 265-7, 288-9, 294, 301, 304, 322, 324, 349, 355-6, 358, 362, 365, 371, 373, 379, 397, 399, 439, 457, 509, 538, 542, 560
–, thing(s) is/ are 173, 294, 560, 580-1
– time 465
– true/ truth 162, 205, 296
–, turn (all) into /make 205, 224, 576
–, turn … into broth 452
– water 201, 549, 550
–, weight is .../ ... weight 269, 272, 581
– white mercury 352
– wins over 164, 170, 326
–, work is 23, 149, 187, 294, 454, 563
– work/ operation 184, 205, 216
open (vb) 68, 79, 98, 137, 154, 165, 240,

283, 337, 530-1
– door 323, 396, 446
– holes 516
–, Opener of mercy 352
–, opening of vessel 235
–, openings 436, 380-1
– the way 144
– vessel 286, 547
operate (vb) 24, 50, 62, 144, 146, 149, 162, 178, 181, 194, 197, 200, 205, 208, 226, 236, 293-4, 302, 349, 355-6, 363, 369, 371, 374-5, 379, 381-2, 386, 396-8, 405, 407, 410, 430, 452, 454, 456-60, 466, 471, 481, 492, 497, 500, 506, 524, 528, 538, 546, 557-8, 562, 567, 571, 577-8, 580
– and cook 405
– badly 528
– bodies 292
– compose, … and cook 205
–, cook-operate 554
– earth 572
–, earth …s on magnesia 369
– every thing 146
– for days 381
–, how to 162
– in first composition 533
– iron 463
– lead-copper 205
–, magnesia 164
– mercury of cinnabar 472
–, mix operated with not-operated 534
–, moist-operate 555
– nature(s) 162, 168, 387
– not 537
– on 245, 247, 256, 277, 281, 349, 534, 561
– on body 214
– on burnt copper 380
– on copper 528
– on fire 494
– on lead-copper 498
– on mercury with white sulphur 379
– on poison 533
– on red/ white/ natures 223, 236
– on stone 381, 367, 508
– on tin 546
– on with fire 254
– on with poison 535
– perfectly 367
– poison 578
– stone 237
– sulphur 455
– this way 510
– well on 272, 558, 565
– with colocynth and vitriol 561
– with eternal water 561
– with fire and sun 532
– with right measure 507
– with vinegar 199
– with white 367
– work 186
operation 28, 46, 53, 120, 129, 143, 146, 154, 164, 179, 183, 187-8, 196, 199, 205, 208, 212-3, 216, 220, 227-8, 235, 243, 246, 253, 267, 273, 275, 277-9, 297-8, 318, 324, 359, 363-4, 366, 379-80, 384, 400, 406, 411, 436, 439, 458, 464-5, 471, 474-5, 477, 480, 483, 485-7, 491, 495-6, 507, 516, 533, 535, 560, 564, 566-7, 573-4, 577
–, (1) one, ... is 45, 216, 355
–, (1) one, ... of 225
–, (1) one complete 288
–, (1) one, operator is 581
–, (2) two ...s 451
–, (3) three ...s 452-3
–, (3) three/ (6) six ...s 452-3
–, (9) nine ...s 323
–, (10th) tenth 529
–, about 165, 188, 477
–, analogy about/ for 387, 166, 524, 537
–, basis of ...s 521
–, beginning of 173, 194, 249, 284, 486-7, 569, 551
–, beneficial for 579
–, be patient with 503
–, Book About the last Operation only and its Weights 80
–, Book About the Other Operation 556
–, Book of Operation 80, 476, 516
–, burning, the composition, and the operation 579
– changes 397
–, combinations, colours, compositions and 526
–, completeness of 571

– completes the work 162
–, correct 474
– covers 201
–, disappear in the 504
–, do persistently in 548
–, doubt about 148
–, do well 447
–, enter/ perform 152
– exhausts 129, 451
–, extract by/ in 214, 382
–, extract poison from body by 520
–, finish 382, 389
–, fire (and water) in 28, 120, 219, 523
–, fire solidified mercury in 372
–, first (other) 183, 560, 572
– for crystal 210
– for/ of copper 207, 398, 481
– for/ of magnesia 207, 377
–, hidden 565
–, ignorance of 63, 221
–, in 184, 164, 188, 257, 481
– in the cooking 174
– is more exalted 152
– is whitening and reddening 498
–, know 375
–, last/ Last Operation; *see also book(s)* 80
–, magnesia makes white in 374
–, make … inaccessible 23, 149
–, many operations 148, 207, 359
–, mercury in 483
–, not seen in 200
– of androdamus 248
– of body of magensia 382
– of composition 507
– of Democritus 552
– of dye 503
– of elixir 548, 577
– of ferment of gold 189
– of fiery/ fire 377-8, 519
– of God 161
– of greatest nature 366
– of head 162
– of iron 320
– of lead 399
– of lead-copper 299, 377, 452
– of litharge 377
– of mercury 151, 432, 500
– of mixing 385
– of nature(s) 454, 512, 524
– of pearls 492
– of pyrite 397
– of sages 317
– of sand 297, 501, 507
– of sea 382
– of secret 537
– of spirit 190
– of sulphur 397
– of tin 377-8
– of vapours 166
– of work 158, 178-9, 387
–, other 547, 556
–, operations 194, 198-9, 207, 219, 288, 320, 323, 328, 344-5, 349-50, 430, 451-3, 456, 480, 491, 519, 521, 526, 547
–, perfcct 411
–, perform 444
–, remain silent about 485
–, rest of 559, 571
–, rotting in 440
–, separate 161, 184, 380
–, soft 504, 505
–, stage of 46
–, strong fire in 28, 523
–, suffer in 304
–, time of 552
– took long time 504
– transforms 177
–, treat gently 505
–, true/ false operations 194
– turns copper into silvery water 379
– turns non-fugitive into fugitive 514
–, unite in … and complete 298
–, use composed in 285
–, whitening, operations as 288
– with eternal water 528
–, wrong 508
opinion 249, 272
–, different opinions 153
–, wrong opinions 144
opium 270
opposites; *see also high-low; fire-water; male-female; precious-cheap; hot-cold etc.; see also two* 29, 227
–, inner-psychic 138
–, mix 487

–, oppose/ opposition 28, 120, 219, 520
–, pair of 59
–, reconcile/ reconciliation of 28-9, 44, 121-4
–, unification 84
–, union of 44, 45, 67, 214
opus alchemicum; *see also work, aim* 10, 45
orbit 252, 253
order (vb) 51, 143, 148, 152, 158, 167-8, 177, 189, 192, 202, 205-6, 219, 225, 227-8, 231, 247, 249, 253, 255-7, 265, 267, 272, 277-8, 280, 283, 286, 289, 291, 295, 297, 299-300, 310, 312, 315, 317, 319, 323-4, 336, 349, 354-6, 360, 364, 366, 369-70, 372, 380, 383, 385, 388-9, 396, 398, 407, 410, 427, 432, 447, 453, 456-7, 460, 465, 467-71, 473, 475, 480-1, 490-1, 493, 495-6, 500, 503-5, 507-9, 511, 516, 520, 523, 528, 534, 536, 538, 540-1, 548-9, 558-9, 562, 567, 571, 574, 578
order (n) of stars 313
ore, zinc 267-8
orientalist(s) 6, 13
orientation 74, 94, 120
origin/ original; *see also beginning* 11, 21, 26, 49, 51, 63, 90, 99, 123, 138, 170, 173, 218, 222-3, 227, 229, 239, 260, 273, 277, 424, 489, 502, 514, 533, 550
– (1) one/ ... is (1) one 160, 178, 359
– (2) two, ... is 265
–, Ancient Egyptian 10, 39, 54, 108
–, Arabic 54, 58
–, Christian-Gnostic 99
–, Greek/ original Greek 24, 52, 68, 115, 119, 135, 137
–, Hellenistic 58
– is blood 485
–, knowledge about/ know not 387, 550
–, Mamluk 98, 99, 110
–, Muslim 124
– of alchemical work 137
– of eternal water/ river is 147, 490
– of India 54
– of magnesia 378
– of (original) Muṣḥaf aṣ–ṣuwar/ text 26, 68, 96, 74, 113-4, 117, 119, 124, 131, 135, 140
– of nature 147
– of ruby 450
– of silver 466
– of stone 368
– of sulphur 407
– of Turba 58, 68
–, Pharaonic 54
–, pre-Islamic 25, 98, 113, 136
osier, Egyptian (Salix aegiptica) 385
Osiris 9, 24, 37, 94, 290, 450
–, corpse of 40
–, osirification 130, 341
Ostanes 27, 184, 201, 220, 246, 285, 326, 398-9
– and Democritus 347
–, book of 202, 572
– is right 463
–, statement of 326-7, 463
ostrich 225
other
– body/ not body 189, 296, 366
– *composition 224, 248, 253, 258, 265, 268-9, 272-3, 277, 282, 285, 287, 384, 410, 538, 548-9, 551, 563, 571, 578, 581*
– cooking 282
–, dissolve … nature 570
– mercury 261, 420, 514, 550
– mixing/ mixture 247, 385
– moist 185
– one 169, 243, 249, 269
– operation 556
– part 558
– power 235
– rotting 279
– spirit(s) 186, 222
– stone 41, 576
– sulphur/ white sulphur 301
–, the other; *see also unknown* 85, 239, 272, 398
– thing(s) 170, 191, 200, 260, 266, 268, 272, 344
– water 146, 282, 549, 562
–, white 549
– work; *see also work, second* 245, 250, 254, 282, 295, 361, 493, 533-4, 563
– world; *see also world* 26, 91, 155, 215, 219
ounce(s) 233, 319-21
–, (1) one 233

–, ($1^1/_2$) one and a half 191, 319
–, (2) two 271, 317, 319, 388, 474
–, (3) three 271, 317-8, 321
–, (4) four 191, 271-4, 319, 506
–, (6) six 501-2
–, (9) nine 317, 474, 505
–, (10) ten 506
–, (21/ 22/ 35) twenty-one/ twenty-two/ thirty-five 500, 506
our
– copper 151, 160, 174, 191, 282, 285, 296, 353, 362, 442, 497, 521, 528, 549, 551, 578
– copper, iron and lead 462
– copper as our lead as our magnesia 220
– gold 277
– gum 174
– silver (of sages) 183, 191, 277, 282-3, 456, 467, 561, 578
– work 362
Ouroboros 109, 113
outer
– appearance 169, 192, 222, 370, 373, 376, 397, 439, 462, 554, 574
– image 161
outlet 440
outside 35, 122, 169, 261, 302, 311, 336, 397, 492, 525
–, make white …. of copper 169
oven(s); *see also furnace, retort* 64-7
overcome
–, (1) one, overcomer and what is ... is 165
– fire 490
– nature …s nature 291
overlook 427
overpowering; *see also conquer* 128, 172
overview 6, 17, 26, 94
overwhelming 32, 35, 118
owner(s) 171, 219
– of bags 488
Oxford 7

–P–

pagan 113
Pagels, E. 11
pain(s) 181, 247, 340
–, of torture 336
paint 180
–, painter(s) 179, 463
pair 59
palm 41-2, 84, 278, 290
Panopolis 9, 17, 73, 92, 121, 130, 132
papyrus 303
–, Papyrus Berolinensis 121
parable(s) 21, 54, 57, 85, 241, 243, 318
paradise 121
parents 182
part; *see also cut; one; pieces; scatter; numbers* 33, 51, 65-6, 197, 225-6, 260, 274, 381, 503
–, ($^1/_2$) half ...(s) 500, 510
–, (1) one 91, 208, 265-6, 268, 270-2, 275, 277, 282, 285, 287, 298, 368, 376, 388, 436, 460, 492, 500, 503-5, 510-11, 547, 563, 566
–, (1) one … from male 265
–, (1) one … of body 268
–, ($1^1/_2$) one and half 510
–, (1st) first 473, 491, 560, 572
–, (2) two ...s 38, 91, 167, 266, 268, 270, 271, 272, 282, 287, 368, 382, 450, 460, 473, 500, 513, 557, 558, 560, 572
–, (2nd) second/ other 206, 558, 560, 572
–, (3) three ...s 153, 265, 266-7, 270, 279, 282, 436, 465, 505
–, (3) three …s from (2) two 265
–, (3rd) third 491
–, (4) four ...s 48, 267, 270-1, 275, 279, 282, 298, 300, 368, 491, 525, 547, 563, 566
–, (4th) fourth 492
–, (6) six ...s 569
–, (24) twenty-four ...s 22
–, burnt 578
–, divide ...s 167
–, essential 476, 477
–, extract subtle ...s 461
–, gentle 369
–, integral 120
–, mix ...s 473
–, no touchable ...s 145
– of air 154
– of bodies/ body 179, 275, 399
– of fire 153, 154
– of natures, thick ...s 520

– of picture 263
– of stone 275
– of their books 214
– of water 153, 154
–, parts 56, 58, 92, 119, 267, 275, 382, 493, 567, 575
–, parts cling, 494, 561
–, parts from silver 282
–, parts of dragon 56, 127, 157
–, pure … of body 166
–, remaining 571
–, rises to its upper 168
–, solid ....(s) 179, 371
–, spiritual 436, 505
–, splashed 579
–, subtle .../ subtle ...s 47, 154, 161, 197, 218, 223, 279, 303, 369, 436, 461, 498, 502, 505-6, 520
–, subtle … as spirit 461
–, subtle … of body 395
–, subtle ... of natures 298
–, thick 161, 190, 214, 218, 223, 395, 498, 514, 521
–, true/ false ...s 147
–, upper 145, 492
parturition 305
pass
–, passage(s) 21, 25, 27-8, 33, 46, 52, 58, 215
–, spirit passes into every body 246
passion 241, 326, 536
– disappears 458
– of virgin 320
–, passionate 29, 320
–, passionately 474
path 74, 559
–, right 260, 356, 361
patience 8, 169, 206, 208, 242, 275, 318, 499, 508, 540, 577
–, impatience/ impatient 486, 507
–, patient (adj) 120, 145, 152, 155, 213, 219, 247, 317, 327-8, 356, 362, 383, 406, 452, 455, 499, 501, 503-5, 510
–, patient (n) 13, 67, 98
Pauli, Wolfgang 98
paws 31
peace 28, 120, 217, 219, 446, 472, 523, 548
–, blackness makes 470
–, peacemaker 238
pearl(s) 167, 171, 176, 347, 388
– appear 492
– Hymn of the Pearl 90
–, mother-of-pearl 280, 324, 297
– of cupulas 492
– of people 492
–, operation of 492
–, The Pure Pearl (book) 116
pedagogic path 74
penetrate (vb) 456, 472, 485, 526
– bodies 570
–, dye 510
–, spirit 547
Peri aretes 27, 41
people(s)
–, books of the 176
–, common 143
–, confuse 147
–, deceive 147
–, gold of the 363, 467
–, ignorant 144, 213
–, lead of 183
–, magnesia of 350
–, magnet of 442
–, mercury of 95, 425, 433
–, metals of 462
– of Alexandria 509
– of Egypt 352
– of experience 159
– of Israel 363
– of Muḥammad 142
– of my time 176
– of Syria 574
– of wisdom 23, 149, 229, 462, 490
– of world 62, 221
–, ordinary 178, 159, 194, 236, 246, 248-9, 258, 277, 280, 286, 288-9, 295, 345, 361, 363, 383, 388, 390, 530, 536
–, pearls of 492
–, silver of 178, 183, 205, 284, 363, 411, 455, 466-7
–, tin of the 546
–, water of 179, 482
pepper 503
perception 10
perch 517
perfect 11, 185, 248, 271, 278, 289, 310-11, 475, 533-4, 547, 557, 577

– colour 280
– dye 295, 567, 573
–, dyeing as … of things 461
– dyeing with female 574
–, perfection 53, 128, 171, 178, 278, 310, 393, 446
–, perfection of metal 461
– poison 566
– work 129, 243, 570
perform 129, 204, 243, 492, 494, 501, 507-8, 560
– well 143
– work 152-3
periods of time, (4) four 522
permanent 212, 497
perplex 394, 418, 442
–, perplexity 410, 447
persevere 158
Persian*; see also Persius* 222
persistent 533
– in reading 145, 203
–, persistence 203, 388
–, persistently 20, 260, 548
Persius; *see Bersīūs; see also Persian*
person
–, (3) three 428-9, 431, 433, 435-6, 442, 444-5, 526
–, (6) six (winged) persons 264, 526, 544
–, dead 290, 310
–, personality 23, 40, 44
phantasies 66-7
Pharaonic 10-11, 24, 29, 39-40, 48, 54
– culture/ knowledge and alchemy 11, 80, 127, 136
– images 10
– Pharaoh 108, 127
Philip, Gospel of 121-3
philosopher 10, 57-8, 62-3
–, Alexandrian 20
–, call togeter 58
–, Greek 58
– head of/ leading 9, 58
–, meeting of 68
–, stone of/ s' stone 40, 62
phlegm 47
phrase 18, 26, 121
physicians; *see also cure, diesease, illness, remedy* 157, 169, 540
Picatrix 94
pick fruits 524
–, pick up 236, 502
picture(s); *see also image; illustration* 19, 29, 31-3, 34-8, 40-3, 64-5, 67, 73-5, 78-9, 81, 84-5, 91, 95, 98-9, 101, 103, 105, 107-11, 119, 134, 136, 179, 230, 264, 313, 331-2, 334, 337, 339, 341-2, 345, 347, 433, 477, 519, 526, 543-4, 557
–, (1st) first 141, 306, 308, 402
–, (2nd) second 404
–, (3) three 80
–, (3rd) third 263, 329, 407
–, (4) four 99
–, (4th) fourth 411
–, (5th) fivth 414
–, (6th) sixth 416
–, (7th) seventh 418
–, (8) eight 421
–, (8th) eighth 81
–, (9th) ninth 425
–, (10th) tenth 426
–, (11th) eleventh 428, 544
–, (12th) twelvth 429, 556
–, (13th) thirteenth 431
–, (14th) fourteenth 433
–, (15th) fifteenth 435, 438
–, (16th) sixteenth 436-8
–, (17th) seventeenth 438
–, (18th) eighteenth 439
–, (19th) nineteenth 440-1
–, (20th) twentieth 442-3
–, (21st) twenty-first 444-5
–, (22) twenty-two 84
–, (22nd) twenty-second 84, 448-9
–, (42) forty-two 75
– and text 19, 74, 81, 84-5, 96-8, 135, 137-8
– as key for understanding 29
– as symbols/ symbolic pictures 31-2, 37, 39, 59, 81, 90-2, 111-3, 118
– at beginning of book/ chapter 75, 526
–, Book of Pictures; *see book(s)*
–, colouring/ coloured 19
–, final/ last 41, 80
– interpretation 12, 31
–, missing (part of) 19, 75, 78-9, 81, 84, 93, 112, 263, 402
– of science 402

– of statue 229
– of tree 448
– of Zosimos and/ or Theosebeia; *see also Theosebeia image/ picture* 92, 101, 141, 276, 347, 391, 402, 439, 444, 477, 517, 555-6
– of Zosimos for Theosebeia 19, 29, 85, 141-2, *210*-2, 336, 341
– series 6, 12, 19, 33, 59, 61, 74-5, 79-81, 84, 111, 115, 135
–, transformation of original 99
piece(s); *see also cut; part; scatter*
–, break into pieces 487
–, cut into pieces 23-4, 56, 127, 149, 157
– of (clean) cloth 215, 394, 473, 568, 572, 576
– of linen 394, 459
pierce 182
piety 433
pious 432
Pistis Sophia 121, 124
pitch 570
pity 216
place (n, vb) 32, 53, 112, 122, 220, 243, 257-8, 299, 313, 325, 356, 360, 382-3, 389, 400, 407, 411, 414, 434, 472, 474, 504, 523, 566
–, (1.000) thousand places 97
–, places (n) 66, 118, 126-7, 260, 274, 345, 364-5, 368, 377-8, 497, 515, 580
plan of Thesobeia 327-8
planet(s) , 229, 357, 450
plant(s); *see also flower; tree* 173, 186, 201, 470, 522, 548, 556
–, cook … in water 502
–, flowers of 554
–, gold plant 129
– of the earth 523
plate 143-4, 293, 299, 320
– and moisture 255
–, dissolved 551
–, mix … with flower of gold 548
– of copper 245
– of glass 319
– of gold 427, 551
– of silver 245, 268, 551
–, solidify 551
plates 141, 234, 250, 293, 364
–, (2) two and (1) one 551
– absorb moisture 529
–, cook 498
–, dissolve 243, 489, 529
–, dry up moisture 529
–, iron into 485
– of copper 489, 536
– of gold 391
– of iron 442
– of male 529
– of truth 427
–, pound/ return 247
–, put … in moisture 548
–, round .... into copper 563
–, swallow 541
–, thin 489
–, turn natures into 381
Plato; *see also Aflatun* 18, 90, 540
–, platonic 29
pleasure 55, 322, 358, 390
plentiful 176
Plessner, Martin 54-6, 58, 94, 125, 131
plough 179, 374
ploughman 358, 374
plug up 173
plurality of colours 571
poem; *see book(s)*
poison 48, 56-7, 126-7, 129-30, 157, 181, 186, 192, 198, 213, 216, 225, 234, 241, 245, 251, 286, 300, 364, 375, 397, 407, 457, 508, 514, 522, 539, 573
–, (1) one composition (of)/ ... and its composition 294, 522
–, (1) one thing, turn ... and mercury into 457
– and ashes 168
– and bitters 255
– and body 232, 281
– and/ of honey 49, 514
– and mixture 293
– and secret 167
– and silver 407
– and veins 520
– as origin 170
– as spiritual dye 566
– becomes red 188
–, body, … and natures 152
–, clean 492
–, complete 224
–, composed 492

–, cook 255
–, cook …, water of sulphur and arsenicd 283
– disappears 293, 454
–, divide 560, 572
–, dry 573
–, dye body with 452
–, dyeing 301
– enters 287
–, extract 232, 440
–, extract body from 520
– falls on body 520
–, fiery 226-7, 254
–, fixed 153
–, girl/ maiden (Giftmädchen) 36, 125, 131
– in woman 55, 157
–, making of 144, 255, 286
–, mercury, body and 151
–, mix/ mixture of 168, 210, 522, 562
–, mix … with nature 298
–, name 530
– of dragon 48
– of sages 282, 520
–, operated 578
–, operate on with 535
– remains 440
–, perfect 547, 566
–, poisons 530, 549
–, pound second 513
–, power of 286-7, 579
–, pure 512
–, purify 167
–, red 281, 533, 538
–, rest of 249, 557
–, roast 579
–, rot 255
–, soak with 578
– submerges into body 265
–, sulphur, stone and 153
–, sweet 129
–, true 255
–, turn copper into 493
–, turn into 474
–, turn mercury, sulphur and gold into dyeing 287
–, turn ... into silver 533
–, turn … sour 304
–, turn ... white 380
– turns bodies into non-bodies 254
– turns into smoke 234
–, washed by the 168
–, water of sulphur and 287
–, white 143, 250, 533
–, whiten with 152
polish 208, 260, 270, 366, 385, 394-5
–, polished earth 250, 395, 397
pollen 254
pollination 166
polluted 215
pomegranate 316
ponder; *see also amplification; contemplate* 5, 85, 143, 177, 188, 196, 298, 326, 341, 366, 377, 395, 404, 499, 539, 548, 550-1, 554, 557
– about/ over/ on/ upon 19, 29, 95, 111, 144, 162, 175, 202, 206, 212, 227, 268, 274, 303, 353, 358-9, 387, 483, 519, 535, 573
–, pondering 23, 40, 66-7, 93, 98, 134, 171, 180, 297, 327, 360, 477
position 276, 556
possess(ed) (vb, adj) 65, 282
–, possessor 470, 473
–, possession (state of/ by archetypes) 31-2, 39, 79, 91
potash 48, 184, 377, 568
pot(s) 168, 323, 436, 460, 474, 487, 503
– and vessel 513
–, cook cover pots 505
–, cover of 503, 512
–, pour onto 512
potters 568
pound (vb) 129, 144, 149, 152, 156, 166, 190, 197, 206, 210, 234, 243, 246-7, 249, 258, 266, 277, 284, 287, 299, 319-20, 323, 325, 362, 367-8, 375, 378, 397, 456-7, 472-4, 482, 489, 492, 500, 502-3, 506, 535, 540-1, 549, 561, 563-4, 568, 573, 575
– all things in sea 380
– and cook 23, 149, 562, 578
– and mix 504, 510
– before dyeing 389
– body 164, 214
– components 501
– copper 559, 566

–, dissolve, … and cook 532
– everything 249
– for days 381
– in sun 364
– lead 395
– mercury with ašqunīa 395
– mixture 407
– mortar 501
– nature(s) 192, 501
– not 549
– plates 247
–, pounded 303, 508
– purple with mortar 503
– repeatedly 573
– saffron 538
– second poison 513
– secret 447, 495
– stone 495
– things with fire 513
– water with body 491
– with fire 533
– with hand 447, 495
– with natron 381
– with nature 447, 495
– with sea 167
– with silver 566
– with sun 129, 395, 564
– with vinegar 511, 564
– with water 317, 400, 469
pounding 143, 145-6, 149, 180, 216, 303, 355, 363, 380, 385, 480, 494, 506, 530, 540, 558, 560, 562, 572
–, (1) one 23, 149, 294
–, aim of 501
– and/ as/ by/ of cooking 145, 198, 254, 399, 532, 560-1, 579
–, burn in 579
– by hand 145, 579
– gentle 482
–, hatching as 554
– of copper 399
– of pounded 379
– of rust 565
– of stone 448
–, subtle 164
– with nature 495
–, without … nothing of looked-for comes into existence 513
pour (vb) 234, 279, 318, 321, 394, 459-60, 464, 489, 503, 560
– copper on dissolved 376
– onto pot 512
– (out) water 141, 460
power(s) 35, 63, 118, 142, 162, 166, 169, 171, 175, 187, 193, 202, 213, 215, 233-4, 237, 243, 270, 310, 322, 336, 350, 362, 393, 401, 436, 462, 470, 481, 488, 498, 519, 543, 547, 559, 581
–, (1) one 326
–, Book of Power 551
– by fire 239
–, different 326
–, feminine 126, 131
–, first 233
–, great 167, 181, 234, 270, 388, 474, 482, 543, 546, 550
– in dusts 375
–, magic 25
– of beyond 136
– of composed/ composed 196, 354
– of copper 512
– of crimson 503, 512
– of female 372, 576
– of glue 474
– of heat 281
– of lead 535
– of male 372
– of mercury 458
– of nature 354-5
– of šuḥaīrah 576
– of poison 170, 286-7, 579
– of sperm 387
– of stone 238
– of substances 326
– of Theosebeia/ Zosimos 340-1
– of vapour/ eternal water 490
– of vinegar 506
– of water 490, 547, 557
– of water of sulphur 286, 490
– of work 170
–, other 235
– serpent 109
–, single sea has no 382
–, thing without 378
– to burn 228
– to hold spirits 483

powerful
–, become more 242
– one (n) 532
–, strong, …, dry and hot 174
praise (vb, n) 9, 26-7, 29, 37, 53 144, 153, 171, 176, 191, 195, 213, 228, 267, 306, 336, 340, 342, 344, 354, 383, 389, 402, 463, 476, 485, 497, 540, 543, 555, 563, 580-1
prayer niche 249, 450
precious 90, 171, 176-7, 219, 222, 232, 237, 249, 279-80, 283, 297, 552, 557, 569, 580
– -cheap 41, 170, 575
– stone 176
precisely 32, 341, 395, 401, 448
preference, give 393
pregnancy 305, 356
–, make itself pregnant 176
–, pregnant 181-2, 311, 530
prejudice 155
prepare (vb) 5, 12, 20, 62, 156, 280, 291, 323, 326, 344, 396, 446, 566
–, preparation for dyeing 490
present (vb) 69, 156, 212, 328, 336
preservation 290
–, preserve/ preserver 190, 235, 290, 536, 570
prevent (vb) 36, 130, 150, 164, 180, 204, 217, 233, 240, 257, 263, 284, 300, 310, 327-8, 339, 342, 390, 402, 410, 420
– appearing of colour 528
– escaping 197, 200, 285, 372, 396, 465, 483, 540-1
– fire (from burning) 397, 490
– him/ her from escaping 164
– knowing 143, 516, 540
– soul coming out 539
price 232, 489
–, priceless 213, 557
priest 20-1, 40, 132, 137, 143, 217, 327, 336
–, priestly one 260
–, priests 229, 472
principium individuationis; see also individuation 32
principle(s); *see also evil; feminine; female; male; self* 11, 32
–, female/ feminine 32, 55, 93, 116, 127
–, guiding 537
–, male/ masculine 92-3, 116
– of evil 31
prisoners 90
problems appear 516
process 32-3, 39-40, 66, 69, 74, 80, 109, 112, 134, 137-8, 234
–, alchemical 24, 41, 74, 80, 101, 117
–, inner/ innerpsychic 40, 44, 98
– of individuation 44, 59
– of projection 39
– of purification 44
– of transformation 37, 39
–, psychological 30
–, right 229
profit 467
progress 278
projection 39, 44
–, project (vb) 33, 39-40, 110
Prometheus 92
–, Lucifer- 32
promise (vb, n) 37, 207, 342
proof 115
prophecy 26, 68
prophet 26, 119-21, 451
–, Jesus as 121
– Muḥammad (master) 119-20, 142, *389*, 581
– Moses 119, 129, 207, 209, 243, 277, 365, 451, 497, 548
– of God 472
–, prophets 142, 222, 237, 323, 328, 516, 556
prostrate 432-3
protect; *see also cover; disguise; keep secret; ruse; scatter; trickery; veil* 204, 450, 507
– from fire 535
– knowledge 27
–, protection 203
–, protective 289
–, protector of work 577
– work 241
proud 334
provision 293
Pseudo-Mağrīṭī 94
psyche 39, 84, 112, 138
– of alchemist 40
psychic 44
– contents 33

– developments 137
– inner-psychic 137-8
– states 117
– system 136
psychiatrist 40
psychological 36, 45, 59, 68, 92-3
– commentary 5, 12, 92
– interpretation 90
– process 30
– transformation 33
psychology
–, depth- 136
–, Research and Training Centre for Depth Psychology 8
psychopompos 39
psychotherapy 138
public, general 98, 118
puff 459
pull 187, 292
pumpkin 462
punish 154, 242
–, punishment 216
pupil; *see also adept; teacher* 117
– of eye 19, 237
pure 48, 53, 164, 166, 185-6, 231, 233, 247, 273, 277, 281, 289, 293, 300, 317, 321, 336, 356, 367, 387-9, 429, 450, 456, 458, 460, 471, 473-4, 477, 480, 502-4, 506-7, 511, 521, 533, 569, 573, 580-1
– and clear 159, 502
–, become 360
– body 146
– copper 563
– flowers 510
– gold 578
–, make 167, 190
– mercury 459
– poison 512
–, purer 281
–, purity 503
– spirit 229
– sulphur 383, 420
– thing 283
– tin 168, 361
– truth 259
–, turn into … water 379
– water 199, 244, 292, 300, 352-3, 395, 454, 487, 489, 502, 531, 550, 560
– water and red sulphur 379
– water of sulphur 261-2, 284, 386, 410, 434, 459-60, 477, 516, 521
–, white 471
– whiteness 53, 484
purification 44, 167, 228, 235, 294, 303, 407, 503
purify (vb) 40, 48, 164, 227, 300, 321, 459, 461, 468, 471, 477, 502, 504, 554, 572
– body 146, 477, 564
– copper 195
– glass 513
– iron 191
– lead 355
– mercuries 416
– poison 167
– shadow 535
– silver 326
–, wash, bleach and 503, 511
– water of its ashes 509
– with water 516
purple 167, 177, 199, 204, 222, 231, 282, 317, 370, 389, 448, 453, 463, 540, 554, 573
–, alumy 473
– aqzal-gold into 528, 538, 558
–, Armenian 503
–, become 165
– branch 448, 495
–, cold dyeing of 453
– colour 36, 341, 347, 447, 470, 557, 562, 574
– dye 168, 248, 316-7, 319, 321, 446, 495, 552, 540-1
– dyeing/ dyeing of 323, 396
–, extract 508
–, ferment of 503
– gold 246, 261, 268, 295, 363-4, 548, 558
–, make/ turn into 248, 323, 473, 495, 509, 552
–, Maltese 503
– metal 451
–, pound … with water 503
– of clothes of king 496
–, purpleness 231
–, purply, purply-black 512
–, red 527
–, saturated 473

– sea 450
– stone 572
–, water alone dyes 554
pursuer of virgin 320
push away 473
put back (into cooking, operation etc.); *see also return; vessel, put in* 379, 480-1, 493, 504, 508, 510-12, 520
pyrite 24, 47, 196, 199, 252, 268, 279, 285, 297, 353, 386, 456, 484, 500, 538, 563, 571
– and copper 572
– as lead 234
– composed with iron 472
–, cook 538
– into ash 486
– mercury, tin, sulphur and 384
–, mix body with 365
–, operation of 397
–, silvery 234
– stone 234, 252
– sulphur and salt 196
–, true 497
–, turn into 279
– turns fine like dust 234
–, vinegar and salt 199
Pythagoras 51

–Q–

qabṣ 457
qalqant; see also colocynth 250, 299, 317, 349, 375, 561
qalqaṭār (copper vitriol)/ *qalqṭār/* quluqṭār 147, 468
qalqṭār; *see qalqaṭār*
qīānūn 187, 451
qibla 120, 286
qintar (a measure), (3) three 471
qirat 278
Qirāṭis; *see Kitāb Qirāṭis; book(s), of Krates*
quality 93-4, 222, 224
– depends on burning and cooking 456
–, divine 33
–, life providing 35
–, shining 35
quantity 171, 208, 258, 489, 504, 506, 546
– of vinegar 510-11
– quantities of works 293
quaternio(n) 44
queen 60, 73
–, moon- 39, 59, 61, 65
– of the heart (Theosebeia) 20
quench 521
quest 69, 90, 132, 137-8, 554
question (n, vb); *see also ask; answer* 7, 19-20, 25, 37, 58, 62, 68, 96-7, 112, 114-5, 117-20, 123, 125, 131, 135, 155, 176, 194, 203, 242, 263, 315, 329, 358, 365, 371, 418, 452, 529, 533, 556
–, (8500) eight thousand five hundred 327
– about burning of copper 365
– about man of wool 539
– about mercury 416
– about mercuries 477
– about mixing of rotten 534
– about relationship 232
– about second work 526
– about winning over the ten 326
–-and-answer; *see also dialogue* 75, 98
–, ashamed of 195
–, ask me! 37, 142, 155, 322, 331, 342, 482, 484, 526, 559
–, Book regarding Questions about the Other Composition 563
–, different 452
–, difficult question 143
–, good 142, 173, 303, 352, 416, 467
–, many 327
–, missing 297
– of Ānṭiqūs 486
– of Hermes' student 231, 571
– of Qusṭūs 486
– of Sīsin to Disqīus 150-1
– of That 150
– other questions 452
–, repeat 328
–, same 197
–, series of 117
–, subtle 226
– to Ābullūn (Apollonius) 402
quick 142, 283
–, body takes spirit quickly 235
–, escape (not) quickly 153
–, quickest 457
–, quickly 175, 222-3, 265, 287-8, 291,

318, 325, 327, 354, 364, 393, 416, 467, 493-4, 500, 504, 507, 520, 562, 569-70, 580
–, solidify quickly 551
quicklime 117
quintessence/ quinta essentia 44, 154
quluqṭār; *see qalqaṭār*
quotation(s) 22, 24, 26, 28, 61
–, quote (vb, n) 24, 27-28, 51, 58, 73, 93, 95, 111, 116-7, 119, 122, 125-6, 129, 136
Qurṭubī 26
Qusṭūs 486

–R–

rain (vb, n) 453
– accepted by earth 548
–, cook in rain-water 453
– water 383, 405, 511
rainbow 37, 256, 342
raise (vb); *see also rise* 48, 218, 261, 300, 321, 436, 505, 520
– in furnace 380
– up by mercury 455
– up into air 509
– (up in) vapour 461, 513, 520
– up (things) 145, 502
–, water/ raising of water 164, 189, 215, 298, 315, 359, 440, 459, 461, 487, 489 494
Ramses II 10
rank, high–ranking 162, 195, 241, 316-7, 379, 406, 486, 515, 537, 542, 550, 552
rarely 128, 151, 213, 242
Ratzinger, Joseph Cardinal 120
raw 247, 383, 484
–, cook 376
ray(s) 218
– of stars 465
– of sun 161, 258
Re 78
reach 33, 53, 143, 150, 158, 171-2, 190, 203-4, 212, 227, 229, 236, 241, 328, 331, 345, 379, 464, 512, 519, 529-30, 547
– goal 370, 560, 568, 571
– intention 262
– knowledge 151
– mixture 223
– not (work, knowledge) 165, 176, 218, 540, 549, 560
– sought-for 380, 560
– ten 273
read 19, 147, 217, 320, 464
– about composition 377
–, how to … books (of sages) 194, 256
–, intensive reading 154
–, persistent in reading 145, 203
–, readership 117
–, reading 5-6, , 180, 242, 337, 537
– repeatedly 19
– statement 386
reality 35, 39
–, bodily 24, 134
– of world 90
realization 560
– of self 39
reason 382
rebind 119
rebirth 127
rebis 44
receiver 440
recognize (vb) 22-3, 28, 93, 115, 175, 236, 275, 285, 345, 368, 393, 399, 540
– tree 448
recollection, projection and 39
recompense 242, 327, 537
reconcile (vb); *see also fusion; coninuction; union* 28, 120, 168, 219, 220-1, 509
–, blackness reconciles 509
– fire and water 28, 120, 123, 137, 220, 523
– opposites/ reconciliation of opposites 28-9, 44, 121-4, 137
–, reconciler 63, 222
reconnect/ reconnection 69
recording 112
recutting 119
red 31, 36, 66, 129, 134, 141, 143, 160, 164, 183, 210, 222, 225, 228, 243, 248, 276, 306, 337, 341, 347, 364, 366, 368, 370, 380, 401, 410, 421, 433, 448, 451, 526, 539, 554, 557, 563, 568-9, 578
– alabaster 561
– and red/ white-red/ red or white 152, 166, 22, 243, 458, 468, 533
– ashes 282
–, become 159, 187, 189, 199, 248, 254, 257,

277, 323, 410, 524-5, 530, 561-4, 567, 571, 576
–, black-red/ make the red black 31, 561, 568
– body of magnesia 379
– branch 448, 495
– cinnabar 373, 535
– clothes 391
– cluster 461
–, colocynth makes 563
– composition 212, 284
– cooking 199
– copper 225, 245, 282, 466, 468, 499
–, copper turns 373
– dog 84, 347
– dust 295, 363
–, dye/ dyeing 205, 420
– dye ... in whiteness 541
– elixir 567
– essence 352
– hands 339
– in appearance 373
– in essence 151, 373, 475, 483, 493, 549, 574
– lead 297, 326, 527, 546
–, make 164-5, 170, 184-5, 197, 207, 212, 236, 245-7, 249-50, 252, 267, 288, 295, 321, 373, 377, 380, 397, 411, 421, 460-1, 468, 498, 525, 532-3, 549, 552, 581
–, make copper 41, 183, 420, 576
–, make natures 147
– male 295
– mercury 256, 430
– poison 188, 281, 533, 538
–, pure water and … sulphur 379
– russet- 199
– sea 129, 450-1, 507
– slave 356
– stone 259, 488, 544, 568
– stripes 36, 81, 341
– sulphur 250-1, 269, 373, 380, 554
– thing 522
–, turn 173, 206, 234, 245, 269, 364, 380, 386, 546
–, turn into … dust 295
– vinegar 507
– viper 263
– vitriol; *see vitriol*
–, white, ... and yellow 199
redeemer 120
redemption 98
reddening 143, 147, 150, 212, 269, 524
–, (1) one, ... and whitening is 498
–, (1st) first 532
–, (2) two 532
–, burning as/ of 288, 523
–, completion of 189
–, mercury of 420
reddish 238, 257, 281, 295, 362-3, 454, 511, 546
– colour(s) 349, 383
–, marine 383
redness 48, 175, 195, 209-10, 216, 226, 277, 295, 303, 323, 355, 357, 379, 396, 446, 493, 527, 557, 560, 564, 570, 575, 580
– and whiteness 183
– appears 277, 491, 547, 558
– as aqzal 493
–, blackness extracts 446, 469, 509
– comes slowly 557
– concealed 493, 542
– covers 360
–, extract whiteness from 542
–, in/ covered by whiteness 533, 541
–, increase 579
– is work 575
–, metallic 411
–, superior 579
reduce (vb) 505
– moisture in winter 511
–, refer back 46-7
– symbols 94
refine/ refining 385, 294, 480
reflect 519
reflection 74, 84, 95
refuse (vb) 158, 240, 357
regions 215
register; *see also level; part; sphere* 34, 64
regret 143, 278, 331, 356, 357, 577
reign (vb, n) 25, 118, 155, 471, 581
reins 238
Reịzenstein, R. 11
reject 28, 44, 50, 63, 123, 158, 196, 268, 354, 454, 455, 487, 496, 503, 514, 526, 557, 580
–, rejected bodies 514
rejoice 164, 200-2, 217, 233, 235, 259, 471

– blood in sperm 387
– female 304
– in each other 168
– in nature 241
–, nature …s in close one 258
–, nature ….s in nature 162, 228, 242, 258, 259, 280, 296, 399, 529
rejuvenate (vb)/ rejuvenation 40, 47, 54, 80, 109
relate (vb) 5, 11, 49, 45, 52, 54, 90, 92, 112, 138, 140, 214, 220, 229, 334, 498
relationship(s) 27, 29-30, 39, 41, 44, 48, 51, 59, 78-9, 81, 101, 109, 111, 117, 122-3, 136-8, 160, 168, 201-2, 223-4, 232, 278, 296-7, 321, 352, 384, 398-9, 442, 462-3, 498, 529, 537, 569, 572
– (2) two pictures, ... of 79
–, individual 59, 64
–, internal 24, 79-80, 133, 137
–, male-female-/ man-woman- 136-8
– of body and nature 393
– of sulphurs and mercury 416
– of teacher and student 79, 84
– of white stone with copper 574
– of Zosimos and Theosebeia 29, 39, 112, 143, 148, 150, 155-6, 173, 212, 242, 315, 322, 559
– to dream-life 23
– with archetypal world 39
relative(s) (n) 63, 221, 278, 295, 339, 355, 382, 569, 580
–, character of 334, 339
–, cloud as 567
–, cloud preserves its 278
– holds cloud 360
– holds/ with relative 278, 284
–, nature holds 284
relief 10, 529
Religion 119
– Christian(ity) 10-11, 19, 29, 37, 99, 110, 113, 118, 120, 124
– Islam(ic) 7, 9-10, 13, 17, 25-6, 54, 69, 73, 98-99, 121, 124-5, 132
–, religious 35, 316
–, symbolic-religious 80, 95, 122
reluctance 305
rely on (vb) 579
remain 144, 164, 177, 184, 190-1, 200, 210, 226-7, 240, 243, 246, 248, 268, 272, 278, 283, 286, 291, 373-4, 394, 400, 432, 436, 474, 487, 502, 506, 508, 540, 569, 579
–, copper remains 374, 496, 501
– in fire 192, 398, 496-7
–, not 304
–, not remaining as sulphurs 398
– of the body 576
– permanent 497
–, poison remains 440
–, remaining (as bodies) 224, 398
–, sediment remains 440, 560
– subtle part of dye 498
–, truth remains 265
– white 459
remedy; *see also cure; disease; doctor; illness; medical* 567, 573
– as water 511
–, a million times proven 39
–, compose remedies 169, 542
–, cook/ dissolve … with tar 158
–, find a 169
–, fire absorbs 486
–, mix remedies 169, 195
–, pound 554
–, remedies 148, 215-6, 463
remember 98, 146, 178, 197, 216, 237, 243-4, 263, 266, 328, 483, 491, 523, 539, 580
remove 167, 187, 217, 251, 282, 362, 477, 551
– air-holes of lead 551
– blackness 168, 283, 482, 565
– dirt 508
– shadow (of copper) 506, 528
– squeaking of tin 565
render 540
renew (vb)/ renewal of 54, 80, 182, 558
– sea 559
– sun 113
rennet 261
repeat (vb); *see also again; put back* 23, 149, 173, 186, 216, 243, 295, 352, 361, 400, 451, 466, ,481, 510, 580
–, pound repeatedly 573
– questions 328
–, repeatedly 26, 39, 45 202, 227, 302, 524

–, repetition 428, 460, 464, 466, 494, 507, 510, 564, 566
–, repetition and truth 368
– statement 467
– washing 167
replace 94, 148
– end with beginning 349
– ferrous with pyrite 500
– second with first composition 287
– something with something else 148
representation
– of teacher and student 78
–, represent 289
–, symbolic 40, 93
research 99, 111, 124, 126, 138
–, Research and Training Centre for Depth Psychology 13
–, researcher(s) 6, 13
resist/ resistance/ resistant
– fire 151, 166, 186, 188, 202, 213, 226, 248, 362, 398, 403, 528, 550
– nature …s not the fire 398
respect 485
response 327, 432
responsibility 23, 149
rest 119, 156, 166, 249, 384, 414, 420, 440, 444, 458, 484, 496, 519, 536-7
–, absorb ... of waters 489
– in dye 495
– of body 217
– of cloud 562
– of composition 184
– of fat 570
– of gum 321
– of life 143
– of operation 194, 559, 571
– of poison 557
– of statement 325
– of things 191, 299, 381
– of water 557-8, 565
– of work 432
result(s) 5, 12, 41, 67, 118, 122, 134, 178, 283, 373
resurrection 81, 98, 177
–, death and 81, 91, 110, 135, 138
–, resurrect 36, 40, 53, 340, 342, 485
retort 65
return 167, 225, 234, 249, 283, 291,317, 357, 359-60, 367, 432, 503, 511, 530-1, 566, 570, 573-5
– aqzal-gold 528
– back 145, 458, 487, 496-7, 507, 524 561
– body to cooking/ moisture 440
– body to heat and moisture 508
– colours 480, 524
– copper 156, 244
– gold/ silver 528, 558
– moisture 283
– plates 247
– residue 512
– sediment on water 244
– soul to body 480, 487
– spirits to body 488
– to ash 504
– to (body/ nature/ soul) 163, 480, 487
– to cooking 145, 480, 503, 512, 557, 565, 573, 576
– to earth/ sea 218
– to Egypt 5
– to eternal water 532
– to fire 482, 573
– to its original nature 502
– to life 48
– to sediment 460
– to teacher 432
– to vessel 283, 509
– wool 510, 542
reveal (vb) 24, 26, 33, 37, 40, 47-8, 69, 74, 80, 84, 91, 98, 113, 111, 117-9, 126, 137-8, 150, 155-6, 171, 257, 259, 342, 344-5, 349, 357, 359, 366, 390, 427, 559
– (not) secret 213, 257, 294, 312, 327, 577
– truth 27, 220, 344, 347, 349, 382, 420, 536
– work 145
review 54, 73-4, 85, 96, 114, 116-7, 125, 133, 135
revive 90, 177, 344
–, (1) one, reviver and revived is 165
– natures 521
–, revivication 228
reward 155, 217
Rīānūsūs 207
Richter, Tonio Sebastian 10, 121, 316
riddles 273
right 41, 53, 146, 150, 158, 191, 197, 205,

210, 213, 229, 231-2, 234, 238, 243, 254, 256, 265, 282, 289, 311, 313, 318-9, 325, 331, 351, 353, 360, 365, 373, 379, 382-3, 396, 398, 416, 431, 433, 444, 446, 462-3, 465, 474-6, 482, 485, 501, 503, 507-8, 540, 572-3
– and left 121
– and wrong 351
–, do work 215
– dye 554
– hand 31-2, 41-2, 263, 391
– measure 365, 396, 403, 523
– path 260, 356, 361, 572
–, sage is/ sages were right 150, 160, 163, 214, 258, 311, 313, 352, 368, 431, 475, 485, 572
– thing 520
– track 318
– way 143, 147, 217, 268, 278, 285, 292, 310, 464-5, 540, 551
– weight 272, 379
– work 147, 153, 535, 565
–, you are right! 144, 175, 182-3, 185, 187, 191, 210, 213, 231-2, 238, 243, 254, 256, 282, 318-9, 351, 353, 373, 382, 396, 398, 446, 476-7, 482, 517, 535, 540, 572-3
rightness 238, 405
– of the work 525
ring(finger) 91
–, stone of 500
ripe/ ripen 122, 156, 498
– compostition 480
–, fruits 572
–, make 469
–, ripen elixir with water 562
–, ripen fruits 236, 278, 524
Risāla; *see also Epistle(s)*
–, al Fakīyāt al-kubrā (the great Epistle of the Spheres) 95
–, fī ḥurūf (The Letters), 43, 407, 411
–, As-sabᶜūna risāla (The 70 Epistles) 18
–, al-ṯāliṯa li-Rūamūs (Third Epistle of Zosimos) 114
rise/ rising (vb); *see also raise* 24, 120, 145, 218, 278, 292, 298, 301, 319, 440, 471, 489
– cloud 198
– dog 494
– in vessel 168, 520
– not 168
–, nothing 512
– (of) sun 356, 450, 530
–, rising of sun/ sun rise 120, 292, 356, 450, 530
–, smoke 223
– to upper 168
– up 48, 502, 533, 560
– up water 272, 400, 509
– vapour 163-4, 513, 519, 533
risk; *see also harm* 501
– of work 368
Ritter, H. 94
ritual 113
–, embalming 39
river 47, 130
–, head of 572
– of running gold 147
–, origin in 147
–, rivers 166
–, water of 426, 458
roast 156, 188, 295, 316, 442, 455, 471-2, 355, 364, 375, 400, 480, 484, 496, 500, 528, 557, 564-5
– and cook 565
– chrysocolla 529
– gold 546
– natron 501
– poison 579
–, roasted 456
–, roasting(s) 23, 149, 164, 369, 379, 481, 530
–, rotting, cooking, soaking and roasting 481
–, šuḥairah 383
– with moisture 573
robe 43, 141
Roberts, A. 123
Robinson, James M. 121
rock; *see also stone* 47-8
– like alabaster 300
– with water 477
role 142
Roman 383
Rome 11
root 63, 122, 201, 218
– and dye 249
–, rooted 36, 130, 337

–, roots 18, 54, 99, 113, 249, 374, 502
–, roots of stone 488
rope(s) 84, 141, 307, 313, 329, 477, 526-7, 544
–, (3) three 141
– of Osiris 290
–, yellow 517
Rosarium philosophorum 59, 61, 136
– and Mushaf as–suwar 59, 61-3
rose 406
–, milk of roses 261
Rosinus (ad Euthiciam) 59, 61-2
rot (vb) 48, 167-8, 177-8, 180-1, 227, 232, 245-6, 248, 261, 300-2, 360, 362, 363, 369, 371, 375, 429, 502, 515-6, 520-1, 532, 551, 558-60, 564, 578
– after soaking of elixir 567
–, become rotten 362
–, body becomes rotten 550
– body (for days) 190, 255
– composition 520
– earth with water 303
– in vessel 560
–, leave to 561
–, make copper rotten 567
–, make earth rotten 303
–, make rotten 151, 156, 218, 232, 515, 567
– metals 302
–, mix rotten and non-rotten 533-4
–, rot in vessel 529
rotting 143, 153, 174, 180, 205, 254, 364, 440, 481-2, 493, 515, 531
–, cooking, soaking and roasting 481
–, dye in 262
–, finish 440
– of silver 466
–, second/ other 279, 567, 572
–, two rottings 254
round 53, 84, 277, 485, 492, 501
– plates 563
–, rounded alum 581
– vessel 231
royal 90, 209, 450
rub (vb) 254, 320, 385, 389, 539
– copper 385
– lead 397
– mercury 394
– plates of iron 442
– with hand 459
– with water 254
ruby 207, 209
–, origin of 450
–, rubies 347
Rudolph, U. 124
Ruelle, Charles Emanuelle 9, 17, 96
ruin (n, vb) 173, 282, 291, 303, 321, 446-7, 456, 459, 492, 495, 498, 524, 535, 549
– composition 490
–, dry iron ...s dissolved silver 442
–, ruining 396, 525
– work/ ruining of work 508, 525
– world; *see also corrupt* 350, 517
Rulandus, Martinus 94
ruler of the Netherworld 24
rulers 219
rungs 208
running of dragon 458
ruses; *see also analogies; cover; disguise; names; trickery; veil* 219, 360
–, all kinds of 144
Ruska, Julius 24, 52, 54-5, 58, 125, 130-1
russet 454
– colour; see also muġra/ muġrāt 349, 406, 454, 511, 569
– -red 199
– -yellow 199
rust 129, 151, 170, 183, 192, 204, 249, 250, 364, 375, 411, 446, 448, 458, 460, 495, 514, 532, 550, 552, 559, 562, 579
– as copper 549
– as poison of honey- 49, 514
–, become/ make/ turn into 189, 269, 379, 411, 487, 549, 580
–, burn copper to 365
–, chrysocolla into 529-30
–, copper into 552, 558
–, copper without 183
– from ashes 283
– into saffron 565
–, iron ...s with moisture 53, 485
–, name 530
– of body 574
– of copper 129, 141, 286, 529, 531
– of copper and chrysocolla 558
– of iron 316, 461, 510
–, operation for 207

–, pounding of the 565
–, rusting 23, 149, 250
–, silver into ... of copper 565
rusty 200, 286, 410, 459
–, become 169, 567
–, burn for turning 580
–, copper 195, 364
–, first composition as making 493
– gold 225
–, make 250-1, 360, 373, 411, 489, 532, 552
–, make copper 216, 303, 355, 379, 493, 551-2
rutl(s) (measure) 269, 471, 501, 503, 509

–S–

sadness 180, 262, 351, 361, 559
safflower 297, 335, 395, 567
saffron 186, 249, 259, 266, 297, 368, 395
– and cloud 498
– becomes water 538
–, copper, chrysocolla, saffron and eternal water 266
–, mercuries with water of sulphur, gum and 430
–, pound 538
–, rust into 565
–, take 565
sagacity 202, 229, 243, 454, 480
sage(s); *see Abīsiqūs; Ābullūn; Africanus, Agathodaimon; Asfīḫās; Alasardus, Badīsios; Bersius; Butitos, Democritus, Disqīus; Hermes, Isis, Maria,* Mīdunah, *Moses, Olympiodoros, Ostanes, Persian, Šīmās,* Taūfīl, *Theodorus, Zosimos; see also philosopher*
–, (1) one/ none of the 158, 249, 311-2, 450, 543, 561
– analogize; *see analogy* 175
–, blame 355
–, burning of 286, 288, 350
–, community of 28, 120, 219, 523
–, composition of 174
– confuse people 383
– differ/ disagreement of 145, 153, 177, 219, 269, 293-4, 380, 401, 519
–, disobey 559
– dispersed and collected 556
–, first 22, 255, 393, 394, 401, 418, 425, 469, 530
– egg of sages 369
–, extract colours from fighter 446
– following/ later 394
–, gum of 285
–, head of 45, 58, 311-2
– hide 388, 410
–, imitate 328
– in/ of Egypt 160, 471
– is/ are right 150, 160, 163, 258, 214, 263, 282, 311, 313, 352, 368, 431, 475, 485, 572
–, juice of 474
– kill 56, 127, 157
–, locks of the 154
–, magnesia of 183
– mercury of 229, 425
–, mixture of 401, 499
–, oath of the 577
– open 165
–, operation of 317
– other 48, 199, 259, 311-3
–, poison of 282, 520
– praise 171, 176, 191, 497
–, sea of 461
–, search for 180
–, secret(s) of 143, 356, 564
–, silver of 183
–, skilfull 180
– stone of 38-9, 44, 62, 117, 129
–, sulphur of the 170
–, sun of 160
–, tree of 84
– way of teaching/ veiling; *see also teaching; veiling* 349-50
–, wax of 287
– work/ works of 47, 91, 153, 214, 246, 293, 315, 469, 500
Sagittarius 494
šaḥīra; *see also vitriol* 147, 250, 299, 316, 349, 406, 454, 468, 511, 561-2, 576
salq (beetroot) 492
salt(s) 196, 199, 210, 272, 291, 442, 465, 468
–, alum, .., natron, lime and makrasīūn 325
–, alum, …, white lead, polished earth and living water 395
– and ash 385
– and copper 442
– and water 400

–, big salting/ saltings 367
–, burn copper with sulphur, … and alum 497
– disappears 487
–, flower of 569
–, Indian 502
–, iron, mercury, vinegar and 320
–, made lean 456
–, mix with salts 468
–, pyrite, sulphur/ vinegar and 196, 199
–, saltiness 509
–, salty 292, 366-7, 568
–, sharp 509
–, sweet from salty 291
–, water becomes 569
–, water of 255, 284
salvation 129, 142, 207, 209, 243, 389, 451, 581
sand 130, 148, 260, 297, 302, 529, 560
–, operation of 297, 501, 507
–, suitable for mixing of 375
–, things named 560
–, turn into 145, 569
–, wash 482
sandarach 248, 468, 411
– and arsenic 411
– and mercury 416
–, arsenic, … and kohl 505
– as sulphurs 467
–, body of magnesia as arsenic 353
–, fight 376
– glue mercury of arsenic and 384
–, mercury from 421
–, mercury from arsenic, … (and pure water/ abšimīt and rest) 287, 353, 420
–, mercury, … and kohl 436
–, murderer of 248
–, pound sulphur with 325
–, sulphur(y bodies), arsenic and 325, 418, 468
– zenderih 411
sands 358
sap 272, 469
sapphire 176, 256
Sartamita/ Sarṭamīṭā/ Sarṭiṭa 111, 249, 261, 315, 389, 414, 442, 540
–, epistle of Zosimos 46, 315
–, Sarṭamīṭā (letter) 411
Satan 11, 28, 31, 121, 123
satisfy 142, 245
–, satisfied 55, 141, 144, 153, 157, 208, 214, 262, 268, 358, 365, 397, 451, 455, 469, 472, 543-4
saturate 156, 286, 317
–, saturated 271, 542
–, saturated purple 473
–, saturation 174
Saturn 252, 305, 311, 357
–, and fighter 305
–, colour of 253
–, Saturnian features 216
scale(s) (yellow) 78, 263-4, 276
scant 550
scarab 19
scatter; *see also break; cut; disguise; keep secret; protect; veil* 22-3, 149, 161, 229, 310, 367, 377, 563
–, put together scattered 384
– statements 384
– work 563
Schäfer, Heinrich 108
science; see also institute 13, 28, 52, 118, 121, 138, 145, 208, 229, 248, 260-1, 290, 293, 312, 328, 354, 359, 401, 432, 450, 454-5, 468, 501, 523
–, Arabic-Islamic 7
–, deter from 23, 149
–, development of 25
–, enter 385, 454
– is nature 143
–, key to 259, 414
–, know them by their 28, 120, 220, 523
–, man skilful in the 154, 155
–, master of 540
–, obscure 206
–, picture of 402
–, seeker of 368, 398, 452
–, students of 147, 152
–, take … from me 257
–, understand 154, 487
–, veil 145
– will appear 25, 155
scorpion 292
sea 91, 146, 162, 166, 209-10, 216, 231, 256, 290, 292, 512, 538, 542, 570
–, animals of 218

–, ash of 509
– becomes hot 218
– born (in, nourished by) 209, 500
–, dew from 291
–, drink salty 292
– dyes 255
–, flower of 231
–, froth of the 442
–, glass into 513
–, mix in some days 380
– mix things with 382
– of cloud 292
– of gold 461
– of sages 461
–, pound (all things) in/ with 167, 380
–, purple 450
–, put airy into 382
–, put nature into 530
–, red sea 129, 255, 450-1, 507
–, renew 559
–, return to 218
–, seas 210
– shell, vinegar, … , and alum 299
–, single sea has no power 382
–, sweeten 292
–, thick 530
–, things marry in 380
–, throw into 360
–, vapour of 513
–, washed 292
–, wash with … water 487
–, water of the 167, 255, 284, 531, 573
–, waves of 358
–, white 167, 450
–, worm of 507
seal (n) 91, 517
–, seal vessel 521
search 135, 143, 180, 299, 389, 464, 526
– for ashes 580
– for natures 147
– not else 558
– search(ed)-for 297-8, 532
season(s)
–, four seasons 236, 299, 522
–, gentleness of 524
second (2nd); *see also "other"* 79, 205, 227, 233, 495, 507, 525, 570
–, about the ... Work 525
–, beginning of … composition 570
– book/ ... Book 212, 344
– burning 288
– century 122, 124
– cinnabar 484
– coagulation 287
– commentary 5
– components 252
– composition 179, 253, 258, 277, 283, 287, 405, 424, 491, 524, 567
– cooking 508, 542
– dog 84
–, dry 569
– elixir 319, 505-6
– figure 31
–, first and second work 517
– making alumy 574
– making lean 572
– part 206, 560, 572
– picture 75, 404
– poison 513
– rotting 279, 567, 572
– season 522
– series 79, 81-3
– solidification 325
– sticking 284
– sulphur 284
– time 47, 206, 212, 506, 538, 551
– treatise 353
– work 205, 295, 301, 361, 364, 386, 405, 420, 490, 511, 526, 554-5, 571
secret(s); *see also reveal* 48, 93, 120, 144, 152, 154, 160, 162, 186, 192-3, 196-7, 204, 210, 213, 217, 227, 233, 257, 275, 282, 295, 320, 358, 469, 475, 532, 556, 559
–, (2) two 152
– and analogies 320
– and poison 167
– appears 57, 157
–, beginning of 561
– comes into existence 373
–, complete 575
–, examples of 473
–, great/ greatest 235, 251, 367, 380, 532
–, hide/ hidden 150, 162, 166, 214, 304, 312, 345, 367, 382-3, 530
– in ashes 580

– in mercuries 427
–, keep; *see also disguise; protect; scatter; trickery; veil* 22, 145, 161-2, 171, 175, 177, 215, 260, 278, 297, 359, 390, 394, 414, 453, 487, 501, 563, 566
– magnesia 463
–, make not clear 529
–, natures of 328
– of composition 279
– of Hermes 48
– of sages 143, 356, 564
– of secrets 399
– of stone 166
– of work 399
–, operation of 537
–, pound 447, 495
–, sacred 429
– seat 458
–, secretly 244
–, soak 538
–, visible 187, 202, 373, 420, 434, 475, 521
– weight 268
sediment 243, 291, 381, 471, 501-2
– and moisture 167
–, dry 493
–, dry, dead, soulless 283
–, extract from sediments 503
–, extract sulphurs from 493
–, extract vapour from 244
–, filings take up 508
– in pot 460
–, leave ...(s) 502, 509
–, marble water, lime, … and fat 381
–, mix with 511
–, name of 167
–, obtain from 512
– remains 560
–, return … on water 244
–, sediments 198, 502-3
–, sediments without spirits 503
–, smashed 204
–, take up 440
–, water of 284
seduce of Saturn 357
see (vb) 43, 49, 148, 164, 185, 189, 235, 251, 336, 374, 378, 455, 484
–, cannot be seen 201
– dreams 143
–, head of seer 319
– picture 37, 342
seed 58, 181, 522
–, mustard seds 401
– of gold 253
– of olives 290
seek (vb) 62, 85, 95, 124, 161, 171, 176, 181, 196, 221, 223, 234, 261, 355, 381, 405, 505
– after 223
– dye 302
– sought-for 380, 481, 489
– stone 367
seeker 120, 360, 370, 398
– and fugitive 166, 232, 278
– and sought 197
– clings to fugitive 384
meets fugitive 465, 468
– mixed with/ takes/ unites with fugitive 152, 166, 466, 468
–, number of seekers 26, 118
– of virgin 473
–, seekers 155, 362, 394, 452
–, seekers of gum 171
–, seekers of science 248, 368, 394, 398, 540
seize 283
–, snow seizes cloud 570
self 32, 39, 41, 44, 122
– and soul 44
– as archetype 92-3
–, realisation of 39
sell (vb) 171, 213-4, 237, 494
semen 248, 481, 485
–, cook … with moisture 481
send epistle/ message/ pages 46, 90, 111, 148, 170, 217, 315, 529, 562
Senior; *see also Ibn Umail* 68
sense(s) 217, 302
separate (vb) 29, 31, 38, 48, 59, 61, 64, 80, 122, 161, 184, 201, 216, 223-4, 232, 238, 240, 273, 292, 298, 301, 355, 357, 370, 380, 488, 504
– (1st/ 2nd) first/ second work 361
– (2) two 254
– bodies and earth 394, 395
– body and soul/ soul from body 370, 436, 438, 514
– body and spirit/ spirit from body 33, 36,

170, 322-3, 339, 439, 476
– divine and profane reality 39
– earth and bodies 394-5
– earth from water 507
– from companion(s) 399, 500, 508
– from moisture 357
– from nature 258
– moisture and sediment 167
– moisture from ashes 511
– nature/ natures 161, 168
– not 301, 344, 473, 513
– pictures 33, 331
–, separation 33, 41, 301, 322
– solid part from earth 371
– sulphur from copper 501
– whiteness and blackness 509
sepulchre 56
series 74, 79-81, 84-5, 135, 137
–, (1st) first series of pictures 75, 80-1
–, (2nd) second series of pictures 81
–, (3rd) third series of pictures 84
– of alchemical images 74, 85
– of chapters 132
– of colours 47
– of dreams 98
– of lectures 12
– of pictures 6, 12, 59, 61, 78, 111, 135, 402
– of questions 117
Serapeion 9
serpent; *see also dragon; Ouroboros* 51, 64, 109, 127
– bird heads 109
– eating/ biting tail; *see dragon* 50, 93, 263, 318, 371
–, ejaculation of 94
– power 109
setting 292
settle 243, 488, 512
seven (7) 145, 229
– colours 465
– cookings 505
– days 156, 234, 283, 367, 488, 503, 531, 568, 581
– Epistles (book) 73, 112, 114, 132
– holes 440
– soakings 561
– stars 450
– things 269, 440, 540-1
– times 120, 156, 158, 278, 283, 436, 471, 483, 489, 500, 505-6, 513, 529, 532, 558-9, 560-1, 569, 575
seventh (7th) 21, 31, 145, 229, 339, 354, 357, 402, 414, 418, 476d
– cooking 436
seventeenth (17th); *see also picture*
– century 31, 67
seventy (70) 10
several times 162, 241, 247, 266, 270, 277, 283, 310, 317, 322, 368, 373, 460, 473, 497, 529, 539, 542, 557, 562
sew (together) 151, 167
sexual intercourse 55, 157, 181-2, 192, 304, 481, 536
Sezgin, Fuat 5-7, 11, 13, 18, 20, 24, 54, 58, 95, 98, 123, 136
shackles 141
shadow 90, 281, 362, 371, 471, 473
– and sun 281-2
–, appear 369
– as colour 528
–, as silvery water 282
– concealed in body 172
–, copper without 24, 197, 201, 379, 381, 386, 410, 497-9, 536
–, disappears/ make disappear/ remove 173, 200-1, 220, 373, 497-8, 410, 420, 506, 528
– figures 31
–, gold without 497, 563
–, invisibile … of copper 373
– of copper 173, 187, 200, 206, 247, 282, 369, 374, 410-1, 420, 506, 528
– of copper and magnesia 374
– of copper concealed in whiteness 373-4
– of copper/ silver 386
–, purify 535
–, shadowy 90
–, turn … into spirit 172
–, without 24, 201, 364, 410, 498, 563
shake 442
shameless 23, 149, 203, 217, 241-2
share 340
sharp 509
–, sharpen 427
–, sharpness 360
sheep 389

sheet(s), winding 36, 217, 341-2
sheikh 569
shell
–, burnt shells 474
– is egg 159
–, moisture, yolk and 159
–, shells of pollen 254
shellfish 511
shield 347
shine (vb)/ shining 35, 47, 63, 160, 168, 209-10, 216, 234, 251, 260, 279, 350, 367, 388, 477, 490, 492, 504, 508, 511, 546, 558
–, shining blood 570
–, shining flame 9
–, shining Indian 499
–, shining spirit 393
–, shining stone 532
ship with many utensils 81, 351
shirt 141
Shiva 32
shore 517
shoulders 66, 79
sick 90, 169, 318-9, 360
–, become 361
–, sickness 362
sid¡n¡((s 509
side(s) 513
–, (1) one 238
–, both 235
–, dark/ bodily 32
–, feminine 39
– of river 47
sieve 146, 482, 487-9
–, made of natures 488
– natures 560
–, sieving 145-6, 208
– water 323
sight 289
– illumine 217
sign/ signs; *see also allegory; codename; symbol* 91, 129, 229, 320, 403, 451, 503, 507, 512
– and symbol 93-95
– of the Zodiac 313, 571
–, signposts 559
significance 74
silent 485
silver 22, 36, 37, 148, 150, 156, 167, 181, 184, 246, 257, 267, 270, 272, 277, 283, 294-5, 302, 316, 326, 339, 363, 375, 410, 431, 466, 469, 493-4, 538
–, (2) two silvers 467
–, absorbs moisture 561
– and copper 220, 566
– and gold 165, 257, 260, 277, 319, 398, 470, 488, 498-9
– and moon 463
– and poison 407
– as mercury 566
– becomes gold 564
–, black 144, 350
–, blackness of 216, 282, 461, 566
–, body of 178
–, Book about the Making of the Silver 550
–, cast 456, 565
–, change and dye 455
–, change/ changing of 205, 292-3, 454, 456, 461, 467
–, changing, colouring, rotting of 466
–, colour(s) (of) 252, 386, 473, 404, 467
–, cook our 493
–, copper and … become water 283
–, copper becomes/ turns into 156, 220
–, copper, … and gold 161, 297, 315, 388, 411, 465, 497, 557
–, destroy 566
– disappears 554
–, dissolve/ dissolved 410, 418, 456, 472, 455, 442
–, dress of 156
–, dye 349, 364, 375
–, dye … into gold 235
–, ferment of 302, 457
–, filings of 500
–, fire enters 246
– for ferment 301
– from iron 385
– from our work 294
–, gold dyes 183
–, gold-silver 195
–, good 156
–, iron, magnesia and filings of 472
–, know our 467
–, loosen 540
–, make black 248, 467

–, make/ making of … (and gold) 166, 260, 280, 349, 357, 377, 379, 400, 420-1, 427, 447, 550, 566, 574
– -man 24
–, mercury from 425
–, milk of moon as 484
–, mix dye with 472
– mixed with litharge 520
–, mix gold with 206, 538, 548
–, mix …, (tar) and copper 469, 499
–, mix ... with 567
–, mix … with water of gum 472
–, mix with 567
–, multiplication of 316
–, name 530
– named lead-copper, copper, salt 294
– of (ordinary) people 178, 183, 205, 248, 363, 411, 455, 466-7
–, operation of and iron 377
–, origin of 466
–, our/ their ... (of our work) 183, 191, 220, 234, 277, 282-3, 456, 467, 493-4, 497, 578
–, parts from 282
–, plate of 245, 268, 551
–, poison into 533
–, purify 326
–, red copper, lead and 468
–, remain 579
–, return 528, 558
–, rubb 385
–, scatter/ mix/ cast 22
–, softening of 456, 461
–, spirit of 37, 345
–, splash … with water of gum 456
–, stone born/ made from copper and 539, 566
–, stone of 484
–, tin and copper into 430
–, transformation of 407
–, turn copper into 231, 372, 493
–, turn gold into 239, 344, 349
–, turn … into 156, 183, 293-4, 362-3, 420, 466, 557
–, turn ... into gold 528, 558
–, turn … into rust of copper 565
–, turn … into stone 156, 564
–, turn ... to black 205
–, vessel of 579
–, water of 78, 128, 172, 243, 289, 426, 457, 517, 527, 556-7
–, white 380, 493
– without shadow 386
–, work of 462-3
silvery 36, 208, 252, 342, 353, 489, 558
– body of magnesia 471
– colour 554
– nourishment 489
– one 37
– pyrite 234
– stone 233, 295, 354, 528
– Theosebeia 37, 344-5
– water 141, 263, 282, 307, 379, 418, 538
Šīmās (ibn Ṭaifun), Simus 62, 187, 195, 221, 249, 254, 278, 375, 456, 497, 514, 560
– and Dīsiqūs 550, 564
–, colocynth and sulphur 552
similar 28, 30-1, 37, 45, 47, 50-2, 63, 98, 108, 125, 130, 160, 174-5, 177, 182, 192, 195, 198, 201-2, 210, 221, 223, 235, 238, 246, 249, 252-3, 258, 267, 280-1, 284, 289, 295, 297, 318-9, 322, 347, 349-50, 353, 355-6, 364, 368, 371, 374, 377, 383, 398, 401, 403, 418, 424, 427, 436, 438, 451-2, 457, 464, 481, 499, 520-1, 529, 532, 558
– crafts 151
–, dissimilar 457, 514
– into water 50, 371
–, mix like with like 46
– name(s) 147, 285
– ones 162, 457, 513
–, similarities 178
–, similarity 64, 67, 81, 134, 151, 182
– spirits 514
– statements 456
– things 197, 294, 334, 383
– to God/ Venus 148, 383
– to truth 147-8, 165
simile; *see also allude; disguise; name(s); similar; veil* 90
Simus; *see Šīmās*
sin 242, 257, 313
sincerity 27, 347
– sincere intention 367
single 187, 215, 240-1, 244, 285, 297, 315,

351, 353, 424
–, become 240
– body 193
– copper 499
– days 155
– into married 397
– lead 289
– nature; *see also composed nature* 393
– one 171
– out 467
– sulphur 284
– thing 173, 186, 399
– -unique 41, 576
– with regard to name 576
sink down 511
Sirirus 494
sister, soror mystica 137
Šit 145, 259
sitting 264
Sīus 150-1
six (6); *see also numbers* 145, 273, 279, 367, 390, 570
–, (660) six hundred and sixty 27, 347
– columns 276
– days 488
– escape 324
– fugitives 324
– hours 473, 502
– months 53, 366, 485
– natures 450
– operations 452-3
– ounces 501-2
– parts 569
– persons/ figures 80, 544
– spirits / spiritual beings 80
– times 299, 486-7, 489, 500, 569
– waters 489
– weights 568
– winged persons 264, 526
sixteenth (16th) 59, 67-8, 436
–, century 119
sixth (6th)
–, (1/6) one sixth 486
–, (2/6) two sixth 267, 268
–, (6/6) six sixth 268
–, (6th) sixth 22, 337, 389, 402, 416, 570
–, (6th) sixth century 93, 96-7, 123, 136
sixty (60)
–, (160) hundred and sixty years 25, 155
–, (660) six hundred and sixty 27, 347
– treatises 158
size 66, 116
– same 134
skill 262
– skilful 180, 488
skin 356
– skinniness 158
sky 38, 58, 198, 217, 244, 256, 291, 298, 311-3, 357, 506
–, colour of 141, 276, 391, 477, 556-7, 571
Skythia 125-6
slag 381, 388, 440
– remains 508
slaughter 370
slave 360, 390, 537
–-girl 310-11, 458
–, red 356
–, virgin 390, 458, 536
–, your 159
sleep; *see also dormant* 47, 216, 331
–, sleeplessness 536
slippers 141
slowness 354
–, slow 283, 291
–, slowly 500, 507, 557
small 32, 43, 64, 66, 78-9, 328, 388, 406, 458, 492
– plant 522
smell 166, 279
smoke 24, 218, 247, 254, 382, 436, 505, 547, 575
– and air 228
– and vapour 223
– and water 505
– can come out 547
–, conceal 192
–, dye is 505
–, earth-smoke 218
– gives water 483
–, heavy dusty 483
–, mix non-body with 483
–, of cinnabar 254
– of earth 218
–, poison turns into 234
– rises 223

–, turn into 200, 233, 251
–, turn … into 483
–, white 254
– with splendour, dye and colour 505
snail 319, 324, 473, 500, 542
–, Egyptian 474
snakes 59
snow 151, 165, 216, 350
– appears 570
– -like soul 370
–, snowy 250, 297, 454
–, snowy earth 151, 395
soak (vb) 156, 161, 180, 231, 272, 278, 295, 363-4, 473, 480, 490, 538, 548, 557-8, 562, 568, 570
–, (7) seven soakings 561
– ash 480, 483
– body 248, 557
– composition 268, 369, 480, 539, 564
– crystal 210
– dust 557
– elixir with eternal water 538
–, increase soaking 570
– in water of sulphur 578
– in/ with vinegar 235, 575
– in/ with water 156, 558
– it! 234, 282, 295, 364, 470, 489, 528-9, 535-6, 557-8, 561, 566-7, 569-72
– ivory 504
– moisture 549
– nature 571
–, rotting after soaking 567
–, rotting, cooking, … and roasting 481
– secret 538
– seven times 529
–, soaking 23, 143, 149, 482, 549, 561, 565, 568, 572
–, soaking of elixir 567, 572
– water and gum 286
– water with rust 565
– with dye 547
– with eternal water 547, 564-5
– with ferment 547
– with moisture 156, 548, 573
– with poison 364, 563, 578
– with tar 568
– wool 318, 322, 473
soft 175, 205, 250-1, 265, 297, 356, 407, 456, 472, 475, 488, 504-5, 537, 572
–, become 157
– body 145
– -cold 175
– one 63
–, softer 480, 564, 570
–, softness 57
– sulphur 296, 501, 506
–, take 161
– yellow stones 167
soften (s.th.) 250, 270, 318, 375-6, 475, 504
– body 301
– casting 376
– fire 494
– iron 551
– of silver 456, 461
– softening 551
soil 126, 395
sold 231
solid 179, 222, 225, 247, 369, 489
– and thick 546
– aqzal 493
–, become 356, 570
–, make 150
– mercury 172
– moist 225
– part 371
solidification 188, 325, 372, 458
– and extracting of purple 508
– of mercury 278
– of sulphur 548
solidify (vb) 40, 44, 151, 156, 159, 179, 188-9, 206, 208, 244, 248, 253, 261, 266, 278, 280, 287, 295, 321, 324-5, 353-4, 364, 483, 490-2, 500, 547, 558, 563, 565, 569, 573-4, 576, 578, 580
– after first dissolving 353, 484
– alum 475
–, and dissolve/ solidifying and dissolving 156, 256, 484
– body and water 569
– body of magnesia with tin 471
–, body …s spirit 491
– chrysocolla 530
– claudianus and matitos 388
– copper …s water 248
– crystal/ lead-copper 210
–, fire solidified mercury 372

– incombustible sulphur 548
– in crystal 319
– in sun 547
– in vessel 508
– iron 485
– magnesia with cloud 378
– mercuries 427
– mercury 225, 251, 256, 363, 372, 416, 424, 430, 457, 513
– mercury in tin 147
– mercury in/ with body of magnesia 344, 349, 351, 353, 372-3, 376-7, 383
– mercury with copper 268
– moisture 213, 366, 537
– plate 551
– quickly/ slowly 500, 507, 551
– red mercury 256
–, solidified 156, 188, 248, 253, 295, 353, 364, 558, 569, 578
– stone 480, 484
– stone with gum 447, 495
– water 209
– water of sulphur 548
solution 501
–, soluble stone 484
–, solve et coagula 41
something
–, elixir and 548
–, from nothing comes 168
– of body 548
son(s) 150, 181-2, 432, 464, 526, 543-4
– and father 37, 182, 342
– and mother 142
– of Adam 145, 203
– of fire 252
– of God 11, 121
– of Ibrahim 25, 155
– of Ismā‘īl 25, 118-20, 155
– turn father into 53, 485
soror mystica; *see sister* 20, 59, 64-5, 67, 137
sorrow 260
soul(s) 37, 44, 59, 81, 92, 164, 214, 227, 262, 334, 342, 350-1, 358, 387, 455, 477, 514, 540, 556
– and body 51, 322, 370, 372, 514, 539
– and cloud 215
– and colour 190
– and self 44
– and sperm 181
– and spirit 122, 154, 218, 302, 322
– and spiritual part of work 436
– as fugitive 487
– as part 226
–, body becomes 146
– comes out (of body/ bodies) 181, 515, 539
–, cure 169, 536
–, delight 157
–, dyeing/ is dyed 225, 370, 539
–, dyer-soul 539, 567
–, egg has 227
–, every 292
–, extract 51, 163, 190, 225, 227, 290, 480, 488, 514
– from the air 521
–, have 382
–, hurt 157
–, improve 539
–, inhaling .. from air 521
–, into body 53, 290
–, killer of 216
– like snow 370
–, listen to 519
–, living 539
– of adept 44
– of copper 226
– of/ from body 162, 477
– of fugitive 489
– of human 226
– returns to body/ return ... to body 480, 487
– separates from/ leaves body 322
–, soulless 283
–, soul, spirit and body 520
–, spirit dries/ enters 154, 218
– spiritual/ with spirit 322, 369, 438-9
–, tie 290
–, tortured ... with body 235
–, transformation of 40
–, vessel of 290
–, without 167, 436, 438
sound 271
– thinking 477
sour 370
– copper, …. water and moisture 493
– ferment 548
– poison 304
– vinegar 234, 355, 370, 456, 470, 531, 561

source 20, 73, 80, 85, 110, 125, 226-7, 458
–, Greek 19
– material 114, 137
– of inspiration 27, 59, 63
–, sources 112, 121, 126
South wind 278
sow (vb) 232, 358
spade 292
sparkling 280
– and cinnabar 281
– and male 281
spatter 467
speak (vb) 33, 63-4, 84, 91, 154, 181, 184, 315, 331, 341, 498
– badly 577
– clearly 27, 274, 347, 349, 394
– right 244
– truth 27, 174-5, 275, 344, 347
– well 153, 256, 291, 351, 356, 363, 366, 370, 383, 396, 398, 416, 420, 452, 482, 516, 532, 540, 577
speech 488
–, speechless 544
speed 278
sperm 160, 174, 176, 181, 304, 318, 357, 480, 485
– and moisture 173
– and soul 181
–, blood decomposes/ feeds 174
–, blood rejoices in 387
–, cook 174
– enters womb 387
–, life of 486
– of dragon 426
–, power of 387
– turns into body with spirit 481
–, wash with 387
sphere, heavenly; *see also epistle* 92
spill 471
spirit(s) 32, 35, 38, 81, 176, 21, 229, 233, 253, 258, 279, 282, 292, 322, 344, 350-1, 371, 396, 402, 446, 493, 498, 537, 559
–, (2) two 310, 323, 438
–, (3) three 322
–, (4) four 546
–, (6) six 80
–, acquire 484
–, airy 362
– and body 233, 235, 323
– and body separated 170
– and cloud 215
– and fire 192
– and male escape 304
– and soul 122, 302
– and spirits 514
– and stone 172
– and vapour/ as vapour 190, 246-7
– appears 33, 35, 332, 336
– arise 200
– as dye 247
– as gum 172
– asks/ talks with spirit 33, 331-2
– as nature 533
– as subtle part 461
–, become 233, 164
– blows 278
–, bodies/ body take(s) ... (on/ quickly) 235 562
–, body solidifies 491
–, body turns into/ bodies become 539, 547
–, burn 379
– clings to body 322
– concealed in body 150, 322
–, conceal spirit(s) 33, 198, 239, 332, 511, 537
–, copper inhales … from moisture 481
– copper with body and 481
–, corrupted 281
– dries/ holds soul 154, 218
–, dryness, moisture, … and cloud 360
–, dyeing 129, 200, 223, 225-7, 436, 524, 543
–, dyeing … disappears 505
–, dyer 255
–, dyer-spirit 579
– dyes 214, 520
– dyes body 178, 233
– enter body 178
– enters soul 154
– escapes not 253
–, evasive 31
–, extract 150, 167, 198, 214, 243-4, 246, 255, 323
–, extract dyeing 521
–, extract … from bodies 190, 305, 496

–, extract … from body 369, 477, 488
–, extract … from hard one 215
–, extract … with fire 520
–, extract ... with spirit 488
–, female … embraces seeker 360
–, fighter turn into 396
–, fire-fighter 215
–, fix spirits 172
–, fugitive 46, 229, 231, 488, 503
– gets not burnt 513
–, hold 483
– holds body 296
–, Holy Spirit 11
–, enters/ is in spirit 154, 336
– in body/ inside bodies 214, 223
–, invisible 371
– leaves body 436
–, magnesia lets not escape 372
–, mix body with 580
–, moist 186, 198, 215, 247, 290, 402, 520-1
–, moist, pure black 580
–, natron and oil 465
–, natures become 539
–, nature turns figther into 446
– of bodies, flowers as 513
– of bodies separate 476
– of chrysocolla 253
– of copper 200
– of dye 168
– of dyeing body 558
– of eternal 231
– of fighter 396, 446
– of lead 461
– of mercury 490
– of nature 396, 446
– of second cinnabar 484
– of silver 37, 345
– of stone 231
– of Theosebeia 33, 332, 336, 340
– of things 246
– of Zosimos 33, 35-36, 331-2, 336, 339
– other 186, 222
– out of water of sulphur 286
– passes into every body 246
– penetrates 547
–, preserve 190
– remains 493
–, return … to body 488
–, sediments without 503
– separates from body 33, 322-3, 332, 439
–, separation of … from body 35
–, shining 393
– similar/ soul and similar 322, 514
–, soul, … and body 520
–, soul with 438
–, sperm turns into body with 481
– submerges in bodies 546
–, subtle; *see subtle* 178, 214
–, sulphur extracts 578
– take(s) 514, 521
–, take (dyeing) … from bodies/ body 246, 521
– turn ... into body 547
– turn ... into spirit 520
–, turn bodies into 521, 567
–, turn body into 164, 170, 179, 259, 296, 468, 491, 537
–, turn composed one into 546
–, turn copper into 41, 536, 576
–, turn into 222, 238, 297, 354, 446
–, turn into body and 369
–, turn nature into 356
–, turn operated into 562
–, turn shadow into 172
–, turn …s into bodies 567
–, turn ... into sulphurs 305
–, vapour extracts 533
spiritual 31, 34, 44, 109, 145, 162, 178, 234-5, 239, 334, 369, 438, 502, 560
– aspect 33
–, become 235, 322
– being(s) 78, 322
– copper 506
– dye 566
– meaning 94
–, nine 269
– part 436, 505
–, spiritual-dyeing 562
–, spirituality 322
– soul 369, 439
–, subtle- 225
– thing 37, 345, 560
–, turn 156, 457
–, turn into … water 501
spittle 226, 258, 535
–, magnesia, kohl and spittle of moon 324

– of the moon 128, 170, 172, 210, 226, 231, 242, 256, 324, 350, 418, 500, 568-9
– of the moon and aqzal 321
– of the moon and gum 454
– of the moon, aqzal (gold) and mercury 472, 500
splash 286, 467, 579
– ivory 475
– silver with water of gum 456
–, splashing natures 397
splendour 36, 37, 55, 157, 270, 280, 310, 336, 339, 342, 436, 523, 554
– of Theosebeia/ Zosimos 341
–, smoke with …, dye and colour 505
split (vb)/ splitting 200, 205-6, 507
spread 389, 399
spring (season) 236, 524
–, offspring 68, 203, 537
–, spring (source of water); see also well 458, 480, 488
sprout (vb) 41, 522
square 223-4, 312
squeaking 234
– disappears 301
– of lead-copper 498
– of tin 250-1, 551
–, remove 498, 565
squeeze out 47-8, 284
s-r-n; see sūrīn/ sūzīn
stable 224
stage; see also level 41, 361, 576
– of operation 46, 328
–, stages of work 61
stagnant 302
stand 49, 171, 344, 337
– upright 264, 276, 313, 329, 334, 414, 418, 421, 439, 442, 445, 477, 526, 544
Starr, P. 6, 8, 13, 26, 320
starry 151, 250, 297, 410
stars 63, 151, 222, 291, 305, 312-3
– and moon 291
–, colours of seven 450
–, rays of 465
–, sun, moon and 175
start 327
– work 281, 304, 349
state 53
statement; *see under books; see names of sages: Abīsiqūs; Ābullūn; Africanus; Agathodaimon; Asfīḫās; Alasardus, Badīsios; Bersius; Butitos; Democritus, Disqīus; Hermes; Isis; Maria; Mīdunah; Moses; Olympiodoros; Ostanes; Persian; Šīmās; Taūfīl; Theodorus; Zosimos; see student Tūīn* 152
– about names 161
– about operation 165
–, alchemical 93, 95
–, clear 519
–, completeness of 451
– confuses 353
–, different 145, 217, 294, 297
–, enigmatic 236, 297
–, extract from 519
–, similar 456
states (n) 544
– of colours 571
– of soul and body 539
statue(s) 37, 141, 229, 270, 276
–, (2) two 404, 448
–, (3) three 425
–, female 270
–, nine winged 517
– of Meritamun 10
– religious 316
steadfast 259
steal 316
steam with sulphur 504
stem 303
stick 47, 459, 469, 477
–, (2nd) second sticking 284
–, sticking 319
stir 321, 460, 504, 511-2
–, up 225, 292
stomach 47-8, 174, 300
–, food changes in 521
–, heat of 174
stone(s); *see also minerals* 41, 66, 93, 112, 148, 153, 167, 170, 176, 179, 197, 207-9, 225, 229, 231, 233, 239-40, 252-3, 254, 256, 259, 274, 280, 289, 294, 302, 304, 319, 321, 350, 358, 376, 387-8, 427, 451-2, 458, 463-5, 488, 507, 532, 539, 557, 566, 575-6
–, (1) one 267, 305, 534

–, (2) two 207
–, (2) two waters from ..., extract 382
–, (4) four corners, ... with 571
– absorbs gum 321
–, acacian/ ašqunī 231
–, amalgamated 564
– and water 464
–, another 571
– are dyed 566
–, become 210, 295, 525, 571
–, birth of 367
–, black 367
–, born every year 481
–, born from copper and silver 566
– breaks quickly 573
–, change 456
–, chrysocolla as 462
–, claudianus–stone 399
–, closed 166
–, coagulate … with water and gum 447
–, colour of 521
–, composition of 456
– contains gum 172
–, cook white … in sun 490
–, copper and 275, 398
–, copper, lead and honoured 265-7, 274, 282, 375, 546
–, coppery 493
–, cracked 317
–, creation of 117
– de-/ increases 166, 173
–, destroy 156, 173, 491, 524-5
– dissolve(s)/ melts 210, 249, 274, 282
– does works 238
–, dry 531
–, dye (of/ for) 204, 256, 319, 375, 492, 496
–, eternal 238
–, etesian 24, 46-7, 212, 252, 282, 304, 325, 368, 464-5, 507, 515, 521
–, existence of 161
–, explanation of 471
–, extract …. from metal 209
–, ferrous 500
–, fiery 201, 380, 398-9
–, fragmented 234, 566
–, frog-stone 361-2
– generated from copper and silver 539
–, glue of 401
–, golden 22, 234, 375, 388, 403, 471, 515
–, greatest 367
–, green 207
–, gummy 388
–, hard 237, 388
–, hard, precious, dry, bitter 237
–, heavy 166
–, hide 259
–, hollow 176, 204, 209, 231, 388, 395, 571
–, honour(ed) 128, 171, 242, 263, 270, 274, 282, 364, 376, 483, 492, 546, 571, 581
–, illuminate 471
–, imprisoned 489
– in cooking 515
–, iron 425
–, know 508
–, kohl- 472, 500
–, lamp-like 209
–, litharge and similar to 464
–, look for/ seek 367, 464-5
–, magnetic stone 581
–, mercury into 356
–, metallic 195
–, moisture dried up of 560
–, mother-of-pearl 280
–, names of/ named 128, 172, 237, 256, 259, 375, 560
–, stone-not-stone 41, 128, 170-1, 176, 213, 225, 231, 236, 238, 281, 575
–, nourish 252
– of copper 483
– of gold 483, 561, 580
– of philosophers 40, 62
– of ring 500
– of sages 39, 44, 117, 128-9
– of silver 484
–, operate on 381, 508
–, origin of 368
–, other 41, 576
–, part of 275
–, pound/ pounding of 448, 495
–, precious 176
–, purple- 148, 572
–, pyrite 196, 234, 252
–, red 259, 488, 544, 568
–, roots of 488
–, round 277
–, royal 209

–, rub 539
–, secret of 166
–, shining, brilliant, splendid 532
–, silvery 233, 252, 295, 354, 528
–, single 240-1
–, soft, yellow 167
–, solidifies 447, 480, 484, 495
–, soluble 484
–, spirit of 231
–, strong 238
–, sulphur, … and poison 153
–, symbol of stone 21, 129
– -tablet 401
–, tin-stone 277
–, turn clod into 161
–, turn copper into 521
–, turn into 145, 243-4, 475, 481, 491, 549, 558, 573, 581
–, turn into honoured 375
–, turn silver into 156, 564
–, turn … into dust 557
–, water-stone 427
–, weights of 274
– which is born every year 571
–, white 173, 233, 490, 530, 565-6, 574
– with water and gum 495
–, work of/ … of/ for work 207-8, 462
stop escaping 16, 465-6
story/ stories 36, 58, 90, 126, 334, 464
strength 63, 161, 222, 238, 249, 340, 491, 523-4, 581
– of fire; see fire
strengthen (vb) 187, 234 ,492, 499, 519, 523, 547, 554, 557
– broth 490
– fire; see fire
stretch hands out 556
stripes 141
–, golden, with red 36, 81, 341
strong 28, 63, 68, 151, 161, 172, 175, 178, 181, 202, 221-2, 224, 233, 239, 255, 286, 297, 311, 313, 317, 323, 329, 331, 355, 357, 364, 380, 382, 398-9, 418, 491-2, 499, 505, 508, 513, 522-3, 524-5, 529, 537, 552, 554
– against fire 169
– and weak 480
–, become stronger 233
–, becomes/ make 192, 569
– body 172
– dye 567
– fire; see fire
– heat 522
– in essence 169
– one/ weak one 35, 336
–, stronger; see also fire, stronger 35, 169, 171, 177, 210, 223-4, 238-9, 254, 249, 275, 287, 311, 336, 364, 370, 474, 481, 486, 491, 493, 499, 508, 522, 525, 557, 561, 566, 570, 572-4
–, strongest 170, 175
– strongly 523
–, strong, powerful, dry and hot 174
–, weak conquers the 169
structure, coherent/ new 85, 115
struggle 225
student(s); *see also Theosebeia* 6, 18, 27-8, 55, 74, 78, 80, 85, 92, 96-8, 109, 112, 114-5, 117-8, 133, 135, 137-8, 146, 152, 158-9, 231, 277, 326, 329, 347, 360, 432-3, 461, 487, 523, 531
– and master/ teacher 33, 35, 51, 78, 118
– Būsīūs 534
– of Agathadaimon 531, 579
– of Democritus 27, 347
– of Hermes 145-6, 148, 231, 299, 329, 451, 468, 571
– of Ostanes 326
– of science 147, 152
–, statement of 534
– Tūīn 534
study (vb, n); *see also read, ponder* 10, 61, 84, 123, 147-8, 260, 303
–, deepen 11
– of alchemy 12
stupidity 577
style 51, 133, 137
subhuman 64
subject 114
submerge 173, 222, 233, 245, 255, 436, 440, 446, 508, 562, 568
– in body/ into bodies 245, 265, 369, 470, 538, 546, 557, 566
– inside of body 509
–, poison 186, 265
– torturer …s in body 470

–, water submerges into body 557
substance(s) 69, 94, 117, 126
–, alchemical 138
–, arcane 74, 81, 84, 130
–, concrete/ symbolic 69, 128
– of body 223
subtle 63, 153, 161-2, 164, 179, 218, 222, 226, 286-7, 317, 369, 427, 436, 469, 575, 578
– and thick 223
– body remains 502
–, dye 510
– dyer 153
– one 227
– part(s) 47, 154, 161, 197, 218, 223, 228, 279, 298, 303, 369, 395, 436, 461, 498, 502, 505-6, 520
– spirit/ -spiritual 178, 214, 225
–, subtlest 179
– thinking 477
– thought 499
– water 282
success 281, 516
– of work and measures of fire 492
–, successful 260
suckle 122
sucks, (body/ bee) 154, 161
Suda 10, 20
Sudanian earth 209
suffer (vb); *see also effort; hardship; harm; disease* 119, 129, 305, 340, 451, 535
–, copper 373
– from work 396
– in operation 304
–, suffering 29, 41, 98, 145, 219, 382, 405, 580
sufficient 294, 387
sugarcane 201, 267, 374
suitability 498
suitable 63, 151, 157, 162, 260, 275, 287, 316, 324, 360, 406-7, 494, 498-9, 540-1, 542, 546, 562, 577
– and harmonious 162
– for marriage 375
– for mixing of sand 375
– one 168-9
sulphur 153, 170, 187, 192, 196, 207, 232, 244, 251, 269, 272, 282, 297, 299, 300, 302, 320, 323, 369, 374, 382, 400, 466, 476, 483, 510, 537-8
–, (1) one 185, 301, 552
–, (1st) first 284, 295, 301
–, (fem.) 373, 467, 509
– acacian/ and āsqūnīa 447, 470
–, amount of 407
– and copper 350
– and dye 247
– and lime 460
– and magnesia 325
– and magnet 321
– and mercury 260, 287
– and slack 388
–, arsenic, ... and sandarach 325, 418
– as cloud 384
–, ascunian 447
as dusts 289
–, ash of 501
– as torturer of her husband 509
– as white cinnabar 373
–, black 568
– blackens body 509
– body 570
–, burn bodies with (soft) 286, 376, 497-8, 506
–, burn/ compose … with copper 288, 501
–, burn copper with 497
– burns 175
– burns not/ gets not burnt 267, 407
–, cinnabar as incombustible 373
–, cloud and water of 288
–, colocynth, sūzīn and 552
–, companions of 552
–, composed/ composition of 296, 320, 384-5, 442, 456, 506
–, contain 513
–, cook (with) (pure water of) 386, 493, 578
–, dark 400
–, dyes/ dyed/ gives colour 251, 461, 504
–, extract from 420
–, extract pure water of 516
– extracts spirit 578
–, ferment of gold as incombustible 386
– fights fire 541
–, firewood of white 507
–, fugitive 365
– gets not burnt 213, 362-3, 493, 513

–, gum, mercury and 407
–, gum, ... and herb 186
–, half of 374
–, hanging 418
–, heavenly 498
– holds sulphur 465
–, incombustible 235, 248, 250, 258, 267, 363, 386, 393, 493, 528, 548
– joins sulphurs 241
– likes all things 540
– makes black 396, 446
– makes copper white 552
–, male 247
– meets sulphur 160, 178
–, mercuries with water of …, gum and saffron 430
–, mercury and pure water of 434
–, mercury turns … into rust 250
–, mix 289, 302, 324, 377, 532, 541
–, mix cloud with water of 189
– mixes with sulphur (and destroys) 284, 323
–, moistures into 515
–, names for water of 247
–, nature of 397
–, nature with 578
– of cinnabar 542
– of sages 170
–, operate on mercury with white 379
–, operated/ operation of 397, 455
–, origin of 407
–, other 301, 554
–, pound white … with sandarach 325
–, power of water of 286, 490
– prevents from escaping 541
–, pure 164, 383, 410, 420
–, pure water of 244, 284, 386, 429, 434, 459, 460, 477, 516, 521
–, pyrite, … and salt 196
–, red 250-1, 269, 373, 379-80, 554
–, second 284
–, single 284
–, soft 296, 501
– solidifies 548
–, solidify water of 548
–, spirit out of water of 286
–, steam with 504
– stronger than fire 254
–, mercury, ... and white lead 260
–, mercury, tin, … and pyrite 384
–, stone, ... and poison 153
–, suzin, ..., colocynth, and pure water 299
–, Treatise of the Sulphur; see also book(s) 185
–, turn body into 258
–, turn mercury, … und gold into dyeing poison 287
– turns fighter into fugitive 446
– turns into dust 528
–, turn ... into water 192
– unites with sulphur 466
–, water of 128-9, 164, 172, 175, 179, 183, 185-8, 192, 198, 199, 210, 224-6, 245, 247-8, 253-6, 261-2, 274, 283-7, 289, 302, 323, 361, 396, 400, 407, 446, 468, 476, 489-90, 521, 540, 548, 551-2, 578
–, water of pure 410
–, water of ..., poison and arsenic 283
–, weight of the 267
–, white 192, 250, 269, 301, 325, 365, 377, 397, 497-8, 541, 552
sulphurs 186, 190-1, 193, 349, 369, 476, 543
–, (2) two 160, 178, 212-3, 284, 301, 457, 459
–, all 552
– and copper 296, 501
– and mercury 416
–, arsenic and sandarach 467
– as fugitives 475
– burn copper 501, 506
–, change 456
– destroy 284
–, disappear 296
–, dry 198
–, dye 190
– escape quickly 467
–, extract (vb) 369
–, fiery 397
–, fire turn … into dyes 494
–, fugitive(s) as 398, 475
– get dyed 475
– hold fugitives 475
– hold sulphurs 199, 225, 227, 232, 241, 325, 515, 532
–, mix … with copper 200
–, mix … with sulphurs 468
–, separate … from copper 501

–, spirits turn into 305
–, sulphur joins 241
–, The Sulphurs (book) 116-7, 132
–, turn … into broth 398
–, turn … into incombustible dyes 522
–, turn … into smoke 200
–, weight of the 191
sulphury/ sulphuric
– bodies, arsenic and sandarach unite with magnesia 468
– body 468, 570
– iron 288
– water 179, 373, 538
summarize (vb) 44, 47-8, 80-1, 133, 196, 199, 294, 344
– work 351
summary 19, 24, 33, 113, 152, 194, 196, 199, 357, 374-5, 452
– of books 261
summer 152, 236, 405-6, 453, 524
– and colour 511
– and moisture 511
– as fire 152
–, heat of 524
sun 10, 34, 36, 38-9, 58-60, 63, 65, 78, 92-3, 105, 120, 129-30, 167, 173, 192, 222, 229, 247, 252-3, 255, 277, 279, 281, 292, 295, 305, 311, 318, 320, 337, 364, 371, 406, 485, 489, 494, 500, 506, 531, 567, 571, 575
– and dew 481, 528, 575
– and fire 494
– and gold 463
– and moisture 318
– and moon 59, 535
– and shadow 281-2
– and water 128, 159, 160-1
–, archetype 39
– as āqusṭus 473
– as gentle fire 522
–, ash of 509
– as red copper 282
–, big 192, 522
–, blackness of 482
–, changeable of 470
–, cook white stone in 490
– descends 281, 367, 570
– disc 108
– dries 501
–, fecundates 128, 242
–, fiery 218
–, fire and 192
–, halo of 429
–, heart of 238, 360, 494, 522-3, 530, 554
– hero 92
–, hot 547
–, interpretation of 473
– -king 39, 59, 61
–, large 305
–, leave in 57, 127, 157, 485
–, light of 305
–, nature of 494, 522, 535
–, nourishes/ nourishment for 218, 512
– of sages 160
– on head 30-2, 35, 37, 64, 67, 84, 78-9, 92, 109-10, 108, 141, 391, 421, 439, 444, 477, 526
–, operate with 532
–, pound with 129, 395, 564
–, rays of 258
–, renewal of 113
– rise(s)/ rising of 356, 450, 530
–, Sol 32, 40
–, sunray 535
–, sun, the moon, and the stars 175
–, sun, water, air 298
–, Sun (zodiac) 58, 311-3
–, transformer of 197
–, turn into ray of 305
–, turn … into silver 173
–, with 305
–, work cannot be completed without 494
Sungod (Re) 54, 78, 80, 92, 109, 127
–, journey of 39, 80, 109
superior 407
– redness 533, 579
supernatural 97
superstitious 455
support 7, 13, 22, 74, 85, 96, 112, 114, 134-5, 390, 395
–, supporter 227
surface 374
– of composition 368
– of water 283, 499
sūrīn/ sūzīn 349, 406, 454, 552
surrender 31, 57, 127, 157

surrounded 130, 146
survey 125
suspend(ed) 48, 300, 339, 488
– furnace 579
–, suspension 32, 328
sustain 363
sūzīn; see *sūrīn*
swallow (vb) 48, 300, 318, 541
swear; see also oath 143, 147, 158, 213, 217, 242, 272, 327, 358, 383, 398, 431, 535, 543
sweat 357
sweet 129, 291, 483, 539
– from salty 291
–, sweeten 575
–, sweeten pyrite 538
–, sweeten sea 292
–, sweeten with sun and dew 575
–, sweetness 509
– water 318, 323, 509, 531
swindler 305
swirl up 513
sword 358
–, of fire 370
symbol(s)/ symbolic; see also allegory; codename; sign 12, 20, 31-42, 54-5, 64, 66-7, 69, 79-1, 108-9, 126-31, 133-4, 135-8, 158, 180, 241, 325, 350, 365, 555
– alchemy/ alchemical 12,33, 92-5, 136, 138
–, amplify; see also ponder 92, 95
– and allegory 85, 91
– and codename 93-5, 126, 131
– chemical/ substance 33, 39, 44, 128
– content 67, 85, 113
– desribe/ explain/ speak/ mention 137, 358, 474, 484, 500, 575
– for process of transformation 37
– for blackness 129
–, key 24, 126
– images/ illustration/ pictures 10, 19, 58, 112-3, 118
–, interpretation as 457
– language/ representation of 40, 93, 500
–, lime as 457
–, material side of 126
–, meaning of 91, 93-5, 111, 126, 138
– name(s)/ name with symbols 22, 138, 350, 365
– nature/ nature of symbols 85, 90, 95, 111, 129, 132, 135, 138
– of alabaster 117
– of ascunia (gum)/ murderess of husband 126, 128-9, 131
– of copper, gold and silver 469
– of inner god-man 109
– of mercurius 130
– of quicklime 117
– of stone 21, 38, 129
–, reconciling 136
– reduce 92
–, religious-symbolic 68-9, 80, 95, 122
– substance 128
–, symbolically 53, 92, 358, 387, 484
–, symbolism 39, 59, 68, 125-6, 130
–, symbolize 31-2, 39, 67, 79, 84, 109, 134
–, symbolon 91
– teaching 98
–, uniting quality of 21
–, write in 138, 241, 345, 387, 555
Syncellus, George 22
synodos 58
Syriac 11, 17-22, 26-7, 94, 97, 99, 135, 137
–, Greek, … and Arabic alchemy 6
– language 21
–, manuscript 21
–, Syria, people of 574
– text(s) 11, 17, 20-1, 23, 27, 125
Syrnas 62

–T–

Tīmīs 529
tablet(s) 91, 259, 401
Tafsir (book) 26
tail 31, 109, 307, 450
–, dragon/ serpent eating its/ with ... in mouth 50, 93, 109, 263, 318, 371
talc 187
–, talcine 233, 376
–, talcous 350
tales; see also fairy tales; story 182, 334, 344
talisman 203, 290, 450, 463
talk 150, 155, 179, 336, 344, 357
–, spirit …s with spirit 33, 332
talqine 395

tar 195, 252, 499, 568
– and gum 277
– and vessel 158
– becomes water 277
–, clear, pure 277
–, cook/ dissolve with remedy 158
–, dissolving of 568
–, mix copper, … and silver 499
–, pure white 581
–, turn into/ become like 293, 320, 325
taste 49, 156, 166, 168, 190, 215, 223, 291, 381, 401, 436, 488, 512, 514
–, different 166
– of body 477
– of companions 191, 497
– of cooking 505
– of copper 200
– of honey 49, 514
– of things 496
Tat (son of Hermes) 150, 543-4
tātlūtā 209
Taūfīl 361, 513, 523
Taurus (sign of zodiac) 494
teach (vb); *see also teaching(s)* 23, 148-9, 176, 258, 284, 352, 365, 393, 398, 463, 533
– companion 362
–, nature ...es 577
–, work ...es 145
teacher; *for Democritus and Zosimos as teachers, see Zosimos* 10, 18, 98, 112, 117, 196, 291, 299, 397, 432, 461, 534
– and student 33, 35, 51, 84, 117
–, Christ as 28
–, inner; *see also guru* 27
–, reaching of 19
teaching(s) 7, 376, 432
–, (1st) first 526
– in (12) twelve steps 81
–, aim of Zosimos' 29
–, authentic 21
–, coherent/ illustated 113
–, enigmatic 111
– Epistle of Teaching 462
–, essence of 11, 134
– of Zosimos 11, 18-9, 21, 26-9, 32, 48, 61, 63, 74, 81, 85, 90, 98, 110-12, 115-7, 124, 132-5, 137, 217, 451, 526, 543
–, personal 117
–, sages' way of …/ veiling 349-50
– symbolic 98
tears, flowing like 401
tease 323
technical 132
temple 10-1, 21, 29, 99, 123
ten (10) 160, 224, 509
–, (1) one wins over 170, 326
–, (10.000) ten thousand 67, 369
– as colours 326
–, become 278
–, Book of Ten Keys 532
– companions 273
– days 531
– Keys (book) 28
– measures 502
– ounces 506
– things 403
– times 158
– -treatise 45
– weights 568
tendency to escape 550
tender 145
tenth (10th) 10, 45, 54, 345, 462, 529, 543, 581
–, (1/10) one tenth 258
–, (10th) tenth century 94, 125, 133
terms, difficult 349
terror 48
test 28, 158, 229, 237, 432, 459, 523, 540, 542
– by touch 557
– glue of gold 535
– with fire 554
testicles, (3) three 473
testimony *28-9, 137, 144, 148, 194*
–, (1) one, ... is 355
–, testimonies of (statment of) sages 144, 148, 194, 580
text(s); *see also book(s); date; letter; origin; original; poeml* 5-7, 12-3, 18-22, 24, 26, 28, 31, 34, 36, 38-9, 44, 46, 49, 51, 55, 58, 60-1, 64, 66, 73, 78, 80-1, 84, 90-9, 107, 109, 111, 113-20, 123-6, 130-8, 140
– and picture(s)/ image(s) 74, 81, 84-5, 96-8, 135-8
–, Arabic 10, 21, 24, 73, 110, 132

–, authentic 9
–, complete 26, 45, 69
–, description of pictures 19
–, edited/ edition(s) 12, 17-8
–, Greek 21, 23-7, 64, 96-7, 117-8, 122, 124, 126, 132-4, 137
–, group of 137
–, illustrated 26
–, known 27
–, Latin 125
–, missing 210, 512
– of extraverted/intraverted nature 132
– of religious–symbolic alchemy 12, 26
– of Zosimos 6, 64, 135, 137
– on alchemy/ alchemical 17
–, Peri aretes 27
–, related 5
–, Syriac 11, 17, 20-1, 23, 27, 125
texture 576
thank 266, 366, 432-3
themselves 356, 492
Theatrum chemicum 130
theme 84, 94, 113, 119, 135
Theodorus 152
Theophilius 54-5, 381, 563
Theosebeia; *see also my lady; Zosimos* 21, 35, 37-8, 45, 73-4, 78-80, 84-5, 93, 97, 110, 112-5, 117-20, 127-8, 132-5, 137-8, 230, 307, 439
– as author 96
– asks for explanation/ desire for understanding/ about dialogue with Zosimos 6-7, 19, 51, 144, 322, 324, 327-8, 331, 345, 357-8, 364-5, 390, 402, 406, 416, 418, 452, 477, 484, 488
–, as queen/ priestess 20
–, divine 35
– afraid of mistakes 454
– embracing Zosimos; see also Zosmos, love for 264
–, big/ greater/ huge/ small 64, 78-9
–, hand of 544
–, head of 444
–, identity of 20
– image/ picture of; *see also picture of Zosimos and/ or Theosebeia* 35-6, 93, 101, 141, 263-4, 276, 306, 313, 329, 332, 337, 342, 345, 347, 391, 402, 407, 411, 414, 416, 418, 421, 425-6, 428-9, 431, 434-6, 439-40, 442, 444-5, 448, 477, 517, 526, 544, 556
–, life of 20
– lived outside Egypt 20
–, name of 61
– offending Zosimos 322, 382-3, 420, 447
–, picture made by Zosimos for her 19, 29, 85, 101, 212
–, plan of 327, 328
–, relationship of Zosimos and 19, 148, 155-6, 173, 212, 242, 315, 322, 559
–, role of (... as interlocutor) 114, 116
–, silvery 37, 345
–, spirit of 33, 332, 336, 340
–, student of Zosimos 18, 74, 78, 80, 84-5, 92, 97-9, 109, 112, 114, 117-8, 133, 137-8
–, tomb of 20
– warned by Zosimos 21
– wins over Zosimos 344
–, with moon on head; *see moon*
thick 145, 163-4, 179-80, 214, 225, 227, 246, 293, 320, 362, 442, 456, 546, 579
– and solid 546
– and subtle 223
–, become 235, 530
– body 178, 226
–, decompose 371
– fat 521
– one dies 476
– part/ parts 161, 190, 218, 223, 395, 498, 514, 520-1
– part into ashes 476
– part of body 214, 395
– sea 530
–, turn 192
thicken(s) 233, 502, 563-4, 575-6
–, nature thickens 558
thickness 246
–, earthly 369
– is destroyed 233
– of body 233
–, remove 254
thief 289
thin 293, 489, 525
–, dye 471
–, making thin 294

thing; *see also things; adjectives of things, e.g. colours; hot; cold; moist; dry; hard; soft; triangular* 63, 85, 143, 155, 164, 173, 175, 179, 204, 241, 254, 257-8, 260, 296, 299, 323-4, 344-5, 358, 393, 446, 450, 453, 460, 466, 469, 484, 486, 489, 494, 520-1, 548, 566
–, (1) one ... / is one ... 50, 62, 160, 162, 170-1, 174, 178, 187, 189, 194-6, 206-7, 210, 221, 224, 227, 247-8, 251, 265-7, 288-9, 294, 301, 304, 322, 324, 349, 355-8, 362, 365, 371, 373, 379, 397, 399, 439, 457, 498, 509, 538, 542, 560, 580-1
–, (1) one ..., become 158
–, (1) one ...., turn into 172, 181, 576
–, (2) two become (1) one 489, 491
–, (3) three names for (1) one 266
–, another 90, 397, 580
–, black/ red 522
–, cast 304
– cooked 189
– despised 144
–, dissolve 535
–, dry 167, 302, 304
–, dyes 195
–, eternal 228
–, every (dry/ moist) 247, 362
–, first 145
– good for dyeing 41, 575
–, hide/ hidden 170, 359
–, insignificant 144
–, know/ known 228, 367
–, luminous 512
–, moist 162, 198, 247, 304
–, single 173, 186, 198, 399
–, spiritual 37, 345, 560
–, terrible 577
–, true 150
– untouchable 258
–, white, pure 283
– without power 378
things; *see also manifold* 29, 129, 142-3, 146-7, 150, 153, 162, 166, 180, 182-4, 187, 197, 202, 206, 221, 226, 239, 241, 243, 247, 250-1, 253-4, 256-7, 261, 265, 273, 275, 284, 289, 299, 301, 310, 329, 334, 341, 344, 349, 353, 358, 365, 374, 382, 400-1, 410, 420, 451, 454-9, 461-3, 468-9, 480, 484, 488, 491, 498, 524, 539, 543-4, 559, 566
–, (1) one ...., all and/ ... are one/ turn into one / one nature and all/ many 81, 161-2, 173, 240, 294, 326
–, (2) two 191, 223, 256, 275, 386, 403, 521, 529
–, (3) three 160, 224, 279, 323, 371, 411, 418, 462
–, mix (3) three 324
–, (7) seven 269, 440, 540, 541
–, (10) ten 403
–, all 63, 81, 157, 162, 244, 324, 397, 540
–, all ... come together in magnesia 351
–, abound ... in water 560
– and analogies/ analogy 153, 178, 281
, any 192
– as indidivual 152
–, asked 331
–, ašqunīā 374
– as sand 560
– as stone 560
– as water 560
–, best of all 26, 157
–, black 317
–, blackness of 167
–, bodily 461
–, burn 496
–, cloud coagulates 252
–, colours of 238
–, compare 223
–, composed 256
–, cook 492
–, crown of all 367
–, describe ... by analogy 174
–, despised 162, 196
–, destroy; *see also manifold* 249
–, different 143, 188, 223-4, 322, 350, 511
–, dissolve 414
– dissolved and transformed by lime 510
–, dry 297
–, dye 461, 481
– enter in work 561
–, equal 272, 440
–, escaping 378
–, evil 122
–, extract from 81, 159

–, extract … from magnesia 156
–, fragment 287, 496
–, fugitive/ as fugitives 49
–, good 154
–, gum of all 401
–, hold on to 490
– in accordance/ agrement (with each other) 152, 418
–, inferior 29, 455
–, invented 206, 559
–, know/ knowledge of 160, 169, 397, 477
–, make yellow 489
–, many 81, 148, 150-1, 162-3, 165, 181, 187, 192, 194, 201, 205, 208, 252, 258, 273, 291, 294, 296, 359, 368, 375, 381-2, 394, 452, 483-4, 439, 542, 580-1
– marry in sea 380
–, mix/ mixing of 144, 146, 159, 246-7, 275, 286, 289, 360, 381, 525, 580
–, moist 198
–, name/ named 212, 224, 304
–, needed 227
– of composition 161
–, other 158, 170, 191, 260, 266, 268, 272, 358, 374
–, pound 318, 513, 533
–, present 156
–, pure/ impure 293
–, put things in context 328
–, raise 502
–, red 252
–, rejected 28, 455
–, rest of 381
– should enter work 434
–, similar 197, 252, 281
–, spirits of 246
–, spiritual part of 436, 505
–, suitable 63, 316
–, taste of 496
–, true 559
–, turn all … into water 399
–, turn red 269
–, turn ... into vapour 531
–, unite 394
–, various 44, 305, 371, 465, 513, 515, 576
–, wash 511
–, wash, bleach and purify 503
–, white 252
– without nature 200
–, work is in 156
–, work on 23, 149
–, worldly 285
thinking; *see also thought* 192, 297, 310, 315, 327, 350
–, determined 477
–, subtle 469, 477
–, think (vb) 227
third (3rd) 159, 275, 495, 525, 570
– book 262, 344
– century 27, 78, 113, 122
– elixir 319, 505-6
– Epistle 111, 115-6, 125
– fire 492
– of weight 484, 510
– one 153
– part 491
– picture 263, 329
– season 522
– series 84, 86-89
– time 506, 570
thirst 364
–, die not of 291
– of fired clay 490
–, thirsty 402, 483
thirteenth (13th) 41, 431, 563, 581
–, books 18
–, century 92, 110, 138
Thomas, Acts of Thomas (apocryphes) 90
thorns 55, 128, 172, 401
Thot 91, 543
– -Hermes–Mercurius 78
thought(s) 11, 21, 115, 118, 180, 331, 397
–, alchemical 123
–, alien 118
–, bad 354
–, birth of 305
–, born in blood 305
–, Gnostic 123
–, head collects the 575
–, pre-Hellenistic/ pre-Islamic (ideas) 136
–, see not 575
–, subtle 499
thousand (1.000) 67, 272, 365, 377, 497, 515, 580
–, (1.000) thousands and thousands 237
–, (1.800) thousand eight hundred 110

– names 128
– places/ answers and questions 97
– times 146, 368
throw on silver 431
three (3); *see also triangular* 31, 74-5, 114, 175, 222, 226-7, 243, 293, 351, 396, 401, 425, 446, 462, 467, 469, 500, 544, 550
–, (1/3) one third 547, 570
–, (2/3) two-third 504, 570, 572
–, (1) one of 325, 508
–, (1) one, ... and 160, 265-6, 424, 439, 473, 513, 547
–, (1) one, ... are/ become/ turn into 273, 325, 452, 550
– (1) one body, ... in 407, 411, 414, 416, 426, 428, 429, 431, 435-6
–, (1) one, mix … to 367
–, (2) two are/ become 263, 265, 325
–, (2) two from three 370, 550
–, (2) two, name 274
–, (2) two, ... and 269, 324, 513
–, (3rd) third 407, 570, 581
–, (3rd) third book 19
–, (3rd) third century 9-10
–, (3rd) third Epistle (of Zosimos) 114-5, 125
– (3rd) third series of pictures 84
–, (3) three and (4) four 224
–, (4) four from 370
–, (4) four, ... and 379, 513
–, (4) four, turn … into 269
– (4th) fourth, ...-fold and 224
–, (5) five turn into 273
–, (360) threee hundred sixty 54
–, (365) three hundred sixty-five 208
– angles 507
– birds 79, 263
– bodies 265, 274
– branches 84, 447-8, 495
– castings 454
– colours 401
– days 188, 293, 320, 475, 503, 519, 568
–, dye … times 473
– dimensional 90
–, divide into 570
– escape not 324
– faces 418, 557
– -fold 224, 231, 280, 319, 351, 372, 452, 472, 475
– -folded bag 472
– -folded changer 470
– -fold with benefit; *see also Hermes* 360, 373, 461, 464, 473
– -fold with letters 475
–, group of 80
–, gum with … colours 401
– -headed 30-2
– legs 440
–, made of 324
– men 141, 407, 411, 414, 416, 421, 426
– mercuries/ mercury 21, 84, 109, 402, 414, 416, 418, 424
–, mix … things 324
–, mortars 406, 454, 511
– names 266, 462
– nights 188
– openings 380, 381
– operations 452-3
– ounces 271, 317-9, 321
– parts 153, 265-7, 270, 277, 279, 282, 436, 465, 505
– persons 428-9, 431, 433, 435-6, 442, 44-5, 526
– pictures 80
– puffs 459
– qintar 471
– ropes 141
– rutl 471
– series of pictures 111, 115, 135
– spirits 109, 322, 439
– statues 141, 425
– sticks 517
– testicles 470, 473
– things 160, 224, 279, 323, 371, 411, 418, 462
– times 31, 457, 465, 503, 546
– trees 556
– versions 117
– waters 473
–, weights of 275
thresh 303
throw (vb) 321, 411, 455, 509
– away 512, 557
– back 47, 300
Thutmosis IV 108
thyme, wild 503

tie 141, 307, 517, 526
– soul 290
– up 142
Timīs 355, 529
time 305, 347
–, (1) one 465
–, (1st) first 212, 505
–, (1) one ..., at 407, 568, 578
–, (2) two times 506
– (2nd) second 47, 206, 506
–, (3) three times 457, 465, 503, 546
–, (3rd) third 506, 570
–, (4/5) four/ five times 504, 471, 511
–, (4) four periods of 522
–, (6) six times 299, 486-7, 489, 500, 569
–, (7) seven times 120, 156, 158, 278, 283, 436, 471, 483, 489, 500, 505-6, 513, 529, 532, 558-61, 569, 575
–, (10) ten times 158
–, (1.000) thousand times 146, 368
–, end of 25, 155
–, few times 493
–, Islamic times 9, 25, 113
–, long 90, 171, 210, 216, 351, 356, 487, 496, 501, 503-4, 508, 512, 542, 569
–, many times 149, 168, 170, 243, 251, 280, 384, 487, 528, 569, 573
– of changing 156
– of completeness 557
– of completion of whitening 189
– of work 487
– of Zosimos 10, 20, 28, 64, 98, 118, 122-3, 130
–, several times 162, 167-8, 241, 247-8, 266, 270, 277, 283, 310, 317, 322, 368, 373, 460, 473, 481, 497, 529, 539, 542, 557, 562
–, uncountable times 150
tin 158, 184, 197, 235, 245, 250-1, 261, 272-3, 277, 288, 298, 378, 398, 458, 460, 466, 530, 546, 565
– and alum 250
– and copper 430
– and human being 235
– and lead 298
– and lead-copper 325
– and mercury; *see also parable of* 21, 226, 399, 426, 466
– and white lead 260
– becomes mercury 541, 546
–, burnt 190
–, cast 394
–, colour of 252
– contains male 235
–, copper, iron, … and lead 287
–, copper, … and body of magnesia 549
– corrupted with lead 394
–, decay of 487
– dyes all bodies 460
–, filings of 278
–, gold, … and mercury 278
–, (heat of) copper, (iron), lead and 293, 301, 403
– leaves not 468
–, loves slave girl 458
–, mercury and copper 455, 472
–, mercury of … clings to cinnabar 403
–, mercury, …, sulphur and pyrite 384
–, mortar of 395
– named lead 273
– of the people 546
–, operation of 377
–, our 546
–, pure 168, 361
–, solidify body of magnesia with 471
–, solidify mercury in 147
–, squeaking of 250-1, 551, 565
– suitable for dyeing 546
–, tinny 208
–, turn … into clod 158
–, (un)touchable 403
–, weight of 274
–, white lead as subtle tin 461
tired 240, 265
title 21-2, 73, 91, 114
–, (un)touchable 403
–, title-names 269
together
–, bring 160, 164, 185, 310
–, come 298, 485, 546
tomb 56, 127, 157, 217, 277, 480
– for the dragon 56, 127, 157
– of Theosebeia 20
– of Zosimos 344
tongue 322, 512
–, burn 512

tool(s) 13, 31, 179
top 66-7, 198, 230, 262, 488
– of stick 517
torture (vb) 40, 323, 334, 336, 339, 358, 396, 439, 470, 536
– body 190
–, nature …s fighter 446
–, natures which 470
– not 447, 509
– of/ with fire 171-2
– soul with body 235
–, stand 171
–, torturing 172, 396
torturer 397, 470
– and dyer 447
– and tortured 396, 446
– enters bodies 192
– in body 233
– kills husband 172
– of (her) husband 128, 172, 233, 277, 354, 363, 427, 509
– submerges in body 470
totality 92
touch 239, 393, 488, 531
–, by 229, 557
–, touchable 258, 393, 403
–, untouchable/ not touchable 145, 214, 258, 393, 399, 403, 482, 520, 543, 562, 566
town(s) 213, 215
track 283
–, right 318
tradition(s) 24, 35, 68, 99, 113, 116, 118
–, alchemical 97
–, iconographic 99
transference 37, 45, 138
–, counter- 138
–, Psychology of Transference 59
transform (vb) 53, 81, 109, 138, 176, 268, 299, 313, 326, 549
– natures 177, 277, 298
– perception 10
– soul 53
– state of things 510
–, work …s natures 299
transformation(s); *see also process* 40, 74, 80, 84, 99, 123, 137-8, 313, 494
– of magnesia 81
– of silver 407
–, process of 39
–, psychological 33, 68
–, weights of the 568
transitions 10
translation 6, 18, 25-6, 58, 73, 90, 128, 140
–, Arabic/ of Arabic text 8, 12, 27, 47, 61, 68
–, directly/indirectly authenticated 132
–, English 5, 13, 74
– from Greek of Greek text /book 7, 25-6, 68, 96-7, *113-5, 118, 122*, 125, 132, 135, 137
– of a Zosimos text 21, 25, 73
– of chrysocolla 243
– of Pyrite 252
–, translate (vb) 5, 12, 112
–, translator(s) 17, 140
transmission of alchemy 17
–, transmit (vb) 22, 96
transpersonal 36, 64
treasure(s) 26, 297, 450-51, 501, 507
–, greatest 370, 556
– house 389
– of God 180
–, treasury 203, 204
treat 300, 324, 464, 579
–, fruits of treating 504
– gently 486, 512
–, treating 324
–, with alum 317-8, 321, 323
treatise; *see also book* 39, 59, 61, 81, 96-7
–, (2nd) second 353
–, (4) four … of Democritus 199
–, (10) ten 45
–, (20th) twentieth Treatise 374
–, (60) sixty 158
–, About the Fire 96-7
–, Greek 40
– of Zosimos for/ to Theosebeia 204, 375
–, Peri aretes 39
– Rosinus ad Euthiciam 59
–, treatises 256
–, Treatise of Magnesia 375
–, Treatise of the Idol 497
–, Treatise of the Sulphur 185
treatment(s) 90-1, 289, 447
tree 43, 52-3, 84, 156, 401-2, 447, 448, 485, 495
–, (3) three trees 556

– with (3) three branches 448
– acacia 128, 130-1
–, eating from … stills hunger 52, 484
–, flowers of the trees 154
–, gum of Arabic 130, 402
–, nature called 52, 484
– of life 41-2
– of sages 84
–, palm 41-2, 84, 278, 290
–, sprouting 41
–, trees 161, 236, 290, 524
–, white 53-4, 485
trembling 388, 477
– and moist one 498
triangle 279
– triangular bag 470, 472-3
trickery; *see also disguise; hide; protect; veil* 56, 127, 157, 159
–, tricks 219, 344
–, trickster 305
triune 31
Trojan war 112
trouble(s) 33, 332, 491, 524
true 29, 37, 255, 259, 297, 305, 357, 397, 453, 500, 506, 554
–, composition 246, 270
– dye 496
– name(s) 144, 170, 212, 221, 237, 269, 349, 368, 418, 424, 442, 483, 571
– nature 162, 223, 291, 352, 355, 557, 571
– natures 206, 215, 466
– one 205, 296, 568, 569, 572
– parts 147
–, pyrite 497
– thing(s) 150, 559
–, untrue 150, 182, 184
–, what you say is 176
– work 500
trunk 447
trustship 367
truth; *see also hide; keep secret; illuminate; protect; reveal; veil* 9, 44, 122, 159, 194, 197, 202, 214, 221-2, 238, 257, 263, 269, 296, 313, 321, 354, 357, 359, 361, 394, 404-5, 418, 432, 453, 455, 463, 471, 559, 562, 566, 570
– and disguised 221, 315
– and names/ similies/ analogies 147-8, 150, 165, 383
– and repetition 368
–, Book of the Truth 19, 78, 141
–, contain the 47, 474
–, copper of 278
– does not become evident 156, 559
–, gather 473
–, guide to 285
– in their/ your hands 196, 565
– is one 162-3
–, key of 358
–, know (not) 154, 270, 278, 383, 410, 420, 482, 541, 551
–, learning of the 144
–, love of 155
–, mercury of 403, 424, 427
–, moisture of 357
–, name 269, 349
–, nature of/ with ... in it 163, 168, 367
–, not 147-8, 165
–, obscure about 148
– of analogy 174
–, plates of 427
–, pure 259
–, reject not 503
– remains 265
–, see (not)/ visible 196, 331, 394
–, similar to 147-8
–, statement of/ say/ speak/ tell 27, 155, 174, 254, 152, 202, 214, 232, 238, 254, 275, 285, 300, 304, 324, 326, 331, 344, 347, 349, 351, 374, 383, 393, 416, 548, 562
–, truthful 186, 232, 242, 244, 254, 304, 368, 535
–, write 202, 217, 261, 345
tube 261, 543
Turba Philosophorum 24-5, 52-6, 58-9, 68-9, 73, 124-5, 131
– and Mushaf as–suwar 52-3, 55-8, 68
– origin of 58-9
turbid 451, 489, 504, 509, 511
–, black turbidity 520
–, turbidity 509
turn (into) 39, 50
– ashes 36, 127
– blood 57, 127, 157
– body into gold 37
– copper into spirit 41

– dialogue 7, 111
– father/ old into sun/ youth 53
– gold 62
– silverman 24
– spirit into silver 37
– s.th. into water 128
twelve (12) 229, 429
–, books 75
– hours 80
– steps of teaching 81
twelvth (12th) 429, 555-6, 563
–, century 108
twenty (20) 278
–, (20th) twentieth 374, 442
–, (21) twenty-one days 21, 381, 400
–, (21st) twenty-first 444-5
– (22) twenty-two 84
–, (22nd) twenty-second 448
–, (24) twenty-four 22
–, (25th) twenty-fifth 366
– (28) twenty-eight 20, 47
– years 5, 154, 508
two (2); *see also mysterium coniunctionis; opposites; unite; union* 28, 30, 32, 35, 43, 58-9, 63-4, 158, 161, 173, 176, 182, 198, 200, 207, 218, 222-3, 226, 232, 234, 238, 243, 259, 263, 272-4, 277, 280, 293, 305, 311, 318, 321, 326, 345, 355, 359-60, 389, 399, 416, 457, 462, 469, 482, 534, 569-70, 580
–, (2/3) two-third 504, 570, 572
–, (2/6) two-sixth 267, 268
–, (1) one from 370
–, (1) one, turn … into 210, 268, 298, 404
–, (1) one, ... and 122, 155-61, 160-1, 174, 178, 184-5, 192, 207, 210, 269, 275, 325, 420, 446, 482, 489, 491, 509, 534, 550-1, 554, 581
– ,(1) one, ... become 159, 301
–, (1) one, …, one 513
–, (2nd) second , 313, 404
–, (2nd) second book 29, 61, 63, 68
–, (2nd) second picture 65
–, (2½) two and a half ounces 319
–, (3) three, name 274
–, (3) three parts from 265
–, (3) three, ... and/ are 263, 265, 269, 324, 513
–, (3) three, ... become 325
–, (3) three, ... from 370, 550
–, antimony and etesian 376
– Arabic manuscripts 133, 137
–, Ars/ Saturn and fighter/ Aqrunis 305
–, arsenic and mercury of cinnabar 235
– ashes 254
– balances 79
– birds 263, 517
–, black and body of magnesia 366
–, blond and white woman 356
– bodies 195, 274, 468
– books 30, 114, 550
–, born from 156
– castings 454
– clouds 360
– colours 161, 270, 296, 506
– columns 306
– components of magnesia 310
– composed things 256
– compositions 212, 272, 360, 551
–, cook 321
– cookings 199, 508
–, copper and fiery stone 398
–, copper and plates 563
–, copper and water 558
–, crystal and gum 319
– days 188, 470, 519
–, dissolve 256, 275, 321
–, divide in … parts 167
– dogs 84, 347
–, dust and marble 284
– dyes 184, 464
–, earth and water 304
–, Eastern and Western 450
– enter 534
–, eternal water and copper/ body 529
– figures 31, 80
–, first day becoming 570
–, flower of barley and alum 504
–, flowers of gold and glassy natron 511
– -folded vessel 549
–, from Cyprus/ India 249
–, fugitive and fighter 470
– halves 91
– hand(s) 23-4, 149
– heads 109, 276
–, herbs 389

– human beings 32-3, 78-9
– images 434
– knots 263
–, legs 339
– letters 279
– levels 64
–, litharge and ašqunīān lime 317
–, male and female 53, 364, 485, 530
–, male and female/ moisture 576
– men 79, 141, 391
– mercuries 261 , 352, 420, 461
–, mercury and cinnabar 542
–, mix and cook 295
– mixings 385
–, mix lead and claudianus 399
–, mix/ mixture of .. (works) 298, 324, 404, 473, v
– moistures 173
– months 160
– natures 160, 174, 214, 236, 249, 534
– -oneness 44
– openings 380
– operations 451
–, origin is 265
– ounces 271-2, 317, 319, 388, 474
– parts 38, 91, 266, 268, 270-2, 275, 282, 287, 368, 382, 450, 460, 473, 500, 513, 557-8, 560, 572
– pictures 35
– plates 551
– poisons 533
– -pronged;see also iron 48, 300
– puffs 459
–, pyrite and androdamus 456
–, pyrite and copper 572
–, reconcile 28, 523
– reddening 532
– reports 48
– rottings 254
– sages 204
– secrets 152
–, separate 254
– series 6
– silvers 467
–, smoke and non-body 483
– spirits 310, 322, 323, 438
–, spiritual 439
– statements 268
– statues 404, 448
– stones 207
– subjects 402
–, sulphur and sulphur 537
– sulphurs 160, 178, 212-3, 284, 301, 457, 459
–, sun and moisture 318
–, sun and shadow 282
– texts 6
–, Theosebeia and close one 334
– things 191, 275, 386, 403, 521, 529
– ties 141
– time 506
–, tin and lead 394
–, tin and mercury 466
–, twice 270, 320, 474, 505, 506
–, unite 189
– vipers 78-9, 141-2, 158, 182, 307
– water and companions 480
– waters 243, 382, 474
– weights 272, 275, 382 581
–, white lead and burnt copper 535
–, whiteness and blackness 509
– whitening 532
–, whites 370
– wings 34-5, 141, 276, 313, 329, 332, 334, 339, 342, 391
–, woman and man 58, 311-2
–, work is from 360
– works 46, 150, 205, 383, 397, 405, 421, 536
– worlds 262, 275, 389
–, youth and slavegirl 310
–, Zosimos and Theosebeia 33, 37-8, 263, 307, 331, 342

–U–

ugly 355
unchangeable 567
uncooked 282
uncorrupted
– urine 400
– water 505
Ullmann, Manfred 9-10, 18, 20, 44, 94, 99, 124
Umar 26
unconscious (adj, n) 2, 44, 67, 91-4, 130, 136

–, collective 40, 44
– instincts 32
–, reactions from the/ relate to the 5, 39
–, spirit of 31
understand (vb) 10, 12, 24, 26-7, 29, 35, 37, 41-3, 53, 63, 68-9, 74, 85, 90-3, 95, 113, 116, 119, 120, 123, 125, 130, 137146-9, 151-3, 156, 158, 162, 165, 174, 176, 179, 203, 208, 212, 215-6, 225, 228, 231, 236, 238-9, 243, 248, 250, 253, 263, 278, 280-2, 295, 297-8, 303, 305, 310, 315, 325-6, 328, 336, 342, 347, 349-51, 356, 358-9, 361, 363, 366-7, 371, 378, 383-4, 386, 394, 399-400, 405-6, 416, 450-2, 457, 463, 466, 468-9, 474-5, 484-5, 488, 492, 497, 501-2, 515-6, 519, 525-6, 536-7, 539, 541, 546, 561, 573
– -able 115
– benefit of nature 387
– by comparing 158
– meaning 33, 291, 300
– measures 519
– not! 37, 90, 111-2, 145, 151-2, 173, 186, 195, 202, 208, 227, 254, 268, 279-80, 286, 315, 326, 328, 331, 336, 342, 344, 350, 352-3, 356, 358, 362, 370, 383-4, 401-2, 405-6, 410-11, 447, 451, 462, 465, 469, 487-8, 495, 537, 546, 550, 573-4, 579
– picture 31
– science 154, 487
– symbols 93
– teaching 98
– well 144, 154, 184, 232, 253, 399, 546
– work 179
understanding 5, 12, 68-9, 93-4, 112, 119, 126, 130-3, 135, 138, 140, 152, 175, 178, 196, 202-3, 208, 241-2, 271, 281, 303, 310, 315, 326-7, 329, 331, 344, 347, 359, 361, 365, 370, 381, 394, 451, 464, 499, 519, 541, 559
–, key to 93
–, method of 92, 138
–, no 27, 370, 519
–, weak 241-2, 281, 450
unfold (vb) 93, 489
union/ unification; *coniunction; fusion; reconcile* 35, 61, 129, 185, 311, 344, 350, 396, 491, 493, 567
– of natures 454
– of opposites 44-5, 67, 84, 214
– of soul and eternal/ with Gold 40
– of things 531
–, unify 44, 84
unique/ single unique 41, 118, 133, 137, 576
unite; *see also connect(ing); reconcile* 40, 44, 58, 122-3, 189, 223-4, 241, 249, 256, 276, 289, 301, 311, 371, 396, 403, 446, 458, 465, 468, 474, 550, 567
– bodies 424, 454
– body of magnesia and components 376
– components 577
– dust and water 298
– male and female 175, 177
–, mix escaping and non-escaping 378
– nature(s) (and relative) 174, 328, 355, 387
–, sulphury bodies with magnesia 468
– thing 394
–, united bodies 524
–, uniting quality of symbol 21
–, unity 114-5, 121
– with air 334
unjust(ly) 48, 300, 464
unknown; *see also unconscious* 85, 90-2, 94-5, 126, 454, 524
–, kown-unknown 128, 172, 225
unmixed 48, 300
unoperated 405
unpounded 482
upper 121, 168
– divine 31, 59
– level 34-5, 64
– light 28
– luminaries 78
– part 66, 145, 492
– world 64
uplifted 31
upright 48, 300, 404, 407, 411, 418, 421, 425, 428-9, 444, 448, 462, 477, 544, 555
–, standing 264, 276, 313, 329, 334, 414, 418, 421, 439, 442, 445, 477, 526, 544
urge (vb, n) 36, 182, 185, 193, 204, 214, 341, 442, 573
–, bodily 29, 66

urine 405, 418, 459, 502
–, alum, … and water of lime 324
– and crimson 512
– and natron 323
–, cook with 511
–, inferior than 176
–, mix garment with … and dye 512
–, natron, alum and water 323
– of boys 156, 573
– of calf 547, 558
– treat (not) with 324
–, uncorrupted 400
–, urinate 465
–, water of 284
–, whiteners 515
–, your own 465
uroboros 109, 113
use 244
–, make ... of 258, 354, 359, 390, 453, 522, 542, 551
– up moisture 542, 564
– up water 282, 560, 564, 566, 573
–, useful 63, 128, 156, 158-9, 283-4, 300, 315, 359, 462, 542
usṭam 250
Ūṭarīq (mercury) 462
utensils, ship with many 81, 351
uterius capax 31
uterus 304, 318

–V–

Valentine 123
Valentius, Basilius 81
value 13, 116, 123, 171
– of work/ stone 213
vanish (vb) 205, 255, 286, 325, 446
–, book that does not 473
–, colours 323, 454
–, dye vanishes (not) 370, 468, 539
–, not 446, 454
–, vanishing 37, 301, 470, 509
vanities 352, 359, 561
vaporisation 23, 149
vapour(s) 143, 164, 166, 190, 197, 200, 223, 234, 241, 244, 253-4, 270, 288, 301, 317, 410, 418, 482, 505, 543, 549, 570
–, all work is 246
– and/ as spirit 190, 246-7
– and smoke 223
– and wind 227
– as things turned into dust 482
–, benefit of 240
–, composition of 45
–, extract 190, 244
–, extract mercury by/ from 424, 493, 503
– extracts spirit 533
–, feminine 490
– mixed with thin 241
–, mix with male 490
– of arsenic 247
– of bodies 386
– of body 292
– of copper 244
– of dry things 198
– of metals 223
– of moisture 198
– of sea 513
– of vapours 166
– performs whole work 490
–, pounds 234
–, power of 490
–, raise (up) (in) 461, 513, 520
– rises (up) 163, 519, 533
–, turn copper into 410
–, turn into 164, 254, 482
–, turn things into 531
–, vapour, cinnabar and cloud 246
–, vapoury 482
–, water-vapour 218
–, white 232, 244, 246
variety 406
various; *see also many* 151, 274, 424
– bodies 166
– colours 557
– names 249, 539
– natures 166
– things 44, 305, 371, 465, 513, 515, 576
veil something; *see disguise; cover; hide; keep secret; protet; scatter; similes* 22, 53, 144, 178, 203-5, 393-4, 484, 496, 530, 536
– and disguise 350, 516
– nature 127, 159
–, sages' way of teaching/ veiling 349, 350

– science 145
– work 517
veins 23-4, 149, 157, 161, 173, 180, 290
–, mix poison with veins 520
– soaked by liver 173
–, soften 318
venerators 219, 556
–, venerated 128, 172
venom 56-7
Venus 58-9, 252, 279, 305, 311, 383, 494, 571
–, body of 279
Vereno, Ingold 95
vertical 434
–, vertically 427, 439
vessel 32, 35, 64, 145, 216, 260, 268, 277-8, 281, 283, 292, 323, 332, 362, 364, 366-7, 381, 406, 418, 427, 459-60, 465, 474, 486, 489, 491, 500, 502, 504-6, 519, 525, 529-31, 542, 549, 559-60, 562, 565-6, 568-9, 575, 581
– and pot 513
– and tar 158
– as composition 568
–, big 267, 568
–, Book of the Vessels 460
–, bottom of 145, 167, 243, 285, 540, 568
–, burn in 288
–, close (top of) 317, 436, 513
–, half of 579
–, head of 519
– imprison in 360
–, mix in 511
–, mouth of 277, 355, 505, 507, 531, 564, 567, 581
– named me (ana) 459
– of copper 442
– of glass 234, 286, 427, 462, 492, 525, 539
– of silver 579
– of soul 290
– on fire 469
–, open/ opening of the 235, 286, 547
–, put in 145, 288, 491, 525, 534, 561, 581
–, raise in 436, 459
–, return to 283, 509
–, rise 168, 520
–, seal 521
–, solidify in 508
–, top of 317
–, vessels 35, 66, 231, 519
– with moisture 549
–, yellow 34-5, 332
victory, crown of 487
view, point of 135
vile 355
vinegar 199, 233-4, 247, 266, 294, 299, 317, 405, 442, 459, 489, 500, 502, 506
– and flowers of gold 504
– and mercury 394
– and water 400
–, clear and pure 504
–, cook with/ cooking of 453, 507, 511
–, disappears 234-5
–, Egyptian 549
– fat, … and honey 199
–, flowers of gold, (ash), glassy natron and (Egyptian) 504, 511
–, iron, mercury, … and salt 320
–, large quantity of 510
–, lead, ferment, eternal water and sour 355
–, mix stone and 234
–, mix with water and 400
–, moisture of 531
–, old 505
–, operate with vinegar and natron 561
–, pound with 564
–, power of 506
–, pure 511
–, pyrite, … and salt 199
–, red 507
–, soak with 575
–, sour 234, 355, 370, 456, 470, 531, 561
–, turn … into smoke 233
–, vinegar, cinnabar and all moistures 552
–, vinegar, gold and fat 457
–, vinegar, sea shell and alum 299
–, wash with water and 400
–, water of 507
–, white 502
–, without 524
–, wondrous 569
violence, no 321
viper(s) 158, 181
– (2) two 78-9, 141-2, 182, 307
–, mix 158
–, red 263

–, yellow 141, 263
virgin 320, 356, 537
–, love of 473
–, seeker of 473
– slave 390, 458, 536
Virgo (sign of zodiac) 571
virtue 154, 213, 215, 236, 310, 354
visible 172, 178, 204, 214, 219, 239, 322, 336, 345, 357, 394, 450, 502, 508
– colour 436
– invisibile 362
– secret 187, 373, 420, 434, 475, 521
– work 466
vision 331, 357
–, great 110
– of Zosimos 40, 133
visit 112, 173
vitriol (šaḥīra) 147, 250, 299, 349, 406, 454, 468, 511, 552, 561-2, 576
–, copper vitriol (qalqaṭār) 147, 316
–, power of 576
–, red 147, 299, 316, 349
–, roasted 316, 383
–, uncooked 383
von Franz, Marie-Louise 5, 7, 11-2, 14, 40
–, Foundation 13
vulgar (vb, adj) 128, 172

–W–

waking state 143
walls 306
warmth 387
– of air 524
–, warm (vb) 290
warn (vb) 28, 120, 219, 289, 456, 505, 508, 523-4, 530
– about escaping 371
–, warned/ warning(s) 491, 503, 579
wash (vb) 164-5, 167-8, 216, 231, 277, 318, 366, 381, 389, 394, 397, 493, 502-3, 531, 543
– bodies 247
– by poison 168
– egg with sea water 487
–, increase washing 569
– it! 389, 400, 470, 480, 509, 538, 569
– pure 506
–, repeated washing/ several times 167
– sand 482
– sea/ with sea 167, 292, 380, 542
– things 511
– with hot water 507
– with pure water/ eternal water 560, 564
– with sperm 387
– with water 385, 400
–, wash, bleach and purify 503, 511
–, washing 168, 228, 380, 486, 489, 494, 564
water 48, 54, 90-1, 93, 146, 153, 157, 159, 176, 178, 201, 208, 218, 223, 239, 244, 254, 265, 271, 277, 282, 292, 298, 300-1, 311, 318, 321, 323, 325, 358, 362, 405, 436, 450, 457, 459, 470, 475, 491, 501, 503-4, 510, 520, 528, 534, 539, 565, 567, 576
–, (1/3) one third or (2/3) two third of 570
–, (1) one 201, 208, 473, 549, 558
–, (1) one ..., body into 550
–, (3) three mercuries as coppery 414
–, abound things in 560
–, above 145
–, absorb 558, 561, 570, 572
–, accept 321
–, achieve … by eternal 490
–, afraid of 209
–, airy 161, 291-2, 382, 538, 565
–, amount of 568
– and aqzāl 209
– and body 263
– and cloud 189, 197
– and companions 480
– and dragon 48
– and dust 146, 192
– and earth 304
– and every body 262
– and fire 28-9, 120, 122-4, 137, 193, 219-20, 228, 523
– and gum 286
– and honey 49, 514 49
– and male 363
– and milk 400
– and rust 565
– and smoke 505

– and stones 464
– and sun 160
– and salt 400, 569
– and vinegar 400
–, aqzaline, black melted 493
–, arsenic into 548
– ascends 492
– as dyer 304
– as gum and broth 384
– as life 53, 485
– as remedy 511
–, bad/ not bad 436
– becomes air 520
– becomes firm 564
– become (like) 146, 295, 359, 531, 569
– becomes like glass 317
–, black 145, 578
–, blackness of 559
–, body absorbs 249, 574
–, blue 79
–, body and 265
–, body coagulates 265
–, body dissolves 482
–, body mixed with 361
–, body turns into/ becomes 146, 159, 244, 482
–, burn copper with … and flowers 497
–, burnt by 569-70
– comes down 145, 488, 568
–, change tail into 50
–, chrysocolla, body of magnesia and eternal 266
–, clear 489
–, cloud and raising of 164, 272, 359, 400
–, cloud draws 162
–, coagulate stone with .. and gum 447
–, cold 209, 447, 495
–, colour of the … of gold 78
–, composed 552, 541, 554
– composed with alum 552
–, composition of 268
–, concealed inside/ concealed spirit in 198, 549
–, cook alone 460
–, cook herb with … and alum 475
–, cook in/ with 453, 474, 511
–, cook plant/ dye in 502
–, cook with eternal 295
–, cooked … with bodies 49, 514
–, copper and eternal 528
–, copper and silver become 283
–, copper into 558, 563
–, copper solidifies 248
–, copper, sour … and moisture 493
– coppery 129, 414
–, cover dust with 531
–, descend in 512
–, dissolve 159, 360, 569
–, divide 558
–, divine 19, 24, 38, 44, 91
–, dog of the 517
–, dragon, egg and 159
–, drink from resurrecting 53, 485
–, dry up 562
–, dust,… and herbs 286
–, dyeing of 209
– dyes/ dyes purple 248, 554
–, earth absorbs 278
–, (earth) air, water, and sun (fire) 222, 298, 359, 51
–, earth becomes/ turns into 228, 370-1, 520
–, earth separates from 507
–, earth turns into 548
– earth, wind and light 122
– elixir and eternal water 538
–, enemy of 28, 120, 219, 523
– escapes 436
–, essential part 477
–, eternal 171, 160, 213, 266, 277-8, 295, 319, 363-4, 480, 482, 490-1, 528-9, 531-2, 537-8, 546-7, 558, 560-1, 564-5, 567, 571-2, 576-7
–, everything becomes 147
–, everything moist as 497
–, extract from 493, 567
–, extract white; *see white* 284
–, fall into 146, 482
–, ferment 180
– ferments copper 558
–, fiery 482
–, fix 480
–, flowers of eternal 567
–, flowery 538
– flows 325
– for defeating dragon 47
– four elements; *see also water, earth; water, airy; water, fiery 92, 122, 222, 515*

–, fragmented plates become 364
– from rock 477
–, golden 141, 164
–, gold with eternal 548
–, gum as living 400
–, higher/ lower 487
–, honoured body and eternal 529
–, hot 286, 389, 556
–, increase 542
–, iron absorbs 485
– is moisture 159
–, lake with 391
–, lead, ferment, eternal … and sour vinegar 355
–, living 401-2
– makes alumy 170
– makes lean body 549
–, marble … with lime, sediment and fat 381
–, melted 493
–, mercuries mixed with/ in 490, 459
–, mercury from arsenic, sandarach and pure 353
– mix copper and 248, 528
–, mix dye with alum and 452
–, mixed 503
– mixes with body 549
– mixes with honey 520
–, mixing of …with water 566
–, mix silver with … of gum 472
–, mix sulphur with 289
–, mix … with bodies 49
–, mix … with honey 534
–, mix with/ in the 153, 401
–, mix with vinegar and 400
–, moist water and dry sulphur 198
–, moisture as/ of 288, 539
–, names for … of sulphur 247
–, name things water 560
–, not composed 516
–, no weight for 268
– of air 382, 489
– of alum 284, 507
– of androdamus 208
– of ashes 284
– of ash of firewood of white sulphur 507
– of blackness 206
– of cinnabar 568
– of copper 426, 569
– of dew 540
– of dragon 426, 474
– of earth 501
– of ferment 503
– of glass 418
– of gum 456
– of gold 78, 428-9, 457, 482, 526-7, 544
– of lead 418, 425
– of life 54
– of lime 324
– of male 529
– of natron/ natrun 233, 284, 293, 535, 549
– of Nile 418, 489
– of people 179
– of pure sulphur 410
– of rain 383
– of river 426, 458
– of sages 248
– of salt 255, 284
– of sea 167, 255, 284, 531, 573
– of saffron 186
– of sediment 284
– of silver 78, 128
– of silver of cinnabar 564
– of sulphur 128-9, 164, 172, 175, 179, 183, 185-9, 192, 198-9, 210, 224-6, 243, 245, 248, 253-6, 261-2, 274, 287-9, 284, 302, 323, 361, 386, 396, 400, 407, 426, 430, 446, 457, 461, 468, 476, 489-90, 516-7, 521, 527, 540, 548, 551, 552, 556-7, 578
– of sulphur, poison and arsenic 283
– of sulphur, solidify 548
– of urine 284
– of vinegar 507
– of white sulphur 379-80
–, operate with eternal 528
–, origin of eternal 490
–, other 146, 282, 482, 562
–, out of 170
–, part of 153-4
–, pound purple with 503
–, pound … with body 491
–, pound with 317, 400, 469
–, pour 460, 489
–, power of 490, 547, 557
–, pure 199, 244, 292, 352, 395, 450, 454, 487, 489, 502, 531, 550, 560

–, pure eternal 573
–, pure …. and red sulphur 379
–, pure … of sulphur 244, 261-2, 284, 386, 429, 434, 459-60, 477, 521
–, pure …., sulphur, suzin, colocynth 300
–, purify 509
–, purify with 516
–, put back 487
–, put dye in its water 511
–, rain water 405
–, raise 164, 189, 215, 298, 315, 440, 487, 489, 494
–, raise in vessel 436, 459
–, rest of the 557-8, 565
–, return … on sediment 244
–, ripen elixir with 562
–, rise up 509
–, rot earth with 303
–, salt, alum, white lead, polished earth and living … 395
–, second work made … eternal 490-1
–, sieve 323
–, silvery 141, 263, 282, 307, 379, 538
–, smoke gives 483
–, soak in/ with 156, 248, 547
–, solidify body and 569
–, spirit out of .. of sulphur 286
–, squeeze out 284
–, stagnant 302
– stone 427
–, stone with … and gum 495
–, submerge in 559, 562
–, subtle/ spiritual 282, 436, 505
–, sulphuric 179, 373, 538
–, surface of 283, 499
–, sweet 318, 323, 509, 531
–, tar becomes 277
– to thirsty-one 483
–, turbid 509, 511
–, turn all things/ everthing into 399, 482
–, turn body into 156, 535, 549, 564
–, turn copper and silver into 566
– turns copper into rust 558
–, turn s.th. into 128, 145-6, 150, 172, 353, 363-4, 399, 481, 530, 572-3, 576
–, turn into gentle 368
–, turn into pure 379
–, turn into spiritual; *see spiritual* 501
–, turn iron into 386
–, turn nature and poison into 298
–, turn plates into 529
–, turn sulphur into 192
–, turn … into air 370, 371
–, turn … into dust 529
–, turn … into saffron 538
–, uncorrupted 505
–, urin, natron, alum and 323
–, use up/ used up 282, 538, 560, 564, 566, 573
–, -vapour 218
–, wash with 385
–, wash with eternal 564
–, wash with hot 507
–, wash with sea 487
–, wash with vinegar and 400
– water-air 464
–, weight of 484
–, white 143, 151, 199, 380, 450, 529, 568, 572
–, white … of sulphur 199
– with different moistures 284
waters; see also water; 148, 215, 349, 460-1, 549
–, (2) two 243, 382, 474
–, (2) two … from stone, extract 382
–, (3) three 473
–, (6) six, absorb rest of 489
–, acid 396
– and body/ bodies 362
–, dye comes from 473
–, escaping, dyeing, fugitive 488
–, extract … from ashes 461
–, master of 558
–, mixed 453
–, natruny 396
– remain from dye 302
–, salty 396
–, whitening 231
waves 530
– of sea 358
wax, mix lead, iron and 155
– of sages 287
–, sealing 502
way 17, 21, 29, 39, 51, 59, 61, 69, 144, 501, 510, 519, 547, 559, 562, 565, 568-9
–, beginning of 531

–, condensed 380
– find a 237
–, lasting 293
–, loose 349, 458
– of doing work/ clear … to work 349, 407, 511
–, right 217, 268, 278, 285, 292, 310, 464-5, 476, 540, 551, 568
– straight 217
– to secret 193
–, work this 497
–, wrong 454, 551
weak 26, 36 169, 175, 241-2, 281, 310, 315, 334, 342, 450, 522
– and strong/ weak one and strong one 35, 336, 480
– conquers the strong 169
– in appearance 169
–, mix … one with fire-resistant one 202
–, moist, ... and cold 174
– of understanding 327
–, weaken (vb) 158
–, weakest 170
–, weak-minded; *see also mind, feeble* 329
–, weakness 504, 550
wealth 556
–, destroy 352
weapons 35-6, 56
–, weapons, woman (spirit/inside) is full of 35-6, 56, 127, 157, 336
weave with gold 36, 215, 341, 474
Wehr, Hans 347
weight; *see numbers; measures; rutl* 191, 265, 269-70, 272-4, 276, 374
–, (1) one/ is one 269, 272, 277, 581
–, (1st) first 270
–, (3) three parts 267
–, (3rd) third of 484, 510
–, (4) four/ (4th) fourth parts 267, 269
–, (9) eight 269
–, apparent 268
– as basis, key and completion 262
–, clear 271
–, decreases 189
–, equal 263, 271-2, 274-5, 280
–, hide 265, 267, 268
–, know 221
–, little 171
–, measures of 158
–, mix according to 269
–, no 268, 272, 298
– of body of magnesia 382
– of composition 568
– of lead 274
– of sulphur 191, 267
– of tin 274
– of zinc ore 267, 268
–, original 489
–, ponder over 268
–, right 272, 379
–, same 270
–, secret 268
–, weigh (vb) 345
weights; *see also parts* 143, 166, 219, 262, 266-7, 269-70, 272-5, 328, 344, 350, 359, 365, 379, 491
–, (1/8) one eighth 267
–, (1/3) one third/ (2/6) two sixth 267-8, 484
–, (1) one/ (6/6) six sixth 268-9, 272-3, 277, 581
–, (2) two 272, 275, 382, 581
–, (3) three (parts), ... of/ is 266-7, 275
–, (4) four 267, 272-3, 275
–, (4th) fourth Epistle about the Weights 112
–, (5) five 269
–, (6) six 568
–, (9) nine 269, 279
–, (10) ten (times the) 158, 568
–, Book of the Weights 262, 275
–, composition and weights 531
–, dispersed 263
–, equal 298
– differ 269, 271, 276
– do not matter 406
–, images of 276
–, know natures, combination and 519
–, named … bodies 267
– of copper 274
– of mercury 129, 447, 451, 495, 507
– of other operation 556
– of things 191
– of transformation 568
– of water 484
–, ponder over 268
–, throw 385
–, true 265, 267, 519

– up 311, 458
well; *see also fountain; spring*
– of mercury 129, 447, 451, 495, 507
– up 311, 458
Weltinnenraum 39
West 59, 310-3, 390, 458
–, goddess of the 54-5
–, western 13, 69, 450, 489
wet 470
– clay 568
–, make 475
whale 64, 229
–, blood turns into 302-3
–, glue of 401, 474-5
–, whalefish 525
wheat 181, 358
– brings forth wheat 551
–, extract grain of … from ear 303
–, field of 293
white 35, 48, 54, 143, 164, 183, 204, 222-3, 228, 232, 245, 255, 270, 282, 297, 303, 307, 310, 316, 332, 355, 366, 368, 374, 401, 436, 444, 448, 460-1, 512, 571, 574, 576
– (1) one 367, 395
– alabaster 561
– and black 506
– and red/ or red 152, 166, 243, 416, 458, 533
– arsenic 541
– ash 515
–, becomes 168, 192, 231, 235, 254, 257, 283, 288, 353, 369, 507, 576
– body 216, 468
– bones 474
– branch 448, 495
– broth 434
–, burn in making 579
– cluster 366, 382
–, colour 575
–, compose … with remedies 542
–, composition 212, 326
–, composition of black and 296
– cooking 199
– copper 244, 363, 473, 494, 499
– dog 84
– dust 284
–, dye/ dyeing 205, 420, 541
– earth 126, 293
–, extract … body 468
–, extract … water 284
– female 388
– fermented cluster 475
– firewood 459
– froth 173, 485
– golden 451
– gravedigger 292
– -green 35, 332
– gum 547
– in appearance 151, 222, 370, 373, 458, 475, 483, 493, 499, 533, 549, 574
– in its nature 574
– interior 465
– lead 183, 260, 272, 350, 395, 461, 475, 535, 541, 581
– litharge 395, 541
– magnesia 367
–, make arsenic 548
–, make themselves 396, 444
–, make/ making/ turn 165,170, 183-5, 187, 195, 197, 199, 207, 212, 234, 236, 244, 246-7, 250-2, 254, 267, 272, 283, 288-9, 292, 294-5, 297, 354, 362, 364, 373, 377, 379, 384-5, 397, 402, 411, 421, 444, 460-1, 465, 468, 494, 498, 532-3, 549, 552, 573-4, 577, 579
–, make/ turn .. . (inside/ outside of) copper 41, 169-70, 173, 200, 232, 244, 250, 261, 283, 353, 362, 374, 380, 382, 386-7, 397, 420, 508, 532, 536, 550, 552, 576, 578
–, make …. every body 226, 399
– mercury 352-3, 362, 459, 528
– nature 363, 367, 372
– on white 370
–, other 549
– plant 173
– poison 143, 250, 380, 533
–, pure 471
– -red 222
– -red copper 468
–, red, white and yellow 199
–, remain 459
– sea 167, 450
– silver 380, 493
– smoke 254

–, soft- 250
– soil(s) 395
– stone 173, 233, 490, 530, 565-6
– sulphur 165, 192, 250, 269, 301, 325, 365, 377, 379, 397, 497-8, 507, 541, 552
–, turn gold 442
–, turn into … froth 387
– tar 581
– thing 283
– thorn 401
– tree 53, 485
– vapour 244, 246
– vinegar 502
– water 143, 151, 199, 450, 529, 568, 572
–, water of … sulphur 380
–, whiteners, galls, urines, virtous mineral natures 515
–, whitened 183, 375, 397, 455, 498
–, whitened body 152, 166, 301, 368, 554
–, whitened by ferment 502
–, whitened cloud 197
–, whitened copper 191, 220, 378-9, 498
–, whitened magnesia 369, 372, 374
–, whitened tin 546
– woman 356, 358
– wool 473
whiteness 40, 48, 53, 151, 175, 226, 234, 238-9, 261, 289, 319, 350, 357, 379, 466, 499, 542, 580
– and redness 183
– appears 566
–, burning as/ of 288, 523
– concealed inside blackness 509
– conquers shadow of copper 374
–, extract … from blackness 509
–, extract … from redness 542
–, intense 40, 575
– of magnesia 374
–, pure 53, 484
–, red dye in 541
–, redness concealed in/ covers 533, 541-2
–, shadow of copper concealed in 373-4
– wents away with fire 56, 127, 157
whitening 23, 143, 149-50, 188, 199, 212, 216, 250, 269, 499-501, 524, 561
–, (1) one, ... and reddening is 498
–, (2) two ...s 532
– as beginning of work 192
–, completion of 189
–, end of 355
–, finished 269
–, first 167, 532
–, mercury of 420
– waters 231
whole
– secret of the sages 564
– work 498
widow 530
wife 10, 375
– of blond one 357
– of dragon 47, 56
will 28, 120, 219-20, 416
– of God 215
willow, Egyptian (Salix aegiptica) 385
wilt 554
win 162, 228, 296, 556
–, (1) one ...s over 10 (ten)/ all 164, 170, 326
– by heat 239
– over everything 258
– (nature) …s over nature 162, 195, 229, 241, 258-9, 285, 296, 326, 354, 393
–, spirit ...s over 35, 336
–, Theosebeia ...s over Zosimos 344
wind 57, 157, 400, 484
– and vapour 227
– of fire 489
– north/ (from) North 127, 159, 278, 292
–, South 278
–, water, earth, … and light 122
–, winds 513
winding 78, 141
– sheet(s) 36, 217, 290, 341-2
wine 383, 460
–, cook in 453
winged 339, 442, 444
–, (6) six … persons 264, 526
–, (9) eight … statues 517
– body 407, 411, 414, 416, 418, 421, 426, 428-9, 431, 435-6
– man 477
– men 544
–, wings 34-5, 141, 276, 307, 313, 329, 332, 334, 342, 391, 421, 426, 428-9, 431, 435-6, 442, 444-5, 526
winner 296
winter 152, 236, 360, 405-6, 453, 522, 524

– and moisture/ moisture of 511, 524, 548
– as cold one 152
wipe off 568
wisdom 22, 33, 116, 124, 150, 161, 176, 240, 332, 567
–, amount of 142
–, dilute with 488
–, extract 469
–, gate of 165
–, glue of 474
–, head of 242
– of the earth 67
–, people of 229, 490
–, wiser 35, 336
wither 523
without 229
– body of gum dyeing becomes not good 547
– lead nothing could/ can be 376, 546
– moisture nothing comes to existence/ be done 294, 298
– pounding nothing of looked-for comes into existence 513
– which nothing could come into being 236, 256, 293
– which nothing is good 214
– which we had no forms with benefit 395
witness 19, 40, 49, 130, 294, 334, 432, 456
woe 155
wolf/ wolves 192
– and dog 289, 498
woman; *see also lady* 38, 41, 43, 55-7, 67 127, 150, 157, 174, 195, 305, 310-1, 315, 327, 357, 387, 418, 490, 537, 543
– and dragon 56, 127, 157
– and man 310-11, 320, 326
–, barren 156
–, colour of 475
–, daughters of men 22
–, great(er); *see also god–man, Other-One, psychopompos, self* 41, 43, 59
–, manly/ warrior 125
– -man relationship 136-8
–, mind of; *see also mind, weak* 150, 315
– murderous to/ kills husband 54, 56, 127, 157, 213
–, noble 20-1
– upright 556
–, very old 168
–, white 356, 358
–, women 126, 178, 310, 315, 477, 536
–, work of woman 487
womb 160, 174, 182, 357, 387, 481, 485-6
–, blood of 485
–, cook in 173
wonder(s) (n) 10, 116, 176, 223
–, about 23, 143, 150, 170, 176, 182, 203, 447
–, wonderful 53, 56, 127, 130, 157, 176, 202, 231, 291, 389
–, wonders, I (Asfihas) am the 166
wood 151
wool 168, 204, 316, 318, 320, 323-4, 388-9, 453, 470, 502-3, 554
– and alum 271, 324
– and broth 552
–, boil 509
–, burn 510
–, dye (of/ from) 204, 271, 406, 512, 539, 541, 552
–, man of 539
– mix with dye 471
–, moisture flows over 542
–, moisture should cover 510
–, pure 293
–, put … back into alum 510
–, return 510, 542
–, return … to alum 317
–, soak 322, 473
–, turn … purple 495
–, white 473
word(s) 11, 26, 40-1, 85, 90, 94-5, 108, 112, 115, 123, 140, 178-9, 192, 194, 202-3, 214-5, 245, 271, 311, 331, 382-3, 463, 575, 580
– and image(s) 19, 29
– by word 5
–, first 349
–, magical 203
– of Democritus; *see also Democritus* 37, 344-5
– of Zosimos 203
–, repletion 576
–, true/ false 259
–, without 64
work; *see also art* 23, 85, 143, 162, 175, 181, 208, 213-4, 216-7, 219, 225, 228, 248,

252-3, 256, 262, 278, 280, 283, 290, 294, 302, 313, 317, 319, 322, 345, 359, 371, 379, 398, 424, 472, 477, 481, 549, 554, 557, 572, 576, 580
–, (1) one, ... is 23, 149, 184, 187, 216, 294, 454, 563
–, (1) one colour, turn … into 405
–, (1st) first 192, 205, 253, 301
–, (1st) first ..., extract from 386
–, (1st) first ..., names of 526
–, (1st) first and (2nd) second; *see also second work* 150, 361, 405, 517
–, (2nd) second/ other 205, 245, 250, 295, 301, 364, 420, 490-1, 493, 511, 526, 543, 554, 563, 555, 571
–, (2nd) second Work, About the 525
–, (2nd) second ..., mix with gold in 386
–, achieve/ obtain 85, 152, 172, 241, 450, 490
– against 519
–, aim (of alchemy/ of the alchemical work); *see also goal* 24, 29, 45, 192
–, alchemical (opus alchemicum) 10, 22, 28-9, 35, 44-5, 63-4, 74, 80-1, 84, 90-1, 98, 113, 119, 134, 137-8
–, all 199, 251, 246
–, analogy for 153, 174, 228, 318, 370, 438, 463, 480, 508
– and cloud 489
– and four natures 218
–, ask about 351
–, basis of 22, 237, 390, 395, 414, 503, 511, 560
–, beginning/ end of 32-3, 128, 171, 181, 187, 192, 213, 220, 229, 250, 253, 287-8, 316, 331, 349, 456, 458, 462, 487, 490, 541, 579
–, book about 27, 221, 347
–, burn 524
–, burning as head of 288
– cannot be completed without it/ sun/ fire 226, 494
–, centre of the 39
–, colours of the work 176
– comes from cloud and raising of water 359
– comes from nature 356
– comes from them 515
–, complete (alchemical)/ entire/ whole 81, 120, 164, 177, 192, 219, 224, 236, 242, 363, 384, 432, 493-4, 498, 561, 579
–, completeness/ completion of 165, 259, 296, 476, 508
–, composition in/ of 215, 265, 427, 554
–, cooking and pounding is 399
–, corrupt 159
–, crown of 251
–, describe … with allusions 474
–, destroy 522
–, disguise 349
–, divide 153
–, do … (promptly/ quickly/ right/ well) 189, 215, 265, 407, 501, 562
–, easy 496
–, enemy of 491
–, enter 28, 37, 62, 152-3, 166, 169, 188, 190, 194, 208, 221, 223, 229, 246, 280, 284, 315, 345, 359, 365, 368, 370, 389, 397-8, 434, 451, 454-5, 459, 487, 491, 499, 524, 537, 561, 565
–, exalted 539
– exist not (without fire) 327, 491
–, experience 497
–, find 562
–, fire destroys 171
–, give birth to 356
–, goal of; *see also aim* 41, 80, 84, 137-8, 278, 560, 568
–, good 28, 120, 220, 523
–, great 44, 132, 138, 219, 261, 365, 375
–, guide(d) to; *see also guru* 84
–, half of 440
– happens through measures of fire 524
–, harm from 169
–, head of 189, 251, 317, 395, 444, 577
–, hide 203, 365, 368, 383
–, how to do 154, 158, 236, 358, 360, 367
– in detail 476
–, individual 81
–, inspire 352
– is completed by operation 162
– is in it (thing, nature, unoperated) 153, 156, 405
– is right 153
– is simple 150
–, is true 327
–, keep … secret 193

–, key to 414, 521
–, know 260, 454, 467
– like glass making 145
– like ignorant 519
–, look for 299
–, make 145, 425, 469
–, make … in obedience to God 556
–, male, female and 249
– many days 505
–, mercuries 432
–, mercury and 425, 469
–, no … without fire 516
–, obtain 536
– of bleacher 387
– of fire 254, 397
– of gold 462-3
– of silver 462, 463
– of stones 462
– of woman 487
– on bodies 543
– only exists by moisture 565
–, operate/ operation of 158, 178, 186, 387
–, our 154, 161, 174, 183, 189, 216, 220, 234, 255, 267, 291, 360, 362, 398, 405, 493-4, 497, 546, 549, 555, 566
–, patience of/ for 540
–, people of 316
–, perfect 129, 243, 271, 570
–, perform 152-3, 147
–, power of 170
–, protect 241
–, pure copper from 563
–, put … in its vessel 525
–, put your hand in 525
–, reach goal of 568
–, redness is 575
–, rest of 432
–, right/ rightness of 525, 535
–, risk of 368
–, Royal 90
–, ruin 508
–, secret 215
–, silver from our 294
–, stages of 61
–, start 281, 304, 349
– starts/ is completed 354
–, stones of 207-8
–, success of … and measures of fire 492
– supported by nature 22
–, teach 145
–, things enter 434, 454-5
–, this/ another 237
– this way 497
–, time of 487
–, transforms natures 299
–, true 500
–, upon 24, 37, 164, 170, 231, 557
–, useful for 166, 284
–, vapour performs whole 490
–, veil 517
–, visible 299, 466
– was completed 6, 579
–, ways of doing 511
– with gentle fire 524
– without error 267
–, working of spirit 41
– would appear to people 164
works 464
– (1st) first sages, ... of 469
–, (2) two 46, 205, 360, 383, 405, 421, 554
–, (2) two ...s, mixing of 404, 554
– come into existence 532
–, hide both 420
– of sages 47 293, 315
– of Zosimos 48
–, see 378
–, stone does 238
world 32, 44, 50, 62, 67, 92, 121-2, 130, 162, 166, 180, 214, 221-2, 227-8, 286, 305, 359, 459, 464, 480, 571
–, (2) two worlds 262, 275
–, Arab(ic) 13, 59
–, archetypal 39, 64, 65
–, corrupt/ destroy/ ruin 23, 145, 149, 215, 217, 236, 259, 350, 517
–, blessings of 484
–, core of 345
–, day-/ night-world 39, 50, 78-9, 371
–, dream-world 41, 137
–, head of the 236, 295, 546-7
–, inner/ outer 90-1
–, invisible 10
–, mix nourishment with 489
–, natures of 50, 371
–, people of 62
–, scientific 17

–, this/ other 26, 31-2, 90-1, 93-5, 119, 126, 130, 155, 215, 219, 241-2, 484
–, unconscious 67, 91, 130
–, Western 7, 59, 63
–, wonder of 10
–, worldly 285
worldview 11
worm(s) 319, 356, 500
– of sea 507
worried 420
worth 285
–, morc worthy 267
–, worthless 173, 188, 228
wrap (vb) 36, 217, 290, 341-2
wring (vb) 576
write 22, 32, 63, 73, 92, 96, 116, 119, 138, 142, 144, 147, 150, 158, 160, 177, 182, 188, 196, 202-5, 221-2, 228, 234, 241, 259-61, 268, 271, 273-4, 290, 292, 297-8, 302, 313, 321, 327, 347, 349, 361, 365, 374-5, 381, 386-7, 390, 411, 414, 434, 450, 460, 477, 487, 491, 501-3, 537, 552, 556, 559
–, about 400
– books 22, 209, 393-4, 398, 427, 526
– clearly 271, 273
–, Democritus 249, 256
– in symbols 85, 345
–, no-one has written about this secret before Zosimos 202, 327
–, sage(s) 165, 169, 265, 272, 305, 315, 318, 323, 327, 350, 462
–, summary of written 261
– truth 217
–, write/ written in books of sages 162, 367, 410, 430
–, writer(s) 19, 27
–, writing of Zosimos/ Zosimos writes to/ for Theosebeia; see Zosimos
wrong 147, 201, 205, 305, 354, 375, 385, 487, 496, 508, 540, 554, 579
– and right 351
– opinions 144
– way 454, 551

–Y–

year(s) 5, 12-3, 236, 242, 299
–, (20) twenty 154, 508
–, (40) fourty 10
–, (100) hundred 53, 485
–, (140) hundred and fourty 25, 118, 155
–, (160) hundred and sixty 25, 118, 155
–, (660) six hundred and sixty 27, 347
–, (1800) thousand eight hundred 110
–, born every year 46, 325, 368, 481, 507, 571
–, every year/ once a year 46, 212, 252, 305, 565, 571
yeast 502
yellow 35, 38, 43, 141, 164, 270, 276, 307, 361, 388, 421, 477, 554
– and black 166
– colour 499
– flowers 259
– (-green) birds 263, 517
– head 279, 280
– in essence 499
–, make things 489
– red and white 199
– ropes 517
–, russet- 199
– scales 263, 264, 276
– soft stones 167
– vessel 34-5, 332
– viper 141, 263
–, yellowness 248, 455, 499, 527, 557
yolk 374
–, dragon is 159
–, moisture, … and shell 159
young 26, 47, 119, 300
– and dragon 51
– man 47, 48
–, old into 53, 485
youth 53-4, 177, 310, 485
– and slave-girl 310-11

–Z–

zandarig, zandarīḥ 574
Zetzner; *see Theatrum chemicum*
Zeus 305, 312-3

zinc ore 267-8
Zodiac 313, 525, 571
–, sign of 571
Zosimos; *see also books of; texts of; origin of Mushaf as-suwar* 9, 12, 18, 21-2, 24, 26, 38, 51, 68, 73-4, 78, 84, 91-6, 105, 107-11, 113, 115, 117, 119-20, 122, 124-6, 129-31, 135, 138, 141, 144, 148, 199, 202, 266, 270, 307, 310, 360, 477, 543
–, about the teachings of other sages 344-5, 349-50, 349, 365, 369-70, 383, 394, 420, 469, 474
–, about his way of learning alchemy 158, 180, 299, 300, 347
– and Gnostic thoughts 122-3
– and Theosebeia 92, 135-6, 331, 416
–, Alexandrian 10
– Arabus 73, 92, 119, 125, 132
– as student of Democritus 347
–, authentic 21, 24
–, body/ corps of 31, 36, 38, 339
–, Book titles; *see book(s)*
–, books/ texts of 97, 114, 133, 135, 137
–, collector of dispersed 9
–, composition of 113
–, criticises Theosebeias question/ understanding/ angry 195, 242, 315, 322, 324, 327, 329, 358
–, dead/ killed/ death of/ dying 36, 80-1, 93, 336, 342, 439, 477
– dedicates epistles to Theosebeia 46, 315
–, destroyed 36, 339-40
–, development of teaching/ psychological development 81, 112, 115-6, 137
–, divine 35
–, dream-life of/ dream of; *see dreams* 6, 20, 23-4, 40, 47-8, 149, 300, 514
– embracing Theosebeia 264
–, epistles of 46 315
– explains how sages confused people 383
–, following of; *see following* 68
–, golden 37, 345
–, greater/ large 78-9
–, guide of 47
–, hand of 141, 307, 329, 544
–, head of 444
–, identity of 9
–, image/ picture of 29, 35, 141-2, 212, 263-4, 276, 313, 329, 332, 337, 342, 345, 347, 402, 404, 407, 411, 414, 418, 421, 425, 426, 428, 429, 431, 434-6, 439, 440, 442, 444-5, 448, 477, 517, 544
–, intention of 28, 143-4, 158, 159, 242, 257, 559
– in vessel 34-5, 332
–, last book/ text of 116
–, life/ dating/ lifetime of 9-10, 27, 96, 109
–,' love for 49, 111, 117, 132, 137
–, name of 51, 61
– nickname/ epithet of 9
– of Panapolis 9
–, original 26
–, reasons to write the Book of Pictures 19
–, relationship to Theosebeia 39, 148, 155, 156, 173, 212, 242, 315, 322, 559
–, revealing what no-one has written before 202, 327
–, school of 21, 25, 219
–, small 78
–, spirit of 33, 35, 336, 339
–, teacher of 27, 84-5, 291, 347
–, teaching of/ teaching alchemy to others/ way of teaching 18, 21, 26-8, 32, 48, 61, 63, 74, 81, 85, 90, 110-2, 117, 124, 132-5, 137, 194, 196, 217, 299, 331, 350, 359, 381, 382, 390, 414, 427, 451, 464, 477, 484, 526, 543
–, thoughts of 112
– time of 10, 20, 28, 64, 98, 118, 122-3, 130
–, tomb of 344
–, vision(s) of 40, 112
– with bull 35
– with sun on head 30-1
–, worldview of 11
–, writes book/ text/ letter to/ for Theosebeia 6, 20, 39, 46, 111, 170-1, 194, 204, 212, 216, 242, 260, 274, 289, 299, 315, 318, 375, 388, 407, 411, 414, 434, 454, 510, 529, 536, 544, 555, 559, 581
–, Zosimos' pictures for Theosebeia; *see pictures*

4. Diacritical Signs: Pronunciation

͗	glottal stop
ā	long a
ṯ	th, unvoiced, as in 'thing'
ğ	voiced g, as in 'gentleman'
ḥ	aspirated h, pronounced in the back of the throat
ẖ	fricative h, as in Scottish 'loch'
ḏ	voiced th, as in 'there'
š	sh, unvoiced, as in 'sheep'
ṣ	dark s
ḍ	dark d
ṭ	dark t
ẓ	dark z
͑	very deep a, pronounced in the throat
ġ	gutteral r
ū	long u
ī	long i